Assessing Students with Special Needs

Fourth Edition

John J. Venn
University of North Florida

PEARSON

Merrill
Prentice Hall

Upper Saddle River, New Jersey
Columbus, Ohio

KH

Library of Congress Cataloging-in-Publication Data

Venn, John.

Assessing students with special needs /John J. Venn.—4th ed.

p. cm.

ISBN 0-13-171296-9

1. Children with disabilities—Education—United States.   2. Educational tests and measurements—United States.
3. Children with disabilities—Psychological testing—United States.   4. Behavioral assessment of children—United States.   I. Title.

LC4031.V46 2007

371.9'043—dc22   2005037525

Vice President and Executive Publisher: Jeffery W. Johnston
Executive Editor: Ann Castel Davis
Development Editor: Heather Doyle Fraser
Editorial Assistant: Kathleen S. Burk
Production Editor: Sheryl Glicker Langner
Production Coordination: Jolynn Kilburg
Design Coordinator: Diane C. Lorenzo
Photo Coordinator: Valerie Schultz
Cover Design: Candace Rowley
Cover Image: Getty One
Production Manager: Laura Messerly
Director of Marketing: David Gesell
Marketing Manager: Autumn Purdy
Marketing Coordinator: Brian Mounts

This book was set in Berkeley Book by Carlisle Publishing Services. It was printed and bound by Hamilton Printing. The cover was printed by The Lehigh Press, Inc.

Photo Credits: Karen Mancinelli/Pearson Learning Photo Studio, 3; Todd Yarrington/Merrill, 20; Patrick White/Merrill, 351; Tom Watson/Merrill, 42; Anne Vega/Merrill, 65, 217, 275, 324; Laura Bolesta /Merrill, 92, 241, 307; Scott Cunningham/Merrill, 113, 378; Anthony Magnacca/Merrill, 143, 175, 405, 422, 444.

Pearson Education Ltd.
Pearson Education Singapore, Pte. Ltd.
Pearson Education Canada, Ltd.
Pearson Education—Japan

Pearson Education Australia Pty, Limited
Pearson Education North Asia Ltd.
Pearson Educación de Mexico, S.A. de C.V.
Pearson Education Malaysia, Pte. Ltd.

10 9 8 7 6 5 4
ISBN: 0-13-171296-9

10/13/09

Preface

The processes and procedures for assessing students with special needs are constantly changing. Changes include new and revised strategies, instruments, legislation, and approaches. Many changes have occurred since the publication of the third edition of this book. This fourth edition contains the following new information:

- Additional information about high-stakes testing
- More information about accommodations in testing
- Expanded information about curriculum-based assessment strategies and procedures
- Descriptions of revised tests reflecting the newest approaches to assessment
- Revised information about IEPs and assessment reflecting the new mandates in IDEA 2004
- Descriptions of new tests and deletions of older tests
- A complete listing of all curriculum-based assessment procedures and major tests that appear in the book (see inside front and back covers)

The fourth edition also includes reflection questions in all chapters. This useful new instructional feature will help students think critically as they develop their understanding of how to use assessment. Because the reflections make use of different perspectives, they encourage students to discover new ways of using assessment in the teaching and learning process.

Although the book includes new and updated features, it retains the best of the existing elements, including the following:

- Expanded and enhanced coverage of classroom-based assessment throughout the text
- Expanded Multicultural Considerations features with emphasis on how to evaluate students from culturally and linguistically diverse backgrounds
- The latest resources on technology and assessment, focusing on practical information that teachers can use in their classrooms
- Extensive coverage of learning styles and modality assessment
- Expanded treatment of processes and procedures for assessing students with attention deficit hyperactivity disorder (ADHD)
- Assessment instrument review tables at the end of chapters 7–17 that provide summaries for instruments discussed in each chapter.
- Sections in each chapter linking assessment with instruction
- Numerous vignettes illustrating assessment from practical, applied perspectives
- Abundant examples, illustrations, checklists, charts, and graphs
- Focus boxes highlighting special assessment considerations
- Opportunities for students to check their comprehension of essential facts and concepts in each of the chapters
- Meeting Performance Standards and Preparing for Licensure Exams sections at the end of each chapter correlate chapter content with CEC Standards and PRAXIS™ knowledge and skills

The fourth edition continues with comprehensive coverage of assessment in a single volume. To achieve this, it covers processes and procedures for assessing students at all age levels with materials for conducting assessment across a broad range of performance levels. College and university students, teachers, and others who read this text and learn the material will acquire essential knowledge and skills that will help them meet the unique assessment needs of children and youth with disabilities.

Organization of the Text

The textbook is divided into four parts. Part I, Chapters 1 through 3, provides the foundation necessary for assessing students with special needs. This section introduces assessment, covers the steps in the assessment process with special emphasis on IEPs and assessment, and includes a complete chapter on inclusive assessment.

The second part, Chapters 4 through 6, introduces practical applications and considerations in assessment including test scores and their meaning. This section explains how to select and evaluate assessment instruments and discusses procedures for giving, scoring, and interpreting tests. Practical tools, including an assessment proficiency checklist and an assessment instrument review guide, appear in this section of the book. Part III, Chapters 7 through 13, covers general assessment considerations, including intelligence testing, evaluating student behavior, developmental assessment, and career assessment. The fourth part, Chapters 14 through 18, focuses on assessing academic achievement. This section emphasizes curriculum-based procedures including portfolio assessment. Classroom-based strategies covered in the achievement chapters include using diagnostic checklists of oral and silent reading, taking running records, and conducting error pattern analysis. Part IV also covers the information that teachers must know about norm-referenced testing of academic performance.

Helpful Supplementary Material to Accompany This Edition

Discover My Website: *Assisting Teachers with Student Assessment*

Technology is a constantly growing and changing aspect of our field that is creating a need for new content and fresh resources. To address this emerging need, I have developed an online learning environment for teachers, prospective teachers, and professors dedicated to assessing students with special needs. Discover my Website at **www.johnvenn.com.**

Instructor's Manual with Test Items

The Instructor's Manual has several useful features, including:

- A summary of each chapter with a concise overview of the content and a description of important points
- Learning activities that the instructor can use in class or out of class

- A test bank with multiple-choice and essay questions—all items are referenced to the page in the text where the content is located
- An entire section with selected checklists, guides, and forms from the text that instructors may use in class activities and assignments

Companion Website

The Companion Website at **www.prenhall.com/venn** provides additional information and interactive learning experiences with the following links for each chapter:

- An overview of the chapter
- Terms to know and the page numbers where they are defined and discussed
- Multiple-choice and essay questions for review so that students can check their comprehension
- Links to other websites and resources that have important information on the chapter topic

Acknowledgments

Many individuals deserve to receive special recognition for their contributions to the development of this book. First, I extend sincere appreciation and thanks to the following reviewers: Susan M. Bruce, Boston College; Dorota Celinska, Roosevelt University; Sharian Deering, University of North Florida; Debi Garland, Towson University; Barbara Morganfield, Southern Methodist University; and Jim Persinger, Emporia State University.

Special thanks are due to my students and colleagues who provided many valuable suggestions for improving this edition. I especially want to thank Sandra Bacchus, senior secretary at the University of North Florida, who helped with formatting the chapters. The talented, perceptive, caring, and dedicated personnel at Merrill/Prentice Hall deserve individual thanks, including Allyson Sharp, Acquisitions Editor, who provided continual support, encouragement, and guidance throughout the revision process; and Heather Fraser, Development Editor, whose knowledge, skills, commitment, creativity, problem-solving ability, and enthusiasm helped to make this fourth edition a reality. I also acknowledge the assistance provided by Kathy Burk, Editorial Assistant; Sheryl Langner, Production Editor; and Jolynn Kilburg, Project Editor.

Finally, I wish to express genuine gratitude to my children Jeffrey, Sarah, and Jason for their support and understanding during this project. However, it is my wife, Janelle, who once again should receive singular acknowledgment for her loving assistance, reassurance, loyalty, and inspirational faith. I continue to be most appreciative to her for her generous and gracious help. Janelle carefully reviewed the chapters before I submitted them, and she provided me with special assistance in developing the reflection questions. I am pleased to once again dedicate this book to her.

Teacher Preparation Classroom

**See a demo at
www.prenhall.com/teacherprep/demo**

Your Class. Their Careers. Our Future. Will your students be prepared?

We invite you to explore our new, innovative and engaging Website and all that it has to offer you, your course, and tomorrow's educators! Organized around the major courses preservice teachers take, the Teacher Preparation site provides media, student/teacher artifacts, strategies, research articles, and other resources to equip your students with the quality tools needed to excel in their courses and prepare them for their first classroom.

This ultimate online education resource is available at no cost, when packaged with a Merrill text, and will provide you and your students access to:

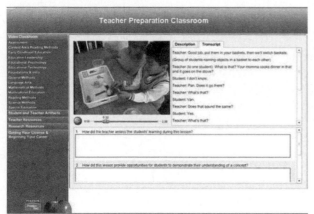

Online Video Library. More than 150 video clips—each tied to a course topic and framed by learning goals and Praxis-type questions—capture real teachers and students working in real classrooms, as well as in-depth interviews with both students and educators.

Student and Teacher Artifacts. More than 200 student and teacher classroom artifacts—each tied to a course topic and framed by learning goals and application questions—provide a wealth of materials and experiences to help make your study to become a professional teacher more concrete and hands-on.

Research Articles. Over 500 articles from ASCD's renowned journal *Educational Leadership.* The site also includes Research Navigator, a searchable database of additional educational journals.

Teaching Strategies. Over 500 strategies and lesson plans for you to use when you become a practicing professional.

Licensure and Career Tools. Resources devoted to helping you pass your licensure exam; learn standards, law, and public policies; plan a teaching portfolio; and succeed in your first year of teaching.

How to ORDER Teacher Prep for you and your students:

For students to receive a *Teacher Prep* Access Code with this text, instructors **must** provide a special value pack ISBN number on their textbook order form. To receive this special ISBN, please email **Merrill.marketing@pearsoned.com** and provide the following information:

- Name and Affiliation
- Author/Title/Edition of Merrill text

Upon ordering *Teacher Prep* for their students, instructors will be given a lifetime *Teacher Prep* Access Code.

About the Author

John Venn has over 30 years of experience as an educator and has held various positions during this time, including classroom teacher, professor, administrator, and diagnostician. John currently serves as professor in the Special Education Department at the University of North Florida. His research and writing interests focus on testing and measurement of students with special needs. He is especially interested in classroom-based assessment. John's interests extend to computers and technology as well. For example, he maintains a Website dedicated to assisting teachers with student assessment. John is deeply committed to finding solutions to the problems and issues in teacher preparation. Because of his dedication to excellence in teacher education, he spends considerable time at several schools. In the schools, he learns how teachers and schools are implementing programs in assessment, standards-based education, inclusion, and literacy instruction. John takes his school experiences back to the university, where he incorporates what he learns into his classes, curricula, and programs. To learn more about John's work in assessment and his activities in technology visit his Website at **www.johnvenn.com.**

Brief Contents

Contents

Chapter 3

Inclusive Assessment   41

PART II
Assessment Concepts and Skills   63

Chapter 4
Practical Measurement Concepts   64

Chapter 5

Test Scores and What They Mean   91

Chapter 6

Selecting and Using Assessment
Instruments   112

Chapter 9
Assessing Motor Proficiency, Perception, and Learning Styles   216

Chapter 12

Assessing Adaptive Behavior   306

Chapter 13

Career and Vocational Assessment   323

PART IV

Assessing Academic Achievement   349

Chapter 14

Assessing Academic Achievement: Curriculum-Based and Norm-Referenced Strategies   350

part I

The Assessment Process

chapter 1

Defining and Describing the Assessment of Students with Special Needs

Objectives

After reading this chapter, you will be prepared to do the following:

- Define *test*, *measurement*, and *assessment* and discuss the similarities and differences among these terms.
- Describe the effect of historical events on current assessment practices.
- Fulfill legal obligations when assessing students with special needs.
- Promote the ethical use of assessment.

Overview

Perhaps one of the most valuable tools available to the teacher of students with special needs is assessment, the process of using tests and other formal and informal means of measurement to make educational decisions. Teachers of students with disabilities need a working knowledge of assessment to effectively and efficiently address student needs and to provide a full range of appropriate educational services.

In this chapter, we investigate assessment basics beginning with the key terms, concepts, and evaluation processes. We also review the evolution of testing as it applies to students with special needs from the early 1900s through current federal legislation, and we consider legal and ethical considerations that influence present assessment practices.

From this point, we proceed in Chapter 2 to investigate the various stages of assessment, including screening, determining eligibility, educational intervention, and measuring progress. We see how the initial assessment stages differ from the subsequent stages and how all the stages connect. In Chapter 3, we explore procedures for assessing students with disabilities in inclusive settings. Chapters 4, 5, and 6 cover practical measurement concepts. In Chapters 7 through 13, we learn how to assess students specifically for intelligence, for developmental progress, for perception and motor proficiency, for classroom behavior, for adaptive behavior, and for career and vocational skills. We also learn how to use the information gathered from these tests as groundwork for building individual education programs that will guide student learning. Finally, in Chapters 14 through 18, we examine assessment of academic

achievement, including overall achievement, reading, mathematics, literacy, and special considerations related to portfolio assessment.

As you can see from this overview of the chapters, a true understanding of assessment goes far beyond giving a test to a student. This book provides that understanding. First, however, we must cover the basics—what assessment is and why it is important.

Defining Assessment

All of us know about assessment from personal experiences. We have all taken tests, ranging from teacher-made tests in the classroom to formal tests such as college entrance exams. Our skills and abilities have also been assessed with checklists, observations, and interviews. Although personal experiences help us understand the definition of assessment, personal experiences fail to convey fully the meaning of assessment.

Assessment

Broadly stated, **assessment** is the process of using measures of student performance and behavior, including tests, to make educational decisions. Assessment consists of an assortment of techniques and procedures for evaluating, estimating, appraising, testing, and drawing conclusions about students. Unlike typical assessment, assessing students with special needs takes into account unique needs; therefore, it becomes different for each student. The goal is to adapt the process to fit individual needs rather than fitting students into particular assessment procedures. For example, using an intelligence test that contains mostly language items with students who are hearing impaired or who have language problems fails to take into account unique needs. An appropriate modification in this situation involves using a specially designed intelligence test that omits verbal language items.

Reflection
When you hear the word *assessment*, what thoughts come to your mind? In your own words, write three brief phrases that describe what assessment means to you.

 To answer this reflection online, go to the *Teaching and Learning* module on the Companion Website at *www.prenhall.com/venn.*

Measurement

Measurement is the process of determining the ability or performance level of students. Testing is one type of measurement, but other measures include behavior observations, interviews, rating scales, checklists, and clinical evaluations. Teachers usually give some measures of performance (such as tests) only once, but they conduct other measures (such as observations of student behavior) repeatedly. The purpose of measurement is to produce objective information such as numbers, scores, or other quantitative data. Like testing, measurement plays a key role in the process of assessing students with disabilities.

Testing

Testing is a specific type of assessment. A **test** is usually given once, and it contains a standard set of questions. Tests produce scores, sets of scores, or some other numerical results. Most tests are given in a prescribed manner and in a structured manner. Types of tests include informal, teacher-made tests and formal, standardized tests. Many tests produce anxiety and worry among test takers. As a result, some students do not perform well on tests, in part due to nervousness and concern. Test anxiety and fear of failure is especially prevalent among students with disabilities.

☑ Check Your Comprehension

Although the terms *assessment*, *measurement*, and *testing* are often interchangeable, specific differences do exist among them. In fact, the differences actually involve the relationship of all three to one another. Assessment is the broadest term, and it subsumes measurement and testing. It involves using a variety of measures, including tests, to make educational decisions about students with disabilities. Assessment is the most general term because making educational decisions about students with special needs requires many different measurements and tests. Measurement is less general than assessment, and it includes testing as well as many other procedures for quantifying behavior and gauging student performance. Testing is the most exact term because it refers to a set of questions given once in a structured setting. Figure 1–1 illustrates the relationship between these terms. The figure shows assessment at the top because it is the most comprehensive term. Measurement appears underneath assessment. Testing is the most exact term, so it is at the bottom.

Figure 1–1
Assessment
terminology

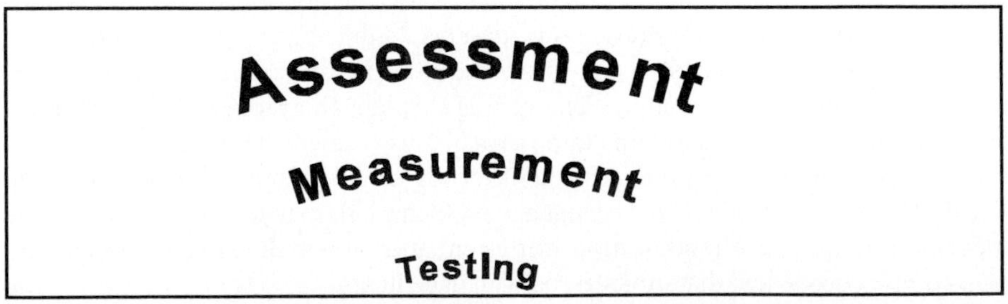

Importance of Assessment

One of the best ways to discover the importance of assessment is through the eyes of teachers, parents, and students with special needs. The following narrative sketches illustrate the importance of assessment in the lives of real people.

Shamikah's mother, Ms. Tisdale, was scared and worried because of her daughter's behavior problems in school. Shamikah often brought home notes describing behaviors such as disturbing other students, refusing to complete work, and other disruptions. Shamikah also brought home incomplete and incorrect papers. Ms. Tisdale, although unsure about the source of the problem, wanted to do something about it.

Shamikah's teacher, Ms. Garcia, was also concerned about Shamikah's behavior and grades, so she scheduled a conference with Ms. Tisdale to discuss the situation. At the conference, the teacher suggested referring Shamikah for assessment to help determine the nature and extent of her problem. The assessment results revealed that Shamikah was performing significantly below average in academic achievement. More important, the results indicated that Shamikah had a visual processing deficit, which explained much of her difficulty with tasks such as copying from the board, completing worksheets, and reading. After reviewing the results, the mother and the teacher agreed that Shamikah's academic and behavior problems were due, in part, to her visual processing deficits.

Based on the assessment, Ms. Garcia implemented instructional modifications to accommodate Shamikah's visual learning deficiencies. Shamikah also received assistance from a special education teacher, and Ms. Tisdale arranged for tutoring after school. As a result of these changes, the teachers and the parent noticed improvements in Shamikah's academic performance and behavior, although she still experienced problems from time to time.

This scenario illustrates the importance of assessment in identifying a student's learning problems and in selecting instructional intervention strategies that respond to specific problems. The following vignette illustrates the importance of assessment in meeting the needs of a student with a severe disability.

Juan was born with Down syndrome, a condition that causes severe mental retardation. Knowing Juan's condition, the special education teacher used assessment to develop an individualized family service plan for Juan when he enrolled in a preschool program at age 3. Assessment assisted the teacher in identifying Juan's current levels of performance, selecting priorities for educational intervention, developing learning objectives, and measuring progress.

In these sketches, assessment played a key role in identifying learning problems and in developing intervention strategies. In both cases, assessment was essential in developing appropriate individualized education programs. Although not all situations are resolved so easily, the cases of Shamikah and Juan illustrate the importance of assessment and demonstrate that understanding assessment is critical for teachers of students with disabilities.

Assessment Influences

The process of assessing learners with special needs includes a complex and far-reaching collection of procedures and practices that reflects the influence of a

Reflection
What are some ways teachers can use assessment to either hinder or help a student's performance?

To answer this reflection online, go to the *Teaching and Learning* module on the Companion Website at *www.prenhall.com/venn.*

Figure 1–2   Assessment influences

number of disciplines and points of view. Indeed, the variety of influences affecting assessment accounts for the complexity and multiplicity of the process. For example, many tests in the assessment pool originated from models designed in other disciplines; this accounts for the diversity of instruments. In addition, federal laws and state procedures that mandate assessment practices, along with the ethical obligations and professional standards that dictate professional concerns, complicate the assessment process significantly. Furthermore, assessment includes implementation of a storehouse of formal and informal measures appropriate to different levels of evaluation. This requires a multilayered structure, which belies the simplicity of a single test. A summary of assessment influences appears in Figure 1–2.

Historical Perspective

One of the best ways to understand assessment influences is to examine assessment from a historical perspective. The history of assessing students with special needs encompasses contributions from many disciplines, including psychology, medicine, and educational measurement. Court decisions and federal laws have also shaped assessment. Ethical obligations and professional standards are another important contributing factor. Contemporary assessment has emerged from these influences. A list of historical landmarks appears in Table 1–1. This is followed by a discussion of the historical significance of each landmark.

Table 1–1   Historical Landmarks

Intelligence Testing

1905   Binet and Simon published the first intelligence test, which later became the Stanford-Binet Intelligence Scale.

1908   The revised Binet and Simon Intelligence Test introduced the concept of mental age.

1949   Wechsler published the Wechsler Intelligence Scale for Children (WISC), the first edition of what has become the foremost intelligence test.

2003   Roid authored the Stanford–Binet Intelligence Scale, Fifth Edition.

2003   Wechsler developed the Wechsler Intelligence Scale for Children, Fourth Edition Integrated.

Testing Groups

1914   The U.S. Army used the Army Alpha and Army Beta tests in World War I, marking the first widespread use of a group intelligence test.

1923   The Stanford Achievement Test (SAT) was published. This was the first widely used group achievement test.

1933   The California Achievement Test, a group achievement test, was published.

1936   The Iowa Test of Basic Skills, a group achievement test, was published.

Assessing Adaptive Behavior

1935   Doll published the Genetic Scale of Social Maturity, a measure of adaptive behavior.

1984   Sparrow, Balla, and Cicchetti published the most recent revision of this instrument, titled the Vineland Adaptive Behavior Scales.

Developmental Assessment

1941   Gesell and Armatruda published Developmental Diagnosis, containing one of the original developmental scales for children from birth to 6 years of age.

Individual Diagnosis and Prescription

1876   Seguin, a medical doctor who developed diagnostic procedures for assessing children with disabilities, established one of the first professional organizations for individuals with disabilities, now known as the American Association on Mental Retardation.

Assessing Individual Achievement

1959   Dunn wrote the original Peabody Picture Vocabulary Test (PPVT), an individually administered test of receptive language vocabulary. The PPVT was the prototype for other individually administered tests.

Table 1–1 *continued*

1970	Dunn and Markwardt created the first edition of the Peabody Individual Achievement Test (PIAT).
1971	Connolly, Nachtman, and Pritchett published the first version of the KeyMath Diagnostic Test of Arithmetic, a comprehensive inventory of essential mathematics.
1998	The American Guidance Service published new editions of the PPVT, the KeyMath Diagnostic Test of Arithmetic, and the Peabody Individual Achievement Test.

Assessing Behavior

1968	B. F. Skinner, the preeminent behavioral psychologist, published *The Technology of Teaching*. Skinner's behavior modification techniques led to the development of behavioral assessment procedures.

Nonbiased Assessment

1978	Mercer introduced the System of Multicultural Pluralistic Assessment (SOMPA). Mercer's assessment approach includes consideration of sociocultural and health factors as an integral part of the assessment process.

Curriculum-Based Assessment

1982	Gronlund wrote about developing curriculum-based assessment procedures using teacher-made tests that offer high accuracy and validity.
1985	Blankenship described the use of curriculum-based assessment data to make instructional decisions.

Inclusive Assessment

1975	The term *mainstreaming* emerged and gained general usage with the passage of Public Law 94–142 in 1975. Mainstreaming grew out of the least restrictive environment requirement in the law.
1985	The Regular Education Initiative (REI), a proposal advocating that general education accept primary responsibility for educating students with disabilities, was introduced. REI called for significant changes in assessment practices for students with special needs.
1988	The concept of inclusion was introduced. Inclusion calls for placing students with disabilities in general education classrooms in neighborhood schools.
1997	The Individuals with Disabilities Education Act of 1997 (IDEA) mandated the participation of students with disabilities in statewide testing programs with accommodations as necessary. IDEA also required Individualized Education Programs (IEPs) to include an explanation of the extent to which a student will not participate in general education.

Information Technology and Assessment

1978	Apple introduced the floppy disk drive, allowing Apple II users to store information including assessment data on something other than cumbersome and unreliable tape cassettes.
1981	IBM introduced the IBM PC, a product that validated the PC as a legitimate education tool for instruction and assessment.
1985	Weiss published a paper on adaptive testing by computer.
1999	The percentage of schools connected to the Internet reached 95%.

Intelligence Testing

The development of intelligence tests was a major historical contribution to assessing students with special needs. In 1905 Alfred Binet, a psychologist, and Theodore Simon, a physician, published the first effective intelligence test. Used in French schools to identify students who could not benefit from educational instruction, the test consisted mostly of verbal items, including (1) naming objects and pictures of objects, (2) supplying missing words at the end of simple sentences, and (3) answering questions such as "What is the thing to do when you are sleepy?" and "What do you do when you are cold?"

When Binet and Simon published an expanded and revised edition of this test in 1908, they introduced the concept of mental age as a way of reporting test results. Roid developed the most recent revision of this test, the Stanford–Binet Intelligence Scales, Fifth Edition, in 2003. Although the Stanford–Binet is still in widespread use, the Wechsler Intelligence Scale for Children, Fourth Edition Integrated (WISC-IV Integrated) (Wechsler, 2003) is currently the most frequently used test of this type. First published in 1949 as the Wechsler Intelligence Scale for Children (WISC), the WISC built on the Binet–Simon intelligence-measuring procedure by adding a wider variety of items and providing separate scores for individual parts of the test.

Assessing Large Groups

The U.S. Army first introduced the practice of assessing large groups during World War I when millions of recruits took the Army Alpha and Army Beta mental ability tests. Literate recruits took the Alpha test, and illiterate recruits took the Beta test. Army staffing specialists used the results to place the recruits in various roles. Those receiving high scores received training for technical jobs or served as officers, whereas those with low scores became foot soldiers.

Although the testing was an overall success, a major problem surfaced. The authors failed to consider ethnic and cultural diversity in selecting items or interpreting results. Consequently, the tests were unfair to soldiers from minority groups and to those with limited English proficiency. This meant that some men received low scores due to test bias rather than low ability. Despite the significant bias problem, this was the first time in history that large groups of people were placed according to their test scores. Eventually, psychometricians refined and expanded these initial mental ability tests for use during World War II. In addition, specialists developed other types of group tests after World War I, including the first of the group achievement tests.

Published in 1923, the Stanford Achievement Test (SAT) was the original large-group achievement test. Two similar tests, the California Achievement Test and the Iowa Test of Basic Skills, appeared in 1933 and 1936, respectively. These timed tests use multiple-choice questions to measure attainment of academic skills such as reading, math, and language. Measuring the achievement of large groups of students with paper-and-pencil tests is standard procedure today. Similarly, business, industry, and government now routinely use large-group tests for a variety of purposes.

Assessing Adaptive Behavior

Adaptive behavior is the ability to adapt to the environment by developing independent personal and social behavior and by adjusting to changes in the environment.

Unlike the concept of intelligence, which focuses on mental abilities, and the concept of achievement, which focuses on academic abilities, adaptive behavior concentrates on functional and practical abilities such as communication, activities of daily living, and social interaction. In 1935, Doll used the Genetic Scale of Social Maturity to introduce the concept of assessing the adaptive behavior of children and adults with mental retardation. Over the years, this scale has remained one of the most widely used measures of adaptive functioning. Sparrow, Balla, and Cicchetti published the current revision of the instrument, the Vineland Adaptive Behavior Scales, in 1984. The ideas introduced by Doll are still in widespread use, and many instruments for assessing functional and practical abilities are available.

Developmental Assessment

Developmental psychologists introduced the notion of assessing the developmental skills of young children from birth through 6 years of age. These psychologists included a group at Yale who studied the developmental patterns of young children and found a remarkably predictable sequence of skill development and learning. In 1941, Gesell and Armatruda, two psychologists in the Yale group, published Developmental Diagnosis. This test measured development in motor, language, personal–social, and adaptive skills. This work inspired others to design additional scales. A large number and variety of developmental scales are now available.

Individual Diagnosis and Prescription

Pioneers from many disciplines, especially medicine, developed the assessment concept of individual diagnosis and prescription. Early work by physicians established clinical procedures for diagnosing disabilities that cause mental retardation, physical handicaps, and health impairments. Edouard O. Seguin, a medical doctor, played a major role in developing these diagnostic procedures. In 1876, Seguin helped to establish the American Association for the Study of the Feebleminded, one of the first professional organizations for individuals with disabilities. This organization later became the American Association on Mental Deficiency (AAMD) and it is now the American Association on Mental Retardation (AAMR).

More recently, medical doctors and physical and occupational therapists have created new methods for individual diagnosis and treatment of neurological disorders. Individual diagnosis and instruction is a cornerstone of assessing students with disabilities. The process resembles the procedures physicians follow in diagnosing and treating medical conditions. Physicians observe the patient's symptoms, conduct medical tests to diagnose the cause, and then write prescriptions to treat the condition. In a similar way, teachers of students with special needs use individual diagnosis and prescription to develop individual instructional plans based on observation and other forms of assessment. Both physicians and teachers rely on direct observation as well as tests and other measures in the assessment process. In both cases, they use assessment to meet individual needs.

Individual Achievement Testing

Special educators established procedures for individual diagnosis and prescription using individually administered tests of academic achievement with the introduction of two tests: the Peabody Individual Achievement Test (PIAT) (Dunn & Markwardt, 1970), and the KeyMath Diagnostic Test of Arithmetic (Connolly, Nachtman, & Pritchett, 1971). These tests and other similar measures gave diagnosticians and teachers formal tools for assessing individual learning needs and developing specific intervention objectives. Unlike group achievement tests, which report results as test scores and general levels of performance, these individually administered tests provide specific data and information for diagnosing remediation needs and for prescribing explicit intervention activities. Many teachers of students with special needs use the current versions of the PIAT (Markwardt, 1998) and the KeyMath (Connolly, 1998).

In 1959, Lloyd Dunn created the Peabody Picture Vocabulary Test, the prototype for the PIAT, the KeyMath, and other individually administered tests. Special educators, psychologists, and speech pathologists use the current edition of the Peabody Picture Vocabulary Test, Third Edition (PPVT-III) (Dunn & Dunn, 1997) to measure the receptive language vocabulary skills of students.

These instruments are significant, in part, because they were among the first tests developed by special educators for use with students who have disabilities. These assessment tools illustrate the importance of individual rather than group testing for students with special needs.

Assessing Behavior

Behavioral psychologists contributed the idea of assessing behavior over time using direct observation and continuous data collection. B. F. Skinner was the pioneer among these psychologists. The discipline was in its infancy in the late 1920s when Skinner shaped behavioral psychology as both a science and a philosophy. Skinner's voluminous research and writings included a book entitled *The Technology of Teaching* (1968). In this book, Skinner described a behavioral approach to education emphasizing direct assessment of student behavior by charting rather than indirect assessment using pencil-and-paper testing. Skinner also recommended developing teaching machines to provide information in small, well-sequenced steps, to give immediate feedback, and to measure progress continuously. Computers now perform many of the functions of Skinner's teaching machines.

Evaluation techniques based on Skinner's principles have become an integral part of assessing students with behavior problems. The behavioral approach utilizes direct observation rather than indirect testing. Direct observation involves listening to or watching a student over time in a structured, systematic manner. Direct observation incorporates repeated measurement of performance rather than one-time testing. This type of assessment provides a more realistic and practical picture of behavior than indirect testing. Examples of inexpensive and unobtrusive behavioral assessment techniques include keeping progress graphs, teaching students how to chart their own performance, counting incidents of misbehavior to establish a baseline, and using audio- and videotapes to measure change in behavior over time.

Bias in Assessment

Bias in assessment has been a critical concern for some time. One of the most significant historical contributions to reducing bias is an approach called the System of Multicultural Pluralistic Assessment (SOMPA) developed by Jane Mercer (Mercer & Lewis, 1978). SOMPA evaluates language and cultural differences as an integral part of the assessment process and attempts to minimize racial and cultural bias in measuring learning ability. SOMPA accomplishes this goal by enabling evaluators to consider sociocultural and health factors in estimating learning potential.

SOMPA includes two major components and requires administration by a team of certified professionals. A social worker gives the parent interview components to the pri-

MULTICULTURAL CONSIDERATIONS

Bias in Assessment

Since the introduction of the original group tests, the problem of bias in testing has appropriately received a great deal of attention. The bias problem applies to individuals whose experiences and culture differ from those of the general population. In a concerted effort to eliminate bias, the major test publishers now invest significant resources in making their tests fair for members of diverse groups. This includes individuals from ethnic and linguistic minority groups and students with disabilities. Significant progress has been made in finding solutions to the issues related to deciding what test modifications yield the most accurate and equitable decisions for all. However, much more needs to be done to ensure that assessment is as fair and unbiased as possible. Further discussion with specific information about fairness in testing appears in later chapters.

Use your own words to develop a definition of bias in testing. Explain your definition and give examples to support your view.

 To answer this reflection online, go to the *Multicultural Considerations* module on the Companion Website at **www.prenhall.com/venn**.

mary caregiver in the home. A psychologist or educational diagnostician gives assessment components to the student in a school setting. In addition to using the resulting test scores in a traditional manner, SOMPA also uses an innovative scoring system that accounts for social and cultural differences. This creative system produces an estimated learning potential score. The estimated learning potential score compares the student with other students who have similar backgrounds. Mercer makes a compelling argument for the use of culturally sensitive assessment measures such as these to reduce bias.

   Assessment approaches such as SOMPA have been especially helpful in protecting students, especially students from minority groups, from incorrect diagnosis. When Mercer introduced SOMPA in the late 1970s, it provided a procedure for responding to a major bias-in-testing issue: the disproportionate number of students from minority groups who receive low scores on ability tests. Additional information about the problem of bias in testing appears in Multicultural Considerations.

Curriculum-Based Assessment

Curriculum-based assessment is an evaluation approach that measures performance based on progress in the curriculum rather than in relation to scores on tests. Also referred to as authentic assessment or performance assessment, curriculum-based assessment relies on teacher-made tests, classwork, homework assignments, and teacher impressions to formulate assessment decisions. In 1982, Gronlund wrote about developing curriculum-based assessment procedures using teacher-made tests that offer high accuracy and validity. In 1985, Blankenship described the use of curriculum-based assessment data to make instructional decisions. The primary advantage of curriculum based assessment is its ability to evaluate student performance in direct relation to what has been taught in the curriculum. Teachers of students with disabilities are especially interested in this type of assessment because it provides a direct link between evaluation and instruction.

Inclusive Assessment

Inclusion involves participation of children and youth with disabilities in the general education classroom and in the general curriculum with appropriate aids and services. Inclusion is a controversial issue, with some advocating full inclusion of all students and others supporting inclusive placement as one alternative in a continuum of services. The inclusion movement can be traced to mainstreaming, which emerged with the passage of Public Law 94–142 in 1975 and the Regular Education Initiative (REI) introduced in 1985. **Mainstreaming** refers to retaining students with disabilities in the "mainstream" of education rather than placing them in separate programs. REI encouraged general education to accept primary responsibility for educating students with disabilities (Davis, 1989). The initiative called for radical change in the treatment of students with special needs and contained two key elements: complete integration of students with disabilities into regular classes and removal of labels for students with disabilities (Kauffman, 1989).

Inclusive education has resulted in new opportunities for special educators to share and expand their expertise. Skill in assessing students with disabilities in inclusive settings has become essential for all educators. For this reason, this book includes a complete chapter on inclusion designed to help you acquire a knowledge base in this increasingly important subject.

Information Technology

Widespread use of computers and related electronic technology has produced an information technology transformation in assessment, in education, and in society in general. This transformation has historical roots in the introduction of the floppy disk drive on the Apple II computer in 1978. The floppy disk allowed users to store information, including assessment data, on something other than cumbersome and unreliable tape cassettes. In 1981, IBM introduced its version of the personal computer. The IBM PC validated the computer as a legitimate education tool for instruction and assessment.

In 1985, Weiss published an article about adaptive testing by computer. Adaptive assessment procedures have since become commonplace, and they are an example of the transformation taking place in information technology. Information about computer adaptive testing appears in the Technology Focus box and in Chapter 14. More recently, most schools have connected their computers to networks with access to the Internet and to other services such as e-mail. Networking enables new forms of computer-based assessment that help teachers help students. Information technology innovations such as adaptive testing and networking are changing the way teachers assess their students.

Teachers are already using test-generation programs, IEP writing software, computer-based behavior assessment programs, grading software, and many other digital tools to help students with special needs. In the future, we can expect widespread use of computer adaptive testing, multimedia assessment, online testing, computer-based test interpretation, and other advanced information technology assessment processes and procedures.

Reflection
Information technology has already changed teaching and assessment in many ways. What future changes do you foresee?

 To answer this reflection online, go to the *Teaching and Learning* module on the Companion Website at *www.prenhall.com/venn*.

TECHNOLOGY FOCUS

Computer Adaptive Testing (CAT)

Computer adaptive testing (CAT) is a recent advance in computer administration that enables interaction between the test and the test taker. D. J. Weiss (1985) was one of the first specialists in assessment to write about this technological innovation. CAT matches a test's difficulty with a test taker's ability. By interacting with test takers, adaptive tests provide an optimal number of test items for each test taker. CAT produces a different set of test items for each test taker based on the test taker's responses. For example, when a test taker correctly answers an item, the test responds by providing a more difficult item. In contrast, when a test taker answers incorrectly, the test adapts by giving an easier item. Adaptive tests use fewer items than conventional tests, and this makes them faster, easier to take, and more accurate. As more adaptive test development programs become available for personal computers, teachers will be able to use them to great advantage with students who have special needs.

☑ Check Your Comprehension

Significant contributions by professionals from many disciplines, including medicine, psychology, and educational measurement, have shaped current assessment practices with students who have learning difficulties. For example, Binet and Simon developed the concept of intelligence and published the first effective intelligence test in 1905. Similarly, U.S. Army psychologists first introduced procedures for assessing large groups during World War I. This led to the development of the Stanford Achievement Test and other large-group tests. In the 1800s, pioneers such as Seguin introduced clinical procedures for individual diagnosis and prescriptive treatment. Lloyd Dunn, a special educator, created the prototype for individually administered testing with the publication of the Peabody Picture Vocabulary Test (PPVT) in 1959. Finally, behavioral psychologists, including B. F. Skinner, created procedures for assessing performance using direct observation and continuous data collection techniques. These contributions provided the foundation for contemporary assessment practices and procedures for students with special needs. Improvements and innovations such as curriculum-based assessment and assessment in inclusive settings continue.

Legal Considerations

Several federal laws have influenced assessment of students with special needs. Protecting the privacy of the student and the family in connection with assessment in general and testing in particular is one of the major legal and ethical considerations. Both the Family and Educational Rights and Privacy Act (FERPA) and the Individuals with Disabilities Education Act (IDEA) affirm the right to privacy by carefully limiting legal access to a student's test scores and results. In addition, IDEA requires schools to obtain specific permission from the parents or legal guardian before testing to determine eligibility for special education. Finally, the requirements of the

Table 1–2 Federal Legislation

Law	Impact
Family and Educational Rights and Privacy Act	Guarantees privacy and access rights for students and parents
Individuals with Disabilities Education Act (IDEA)	Requires permission for testing, mandates an IEP, and calls for participation in general education
Infants and Toddlers Program	Requires assessing family needs and developing an individual family service plan

Infants and Toddlers Program, which is part of IDEA, mandate assessment of family needs and the development of an individual family service plan (IFSP). A summary of these legal requirements appears in Table 1–2.

IDEA

IDEA is the acronym for the Individuals with Disabilities Education Act. Under this federal law, millions of students with disabilities receive special education services. The services include early intervention for infants and toddlers and special education through school systems for children and youth from age 3 through 21. These programs and services are vital in helping children and youth with disabilities grow, develop, learn, achieve, and succeed, and they include an array of tests and assessments. However, the IDEA is not a static law. It has changed over time as we learn more about the education and support services students with disabilities need, and what school systems need in order to respond. Many factors influence changes in the law over time, including an ongoing dialogue on possible reforms among politicians, policy makers, and advocates (National Dissemination Center for Children, 2004).

The IDEA has a long history beginning with the original law passed by Congress in 1975. The IDEA substantially changed in 1997, and some of the changes had to do with testing and assessment. These included new requirements for participation of students with disabilities in state and district assessment (testing) programs, and more flexibility in conducting reevaluations. The most recent reauthorization of the IDEA (IDEA, 2004) also contains significant changes that impact how we test and evaluate students with special needs. These changes include the following:

- Paperwork reduction eliminates many of the requirements for developing short-term learning objectives in the IEP process. Chapter 2 details the specifics of the IEP process, including the newest requirements.
- Changes in the requirements for reevaluations providing additional flexibility designed to meet student needs.

Ethical Considerations and Professional Standards

In addition to understanding the legal mandates for assessment, teachers should also be familiar with the ethical considerations and professional standards. The *Standards for Educational and Psychological Testing*, published by the American Educational Research Association (1999), includes comprehensive descriptions of ethics in testing. The *Code of Professional Responsibilities in Educational Measurement*, published by the National Council on Measurement in Education (Schmeiser, Geisinger, Johnson-Lewis, Roeber, & Schafer, 1995), is another excellent source of information on the ethical responsibilities of professionals who develop and use tests. The eight areas in the Code describe professional assessment responsibilities of those who: develop; market and sell; select; administer; score; interpret, use, and communicate results; educate; and evaluate programs and conduct research. The standards from these professional organizations include guidelines that explain many of the basic assessment principles, including permission for testing, the privacy of test results, and the importance of standardized administration procedures.

The *Standards for Educational and Psychological Testing* contains an entire section on testing individuals with disabilities. This section focuses on the accommodations, modifications, and adaptations needed when testing students with special needs. Specific accommodation strategies include standards for modifying and adapting test administration, media, timing, settings, and content.

Recent advances in knowledge, practices, and social policies have resulted in more inclusive participation of individuals with disabilities in education and employment. These advances have raised new assessment issues and created considerable debate. In particular, many questions are associated with modified administration of large-scale standardized tests for students with disabilities. The problem is that in the past, score reports from some large-scale standardized tests included an asterisk next to the score report or some other designation or flag that denoted modified test administration. The controversy centers around the efficacy of adding a flag on a test score to indicate an accommodation for a disability. Such flags conflict with legal and social policy regarding fairness in testing individuals with disabilities. For this reason, score reports from modified administrations should avoid flags or other indicators in most situations.

Permission for Testing   Specific regulations for obtaining permission for testing appear in the federal regulations for implementing the IDEA. This legislation refers to testing used selectively to determine if a student has a disability and to identify needs for special education and related services. It excludes basic tests given to all students in a school, grade, or class. The IDEA requires the school to fully inform parents of all information relevant to the testing. Parents must receive the information in their native language or in another appropriate mode of communication. The parents must give informed written consent for testing prior to the evaluation. Furthermore, parents must understand that granting of consent for testing is voluntary on their part and may be revoked at any time.

Specific regulations regarding permission for testing such as those in IDEA apply in many testing situations. In fact, obtaining permission for testing is one of the broad principles of assessment that is widely accepted and often mandated by law. Even when permission is not required, test givers should make sure that test takers have relevant information regarding the testing. This means that the test giver is responsible for ensuring that test takers understand relevant information about the test, such as the purpose for testing, the type of testing, and the application of the test results (Schmeiser et al., 1995).

Privacy of Test Results   Ensuring the privacy of test results is another of the basic assessment standards. This standard prohibits the release of test results identified by the names of individual test takers to any person or institution without the permission of the test taker, parent, or legal guardian. The need for privacy also includes test results on file that should be protected from inappropriate disclosure (Schmeiser et al., 1995).

Standardized Test Administration   In order to ensure accurate results, tests should be given and scored using the developer's instructions. For this reason, virtually all formal tests are standardized with specific administration and scoring procedures. It is important for test givers to carefully follow the standard procedures including the protocols for giving instructions, setting time limits, presenting the test items, and using test materials. Though standardized procedures should be followed whenever possible, test givers sometimes have situations in which it is advisable or legally mandated to modify the administration. This includes testing students with some disabilities and students with limited proficiency in the language of the test. In these and other situations appropriate accommodations may be needed. For students with disabilities the IEP is the document that specifies the appropriate accommodations in testing for individual students (American Educational Research Association, 1999). Information about specific accommodations in testing appears in Chapter 3.

✓ Check Your Comprehension

Federal legislation, along with various ethical concerns, makes assessing students with disabilities particularly complex and demanding. Because laws and ethics are vital to protect the rights of students, teachers of students with learning problems must understand and apply them. When teachers do this, students are safeguarded from the potentially negative effects of testing.

Summary

Assessment, the use of tests and other measures to make educational decisions, is an elaborate process with a multifaceted structure. Contributions from specialists representing many disciplines account for much of the diversity in the assessment process. Specific legal mandates and ethical considerations further contribute to the complex nature of assessment. For this reason, a generic model fails to meet unique needs; therefore, appropriately assessing students with special needs requires a combination of approaches to fit the individual and to provide accurate data for making educational decisions. Because it is so complicated, those who serve students with special needs should be well versed in available assessment procedures and the appropriateness of those procedures in given situations. Assessment can have a significant positive or negative effect on the lives of students. Therefore, it is imperative to understand assessment procedures, select appropriate measurement instruments, conduct assessment skillfully, and make proper educational decisions. Assessment is an essential tool for providing the best possible education and related services to those who require and are entitled to them.

 To check your comprehension of chapter contents, go to the *Quiz* module in Chapter 1 of the Companion Website, *www.prenhall.com/venn*.

Meeting Performance Standards and Preparing for Licensure Exams

The Council for Exceptional Children (CEC) has established a Common Core of Knowledge and Skills Essential for All Beginning Special Education Teachers. Organized in 10 domain areas, the CEC developed these standards in collaboration with several other professional groups and organizations, including the Interstate New Teacher Assessment and Support Consortium (INTASC). The CEC Standards also serve as the basis for curriculum content in teacher preparation programs approved by the National

Council for the Accreditation of Teacher Education (NCATE). In addition, the PRAXIS™ tests, developed by the Educational Testing Service (ETS), assess content knowledge related to the CEC Standards. The PRAXIS™ tests in special education are part of the Subject Assessment/Specialty Area Tests of the PRAXIS™ Series of Professional Assessments for Beginning Teachers. Although teacher licensure and certification standards vary from state to state, all special educators should demonstrate the competencies in the CEC Standards and the PRAXIS™ material. In addition, many states require passing one or more PRAXIS™ tests as part of certifying and licensing special education teachers.

Through agreements with CEC and ETS, Performance Standards for Special Education Teachers sections appear at the end of each chapter in the text. These sections specify the CEC Standards and the PRAXIS™ material that link to content covered in the chapters. The PRAXIS™ material is from the Education of Exceptional Students: Core Content Knowledge test. Look for the Performance Standards sections at the end of each chapter in the text. The CEC Standards and PRAXIS™ material listed next connects with significant content in Chapter 1. The information in parentheses identifies where to find the particular standard in the CEC Standards and the content reference in the PRAXIS™ materials.

CEC Standards for Beginning Special Education Teachers
- Basic terminology used in assessment (CC8K1)
- Legal provisions and ethical principles regarding assessment of individuals (CC8K2)
- Historical points of view and contribution of culturally diverse groups (CC1K8)
- Historical foundations, classic studies, major contributors, major legislation, and current issues related to knowledge and practice (IC1K2)

PRAXIS™ Education of Exceptional Students: Core Content Knowledge
- Federal laws and legal issues related to special education, including Public Law 105–17 (IDEA 97) (0353 I)
- Historical movements/trends affecting the connections between special education and the larger society (0353 II)
- Assessment, including use of assessment for screening, diagnosis, placement, and the making of instructional decisions (0353 III)

chapter 2

Steps in the
Assessment Process

Objectives

After reading this chapter, you will be prepared to do the following:

- Assess students to screen for potential learning problems.
- Assess students to determine eligibility for special services.
- Integrate assessment into the IEP process.
- Use assessment as part of instructional intervention.
- Use assessment to measure student progress.

Overview

Assessing students with special needs occurs in several steps and consists of multiple layers. In this chapter, we investigate the different steps in the process. Our study begins with assessment as it relates to screening students. Next, we study the process of determining eligibility for special services. We also focus on the relationship between assessment and individual educational plans (IEPs). The IEP information includes quality indicators for IEP assessment and sample IEPs with evaluation criteria and appraisal procedures. Later in the chapter, we consider the kinds of assessment associated with instructional intervention and measuring student progress. This step-by-step examination will help you understand the complex, multifaceted layers in assessment. Our study also provides the basis for learning about specific appraisal procedures and tests in later chapters. This chapter includes four case studies, one for each step in the process. These biographical cases link assessment theory and instructional practice. Later chapters refer to these cases; therefore, these profiles establish the foundation for more specific information in subsequent chapters.

The Assessment Process

Each step in the assessment process has different goals and produces specific types of data or information. Because assessment is so complex, overlap among stages occurs with certain procedures and tests. Despite this overlap, grouping assessment into stages produces an orderly sequence that matches the steps taken to identify students with special needs and provides appropriate intervention for those students who qualify for services.

The first step, screening to identify potential problems needing further assessment, naturally leads to the second stage, called determining eligibility. This stage

occurs when screening reveals a problem requiring additional evaluation. It is the testing and assessment during eligibility that helps identify students who qualify for special education and related services. After identifying students as disabled and arranging to provide appropriate services, the next step is to obtain the assessment data needed to develop an instructional intervention program. The final phase in the process is measuring student progress, which includes assessing student performance and monitoring program effectiveness. A description of the purpose of each step appears in Table 2–1.

The Screening Process

Many assessment activities occur as part of the **screening process**, including the procedures schools must follow to identify students with potential learning problems. School screening begins when a professional or a parent observes a student whose

Table 2–1   Steps in the Assessment Process

Step	Purpose	Assessment Question
Screening	To identify general performance levels	Does a potential problem exist requiring further assessment?
Determining eligibility	To decide who qualifies for services	Does the student have a disability?
Instructional intervention	To obtain data for making instructional decisions	What interventions are appropriate? What are the intervention priorities?
Measuring progress	To assess performance; to see if the student is achieving IEP goals; to monitor program effectiveness	Is the student making progress? Do the services meet the student's needs?

performance or behavior is so different that it causes significant concern. In most cases, teachers make the initial referral. The purpose of screening is to determine if a student's general level of performance or behavior falls outside average or normal ranges. Screening helps alert parents and professionals to students who may have serious learning or behavior problems. Like all assessment processes, screening relies on specialized tests and evaluation procedures. These assessments provide a sketch or an overall picture of performance rather than a detailed analysis. Screening focuses on one question: Does a potential problem exist that requires further attention? The screening process takes many forms, including use of the following:

Formal screening tests
Informal screening checklists, scales, and inventories
Observations of behavior, speech, and language
Vision and hearing test results
Medical reports
Progress records
Intervention records
Educational history
Attendance history
Parent contacts and conferences

Special Considerations and Precautions

Like all assessment, screening requires consideration of many factors. Screeners must take special precautions to protect students during the process. Peterson (1987) and Gargiulo and Kilgo (2000) identified the following considerations and precautions:

- The best screening programs check all aspects of child growth and development and include follow-up services. Without follow-up services, screening serves no practical purpose. Child Find is perhaps the best example of a screening program that meets these criteria. All states offer Child Find services, including screening programs designed to identify students with special needs and to arrange for follow-up services in response to identified needs.
- Screeners should plan specific procedures based on the number and the ages of the children (individual, small-group, or large-group screening).
- Screeners should use suitable surroundings. Familiar environments may help children feel most comfortable.
- Screeners should carefully consider cultural and language factors including ethnic or racial background, native language, geographic region (urban, suburban, or rural), and family income level.
- Screeners should ensure that screening is part of a continuum of services including diagnostic follow-up assessment and treatment or intervention.
- Professionals should be aware of and responsive to family concerns.
- Parents or guardians must receive enough information to ensure their full participation in the screening process.
- Professionals must avoid labeling as a result of the screening. Classification and labeling should occur only after comprehensive assessment.

Child-Study Teams

Most schools rely on a core team of professionals, often called **child-study teams**, to coordinate screening and other activities associated with identifying students with special needs. Prereferral teams, teacher assistance teams, and student assistance teams are other names for these groups of professionals. The teams usually consist of a school administrator, a counselor, general education teachers, and special education teachers. Referrals to child-study teams put into motion a series of screening activities, including the following:

- Observing student behavior
- Meeting with parents
- Documenting intervention efforts
- Administering screening tests
- Completing behavior rating scales

After completing these screening activities, child-study teams review the data and decide whether to forward the case as a referral to a staffing team. If a child-study team sends a referral forward, the staffing team conducts comprehensive eligibility testing to determine if the student qualifies for special education and related services or for other special services such as those provided under Title 1 and Section 504.

Screening Instruments

Screening instruments are brief, easy-to-administer tests, rating scales, checklists, and direct observation techniques given individually or in groups. Because they provide an overview or a sketch of behavior rather than a detailed analysis, screening instruments measure performance with a limited number of items. Limiting the items makes it possible to administer screening instruments in a short time. Evaluators usually need about 15 or 20 minutes to give and score a screening test, fill out a rating scale, complete a checklist, or record the results of a direct observation session.

Limitations of Screening

Screening tests measure overall performance rather than specific strengths and weaknesses. For this reason, professionals must avoid using screening tests in place of comprehensive assessment. Instead, screening helps to identify students who need more in-depth assessment and obtain ideas about where to begin intervention while awaiting comprehensive diagnostic evaluation.

Reflection
As a teacher, what behaviors do you see that would lead to a recommendation for screening?

 To answer this reflection online, go to the *Teaching and Learning* module on the Companion Website at *www.prenhall.com/venn.*

Why Do We Screen Students?

Several reasons exist for screening students. First, when we suspect that a student may have learning problems, we use screening to confirm our observations and impressions. Second, we use screening to document that a student has a potential problem. For example, if a student receives a low score on a screening test, that low score can serve as evidence of a possible disability. Third, we use screening as the basis for deciding whether to conduct more extensive evaluation to identify a student as having a particular disability. A summary of the reasons for screening students appears in Focus 2–1.

Prereferral Activities

One of the most common and important types of screening involves prereferral activities. The purpose of prereferral is to screen students with potential problems to determine the need for comprehensive testing. The following narrative documents this process.

F OCUS 2-1

Why Do We Screen Students?

- To confirm our observations and impressions
- To document potential problems
- To decide if further testing is needed

Jerrold Johnson, a bright, energetic child, has been a student at Davis Elementary School since kindergarten. Although Jerrold occasionally displays acting-out behavior, he has earned a reputation as a hard-working student who is well liked by his teachers and peers. Unfortunately, Jerrold has experienced academic difficulty in prereading and reading tasks since beginning school. Although Jerrold's mother and his teachers had noticed this, they attributed the difficulty to developmental delay and hoped he would catch up without the need for special services. Unfortunately, Jerrold continued to have reading difficulty in the second grade. Mrs. Romero, Jerrold's second-grade teacher, described Jerrold as one of the poorest readers in her class based on his reading group performance. In particular, Mrs. Romero noticed that Jerrold had the most difficulty with word recognition, such as learning new words and remembering previously learned words.

Because of his continuing reading difficulties, Mrs. Romero decided to confirm her observations and impressions by asking the school's child-study team to screen Jerrold for a possible reading disability. Mrs. Romero was familiar with the child-study team screening process and knew that the team would require specific prereferral information if she brought his case to them. This information included observations of Jerrold's behavior, evidence of meetings with parents to discuss the problem, and documentation showing that the teacher had tried educational interventions in an attempt to solve the problem.

Mrs. Romero obtained one observation of Jerrold's behavior by having another second-grade teacher observe during a reading lesson. The teacher documented her observations by writing the brief narrative that appears in Figure 2–1. Mrs. Romero obtained a second observation by asking Jerrold's first-grade teacher to complete the rating scale that appears in

Figure 2–1   Observation of behavior

Name of Student	*Jerrold*
Name of Observer	*Ms. Breslau*
Length of Observations	*55 minutes (11-2) & 40 minutes (11-4)*
Location of Observation	*Jerrold's classroom*

Observation Notes

I observed Jerrold because of his difficulty in reading. For this reason, I planned my observations during the regular morning reading lesson. Jerrold exhibited some acting-out behavior during my observations. Specifically, Jerrold seemed to become restless and distracted when he had difficulty with the assigned reading tasks. However, he tried to complete all of his work, and his overall conduct was acceptable.

Figure 2–2. The observations indicated that although Jerrold displayed occasional behavior problems, his behavior was generally acceptable.

Mrs. Romero knew that her meetings with Jerrold's mother to discuss her son's reading problems were a critical step in the referral process. She knew that she must convince Jerrold's mother to consent to any testing that might be needed if the child-study team used the screening information to recommend eligibility testing. The conference notes from Mrs. Romero's two meetings with Jerrold's mom appear in Figure 2–3.

Mrs. Romero had attempted a number of different educational interventions in an effort to help Jerrold overcome his reading problems. As part of the child-study team screening and prereferral process, she documented these attempts in a written narrative description. Her description of educational interventions appears in Figure 2–4.

After completing these screening activities, the child-study team met with Mrs. Romero to decide whether to forward the case to a staffing team for comprehensive testing. As a result of the thorough and precise screening information provided by Mrs. Romero, the team decided to recommend in-depth eligibility testing to determine if Jerrold qualified for classification as a student with a disability who could benefit from special education services to help remediate his reading difficulties.

Jerrold's case study illustrates one role of assessment in the screening process. We will revisit Jerrold's case later in this chapter as we investigate IEPs, and we will see Jerrold in Chapter 7 as we examine other types of tests.

Figure 2–2   Checklist of classroom conduct

Student _____ *Jerrold* _____

Rater _____ *Mrs. Kelly* _____

Date _____ *November 3* _____

How often did you observe these behaviors?	1 = never 5 = always				
	1	2	3	4	5
Often fidgets, squirms, or displays restlessness				✓	
Has difficulty remaining seated		✓			
Is easily distracted		✓			
Often blurts out during class		✓			
Has difficulty paying attention in class				✓	
Often talks excessively				✓	
Often interrupts others		✓			
Has difficulty listening		✓			
Often plays loudly		✓			
Other notable behavior (specify)					

Comments Jerrold was a student in my first-grade class last year. I filled out this rating scale based on his behavior in my class.

Figure 2–3 Conference notes

> **Conference One**
> **Date** November 4
> *During the conference with Mrs. Johnson, we discussed Jerrold's difficulties in reading and the educational interventions (see Figure 2-4) that we have used to help Jerrold improve his reading skills. I mentioned to Ms. Johnson that the school might ask her for permission to test Jerrold for a possible reading disability if Jerrold continued to experience difficulties.*
>
> **Conference Two**
> **Date** December 12
> *During this conference, I told Mrs. Johnson that the school was going to ask for permission to test Jerrold, and I asked her if she would sign the permission forms. Mrs. Johnson said that she would go ahead and sign the forms.*

Figure 2–4 Educational interventions

> **Intervention One**
>
> *One of the main interventions designed to help Jerrold improve his reading skills was placement in a special reading group. This group was specifically designed to have a smaller number of students so that Jerrold could receive additional help from the teacher.*
>
> **Intervention Two**
>
> *A second intervention was to provide Jerrold special help with new vocabulary words and words he was having difficulty with prior to introducing the words in Jerrold's reading group.*
>
> **Intervention Three**
>
> *Several other interventions have been provided, including special seating for Jerrold next to the teacher so he could receive extra help, assignment of a peer to help him with his reading, help from a teaching assistant 2 days a week, and special homework for Jerrold. The homework was arranged with Jerrold's mother, Mrs. Johnson. Mrs. Johnson asked for the special homework so that she could reinforce what he was learning at school.*

☑ Check Your Comprehension

Screening, the first step in the assessment process, provides a sketch or overall picture of performance focused on one question: Does a potential problem exist that requires further attention? Answering this question involves using rating scales, checklists, direct observation techniques, and brief, easy-to-administer tests. Screening helps to identify students who need in-depth assessment and to obtain ideas about where to begin intervention and what to do while awaiting comprehensive diagnostic evaluation. Comprehensive diagnostic evaluation occurs at the next level of the assessment process: deciding eligibility for special education services.

The Eligibility Process

The **eligibility process** involves determining the nature and severity of a learning problem and deciding eligibility for special education services. Federal law mandates

Reflection
Parents sometimes resist the screening process. Explain why parents might resist screening for their children.

 To answer this reflection online, go to the *Teaching and Learning* module on the Companion Website at *www.prenhall.com/venn.*

general eligibility procedures, and each state has specific regulations. For example, some states rely on the traditional classification categories such as learning disabilities, emotional disturbance, and mental retardation. Other states use generic systems with categories such as educationally handicapped and severely handicapped.

Regardless of the classification system, federal law and state regulations include specific rules concerning assessment. For example, certified specialists must conduct the testing according to specific regulations. Full parent participation is required and parents have specific rights and responsibilities. These include parent permission for testing, parent participation in meetings, and informed consent regarding classification and placement decisions. For example, in the case study involving Jerrold, the mother, Mrs. Johnson, had the right to refuse to sign the forms giving permission for testing. Without permission the school system could not have proceeded with the referral. For this reason the teacher in the case, Mrs. Romero, held special conferences with Mrs. Johnson to discuss Jerrold's reading difficulties and to describe the benefits of special services. The law also includes procedural safeguards to protect parents and their children. These safeguards include the right to independent evaluations and due process procedures for resolving disagreements. Additional procedural safeguards are in place for students and parents from culturally and linguistically diverse backgrounds. Information about these safeguards as they apply to parents appears in Multicultural Considerations.

The eligibility process requires use of an interdisciplinary assessment team. Depending on the disability, various specialists work together to obtain a complete diagnosis and prescribe needed services. A physical therapist working in concert with a physician, for example, may diagnose the nature and extent of a physical impairment. Based on the diagnosis, the IEP may include physical therapy services. Similarly, an audiologist may conduct specific tests to identify the type and degree of a hearing loss. In almost every case, a psychologist or an educational diagnostician administers a test to identify intellectual ability and developmental status or scholastic ability. Other specialists, including speech and language pathologists, occupational therapists, and health-related professionals, may also participate as members of the assessment team, depending on the reason for testing and the nature of the problem.

MUTUAL CONSIDERATIONS

Assessing Students with Limited English Proficiency

For parents with limited English proficiency, the school system is responsible for providing all information in the native language. This means permission forms and other paperwork must be in the parent's native language. Likewise, the school must provide parents with an interpreter at meetings. This also applies to parents who are deaf and need a sign language interpreter.

Having interpreters for parents is important; however, this requires planning ahead. What ways can teachers in the classroom facilitate communication with parents from different cultures?

To answer this reflection online, go to the *Multicultural Considerations* module on the Companion Website at **www.prenhall.com/venn.**

Assessment Instruments for Determining Eligibility

Assessment at this level involves the use of comprehensive diagnostic tests and procedures administered by psychologists, educational diagnosticians, and other certified professionals. Unlike brief screening tests, these tests are in-depth, complex instruments and measurement systems that take several hours to administer, score, and interpret. In most cases, evaluators give a battery of formal, individually administered diagnostic tests. Depending on the student's needs and the reasons for the evaluation, the battery may include instruments to assess intelligence, achievement, behavior, and perception. The battery takes several hours to administer.

Limitations of Eligibility Determination

The eligibility process relies heavily on test scores. Although scores are dependable, they sometimes fail to accurately predict true behavior and ability. Problems with scores occur for various reasons. For example, some students perform poorly on tests, especially pencil-on-paper tests given in testing situations. Other students, however, perform well on tests but display learning or behavior problems in the classroom. Furthermore, scores indicate—but do not prove—students' ability levels. For these reasons, we should use test scores cautiously while keeping the limitations in mind at all times. Despite limitations, federal and state laws require the use of scores derived from formal assessment instruments. Such scores provide an objective measure to protect students from decisions based on the subjective impressions of professionals. Subjective impressions, such as opinions and judgments about student ability, performance, and behavior, are difficult to quantify and can result in biased and unfair decisions about students.

Why Do We Use Assessment to Determine Eligibility?

We assess students to determine eligibility for several reasons. The primary reason is to obtain a comprehensive diagnosis of student strengths, weaknesses, and learning needs. We use this diagnosis as a basis for making classification decisions that respond to the student's individual and unique needs. Second, we use assessment in response to legal requirements and state and district regulations. Third, and perhaps the most important, we use assessment to protect the rights of children and their families. The purpose of this type of assessment is to determine if a student has a disability, and, if so, to decide the types of special education or related services needed to provide an appropriate education. These are legal decisions that label a student, and, because of the legalities involved, they rely heavily on test results. In the vast majority of cases, parents agree with the school system regarding eligibility recommendations, but parents can challenge a recommendation, and schools can dispute parent requests. When such disputes cannot be resolved, they must be decided in a due process hearing or a court of law. For this reason, eligibility procedures follow procedural safeguards to protect students, parents, and school systems. These necessary and important safeguards sometimes make the process lengthy and cumbersome. A summary of the reasons for using assessment to determine eligibility appears in Focus 2–2.

Practical Application of the Eligibility Process

Let's take a look at the story of Mrs. Sharon Pinkney and her daughter Angel.

Mrs. Pinkney had long suspected that her daughter had learning problems, and her suspicions were confirmed when she met with Angel's teacher. In the meeting, the teacher

Focus 2-2

Why Do We Use Assessment to Determine Eligibility?

- To diagnose learning needs
- To meet legal requirements
- To protect students and their families
- To determine eligibility for services

described Angel's learning problems and asked for permission to refer Angel to a school-based child-study team for advice on ways to help. Mrs. Pinkney, who was both concerned about Angel's academic difficulties and relieved that the teacher had also identified them, agreed. The teacher indicated that the team might recommend testing to determine if Angel needed special help. About a month later, the teacher called Mrs. Pinkney to inform her of the school team's recommendation for further testing. When she received the permission forms, she signed and returned them.

Another month later, the counselor called to ask Mrs. Pinkney to come in for a meeting to discuss the testing results. The counselor began the meeting by introducing Mrs. Pinkney to the other attendees: a psychologist, a staffing specialist, an assistant principal, and the teacher who chaired the school's child-study team. After the introductions, the school counselor asked Mrs. Pinkney several questions about Angel's achievement and behavior. This gave Mrs. Pinkney the opportunity to describe her daughter to the professionals and to talk about Angel's academic difficulties. Next, the school psychologist gave her report. In her assessment of Angel, she identified a "significant discrepancy" between Angel's ability to learn, which was "normal" (as measured by an intelligence test), and her achievement, which was "below average" (as measured by an achievement test). The psychologist indicated that Angel had the most difficulty with reading, especially reading comprehension. During testing, Angel had difficulty answering specific questions about passages she had read, such as "What was the dog's name?" She was unable to tell the sequence in stories read, and she failed to recall the main idea in stories. After explaining the testing results, the staffing team indicated that Angel was eligible for special education and related services including reading instruction with an emphasis on building comprehension skills such as remembering basic facts, recalling sequences, and recognizing main ideas in passages. Mrs. Pinkney had an opportunity to participate with the professionals as they developed their program placement recommendation and designed the initial IEP.

When the staffing team indicated Angel would receive help from a teacher who specialized in reading disabilities, Mrs. Pinkney was relieved. She learned that she could review the special education services each year and approve any changes. The conference made Mrs. Pinkney feel much better about Angel's disability and the possibility that she could learn to compensate for it. Several weeks later, Angel began receiving her new services, and, over time, the extra instruction helped Angel improve her reading comprehension and build her self-confidence.

✓ Check Your Comprehension

Angel's vignette shows many of the steps in the second level of assessment: the eligibility process. Because of the number of steps involved, this process can take 6 months or longer in some situations. Eligibility testing enables diagnosis of specific disabilities, which serves as the basis for providing special services. As part of the eligibility process, the staffing team develops an initial IEP. Developing specific intervention activities falls into a third level of assessment: instructional intervention with students. However, before initiating an intervention program, students with disabilities must have an IEP that responds to their unique learning needs.

The Individual Education Plan (IEP)

The **individual education plan** (IEP) is the document that guides the development and implementation of the instructional intervention program and the process of measuring student progress. The IEP, which is mandated by the Individuals with Disabilities Education Act (IDEA), is a written document developed jointly by parents, professionals, and, if appropriate, the student. The staffing team develops an initial IEP as part of the eligibility process, but once a student begins to receive special education services, a school-based team develops subsequent IEPs. By law the IEP must include certain components that describe an appropriate education for a student who receives special education services. The law requires that teachers join with parents and other professionals as part of a team to develop the IEP. A list of the IEP components is given in Table 2–2.

IEPs and the Diagnostic-Prescriptive Model

The IEP components clearly set forth several legal mandates, including specific guidelines for assessing students who receive special education services. The basis of assessment in the IEP process is an appraisal method known as the **diagnostic-prescriptive model**, an approach that involves the following:

- Conducting an initial evaluation to identify present levels of performance (diagnosis)
- Using the results to determine appropriate annual goals and benchmarks or short-term objectives (prescription)
- Measuring progress toward meeting the annual goals and determining the extent to which that progress is sufficient to achieve the goals by the end of the year (diagnosis)
- Revising the annual goals and benchmarks based on the progress that has been made (prescription)

Perhaps a better name for this model is the test-teach-test-teach method. When teachers use this approach, they pretest students to determine learning needs and then teach using a curriculum based on those needs. After instruction, teachers posttest their students to measure progress and revise their teaching as appropriate. As specified in the IEP, implementing this approach involves a series of steps. A diagram of the steps in the diagnostic-prescriptive model appears in Figure 2–5; Table 2–3 lists and describes each step in the process along with matching IEP components.

Individual Family Service Plans and Transition IEPs

For children younger than age 3, IDEA's Infant and Toddler Program mandates a specialized IEP called an individual family service plan (IFSP). The IFSP requirements include procedures for assessing not only the needs of the child but the needs of the family as well. Similarly, IDEA calls for a specialized transition IEP for students beginning at age 16. The transition IEP facilitates movement from school to postschool activities.

Table 2–2   Individual Education Plan (IEP) Components

1. A statement of the child's present levels of academic achievement and functional performance, including (a) how the child's disability affects the child's involvement and progress in the general education curriculum; (b) for preschool children, as appropriate, how the disability affects the child's participation in appropriate activities; and (c) for children with disabilities who take alternate assessments aligned to alternate achievement standards, a description of benchmarks or short-term objectives.

2. A statement of measurable annual goals, including academic and functional goals, designed to (a) meet the child's needs that result from the child's disability to enable the child to be involved in and make progress in the general education curriculum; and (b) meet each of the child's other educational needs that result from the child's disability.

3. A description of how the child's progress toward meeting the annual goals described in component 2 will be measured and an explanation of when periodic reports on the progress the child is making toward meeting the annual goals (such as through the use of quarterly or other periodic reports, concurrent with the issuance of report cards) will be provided.

4. A statement of the special education and related services and supplementary aids and services, based on peer-reviewed research to the extent practicable, to be provided to the child, or on behalf of the child, and a statement of the program modifications or supports for school personnel that will be provided for the child (a) to advance appropriately toward attaining goals; (b) to be involved in and make progress in the general education curriculum in accordance with component 1 and to participate in extracurricular and other nonacademic activities; and (c) to be educated and participate with other children with disabilities and nondisabled children in the activities described in this subparagraph.

5. An explanation of the extent, if any, to which the child will not participate with nondisabled children in the regular class and activities described in component 4.

6. A statement of any individual appropriate accommodations that are necessary to measure the academic achievement and functional performance of the child on state- and district-wide assessments, and if the IEP team determines that the child shall take an alternate assessment on a particular state- or district-wide assessment of student achievement, a statement of why the child cannot participate in the regular assessment; and the particular alternate assessment selected is appropriate for the child.

7. The projected date for initiation of services and modifications described in component 4, and the anticipated frequency, location, and duration of the services.

8. Beginning not later than the first IEP to be in effect when the child is 16, and updated annually thereafter (a) appropriate measurable postsecondary goals based upon age-appropriate transition assessments related to training, education, employment, and, where appropriate, independent living skills; and (b) the transition services (including courses of study) needed to assist the child in reaching those goals.

A team that includes the parents develops IEPs, IFSP, and transition IEPs. The plans must be based on assessment of the student's individual and unique needs. The plans, developed at a team meeting, include annual goals and evaluation criteria, procedures, and schedules. Virtually all school systems use software to assist in the IEP development process. Information about this software appears in the Technology Focus box.

Figure 2–5   Illustration of the diagnostic-prescriptive model

Test

Teach

Diagnostic-
Prescriptive
Model

Teach

Test

Table 2–3   IEPs and the Diagnostic-Prescriptive Model

Assessment Step	IEP Component
Diagnose/Test	1. Identify the child's present levels of academic achievement and functional performance and develop goals.
Prescribe/Teach	2. Teach the child based on the annual goals.
Diagnose/Test	3. Measure progress toward meeting the annual goals.
Prescribe/Teach	4. Review the IEP at least annually and revise the goals as appropriate.

TECHNOLOGY FOCUS

IEP Software

Most school systems have purchased or developed special education management software to help teachers and administrators prepare IEPs, evaluations, and reports for state agencies. To find out more about this software, conduct an Internet search using "IEP software" as the key search words. Many systems have installed this software on their networks so that it is accessible from any connected computer.

Assessing IEP Quality

The Florida Department of Education (Burke & Beech, 2000, pp. 169–171) developed a set of indicators for assessing IEP quality. These IEP indicators include items for measuring IEP objectives and assessment procedures, including present levels of performance, annual goals, short-term objectives, student progress, and student participation in high-stakes testing programs. Selected items from this valuable guide appear in Figure 2–6.

Figure 2–6 IEP quality indicators

	Meets Criterion	Doesn't Meet Criterion
Present Level of Performance		
Statements represent input from a variety of sources.		
References to specific assessments are excluded unless easily understood without teacher or test manuals.		
The narrative statement of student strengths and needs includes descriptive information that is usable by school personnel and understood by parents and the student, as appropriate.		
Statements are free of jargon.		
Statements of needs are expressed in observable or measurable terms.		
Priority educational needs of the student are reflected in the present level of educational performance statements.		
Statements describe the student's abilities and needs in relation to the student's desired school/postschool outcomes.		
Statements reflect the student's abilities or behaviors in home, school, community, and work settings.		
Statements reflect coordination of priority educational needs across all areas of the student's needs.		
Measurable Annual Goals		
Annual goals are related to desired school/postschool outcomes and priority educational needs.		
Educationally relevant therapies are reflected in classroom goals, as appropriate.		
Community-based instruction or community experiences are reflected in the goals.		
Instructional responsibilities are addressed for each annual goal.		
Short-Term Objectives or Benchmarks		
Objectives or benchmarks focus on specific needs identified in present level of performance statements rather than on curriculum scope and sequence.		
Objectives or benchmarks are achievable in relation to the student's identified strengths and needs.		
Objectives or benchmarks reflect progress to more complex skills or mastery of behavior.		
Objectives or benchmarks are written in easily understood, jargon-free language.		

	Meets Criterion	Doesn't Meet Criterion
Objectives or benchmarks reflect integration and use of skills needed in the classroom, community, and home.		
Objectives or benchmarks are chronologically and developmentally appropriate for the student.		
Student Progress		
Evaluation procedures include ongoing and frequent measurement of objectives or benchmarks.		
Criteria for mastery describe the expected performance in terms of how well and over what period of time.		
Criteria for mastery are attainable yet challenging in relation to the student's ability.		
A variety of evaluation methods and procedures are provided.		
Evaluation procedures include home, work, community, and school settings for measuring objectives or benchmarks logically carried out in a specific setting.		
Documentation of mastery of short-term objectives or benchmarks is included on the IEP.		
Participation in State- and District-Wide Assessment Programs		
Modifications, accommodations, and supports for personnel are related to meeting priority educational needs and attaining the desired school or postschool outcomes identified in the IEP.		
A positive correlation between accommodations in the instructional program and in the state- or district-wide assessment program is reflected.		
Input from a variety of sources (e.g., parents, student, basic or vocational teacher, employment specialist, agency representative) is reflected.		
Accommodations that support participation in the instructional and assessment program are understood by parents, the student, and individuals involved in implementation, and those modifications are specified in detail.		

IEPs and Participation in General Education

The IDEA requirements emphasize participation in the general education curriculum and call attention to the accommodations and adjustments necessary for students with disabilities to access the regular curriculum and participate in extracurricular and other nonacademic activities. These requirements highlight the need for special services that facilitate appropriate participation in particular areas of the curriculum. This requirement provides the legal basis for inclusion programs and procedures.

Comprehensive information about assessment in inclusive settings appears in Chapter 18, which is an entire chapter describing this increasingly important aspect of education.

☑ Check Your Comprehension

For students with disabilities, the IEP guides the development and implementation of instructional intervention programs and the process of measuring progress. An IEP is a written plan developed jointly by parents, professionals, and, if appropriate, the student. The IEP is also the legal document that describes the elements of an appropriate education for students who receive special education services. The basis of assessment in the IEP is an appraisal method known as the diagnostic-prescriptive model, which uses a test-teach-test-teach instructional approach. IEP guidelines emphasize the participation of students with disabilities in general education and with appropriate supplementary aids and services.

Instructional Intervention

The instructional intervention process provides the information necessary for making educational decisions related to developing instructional objectives, establishing intervention priorities, and evaluating the effectiveness of curricula and materials. **Instructional intervention** uses the curriculum-based assessment that is a regular part of daily instruction. This enables evaluation of student performance in relation to specific instructional objectives articulated in the IEP. For the teacher of students with special needs, instructional intervention is the most important assessment process. Without it, teachers have difficulty developing and tailoring programs that respond to individual performance levels, learning needs, and performance standards.

Assessment Instruments for Instructional Intervention

Instructional intervention relies primarily on curriculum-based, teacher-developed assessments. Use of formal tests is less prevalent. Curriculum-based assessments are measures such as checklists of student performance, rubrics, teacher-made tests, observations, and impressions. Teacher observations include systematic procedures for listening and watching students for the purpose of gathering information to help make intervention decisions. For example, structured observations help teachers develop behavior charts to illustrate and measure student behavior. Behavior charts provide valuable assessment data that inform behavior management programs. Impressions are less structured and systematic, but they can lead to valuable conclusions and judgments. Impressions usually evolve after teachers interact with students over time. For example, a teacher may decide to use a particular intervention based on an impression formed after working directly with a student and consulting with other teachers (Salvia & Yssledyke, 2004).

Limitations of Assessment in Instructional Intervention

Assessment for instructional intervention often relies on subjective evaluation derived from impressions and opinions. Although subjective information is valuable in making instructional intervention decisions, it can be arbitrary and biased. For this reason, assessment should include more than subjective appraisal. A teacher might, for example, combine impressions with clinical judgment along with results from a checklist of skills and a score from a standardized test to ensure a fair, objective decision that leads to developing the best possible IEP goals and intervention strategies.

Why Do We Use Assessment in Instructional Intervention?

We use assessment as part of instructional intervention for many reasons. First, assessment helps identify student readiness for instruction and helps determine strengths, weaknesses, interests, motivation, and learning style. In many situations, we rely on teacher-made measurements such as classroom quizzes, direct observations, or checklists of skills to accomplish this goal. Second, as teachers we need to know what students have already learned. This knowledge then helps us determine what students need to learn next. The purpose of this type of diagnostic assessment is to obtain information for planning instructional interventions that respond to the needs of the students who will be receiving the instruction. In other words, appropriate assessment is necessary to make the best possible intervention decisions. These decisions include establishing intervention priorities, developing instructional objectives, and evaluating curriculum and materials. A summary of the reasons for using assessment in instructional intervention appears in Focus 2–3.

Practical Application of Assessment in Instructional Intervention

Brenna Bateh is an outstanding teacher who has earned a reputation for innovative, student-based, individualized instruction. One of the ways she accomplishes this is with curriculum-based assessment that helps her continually measure the academic performance and interests of her students. She also seeks new ways to measure achievement and motivation by reading about the latest assessment procedures and using her own creativity and experience to devise new evaluations.

Ms. Bateh learned in her teacher education classes that assessment as part of instructional intervention could help her establish learning benchmarks and plan ways to help students achieve their IEP goals. When Ms. Bateh began her teaching career, she practiced answering the following questions as part of instructional planning: What do my students need to learn in my class? What are the benchmarks for this learning? How much of this material do they already know? How can I best determine if my students have accomplished

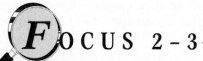

FOCUS 2-3

Why Do We Use Assessment in the Instructional Intervention Process?

- To identify instructional needs
- To establish intervention priorities
- To develop instructional objectives
- To evaluate curriculum and materials

these goals? What are my students' skills and knowledge as they enter the class? What level of motivation and interest do my students bring to class?

To decide what students should know, Ms. Bateh relies on a variety of sources: her experience, other teachers' experiences, curriculum requirements, performance standards, instructional and curriculum materials, and student interests. After deciding what students should learn, Ms. Bateh pretests the students to identify how much they know. She usually does this by preparing simple teacher-made tests. Results from these pretests divulge what the students already know and show the students what they will be responsible for learning. Ms. Bateh also uses posttest probes at the end of some lessons to decide if the students have learned the material and to summarize the material for the students. The information she receives from the probes provides essential data about student needs and their strengths and weaknesses—an important goal of instructional intervention. Pretest results from Ms. Bateh's classes often reveal that her students have diverse needs requiring many opportunities to practice skills, followed by extensive feedback. Ms. Bateh knows that she needs to individualize instruction as much as possible because all students have unique learning styles at different levels of performance and motivation.

When Ms. Bateh first began teaching, she felt overwhelmed by the challenge of meeting the needs of all her students. She tried conventional methods such as individualizing instruction within the group, peer teaching, and cooperative learning. These helped, but she decided that she needed to incorporate additional reflective teaching and learning activities to motivate her students. Portfolio-based instruction and assessment activities such as portfolio conferences really helped her students learn reflection and self-evaluation.

As you can see, Ms. Bateh continually strives for improvement. Even after she finds solutions to instructional dilemmas, she searches for even better ways to help her students. Ms. Bateh has learned how to use assessment as a regular part of instruction rather than as an extra element added on to meet state and district guidelines.

☑ Check Your Comprehension

Conducting assessment as part of instructional intervention helps teachers obtain the information they need to make educational decisions related to instructional objectives, intervention priorities, and the effectiveness of curricula and materials. Teachers also conduct assessment during instructional intervention to obtain data for IEPs. For teachers, this is the most important of the assessment processes. Without it, teachers have difficulty developing individual programs that respond to the performance levels and learning needs of their students. Assessment as part of instructional intervention relies primarily on classroom-based, teacher-designed assessment instruments and procedures.

The Progress-Measuring Process

The process of **measuring progress** involves ongoing evaluation and periodic measurement of overall performance. Educators also assess student progress to gauge program effectiveness and to ensure that services respond to individual needs.

Assessment Instruments for Measuring Progress

Ongoing evaluation of student progress relies primarily on informal, curriculum-based evaluation procedures that relate directly to instruction. Examples include the following:

Progress on daily lessons
Scores from class tests, worksheets, and papers
Results of task- and error-pattern analysis
Teacher observations and impressions
Information from student portfolios
Behavior management data

In order to reliably measure progress, teachers keep records of these data and information sources. Teachers maintain these records in grade books, graphs, charts from behavior management programs, portfolios, narrative reports from observations and impressions, and, increasingly, in digital storage formats on computers.

Measuring the overall progress of students, usually on an annual basis, is best accomplished with more formal measures such as achievement tests and standardized behavior rating scales. Measuring global progress using formal assessment provides information for making decisions about program effectiveness and supplies data for comparing the performance of one student to others.

Limitations of Measuring Student Progress

Measuring student progress can be a time consuming process that takes away from instructional time. This is especially true at the end of the school year when teachers must give high-stakes tests as part of statewide and district testing programs. In the classroom and in other instructional settings, teachers often manage the time problem by using an evaluation approach called curriculum based assessment (CBA). CBA is specifically for teacher use in instructional situations. CBA helps teachers measure progress as a regular part of instruction rather than as a separate activity. In other words, CBA is an instructional ingredient instead of a disconnected requirement, such as high-stakes testing. Thus, teachers use CBA to measure what they are teaching in ways that contribute to student accomplishment. This practical solution minimizes loss of valuable instructional time to testing. Details about specific CBA methods and procedures appear in later chapters.

Why Do We Assess Student Progress?

Measuring student progress is an essential element in the assessment process for several reasons. First, progress measurement provides data and information for making decisions regarding student performance during daily instruction and throughout the year. Assessment also gives feedback about progress, or lack of progress, to students and parents. Measuring progress is certainly an essential element in the IEP process. Finally, student progress data and information help measure program effectiveness.

Because of the importance of measuring student progress, the need for reliable and valid assessment is significant. Teachers must know how their students are performing to determine when they achieve benchmarks, goals, and performance standards. This knowledge, gained from assessment, helps to make decisions about what to teach next and how to teach it. Likewise, teachers must identify students who fail to achieve their objectives. The decision for these students involves how to develop

FOCUS 2 - 4

Why Do We Measure Student Progress?

- To assess progress on daily lessons
- To assess progress over time
- To assess general progress
- To monitor program effectiveness
- To ensure that special education services respond to individual student needs
- To determine how well the IEP is working

the best possible remediation plans. Accurate progress measurement also provides a way to document student accomplishments. This documentation enables accountability for instructional programs. A summary of the reasons for measuring student progress appears in Focus 2–4.

Practical Application of the Progress-Measuring Process

It took Keisha, a student in Deidre McDowell's class, several weeks to get used to all of the self-grading tasks that she had to do. Keisha was accustomed to getting class grades, but she was not familiar with all of the self-assessment activities required by Ms. McDowell. Keisha remembered that when she first joined the class, Ms. McDowell explained that all students were going to keep up with their own assignments and grades, but at the time she did not really understand what this meant. Ms. McDowell told the class how important it was for students to know how much progress they were making and that the best way to do this was to have students help measure their own learning. As Keisha got to know the other students and discovered that Ms. McDowell's expectations were easy to follow, she started enjoying all of the new requirements. These requirements included the following:

- *Maintaining her own grade book that listed all her homework, classwork, and test grades. Ms. McDowell checked this on a regular basis.*
- *Keeping her own behavior charts that she had to fill out at the end of each school day. Ms. McDowell checked these charts every day. Keisha was glad that she had to do this only at the end of the day because some of the worst students in the class had to fill them out several times during the day. One of Keisha's behavior charts appears in Figure 2–7.*
- *Keeping up with her student portfolio checklist, which listed each item in her portfolio with spaces for Keisha to record completion dates.*
- *Keisha also met with Ms. McDowell at the end of each grading period to go over her grades and to answer Ms. McDowell's questions, such as "Are you happy with your grades?" "Could you have done better?" "How?" "What school work did you like best and why?" and "What schoolwork did you like least and why?" At first, Keisha did not like all the questions, but as she became used to them, she could see how they really did help her measure her own progress.*

☑ Check Your Comprehension

The progress-measuring process includes ongoing evaluation of student accomplishment on daily lessons, frequent appraisal of progress toward

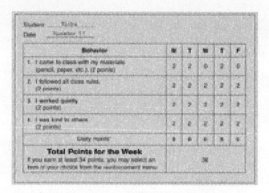

Figure 2–7 Student attainment report

meeting IEP benchmarks, and an occasional (at least annual) review of general progress. Most progress assessment is informal, consisting of teacher-made tests and other measures, such as checklists and teacher judgments that relate directly to the instructional curriculum. Measuring student progress provides information for making instructional decisions, monitoring the IEP, and giving feedback to students. Measuring student progress also provides a way to gauge program effectiveness.

Summary

The process of assessing students with special needs involves several steps, including the following

- Screening
- Determining eligibility
- Instructional intervention
- Measuring progress

Although distinctions and differences exist among these assessment steps, similarities exist among the stages as well. The differences involve the purpose of assessment at each level and the type of assessment procedures in each step. Screening is generally the initial phase of assessment, and is usually a brief and relatively uncomplicated process. In contrast, determining eligibility usually involves lengthy, complicated, and formal diagnostic testing procedures. For students with disabilities, the IEP guides their instructional intervention programs and helps to measure progress. IEP development occurs during several steps in the assessment process. Both instructional intervention and measuring progress rely on informal, curriculum-based assessment directly tied to instruction. The similarities among the assessment categories involve the goal of all assessment: to contribute information for designing an appropriate education for students with special needs.

To check your comprehension of chapter contents, go to the *Quiz* module in Chapter 2 of the Companion Website, *www.prenhall.com/venn*.

Reflection
As a teacher, which step in the process of assessing students with disabilities do you think is most critical? Explain your answer.

 To answer this reflection online, go to the *Teaching and Learning* module on the Companion Website at *www.prenhall.com/venn.*

Meeting Performance Standards and Preparing for Licensure Exams

After reading this chapter, you should be able to demonstrate the following CEC standards and PRAXIS™ test knowledge and skills. The information in parentheses identifies where to find the particular CEC standard and PRAXIS™ content reference.

CEC Standards for Beginning Special Education Teachers

- Issues, assurances and due process rights related to assessment, eligibility, and placement within a continuum of services (CC1K6)
- Screening, prereferral, referral, and classification procedures (CC8K3)
- Use and limitations of assessment instruments (CC8K4)
- Use assessment information in making eligibility, program, and placement decisions for individuals with exceptional learning needs, including those from culturally and/or linguistically diverse backgrounds (CC8S6)
- Evaluate instruction and monitor progress of individuals with exceptional learning needs (CC8S8)

PRAXIS™ Education of Exceptional Students: Core Content Knowledge

- Curriculum and instruction and their implementation across the continuum of educational placements, including the individualized family service plan (IFSP)/individualized education program (IEP) process (0353 III)
- Assessment, including use of assessment for screening, diagnosis, placement, and the making of instructional decisions; for example: how to select and conduct nondiscriminatory and appropriate assessments; how to interpret standardized and specialized assessment results; how to effectively use evaluation results in individualized family service plan (IFSP)/individualized education program (IEP) development; how to prepare written reports and communicate findings (0353 III)

chapter 3

Inclusive Assessment

Objectives

After reading this chapter, you will be prepared to do the following:

- Define inclusive assessment.
- Modify assessment practices for students with disabilities in inclusive settings.
- Work together with other teachers in assessing student performance and assigning grades.
- Use alternative grading strategies.
- Modify teacher-made tests.
- Assess teamwork in cooperative learning.

Overview

In this chapter, you will explore procedures for assessing students with disabilities in inclusive settings. Your study of this increasingly important topic begins with questions teachers have about inclusive assessment. Next, you will investigate the definition of inclusion as it relates to assessing students with special needs. Your study of inclusive assessment includes review of new approaches, including assessment design modifications and test accommodations for students with disabilities. You will also explore the alternative grading criteria that teachers use in response to unique student abilities, interests, behavior, and educational goals.

Questions Teachers Ask About Inclusive Assessment

The following narrative illustrates some of the questions teachers have about assessment in inclusive settings.

Maria Aspera, a special education teacher recently assigned to an inclusion class, has never assessed children with special needs in a general education setting. As a result, she has some questions. For instance, what assessments are best in inclusion classrooms? Are there special tests for inclusion settings? How much do teachers need to modify traditional classroom testing for students with disabilities? In addition, how useful is curriculum-based assessment, especially portfolio assessment, in evaluating students with special needs in general education classes?

Maria decides to find answers to these questions by doing some research. She finds a lot of information on inclusion in general and on methods for successful inclusion, but she finds very little information about assessment in inclusive settings. She discovers that she needs to learn

more about accommodations and modifications in testing and that assessment in inclusive settings requires teamwork and ongoing communication between the general and special education co-teachers. She locates some helpful suggestions regarding the most frequently occurring testing and grading problems of students in regular classes and learns that not all students with disabilities require extensive modifications in assessment. To her relief, Maria realizes that most modifications for students with special needs involve minor alterations of procedures rather than major adjustments. As she begins her new teaching assignment, she decides that her goal is to provide appropriate assessment in ways that are as similar as possible to the testing and grading used with the general education students in the class.

Growth of Inclusive Education

Keeping pace with changes in assessment practices and services for students with disabilities is challenging. Many innovations have occurred, one of the most significant of which has been educating students with disabilities in general classrooms. As a result, assessment practices are also changing, although not as quickly as some educators would prefer.

Definition of Inclusion

The 2004 amendments to IDEA (IDEA 2004) define **inclusion** as the education of students who have disabilities with students who are nondisabled. IDEA 2004 further states that special classes, separate schooling, or other removal of students with disabilities from the regular educational environment should happen only if the nature or severity of the disability precludes education in regular classes with appropriate supplementary aides and support services. Inclusive education involves placement in the local school and in the general education setting with appropriate supports and curricular adaptations designed individually for each student eligible for special education services. The related concept of **full inclusion** refers to attaining the greatest integration possible for all, including students with severe disabilities. The philosophy is that all students are active, fully participating members of the school community, and that schools understand the benefits of inclusive education for all students. More specifically, full inclusion refers to full membership in the general classroom with all of the supports necessary for successful inclusion. Inclusion also encompasses placement in a variety of educational settings. In addition to the general education classroom, inclusion extends to community-based instruction and educational activities such as school clubs and athletics that occur outside the classroom.

Inclusion gives students with disabilities the opportunity to participate in typical school activities with their peers who are not disabled. Experts expect that inclusion will result in classrooms that serve much more diverse student groups. As a result, teachers need to develop new instructional methodologies and assessment procedures that respond to the greater diversity of student needs. In other words, the concept of the general education classroom is changing; therefore, the notions of teaching, learning, and assessment are changing as well.

Although assessment in inclusive settings requires changes, many current evaluation practices work well in inclusive settings. For example, curriculum-based assessment procedures, such as teacher-made testing, grading of homework assignments, and grading of classwork, already occur in the same way in most classrooms. In fact, teachers should use established assessment procedures whenever possible as long as they meet the increasingly diverse needs of the students.

Assessment Issues in General Education

Key issues in general education include concerns about standards and assessment in inclusive settings because many general education teachers feel that required modifications for students with special needs lower curriculum standards. In contrast, special education teachers often express concerns about the emphasis in general education on testing as a means of accountability. General educators often feel pressured to make sure that their students perform well on tests. Because students with special needs tend to perform poorly on tests, general educators may be hesitant to accept inclusion due to fears about a negative impact on the testing performance of the total class. According to Elliott (2001), including students with disabilities in standardized assessments is an important goal. However, including all students in educational accountability systems raises concerns about performance standards for students with disabilities, the use of accommodations in testing, the effects of accommodations on assessment validity, and the reporting of scores when accommodations have been used. These are examples of the issues that educators are dealing with as they develop strategies for assessing students with disabilities in inclusive settings. Although many of the basic procedures for successful inclusion are well established, not all processes surrounding inclusion have been resolved. Unresolved issues include inclusion of students with severe disabilities, co-teaching, support services, and assessment. Teachers are still in the process of developing the best possible solutions to these issues and concerns.

Why Do We Modify Assessment in Inclusive Settings?

The following narrative illustrates why we modify assessment for students with disabilities in inclusive settings. The scenario depicts some of the most commonly used assessment modifications and shows how assessment modifications help students with disabilities succeed in inclusive classrooms.

Ms. McBride, a general education teacher in a newly formed inclusion class, was disappointed by the student performance on her teacher-made tests. In class discussions and activities, her students appeared to understand the material. On the tests, however, many students received grades of Cs, Ds, and Fs. The scores of several students with disabilities were especially low. Confused and frustrated, Ms. McBride asked her students why they were having difficulty. They responded with the following comments: "I didn't understand some of the questions." "I skipped some questions because there were too many on the page." "The directions were confusing." "I lost my place on the answer sheet." "I didn't have enough room for my answers." "I thought the true-false questions were tricky."

After discussing the problem of low test grades with the special education co-teacher, Ms. McBride decided to try out some test design modifications suggested by her colleague. Together the teachers implemented several accommodations, including an improved test format, explicit directions, revised response modes, a greater variety of items, and better test readability. Although some students continued to score poorly, the teachers noted a marked improvement in the performance of many students. The teachers and the students were pleased with the results because the testing modifications allowed the students with disabilities to demonstrate what they had learned, and the improved tests benefited all of the students in the class.

This account illustrates the effectiveness of modifying assessment by making design modifications to teacher-made tests. Because performance on teacher-made tests is a key element in evaluating achievement and assigning semester grades, classroom tests must be well designed and sensitive to unique learning needs.

New Approaches to Inclusive Assessment

Modifying assessment by redesigning teacher-made tests is just one example of the new approaches teachers are using in inclusive settings. Other approaches include team assessment, assessing teamwork in cooperative learning, and portfolio assessment. New assessment procedures are necessary to meet the needs of the increasing numbers of students with disabilities who receive all or part of their education in general classes. Inclusive classes must also respond to the needs of increasingly diverse groups of students. Though inclusive educational practices focus on students with disabilities in general education, schools need to be restructured so that they meet the needs of all students, including students from culturally and linguistically different backgrounds. Information about ways to differentiate cultural and language differences from learning problems appears in Multicultural Considerations. Information about inclusive assessment also appears in Chapter 6, especially in the section on accommodations in test administration.

Team Assessment

One of the most useful assessment approaches in inclusive classrooms is **team assessment,** a process that involves all teachers in the evaluation process, not just special education teachers. Team assessment helps general education teachers, in particular, who have many concerns about testing and grading students with disabilities. Some concerns result from a lack of training and experience in appropriate techniques for modifying evaluation procedures with mainstreamed students. Other concerns arise from the resistance of a few teachers to altering their traditional testing and grading practices. However, successful inclusion depends in part on the willingness of teachers to modify their measurement procedures in response to the needs of individual students.

MULTICULTURAL CONSIDERATIONS

Differentiating Cultural and Language Differences from Learning Problems

With students for whom English is their second language, it is important to try to differentiate cultural and language differences from learning problems. The dilemma is that learning a second language is difficult and the behaviors associated with the process of second-language learning are similar to the behaviors linked to learning problems. Because these behaviors are similar, students who have trouble acquiring their second language may be inappropriately identified as disabled.

Assessing native-language and second-language proficiency is one of the keys to successful differentiation. Most second-language learners with at least some proficiency in their native language do not have a disability even if they are struggling with second-language acquisition. In these situations, students often benefit from participation in bilingual education programs. Students who fail to make satisfactory progress over a long period even with an appropriate curriculum provided by a qualified teacher may have a disability. This is especially true when assessment data and information indicate that a student has deficits in both the native language and the second language coupled with delays in academic and social behaviors. Students who qualify as disabled may benefit from special education services that address their individual linguistic, cultural, and experiential learning needs.

Describe some behaviors a teacher would look for when considering a referral to screen a bilingual student for a possible disability.

To answer this reflection online, go to the *Multicultural Considerations* module on the Companion Website at www.prenhall.com/venn.

Team assessment is necessary because the inclusion classroom is different from the traditional classroom. The goals, teachers, curriculum, and assessment procedures all differ (Tiegerman-Farber & Radziewicz, 1998). Because the inclusion classroom changes assessment, general and special education teachers as well as the other members of the assessment team must work together in implementing new assessment procedures. Fortunately, most teachers are willing to collaborate as co-teachers in developing and implementing new assessment techniques that benefit all students while accommodating the needs of students with disabilities.

One of the assessment elements that teachers should consider is how well the members of the team work together. Teachers can use the team analysis checklist in Figure 3–1 to assess team collaboration and effectiveness. The 25 items in the checklist cover the most important aspects of team success, including team goals, structure, interpersonal relations, resolution of conflicts, information exchange, consensus, assignment of responsibility, and team assessment. The checklist is an informal tool for evaluating overall team effectiveness and identifying specific problems that the team needs to address. The checklist is useful in a variety of settings and situations in which professionals work together as a team.

Figure 3–1 Team analysis checklist

Team Analysis Checklist		
Item	Yes	No
Team Purpose		
1. I understand the purpose of the team.		
2. I believe it is possible to accomplish the team purpose.		
Team Structure		
3. I know the expertise of each team member.		
4. I know the major tasks associated with the team objectives.		
5. I know who serves as team leader.		
6. I accept the leadership of the team leader.		
Interpersonal Relations		
7. Fellow team members accept me as a valuable contributor.		
8. I perceive most of the other members as valuable team contributors.		
9. All team members can fully express their views.		
10. Team members listen to and consider the views of others.		
11. The team avoids domination by one individual member.		
Resolution of Conflicts		
12. The team solves conflicts together.		
13. The team strongly discourages personal attacks.		
14. I accept team decisions even if they conflict with my own view.		
Records, Reporting, and Responsibility		
15. The team has a process for recording activities and decisions.		
16. The team members share recording and reporting duties.		
Information Exchange		
17. I have regular opportunities to contribute my professional knowledge to the team.		
18. Other team members have regular opportunities to contribute their professional knowledge to the team.		
19. The team frequently seeks information from outside sources.		

Gaining Consensus		
20. The members have opportunities for input in making team decisions.		
21. The members reach consensus prior to making team decisions.		
Assigning Responsibility		
22. After the team makes a decision, members accept responsibility for specific follow-up and implementation activities.		
23. The team shares follow-up and implementation responsibilities appropriately.		
Team Assessment		
24. The team assesses the program on a regular basis.		
25. All team members have opportunities to participate in program change and program evaluation activities.		

Team assessment requires a substantial amount of time, professional commitment, and interpersonal communication. Active participation of all team members in gathering and interpreting assessment data is a key element. Team assessment is a decision-making approach that results in a more complete assessment of student needs based on discussion among team members with diverse expertise.

☑ Check Your Comprehension

Of the many changes that have occurred in educating students with special needs, one of the most significant has been the inclusion of students with disabilities in general education. As a result, assessment practices are also changing. Key issues in general education include concerns about performance standards, accommodations in testing, and the best ways to include all students in educational accountability systems. Teachers in inclusive settings are learning new assessment techniques, including how to redesign teacher-made tests and how to use team assessment in which general and special education teachers work closely together in the educational decision-making process.

Alternative Grading

Mr. Chuma, a middle school science teacher, and Mr. Staub, a special education teacher, recently began working together as a cooperative instructional team. At the end of the first grading period they were still adjusting to each other when they had to decide how to assign grades. Mr. Chuma felt all students should be graded in the same manner and believed he should assign all of the grades himself. Mr. Chuma's grading system was based primarily on test scores with little emphasis on other measures of student performance and achievement. Mr. Staub felt the two teachers should cooperatively assign grades and give individual consideration when grading students with disabilities. Mr. Staub believed in using alternative grading with individual students when necessary and appropriate. Mr. Staub felt that the integrity of the curriculum and the standards could be maintained even with the use of alternative grading.

Reflection
As a general education teacher, what would be some of your concerns with having an inclusion classroom? How would you do to deal with each of your concerns?

 To answer this reflection online, go to the *Teaching and Learning* module on the Companion Website at *www. prenhall.com/venn.*

Table 3–1 Alternative Grading Strategies

- Pass/fail grading
- Multiple grading
- Grading for effort
- Portfolio-based grading
- Competency-based grading
- Point systems
- Contract grading
- Descriptive grading
- Level grading
- IEP grading
- Mastery level/criterion grading
- Shared grading
- Progressive improvement grading

This brief scenario, based on a vignette by Salend and Duhaney (2002), illustrates the complexities associated with grading, especially with students who have disabilities placed in inclusive classes. As more students with disabilities receive their education in general education classes, teachers are grappling with the challenging and complex issues associated with assigning grades. In some situations, the IEP team includes alternative grading procedures in a student's IEP. In other situations, students receive alternative grading consideration as needed without specifying a particular procedure in the IEP. Regardless of whether **alternative grading** appears in a student's IEP, the general education teacher and the special education teacher should work together as a team in the grading process. This means that teachers need to reach agreement on the type of grading system they will use and the grading responsibilities of each teacher before assigning grades.

Results from a comprehensive study of class grading (Bursuck et al., 1996) indicated that most teachers support the use of alternative grading with students who have special learning needs. The most common alternative grading procedures identified in this study were pass/fail grades, multiple grades, grading for effort, and portfolio-based grading. An explanation of how to use these and other alternative procedures follows (Mercer & Mercer, 2005; Salend, 2005; Salend & Duhaney, 2002; Wood, 2006). A list of alternative grading strategies appears in Table 3–1.

Pass/Fail Grading

Pass/fail grading involves establishing minimum criteria for receiving a passing grade. Students who successfully meet the criteria receive a grade of "pass," and those who fail to demonstrate the required skills and knowledge receive a grade of "fail."

Multiple Grading

Multiple grading enables teachers to assign grades in more than one area. For example, students can earn two grades: one for effort and one for performance. Multiple grading also provides a way to grade students based on ability.

Grading for Effort

Some teachers use **grading for effort** with students whose ability is so low that they are unable to meet even minimum performance standards.

Portfolio-Based Grading

Portfolio-Based grading is another technique for evaluating students with special needs in inclusive settings (Mercer & Mercer, 2005). Teachers assign portfolio grades based on evaluation of the authentic samples of student work that appear in a portfolio. Rather than emphasizing grades such as test scores, the portfolio approach relies more on holistic grades. This encourages reflective teaching, learning, and assessment. As a result, students have many opportunities to evaluate their performance, receive feedback during portfolio conferences, and think about their learning experiences and progress. Portfolio grading has the potential for expanding measurement into new and challenging areas. Details about portfolio grading appear in Chapter 18, which is an entire chapter devoted to this exciting and useful approach to evaluating student performance.

Competency-Based Grading

With **competency-based grading**, students demonstrate attainment of required skills. Teachers should establish criteria for successful attainment of competencies prior to instruction so that students know what is expected. Students then receive grades based on their progress in reaching specified criterion levels for each competency or skill. Teachers often list the required competencies on a checklist, which helps monitor student progress. Teachers assign grades according to the number of successfully mastered skills.

Point Systems

Point systems assign points for successfully completing learning activities, tests, and assignments. A sample point system may consist of the following:

10 points for each of 10 homework assignments completed
20 points for each of five class quizzes
50 points for completing the class project or paper
10 points for daily participation in class

Students can earn all the points or partial points for a particular assignment depending on their level of performance. At the end of the grading period, students receive grades corresponding to the total number of points earned. Students with the highest number of points earn a grade of "A"; students with lower point totals earn lower grades.

Contract Grading

Contract grading involves having the teacher and the student sign a contract that describes the work that the student will complete within a specified time. Students may contract for grades of "A," "B," or "C," depending on the amount or quality of work they complete. For example, students who contract for an "A" may write an extra paper during the grading period or complete specific enrichment activities such as documenting books, articles, or chapters read on a particular topic. The student and the teacher sign the contract prior to instruction. The teacher and the student then monitor progress in fulfilling the contract, and the teacher assigns a final grade at the end of the grading period.

Descriptive Grading

Descriptive grading relies on descriptive comments that the teacher writes to describe the quality of a student's performance. Descriptive grading avoids numbers such as point totals. Instead, the narrative statements describe student performance, effort, attitude, behavior, interest, and learning style. For example, team teachers in an inclusion class may decide to evaluate the performance of a student with a severe disability using descriptive grading. Teachers often use examples of completed student work to support the qualitative statements.

Level Grading

In **level grading,** the teacher individualizes grading by indicating the level of difficulty (1, 2, or 3) for each grade. A 1 indicates above-grade-level difficulty, a 2 indicates on grade-level-difficulty, and a 3 denotes below-grade-level difficulty. For example, a grade of C2 indicates the student is doing average work on grade level. Likewise, a B3 indicates above average performance on work that is below grade level in difficulty.

IEP Grading

IEP grading reflects student attainment of IEP goals. The teacher measures progress and assigns grades using the evaluation criteria for each IEP objective. The teacher individualizes IEP grading for each student.

Mastery Level/Criterion Grading

Students reach mastery level when they reach a criterion level on specific skills. Thus, **mastery level/criterion grading** relies on content or skills divided into specific components. Mastery level/criterion grading normally involves pretesting students to determine level of performance on each skill in the curriculum, instruction on skills not yet mastered, and posttesting to identify skills mastered after instruction.

Shared Grading

Shared grading involves collaboration among two or more teachers to assign a grade. Shared grading often occurs when teachers instruct the same student in a subject or content area, such as in a co-teaching situation in an inclusion class with a general and special education teacher.

Progressive Improvement Grading

Progressive improvement grading involves giving students feedback and instruction on tests and learning activities throughout the grading period. However, grades are based on the results from the cumulative tests and learning activities occurring at the end of the term.

Questions Teachers Ask About Alternative Grades

Because so many alternative grading and testing procedures exist and new practices appear frequently, teachers have many questions about how to best modify grades and provide appropriate testing accommodations. Among the many questions that teachers ask are these:

- How can I make sure that grading modifications and testing accommodations maintain the integrity of the test, the course, and the curriculum?
- Do alternative grading and testing give students with disabilities an advantage over other students?

- How can I find the time and locate the necessary resources to implement testing accommodations?
- Should students with disabilities be graded using the same grading system as their peers without disabilities?
- Should grades reflect student competence?
- Should grades reflect student growth, progress, and effort?

Responding to these questions is challenging, and teachers have a variety of opinions about the best answers. For this reason, IEP teams rather than individual teachers should make decisions about needed adaptations. Further, experts (Salend, 2005; Thurlow, 2001) point out that the IEP is the legal document that defines an appropriate educational plan. As a result, student IEPs should outline the decisions of the team regarding needed modifications in grading and testing. Students with disabilities also have a legal right under IDEA to take large-scale and statewide assessments (Shriner & DeStefano, 2001; Thompson & Thurlow, 2001). However, because these types of assessments can create problems for students with disabilities, educators must consider procedures for reducing the possible negative effects. Again, it is the responsibility of the IEP team to address the problems and issues, and when students need accommodations or exemptions from these assessments, IEPs should include appropriate plans for providing these services.

On a more practical level, most teachers rely on a variety of support services in providing students with needed accommodations. Although many programs have well-established support services, teachers often find that they must also develop their own support systems. For example, teachers may use paraprofessionals, resource teachers, parent volunteers, or community volunteers to assist students with accommodations by giving oral tests, tape-recording instructions, transcribing tape-recorded test responses, and monitoring students who take tests in alternative settings. Teachers also use computers and other forms of technology to help support students with disabilities. See the Technology Focus box for a discussion of technology-based assessment processes and procedures useful in inclusive classrooms.

TECHNOLOGY FOCUS
Technology-Based Assessment

Innovations in technology and multimedia hold much promise for improving assessment in inclusive settings. Teachers are discovering innovative ways to use technology and multimedia for curriculum-based assessment, IEP development, records management, grading, and tracking student progress. As costs decrease and capabilities increase, use of computers and related technology in assessment will become even more widespread. Implementation of computers and related technology will enable teachers to assess students with special needs in new and exciting ways and may help reduce existing assessment barriers. Advances have occurred in many computer applications, including software programs for IEP development.

School systems routinely provide teachers with computer programs to assist in developing IEPs and measuring student progress in achieving IEP goals. Teachers and IEP teams use these programs to formulate benchmarks and to accomplish other IEP development tasks, such as completing the cover page.

Technology-Based Assessment (continued)

Teachers can create objectives or select them from a data bank and modify them as necessary to fit individual students. Although computer-based IEPs hold much potential for the future, certain limitations may reduce the usefulness of such programs. For example, teachers may need extensive and expensive technical support. Technical support needs include assistance with the hardware and software problems that frequently arise, especially with new systems and programs. Teachers also need technical support in learning to use new IEP software efficiently.

Computerized records-management and grade-reporting programs enable teachers to keep student records in a manner comparable to the traditional student record booklet. Teachers maintain attendance, test scores, grades on papers, homework assignments, and other information in this way. Records-management software also averages test score grades and produces weighted averages. Teachers can track the progress of individual students and measure group performance using these programs. Available software programs for grading include Grade Point by Paper Trail Software and ThinkWave Educator by ThinkWave. Teachers can use grading software programs like these to create progress reports, average grades, prepare report cards, prepare for conferences, develop parent reports, plan for remedial instruction, track assignments, and create checklists. Teachers can also use grading software as a motivating tool by giving students daily access to their grades. More teachers are also using online grade-reporting software to keep students and parents up-to-date on student performance and achievement. Online grading software provides individual, secure, and password-protected access to grades, attendance, assignments, and lessons. Software such as Grades Online! by ThinkWare enables secure publishing of information on the Internet, including upcoming tests and assignments, results with individual comments, lesson plans, absences, and announcements. Students and parents log in using password-protected accounts to see individual information.

According to Amaro (1997), giving this type of access to grades helps eliminate surprises for students who think they have good grades but don't, and it makes it possible for students to set exact goals for raising their grades. As a result, students with low grades will be motivated to work harder to boost their averages; students with high grades will be encouraged to continue to work hard to maintain their grades. This approach to grading makes averages real to students with special needs because they often fail to understand how averages work and may see grading as a process under the control of the teacher.

Because electronic tracking software is so new, it has several drawbacks, including limited availability of programs and a lack of laptop and handheld computers for teachers to use in the classroom. Improved versions of tracking software along with greater availability of portable computers may make this technology more useful in the future. Overall, these programs give teachers greater control over and better organization of student and group data and information.

Although few teachers question students' rights to reasonable and appropriate modifications and accommodations, most agree that schools should use alternative testing and grading only when necessary. Further, teachers should wean students from modifications whenever possible. This helps to ensure maximum success and independence in the general education setting for students with special needs.

☑ Check Your Comprehension

As you can see from our description of alternative grading procedures, teachers can select an appropriate grading procedure from an array of available options. Sometimes teachers combine two or more grading procedures. The particular alternative grading system that the teacher develops will depend on the needs of the individual student with consideration given to student ability, motivation, interest, behavior, and educational goals.

Reflection

From the list of alternative grading, choose one method you would like to use and explain the reason for your choice. Also select a method you would not like to use and explain why.

 To answer this reflection online, go to the *Teaching and Learning* module on the Companion Website at *www. prenhall.com/venn.*

Modifying Teacher-Made Tests

Almost all teachers assess student performance using teacher-made tests. The problem is that teacher-made tests may fail to give students with learning and behavior disabilities the opportunity to demonstrate what they have learned. This occurs because students with disabilities may have deficits in attention, memory, organization, reading, or writing that hinder performance on teacher-made tests. For these reasons, teachers need to incorporate test design alterations to minimize the effect of attention and memory problems. Although teachers are continuing to develop new testing modifications for students in inclusive settings, a number of appropriate and effective techniques already exist.

A recent study by Bielinski, Ysseldyke, Bolt, Friedebach, and Friedebach (2001) on the use of accommodations found that extended time, small-group administration, and read-aloud were used most often. Read-alouds involve having a proctor read the test items to the examinee. The results also indicated that accommodations were rarely used in isolation. Students were likely to use at least two accommodations together.

Fortunately, not all students with disabilities require assessment adaptations. Furthermore, appropriate modifications for students who require them usually involve minor alterations of procedures rather than major adjustments. The goal is to provide appropriate evaluation using techniques that are as similar as possible to the testing and grading used with all students in the class. In addition to the accommodations just described, test design modifications may also include changes in format, directions, response modes, test items, test setting, and test timing (Mercer & Mercer, 2005; Salend, 2005).

Test Format

Students with disabilities sometimes master the academic content necessary for successful performance on a test but perform poorly on the test due to problems with the **test format.** Long, poorly designed, cluttered, or distracting tests can negatively affect student performance. Teachers can reduce format problems by giving tests that have these features:

- Are clean and printed darkly on a solid, clear background
- Are typed (not handwritten) in a familiar style

- Have proper spacing and sequencing of items
- Avoid separate answer sheets that require students to transfer responses
- Present questions in a structured, stable, predictable sequence (this helps students make the transition from item to item)
- Provide adequate space for responding to each item
- Have a reading level that is not too high for the students

In addition to these test format considerations, some students may need specialized equipment. Students who are visually impaired, for example, may need large-print or braille versions of tests. Students with hearing impairments may need the services of an interpreter. Likewise, students with reading disabilities may need audiocassettes of tests and markers to focus attention and maintain their place.

Test Directions

In some situations, students with special needs may receive poor marks on a test due to difficulty in following the **test directions** rather than lack of knowledge of the test content. Teachers can minimize this problem by using cues that help students understand and follow test directions. Cues include color coding, font variations, underlining, bolding, symbols, and enlarging the print. Cues can highlight key parts of items and emphasize changes in specific items. For example, a model showing changes in item type or test directions can be placed in a box. Symbols such as arrows or "go" signs can delineate continuations, and "stop" signs can indicate the end of a section. Teachers, paraprofessionals, or class volunteers can also provide cues. For example, some students need a proctor to read test directions and questions.

Response Modes

Teachers may need to modify the **response modes** of test items for students with written or verbal communication difficulties. For example, when the mechanics of written language are not important in grading answers, students can record responses on an audiocassette, or they can take an oral exam. Students can also dictate answers to a scribe, review their answers, and then direct the scribe to revise grammar, punctuation, and word choices in the responses. Word processors, pointers, communication boards, typewriters, and other adaptive devices also can assist students. Finally, some students may need aids such as calculators, word lists, or arithmetic tables.

Test Items

Teachers should consider the needs of their students with disabilities when selecting the types of items to include on tests. With multiple-choice items, for example, teachers can improve student performance by adhering to the following guidelines:

- Present response choices in a vertical format.
- Avoid double negatives.
- Keep the response choices as brief as possible.
- Avoid potentially confusing choices such as *all of the above* or *none of the above.*
- Limit the number of choices to no more than four items.

Students who have difficulty recording their answers should have the option of circling their response selection.

With matching items, teachers should keep several design features in mind, including the following:

- Limit sections to no more than 10 item pairs.
- Provide an equal number of choices in both columns, with one correct response for each pair.
- Present longer items in the left-hand column.
- Organize matching items so they all appear on the same page.
- Place an answer space next to each item instead of having students draw lines.

Other test formats include true–false, fill-in-the-blank, short answer, and essay. Appropriate modifications for these items include the following:

- Require only a brief response or an outline for short-answer or essay questions.
- Define unfamiliar or abstract vocabulary.
- Provide a group of possible answers for fill-in-the-blank questions.
- Avoid the use of *never, not, sometimes,* and *always* in true–false questions.
- Provide subsections that break up essay questions into manageable sections.

Modifying the Test Setting and Timing

Some students may need to take tests in an alternative setting such as alone in a quiet room, in a study carrel, in a small group, or in a resource room. Sometimes students also benefit from extended time to complete a test by giving breaks during testing or by testing over several sessions instead of one long session.

Test Anxiety

Teachers should also consider the impact of **test anxiety** and embarrassment on performance. Wood (2006) developed the following guidelines to minimize student apprehension.

1. Avoid pressuring students by telling them to "finish quickly" or "this counts as half of your 9-weeks' grade."
2. Avoid using testing as punishment for students who exhibit behavior problems.
3. Give as many practice tests as possible.
4. Allow students to take retests as needed.
5. Avoid threats of unreasonable consequences for poor test performance.
6. For students who take tests slowly, grade only the completed items.
7. Adapted tests for students should be given in a resource room.
8. Adapted tests should closely match regular tests so that students are not self-conscious.
9. Mainstreamed students should be assisted without being labeled.
10. Work with students individually to arrange testing accommodations.

Students with disabilities can benefit from and have a right to testing modifications such as these that enable them to successfully demonstrate their knowledge and skills in general education classes. Reasonable modifications are essential so that capable students with special needs are tested fairly in ways that give them the opportunity to earn good grades.

☑ Check Your Comprehension

Students with disabilities have learning and behavior problems that limit their ability to perform well on teacher-made tests. As a result, teachers need to incorporate test design alterations that minimize the effect of attention, memory, and behavior problems. A number of appropriate and effective techniques already exist, and teachers are still developing new modifications specifically for students with disabilities in inclusive settings. Test design modifications include changes in format, directions, response modes, test items, test setting, and test timing. Teachers also use a number of strategies to reduce student test anxiety and embarrassment.

Cooperative Learning Assessment

Cooperative learning is an instructional strategy in which students learn together in teams. Experts (Cohen, 1994; Pomplan, 1996; Webb, 1995) indicate that students with disabilities who participate in cooperative groups are more likely to make successful transitions into general education classes. Some students with disabilities, however, need social and group skills training to ensure successful participation in cooperative learning groups. Research studies by Pomplan (1997) and Carlson, Ellison, and Dietrich (1988) provide evidence supporting the effectiveness of cooperative learning in inclusive classrooms. These studies suggest that nonroutine, open-ended tasks maximize the participation of students with disabilities in heterogeneous cooperative groups.

Appropriate assessment is one of the key components in cooperative learning. Further, assessing teamwork in cooperative learning is as important as assessing individual student work. The following cooperative learning assessment procedures, developed by Johnson, Johnson, and Holubec (1998), include ways to assess teamwork and individual work. Teachers can easily adapt these procedures for use in inclusive classrooms.

When teachers use cooperative learning, they are responsible for ensuring that appropriate assessment takes place. The steps in assessing cooperative learning are similar to those in assessing any lesson:

- Specify the objectives.
- Develop the assignment.
- Determine grading criteria.
- Explain the assignment and share the grading criteria with students.
- Monitor the efforts of the cooperative groups.
- Intervene and provide support as necessary.
- Evaluate the results.

Teachers may use several assessment strategies to evaluate results, including the following:

- Observing group performance as it occurs
- Interviewing individual students and groups of students
- Evaluating individual and group performance on classwork and homework
- Grading teacher-made tests given to individuals or groups

Although these strategies are familiar to most teachers, Johnson et al. (1998) have also designed specialized approaches to assessment in cooperative learning situations. Specialized assessment approaches include peer editing, peer assessment of class presentations, self-assessment, peer assessment, group assessment, and group celebration. An explanation of each approach follows.

Peer Editing

Peer editing involves having the other members of the cooperative group edit the compositions of individual students. In peer editing, all group members certify that each member's paper meets the criteria set by the teacher. Group members work together in developing their papers, and each group member receives two grades. One grade is an individual grade based on the quality of the manuscript. The other grade is a group grade that reflects the sum quality of the group's papers.

One way to structure peer editing uses the following steps. First, the teacher assigns students to cooperative learning pairs with at least one good writer in each pair. Second, the teacher gives the students individual writing assignments. Third, the teacher has the students describe what they are planning to write to each other. Fourth, students work individually on their papers, but they also share material with each other and help their partners. The teacher monitors the work of the pairs and assists as necessary to help students develop their writing skills and their cooperative skills. Finally, when the assignments are complete, the teacher helps the students do the following:

- Discuss how well they worked together by describing specific actions they engaged in to help each other
- Plan what behaviors they are going to emphasize in future cooperative writing assignments
- Thank each other for the help they received

Students with special needs may require additional instruction, support, coaching, and encouragement to develop peer-editing skills. The special education teacher can often provide this support directly. Teachers may also arrange for teaching assistants, peer tutors, or volunteer tutors to provide extra support while students learn how to work with others on cooperative writing assignments.

Peer Assessment of Class Presentations

Peers can evaluate presentations given by fellow students. One way to encourage group interdependence and to foster **peer assessment** is to structure class presentations so that all members must learn the material presented. Teachers can accomplish this by assigning students to cooperative groups of four, giving each group a topic, and requiring each group to develop a presentation that every group member can give in its entirety. The presentation criteria should include a specific period of active participation by the audience. The groups should have sufficient time to prepare and rehearse so that all group members can give the presentation. The teacher then divides the class into four sections (one in each corner of the classroom). One member of each group goes to each section and gives the presentation to the audience in their section. Assessment involves having the audience rate the presentation using a rating form. The rating form should include items for assessing the quality of the information; the interest generated by the presentation; the ease of understanding; the organization, creativity, and originality; and audience participation. The students give one copy of the completed rating form to the presenter and one copy to the teacher. The teacher also observes parts of all the presentations. Finally, the groups meet to evaluate the effectiveness of the presentations, to celebrate their successes, and to discuss ways to improve their presentation skills in the future.

Self-Assessment and Peer Assessment

Arranging for students to assess themselves and each other should be an element in most cooperative learning lessons. Students with special needs in inclusive settings may need considerable guidance to develop **self-assessment** and peer-assessment skills. Students who lack these skills need opportunities to develop them over time. Teachers may accomplish this in many ways, including modeling, role playing, coaching, and direct instruction. The goal is for students to discuss and reflect on their learning and that of others.

Teachers can use cooperative learning assessment checklists such as those in Figures 3–2 and 3–3 to help students develop self-assessment and peer-assessment competencies. The checklist in Figure 3–2 is for student self-assessment. Teachers should help students learn how to rate their own collaboration skills with the self-assessment checklist. The checklist in Figure 3–3 is for peer assessment. Teachers should give students instruction in using the peer-assessment checklist in Figure 3–3 to rate the participation of their peers in their cooperative group. Students can use the completed checklists to compare their self-ratings with the ratings from their peers. The checklists provide data that teachers and students can use to ensure they are making positive contributions to the learning of all group members. Teachers can also use the results in grading individual students and cooperative learning groups, or teachers may develop their own assessment checklists to fit particular cooperative learning assignments. For example, teachers of young students should develop simplified checklists and rating scales.

Group Assessment

Because individual assessment is more common in the classroom than **group assessment,** the typical cooperative learning group has students learn in a group but

FIGURE 3–2   Cooperative learning assessment checklist—self-assessment form

Your Name_____
Rate yourself using the following scale:

        4—Excellent, 3—Very Good, 2—Good, 1—Poor

Assessment Item   Rating

1. I was on time.   _____
2. I was prepared.   _____
3. I contributed to the learning of others in my group.   _____
4. I listened to the other members of the group.   _____
5. I worked together with others in my group.   _____
6. The other members would like to work with me again.   _____

Comments

_____
_____
_____

FIGURE 3–3   Cooperative learning assessment checklist—peer-assessment form

---

Person Being Rated_____Rater_____

Rate the group member using the following scale:

4—Excellent, 3—Very Good, 2—Good, 1—Poor

Assessment Item   Rating

1. The group member was on time.   _____
2. The group member was prepared.   _____
3. The group member contributed to the learning of others. _____
4. The group member listened to others.   _____
5. The group member worked together with others.   _____
6. I would like to work with this group member again.   _____

Comments

_____

_____

_____

_____

---

individually demonstrate what they have learned. In real life, most organizations focus on the success of the organization as a whole. The emphasis is on the success of departments in the organization and teams in departments rather than the success of individual employees. For this reason, cooperative learning assignments in school should require group reports, exhibits, performances, and presentations in which the students work together and teachers grade the performance of the group.

Group Celebration

Group celebrations should occur at the end of cooperative learning lessons after completion of assessment and grading. Celebrations may be simple, such as having students congratulate each other, or they can be more elaborate, such as a group cheer, a dance, a song, or an event. Group celebrations give students the opportunity to salute their success and reflect on how well they collaborated to achieve their learning goals. One way to celebrate success is to arrange an activity in which students share how well they are achieving their academic goals and what they learned through collaboration. Recognizing the learning efforts of group members and their contributions to the learning of others is an important element in rewarding and reinforcing group interdependence.

Assigning Grades in Cooperative Learning

The way teachers assign grades in cooperative learning depends on the amount of interdependence they wish to develop among students. Teachers have a number of options for assigning grades. Examples of some of the available options follow.

• *Individual grading with extra points based on all members reaching criterion*: This grading procedure encourages group members to study together so that everyone learns the material. Students are graded individually but also receive extra points if all group members achieve a preestablished criterion level. An example of this procedure is as follows:

Group Member	Individual Points	Extra Points[1]	Total Points
Jaros	95	3	98
Marinko	92	3	95
Tammy	90	3	93

[1] Criteria for Extra Points: If all group members receive at least 90 individual points, all group members receive 3 extra points.

• *Individual grading with extra points based on the lowest score*: In this grading system the group members prepare with each other to take the exam. The group members receive extra points based on the lowest individual score in the group. An example is as follows:

Group Member	Individual Points	Extra Points[2]	Total Points
Jaros	99	4	103
Marinko	87	4	91
Tammy	80	4	84

[2] Criteria for Extra Points: 90–100 = 5 points, 80–89 = 4 points, 70–79 = 3 points

• *Individual grading with extra points based on the group average*: After group members help each other study for the test, students take the exam individually and receive individual scores. The scores of all group members are then averaged, and the average is added to each student's score. An example is as follows:

Group Member	Individual Score	Average Score	Total Score
Jaros	88	82	170
Marinko	82	82	164
Tammy	77	82	159

• *Random selection of one group member's work to grade*: The students in the group complete the assignment individually and then help each other to make sure all the papers are correct. Because the group certifies all papers as correct, it matters little which paper is randomly selected by the teacher for grading. All group members receive the same grade.

• *Assigning the lowest member's grade to all members of the group*: The group members help each other study for the exam. Then students take the exam individually, but all group members receive the lowest grade in the group. This grading procedure helps group members encourage, support, and assist the low-achieving members of the group. This sometimes results in significant increases in the performance of low-achieving students. Teachers can avoid the problem of penalizing advanced and high-achieving students by using group grades like this only for extra credit or rewards. Thus, a low grade from a group exam can potentially increase but never reduce a student's individual grade.

• *Averaging individual grades with a collaboration score*: The group members work together to learn the assigned material and then take individual exams. The grades of the group are then averaged. The teacher also observes the group to determine the level of collaboration (e.g., leadership, shared decision making, listening). The group then receives a collaboration grade that is added to their average grade to arrive at a total score.

- *Individual grading with celebration rewards:* The members of the group help each other study for the exam, but they take the test individually and receive individual grades. The group is rewarded with free time, extra time in the yard, snacks, stickers, or other appropriate reinforcers if they all achieve a predetermined level of success.

Johnson et al. (1998) developed these procedures for assessing the performance of students in cooperative learning groups. Teachers should select a particular procedure from these available options depending on the nature of the assigned task and the amount of interdependence they wish to foster in the group.

Peer-Tutoring Assessment

Another evaluation strategy that is useful in inclusive settings is **peer-tutoring assessment.** Peer tutoring is an instructional strategy in which a student tutor teaches another student in a tutor-tutee relationship designed to promote academic learning and social skill development. Successful peer tutoring involves planning, tutor training, teacher support, and assessment. Some teachers assess the progress of tutees by having tutors complete daily progress sheets. Teachers can also monitor progress by observing tutor–tutee pairs, conducting interviews, and having tutors and tutees complete simple questionnaires.

☑ Check Your Comprehension

Cooperative learning is a major element of many inclusive classrooms. Appropriate assessment is one of the key components of cooperative learning success. Cooperative learning assessment includes a variety of procedures, such as peer editing, self-assessment, peer assessment, group assessment, group celebration, and peer tutoring. Teachers may select from several available strategies for assigning grades in cooperative learning. The particular approach to grade assignment depends on the amount of interdependence and cooperation teachers wish to develop among students.

Summary

Inclusion of students with disabilities in general education means that regular classrooms are composed of much more diverse student groups than in the past. As a result, teachers in inclusive settings must provide significant testing modifications to meet individual needs. Although most teachers are familiar with inclusion in general, they have many questions about inclusive assessment. Furthermore, the wide variety of alternative testing procedures makes inclusive assessment complex and challenging. On the other hand, this variety also provides a range of options from which to select the best test procedure for each student.

Clearly, teachers should continue efforts to improve assessment procedures for students with disabilities in inclusive classrooms. In order to achieve this goal, teachers need to be familiar with appropriate procedures for assessment in inclusive settings. Teachers equipped with this knowledge can make sure that their students receive fair and accurate assessment regardless of the setting in which they receive their education.

To check your comprehension of chapter contents, go to the *Quiz* module in Chapter 3 of the Companion Website, *www.prenhall.com/venn.*

Meeting Performance Standards and Preparing for Licensure Exams

After reading this chapter, you should be able to demonstrate the following CEC standards and PRAXIS™ test knowledge and skills. The information in parentheses identifies where to find the particular CEC standard and PRAXIS™ content reference.

CEC Standards for Beginning Special Education Teachers

- Teach individuals to use self-assessment, problem solving, and other cognitive strategies to meet their needs (CC4S2)
- Strategies to prepare for and take tests (GC4K2)
- Methods for ensuring individual academic success in one-to-one, small-group, and large-group settings (GC5K3)
- Develop or modify individualized assessment strategies (CC8S4)
- Evaluate instruction and monitor progress of individuals with exceptional learning needs (CC8S8)
- Implement procedures for assessing and reporting both appropriate and problematic social behaviors of individuals with disabilities (GC8S1)
- Use group problem-solving skills to develop, implement, and evaluate collaborative activities (CC10S7)

PRAXIS™ Education of Exceptional Students: Core Content Knowledge

- Historical movements/trends affecting the connections between special education and the larger society; for example: inclusion, application of technology, accountability, and meeting educational standards (0353 II)
- Background knowledge, including placement and program issues such as least restrictive environment; continuum of educational and related services (30353 III)
- Assessment, including use of assessment for screening, diagnosis, placement, and the making of instructional decisions (0353 III)

part II

Assessment Concepts and Skills

chapter 4

Practical Measurement Concepts

Objectives

After reading this chapter, you will be prepared to do the following:

- Understand and use the basic statistical concepts of distributions, central tendency, and variability.
- Understand reliability and give examples of the four major types of reliability.
- Understand validity and give examples of the three major types of validity.
- Describe norm-referenced and criterion-referenced measurement.
- Understand norms and describe the norm-development process.
- Understand the process of standardizing assessments.
- Use practical measurement concepts to assist in selecting and evaluating assessments for students with special needs.

Overview

The basic concepts of measurement are essential to understanding assessment of students with special needs. This chapter aids you in developing your knowledge in this critical area. To achieve this goal, you will examine the key measurement concepts of basic statistics, accuracy in assessment, and the effectiveness of tests and evaluation procedures. You will also investigate the meaning of criterion-referenced and norm-referenced measurement and consider the uses, advantages, and disadvantages of each. At the conclusion of this chapter, you will review practical measurement concepts and procedures for evaluating tests from an applied, functional perspective.

Introduction to the Measurement Concepts

The basic concepts of measurement are a fundamental element of all assessment processes and procedures. These concepts provide the basis for quantifying the abilities, skills, and behaviors of students. As a special educator, you will benefit from knowledge of these concepts in several ways. Understanding the concepts of measurement enables you to use test manuals properly, especially the technical sections on scoring and interpreting results. Teachers and other professionals rely on the measurement concepts to communicate assessment information with colleagues, students, parents, and others. The concepts also help in selecting assessment procedures that fit the individual needs of particular students. Finally, appropriate application of

measurement procedures helps ensure the collection of accurate and meaningful instructional data and information.

Definition of Statistics

The basic concepts of measurement all center on statistics. **Statistics** are special kinds of numbers that summarize and give meaning to large groups of data by putting them into manageable form. Examples of statistics in our daily lives include the interest rates on credit cards, the rate of inflation, and the unemployment rate. Teachers routinely use statistics in grading and scoring. Examples of classroom statistics include percent correct scores on teacher-made tests, percentile ranks on high-stakes tests, and the number of items mastered on skills checklists. Teachers also rely on statistics to summarize scores of groups of students who take class tests. To illustrate this point, a large set of hypothetical test scores from several of Ms. Street's classes appears in Table 4–1. This random listing of scores has little meaning, demonstrating the difficulty of drawing conclusions from large groups of unorganized numbers. However, statistics summarize the scores and give meaning to the numbers by converting the data into practical form. Three of the basic statistics frequently used in education are

- distributions, which are often graphed;
- measures of central tendency, also called averages; and
- measures of variability sometimes referred to as dispersions.

Distributions

One of the best ways to describe large groups of numbers such as test scores is to establish distributions. **Distributions** are helpful because they classify large sets of scores into meaningful arrangements that visually summarize and illustrate the relationship among the scores. The procedure for establishing distributions involves organizing scores in rank order from highest to lowest, grouping them in intervals,

Table 4–1 Random List of Test Scores from Ms. Street's Classes

Student	# of Correct Answers	Student	# of Correct Answers
Robert	38	Vicki	29
Kevin	24	Chiquita	29
Charmane	36	Lisa	25
Nadira	40	Grant	36
Todd	37	Nat	41
Julie	37	Clint	24
Blythe	29	Patrick	33
Debbie	44	Lynne	41
Jason	44	Lib	39
Jeffrey	35	Sharian	44
Lasonya	38	Latanya	32
Nathan	34	Kathe	43
Karly	27	Molly	29
Asher	46	Johnny	31
Katrina	35	Justin	34
Soo	46	Elliot	26
Bob	32	Lanier	37
Donna	39	Charlene	35
Connie	32	Qadi	33
Eli	33	Rossi	35
Chris	26	David	36
Ann Marie	40	Carver	35
Casey	29	Mary	40
Lacy	42	Sebastion	39
Peggy	35	Sharon	37

and graphing them. This arrangement displays the pattern of the scores and organizes them for easy graphing. To illustrate this procedure, the random list of scores from Ms. Street's classes (Table 4–1) appears in Table 4–2 in rank order and in groups spanning three intervals. Graphing distributions with bar or line charts visually depicts the pattern of the scores. Graphs of the scores from Ms. Street's classes appear in Figure 4–1. The vertical axis of the line graph displays the frequency of occurrence of each group of scores, and the horizontal axis displays the individual scores.

These test scores fall into a pattern called a normal distribution. In a **normal distribution** most of the scores cluster around the average score. The scores also follow an even pattern with about an equal number of scores falling above and below the average score. Because the shape when graphed looks somewhat like a bell, another name for the normal distribution is the bell-shaped curve or **bell curve**. Use of normal distributions is based on the concept that cognitive, psychological, and emotional characteristics are evenly distributed in the population. This is an important theoretical assumption in test development. When developers create new norm-referenced tests, they expect the scores to fall into a normally distributed pattern. Similarly, when teachers create curriculum-based assessments, they usually expect the resulting scores to be distributed in a normal curve with a few high scores and a few low scores but with the majority of scores in the midrange.

Table 4-2 Rank Order of Test Scores from Ms. Street's Classes

Student	Correct Answers	Scores in Group	Student	Correct Answers	Scores in Group
Asher	46		Jeffrey	35	
Soo	46		Katrina	35	
Debbie	44	5	Peggy	35	
Jason	44		Rossi	35	
Sharian	44				
			Justin	34	
Kathe	43		Nathan	34	
Lacy	42	4	Eli	33	
Lynne	41		Patrick	33	
Nat	41		Qadi	33	8
			Bob	32	
Nadira	40		Latanya	32	
Ann Marie	40		Connie	32	
Mary	40				
Lib	39		Johnny	31	
Donna	39	8	Casey	29	
Sebastian	39		Chiquita	29	6
Lasonya	38		Molly	29	
Robert	38		Blythe	29	
			Vicki	29	
Sharon	37				
Lanier	37		Karly	27	
Julie	37		Chris	26	3
Todd	37		Elliot	26	
Charmane	36				
David	36		Lisa	25	
Grant	36	13	Kevin	24	3
Carver	35		Clint	24	
Charlene	35				

Abnormal or **skewed distributions** occur when scores cluster at either the high or the low end rather than at the middle or average of a distribution. This happens, for example, when teachers give easy or difficult tests in which most students receive very high or very low scores, respectively. With a positive skew, scores cluster around the low end, and with a negative skew, scores bunch up at the high end. An illustration of positive skew appears in Figure 4-2. This type of distribution characterizes scores, such as those from a class test, in which almost all the marks range from 60 to 70 (when the highest possible score is 100). In contrast, a negative skew, as appears in Figure 4-3, occurs when most scores on a class test fall in the 90 to 100 range.

In most situations, a normal distribution is desirable. Skewed distributions are generally undesirable. For this reason, teachers usually avoid giving tests that produce skewed results because if most students score 100% on a test, not only is the test probably too easy, but the results fail to discriminate among the students. Similarly, if most

Figure 4–1 Line graph of the test scores from Ms. Street's classes

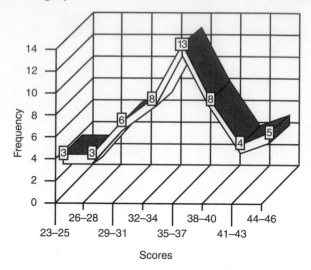

Figure 4–2 A positively skewed distribution

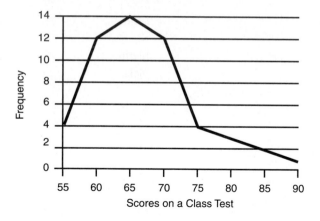

Figure 4–3 A negatively skewed distribution

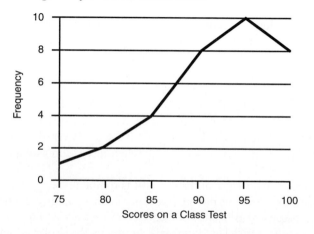

students receive low marks on a test, the skewed results fail to distinguish among the students.

Establishing distributions provides a method of describing groups of scores; graphing distributions produces a visual picture of the pattern of the scores. Another way to describe large groups of numbers with statistics is by measuring the central tendency.

Measures of Central Tendency

The **measures of central tendency** are statistics that describe the typical or representative scores in a group. These measures are usually referred to as averages because they summarize the overall trend or the most frequently occurring scores in distributions. The commonly used averages or measures of central tendency are mean, median, and mode. The **mean** denotes the average number in a distribution and is the most commonly used measure of central tendency. In most instances, the term *average* refers to the mean rather than to the other specific measures of central tendency. The **mode** indicates the most frequently occurring score in a distribution. The **median** marks the midpoint, or middle figure, in a distribution.

When teachers give class tests, they usually describe the performance of the group by reporting the mean, or average, score. Teachers also rely on the mean to characterize the performance of individual students by averaging scores across several class tests. The formula for calculating the mean involves summing all of the scores and dividing by the number of scores, as follows:

$$\text{Mean} = \frac{\text{Sum of the scores}}{\text{Number of scores}}$$

Mathematical calculations rely on symbols as a form of notation for each of the operations in a formula. The formula for the mean uses the following mathematical symbols:

$\bar{x}$ = mean
X = any score
Σ = sum
N = number of scores

When the formula is depicted with these symbols, it appears as follows:

$$\bar{x} = \frac{\Sigma X}{N}$$

Using the scores from Ms. Street's class tests, the calculation for the mean is

ΣX = 1,761 (the sum of the test scores)
N = 50 (the total number of test scores)
$\bar{x}$ = 1,761/50 = 35 (the mean or average score on the test)

The number of scores in the distribution is an important characteristic in calculating the mean because as the number of scores increases, the accuracy of the mean increases. Conversely, as the number of scores in a distribution decreases, the accuracy also decreases. This happens because with only a few scores in a group, an extreme score significantly changes the mean. However, with many scores in a distribution, an extreme score fails to significantly alter the mean.

Table 4–3   Effect of an Extreme Score on the Mean

Scores in Distribution A	Scores in Distribution B
90	90
95	95
90	90
95	85
15	90
$X = 385$	95
$N = 5$	90
$\bar{x} = \dfrac{\Sigma X}{N} = \dfrac{385}{5} = 77$	85
	90
	85
	90
	95
	85
	95
	15
	$\Sigma X = 1{,}275$
	$N = 15$
	$\bar{x} = \dfrac{\Sigma X}{N} = \dfrac{1{,}275}{15} = 85$

The examples in Table 4–3 illustrate the effect of an extreme score on the mean. Distribution A contains only five scores, including one extreme score. In this small distribution, the extreme score significantly lowers the mean. Distribution B contains 15 scores, including the same extreme score. Because this is a larger distribution, the extreme score has little effect on the mean.

Because the number of scores in a distribution is such an important characteristic, experts recommend cautious use of the mean with small groups of scores, especially with extreme scores. According to most authorities, small distributions contain fewer than 15 scores. Although distributions with at least 15 scores are generally sufficient for calculating accurate means, distributions with 30 or more scores are ideal in size. For example, there are 50 scores from Ms. Street's classes. Thus, the mean score of 35 accurately describes this distribution. The measures of central tendency, especially the mean, provide highly useful statistics for describing groups of scores. The measures of variability supply a complementary method for characterizing large sets of numbers.

Measures of Variability

Unlike the mean, which describes central tendency, the **measures of variability** summarize the spread or dispersion of distributions. The two most important measures of variability in assessment are the standard deviation and the standard error of measurement. The **standard deviation** summarizes the variability of groups of scores by measuring the average distance of individual scores from the mean of the distribution. In other words, the standard deviation describes the magnitude of the distance of individual scores from the average score. Distributions with higher variability yield larger standard deviations than distributions with lower variability. Educators rely on the standard deviation, by far the most common measure of variability, for functions such as interpreting the meaning of test scores, determining the amount of error in test scores, and reporting scores derived from formal standardized tests.

Standard Deviation

The statistical notation for standard deviation is SD, S, s, or σ (the Greek letter sigma). To calculate the standard deviation, use the following formula:

$$SD = \frac{\sqrt{\Sigma(X - \bar{x})}}{N}$$

where SD = standard deviation

$\sqrt{}$ = square root

Σ = sum

X = raw score on the test

$\bar{x}$ = mean of the test

N = number of test scores

Calculating the standard deviation (using the scores from Ms. Street's classes) involves several steps, as outlined in Table 4–4. The first step is to find the mean by adding all the scores and dividing the total by the number of scores. The mean from the scores in Ms. Street's classes is 35 (1,761/50 = 35.22). The next step involves

Table 4–4 Calculating the Standard Deviation of the Scores from Ms. Street's Classes

Student	Test	Score X − x	(X − x̄)²
Asher	46	46 − 35 = 11	11 × 11 = 121
Soo	46	46 − 35 − 11	11 × 11 = 121
Debbie	44	44 − 35 = 9	9 × 9 = 81
Jason	44	44 − 35 − 9	9 × 9 = 81
Sharian	44	44 − 35 = 9	9 × 9 = 81
Kathe	43	43 − 35 = 8	8 × 8 = 64
Lacy	42	42 − 35 = 7	7 × 7 = 49
Lynne	41	41 − 35 = 6	6 × 6 = 36
Nat	41	41 − 35 = 6	6 × 6 = 36
Nadira	40	40 − 35 = 5	5 × 5 = 25
Ann Marie	40	40 − 35 − 5	5 × 5 = 25
Mary	40	40 − 35 = 5	5 × 5 = 25
Lib	39	39 − 35 = 4	4 × 4 = 16
Donna	39	39 − 35 = 4	4 × 4 = 16
Sebastian	39	39 − 35 = 4	4 × 4 = 16
Lasonya	38	38 − 35 = 3	3 × 3 = 9
Robert	38	38 − 35 = 3	3 × 3 = 9
Sharon	37	37 − 35 = 2	2 × 2 = 4
Lanier	37	37 − 35 = 2	2 × 2 = 4
Julie	37	37 − 35 = 2	2 × 2 = 4
Todd	37	37 − 35 = 2	2 × 2 = 4
Charmane	36	36 − 35 = 1	1 × 1 = 1
David	36	36 − 35 = 1	1 × 1 = 1

(continued)

Table 4–4   continued

Student	Test	Score $X - \bar{x}$	$(X - \bar{x})^2$
Grant	36	36 − 35 = 1	1 × 1 = 1
Carver	35	35 − 35 = 0	0 × 0 = 0
Charlene	35	35 − 35 = 0	0 × 0 = 0
Jeffrey	35	35 − 35 = 0	0 × 0 = 0
Katrina	35	35 − 35 = 0	0 × 0 = 0
Peggy	35	35 − 35 = 0	0 × 0 = 0
Rossi	35	35 − 35 = 0	0 × 0 = 0
Justin	34	34 − 35 = −1	−1 × −1 = 1
Nathan	34	34 − 35 = −1	−1 × −1 = 1
Eli	33	33 − 35 = −2	−2 × −2 = 4
Patrick	33	33 − 35 = −2	−2 × −2 = 4
Qadi	33	33 − 35 = −2	−2 × −2 = 4
Bob	32	32 − 35 = −3	−3 × −3 = 9
Latanya	32	32 − 35 = −3	−3 × −3 = 9
Connie	32	32 − 35 = −3	−3 × −3 = 9
Johnny	31	31 − 35 = −4	−4 × −4 = 16
Casey	29	29 − 35 = −6	−6 × −6 = 36
Chiquita	29	29 − 35 = −6	−6 × −6 = 36
Molly	29	29 − 35 = −6	−6 × −6 = 36
Blythe	29	29 − 35 = −6	−6 × −6 = 36
Vicki	29	29 − 35 = −6	−6 × −6 = 36
Karly	27	27 − 35 = −8	−8 × −8 = 64
Chris	26	26 − 35 = −9	−9 × −9 = 81
Elliot	26	26 − 35 = −9	−9 × −9 = 81
Lisa	25	25 − 35 = −10	−10 × −10 = 100
Kevin	24	24 − 35 = −11	−11 × −11 = 121
Clint	24	24 − 35 = −11	−11 × −11 = 121
	$\Sigma = 1{,}761$		$\Sigma(X - \bar{x})^2 = 1{,}635$

subtracting the mean from each score. This procedure is shown in the third column. Next, the differences from the mean in the third column are squared, as shown in the fourth column. The subsequent step is to sum the squared differences from the mean, which in this case is 1,635 (this number appears at the bottom of the fourth column), and divide by the number of scores (there are 50 scores). Thus 1,635 divided by 50 equals 32.7 (1,635/50 = 32.7). The resulting value of 32.7 is the variance, defined as the average squared deviation of scores from the mean. One more calculation is necessary to obtain the standard deviation. The variance is the average squared deviation from the mean. The standard deviation is the average deviation from the mean. To obtain the standard deviation, the square must be eliminated from the variance by determining the square root of the variance. In this case the square root of 32.7 is 5.72. The square root of a specific number is the number that, when multiplied by itself, produces that specific number. For example, the square root of 100 is 10, and the square root of 36 is 6. Most mathematics books contain a table of square roots for the numbers 1 through 100. Most calculators also provide a square root function.

Standard Deviation and the Bell-Shaped Curve

One of the best ways to explain standard deviation is by relating it to the normal distribution or the bell-shaped curve. In a normal distribution, a precise relationship exists between the standard deviation and the scores in the distribution. This relationship depends on the percentage distribution of scores in the normal curve, as illustrated in Figure 4–4. Here standard deviation units appear on the line under the curve marked to show 1, 2, and 3 standard deviations (SDs) from the mean, which is marked with a 0. The percentage of scores falling within each standard deviation unit also appears in Figure 4–4. For example, the percentage of scores between the mean (0) and +1 SD is 34.13%. The same percentage of scores, 34.13%, occurs between the mean and −1 SD from the mean. A majority or 68.26% (34.13 + 34.13 = 68.26) of the scores occur between +1 and −1 SDs from the mean. In other words, in a normal distribution most of the scores cluster around the mean, or average. Almost all, or 95.44%, of the scores occur between +2 and −2 SDs from the mean.

Understanding the percentage distribution of scores in a normal curve helps in interpreting norm-referenced scores. For example, characteristics such as achievement tend to be normally distributed among students in the school population. Most students have average achievement, and their scores cluster around the middle of a bell-shaped curve. Relatively few students have significantly high or low achievement, and their scores fall near the ends of the bell-shaped curve.

Many, but not all, students with disabilities have low achievement. Therefore, the distribution of achievement with students who have disabilities takes on a positive skew. In other words, the test scores of students with disabilities usually fall at the low end of the bell-shaped curve. Further, students with disabilities often score in the bottom 2% on standardized tests. This is more than 2 SDs below the mean. In fact, in order to qualify for most special education programs, students must score at least 2 SDs below the mean on the appropriate measures of achievement or ability. Therefore, teachers in special education instruct a significant number of students whose scores on standardized tests are lower than 98% of all students in the school. In contrast, students who are gifted rise to the high end of the bell-shaped curve. The scores on norm-referenced intelligence and achievement tests of students who are gifted are usually in the top 2%, or higher than 98% of all students.

Specialists in statistics indicate that the standard deviation along with the mean represent the two most important basic statistics. As a result, testing experts often report these two statistics together because of the special relationship between them.

Reflection

Looking at students' test scores, how would measures such as the standard deviation and the mean help you in understanding your class as a group?

 To answer this reflection online, go to the *Teaching and Learning* module on the Companion Website at *www.prenhall.com/venn.*

Figure 4–4 Distribution of cases in the normal curve

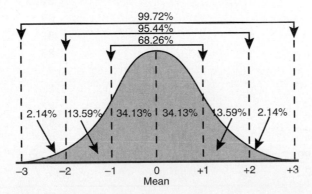

Relationship Between the Standard Deviation and the Mean

An illustration of the relationship between the standard deviation and the mean appears in Table 4–5. For demonstration purposes, the example relies on a small group of 10 scores rather than a larger set of scores. In this example, both sets of scores produce the same mean, $\overline{x} = 90$. In other words, the central tendency of the two sets of scores is identical. However, the mean describes only the average scores for the two sets. The mean does not describe the variability of the scores, and there is a large difference in the standard deviation, or variability, of the two groups of scores. The standard deviation of the scores in Group 1 is 2.2, and the standard deviation of the scores in Group 2 is 7.3. In other words, the variability of the scores in Group 2 is significantly greater than that of the scores in Group 1.

The normal distribution provides the basis for interpreting the differences in the standard deviations of the two groups. In a normal distribution approximately 68% of the scores fall between 1 SD below the mean and 1 SD above the mean. In Group 1 the mean score is 90 and the standard deviation is 2.2. One standard deviation below the mean is 87.8 (90 − 2.2 = 87.8), and 1 SD above the mean is 92.2 (90 + 2.2 = 92.2). Therefore, 68% of the scores in Group 1 occur between 87.8 and 92.2. In Group 2 the mean is also 90, but the standard deviation is 7.3. For this group, 1 SD below the mean is 82.7 (90 − 7.3 = 82.7), and 1 SD above the mean is 97.3 (90 + 7.3 = 97.3). Therefore, 68% of the scores in this group occur between 82.7 and 97.3.

The mean and the standard deviation for the scores from Ms. Street's classes further illustrate the interpretation of standard deviation and the relationship between the standard deviation and the mean. The mean score from Ms. Street's classes was 35, and the standard deviation was 5.72. Therefore, 1 SD below the mean is 29.28 (35 − 5.72 = 29.28), and 1 SD above the mean is 40.72 (35 + 5.72 = 40.72). Therefore, 68%, or more than two-thirds, of the scores from Ms. Street's classes were between 29.28 and 40.72. In other words, a majority of the scores fell within the range of 29 to 40 and clustered around 35. Relatively few students scored above 40 or below 29.

In many situations, the mean and the standard deviation are the best statistics for describing groups of numbers. Statisticians suggest that if you can report only two

Table 4–5 Illustration of the Relationship Between the Standard Deviation and the Mean

Scores from Group 1	Scores from Group 2
90	98
88	82
90	98
94	82
86	85
92	95
90	82
88	97
90	83
92	98
Mean = 90	Mean = 90
SD = 2.2	SD = 7.3

statistics to describe a group of numbers, you should probably select the mean and the standard deviation. However, another statistic, the standard error of measurement, also has special meaning in assessment.

Standard Error of Measurement

The **standard error of measurement** is an estimate of the variability of individual test scores. This statistic is also referred to as the standard error of a score. Testing specialists use this statistic as a measure of the accuracy or reliability of tests. The essential notion of standard error of measurement originates from the idea that giving a test many times to the same student (assuming no learning occurs from the repeated testing) produces scores that vary somewhat each time. All test scores contain some measurement error or variability, but some test scores contain more variability or error than others. A test score with higher variability yields a larger standard error of measurement than a test score with lower variability.

The statistical symbols for expressing standard error of measurement include the notations SEM and SE_{meas}. The formula for the standard error of measurement is as follows:

$$SE_{meas} = S_x \sqrt{- r_{xx}}$$

where

$$
\begin{array}{ll}
SE_{meas} & = \text{the standard error of measurement} \\
S_x & = \text{the standard deviation of the test} \\
\sqrt{} & = \text{the square root} \\
r_{xx} & = \text{the reliability coefficient of the test}
\end{array}
$$

The following example explains the concept of standard error of measurement from a more practical viewpoint. Assume that a test developer gave an intelligence test to a single student 100 times. If it were possible to give a test this many times, the developer could calculate the mean and standard deviation of the resulting 100 test scores to provide an index of the amount of error in the scores. Because of measurement error, the 100 individual scores would vary each time in the pattern of a bell-shaped curve, or normal distribution. The mean of the distribution of these 100 scores would represent the true score. In other words, the true score refers to the average of the 100 individual scores. The standard deviation would represent the amount of variability in the scores around the true score. Unfortunately, it is not feasible to give the same test to a single student 100 times because of constraints such as student fatigue and the learning that takes place during repeated testing.

Because actually giving a test repeatedly is not possible, mathematicians developed the standard error of measurement statistic to estimate the amount of error in a test score. This statistic defines a confidence band, or confidence interval, that delineates a student's true score and accounts for any measurement error. Teachers rely on the confidence band concept when they use test scores as estimates of student performance rather than as exact scores. The idea of a confidence band encourages reporting performance as a range of scores rather than as a single score.

A practical example of the confidence band involves a situation in which a student receives an intelligence quotient (IQ) score of 70 on a test of mental ability. If the standard error of measurement for the test were 5 IQ points, then placing 5 points on either side of the score of 70 (70 +/− 5 = 65 to 75) would define the confidence interval. In this example, the confidence band ranges from 65 to 75. This means that the student's true score falls somewhere within the interval of 65 to 75 IQ points but may not be exactly 70. In other words, if a student took the same test over again, it is likely that the resulting score would be somewhere between the interval of 65 to 75, but probably not exactly 70, on the second administration. Likewise, if a student received a score of 85 on an intelligence test and the standard error of measurement for the test was 4, then the confidence band would extend to 4 points on either side of 85, or 81 to 89.

The standard error of measurement provides an indication of the technical quality of a test and helps in interpreting results. The concept suggests interpreting individual test scores within a band or range of possible scores rather than as one absolute number. Each test produces a different standard error of measurement, and most test authors report this statistic in the technical section of their manual. Most well-developed, norm-referenced tests report confidence bands in the approximate range of 4 or 5 points. The confidence band with extreme scores is usually more than 4 or 5 points.

Teachers, psychologists, diagnosticians, and other professionals rely on the standard error of measurement statistic when they judge the accuracy of a student's score with respect to the test taken. For example, professionals must be cautious when they interpret the meaning of the student's performance on tests that exhibit a high standard error of measurement. In such cases, professionals often interpret the test score result as falling within a band of possible scores rather than as an absolute score. On the other hand, they can be more confident when interpreting scores from tests that display a low standard error of measurement. Furthermore, because the standard error of scores increases at the extremes of a test, professionals must be careful when interpreting student scores that fall into high and low ranges.

☑ Check Your Comprehension

Knowledge of the statistical concepts of distributions, central tendency, and variability sets the groundwork for considering additional measurement topics. Distributions visually summarize and illustrate the relationships among scores. The measures of central tendency, consisting of the mean, the median, and the mode, describe the average score or most numerous score in a distribution. The measures of variability summarize the spread, or dispersion, of distributions. The next section uses these concepts in considering the process of measuring reliability.

Reliability

Reliability is an essential technical quality of assessment instruments. The concept of **reliability** refers to the accuracy and consistency of scores from tests and from other assessments that measure student achievement, performance, and behavior. Reliable assessments produce similar results across various conditions and situations, including different evaluators and environments.

A helpful way to grasp the concept of reliability is to think of scores as consisting of two parts: error and true score. Error is random, unexplained variation in scores that reduces reliability. True score is nonrandom, or explainable, variation in scores that increases reliability. Although error exists in all scores, reliable tests minimize the amount of error. One method for estimating the amount of error and true score is the standard error of measurement statistic. Test authors use this statistic and

Table 4–6   Methods for Estimating Reliability

Type of Reliability	Process	Source of Variability
Test-retest	Give the test twice	Time between tests
Alternate-form	Give two forms of the test	Variation between tests
Split-half	Divide the test in half	Variation between test halves
Standard error of measurement	Calculate a confidence interval	Individual scores
Interrater	Use two observers	Reliability across observers

other measures in developing new tests, and they report these statistics in the technical sections of test manuals.

The most widely reported statistic for expressing reliability, the reliability coefficient, consists of values from 0 to 1.00. The mathematical notation for reliability is r, and a reliability coefficient of r = 0 indicates a total lack of reliability, whereas a coefficient of 1.00 represents perfect reliability. In general, acceptable reliability coefficients begin at r = .90 and rise to as much as r = .98. Coefficients below r = .90 may indicate inadequate reliability, except in special circumstances involving assessment of difficult-to-measure behaviors such as social interaction, self-concept, and behavior problems. One way of describing reliability coefficients involves thinking of a coefficient such as r = .90 as an expression of the accuracy of a test in which 90% of the variability of a score consists of true variability and 10% consists of error or unexplained variance. In most testing situations, accuracy ratings of 90% or more represent an acceptable level for making educational decisions; thus, coefficients of r = .90 and above indicate adequate test reliability. However, instruments with reliability coefficients of r = .75, for example, fail to provide acceptable reliability because approximately 25% of the score may be due to error or unexplained variance.

Test developers may select from different methods for estimating the reliability of assessment instruments. These include test-retest, alternate-form, split-half, standard error of measurement, and interrater reliability. A summary of these types of reliability appears in Table 4–6.

Test-Retest Reliability

Test-retest reliability is a process for estimating accuracy that involves giving a test twice to a carefully selected group and using the resulting scores to calculate a reliability coefficient. The reliability coefficient is the statistic that describes the consistency among the two sets of scores. In other words, this statistic expresses the correlation between the scores obtained by the same students on two administrations of a test. A critical factor with test-retest reliability is the length of time between testing and retesting. Too little time between testing and retesting inflates the reliability coefficient, whereas too much time deflates the reliability coefficient. In most situations, a 2-week interval allows enough time to adjust for any learning that may take place from the first testing experience. Longer intervals may reduce the reliability estimate due to maturation of the students or the influence of outside events. However, the length of time between testing also depends on the type and nature of the test. Because it requires two administrations of a test, the procedure for estimating test-retest reliability is time consuming, expensive, and error producing. For these reasons, test developers often prefer other methods for measuring reliability, including alternate-form reliability.

Alternate-Form Reliability

Alternate-form reliability, also called *equivalent-form reliability*, is a process for estimating accuracy that compares the scores from two forms of the same test. Estimating this type of reliability involves writing two forms, giving both forms to a carefully selected group, and comparing the resulting scores. The reliability coefficient in this case describes the correlation between the scores obtained by the same students on the two forms. This type of reliability avoids the problem of giving the same test twice, as in test-retest reliability. The use of equivalent forms also provides the advantage of a second form for use when a student needs testing twice within a short time frame.

A disadvantage of this type of reliability estimation is the necessity for making two equivalent forms. Making two equal forms is not usually a problem with large-scale, commercial tests. However, preparing two equal forms is often difficult for authors of specialized tests. The process involves developing two forms, such as Form A and Form B, and requires developing twice as many items with the items equally arranged. This process introduces random error, and it entails extra expense and difficulty in test development; thus, test developers sometimes turn to a third type of reliability, split-half reliability, that avoids these obstacles.

Split-Half Reliability

Split-half reliability is a procedure for determining accuracy that involves correlating two halves of the same test. The steps in the process include giving a test once, splitting the items in half, and comparing the results of the two halves to each other. The reliability coefficient obtained is an estimate of the correlation between the items in each half of the test. Test researchers split the test in half in several different ways. One technique involves comparing even-numbered and odd-numbered test items. Another procedure consists of comparing the first half of the test to the second half. Dividing the test items randomly into two halves also splits the test for comparison purposes. The method of dividing a test depends on the type of test; however, most developers use an odd-even split.

Because it relies on a single administration of one test, split-half reliability actually involves measuring the internal consistency of an assessment tool. For this reason some experts refer to split-half reliability as a type of internal consistency reliability. Testing specialists also use the standard error of measurement statistic described earlier to estimate the internal consistency of tests. The essential concept of both split-half reliability and standard error of measurement is that all tests have some measurement error within themselves, but tests with the best internal consistency minimize this type of variability.

Split-half reliability offers several advantages over the other types of reliability. Giving a test once is less expensive, faster, and easier. Because it uses only one administration and one form, split-half reliability produces more accurate results than other techniques by reducing the chances for error. With the other types of reliability estimation, test developers face many more uncontrollable events resulting from giving a test twice or from giving two forms of the same test. For these reasons, many test authors prefer split-half reliability.

Interrater Reliability

Interrater reliability, often referred to as *interobserver reliability*, is an estimate of the observations from two observers who directly watch or listen a student. Many applications exist for interrater reliability in special education, including assessment related to behavior-management programs. The reliability coefficient obtained in this case correlates the observations of two independent observers. The procedure involves having two raters independently observe and record specified behaviors, such as out-of-seat or off-task behavior, during the same time periods. Comparing the ratings of the observers produces an estimate of the percentage of agreement between the two observations. One of the widely used procedures for measuring interrater reliability involves calculating the percentage of agreement using the following formula:

$$\frac{\text{Number of agreements}}{\text{Number of agreements + Disagreements}} \times 100 = \text{Percentage of agreements}$$

However, estimating interrater reliability involves more than simply collecting and calculating the percentage of agreement between two raters. Establishing interrater reliability actually involves a series of steps, including:

- Identifying observable behaviors
- Determining appropriate data-gathering procedures
- Selecting a method of data analysis
- Adjusting the data-gathering process as needed

Following these steps helps to ensure the collection of consistent, accurate data that professionals can rely on for making the best possible educational decisions.

☑ Check Your Comprehension

Reliability refers to the consistency or accuracy of test scores and other measures of behavior. Although reliability plays an essential role in the basic measurement process, verifying the technical adequacy of a test also involves providing evidence of test validity.

Validity

Measurement experts consider validity, the effectiveness of assessment instruments, to be the most important technical characteristic. The basic question of validity is, "How well does the instrument measure what it was designed to measure?" or "Does the instrument do what it is supposed to do?" Developers establish initial validity as part of the test-development process, but validity research often continues after publication of an assessment tool. The concept of validity includes the notion that the uses of a test should be validated, not just the test itself (American Educational Research Association, 1999; Rubin, 1988). This view points out the importance of considering the consequences of tests as part of the process of determining the effectiveness of a test. The five major types of test validity are content validity, criterion-related validity, construct validity, face and cash validity, and consequences of testing.

Content Validity

Content validity refers to how well a test covers the domain or learning area measured by the test. A test with good content validity includes a representative sample of the behavior in the domain or learning area. A valid test of language, for example, includes items that measure performance in the relevant language skills. Likewise, a valid test of reading consists of items to assess the proficiency of relevant reading skills. The process of establishing content validity involves several steps, including the following:

- Developing test specifications based on a complete review of the content area
- Writing test items to fit the test specifications
- Conducting field tests by giving the test to carefully selected groups
- Reviewing and revising the test after the initial field tests
- Compiling the final test

These steps rely heavily on the expert opinion of professionals in the field, including teachers, curriculum experts, professors, and test-development specialists. In most cases developers use a team of professionals. Several test-development teams may work together to develop large commercial tests; small teams consisting mainly of the test authors develop most noncommercial tests. In the classroom, teachers validate the test content when they evaluate the quality of the items before giving a test. Test developers use a similar process. In fact, many test developers hire teachers to review tests before publication as part of the content validation process. Test users can evaluate content validity by reviewing the information provided by the test developer in the test manual. Test users can also evaluate content validity by conducting their own review of the quality and relevance of test items. Other measures of test effectiveness related to content validity include face validity and cash validity.

Face and Cash Validity

Face validity, a superficial type of nontechnical validity, involves quickly reviewing a test to determine whether it appears valid on the surface. Although it is a desirable feature, face validity fails as a substitute for well-established content validity. Tests that sell well have **cash validity,** another type of nontechnical validity. However, high sales volume is not an appropriate criterion for evaluating test effectiveness, and test users should avoid selecting an instrument on this basis. Furthermore, just because a test sells well and is therefore readily available, it is not necessarily valid for use in a particular situation.

Criterion-Related Validity

Criterion-related validity involves analyzing the relationship between a test and other independent criteria of effectiveness. Criterion-related validity includes predictive validity, which entails measuring the effectiveness of a test in predicting future performance, and concurrent validity, which involves correlating a test with a comparable test or other measure of proven validity. Establishing predictive validity entails evaluating student performance against a directly related but independent criterion. For example, the criterion for an achievement test might be the grade-point averages of the students during the following year. The criterion for a vocational aptitude test might be performance on the job. Predictive validity consists of correlating test performance with performance on the predictive measure. Highly positive correlations indicate good predictive validity. Inadequate predictive validity results from scores that fail to correlate with scores on the predictive measure. Educational decisions, such as classifying students as disabled and placing them in programs, require tests with good predictive validity.

Educational decisions related to instruction and program planning rely on tests with good concurrent validity. Concurrent validity entails comparing scores from a new test with scores from a valid test that measures the same content. In this case, the

TECHNOLOGY FOCUS
Validity of Computer-Based Testing

Many tests are now available in pencil-on-paper and computer-based administration formats. When both forms are available, it is important that the scores from both administration formats yield equivalent or parallel results. Validity research comparing both sets of scores is necessary to establish equivalency. This research is necessary because computer-based assessment alters the mode of administration and thus changes the test. Therefore, conventional tests cannot simply be transferred to the computer. For example, most paragraphs measuring reading comprehension fit on one page in a conventional response booklet, but on the computer, the paragraph fills up more than one computer screen. Therefore, with computer-based assessment, the test taker must scan back and forth on the screen to read a paragraph and answer the comprehension questions. This makes a computer-based test different from the same test in pencil-on-paper format. Furthermore, reading a paragraph from a computer screen is unlike reading the same paragraph from a test booklet. For these reasons, developers of computer-based tests have established procedures to validate equivalence.

developer gives both tests to a carefully selected group of students and compares the results. Results that produce highly positive correlations between performance on the new test and performance on the concurrent measure indicate good validity. Results that fail to show a correlation between the new test and the concurrent measure suggest poor concurrent validity. Another method for establishing concurrent validity involves comparing a test with some currently available criterion other than another test score. For example, correlating student performance on a test of social skills with a teacher's ratings of a student's social skills provides a means for establishing concurrent validity without the use of another test.

As more computer-based versions of tests are becoming available, test publishers are developing procedures for validating the computer-based versions of tests. Information about this validation process appears in the Technology Focus.

Construct Validity

More abstract than the other types of validity, **construct validity** refers to how well a test measures a theoretical construct, or attribute. Examples of constructs include traits such as intelligence, mathematical reasoning ability, receptive language vocabulary, and gross motor skills. The lengthy process of establishing construct validity entails synthesizing scientific research data about the relationship between test performance and the theoretical construct measured by the test. However, no specific step-by-step procedures exist for establishing this form of validity. In fact, Angoff (1988), who described construct validity as an evolving concept rather than a set of techniques, suggested that the essence of construct validity relates to the interpretation drawn from the test scores. According to Angoff, examining construct validity includes the following types of research: "correlational studies, factorial studies, studies of differences with respect to groups, situations, tasks, and times, observational studies of change, and studies of experimentally induced change" (p. 30). In other words, construct validity is a process involving systematic review of research and careful accumulation of evidence to support the adequacy of a test.

Tests such as the Wechsler Intelligence Scale for Children, Fourth Edition (WISC-IV; Wechsler, 1991) demonstrate construct validity based on hundreds of research studies covering a variety of topics. The accumulated knowledge from these studies provides clear evidence that the WISC-IV measures the construct called intelligence. Other tests, however, lack evidence to support construct validity. For example, accumulated knowledge from research studies with the Wide Range Achievement Test—Expanded Edition (WRAT-EXPANDED; Robertson, 2002) suggests that this particular instrument fails to measure the construct called wide-range achievement.

Because establishing construct validity entails a long and involved process, most tests provide little information about this type of validity. Only the most well-established tests present solid evidence of construct validity. On the other hand, all but the most informal tests provide information about the other two types of validity: content and criterion related.

Consequences of Testing

A relatively new validity question concerns the **consequences of testing**. This type of validity is important to consider when the goals of testing are to improve classroom instruction, upgrade educational standards, or clarify expected achievement levels for students (American Educational Research Association, 1999). When the goal is to improve classroom instruction, then improvements should be documented as part of the test validation process. The validation should ensure that the testing results in positive improvements. Likewise, when the purpose is to help clarify expected student achievement levels, then the effectiveness of testing in clarifying expectations should be examined as part of the validation process.

The need to consider the consequences of testing is especially important given the increasing emphasis on high-stakes testing programs. A major concern is that politicians and policy makers often mandate high-stakes testing programs without validation. **High-stakes tests** are given to students in a school, school district, or in an entire state for accountability purposes. These programs are "high stakes" when the results are used to make significant decisions about students, teachers, and schools. For example, schools may be judged according to the average scores of their students. According to the American Educational Research Association (2000), high scores may result in praise and rewards for schools. Low scores may bring public criticism and significant sanctions. Individual students who score well may receive special diplomas for their academic accomplishments. Students with low scores may be retained or denied a high school diploma.

High-stakes testing programs are often touted by politicians and by policy makers as having a beneficial effect on classroom instruction and student achievement levels. However, the American Evaluation Association (AEA) recently questioned the validity of high-stakes testing. According to the AEA (2002), evidence indicates that high-stakes testing may fail to improve classroom instruction. Even worse, the AEA contends that testing may lead to negative consequences and inappropriate instructional practices. The negative consequences may include increased student and teacher attrition, mismatch with the curriculum, cultural bias, overallocation of resources into testing, and bias against students with disabilities. Because of these concerns, the AEA has called for further study of the consequences of high-stakes testing.

Table 4–7   Characteristics of the Types of Validity

Type of Validity	Technical Question	Practical Question
Content	Do the test items represent the behavior being assessed?	Do Sarah's scores correspond with her performance in the domain?
Criterion-related (predictive)	Do the test scores predict future behavior?	Do Jason's scores indicate how well he will perform in math next semester?
Criterion-related (concurrent)	Do scores from the new test correlate with scores from a valid test in the same content area?	Do Jeffrey's scores on the current test correspond with his scores on the new test that will be used next year?
Construct	Does the test assess the theoretical trait it was designed to measure?	Is the test useful for measuring Logan's intelligence?
Consequences of testing	Are improvements in classroom instruction documented?	Does the testing improve classroom instruction?

In the meantime, the AEA opposes high-stakes testing until evidence is provided to demonstrate the effectiveness of the practice.

☑ Check Your Comprehension

Validity, the most important of the technical characteristics of tests, includes four major types: content, criterion-related, construct, and consequences. A summary of the distinctive characteristics of each type appears in Table 4–7. The process of validating a test cannot be separated from the process of determining test reliability. In fact, an unusual and surprising relationship exists between the two concepts. Tests can be reliable without being valid but cannot be valid without being reliable. In other words, reliability must be established before validity. One way of explaining this relationship is by analogy with a clock. For example, it is possible for a clock to be reliable without being valid, in that a clock can be consistently 43 minutes slow. In this case, the slow clock is reliable but not valid. This is analogous to a test that consistently underestimates student achievement by two grade levels. In this instance, the test is reliable but it is certainly not valid.

Norm-Referenced and Criterion-Referenced Assessment

Norm-referenced and criterion-referenced assessment represent two fundamentally different ways of interpreting performance. Norm-referenced assessment involves interpreting the performance of individuals and groups in relation to the performance of others. Criterion-referenced assessment, on the other hand, refers to interpreting performance in relation to some functional level or criterion.

Reflection

Everyone has been affected by high-stakes testing. Describe an experience you have had.

 To answer this reflection online, go to the *Teaching and Learning* module on the Companion Website at *www.prenhall.com/venn*.

Norm-Referenced Assessment

Norm-referenced assessment relates individual scores or groups of scores to the scores of those in comparison groups, called norm groups or norm sample groups. Norm groups consist of carefully selected groups of students who take the test in a precise manner. The norms constitute sets of scores for each age or grade level based on the average scores of the students in the norm group. With norm-referenced testing, the criterion of reference is the "place" or "rank" of a student compared with other students. A student with a percentile rank of 25 on a norm-referenced test, for example, ranks in the lowest 25% compared with the norm group. This ranking procedure illustrates how norm-referenced scores show relative standing. Although many uses exist for norm-referenced testing, it is most useful for making classification and placement decisions about students with special needs.

Criterion-Referenced Assessment

Criterion-referenced assessment involves interpreting performance in relation to a specific functional level or criterion. Criterion-referenced assessment is closely related to instruction and it is ideal for measuring student knowledge on relatively small and discrete units. When the criterion of reference relates to content, performance is compared to a standard of mastery or proficiency for a skill or set of skills. For example, the Comprehensive Inventory of Basic Skills, Revised (CIBS-R, Brigance, 1999), a criterion-referenced test of academic skills, measures competencies such as word-attack skills, phonetic skills, subtracting two-digit numbers, and solving mathematical word problems. Giving the CIBS-R entails evaluating performance in terms of student mastery of specific skills. The criterion-referenced assessment information produced by the CIBS-R is most helpful for making instructional decisions, such as determining what skills a student has mastered and which skills a student needs to learn next.

The criterion of reference can also be the individual student. When the criterion of reference is the individual, a student's performance is related to an earlier performance on the same measure. For example, giving the CIBS-R at the beginning and again at the end of the school year enables measurement of progress over time. In this case, the comparison involves performance on the first and second administrations of the CIBS-R.

Test Norms

Test norms are sets of scores developed from the scores of the subjects in the norm group, which consists of a carefully selected sample of students who take a test in a precise manner. Many types of norms exist, including national, state, and local norms.

National norms exist for virtually all norm-referenced tests. Good national norms, calculated from the results of testing a large sample group of students from all parts of the country, represent all students in the U.S. population. A well-selected national norm group includes students who represent a variety of socioeconomic circumstances, ethnic backgrounds, and geographic areas. National norms are useful for comparing the performance of individuals and groups with the performance of similar students from the norm sample group. For students with learning problems, this comparative information helps determine the nature and severity of the problem. For example, for a student with a reading problem, norm-referenced test results can reveal how far behind the student is in reading compared with other children of the same age and grade. Likewise, if students are making excellent progress in reading

FOCUS 4 – 1

Classroom Norms

Many teachers develop informal but highly useful classroom norms for frequently taught courses. The process for developing teacher-made norms involves collecting the results of a series of frequently used class tests and other curriculum-based assessments. These results, when collected over time, serve as the basis for comparisons among students and across classes. Although classroom norms cannot be used to place or label children, teachers find them helpful for evaluating the instructional program and the performance of individuals and groups.

achievement, norm-referenced test results can help determine how much progress the students have made in relation to similar children.

State, local, and class norms exist for some but not all tests. However, state and local norms, which compare the performance of an individual with those of other students in the same state, school system, or class, may be more valuable than national norms, depending on the purpose of testing (Brown, 1980). Local norms developed from a representative sample of students in a specific school or district, for example, allow comparisons with other local students rather than comparisons at a national level. Information about classroom norms appears in Focus 4–1.

The soundness of norm-referenced scores depends on the soundness of the norm group. Valid comparisons occur when the characteristics of the norm group represent the characteristics of the student. On the other hand, invalid comparisons occur when the characteristics of the norm group differ from those of the student. Sattler (2001) identified three important factors in evaluating the validity of a norm group: representativeness, size, and relevance.

Representativeness refers to whether a norm group typifies the particular group of students for whom the test was designed, and includes characteristics such as age, grade level, gender, geographic region, ethnic group, and socioeconomic status. Size refers to the number of subjects in the norm group. According to Sattler, adequate norms include at least 100 subjects for each age or grade level on the test. Relevance concerns the applicability of the norm group to the student taking the test. Some tests provide more than one norm group for comparison purposes, such as norms for students from disability groups. Information about norms for students with disabilities appears in Focus 4–2.

Standardization

Standardization refers to structuring test materials, administration procedures, scoring methods, and procedures for interpreting results. Standardization makes it possible to give, score, and interpret tests in a controlled manner that minimizes erratic, unpredictable results. This helps to ensure accuracy and consistency in measuring progress, determining levels of performance, and comparing performance to others.

All norm-referenced tests include standardized procedures that evaluators must follow. Giving a normed test in a nonstandard manner invalidates the norms because the individual student receives a score based on modified testing conditions whereas the norm group received their scores based on standard testing conditions. Although

> ## FOCUS 4-2
>
> ### Norms for Students with Disabilities
>
> Specialized norms for students with disabilities are generally not available except with a few of the most widely used tests. For example, the Vineland Adaptive Behavior Scales offer regular norms plus supplementary norms derived from samples of children with mental retardation, emotional disturbance, visual impairments, and hearing impairments. Although specialized norms are useful in some specific situations, the appropriate standard of comparison when making eligibility and placement decisions is the performance of students in general education classrooms. Therefore, regular norms serve as the basis for determining when students have achievement or performance problems that qualify them for special education services. Specialized norms supplement regular norms by providing additional diagnostic information.

some criterion-referenced tests include standardized procedures just like norm-referenced tests, most criterion-referenced tests include adaptable administration procedures that encourage flexibility in testing. This flexibility gives an evaluator opportunities to fit the test to the needs of the student.

Standardization helps to prevent bias in testing against certain students. However, standardizing a test fails to completely eliminate the possibility of bias, especially bias against students with disabilities. Standardized tests that require manipulation of materials such as blocks, for example, set up a barrier to students with physical impairments. In the same way, standardized tests that measure cognitive ability primarily through language and vocabulary skills introduce bias against students with hearing impairments and students who are English language learners.

☑ Check Your Comprehension

Distinct differences exist between criterion-referenced and norm-referenced testing. The differences center around the purpose of testing. The purpose for norm-referenced testing involves comparison to others whereas the goal of criterion-referenced testing involves measuring performance in relation to a functional criterion. Both types of testing serve necessary and important functions as part of assessment in special education. Although it is important to understand these technical measurement concepts, it is also important to consider certain practical measurement concepts.

Practical Measurement Concepts

The practical measurement concepts focus on the applied functional features of assessment instruments. This includes consideration of the ongoing assessment issue of fairness in assessment, especially for students with learning problems who are at-risk for school failure due to special needs, diverse backgrounds, and language differences. Experts in testing and professional associations (Cronbach, 1988; Drummond & Jones, 2006, Joint Committee on Testing Practices, 2004; Messick, 1988) suggest including the practical aspects, including fairness, in assessment in the validation process. Teachers are especially sensitive to the practical perspective because they see firsthand the effects of testing.

Checklist of Practical Measurement Concepts

The practical considerations described by Drummond and Jones (2006) appear in checklist form in Table 4–8. The items focus on concepts applicable to tests in general with special considerations specific to assessing students with learning problems. The checklist of practical concepts is followed by an in-depth discussion of the issue of fairness with a focus on what can be done to eliminate or reduce bias in assessment.

Fairness in Assessment

Fairness in assessment refers to equity of tests for all students regardless of race, ethnicity, language, gender, or cultural background. Fairness is required by federal law, but bias still occurs for several reasons (Macmillan & Reschly, 1998; Murtagh, 2003). The complexities associated with developing fair assessments account for much of the problem. The continuing increase in diversity among school-age children is also a key factor. Another consideration is the need for psychologists and diagnosticians to continue building their skills in testing students from various cultural and linguistic backgrounds. Because assessment professionals are often not proficient in the languages spoken by the students, they must use interpreters during test administration. Unfortunately, interpreters may not be familiar with assessment procedures. Thus, problems arise when assessment experts and interpreters

Table 4–8 Checklist of Practical Measurement Concepts

Item	Yes	No	Comments
1. Is the time involved in testing reasonable, given the purpose of the testing and the expected benefits?			
2. Is the cost of the test reasonable?			
3. Is the test well designed in an attractive and durable package with high-quality materials?			
4. Is the reading level of the test appropriate?			
5. Are the administration procedures clearly described and easy to follow?			
6. Are the response booklets and scoring sheets well designed with sufficient space for student responses?			
7. Are the scoring procedures clearly described and easy to follow?			
8. Are the interpretation procedures explained with examples and case studies?			
9. Are aids available for the evaluator (e.g., audio cassettes, computer software)?			
10. Is the manual clear and complete?			
11. Does the test include enough items to obtain an accurate estimate of skills and abilities?			

work together without the benefit of common training and expertise. The goal is to continue improving assessment approaches to account for diversity by addressing these types of issues. Further, experts and policy makers must agree on the test procedures and interpretations that are appropriate for students from diverse backgrounds and experiences.

Forms of Assessment Bias

In a discussion of fairness as it relates to the technical qualities of tests, Rust and Golombok (1989) described three forms of bias: item bias, internal bias, and external bias. **Item bias** refers to unfairness that exists within individual items on a test, an example of which is a question about temperature based on the Celsius scale in countries that use the Fahrenheit scale. Item bias is the easiest form of bias to correct. Test developers usually rely on various forms of error pattern analysis to identify questions that are unfair to groups of individuals. After identifying unfair items, the developers either modify or eliminate the biased questions. Information about what teachers can do about assessment bias in their own classrooms appears in Multicultural Considerations.

MULTICULTURAL CONSIDERATIONS

Eliminating Bias in Curriculum-Based Assessment

Bias in assessment is such a serious problem that educators should consider the potential for bias a key element in all assessments, including curriculum-based assessments (Popham, 2002). The most important step in considering bias is making a commitment to be sensitive to the possibility of bias. After making this commitment, educators can take a number of steps to reduce or eliminate bias. One step is to think seriously about the impact of differing backgrounds on the way students respond to assessments. For example, even if you are an Asian American and you have mostly Asian students, this does not mean that your background is similar to the background of your students. If you have a White, middle-class background and you teach mostly Asian students, your background is almost certainly different from the background of your students. Another step is to review every teacher-made test and classroom assessment to determine if any items might offend or unfairly penalize any students. For example, for many of us who grew up in large cities a "range" is a kitchen appliance. In contrast, those with rural backgrounds in ranching have an entirely different understanding of the meaning of the word "range." In other words, classroom tests made by teachers from the city may contain items that are confusing to students from rural farming or ranching backgrounds. If unfair items are identified, then the items need to be revised or eliminated. Though it is probably impossible to remove all bias from classroom assessments, teachers committed to eliminating as much bias as possible are much more likely to create less-biased assessments.

What are some ways you could determine if you have biased questions on your test?

To answer this reflection online, go to the *Multicultural Considerations* module on the Companion Website at **www.prenhall.com/venn**.

Internal bias refers to differences in average scores among two or more groups due to the qualities of a test rather than actual differences among the groups. Internal bias has received the most attention from both experts in testing and policy makers. As a result, many developers include evidence to show that their tests avoid internal bias. For example, when developers prepare a new test, they compare scores from the new test with those from an existing test that is free from internal bias. This comparison includes scores from specific groups of students, such as students from minority groups and students with disabilities. If scores from the new test are consistent with those from the existing test across the various groups, the new test avoids internal bias. On the other hand, if scores from the new test fail to match scores from the existing test, internal bias may exist. Test developers are responsible for correcting bias problems prior to publication.

The third type of bias, **external bias**, occurs when decision makers use test results in an unfair manner. External bias can occur when school systems place students unfairly based on test scores. For example, this happens when the placement procedure creates a staffing pattern in which students from minority groups are under- or overrepresented in certain classes. In an attempt to avoid this type of bias, the law requires schools, agencies, and institutions to follow established guidelines that incorporate rules designed to eliminate external bias and ensure fairness.

☑ Check Your Comprehension

The pragmatic, functional features of assessment instruments are an important aspect of the measurement process, especially for practitioners. In addition, the practical measurement concepts complement the more technical aspects of measurement by providing an applied viewpoint. Comprehensive analysis of the measurement features of assessments involves both practical and technical considerations. Because it is so important for tests to be fair—and for students, parents, and teachers to believe that tests are fair—efforts must continue to eliminate discrimination in assessment. Fortunately, test developers and policy makers are continuing to improve testing and measurement so that it is as fair as possible for all students.

Summary

Knowledge of measurement concepts and techniques serves as a foundation for understanding the assessment of students with learning problems. The measurement concepts include the basic statistics for describing scores and procedures for evaluating the reliability and validity of assessment instruments. Furthermore, measurement concepts define two distinct types of testing: criterion-referenced and norm-referenced testing. Considering the practical aspects of the validity of tests and measurements is also an important part of effective measurement. In other words, many aspects of assessing students with special needs are based on measurement principles and practices.

Teaching students with disabilities requires skillful measurement of student behavior and proper selection of accurate measurement tools in each situation. The method educators use to measure performance influences, either beneficially or harmfully, the lives of students with disabilities. By using measurement techniques carefully, cautiously, and correctly, teachers support the rights of students and their families to receive appropriate educational assessment and services.

In Chapter 5, the basic concepts of measurement are applied to the topic of test scores and their significance. Later chapters apply measurement concepts in the process of examining the wide range and variety of tests and other evaluation procedures involved in assessing students with learning problems.

 To check your comprehension of chapter contents, go to the *Quiz* module in Chapter 4 of the Companion Website, *www.prenhall.com/venn*.

Meeting Performance Standards and Preparing for Licensure Exams

After reading this chapter, you should be able to demonstrate the CEC standards and PRAXIS™ test knowledge and skills. The information in parentheses identifies where to find the particular CEC standard and PRAXIS™ content reference.

CEC Standards for Beginning Special Education Teachers

- Basic terminology used in assessment (CC8K1)
- Interpret information from formal and informal assessments (CC8S5)
- Report assessment results to all stakeholders using effective communication skills (CC8S7)
- Factors that influence the overrepresentation of culturally/linguistically diverse students in programs for individuals with disabilities (GC1K7)

PRAXIS™ Education of Exceptional Students: Core Content Knowledge

- Assessment, including use of assessment for screening, diagnosis, placement, and the making of instructional decisions; for example: how to select and conduct nondiscriminatory and appropriate assessments; how to interpret standardized and specialized assessment results; procedures and test materials, both formal and informal, typically used for prereferral, screening, referral, classification, placement, and ongoing program monitoring

chapter 5

Test Scores and What They Mean

Objectives

After reading this chapter, you will be prepared to do the following:

- Explain the standards for scoring, including procedures for accurately reporting results.
- Understand and use raw scores.
- Understand the purpose and use of norm-referenced and criterion-referenced scores.
- Interpret and use criterion-referenced scores, including simple numerical reports, percent correct scores, letter grades, and graphs.
- Interpret and use age- and grade-equivalent scores.
- Interpret and use percentile ranks.
- Interpret and use the standard scores, including intelligence quotients, stanines, and normal curve equivalents.
- Apply the principles of using test scores.

Overview

Assessing students with learning problems requires the use of an assortment of scores. In this chapter, you study the various scores used in assessment, discover what they mean, and consider how to interpret them. You also investigate more fully the two fundamentally different categories of scoring: criterion-referenced and norm-referenced. The scoring associated with each category is the focus of the chapter, and for every score there is a definition, a practical example, a description of advantages, and a discussion of limitations. At the conclusion of the chapter, you will consider practical principles for using scores in educational settings.

Using Scores Properly

Mrs. Weinroth teaches students with mild and moderate disabilities. With the increasing emphasis on standards-based education, she has become much more interested in interpreting test scores. Because of standards-based education, she wants to learn even more about how to use scores to help her students. In her investigation she first asks herself, what scores are

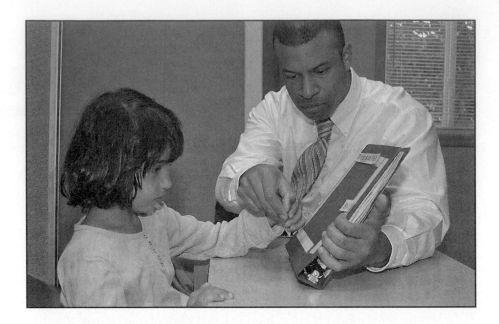

available, and what kinds are best? How many different kinds are there? Next, she asks, why use scores? How valuable are they to teachers, and can they really make a difference in learning and teaching? What can they do for her that other sources do not? What about her students—what can test scores do for them?

Mrs. Weinroth does some research, consults other educators, attends an inservice work-shop on interpreting scores, and decides she really would like to learn even more. She gets helpful information from these activities, but she still wonders about differences between scores of students with disabilities and those of "typical" students. She decides to continue her quest by visiting with the district's diagnostic teacher and talking with a teacher in another school who uses test scores with success.

Definition of Scores

Simply defined, **scores** are the numerical result of assessment. Scores summarize test results and results from other assessments using numbers, and these results provide an effective and efficient way to describe student performance in an objective manner. Educators rely on scores for a variety of purposes. Psychologists and diagnosticians use test scores to classify and place students in special education. Teachers depend on scores from curriculum-based measures, such as class tests, to plan and evaluate instruction. Administrators use them to evaluate programs. Counselors and others relate test scores to student performance in communicating with parents about the progress or lack of progress of their children. In all of these situations, professionals use scores to make educational decisions and to communicate information about those decisions.

Although scores provide essential information, mistakes may occur unless other factors are considered. For this reason, experts caution against the use of scores in isolation as the sole decision-making criterion. Instead, testing specialists recommend using scores together with qualitative information about students and the setting in which students are expected to perform. Qualitative information includes teacher judgment about what is best for students and subjective impressions based on observing and interacting with students.

FOCUS 5-1

Standards for Scoring Educational Tests

The American Psychological Association published the revised *Standards for Educational and Psychological Testing* in 1999. The new standards include the following guidelines:

- Accurate test scoring requires test administration and scoring according to the test developer's instructions.
- Test scores should be interpreted with other information, including norms, measurement error, and descriptions of test content.
- Computer interpretation of test scores requires validation to ensure accuracy.
- Evaluators should provide score reports in a form that is easily understandable to those receiving the report.
- The test giver is responsible for explaining the limitations of test scores and the relationship of test scores to other information.

The standards also require that the test giver ensure accuracy in scoring and interpreting results. This means that test givers should check all steps in the testing process, including spot checking computer- or machine-scored tests. Accuracy is essential because even a small scoring error can ultimately result in making the wrong educational decision. For example, if a test giver calculates the chronological age of a student incorrectly when scoring a norm-referenced test, the resulting test score will be inaccurate. Likewise, if a test giver calculates a raw score incorrectly, the resulting transformed score will be inaccurate. For this reason, test givers must make sure that the test administration and scoring process is error free.

The goal is to strike a balance between quantitative and qualitative information. This is not easy, but it is necessary to make decisions in the best interests of the student, the parents, and the teacher. Fortunately, published standards (American Psychological Association, 1999; International Test Commission, 2000a, 2000b) serve as guides for scoring and interpreting tests in equitable and accurate ways. Focus 5–1 describes some of these published standards.

Problems with Test Scores

Mary Beth once had a teacher who told her parents that she was profoundly retarded with an IQ of 25 or lower. This test score meant, according to the teacher, that Mary Beth could not progress beyond a very low level of functioning. Furthermore, the teacher said that Mary Beth was progressing so slowly that her developmental age as an adult would be no higher than that of a 5- or 6-year-old child. Last year Mary Beth enrolled in a supported employment program and, with the help of a job coach, began work at a print shop, running a copy machine. After extensive training, Mary Beth learned to operate the copy machine and is now successfully employed.

This true story and the one that follows show some of the problems with test scores as illustrated by the following questions: Were the scores correct? Were they fair and unbiased? Did the teacher interpret test scores accurately? Do test designers fail to delineate limits of their tests to predict future performance? Do teachers sometimes use scores to forecast potential or lack of potential without carefully limiting the validity of their estimates?

Jose, a successful teacher of Mexican-American descent, tells this story about himself: As a youngster, he received a low score on an intelligence test in elementary school. The school district labeled him as mentally retarded and placed him in a special education class. The school district psychologist told his parents that his intelligence was so low that he would never progress any higher than the fifth- or sixth-grade level in academic learning. Ultimately, Jose earned a doctorate, and he is now a professor at a junior college.

Unfortunately, teachers sometimes use test scores inappropriately, as illustrated in the following example.

Janet has a severe learning disability. In high school, her special education teacher told her that she could never succeed in college because test scores showed she could not score high enough on the entrance exam, and her learning disability was too severe. Today Janet is a school psychologist with a doctoral degree, and she often lectures in college classes on assessment in special education.

All of these cases involve real people, and each is based on an actual testing situation. The scenarios portray situations in which teachers and others in decision-making positions failed to interpret the meaning of test scores accurately. Although most professionals strive to avoid such mistakes, the cases illustrate how easy it is to misinterpret test scores. This occurs because of the misconceptions and myths that surround such results. Fortunately, college students preparing for careers in teaching learn about test scores in personnel preparation programs, and after accepting positions, teachers continue to expand their knowledge of the subject. Learning as much as possible about test scores is necessary because of the complexity of the topic and the continuing changes in their use. Surprisingly, even specialists in assessment have trouble keeping up to date with this complicated subject.

Fortunately, in most situations professionals interpret test scores accurately, and the cases just cited are exceptions rather than typical occurrences. The following account shows one of the many positive ways in which professionals use test scores.

Accurately Interpreting Test Scores

Joseph's difficulty with schoolwork started in kindergarten, but his problems intensified in the first grade when the curriculum focus shifted from developmental to academic skills. Concerned about his severe lack of progress in academics, Joseph's teacher referred him to the child-study team. After completing the initial steps in the referral process, the team arranged for an assessment specialist to evaluate Joseph with a battery of diagnostic tests. In the diagnostic report, the specialist reported test scores in reading, math, and writing that fell into the significantly below-average range. Likewise, the specialist reported an intelligence quotient (IQ) that fell below the cutoff level for mental retardation. In addition, the specialist described adaptive behavior scores that were also significantly below average. The placement team relied on these test scores as critical information in identifying Joseph as mildly retarded and recommending special education services. In fact, the law required the team to obtain these test scores as part of the process of identifying Joseph as disabled. As is often the case, the special services were well suited to Joseph's individual learning needs, and after a few weeks, he began to succeed in schoolwork for the first time.

The cases cited emphasize the need to understand the diverse collection of available test scores, starting with the meaning of test scores in general. The ultimate intent of this chapter is to develop an understanding of the different scores, what they mean, when to use them, and how to interpret them.

✔ Check Your Comprehension

Scores provide an efficient and effective way to describe student performance. As educators, we use a variety of scores for a variety of purposes, and interpreting scores involves many considerations. We should follow the professional standards for scoring to ensure the highest possible accuracy with all types of scores. The goal is to obtain the best possible descriptions of performance and to maintain accuracy in all scoring activities.

Types of Scores

Teachers rely on many types of scores. Most scoring begins with calculating a raw score. Thus, the raw score is usually the first score obtained in assessment.

Raw Scores

A **raw score** is the simple numerical result of assessment, typically the number of items answered correctly. In most situations, evaluators avoid using raw scores to report results. Instead, they convert raw scores into various types of transformed scores because most raw scores, such as 39 on a mathematics test, are meaningless in isolation. Likewise, a raw score of 128 on a vocabulary test gives no information for making educational decisions. Further, raw scores from different tests are not comparable. For example, if a student takes two tests, in which Test 1 consists of 50 items and Test 2 consists of 100 items, a raw score of 10 correct on the first test does not mean the same thing as a raw score of 40 correct on the second test. In this example, the two raw scores are not comparable because the tests are of different lengths, and they may differ in level of difficulty. For these reasons, most tests provide a procedure for converting raw scores into various other scores.

The two major categories of transformed scores, norm-referenced and criterion-referenced, represent fundamentally different ways of describing student performance. Whereas norm-referenced scores are formal and standardized, criterion-referenced scores are less formal and more flexible.

Norm-Referenced Scores

A **norm-referenced score** interprets student performance in relation to the performance of others by comparing an individual score with the average score of corresponding students in a norm sample group. The soundness of a single score depends on the soundness of the norm group scores. A score is sound when compared to scores from a representative norm group with similar characteristics; a score is unsound and of limited value when compared to scores from an unrepresentative norm group.

Reflection
Using scores appropriately presents many unique professional challenges. What steps can you take to ensure you use test scores appropriately and avoid the pitfalls that lead to misinterpretation?

 To answer this reflection online; go to the *Teaching and Learning* module on the companion Website at *www.prenhall.com/venn*.

For example, when evaluators test students with the Wechsler Individual Achievement Test, Second Edition (Wechsler, 2001), they compare an individual's score to scores from an equivalent sample group of students who were tested to establish the norms. Fortunately, this test has excellent norms based on a representative sample group of students, which includes youngsters from a wide range of cultural, ethnic, geographic, and economic backgrounds.

Some widely used tests, however, have inadequate norms. For example, a test that was widely used throughout the United States and internationally for many years had a norm sample consisting almost entirely of students from suburban, middle-class backgrounds. Giving the test to a student from this background produced a valid score because the student's performance was compared to that of others from similar circumstances. However, giving the test to students from rural, poor backgrounds or to students with disabilities produced invalid, biased scores because the norm group failed to include students from similar backgrounds. This shows that the usefulness of an individual score depends on the adequacy of the norms.

Criterion-Referenced Scores

A **criterion-referenced score** interprets performance from a different viewpoint. It explains results in relation to a functional level of performance rather than in relation to the performance of others. When the criterion of reference is content related, the soundness of an individual score depends on the soundness of the content of the test or other assessment. If the test items accurately reflect the instructional content, then the test score is sound; if the content of the test fails to represent the instructional content, then the value of the score is limited. For example, if after teaching addition skills the teacher gives a teacher-made test covering those addition skills, the resulting test scores will be sound. If, on the other hand, the content of the teacher-made test includes addition and subtraction, the value of the resulting scores will be limited. Virtually all scores from curriculum-based assessments, including teacher-made tests, are criterion-referenced.

When the criterion relates to the student over time, the soundness of the score depends on administering and scoring the test in the same manner for each administration of the test. For example, if a teacher uses a test to measure proficiency in a certain skill area before and after instruction, the soundness of the score depends on administering and scoring the pretest and posttest in the same manner.

Teachers sometimes use norm-referenced scores in a criterion-referenced manner. A discussion of this use of norm-referenced scores appears in Focus 5–2.

☑ Check Your Comprehension

Norm- and criterion-referenced scores define the two broad categories of scores. The difference in the categories involves the purpose for testing and the methods of scoring and interpreting the results. Though educators use a variety of specific scores from each category, teachers rely primarily on criterion-referenced scores in the classroom.

Specific Criterion-Referenced Scores

Educators routinely use a variety of specific criterion-referenced scores. These include simple numerical reports, percent correct scores, and letter grades.

F OCUS 5 – 2

**Using Norm-Referenced Scores
in a Criterion-Referenced Manner**

Teachers sometimes use scores from norm-referenced tests in a criterion-referenced manner by giving tests at the beginning and again at the end of the year to measure individual student progress over time. In this situation, previous performance rather than the performance of students in the norm group serves as the criterion of reference. Although it is appropriate to use norm-referenced tests in this manner, and many test manuals suggest that teachers do so, such use may jeopardize reliability. The problem occurs because most norm-referenced tests measure only a few items corresponding to a given instructional objective, making it difficult to determine whether those items serve as a representative sample for any given objective. Therefore, deciding whether a student demonstrates competency by using a few items from a norm-referenced test is not the best way to determine skill level. In most situations, teachers should determine mastery of content with criterion-referenced, curriculum-based assessment tools that assess students with many items.

Simple Numerical Reports

Transforming a raw score into a simple numerical report produces one of the most useful and often used criterion-referenced scores. The most common numerical report is the number of right and wrong answers on a test. An example of this type of score is 45 of 50 correct responses, often expressed as 45/50. Teachers frequently report this type of score on class tests, papers, worksheets, and homework assignments. The score is also useful with skills checklists, task analysis, minimum competency tests, and other curriculum-based assessment procedures.

Percent Correct Scores

A **percent correct score** is a criterion-referenced score that describes performance as the percentage of correct answers on a test. Calculating a percent correct score involves dividing the number of correct answers by the total number of items on the test. For example, if a student answers 8 items correctly on a test with 10 items, then the percent correct score is 80%. This score provides a convenient and straightforward way to convert raw scores into a more useful form. Like the simple numerical report score, the percent correct score is useful with class tests, checklists, minimum competency tests, and a variety of other curriculum-based assessment instruments.

Teachers should avoid using percent correct scores to compare performance across tests. This limitation is necessary because a percent correct score of 87% on an easy spelling test, for example, is not equivalent to a score of 87% on a difficult spelling test. Likewise, a score of 68% on a math test is not equivalent to a score of 68% on a reading test. This same limitation applies to numerical report scores.

Letter Grades

Letter grading is the classic means of describing student performance. Many teachers derive **letter grades** from percent correct scores and assign them according to a grading

Table 5–1   Sample Grading Scale

Percent Correct	Grade
90–100	A
80–89	B
70–79	C
60–69	D
Less than 60	F

TECHNOLOGY FOCUS

Online Gradebook Programs

Online teacher gradebook programs allow teachers to log in and work on their gradebooks at any time from any computer connected to the Internet. Gradebooks programs are useful for recording and reporting scores and grades, and enhancing communication between teachers, students, and parents. Teachers can assign passwords to students and parents so that they can view their own grading and attendance summaries. Available gradebook programs include mygradebook.com, Making the Grade, and Thinkwave Web Educator. The advantages of online gradebooks include increased parent communication, more feedback to students about their performance, and improved organization of class scoring, grading, and management tasks. Disadvantages include lack of Internet access for some, slow connections for others, the extra time it takes to set up and maintain electronic gradebooks, technical support issues, and the difficulty in viewing information on the computer, especially with programs that require frequent switching between screens.

scale. An example of a letter-grade scale based on percent correct scores appears in Table 5–1. Sometimes subjective information, such as teacher opinion or impressions, serves as the basis for grade scores rather than objective data. Such arbitrary assignment limits the value of letter grades. Although not scores in a technical sense, letter grades provide a way to describe student performance quickly and easily in a manner familiar to most people. Within this context, letter grades serve as practical tools for describing student performance. Many teachers rely on alternative grading procedures to meet the unique needs of students with disabilities. Widely used alternative grading procedures include pass/fail grading, multiple grading, grading for effort, and portfolio-based grading. Many teachers are using Web-based gradebook programs to record and report student scores and grades. Information about online gradebooks appears in the Technology Focus box.

Graphs

Converting raw scores into **graphical reports** produces profiles or visual representations of performance. Graphs show progress over time and help with analysis of strengths and weaknesses across skills. Like letter grades, graphs technically are not scores but they do show student outcomes using various scores and assessment

Figure 5–1 Student classroom progress graph

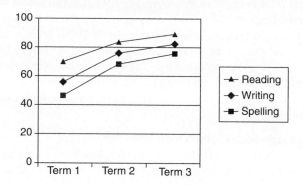

results. Frequently used graphs include profiles illustrating test results, student progress in the classroom, and student behavior. A sample student classroom progress graph is shown in Figure 5–1. This profile depicts a student's performance across grading periods in an intensive reading class.

Data sources for graphs include test scores, scores from written work, homework grades, data on student behavior, and simple numerical reports from checklists. Plotting data on profiles visually illustrates student performance and simplifies the process of communicating assessment information to students, parents, and others. The use of profiles is not limited to criterion-referenced scores. Profiles serve an equally useful purpose with norm-referenced scores.

✓ Check Your Comprehension

Criterion-referenced scores range from simple numerical reports to more complex graphical reports. Teachers frequently rely on this type of scoring in the classroom and in other instructional settings. Criterion-referenced scores help to plan intervention programs, measure student progress, and report performance. The essential notion of criterion-referenced scoring is interpreting performance in relation to a functional level such as progress in learning the skills in a curriculum. In contrast, the basic idea of norm-referenced scoring is interpretation of performance in relation to others.

Specific Norm-Referenced Scores

Norm-referenced scores include age scores, grade scores, percentiles, and standard scores. All norm-referenced scores, sometimes called derived scores, originate from norms. With most norm-referenced tests, the test giver chooses the score to report from a selection of several scores. Understanding all the available scores makes it possible to select the most appropriate score in a given situation. The appropriate score in one situation may not be appropriate in another. The goal is to select the score that fulfills the purpose of testing and fits the needs of the individual student.

Age Scores

An **age score** describes the typical or average performance of different age groups. For example, if a 6-year-old receives an age score of 5 years on a developmental test, the age score of 5 symbolizes the highest average age level of performance on the test.

Reflection
Which criterion-referenced scores did you like best when you were a student in high school and college? Have your experiences with scores as a student influenced the scores you use or plan to use as a teacher?

 To answer this reflection online, go to the *Teaching and Learning* module on the companion Website at *www.prenhall.com/venn*.

Test developers can formulate age scores for tests measuring any characteristic that changes with age. However, the most common use of age scores is with intelligence and achievement tests. Binet and Simon originally developed the mental age (MA) concept and score when they revised their intelligence test in 1908. An MA score represents mental ability in relation to the average performance of the individuals in the norm group at each successive chronological age. For example, one way to describe a child's mental age is as follows: *Three months ago, Timmy, whose chronological age was 6 years, 2 months (expressed as 6.2), received an MA of 9 years, 9 months (expressed as 9.9) on an intelligence test.*

Developmental Age Scores   **Developmental age** is a type of age score designed to measure the performance of infants, toddlers, and preschoolers in a range from birth through 6 years of age. A few developmental scales measure skills after 6 years of age, but most end at age 6.

When tested with a developmental scale, Jason, who was 3 years old at the time, received the following developmental age scores: 1 year in language development, 4 years in gross motor development, 4 years in fine motor development, 3 years in social skills, and 3 years in self-help skills.

Quotient Scores

A **quotient score** is an extension of an age score. The most common quotient score is a ratio intelligence quotient (ratio IQ). A ratio IQ is an age score derived from an intelligence test that expresses mental ability based on the ratio of a student's mental age (MA) to chronological age (CA). The formula for calculating a ratio IQ is:

$$\frac{MA}{CA} \times 100 = \text{Ratio IQ}$$

When Warren was 11 years, 9 months old, he received an MA score of 9.9 on an intelligence test. A ratio IQ score was obtained by dividing the MA of 9.9 by Warren's chronological age of 11.9. The resulting number, 0.83, was multiplied by 100 to obtain a ratio IQ of 83.

$$\frac{9.9}{11.9} \times 100 = 83$$

Warren's ratio IQ of 83 is interpreted in relation to an average IQ, which is 100. A score of 100 indicates a student with average intelligence. Warren's score is 17 points below the average and reflects below-average intellectual development. If Warren had obtained an MA of 11.9 on the test, his ratio IQ would have been normal, or average.

$$\frac{11.9}{11.9} \times 100 = 100$$

Although the logic of this type of test score is straightforward and seems reasonable, this score and all similar age-based scores are subject to misinterpretation for reasons explained later in this chapter in the section listing the disadvantages of such scores. Developers use a variety of names to describe age scores from different tests, including *developmental age, developmental quotient, social age, social quotient, learning quotient,* and *achievement quotient.*

Grade Scores

A **grade score** describes student performance according to scholastic grade levels. However, it is actually a specific type of age score rather than a separate score. In other words, grade scores express achievement in association with scholastic grades rather than chronological ages. Other terms for grade scores include *grade-equivalent scores, grade-referenced scores,* and *grade-placement scores.* For example, if a seventh grader receives a grade score of ninth grade on an academic test, this signifies the highest average grade level of attainment on the test.

Sarah received an overall grade-level score of third grade, fifth month (3.5) on an academic achievement test. She received scores of 4.4 on the reading recognition subtest, 4.1 on the reading comprehension subtest, 2.3 on the mathematics subtest, and 2.6 on the spelling subtest.

The overall score placed Sarah at the third grade, fifth month in academic achievement. More specifically, Sarah's academic strength was in reading, where she scored at a fourth-grade level. She was weaker in the academic areas of mathematics and spelling. In these areas she scored at about one grade level behind her overall average level of achievement.

Although generally correct, this interpretation is not necessarily accurate, depending on the age of the student. For a 21-year-old student, these scores would indicate a significantly low level of functioning; for a 4-year-old child, these scores would indicate a significantly advanced level of performance. In addition, the actual academic performance in a classroom situation of a 21-year-old and a 4-year-old with these scores would be much different, and the intervention approach would also vary considerably.

Advantages of Age and Grade Scores Age and grade scores seem more practical and appealing than most other scores because it makes so much sense to think of scores in these terms. The concept of age and grade scoring appears easy to understand, making it possible to describe test performance in a more concrete way than with other scores. In addition, more people recognize age scores than the other norm-referenced scores. Although advantages exist in the use of age scores, especially with tests for very young children, the scores also have many disadvantages.

Disadvantages of Age and Grade Scores Despite the widespread use of age and grade scores, specialists continue to document the disadvantages of age and grade scores with convincing evidence that seriously questions further use in most situations (American Guidance Service, n.d.; Linn & Miller, 2005; McLoughlin & Lewis, 2005; Nitko, 2004). Furthermore, the Standards for Educational and Psychological Testing (American Psychological Association, 1999) advocate the elimination of age and grade scores altogether. Criticism of grade scores occurs because of the many drawbacks associated with these scores. As a result, when professionals use age and grade scores, they should do so cautiously with a full understanding of the possibilities for misinterpretation. A list of the disadvantages that lead to misinterpretation appears in Table 5–2. The following paragraphs provide a description of each drawback.

Inaccurate Generalizations. Experts point out that age and grade scores may lead to inaccurate generalizations about overall performance. This serious limitation exists in particular with students who have special needs because they often receive extremely low scores. For example, describing the performance of a 10-year-old who receives an age score of 3 on a developmental test as "performing like a 3-year-old" is

Table 5–2 Disadvantages of Age and Grade Scores

- Age and grade scores lead to inaccurate generalizations.
- The reliability of age and grade scores decreases as the student's age increases.
- Age and grade scores shrink independent of behavior change.
- Age and grade units are not equal.
- Age and grade scores from different tests are not comparable.
- Age and grade scores cannot be averaged.
- Some tests estimate certain age and grade scores.
- Age and grade scores may not indicate skill development.

an inaccurate generalization. Although a 10-year-old may receive an age score of 3 on a test, the pattern of development of a 10-year-old with this score is usually much different than the pattern of development of an average 3-year-old. A more accurate description of a 10-year-old who receives a developmental age score of 3 is that the student performs some skills typical of a child younger than age 3, some skills typical of a 3-year-old, and some skills above the 3-year-old age level. In contrast, a typical 3-year-old performs most skills at the 3-year-old level and few skills above or below the 3-year-old age level. The problem, in part, is the difficulty of explaining subtle details like these when reporting test score results. Another example of the problem is a 12th grader who receives a score of third grade on a reading test. In this instance, the 12th grader probably does not read like a typical third grader. Thus, describing the reading performance of a high school senior as "reading like a third grader" is an inappropriate generalization. These examples illustrate how age scores lead to inaccurate generalizations.

Decreasing Reliability. The reliability of age and grade scores tends to decrease with age because as children grow older, their pattern of skill development becomes less predictable. Although the age scores of preschoolers tend to be reliable and stable, the age scores of adolescents and adults are difficult to assess accurately. This occurs because children up to the age of about 6 years learn most skills in a remarkably similar sequence and pattern. This predictability in skill development fades with children above age 6.

Independent Decline. Age scores and grade scores decline or shrink with increasing chronological age. This decrease in scores occurs independent of behavior change because as students age, it becomes easier for them to fall farther and farther behind. Although a 1-year-old cannot fall more than 1 year behind in development, a 12-year-old can easily fall more than a year behind in development. In fact, a 12-year-old can be as much as 12 years behind. Likewise, a first grader cannot fall more than one grade level behind, but a 12th grader can be as many 12 years below grade level. This shrinkage is more pronounced with scores at older age levels. It is less of a problem with young children because behavior change is relatively rapid in infants, toddlers, and preschoolers. For this reason, experts support use of developmental age scores in the birth-to-6-year-old range, but caution against using such scores for students as they become older.

Unequal Units. Another problem concerns the inequality of age- and grade-score units. For example, a larger difference exists among the reading behaviors of first and second graders compared with the reading behaviors of 11th and 12th graders. Likewise, larger differences exist in the language development of 1- and 2-year-old infants compared with the language development of 9- and 10-year-old children. These examples illustrate the inequality of age-score units, which make the scores less effective measures of behavior than some of the other norm-referenced scores.

Score Comparison Limitations. Age and grade scores from different tests are not directly comparable because of differences in content and standardization procedures among the tests. This means that if a child has age scores from several different tests, comparisons across the tests may not be valid. Although all comparisons across tests should be made cautiously, comparisons using age scores tend to be especially problematic.

Averaging Distorts Performance. Age and grade scores show relative standing, not absolute differences; therefore, averaging the results of various scores to show overall achievement distorts performance. For example, averaging a reading score of second grade and a math score of eighth grade for an overall average level of achievement of fifth grade misrepresents achievement. Although the overall average is fifth grade, a student with these scores does not perform at all like a fifth grader in reading and mathematics.

Estimation of Certain Scores. Some tests estimate certain scores because it is too difficult to include students from every specific grade level and month in the norm sample group. For example, if a group of third-grade students takes a tests at the beginning of the school year as part of the norm development process and a group of fourth-grade students takes the test in the middle of the school year, then the test developer must estimate grade scores for the months in between. For this reason, grade scores from tests may not fit with informal teacher observations about the specific grade-level skills of a student. Therefore, teachers should use grade scores cautiously, especially when placing students in instructional groups.

Scores May Not Indicate Skill Development. Age scores often fail to indicate skill development because obtained scores do not always reflect students' present levels of performance. The following scenario illustrates this dilemma: If a second grader scored sixth grade on a math test, it does not necessarily mean that the student functions at the sixth-grade level in math. How can a second grader perform sixth-grade math when the student has not been taught sixth-grade skills? The technically appropriate interpretation of this result is that the second grader obtained a grade-equivalent score of sixth grade on the second-grade test using the norms for second-grade students. It does not mean that the second grader performed math like a typical sixth grader. If the performance of the second grader was scored using the norms for sixth graders, the resulting score would be lower.

☑ Check Your Comprehension

Age and grade scores are widely used because they are practical, easy to interpret, and suitable for communication with others, especially parents. Unfortunately, experts caution against their continued use because misinterpretation occurs so frequently. For this reason, some test developers omit such scores from new tests and from revisions of older tests. Test users should also begin to report other scores whenever possible. The exception to this rule remains in the use of developmental age scores for describing the performance of infants and young children. Fortunately, more accurate, norm-referenced scores exist as replacements for age scores.

Reflection

Given the disadvantages of grade scores, why do you think educators continue to use them so frequently instead of using other norm-referenced scores?

 To answer this reflection online, go to the *Teaching and Learning* module on the companion Website at *www.prenhall.com/venn*.

Percentile Ranks

In response to the many problems associated with grade and age scores, most experts recommend use of **percentile ranks** instead of grade and age scores. Percentile ranks or percentile scores are one of the most widely used and easily understood measures of test performance. Percentile ranks show relative standing by ranking students in comparison to similar students in the same age or grade norm group. Thus, a student with percentile rank of 40 on a reading test performed better than 40 percent of the students and worse than 60 percent of the students in the appropriate norm group. A percentile is any 1 of 99 scores divided into a distribution of 100 equal ranks ranging from 1 to 99. The 50th percentile signifies the average ranking or average performance.

Mary received a percentile score of 50 on a test of vocational skills. This score ranks in the middle range and indicates average performance.

Noah received a percentile score of 20 on a test of vocational skills. This score ranks in the bottom fourth or bottom 25% and signifies below-average performance.

Gail received a percentile score of 82 on a test of vocational skills. This score ranks in the top fourth or top 25% and denotes above-average performance.

Several test publishers use an application of percentile ranks called the percentile band. The percentile band is a range of percentile ranks. **Deciles**, a type of percentile band, divide scores into tenths or 10 equal units: 1–9, 10–19, 20–29, and so forth. Quartiles, another type of percentile band, divide scores into 4 units or fourths: 1–24, 25–49, 50–74, and 75–99. The fourth or highest quartile (75–99) designates the top quarter or top fourth of all scores. The first or lowest quartile (1–24) marks the bottom quarter or bottom fourth of all scores. Percentile bands call attention to the measurement error that exists in each individual score. Rather than interpreting scores as precise values, percentile bands allow for interpretation of performance within a band or range of percentile ranks.

Care should be taken to avoid confusing percentiles with percent correct scores. Percent correct scores are informal, criterion-referenced measures. In contrast, percentiles are formal scores used in norm-referenced testing. For example, if a student receives a percent correct score of 90% by answering 90 of 100 questions correctly on a test, this does not mean that the score ranks in the 90th percentile. It means that the student correctly answered 90% of the test questions. A percent correct score like this fails to provide information about relative standing in relation to the scores of other students.

Advantages of Percentile Ranks

The advantages of percentiles include applicability to all age levels and suitability for scoring performance across domains, including intellectual, academic, social, and physical. Percentile ranks are reasonably easy to understand and are less susceptible to misinterpretation than age scores.

Disadvantages of Percentile Ranks

The major drawback of percentiles involves the unequal length of percentile units, especially at the extremes. This characteristic results in a tendency to underemphasize differences near the middle and overemphasize differences near the ends. In other words, the difference between 50 and 55 is less than the difference between 90 and 95. This inequality occurs because percentiles, which are calculated from ranked data, designate relative standing, not absolute differences. This characteristic problem is not limited to percentiles. Instead, it is a characteristic shared among most test scores in that most scores are less accurate at the extremes.

☑ Check Your Comprehension

Most experts agree that percentile ranks are probably the best all-around norm-referenced score for general use. Percentiles display many advantages and few limitations. Percentile scores indicate relative standing by comparing individual student performance with the performance of students in a corresponding norm group.

Standard Scores

Standard scores express performance by comparing the deviation of individual scores from the mean or average score with the scores of students in a norm group of the same chronological age or scholastic grade level. The standard deviation, or average variability, of the scores in the norm group provides the basis for calculating standard scores. Standard scores have the advantage of enabling comparison of performance across tests. This makes them especially useful in the process of classifying and placing students. Although test developers have the option of creating standard scores with various means and standard deviations, the most widely used standard scores have means (x) of 100 and standard deviations (SDs) of 15. Originally designed for intelligence testing, test developers routinely use standard scores with a variety of tests.

Quotient Scores

When used with intelligence tests, a standard score with a mean of 100 and a standard deviation of 15 is usually called an intelligence quotient (IQ). The more technical name for this particular standard score is deviation IQ. A deviation IQ is a standard score that provides an index of general mental ability based on the deviation between an individual score and the average score in the norm group of the same age or grade level. Other tests use similar quotient scores. For example, some achievement tests use an achievement quotient (AQ), and certain developmental tests rely on a developmental quotient (DQ).

Standard Scores and the Normal Distribution

The basis for interpreting standard scores, including those with means of 100 and standard deviations of 15, is the normal distribution or bell-shaped curve. An illustration of this distribution appears in Figure 5–2. In a normal distribution, most scores fall into the average range, which is within 15 points of the mean, or between 85 and 115 (100 − 15 = 85 and 100 + 15 = 115). More specifically, about 68% of all scores in a normal distribution occur between 1 SD below the mean (85) and 1 SD above the mean (115). Relatively few scores (about 16%) rise above 1 SD (above 115) or fall below 1 SD (below 85).

The following examples describe the process for interpreting standard scores with a mean of 100 and a standard deviation of 15, using this bell-shaped distribution pattern.

Figure 5–2 Relationship among scores and the normal distribution

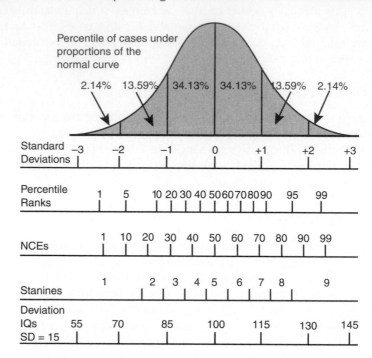

Percentile of cases under proportions of the normal curve

2.14% 13.59% 34.13% 34.13% 13.59% 2.14%

Standard Deviations −3 −2 −1 0 +1 +2 +3

Percentile Ranks 1 5 10 20 30 40 50 60 70 80 90 95 99

NCEs 1 10 20 30 40 50 60 70 80 90 99

Stanines 1 2 3 4 5 6 7 8 9

Deviation IQs SD = 15 55 70 85 100 115 130 145

Jeffrey received a standard score (in this case an IQ score) of 95 on an intelligence test. This placed Jeffrey's score in the average range (about the middle of the bell-shaped curve) of intellectual ability compared with other students.

Angelo received a standard score of 105 on an intelligence test. This placed Angelo's score in the average range (about the middle of the bell-shaped curve) of intellectual ability compared with other students.

Tom received a standard score of 120 on an achievement test. This placed Tom's score in the above-average range (toward the higher end of the bell-shaped curve) of academic achievement.

Bob received a standard score of 80 on an achievement test. This positioned Bob's score in the below-average range (toward the lower end of the bell-shaped curve) of academic achievement.

Standard scores between 115 and 130 are above-average scores because they are 1 SD above the mean (100 + 15 = 115). Likewise, standard scores between 70 and 85 represent below-average scores because they are 1 SD below the mean (100 − 15 = 85).

Sharian received a standard score of 135 on a test of creativity. This indicates that Sharian scored in the significantly above-average range (at the extreme positive end of the bell-shaped curve) in creative ability.

Nancy received a standard score of 65 on an intelligence test. This score indicated that she performed in the significantly below-average range (at the extremely negative end of the bell-shaped curve) in intellectual ability.

Standard scores of 130 or higher are in the significantly above-average range because they are 2 SDs above the mean (100 + 30 = 130). In contrast, standard scores of 70 or below fall into the significantly below-average range because they are 2 SDs below the mean (100 − 30 = 70). Although the standard scores with a mean of 100 and a standard deviation of 15 are the most common standard scores, other valuable and widely used standard scores exist as well, such as z-scores, t-scores, stanines, and normal curve equivalents.

Z-Scores and T-Scores

A **z-score** is a standard score with a mean of 0 and a standard deviation of 1. A z-score of 0 is average whereas a z-score of +1 is 1 SD above the mean or above average. Likewise, a z-score of −1 is 1 SD below the mean or below average. Unfortunately, z-scores employ negative numbers, making them difficult to understand and communicate. Although researchers frequently use z-scores, they rarely appear in other situations.

Similar to the z-score without the negative numbers, the **t-score** is a standard score with a mean of 50 and a standard deviation of 10. A t-score of 50 is average whereas a t-score of 40 is 1 SD below the mean or below average, and a t-score of 60 is 1 SD above the mean or above average. Because t-scores do not use negative numbers, interpreting them is not as difficult as interpreting z-scores. A t-score of 50 represents the performance of a typical or average child. A score of 40 indicates that the student performed at a level below approximately 84% of the students in the norm group based on interpreting the score in relation to the bell-shaped curve. A score of 60 suggests superior performance and indicates a score better than approximately 84% of the students in the corresponding norm group. Whereas z-scores rarely appear except in research, subtests on intelligence and achievement tests often use t scores as the unit of measure.

Stanines

Stanines are standard scores with a mean of 5, a standard deviation of 2, and a range of 1 to 9. Psychologists originally developed stanines during World War II for use with mental ability tests. The psychologists needed a one-digit score to fit a computer punch card with limited space. Therefore, they set up a scale with a top score of 9. Because they use a scale of 1 to 9 and average scores occur around the mean of 5, stanines are convenient for communicating test results, especially with nonprofessionals. Stanines above 1 SD from the mean (5 + 2 = 7) fall in the above-average range, and stanines below 1 SD (5 − 2 = 3) fall in the below-average range.

Normal Curve Equivalents

Normal curve equivalents (NCEs) are standard scores with a mean of 50 and a standard deviation of 21.06. NCE values within 21.06 points of 50 (50 +/− 21.06, or 71.06 to 28.94) represent average scores. Scores of 28.94 and lower fall more than 1 SD from the mean of 50 and indicate below-average test performance. Scores of 71.06 and higher are more than 1 SD from the mean and represent above-average values.

The researchers who developed this score selected these values so that NCEs would have the same range (1 to 99) and midpoint (50) as percentiles. This match with percentiles helps to make NCEs understandable. The major advantage of NCEs is the equal length of NCE units. This characteristic results in equal intervals between the NCE scores. In other words, the difference between scores at the midpoint such as 50 and 55 is the same as the difference between 90 and 95 or 10 and 15. In other words, NCEs are equal in size from the bottom to the top of the scale whereas percentiles are larger at the ends and smaller in the middle (CTB McGraw-Hill, 2001).

When interpreting NCEs, a score of 50 is at grade level and scores near 50 are also average scores. When using NCEs to measure progress over time, all gains in scores indicate above-average progress. Scores that remain about the same over time indicate average progress. In other words, no change in NCE scores over time, such as at the beginning and at the end of the school year, does not mean that the student or group of students failed to make progress. Instead, no change means that progress occurred at the average, expected rate. Scores that decline indicate below-average progress (CTB McGraw-Hill, 2001).

Advantages of Standard Scores

The major advantage of standard scores is that they maintain their original position of standing relative to the distribution of scores when transformed. This desirable technical quality makes it possible to compare test scores across students on the same test and among students on different tests with a higher degree of accuracy than is possible with other scores. NCEs are even more accurate than the other standard scores when making these comparisons. This accuracy allows the reporting of scores across various age and grade levels with less chance for misinterpretation than with other norm-referenced scores. For these reasons, standard scores are the score of choice when making eligibility staffing and placement decisions about students.

Disadvantages of Standard Scores

Standard scores are more difficult to interpret than the other norm-referenced scores, especially percentiles. Difficulties with interpretation occur because grasping the precise meaning of standard scores requires application of statistical concepts, such as the normal curve. This causes obstacles in the use of standard scores in communicating test results to others, especially with parents and students.

The use of standard scores from different tests with differing standard deviations also causes interpretation problems. For example, a standard score of 70 on a test with a mean of 100 and a standard deviation of 15 is 2 SD below the mean ($100 - 30 = 70$). This score is not directly comparable to a score of 70 on a test with a mean of 100 and a standard deviation of 16. The comparable score on the test with a standard deviation of 16 is 68 ($100 - 32 = 68$). Care must be taken in the use of standard scores to avoid this type of misinterpretation, particularly when classifying students based on test scores and communicating results with others.

☑ Check Your Comprehension

The standard scores are the most accurate of all the norm-referenced scores. Standard scores allow comparison of results across different tests, and this facilitates the process of assessment in special education, especially the difficult step of identifying and placing students with special needs. In fact, many aspects of assessment in special education, including the identification and placement process, prescribe the use of standard scores to provide objective information for making educational decisions.

Table 5–3 Principles of Using Scores

- Understand the score.
- Know the norms.
- Consider all available information.
- Use caution.
- Communicate effectively.
- Ask the experts.

Principles of Using Scores

Lyman (1998) developed a set of important principles for new test users to keep in mind when interpreting and reporting scores. A summary of these excellent practical suggestions for accurate and effective use of test scores appears in Table 5–3. This is followed by a discussion of each principle.

Understand the Score

Make sure to understand the type of score you are using: a standard score, a raw score, a percentile rank, or something else. Misunderstanding results from confusing similar scores, such as percentile rank and percent correct. At times you have no choice in what score to use. In this case be aware of any limitations of the score. At other times you must choose among alternative scores. Knowing the score and what it means assists in making the best choice in each situation.

Know the Norms

Always make sure of the norms for the tests you are using. Some of the norms for tests in wide use in special education are inadequate. For example, the Wide Range Achievement Test—Expanded Edition (WRAT—EXPANDED) (Robertson, 2002) has poorly developed norms. As a result, scores from this test should be used cautiously. Other tests in wide use do not have norms at all. The norm sample must be sound and must represent the tested student; otherwise, the norms are not valid. Failure to meet these conditions results in inappropriate scoring.

Consider All Available Information

Consider all available information when interpreting test results, not just the score. A score reported in isolation has little meaning. Always report the name of the assessment and the date along with the score. Consider all available information related to the test even if it is not derived from the assessment. This may include, but is not limited to, the purpose of testing, the setting for the testing, and the response of the student to the test.

Use Caution

Scores suggest ability and performance level; they do not prove ability. Use scores with caution, keeping their limitations in mind at all times. Careful, cautious use of test scores avoids problems and protects the sensitive egos of students who receive low scores. Review the accompanying Multicultural Considerations feature for a discussion of ways to account for low scores.

MULTICULTURAL CONSIDERATIONS

Accounting for Low Scores

When students receive low scores, it is important to consider the possible contributing factors (Sattler, 2001). It is also important to remember that most scores are obtained during a single period. Therefore, one score may not accurately reflect typical performance. In other words, scores tell us about performance at one point in time under controlled (and often stressful) conditions. In many situations, low scores may simply identify the students who have not yet acquired the requisite knowledge and skills measured by the assessment. The problem is that some students may have knowledge and skills that tests fail to identify. This is often a critical issue, especially with students from diverse backgrounds. For example, some students may have cultural, ethnic, or language experiences that negatively influence scores. Likewise, students who are at risk for school failure may perform poorly on tests even when they know the material. Other considerations include how students respond to the assessment situation and how students handle the demands of a test or an assessment. For example, some students become so anxious during testing that they fail due to anxiety even if they know the material on the test. Because the influence of these factors varies, it is important to try to identify and account for possible influences when interpreting and reporting low scores.

Think of a student, relative, friend, or neighbor who receives low scores. Which of the contributing factors mentioned in the Multicultural Considerations feature may help to account for the low scores? Can you think of other factors not mentioned in the text that may contribute to the low scores?

 To answer this reflection online, go to the *Multicultural Considerations* module on the Companion Website at **www.prenhall.com/venn**.

Communicate Effectively

Give all necessary information and interpret scores in practical, understandable ways. Because many, although not all, students with learning problems score low on tests, use scores carefully in ways that are as positive as possible. Attempt to avoid using scores in ways that contribute to poor self-concept and feelings of failure.

Ask the Experts

Interpreting complicated scores requires specialized knowledge and skills. Most school systems have specialists who should be available to those who would like assistance. If you are not sure about the meaning of a particular score, go ahead and ask for help from a testing specialist.

Check Your Comprehension

The principles of using scores highlight some of the important things to keep in mind when using scores. The goal is to assure accurate scoring and interpretation of all assessments. Additional procedures for scoring tests appear in later chapters, including Chapter 6, which provides a checklist for evaluators to use in assessing their proficiency in conducting evaluations and scoring tests.

Summary

Scoring is an integral step in the process of evaluating the performance of students with learning problems. Scores are the numerical result of assessment, and almost all curriculum-based measures and all norm-referenced tests provide some type of score report. As a result, educators encounter many different kinds of scores. Criterion-referenced scores are a key ingredient in curriculum-based assessment. Norm-referenced scores are a principal component in more formal, standardized testing. Scores perform the essential function of objectively describing student ability and performance levels, but many pitfalls exist in scoring and some aspects of the process confuse even the experts. The pitfalls include misuse of scores, misinterpretation of results, and misunderstanding of the meaning of scores. Fortunately, standards for scoring and principles for using test scores are available as guides to help us avoid these hazards. Following standards and principles ensures accuracy and fairness in scoring. The ultimate goal of assessment is to fairly and accurately measure ability and performance in ways that lead to providing the best possible educational programs and services for students.

 To check your comprehension of the chapter contents, go to the *Guided Review* and *Quiz* modules in Chapter 5 of the Companion Website, *www.prenhall.com/venn*.

Meeting Performance Standards and Preparing for Licensure Exams

After reading this chapter, you should be able to demonstrate the following CEC Standards and PRAXIS™ test knowledge and skills. The information in parentheses identifies where to find the particular CEC Standard and PRAXIS™ content reference.

CEC Standards for Beginning Special Education Teachers

- Basic terminology used in assessment (CC8K1)
- Interpret information from formal and informal assessments (CC8S5)

PRAXIS™ Education of Exceptional Students: Core Content Knowledge

- Assessment, including use of assessment for screening, diagnosis, placement, and the making of instructional decisions; for example: how to select and conduct nondiscriminatory and appropriate assessments; how to interpret standardized and specialized assessment results; procedures and test materials, both formal and informal, typically used for prereferral, screening, referral, classification, placement, and ongoing program monitoring.

chapter 6

Selecting and Using Assessment Instruments

Objectives

After reading this chapter, you will be prepared to do the following:

- Explain the decision model for locating, selecting, and evaluating assessment instruments.
- Understand the wide range and variety of assessment decisions made by special educators.
- Determine the information needed to make the best possible assessment decision.
- Identify what information is already available.
- Identify what additional information is needed.
- Use the sources of test information to locate available assessment instruments.
- Use the assessment analysis checklist in Figure 6–1 to evaluate available instruments.
- Use the assessment instrument review form in Figure 6–2 to appraise various instruments.
- Understand why we use assessment to document teaching and learning.
- Prepare for assessment.
- Establish an appropriate assessment environment.
- Respond to students' needs during assessment.
- Provide reasonable accommodations during testing.
- Use appropriate prompts during assessment.
- Include anecdotal assessment information on score sheets and in written reports.
- Select the best possible assessment tool.
- Prepare written reports.

Overview

Among the necessary competencies in the knowledge base of assessing students with special needs are skills in selecting and using assessment instruments. These skills include locating, selecting, and evaluating assessment instruments and giving, scoring, interpreting, and reporting assessments. As you investigate the processes for selecting and using assessments in this chapter, you will discover that whether a particular test is appropriate depends on many factors, including technical adequacy, the purpose for testing, and the unique needs of the student. Because high-quality tools produce the best possible assessment results, the

quality of the chosen instrument often determines the value of the results. For this reason, this chapter includes specific criteria for judging the test quality.

All teachers administer and score various assessments as part of the instructional process. Therefore, teachers must understand the techniques and procedures for accurate test administration, scoring, interpretation, and report writing. In this chapter, you will explore practical techniques for giving and scoring tests and reporting test results. At the end of the chapter, you will review several case-study examples of written reports.

The Decision Model

A three-phase decision model for test use and selection (Drummond & Jones, 2006) illustrates the processes and procedures for locating, selecting, and evaluating assessment instruments. The phases in the model are preparation, data collection, and evaluation. The first phase in the three-phase model is preparation. The questions in the preparation phase are the following:

1. What specific assessment judgments and decisions have to be made?
2. What information is needed to make the best decisions?
3. What information is already available?
4. What assessment methods and instruments will provide the needed information?
5. How should appropriate instruments be located?
6. What criteria should be used in selecting and evaluating assessment instruments?

These questions show the sequential steps in the preparation phase of the model, beginning with the assessment decision. Explanation of how to respond to each of these preparation questions follows. Discussion of phases two and three of the model appears later in the chapter.

Assessment Decisions

Special education teachers make a wide range and variety of assessment decisions regarding the education of students with special needs, ranging from initial referral decisions to daily instructional decisions. For example, when special educators serve as members of child-study teams and student staffing committees, they help make placement decisions. In contrast, when special educators assess the strengths and weaknesses of students with reading disabilities, they use the evaluation results to help design reading remediation programs. Likewise, when teachers use spelling and math quizzes to help them prepare the lesson for the next day, they are making instructional decisions. Teachers also make many educational progress decisions based on classroom assessment data.

Special education teachers also make important assessment decisions when they help develop individual education plans (IEPs), individual transition plans (ITPs), and individual family service plans (IFSPs). IEPs are planning documents that define the elements of an appropriate education for each individual student with a disability. ITPs are planning documents for students who will soon graduate from school and enter the world of work. IFSPs are for infants, toddlers, and their families. When teachers help develop IEPs, ITPs, and IFSPs, they make vital educational planning decisions that affect the quality of the lives of children and youth with special needs.

These are just a few examples of the many kinds of assessment decisions and judgments that teachers make. Good decisions emerge from information. The key is to determine as clearly as possible the kind of assessment decision that must be made before proceeding to the next step.

Required Assessment Information   The second preparation step involves specifying the required assessment information. This ensures that the assessment provides enough data to make the best possible decision and to avoid unnecessary assessment. For example, most placement and staffing decisions require explicit assessment information. When testing a student for a learning disability, school district procedures define the tests that the evaluators must give and the use of the test results to make the eligibility decision. In other situations, the type of information needed is not mandated. For example, the assessment information needed to place a student in a work-study job in the community includes the student's work experience, job interests, and work aptitudes. Data and information about the student's educational achievement and interests, as well as job openings and appropriate job placement sites, are other dimensions that might be relevant to the placement decision.

Available Assessment Information   The third step is to identify what needed information is already available. In initial referral situations, there are specific activities that must be completed and documented. These include observing the student, attempting educational interventions to help resolve the problem, and meeting with the parents. Some of these assessments may have already occurred prior to the referral. If so, this information should be used to avoid replicating assessments. In most school settings, each student has a cumulative folder that contains a social and an educational history, test results, attendance records, health information, and miscellaneous records, which can be very helpful in the decision-making process. However, when placing students, certain evaluations must be conducted regardless of the amount of prior information. Unfortunately, this sometimes leads to overtesting, especially with students who have special needs. For example, some students have been tested so many times with individually administered, standardized achievement tests that by the time they reach high school they resist and even refuse further testing.

Needed Assessment Information   After identifying the type of information that is needed and the information that is already available, the next step is to determine the methods and instruments for obtaining additional data. For example, if additional information is needed to make curricular and instructional decisions for students in a new class, then testing all of the new students with classroom-based instruments might be appropriate. If the goal is to enroll a student into another program, then individual testing with formal standardized instruments may be necessary. If assessment information is needed to design a behavior-management program for a child with aggressive, acting-out behavior, then the teacher may need to obtain a baseline of the inappropriate behavior. In other words, the particular assessment methods and instruments depend on the purpose for conducting the assessment and the needs of the child.

Locating Appropriate Assessment Instruments

Thousands of tests are available for purchase from test publishers. Many more are developed locally, statewide, or for specific projects. Although no single source exists for all instruments, several popular and widely used sources for locating tests exist.

Tests in Print

Tests in Print VI (Murphy, Impara, & Plake, 2002) provides a comprehensive bibliography to all known commercially available tests that are currently in print. It also functions as an index for the *Mental Measurements Yearbook* (MMY)(Spies & Plake, 2005) test review series by directing readers to the appropriate MMY volume(s) for reviews of specific tests. *Tests in Print* (TIP) can be utilized to determine a test's availability; then the appropriate MMY volume can be referenced for a critical, candid review. TIP contains a reference list of professional literature providing information about specific tests as well. TIP, available in most college, university, and large public libraries, lists more than 3,000 instruments available from commercial publishers.

Noncommercial Assessments

Though TIP is a valuable reference tool, it does not include noncommercial assessments. Noncommercial assessments are not available for purchase; instead, they appear in books and articles in professional journals. Schools, school districts, and state departments of education also publish noncommercial tests and assessments. Locating noncommercial and unpublished assessments can be difficult; however, one of the best sources of information about unpublished tests is *TestLink*, the Educational Testing Service (ETS) Test Collection Database containing descriptions of over 20,000 tests and other measurement instruments. The database contains descriptions of tests in the ETS Tests in Microfiche Collection and tests described in journal articles or book chapters. *TestLink* encompasses virtually all fields, from vocational interest inventories to instruments that measure shyness to assessment of managerial style, as well as education-related achievement and aptitude tests.

Locating Tests for Students with Limited English Proficiency

Locating tests for students from diverse backgrounds, including students with limited English proficiency, is a continuing concern in assessment. This problem is part of a larger issue often referred to as fairness in testing. **Fairness in testing** is one of

MULTICULTURAL CONSIDERATIONS

Fairness in Testing

Fairness in testing issues occur in many forms. One form involves inaccurate referrals for special education as a result of a student's minority status, gender, language, or age. For example, teachers may underrefer students from minority groups for programs serving those who are gifted. In contrast, teachers may also underrefer students from majority groups for programs serving students with mild mental retardation. A critical concern is the disproportionate number of students from minority groups who receive low scores on norm-referenced tests and other assessment instruments. Fairness issues can also occur when evaluators administer and score tests and when teachers give and grade classroom assessments. Common administration and scoring errors include failure to establish rapport prior to assessment and mishandling the administration of a test or interview (e.g., rushing or upsetting a student) because of preconceived ideas based on a student's background, appearance, or language. Other questions about fairness in testing result from technical inadequacies of tests such as normative groups that exclude students from diverse backgrounds and curriculum-based assessments with inadequate reliability and validity.

Critics continue to raise questions about fairness in testing and the many difficult and controversial issues related to nondiscriminatory assessment. Some critics argue that because developers create assessments within the context of their culture, elements of bias are bound to appear. Although it may be impossible to develop entirely culture-free assessments, developers and users must continue efforts to reduce partiality to a minimum and to consider prejudice in the use of test results.

The test performance of students from historically underrepresented groups continues to be a fairness in testing issue (Thorndike, 2005). Some students from minority groups, such as recent immigrants from Southeast Asia, are highly motivated to perform well on individual tasks such as tests of academic achievement. In contrast, some Native American students focus more on group success and group tasks and less on individual performance associated with taking individual tests. The challenge is to refine the overall testing approach to account for differences such as these. This refinement might lead to more adaptive testing based on students' abilities, interests, and experiences. For example, the test scores of majority students may require an interpretation different from the test scores of some minority students. The challenge is to agree on what types of interpretations are appropriate for students from diverse backgrounds. The goal is to incorporate those adjustments that provide the most accurate and fairest test score interpretations and assessment decisions.

In your own words (with your own definition) describe what you consider to be fairness in testing. Do you think your definition is the same as the student next to you? Explain.

To answer this reflection online, go to the *Multicultural Considerations* module on the companion Website at *www.prenhall.com/venn*.

the most significant concerns in assessment. The issue involves students from diverse backgrounds, including students with limited English proficiency. The accompanying Multicultural Considerations feature provides a definition of fairness in testing along with some practical suggestions for avoiding discrimination in assessment.

Other Information Sources

Once a particular test or group of tests has been located, more detailed information is available from several sources. Current textbooks on assessment, available in university libraries, are excellent sources for locating tests and obtaining detailed information about particular tests. Test publishers' catalogues provide another good source of information. Obtaining a catalogue is usually as simple as contacting the publisher and requesting a catalogue. Publishers also host Websites with catalogue information. For example, American Guidance Service, one of the largest and best publishers of tests for students with special needs, provides extensive online information.

Testing centers in local school systems and measurement centers at many universities are another source of information. These centers usually maintain a collection of current catalogues and specimen sets for review. Hands-on examination of the tests themselves, along with a review of the test manuals, provides practical firsthand information about the suitability of particular tests. Test manuals contain descriptions of the purpose of the instrument, directions for administration and scoring, guidelines for interpretation, and information about reliability, validity, and other technical qualities.

Evaluating Assessment Instruments

Catalogues and other materials from test publishers focus on selling tests rather than on critical evaluation by external reviewers. For this reason, it is useful to consider independent sources for external reviews such as professional journals, specimen sets, and newsletters. The Council for Exceptional Children has a division, the Council for Educational Diagnostic Services (CEDS), dedicated to testing and assessing children with special needs. CEDS serves professionals engaged in diagnosing and testing children. CEDS publishes *Assessment for Effective Intervention*, a professional journal on testing, and *Communiqué*, a newsletter, both of which provide helpful information on selecting and evaluating tests for children with special needs. Consulting with teachers and other professional colleagues can also yield valuable information.

Mental Measurements Yearbooks

The *Mental Measurements Yearbooks* (MMY) (Spies & Plake, 2005) are the premier source for in-depth reviews. Published by the Buros Institute for Mental Measurements, the MMYs are large reference books with thousands of test reviews. Each MMY includes timely, consumer-oriented reviews promoting and encouraging informed test selection. MMY entries include descriptive information, two professional reviews of each instrument, and a list of references to relevant literature. The professional reviews provide detailed information about reliability, validity, norms, administration, scoring, and interpretation. Each MMY volume has six indexes for locating tests by title, acronym, subject, publisher, author, and score. These indexes help locate specific tests and groups of tests in a particular category. The MMY series is available in most university libraries, many large public libraries, and online.

Practical Criteria for Test Selection and Evaluation

Professionals should consider several criteria when selecting and evaluating assessment tools. Matching the assessment to student needs is a primary consideration, but evaluators should weigh other factors as well, including the age range of the instrument, test content, and assessment features.

The ultimate test selection and evaluation goal is to choose an instrument or procedure that provides valid and practical assessment information. The assessment analysis checklist in Figure 6–1 is a brief, informal checklist designed to assist in the selection and review process. The checklist contains key factors for reviewers to consider in the evaluation process. Scoring the checklist involves assigning a yes or no to each item. The form contains space to include comments and remarks. The assessment instrument review form in Figure 6–2 contains detailed information for conducting in-depth analysis. The review form, derived from a training manual developed by Graham (1992), helps in conducting formal, comprehensive reviews. Prior to completing the form, reviewers should have a complete specimen set of the test under review that contains all the materials, including the manual. Completing the review form usually takes about 30 to 45 minutes.

Figure 6–1 Assessment analysis checklist

Test Name: _____

	Yes	No
1. Does the instrument match student needs?	_____	_____
2. Is the age range appropriate?	_____	_____
3. Does the content reflect the student's curriculum?	_____	_____
4. Does the instrument provide clear administration instructions?	_____	_____
5. Does the instrument include precise scoring procedures?	_____	_____
6. Does the instrument include specific instructions for interpreting results?	_____	_____
7. Does the instrument include a curriculum or activity guide?	_____	_____
8. Does the instrument exhibit adequate technical qualities?	_____	_____

Additional observations regarding the suitability of the instrument:

_____

_____

_____

_____

_____

Figure 6–2 Assessment instrument review form

Name of Instrument _____

Author(s) _____

Date of Publication _____ Publisher _____

1. List the subtests (e.g., learning areas) addressed.

   _____

   _____

2. Describe the age range. _____

   _____

3. State the purpose. _____ _____

   _____

4. Describe the examiner qualifications. _____

   _____

5. List the available scores. _____ _____ _____

   _____

6. Does the instrument display adequate technical qualities (i.e., validity, reliability, norms, and other research)?

   _____

   _____

7. Is this the instrument suitable (or can it be adapted) for students with limited English proficiency?

   _____

   _____

8. Are the administration procedures well designed and easy to follow?

   _____

   _____

9. What is the approximate administration and scoring time?

   _____

   _____

10. Is the instrument suitable (or can it be adapted) for use with students who have disabilities?

   _____

   _____

Figure 6–2 *continued*

11. Are the scoring procedures well designed and easy to follow?

_____

_____

12. What are the strengths of the instrument?

_____

_____

13. Does the instrument display any weaknesses?

_____

_____

14. Overall summary and conclusion regarding the instrument.

_____

_____

15. Additional comments, information, and observations:

_____

_____

☑ Check Your Comprehension

Teachers of students with special needs should know how to locate, select, and evaluate assessment instruments. Although no single source can list or describe all instruments that might be useful in specific situations, several databases and reference tools are readily available. Sources for evaluating tests include the *Mental Measurements Yearbooks* and reviews in professional journals. Other useful sources of test information include specimen sets, publishers' catalogues, newsletters, and textbooks on assessment.

Using Assessment to Document Teaching and Learning

The second phase in the three phases of the Drummond decision model is data collection. This involves obtaining needed information through testing, observation, and other appropriate methods, including curriculum-based assessment. When providing services to students with disabilities, teachers spend most of their time in direct instructional activities such as teaching lessons, giving instructions, providing assistance, and interacting with students. Teachers must also spend time collecting data to document educational efforts. In some situations, it may seem that the paperwork required for data collection such as IEPs, progress notes, and reports takes time away from direct instructional activities. Assessment, in particular, may appear to be "just more paperwork" that teachers must put in a student's file. Appearances, however, can be deceiving.

Meaningful assessment provides essential information for making educational decisions and ensuring appropriate educational services. Assessment includes methods of measurement for determining present levels of performance, identifying instructional objectives, and gauging progress. Without assessment information, teachers would have to base instructional efforts on personal opinion and guesswork. Although teachers change each year, important assessment results and documentation remain part of a student's permanent record. Practical reasons for using assessment include the following:

- Assessment provides essential information for making educational decisions.
- Assessment ensures the provision of appropriate educational services.
- Assessment helps determine present levels of performance, identify instructional objectives, and gauge progress.
- Assessment provides concrete evidence of learning.
- If a student fails to progress, assessment helps to identify the reasons for poor progress and to revise the instructional program.

Other practical reasons exist for taking the time to assess students and document the results. Assessment provides a basis for comparison when monitoring student progress. Although most teachers feel that their students learn new skills during the year, assessment results provide concrete evidence of learning by showing student progress in comparison to the last assessment. Furthermore, assessment results over several years provide evidence of progress that may not be obvious on a day-to-day basis. On the other hand, if progress fails to occur, teachers need to identify the reasons and revise the instructional program to ensure responsiveness to a student's educational needs. The amount of prior progress provides an index of future progress and enables the teacher to establish realistic long- and short-term learning objectives. For these reasons, special educators find that assessment provides useful comparison information.

Preparing for Assessment

Preparing for assessment involves reviewing cumulative records, gathering information from others, studying an assessment tool, and organizing an assessment session. Although this requires a good deal of work, proper preparation saves time and makes conducting the assessment itself less difficult. Evaluators who fail to prepare adequately may have a frustrating and time-consuming assessment experience. However, with proper preparation, the assessment process usually goes smoothly. Preparation often begins with reviewing a student's record folder.

Reviewing Records   One way evaluators gain knowledge about a student is by reviewing the cumulative record, which includes results from previous evaluations and provides a history of educational services. The records may also indicate recent changes in behavior or medication that can affect performance during assessment. In addition, the records may include details about sensory deficits or medical problems. All of this is important information for the evaluator preparing to conduct an assessment. Even if an evaluator interacts with a student on a daily basis, reviewing records may provide valuable insight into student needs.

Gathering Information   Parents, other caregivers, and school personnel who interact with a student on a regular basis represent another source of information. These people can answer a variety of questions, including when a student seems most alert, cooperative, and attentive, so that the evaluator has the opportunity to schedule the assessment to facilitate optimal performance. The evaluator uses this information to determine things as whether to give an assessment in total all at one sitting or in parts over a couple of days. The evaluator can also obtain information about the language skill of a student and how best to communicate with the student. In addition, parents and teachers can provide background about student reinforcement preferences and potential behavior problems. Parents, in particular, can often provide background about events or activities at home that may explain changes in student behavior or performance. Gathering information about a student from others prior to assessment makes the process flow smoothly and accurately.

Reviewing the Assessment Tool   Another step in preparing for assessment is reviewing the test or evaluation procedure selected for use. Specific information about use of the tool should be available with each assessment instrument. Prior to giving a test, the evaluator should review and practice the administration and scoring procedures. Avoid giving a test without practice. An evaluator who fails to prepare for an assessment may become frustrated, angry, and surrounded by meaningless bits and pieces of information. Most people would refuse to accept mistakes because of an evaluator error if the results affected them personally. Likewise, evaluators should avoid assessment mistakes because decisions based on test results affect students' lives. Evaluators who need help with a new assessment instrument or procedure should seek assistance from a colleague or specialist. Most professionals will gladly help a colleague learn the nuances of administering and scoring a particular assessment instrument.

Organizing the Assessment Session   Organization serves as a key to conducting efficient assessment. It includes careful scheduling, in advance, to prevent the frustration of being ready to test or observe only to discover that a student is out of class. Scheduling involves selecting an appropriate time and date and communicating the assessment plans to the student, to colleagues, and to the parents. The evaluator should also gather the materials needed for the session at the assessment site. This prevents last-minute searches to find missing score sheets, testing equipment, and other items. By organizing materials and equipment when preparing to conduct an assessment, the evaluator saves time and effort.

Another time-saver is to identify a student's present level of performance before testing. This avoids spending time retesting in previously accomplished skill areas. A student's cumulative record should include past assessment results. The individualized plan also identifies levels of performance, and the evaluator should use these data in planning for an assessment.

Finally, the evaluator should know the reason for the assessment and the way the results apply to meet the student's needs. If the goal is to obtain information about whether a student performs certain tasks independently or with assistance, the evaluator should prepare and conduct the assessment to gather this information. If the goal is to identify the skills the student has mastered and those in need of additional intervention, the evaluator should prepare the assessment to provide this information. By knowing the product, the evaluator saves time and obtains better assessment information.

The Assessment Environment

The **assessment environment** refers to the appropriateness of the setting, circumstances, and conditions surrounding an evaluation. By providing an appropriate environment, the evaluator helps to ensure that students perform at their best. All of us remember experiences in which we had to take a test in a noisy room, fill out important papers with a pen that would not write, or deal with interruptions when trying to convey important information to someone. Distracters like these may negatively influence performance. Because assessment results provide the basis for important decisions, careful thought should go into structuring the assessment environment to avoid interruptions and distractions.

The Assessment Setting   An appropriate setting to conduct an assessment is a key consideration. Depending on the type of assessment, appropriate settings include a classroom, a quiet room, or a home. Regardless of the location, the evaluator should make prior arrangements, and whenever possible, the setting should be familiar to the student. Because new settings may cause anxiety and distractions, the evaluator should take the assessment materials to the class, home, or other natural settings whenever possible.

Minimizing Distractions   The evaluator should examine the location for possible distractions that may affect a student's performance. For example, if the assessment takes place in a classroom filled with other students engaged in various tasks, the evaluator should minimize distractions by placing the student close to a wall or in a corner facing away from the classroom activity. In some cases, the evaluator may be responsible for supervising other students while conducting an assessment with an individual student. When this happens, the evaluator should provide the others with appropriate tasks to occupy them constructively during the assessment. The goal is to arrange space and uninterrupted time so that the evaluator can focus on the assessment.

Student Needs During Assessment

Responding to student needs represents a key to assessment success. Student needs during assessment include considerations related to test anxiety and session length. In special education, in particular, the evaluator should assess students in a manner that responds to their individual needs. This includes ensuring that students feel comfortable and relaxed during assessment and that they receive instructions tailored to their level of understanding. These elements set the stage for positive feelings about the assessment process and motivate students to perform at their best.

Test Anxiety   Many students become nervous when tested. In addition, students with special needs often exhibit fear of failure caused by a history of learning problems. This fear may become pronounced during assessment. To help overcome test anxiety, the evaluator should begin whenever possible with known tasks that are easy to complete successfully. This helps a student feel more confident and willing to proceed. Most standardized tests already include a set of relatively easy example items for this purpose. Special educators should also include warm-up tasks as part of curriculum-based assessment.

Session Length   In general, evaluators should avoid assessment sessions longer than 45 minutes to an hour. However, with some students, especially young children, individual sessions may need to be even shorter. To ensure physical comfort and prevent undue fatigue, the evaluator should schedule short breaks within the sessions. Lengthy assessments should take place during more than one sitting. Ensuring physical comfort includes attention to factors such as room temperature. Rooms that are too hot or cold may reduce student concentration and motivation. If factors such as temperature affect a student's performance, the assessor should make a notation of the circumstances on the score sheet and in the assessment report.

Reflection
Test anxiety and fear of failure is common among students with disabilities, but most of us become at least a bit nervous in testing situations, especially if they are new. What are some things you have done in anxiety-producing testing situations to help reduce your nervousness? Which of these strategies are applicable to situations in which students experience extreme test anxiety? How are they applicable?

 To answer this reflection online, go to the *Teaching and Learning* module on the companion Website at *www.prenhall.com/venn.*

Test Accommodations

Students with disabilities have the right to and can benefit from reasonable **accommodations in testing**. Test accommodations are special test administration provisions that give students with disabilities a better opportunity to demonstrate their knowledge and skills. The Individuals with Disabilities Education Act (IDEA) guarantees reasonable test accommodations for students with disabilities. For those students who elect not to receive or are ineligible for special education services, Section 504 of the Vocational Rehabilitation Act ensures their right to reasonable testing accommodations. The Americans with Disabilities Act (ADA) also allows for accommodations in testing.

Testing accommodations should reflect the particular needs of the individual student. A child with blindness, for example, may need a Braille or a cassette version of a test. Other common test accommodations include a reader or a scribe, a sign language interpreter, extra testing time, or adjustable desks for children who use wheelchairs. Test accommodations allow children with disabilities a better opportunity to demonstrate their knowledge and skills, but not all modifications are reasonable or appropriate. The IEP is the document that educators should look to for guidance regarding appropriate modifications for each individual student.

Though no single accommodation may be adequate or appropriate for all students with a given disability, commonly used accommodations include the following (Educational Testing Service, 2004):

Computer-Based Testing (CBT)
- Extended testing time
- Additional rest breaks
- Selectable background and foreground screen colors
- Reader
- Recorder/writer of answers
- Sign language interpreter (for spoken directions only)
- Braille or audiocassette formats
- Computer accessories for those who are familiar with their use
- Trackball mouse
- HeadMaster Plus mouse
- Intellikeys keyboard
- ZOOMTEXT

Pencil-on-Paper Testing
- Extended testing time
- Additional rest breaks
- Reader
- Recorder/writer of answers
- Sign language interpreter (for spoken directions only)

Alternate Test Formats
- Braille
- Enlarged print (14 pt.)
- Large print (greater than 14 pt.)
- Large-print answer sheet
- Audiocassette with large-print figure supplement
- Audiocassette with Braille figure supplement

Practical Considerations in Providing Test Accommodations

Keep the following considerations in mind when testing students with disabilities.

- Keep records documenting a student's history of accommodations. These records will help the student obtain such accommodations in higher education and outside of school.
- Because each student is unique, students with the same disability may need different accommodations. In other words, accommodations for one student may not work for another student with the same disability. The student's IEP or 504 plan should guide decisions regarding specific accommodations.
- Students should become informed consumers. This means that teachers, parents, and children should become familiar with accommodations, especially those that best help each child in the classroom and while taking various types of tests.
- Students should register early for special versions of standardized tests because it may take time to develop a special test format or modification.
- Students should receive special and individualized guidance prior to taking standardized tests. Guidance will help all children, especially those who tend to experience greater than average test anxiety. Students should understand how to take standardized tests, handle different types of test questions, and pace their efforts.
- Students should practice taking standardized tests well in advance. Experience with practice materials before taking the actual test boosts confidence and reduces anxiety. Students should take practice tests with the same accommodations that they would use during the actual testing.
- Advise students of their options concerning testing accommodations. Options include more testing time, longer breaks between sections, and extra time for specific types of materials.

Prompting During Assessment

Prompting during assessment refers to the appropriate use of verbal cues, modeling, and physical prompts while administering a test or conducting another type of assessment procedure. Because some tests specifically prohibit use of prompts and others mandate particular methods of prompting, no absolute guidelines exist concerning prompting during assessment. To find out if a test calls for specific procedures, the evaluator should check the manual for instructions on prompting. If the administration procedures do not prohibit prompting, then evaluators may find the following procedures useful in many situations. However, when evaluators use special prompts, they should clearly note them on the score sheet and in the assessment report to avoid misinterpretation of the results.

Most tests and assessment procedures specify whether a student can perform a skill independently. However, when a student fails to perform a task, the teacher needs to know the amount of assistance the student needs to accomplish the task. This is why special educators often use prompts to determine a student's need for assistance. Levels of assistance include verbal prompts, modeling, and physical prompts. Special educators often refer to these as the "tell, show, guide" prompting techniques.

Reflection
Which two practical considerations in providing test accommodations seem most important to you in responding to the needs of students with disabilities? Explain your choices.

 To answer this reflection online, go to the *Teaching and Learning* module on the Companion Website at *www.prenhall.com/venn.*

Verbal Cues

In most assessment situations, an evaluator administers items by verbally requesting a student to do a task. For example, an evaluator may give a general instruction such as "Complete the math problems on this page in the test booklet." If a student fails to follow the instruction or begins to complete the math problems but stops before finishing, evaluators usually provide a verbal cue or prompt. The evaluator may say, "Keep working until you have finished all of the problems," "Try to complete each problem," or "Do the best you can." If the student completes the task only after receiving multiple cues, then the evaluator indicates that the student failed to complete the tasks independently but successfully performed them when given verbal assistance in the form of prompting to finish the work.

Modeling

Unfortunately, some students fail to perform certain tasks even when given verbal prompts. When this happens, an evaluator may have to model appropriate task completion. When evaluators model a task, they demonstrate how to complete the task and then have the student imitate the performance.

Physical Prompts

In some assessment situations, especially with young students or students with severe disabilities, the evaluator may need to provide physical prompts to enable task completion. Evaluators should use physical prompts only after unsuccessful attempts with modeling and verbal prompting. Physical prompting usually involves actually guiding a student's hand through a task such as using a computer, completing a manipulative activity (e.g., putting together a puzzle), or performing some other task that requires movement.

Anecdotal Assessment Information

Even the most thorough assessment tool does not always ask the "right" questions or provide sufficient space for additional comments. **Anecdotal assessment information** includes notes, comments, and other information about student needs, behaviors, and test performance added to score sheets or included in written reports. Anecdotal information includes important facts that someone not familiar with a student should know. Examples of anecdotal information include a student who has a hearing aid but does not like to wear it even though it improves the ability to follow directions; a student who performs better for men than for women; a student more willing to do a task when asked to do it, rather than when told to do it; a student who becomes red in the face prior to a seizure; or a student who responds best when reinforced with extra time with the teacher.

Behavior Problems

For some students the most important additional information concerns behavior such as noncompliance, aggression, withdrawal, or the need for special reinforcement during assessment. In cases involving severe behavior problems, the anecdotal information should address the specific problem. Regardless of the severity of the behavior, however, most teachers find that additional information is helpful. For example, with a student who has been on a behavior program for several months, an evaluator may decide to attach the resulting program data to the assessment report. This assists others who may work with this student in the future by providing information for developing the best possible intervention plan.

The Importance of Accuracy

When evaluators include additional information, they must avoid opinions or subjective impressions. For example, if a student refuses to follow instructions, an evaluator should ensure this behavior is typical in other settings before including statements about noncompliance as anecdotal information. If an evaluator includes incorrect information that becomes part of a permanent record, it may unfairly limit opportunities for that student in the future. Therefore, evaluators must exercise caution to ensure the accuracy of all assessment information.

☑ Check Your Comprehension

Using assessment to document teaching and learning involves many factors. For example, preparing for assessment takes time, but preparation is an investment that results in time savings during administration, scoring, and interpretation. Providing a suitable environment for optimal student performance is another factor. Regardless of the setting, the goal is to maximize student comfort and minimize distractions. Responding to student needs represents another important practical consideration. Because student performance depends, in part, on how they feel, evaluators should be sensitive to physical comfort, communication preferences, and anxiety levels. Students with disabilities may also need accommodations that will give them a better opportunity to demonstrate their knowledge and skills. In some situations, the "tell, show, guide" method of prompting gives students the opportunity to perform a task with additional assistance. This may help distinguish the difference between a lack of understanding and an actual skill deficiency. For those who fail most tasks, this approach provides a way to identify what students can do with assistance. Finally, providing anecdotal assessment information including written notes helps accurately document actual performance levels and abilities.

Assessment Proficiency

Teachers often give, score, and interpret tests and assessments. In order to ensure accuracy, teachers need to practice giving, scoring, and interpreting new tests. The **assessment proficiency checklist (APC)** shown in Figure 6–3 is a helpful tool for validating competence in test administration and scoring. The APC consists of two parts. Part I measures proficiency in administering tests and assessments. Part II measures proficiency in scoring tests and assessments. Teachers who wish to self-check their administration and scoring skills can use the APC as a self evaluation tool by completing both parts of the checklist after giving a practice test or assessment to a student. Alternatively, an observer may watch a teacher giving and scoring a practice test. After the testing, the observer completes the APC form and reviews the results with the teacher. The APC is also an excellent tool for use in in-service and preservice training activities that involve learning how to administer and score tests.

Figure 6–3 Assessment proficiency checklist

Student _____ Date _____

Evaluator _____ Location _____

Observer _____ Test _____

Part I: Administration Proficiency

Item	Score		
The evaluator:	Yes	No	NA
1. Reviewed prior assessment results and student needs before testing			
2. Prepared a suitable location with necessary materials and equipment			
3. Established and maintained rapport with the student			
4. Explained the purpose of assessment in an appropriate manner			
5. Maintained student attention during the assessment			
6. Used appropriate prompting procedures			
7. Repeated or demonstrated items as appropriate			
8. Administered items in correct order and gave all items			
9. Provided appropriate feedback to student responses to the items			
10. Properly managed behavior			
11. Ended the assessment positively with appropriate praise			

Notes and Comments:

Part II: Scoring Proficiency

Item	Score		
The evaluator:	Yes	No	NA
1. Completed the cover sheet correctly			
2. Established accurate basal levels			
3. Established accurate ceiling levels			
4. Included appropriate notes about student responses to particular items			
5. Calculated accurate raw scores			
6. Calculated and recorded accurate transformed scores			
7. Correctly completed the scoring profile			

Notes and Comments:

Part 1: Administration Proficiency Score
Number of "Yes" Items _____   Number of "No" Items _____   Percent Correct Score _____

Part 2: Scoring Proficiency Score
Number of "Yes" Items _____   Number of "No" Items _____   Percent Correct Score _____

_____   _____
             Signature of Observer   Signature of Evaluator

Score the checklist by marking each item within the Yes, No, or NA column as appropriate. Then divide the total number of Yes items by the total number of No items to produce a percent correct score for each part.

Report Writing

The third and final phase in the Drummond decision model is evaluation, which involves forming hypotheses, making decisions or judgments, and reporting decisions and judgments. Special educators read, interpret, and apply reports by psychologists, diagnosticians, and other professionals, and they write assessment reports themselves. The content and format of written reports depends on a variety of factors, including who will receive the report and the reasons for assessment. Most written reports, however, have similar contents.

Report Outline

This content outline is a guide rather than a fixed, inflexible way of preparing a report.

Identifying Information
Student's Name, Address, Date of Birth, Chronological Age, and Gender
Evaluator's Name
Date or Dates of Evaluation
Location of Evaluation

Background Information
Reason for the Assessment
Relevant Educational, Family, Social, and Medical Histories
Observation of the Student's Behavior
   Including physical appearance, general behavior, responses to the testing session, and specific behavior (e.g., activity level, communication style, unusual conduct)
Brief Description of the Tests

Summary of the Test Score Results
Tests Administered
Total and Subtest Scores
Standard Error of Measurement for the Scores (if available)

Discussion and Interpretation of Results
Description of Student Performance
   Describe relevant areas and interpret student strengths, weaknesses, and gaps in performance overall and in each area assessed

Recommendations
Responses to Referral Questions, Placement Suggestions, and Intervention Recommendations
   Include instructional activities, teaching materials, and equipment considerations

Report Writing Principles

The following writing principles help make reports more readable and effective (Sattler, 2001).

Principle 1 — Focus on Abilities

Reports should focus on student abilities and performance rather than on tests and test scores. This is important because most readers are not familiar with specific tests and may have difficulty interpreting the meaning of particular test scores.

Principle 2 — Describe the Student

Because reports are about real students, they should including interesting images and appropriate examples describing what the student is really like, how the student behaved during the testing, and how the student approached representative assessment tasks. Reports should contain descriptions of specific behaviors, and they may include direct quotes from the student.

Principle 3 — Report Percentile Ranks

When reporting test scores, use percentile ranks whenever possible. Readers may understand percentile ranks more easily than other scores such as standard scores. Because grade scores are easily misinterpreted, avoid them whenever possible.

Principle 4 — Clearly Interpret the Results

Provide a clear interpretation of the results by describing the meaning of the student's performance on tests and other assessments. Avoid simply presenting facts, descriptive information, and test scores. Instead, interpret and give meaning to the facts, information, and scores by developing appropriate conclusions and recommendations.

Principle 5 — Avoid Jargon and Technical Terminology

Most readers will not understand jargon, acronyms, slang, and technical terminology. Therefore, avoid using terms such as "processing ability" and "standard scores" whenever possible. Keeping technical information out of reports will enhance readability.

Principle 6 — Use a Suitable Writing Style

A suitable writing style is essential. Key style elements include organization and grammar. Most reports should be organized around three or four key points and should maintain consistent tense. Observed behavior and student performance during testing should be described in past tense. Discussion of student abilities and description of student characteristics can be written in present tense.

Principle 7 — Proofread the Report

Careful proofreading to eliminate spelling mistakes, grammar errors, missing phrases, and other oversights is an important element in the report writing process. Also, check the final copy to make sure it is formatted correctly.

Sample Reports

Two sample case-study reports illustrating how to describe test performance in narrative form follow. The first report is based on assessment results from the Wechsler Individual Achievement Test—Revised (WIAT—II). This report includes testing results and an instructional intervention plan for a 13-year-old student with a disability. The second report is a computer-generated case study from the KeyMath–Revised/Normative Update: A Diagnostic Inventory of Essential Mathematics (KeyMath—R/NU) (Connolly, 1998). The KeyMath–Revised Automated System for Scoring and Interpreting Standardized Tests (ASSIST) software program (Rodgers, 1998) produced this report. Further information about computer-generated reports appears in the Technology Focus box.

TECHNOLOGY FOCUS

Computer-Generated Reports

The computer-generated case study in this chapter shows how computer software programs generate reports with test score results and descriptions of student performance. The software reporting program for the KeyMath-R/NU, a norm-referenced, diagnostic test, produces sufficient information to create detailed recommendations, including specific learning activities. However, because the report is computer-generated, it fails to include specific observations of the student's behavior during the testing session.

Although computer reports like this one can be highly useful in a variety of situations, concern exists regarding the possibility for misuse of automated test reports. To avoid potential pitfalls, professionals who use computer-based interpretive reports must adjust or modify them to account for individual student needs. Potential problems with automated interpretation include the following:

- Inexperienced professionals who use computerized reports without considering possible limitations and problems,
- Developers of computer-based interpretation programs who fail to provide information about the limitations of such reports, and
- Developers who fail to provide information validating the use of their computer-based report programs.

Diagnostic Assessment Report

Identifying Information
Student: Cindy Rhodes
Age: 13 years, 7 months
Teacher: Ms. Kibby Williams
Testing Location: Riverdale Junior High School
Assessment Instrument: *Wechsler Individual Achievement Test — Revised (WIAT—II)*

Date of Testing: 8-1-2006
Date of Birth: 12-18-1988
Examiner: Lauren Jaffee

BACKGROUND AND RATIONALE FOR THE ASSESSMENT

The purpose for evaluating Cindy's academic achievement with the WIAT-II was to identify her specific strengths and weaknesses in academic achievement and to prescribe an instructional plan that might close any gaps that exist between her potential and actual achievement. A licensed school psychologist recently evaluated Cindy with the Wechsler Intelligence Scale for Children, Fourth Edition (WISC-IV). The results indicated a Full Scale IQ of 95.

Cindy has a congenital condition known as Apert syndrome, which is characterized by premature fusion of the skull and fusion of her hands and feet, and she has had repeated surgeries to correct development issues associated with the syndrome. She receives special education services due to physical impairments, short-term visual memory difficulties, and visual-motor coordination deficits. She takes Ritalin to relieve attention deficit hyperactivity disorder (ADHD) symptoms.

During the evaluation, Cindy put forth strong efforts to answer the questions, although occasionally she seemed to respond impulsively without carefully considering all of her options. Toward the end of the evaluation, Cindy became somewhat frustrated, especially when approaching ceiling levels. Occasionally her answers indicated that she did not totally understand the questions as asked by the examiner (in accordance with the administration instructions). Overall, Cindy's motivation and speed in answering the questions were satisfactory.

Summary of *WIAT-II* Subtest Scores	
Oral language	72
Listening comprehension	72
Written expression	59
Spelling	55
Pseudo-word decoding	66
Word reading	68
Numerical operations	14
Mathematics reasoning	23

INTERPRETATION OF THE RESULTS

Cindy's performance on specific WIAT-II subtests varied. Her strongest skills were in oral language and listening comprehension. On these subtests, she received percentile ranks of 72 and 77, respectively. Cindy also performed almost as well in pseudo-word decoding (66th percentile) and word reading (68th percentile). Her scores in written expression (59th percentile) and spelling (55th percentile) were above average. In contrast, Cindy's performance in mathematics was significantly below these levels as indicated by percentile ranks of 14 in numerical operations and 23 in mathematics reasoning. These scores indicate serious performance deficits. Because her math performance was significantly below average, Cindy's instructional program should emphasize remediation in these areas. Weak mathematics skills may contribute to Cindy falling further behind as she moves into pre-algebra and algebra in the eighth- and ninth-grade curriculum. Therefore, the instructional recommendations that follow focus on building skills in mathematics.

A review of Cindy's performance in the mathematics domains provides insight into some of her difficulties. For example, Cindy needs to master several prerequisite concept skills, specifically in renaming three-digit numbers and place value concepts. These skill deficits explain some of her difficulties in operations. Cindy also appears to need help in mastering the concepts of fractions and percents. An error analysis of her written calculations confirmed this observation. The error analysis revealed that nearly every computational error involved mistakes in regrouping (place value) whole and decimal numbers and renaming fractions prior to performing calculations. Basic algorithm knowledge seemed to be intact, except in division operations and all operations involving fractions. One might also take into consideration Cindy's attention deficits that may affect operations performance, and this is substantiated in that she made some mistakes simply by a tendency to rush to answer impulsively before careful consideration of options and by hurrying to answer problems without careful attention to details. Further investigation revealed weaknesses primarily in problem solving, specifically difficulty in understanding and solving nonroutine problems.

RECOMMENDATIONS

An instructional plan for Cindy should include a review of place value concepts and operational algorithms using methods that will take her from the concrete (using manipulatives) through the semiconcrete (where she will draw pictures to help her solve problems) and finally to the abstract. The same type of instruction will also help Cindy with fractions, decimals, and percentages. Drawing pictures to help solve word problems should be a strategy used often with Cindy to help her focus on the presented information and how it can be used to solve the problem. This approach will build upon her strengths in applying her mathematics concepts to real-life situations.

Cindy also needs to learn strategies for helping her focus on her work and review for accuracy. She should be encouraged to use estimation often to be able to evaluate the reasonableness of her responses. Self-monitoring plans where she sets goals for improving accuracy and she is rewarded for her achievements would be helpful in maintaining her attention to details.

Encouraging Cindy to turn abstract problems into more concrete ones by creating hypothetical stories that describe the conditions for which she must solve the problem a particular way will also help her connect the algorithm to the basic concepts. This activity will allow her to draw upon her verbal strengths to build her mathematics skills.

The learning activities that follow in this report are examples incorporating some of the recommendations just outlined.

LEARNING ACTIVITIES

1. *Using Base-10 Manipulatives to Teach Place Value and Algorithms:* Base-10 blocks (such as Dienes blocks), bundles of toothpicks or Popsicle sticks, different colored poker chips used with a cash box, or any number of concrete manipulatives can be used to help Cindy express multidigit numbers in concrete form. Cindy needs to learn the algorithms for each of the four operations using these manipulatives. The teacher should model the use of the manipulatives to solve the problems, speaking aloud her thought processes as she completes the steps. She should then coach Cindy as she performs the steps on her own. Cindy should use the manipulatives to represent the regrouping necessary in executing the steps of the algorithm, and then she should be encouraged to draw her own pictures to represent the steps. Finally, she should record the steps in the traditional algorithmic format as she solves the problems to help her make the transition from the concrete representation of the concept to the abstract. Problems should be presented to her in word problem format, and she should use the manipulatives to solve the problems. This process will help her apply the concepts to real-life situations. This process should be used until Cindy can solve any of the whole number algorithms using multidigit numbers (to at least the thousands place) with 90% accuracy.

2. *Using Number Lines and Graph Paper to Teach Multiple Representations of Fractions:* Cindy should use number lines and graph paper in working with fractions to help her focus on finding and naming equivalent fractions. This basic idea of using various pictorial ways of representing fractions will help her develop a flexible and multifaceted understanding of fractions. She can then learn the algorithms for the operations involving fractions by shading in and subdividing areas of the graph paper as she works with concepts such as least common multiple. Getting this concrete representation of fractions will help her understand the more abstract algorithms involved with operations with fractions. A sample activity using the graph paper in teaching the addition algorithm for fractions is as follows:

> Use unit regions and parts of unit regions. Let Cindy first represent each addend as fractional parts of a unit region on the graph paper. It will be necessary for her to exchange some of the fractional parts so they are all of the same size (same denomination). The fractional parts can then be used to determine the total number of units. This procedure should be related step-by-step to the mechanics of notation in a written algorithm, probably as an example written vertically so the renaming can be noted more easily, as in the following example:

Problem: 5/12 + 3/8 = ?

Step 1:

Find the lowest common multiple of 12 and 8.

12 (Shown as 4 × 3)

8 (Shown as 8 × 1)

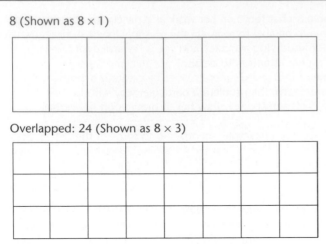

Overlapped: 24 (Shown as 8 × 3)

Step 2: Convert addends to equivalent fractions.

$\underline{5}$ = □ $\underline{3}$ = □

12 = 24   8 = 24

Use a number line to focus on equivalent fractions.

Prepare a number line from zero to one, with rows of labels for halves, thirds, fourths, etc. Have Cindy find and state the many fractions for the same point. State that each point shows a number, and the fractions are different names for the same number.

Step 3: Solve by shading in representations of each addend in the graph as shown in step 1.

Step 4: Record results in algorithm.

3. *Computer Programs:* For additional practice that Cindy can do on her own without direct involvement by the teacher, a computer program such as the Cornerstone Mathematics program is an excellent choice. It would be useful for reviewing the concepts behind the basic operations, stepping Cindy through the mechanics of the algorithms, and then testing her in a standardized format to help her focus on the accuracy of reporting answers. The teacher can assign Cindy just those lessons that will address her weak areas, and the program will not allow her to proceed to a new lesson until she has mastered her currently assigned one. It also uses an arcade-style game format to help drill her on speed and accuracy in executing the algorithms. The program has a default mastery level of 80%, but teachers can change the level as appropriate.

The Mighty Math Series by Edmark is another computer program for reviewing operational concepts and algorithms. Based on NCTM standards and incorporating math as reasoning and math as problem-solving, Mighty Math activities for number concepts, operations, and fractions and decimals will be motivational for Cindy and allow her time to explore concepts and receive drill-and-practice on solving the problems. The teacher can also set a mastery level in the drill-and-practice portion of Mighty Math.

4. *Beat the Calculator Activity:* Before starting this activity, which Cindy can use to practice any of the operational algorithms for either whole or rational numbers, Cindy will complete a self-monitoring worksheet in which she sets a goal for the number of problems she can complete accurately. She and her teacher will determine the appropriate reward for meeting her goal. She can then complete a set number of problems, for example, 10 problems of multidigit division. She works the problems, brings them to the teacher for a quick scan to see if the problems are completed, then checks her accuracy using the calculator. If she correctly worked the problem on her own, she can count the problem as contributing toward her goal. If the calculator's response is different from her own, she reworks the problem, attempting to find her mistakes. She can use this activity over time, and then track her progress on a graph so that she can evaluate how she is doing. This will allow her to use her strengths in applications to help focus on her weaknesses in basic concepts and operations.

5. *Using Equal Fractions to Help Solve Problems Involving Percent:* Write a proportion for each problem involving decimals: one fraction equal to another. With one fraction, show what the problem tells about percent, and with the other show what the problem tells about the number of things. Use *n* whenever you are not told a number. For example: 70 is 14% of what number?

Percent 14 = 70 − part of the amount

   100 = *n* − the whole amount

After Cindy is able to write a proportion for a percent problem, suggest that the two products indicated by an X are equal. Have Cindy supply several pairs of fractions known to be equal, and cross-multiply each pair to see if the rule holds for them. Then apply cross-multiplication to percent problems. Cindy should be able to solve 90% of word problems involving decimals using this procedure.

Computer-Generated Narrative Report from the KeyMath-Revised/NU

01/15/2000   KeyMath-Revised/NU
Name: Bertelli, Brenda   Test Date: 01/05/2006
Age: 9-1   Grade: 4

SCORE NARRATIVE

The KeyMath-R/NU is an individually administered test that provides a comprehensive assessment of important mathematics concepts and skills. The test identifies an individual's strengths and weaknesses in three broad areas—Basic Concepts, Operations, and Applications. These areas are composed of 13 subtests or "strands" (e g , Numeration), which are composed of 43 substrands or domains (e.g., Multidigit Numbers).

This computer-generated report assesses Brenda's KeyMath-R/NU performance and makes instructional recommendations. It is suggested that you prioritize and select those recommendations that best fit Brenda's needs. For a more comprehensive listing of instructional recommendations tailored for Brenda, see the report entitled "Item Objectives and TAP Resources." In planning her instruction, try to capitalize on Brenda's personal strengths to provide developmental support.

TOTAL TEST PERFORMANCE

The total test mean is 100, and the standard deviation is 15. Brenda's total test standard score was 91. Her performance yielded a percentile rank of 27, meaning that Brenda outperformed 27 percent of her age-level peers on the total test. This level of performance is typically achieved by individuals at age 8-2 (i.e., equals an age equivalent of 8-2). Her achievement on KeyMath-R/NU was at the 4th stanine. Collectively, these indicators describe Brenda's overall test performance as average. Brenda recently obtained a standard score of 93 on the DAS GCA Composite. Her actual achievement, based on the Total Test, is lower than the expected achievement score of 95. The percent of the population with the same size of discrepancy or greater is 34.

AREA PERFORMANCE

A mean of 100 and a standard deviation of 15 are also used to analyze an individual's performance in the three broad areas of Basic Concepts, Operations, and Applications. Brenda's performance in each area was compared with the performance achieved by individuals at her age level in the norm group. Her performance in these areas is as follows:

1. *Basic Concepts:* This area addresses the knowledge of quantity and space. Brenda achieved a standard score of 88, a percentile rank of 21, and an age equivalent of 7-9. This is below average and suggests a need for remedial instruction.

2. *Operations:* This area addresses both written and mental computation. Brenda achieved a standard score of 94, a percentile rank of 34, and an age equivalent of 8-5. This is within the average range, but may reflect some specific content on which remedial instruction will be helpful.

3. *Applications:* This area requires the practical use of mathematical knowledge and operational skills. Brenda achieved a standard score of 89, a percentile rank of 23, and an age equivalent of 7-10. This is below average and suggests a need for remedial instruction.

A statistical analysis was completed on the variance present in Brenda's performance among the three areas. Basic Concepts and Operations have a standard score difference of 6 points, which is nonsignificant. Basic Concepts and Applications have a standard score difference of 1 point, which is nonsignificant. Operations and Applications have a standard score difference of 5, which is nonsignificant. The presence of no significant differences is a further indication that Brenda's test performance evidences no major patterns of strengths and weaknesses that should be considered when planning instruction. To be effective, prescriptive instruction will need to focus on strengths and weaknesses that may exist on specific concepts and skills. These become evident through a review of her performance on the different subtests and their respective content.

SUBTEST PERFORMANCE

Brenda's performance on each subtest was compared with the performance achieved by individuals at her age level in the norm group. To make that comparison, her performance on each subtest was reported on a scale having a mean of 10 and a standard deviation of 3, and ranging from 1 to 19. Within that range, the scores from 9 to 11 and slightly beyond are considered average. Compared to her peers on subtests, Brenda displays no specific strengths. She displays the following weaknesses relative to the performance of her peers: Rational Numbers, Geometry, Measurement, Time and Money, and Estimation.

Following is a discussion of how Brenda performed on each of the 13 subtests. Instructional recommendations are included primarily for use with individuals who exhibit specific subtest weaknesses.

1. *Numeration:* Brenda's scaled score of 9 and percentile rank of 37 indicate that in numeration and whole numbers, she is performing at an average level. The content on which Brenda needs to focus is three-digit numbers. Concepts developed with two-digit numbers, including place value, ordering, renaming, and rounding, need to be reinforced here. The place value and renaming concepts are essential to the effective handling of computation involving regrouping. Instruction should involve a variety of manipulative and pictorial models; activities may include base-10 blocks, color-coded cubes, chip trading, hundreds charts, money (dollars, dimes, and pennies), and number lines.

2. *Rational Numbers:* Fractions, decimals, and percents are difficult for many subjects. Brenda achieved a scaled score of 8 and a percentile rank of 25 in rational numbers. These scores indicate that her performance is slightly below average. Brenda's current level of functioning involves constructing and labeling fraction and decimal representations. The instructional emphasis for her work on fractions should be placed on part/whole models, with attention first directed to the denominator value and then to the numerator value. You might say, "A shape is folded into four parts of the same size. Three of the four parts are colored red, so three-fourths of the shape is red." When Brenda can effectively use part/whole models, instruction should progress to part/group models (e.g., two red marbles in a set of five marbles [2/5]; six red marbles in a set of eight marbles [3/4]).

3. *Geometry:* Brenda's scaled score of 7 and percentile rank of 16 reveal that in geometry, she is performing below average. Brenda has generally progressed beyond the recognition of common two-dimensional figures and is now into content involving coordinate planes. The use of grids, geoboards, and dot matrices can be particularly helpful in developing and applying concepts involving symmetry, parallel and intersecting line segments, and angles.

4. *Addition:* A scaled score of 9 and percentile rank of 37 indicate that in addition tasks, Brenda is functioning at an average level. Brenda has general mastery of addition facts and partial mastery of algorithms for whole numbers. Before she can effectively add two- and three-digit numbers with regrouping, she must have mastered the ability to rename numbers. Dimes and pennies are particularly

useful in developing this skill (e.g., using different combinations of dimes and pennies to represent the value 42 cents). It is easy to build on such activities by having her record the value in each of two sets of dimes and pennies, and then represent and record their combined value using no more than nine pennies in the total. When Brenda can represent and record the addition algorithm with numbers at this level, it will be easy for her to transfer to the addition of multidigit numbers.

5. *Subtraction:* Brenda's scaled score of 11 and percentile rank of 83 reveal that in subtraction, she is functioning at an average level. Brenda has achieved general mastery of the subtraction facts and partial mastery of the subtraction algorithm with whole numbers. Before she can successfully subtract with regrouping, she must establish the ability to rename two- and three-digit numbers. This skill is most easily acquired through activities involving dimes and pennies, base-10 blocks, chip trading, and the like. Many individuals find it helpful to begin subtraction by completely renaming the minuend where needed, rather than regrouping during the subtraction process. This allows them to concentrate on one task at a time.

6. *Multiplication:* The scaled score of 9 and percentile rank of 37 reveal that in multiplication, Brenda is functioning at an average level. She needs to work on multiplication models and facts. It may be helpful to have her represent several like sets (e.g., 4 fives) and record them as repeated addition (5 + 5 + 5 + 5 = 20) and as multiplication ($4 \times 5 = 20$). Brenda should also learn to associate such facts with arrays (e.g., four rows with five in each). Multiplication facts with zero are difficult for many individuals. If she is having such difficulty, use slips of paper as place holders for sets. When empty, these slips effectively show that four sets of zero cubes equals zero. When Brenda can represent and record such facts, use frequent oral drills to maintain mastery.

7. *Division:* Brenda's scaled score of 9 and percentile rank of 37 indicate that in division, she is functioning at an average level. Brenda needs to work on division models and facts. Instruction should include separating amounts into equal-sized groups, evenly distributing amounts into a given number of sets, and recording these actions with division number sentences. All division facts should be associated with the inverse multiplication facts, because the latter are easier for individuals to recall and represent. When Brenda can represent and record division facts, provide frequent oral drills to maintain mastery.

8. *Mental Computation:* A scaled score of 10 and percentile rank of 50 reveal that in mental computation, Brenda is functioning at an average level. Brenda's performance suggests that practice with orally presented mental computation chains would be useful in developing number and fact facility. Begin with relatively easy chains such as "four, plus six, minus eight, equals -?-" and progress to more difficult chains such as "nine, minus four, plus twenty, minus ten, equals -?-." (Pause at each comma for about one second.) Provide practice on such chains on a weekly basis for intense 3- or 4-minute sessions in a game-like atmosphere. Adjust the content, speed, and number of computations to conform to Brenda's progress.

9. *Measurement:* Brenda's scaled score of 7 and percentile rank of 16 indicate that in measurement, she is performing below average. Brenda has generally moved beyond making simple comparisons and is now using nonstandard units to measure length, weight, area (space covered), and capacity (amount held). Instruction should include all of these topics as well as the selection of appropriate units for given measurement tasks (e.g., paper clips rather than pencils as a unit for measuring the length of a comb). Related experiences with weights and a pan balance would be helpful.

10. *Time and Money:* In time and money skills, Brenda achieved a scaled score of 8 and percentile rank of 25, indicating that she is functioning slightly below average. Brenda should work on using the monthly calendar to determine days, dates, and time intervals (e.g., "What day is the 17th?" "What is the date of the fourth Monday?" "What is the date 2 weeks after the first Friday?"). She should also work on reading a clock and recording the times to the minute. In the area of money, Brenda should work at using different coin combinations to make values up to one dollar and to make change up to 25 cents.

11. *Estimation:* A scaled score of 8 and percentile rank of 25 indicate that Brenda's ability to estimate is slightly below average. Brenda is still learning to estimate quantities and can benefit from practice using subsets and feedback on prior guesses to improve estimates. She is also beginning to estimate measurements using nonstandard and some standard units. A useful instructional technique is to have

her estimate a measurement (e.g., the room is 24 shoe lengths wide) and, after part of the measurement is completed, allow her an opportunity to "refine" the estimate. Such "refinements" might be allowed two or three times per exercise. These efforts will enhance Brenda's ability to make estimates (judgments) and strengthen her measurement skills.

12. *Interpreting Data:* In interpreting data, Brenda achieved a scaled score of 10 and percentile rank of 50, a performance that is at an average level. Brenda is now ready to make use of charts and tables in practical situations, such as interpreting transportation schedules and simple mileage charts. Instruction should include the construction and use of one- and two-attribute bar graphs, pictographs employing keys, and line and circle graphs.

13. *Problem Solving:* Brenda's performance on the problem-solving subtest yielded a scaled score of 9 and percentile rank of 37, indicating that she is functioning at an average level. Brenda is still working to relate computation with word problems. Practice in determining the "action" in problem situations would be particularly helpful. By identifying the action, she can reliably infer the operation that is required. For example, combining unlike amounts is always done with addition, combining a set of like amounts is most efficiently done with multiplication, separating and comparing amounts is done with subtraction, and separating a large amount into smaller, like amounts is most efficiently done with division.

Brenda can also benefit from practice analyzing word problems to determine key information, extraneous information, and information that is missing but necessary for a problem's solution. Her progress in the development of problem-solving skills will be greatly influenced by the amount of instructional time devoted to such efforts and the diversity of such experiences.

☑ Check Your Comprehension

Teachers often review assessment reports written by others, and sometimes they are asked to write various types of assessment reports that describe the performance of their students. Most written reports contain the following common elements: identifying information, background information, summary of results, discussion and interpretation of results, and recommendations. The content and format depend on a variety of factors, including the student's needs, the writer's preferences, the intended uses of the report, and the nature of the reported assessment.

Reflection
What pitfalls do you see in using a computer-generated report rather than a teacher-written report? Explain your answer.

 To answer this reflection online, go to the *Teaching and Learning* module on the companion Website at *www.prenhall.com/venn.*

Summary

The practical aspects of assessment refer to applied procedures for giving and scoring tests, for conducting other evaluation procedures, and for interpreting, reporting, and using assessment data. These practical considerations are important because accurate administration, scoring, and reporting produce useful assessment data. All special education teachers need to master the practical aspects of testing so that they can administer tests skillfully and interpret the results appropriately. Because teaching students with disabilities includes measurement and evaluation as key components, the practical aspects of the process are an essential element in the knowledge base of assessment in special education. Special education teachers need to understand the theoretical aspects and the practical elements of assessment.

To check your comprehension of the chapter contents, go to the *Guided Review* and *Quiz* modules in Chapter 6 of the Companion Website, *www.prenhall.com/venn*.

Meeting Performance Standards and Preparing for Licensure Exams

The CEC Standards and PRAXIS™ material listed here connect with significant content in Chapter 6. The information in the parentheses identifies where to find the particular standard in the CEC Standards and the content reference in the PRAXIS™ material.

CEC Standards for Beginning Special Education Teachers

- Use and limitations of assessment instruments (CC8K4)
- Administer nonbiased formal and informal assessments (CC8S2)
- Interpret information from formal and informal assessments (CC8S5)
- Report assessment results to all stakeholders using effective communication skills (CC8S7)
- Select, adapt, and modify assessments to accommodate the unique abilities and needs of individuals with disabilities (GC8S3)

PRAXIS™ Education of Exceptional Students: Core Content Knowledge

- Assessment, including use of assessment for screening, diagnosis, placement, and the making of instructional decisions, for example: how to select and conduct nondiscriminatory and appropriate assessments; how to interpret standardized and specialized assessment results; how to prepare written reports and communicate findings (0353 III)

part III

Assessing General
Performance

chapter 7

Assessing Intelligence

Objectives

After reading this chapter, you will be prepared to do the following:

- Explain the term *intelligence* and apply its various definitions.
- Describe the types of behaviors measured by intelligence tests.
- Explain the uses of intelligence testing with students who have special needs.
- Describe how the issues in intelligence testing apply to current decision making.
- Name and describe the uses of individually administered tests of general intelligence.
- Name and describe the uses of the specialized tests of intellectual ability.
- Use the intelligence test guidelines for teachers.

Overview

This chapter helps you to develop knowledge of the content and processes associated with assessing intelligence. You begin by investigating the basic concepts and the critical issues in testing intelligence. Next, you review individually administered tests of general intelligence and specialized tests of intellectual ability. As you explore each test, you will review the purpose of the instrument, the administration and scoring procedures, the technical characteristics, and the uses of the tool. Finally, you will examine practical guidelines for teachers in the use of intelligence tests. The ultimate goal is to help you acquire an understanding of the various intelligence tests—their meaning, their interpretation, and their use with students who have special needs.

Introduction

The following narrative illustrates some of the most frequently asked questions that teachers of students with special needs have about intelligence tests.

An elementary school principal recently asked the school psychologist to meet with the teachers to discuss the types of intelligence testing services she provided to the school. The psychologist decided to focus her remarks on the intelligence tests used most frequently with exceptional students, including children who are gifted. Her presentation emphasized the questions most frequently asked by teachers, such as: What are the group-administered intelligence tests, and how do you use them in screening? What individually administered tests do you use most often, and what purposes do they serve? Are there special tests for very young children and children with severe disabilities? Can teachers use intelligence test results to help plan curricula and to place their students in the most appropriate learning groups?

During the presentation, one of the teachers asked the psychologist to tackle a key issue: "Because we know that many students with special needs have very low or very high intelligence (e.g., mentally retarded and gifted), how sensitive are the intelligence tests to extreme scores at both the high and low ends of the scale?" The psychologist explained that this central question illustrates a critical aspect of intelligence tests and their interpretations. She indicated that because intelligence tests, like all tests, are less accurate at the extremes, caution must be used when interpreting extremely high and low scores.

This chapter answers these important questions and provides other relevant information about intelligence testing with students who have special needs.

Purpose of Intelligence Testing

Most intelligence testing occurs during the classification and placement stage of assessing students with special needs. During this stage, assessment teams use intelligence test results, along with other measures of student ability and performance, to identify students who qualify for special services, including special education. Despite widespread use of intelligence tests, the meaning of **intelligence** and the efficacy of using intelligence tests remains a topic of debate for several reasons. One point of debate involves the initial (and difficult) task of defining intelligence. Developing tests of intelligence based on a particular definition is an even greater challenge. Finally, the central focus of the debate concerns the role and use of intelligence tests in the process of classifying and placing students. Although some critics argue for the elimination of intelligence testing, most contend that no valid substitutes for intelligence testing exist at present. Most experts argue that we must continue to use intelligence tests, along with other valid measurements, to obtain a comprehensive picture of student learning ability and performance.

Defining Intelligence

What is intelligence? Is it the ability to change behavior based upon experience? Is it what intelligence tests measure? Is it a complex theoretical concept that explains

Reflection
Why do you think extreme scores should be treated cautiously? Give an example to support your view.

 To answer this reflection online, go to the *Teaching and Learning* module on the companion Website at *www.prenhall.com/venn.*

certain types of behavior? Is it a score on an IQ test? Is it the measurement of one general trait or the separate measurement of different traits or characteristics? What makes a person intelligent? How should we measure intelligence? These questions illustrate the difficulties in defining intelligence. Answers to these questions provide valuable insight into the challenge of defining the term and understanding the tests that measure it.

Most experts agree on the general definition of intelligence as a trait or construct associated with cognitive or intellectual capacity and directly related to the potential or ability to learn. In other words, intelligence is an abstract quality associated with all types of intellectual processes including abstract thinking, mental reasoning, using sound judgment, and making rational decisions. In defining intelligence, specialists note that the term represents a concept, not an object. A concept is an idea or theoretical construct developed, in the case of intelligence, to describe a behavior or a set of behaviors. A concept such as intelligence is not a thing or concrete object like a chair that can be seen, touched, or moved. A more sensible approach is to describe intelligence according to what a person does or fails to do rather than describing it according to what a person is (Murphy & Davidshofer, 2005).

Gardner (2000) revolutionized our thinking about intelligence with groundbreaking books (Gardner, 1983, 1993) on **multiple intelligences**. A discussion of assessing multiple intelligences appears in the Technology Focus. From this perspective, a reasonable conclusion is that intelligence consists of a range of behaviors requiring mental ability rather than one single behavior. Furthermore, the purpose of intelligence

TECHNOLOGY FOCUS
Assessing Multiple Intelligences

The concept of multiple intelligences (Gardner, 2000) refers to different dimensions of intelligence and recognizes that students have unique cognitive behaviors and learning styles. Although demand exists for standardized pencil-on-paper tests of multiple intelligences, few, if any, such measures exist. Chen and Gardner (1997) suggest that appropriate assessment of multiple intelligences requires significant departures from traditional testing. For this reason, as experts develop measures of multiple intelligences, alternative forms of assessment will emerge that will include new instruments, materials, and frameworks designed to tap the divergent behaviors associated with each intellectual capacity. For example, bodily intelligence can be assessed by recording how well a child learns and remembers a new dance or physical exercise. Likewise, assessing interpersonal intelligence requires accurate measurement of how a child interacts with and influences others in different social situations. Most teachers rely on informal assessment of multiple intelligences using observation of student behavior. One of the commercially available measures is the Teele Inventory for Multiple Intelligences (TIMI) (Teele, 1997). The TIMI includes an intelligence inventory, answer sheets, and a teacher's guide. Teachers can use the TIMI to put multiple intelligences theory into action in their classrooms, identify their students' strengths and talents, and gain valuable information about how to teach more effectively. Another informal measure is the Multiple Intelligences Survey (McKenzie, 1999).

testing is to measure various levels of intellectual ability within and across individuals. Many students served in special programs manifest below-average intelligence and in some cases, students exhibit extremely low levels of intelligence. For this reason, teachers of students with special needs should be aware of the levels of intelligence of their students and, more important, the instructional implications of intelligence.

Instructional Implications of Intelligence

The concept of levels of intelligence suggests that the learning rates and patterns of students with abnormal intelligence are quantitatively and qualitatively different from the learning rates and patterns of students with normal intelligence. Further, students at the same levels of intelligence often display similar learning characteristics. Although intelligence is only one variable in the learning process, teachers use many specialized methods and materials with students who have significantly high or low levels of cognitive ability. For example, students with abnormally low intelligence learn at a slower rate. As a result, teachers use techniques such as overlearning (e.g., repeated practice) and creative repetition to help compensate for the cognitive deficits. Likewise, teachers carefully introduce new tasks only after students have mastered all of the prerequisite skills. Teachers also avoid tasks that are beyond a child's level of mental ability because such tasks quickly become frustrating and often lead to failure for the student and the teacher. In contrast, students with abnormally high levels of intelligence learn at a higher rate than average students. Highly intelligent students also benefit from unique teaching methods and materials. For example, teachers of gifted students use tasks that encourage divergent thinking and creativity. Knowledge of the instructional implications of intelligence helps in understanding the process of assessing the intellectual capacity of children with special needs.

Although psychologists agree about the general meaning of intelligence, they disagree about specific definitions. For example, Wechsler and Binet, two authors of intelligence tests, offer contrasting descriptions of intelligence (Sattler, 2001). According to Wechsler, creator of the Wechsler Scales of Intelligence, intelligence is a global ability to act in a purposeful manner, to think reasonably, and to adjust appropriately to the environment. In contrast, Binet, the originator of intelligence tests, believed that intelligence consists of a group of abilities including judgment, good sense, initiative, and the ability to adjust to changes in the environment. These differing definitions help to explain why different authors construct different types of intelligence tests, depending on their interpretation of the meaning of the term.

Behaviors Measured by Intelligence Tests

Intelligence tests measure learning ability by sampling various behaviors (Salvia & Ysseldyke, 2004). Although similarities exist in the behaviors measured by intelligence tests, different tests measure different behaviors. Because each test relies on a unique sample of behaviors, professionals should always reference a specific test when using intelligence test scores (often referred to as IQ scores). Naming a test is necessary because IQ scores from different tests have different meanings. For example, a screening test of intelligence, such as the Otis-Lennon School Ability Test (OLSAT) (Otis & Lennon, 2002) is derived from a different sample of behaviors than an IQ score from an individually administered, general test of intelligence, such as the Wechsler Intelligence Scale for Children—Fourth Edition (WISC-IV) (Wechsler, 2003). When an IQ score appears in isolation, we must ask the question, "IQ as measured by which test?" The following overview of the behaviors sampled by different types of intelligence tests illustrates the significance of this question.

Intelligence tests can be grouped into two major categories: individually administered general tests and specialized tests. An overview of each category follows.

Individually Administered Tests of General Intelligence

The individually administered tests of general intelligence include subtests sampling a variety of behaviors including verbal language ability and performance skills. The verbal language items require responses to oral questions. For example, tasks such as answering factual and comprehension questions, defining vocabulary words, identifying similarities, and solving arithmetic problems all involve verbal language. Specific examples of such items include these questions: "Who invented the telephone?" "What is a paragraph?" "How are a window and a door similar?" (Wechsler, 1991).

Other verbal language items require definitions of increasingly difficult words, such as *string*, *spring*, *novel*, and *facetious*. Absurdities are another type of verbal language item on some tests. These require students to identify the nonsense aspects in presented pictures (e.g., an elephant with wings).

In contrast are the items measuring performance skills such as fine motor proficiency and perceptual ability. Performance behaviors require students to respond to items using motor and perceptual skills. Performance items rely on language only in the instructions. Many performance items assess ability based on speed of task completion (measured with a stopwatch) and the number of errors. Examples include putting together puzzle pieces to form complete objects, using a pencil to trace a path through mazes of increasing complexity, and arranging blocks according to visually presented designs. Because performance items avoid use of language, they are useful for testing students with intact motor and perceptual processes but impaired verbal language.

The individually administered general tests contain subtests for measuring a variety of behaviors. In contrast, the specialized tests sample a restricted set of behaviors.

Specialized Intelligence Tests

The specialized intelligence tests include screening tests given to individuals and groups of students, tests for students with unique disabilities, and tests for infants, toddlers, and preschoolers. A description of each group of specialized tests follows.

Screening Tests   Most screening tests are designed for administration to individuals or to groups, and they measure cognitive ability by having students pencil in responses to multiple-choice questions on machine-scored answer sheets. The Otis-Lennon School Ability Test (Otis & Lennon, 2002) is one of the widely used screening intelligence tests that rely on this format. The multiple-choice format limits the variety of content. As a result, these tests tend to measure intelligence with a restricted sample of behaviors. In addition, the pencil-on-paper format requires that test takers have good reading skills and experience with "bubble-in" scoring sheets. Although this format is appropriate for most students, it causes difficulties for students with special needs. For example, students with visual perception problems may have difficulty accurately recording answers on scoring sheets.

Intelligence Tests for Students with Unique Disabilities   Like screening tests, tests for students with unique disabilities also rely on restricted samples of behaviors. For example, the Universal Nonverbal Intelligence Test (UNIT) (Bracken & McCallum, 1997) is a test of visual memory and visual reasoning ability that requires no verbal and minimal motor responses. Developed for testing students with hearing impairments,

Figure 7–1   Sample visual-reasoning tasks

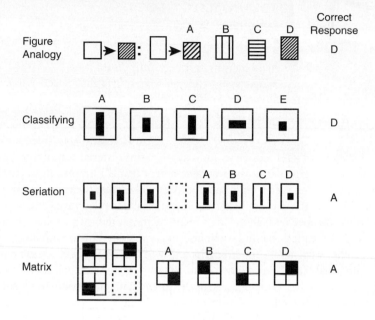

language disabilities, or limited English proficiency, the UNIT does not require reading, writing, or speaking skills. The UNIT consists of pictures and abstract drawings on cards that students respond to by pointing to the correct drawing or, if necessary, using an eye-blink communication system. Tests such as the UNIT sample visual reasoning behaviors that require visual-perception ability to make perceptual discriminations and to remember visual images. Perceptual discriminations involve simple perceptual classifications and abstract manipulation of symbolic concepts. Perceptual classification tasks usually consist of discrimination of colors, shapes, numbers, and objects. Abstract manipulation of symbolic concepts involves tasks such as visual discrimination (recognizing small differences in objects such as geometric drawings), visual sequencing (identifying the progressive relationship in a series of geometric figures), and recognition of details (identifying missing parts in pictures). Visual memory involves tasks such as remembering symbols, memory for designs, and object memory. Illustrations of some visual-reasoning tasks appear in Figure 7–1.

Specialized Tests for Infants, Toddlers, and Preschoolers   Specialized tests for infants, toddlers, and preschoolers estimate learning potential based on samples of the behavior appropriate for very young children. The Bayley Scales of Infant Development, Second Edition (Bayley, 1993), for example, consist of subscales of mental ability, motor skills, and behavior. The mental scale samples sensory and perceptual skills, vocalizations, and early verbal communication; the motor scale measures gross motor and fine motor skills; and the behavior scale is a rating scale completed by a primary caregiver.

Why Do We Assess Intelligence?

The main reason for giving intelligence tests to students with special needs is to identify and classify students. In fact, the law mandates that most students referred for

TECHNOLOGY FOCUS
Why Do We Assess Intelligence?

- To obtain an estimate of learning ability
- To identify students with disabilities
- To classify students according to their specific disability
- To periodically reevaluate the learning ability of students

special education services receive an individually administered test of intelligence to estimate their learning ability. The way assessment teams interpret this estimate depends on the student's suspected disability. When assessment teams suspect learning disabilities, they look for a significant discrepancy between learning ability (as measured by an intelligence test) and achievement (as measured by an achievement test). Students with learning disabilities will also likely display normal intelligence and a learning profile with significant strengths and weaknesses. When assessment teams suspect emotional disturbance, they look for normal intellectual abilities because eligibility requirements exclude students with mental retardation from such programs. When team members suspect mental retardation, they rely on intelligence testing to obtain evidence of significantly below-average learning ability that exists concurrently with deficits in adaptive behavior.

Although many states have replaced the traditional categories of learning disabilities, emotional disturbance, and mental retardation with more generic categories such as educationally handicapped, learning handicapped, and severely handicapped, all states employ some form of intelligence testing in identifying, classifying, and placing students into special programs. In addition, regulations require periodic reevaluation of intelligence to determine if a student should remain in the current placement, transfer to another program, or transfer out of special education entirely. A summary listing of the reasons for giving intelligence tests to students with special needs appears in the Technology Focus box.

You may recall the account of Jerrold Johnson that first appeared in Chapter 2, which illustrated critical steps in the screening and referral process. Because of this process, Jerrold was recommended for comprehensive testing to determine if he qualified for special education services. The following account illustrates how intelligence testing helped to identify Jerrold's reading disability.

When the child-study team forwarded Jerrold's case to a staffing team for comprehensive testing, the psychologist assigned to the case decided to administer the Wechsler Intelligence Scale for Children, Fourth Edition (WISC-IV) (Wechsler, 2003). The purpose was to determine Jerrold's intelligence. His WISC-IV scores were in the normal range, and he received a full-scale IQ score (a standard score) of 97. In addition to giving the WISC-IV, the psychologist administered a diagnostic achievement test, the Wechsler Individual Achievement Test, Second Edition (WIAT-II) (Wechsler, 2001). The WISC-IV and the WIAT-II, developed by the same author, have the advantage of being co-normed. This means that they were standardized using the same groups of children. As a result, scores from the two tests are directly comparable. In order to qualify as learning disabled, Jerrold's scores on these tests had to show a significant discrepancy between intelligence as measured by the WISC-IV and achievement as measured by the WIAT-II. Jerrold's scores on the WIAT-II were much lower than his WISC-IV scores, especially in reading recognition (a standard score of 81) and reading comprehension (a standard score of 77). Because of the significant discrepancy between aptitude and achievement, Jerrold qualified for special education services. As a result, he began receiving services for students with learning disabilities designed to meet his individual learning needs.

Jerrold's case illustrates the role of intelligence testing in identifying a student with a learning disability. In contrast, the next scenario illustrates the role of intelligence testing in identifying a student with mental retardation.

The psychologist evaluated Johnny, a student in Mrs. Johnson's second-grade class, for special education placement due to poor academic performance and inappropriate classroom behavior. When Johnny was tested, he received a full-scale IQ of 64 on the WISC-IV (Wechsler, 2003). This score fell well below the cutoff of 80 for mental retardation used in this particular state. In addition to intelligence testing, the psychologist administered a test of academic achievement and an adaptive behavior scale before making an eligibility and placement decision. Johnny's achievement was consistently low in all academic areas, resulting in a flat profile. His adaptive behavior also fell into the significantly below-average range. In making their recommendation, the assessment team found that the test data clearly supported providing Johnny with services for students with mild mental retardation.

In Johnny's case, the intelligence test results provided clear-cut identification data. In other situations, however, intelligence testing may not provide conclusive information. The next example illustrates this point.

The intelligence test score Walter received (an IQ of 80 on the Stanford–Binet Intelligence Scale, Fifth Edition [SB5]) placed him directly on the eligibility borderline for the mental retardation program. Because the test score fell on the cutoff line, the assessment team turned to other assessment data to help make their decision. Unfortunately, Walter's levels of performance in achievement and adaptive behavior also fell near the borderline for eligibility. Because the assessment data failed to indicate clearly a disability, the team carefully considered Walter's social and family history before making a placement decision. Walter, a minority student, had grown up in a deprived and culturally different environment characterized by poverty and lack of experience. Therefore, the assessment team reasoned that environmental deprivation rather than mental retardation was a possible cause of his poor school performance. In deciding that the test data failed to support placement in special education, the assessment team strongly considered the economic and cultural factors. They recommended continued placement in the first grade and helped Walter's teacher to identify additional interventions to try in class. The assessment team also made arrangements for Walter to enroll in a remedial reading program where he received additional instructional assistance. Finally, the assessment team made plans for retesting Walter in 1 year to obtain another estimate of his learning ability and achievement.

In contrast to the earlier example, Walter's case illustrates a situation in which test data failed to provide conclusive evidence for making a placement decision.

Issues in Intelligence Testing

Although intelligence testing is one of the most important contributions in the field of psychology, it remains controversial in special education. Concerns center on several drawbacks, including limited ability to predict nonacademic and vocational success,

MULTICULTURAL CONSIDERATIONS

Intelligence Testing and the Bell Curve

When *The Bell Curve: Intelligence and Class Structure in American Life* (Herrnstein & Murray, 1994) was published, intelligence testing received much attention in the popular press. A basic argument of the book is that widespread intelligence testing creates a class of intellectual elites in positions of political and economic power. According to the authors, the problem is that economically and socially disadvantaged children (many of whom are from minority groups) are excluded from this elite class. The bell curve controversy raises continuing social and political arguments. As educators we need to be aware of and sensitive to these arguments because children from minority groups are overrepresented in special education classes due to low scores on intelligence tests. Thorndike (2005) suggested we ask what the research data say about measuring intelligence to predict academic success. Because the data show such a strong positive correlation between intelligence and academic success, we rely on intelligence testing to identify students with disabilities. However, if we eliminate intelligence tests, accurate identification would be even more difficult. Our goal as special educators should be to eliminate bias in the use of intelligence tests so that all children are treated fairly and equally.

The *Bell Curve* was written to explain, using empirical statistical analysis, the variations in intelligence in American society, raise some warnings regarding the consequences of this intelligence gap, and propose a national social policy with the goal of mitigating the worst of the consequences attributed to this intelligence gap. Many of the assertions put forth and conclusions reached by the authors are very controversial, ranging from the relationships between low measured intelligence and antisocial behavior to the observed relationship between low African American test scores (compared to Whites and Asians) and genetic factors in intelligence abilities. When the book was released, it received a large public response. In the first several months 400,000 copies of the book were sold around the world. Several thousand reviews and commentaries have been written in the short time since the book's publication.

In your own words explain why you think intelligence testing is so controversial.

 To answer this reflection online, go to the *Multicultural Considerations* module on the Companion Website at *www.prenhall.com/venn.*

inaccuracy of IQ scores at the extremes, and cultural bias against minority groups. Many of these issues were highlighted in Herrnstein and Murray's 1994 book on intelligence testing and the bell curve. Information about the bell curve controversy appears in the accompanying Multicultural Considerations feature.

Effectiveness in Predicting Nonschool Behavior

Little evidence exists to support using intelligence test results to predict nonschool behaviors, such as potential for vocational success and preferred learning style. The problem stems, in part, from misunderstanding the purpose of intelligence testing.

Most people, including some psychologists, believe that intelligence testing measures natural ability or potential. However, this theory is difficult to support. Clearly, the originators of intelligence testing designed the tests to predict school behaviors. In 1905, Binet and Simon wrote the first intelligence test as a tool for identifying students with limited potential for success in school. As a result of testing, educators excluded students with low scores from the school system. Thus, the original purpose was to predict school success. More recently, however, psychologists and others have come to rely on intelligence test results to predict learning style, vocational aptitude, and other abilities, even though the validity of such practices is questionable.

Accuracy

Another issue concerns accuracy at the extremes of high and low performance. The problem is that IQ scores, like all test scores, lose accuracy at extremely high and low levels of performance. This creates a dilemma with students who have special needs because they often receive scores in the extreme ranges. For example, students with mild disabilities often receive IQ scores in the below-average range of 70 to 85, whereas students with severe and profound disabilities typically receive IQ scores of 55 and lower. On the other end of the IQ scale, students who are gifted typically score in the IQ range of 130 and above. The standard error of measurement (an estimate of the accuracy of a score) in these extreme ranges is much higher than for scores in the midrange of intelligence tests (around 100 IQ points). For this reason, assessment teams must treat extreme scores with caution to avoid misuse in identifying, classifying, and placing students.

Bias

A third issue, bias against certain groups of students, represents the greatest area of concern in intelligence testing. The long running debate about bias pertains to the correct use of intelligence tests with students from deprived and culturally different backgrounds. This includes students with limited English language proficiency as well as students with disabilities. Many experts point out that intelligence tests are not culture fair. **Culture fair** refers to equity for all students regardless of cultural background. Culture-fair tests attempt to provide students of different cultures and life experiences equal opportunities for success. As a result, developers of culture-fair tests must limit test content to material that is common to all cultures or that is unfamiliar or new for students from various different cultural backgrounds. Although developing a completely culture-fair test may be impossible, most test writers reduce, as much as possible, the influence of cultural factors in testing. Test writers accomplish this goal by eliminating "culturally loaded" items, such as pictures or vocabulary that are unique to a specific cultural experience. The classic example of such an item is a question from an early edition of the Wechsler Intelligence Scale for Children. The question involved asking children what they should do if a much smaller child hit them. "Correct" answers included telling an adult or ignoring the smaller child. "Incorrect" answers included hitting the child back. The question is culturally loaded because children in some cultures learn that hitting a much younger child back is appropriate whereas children in other cultures learn the opposite.

Despite efforts to eliminate bias in intelligence testing, evidence suggests that intelligence tests favor students from middle-class backgrounds and discriminate against students from low-socioeconomic backgrounds, rural areas, and minority

MULTICULTURAL CONSIDERATIONS

Intelligence Testing with Students from Diverse Backgrounds

Many issues and concerns surround intelligence testing with students from culturally and linguistically diverse backgrounds (Sattler, 2001). The issues and concerns center on the fact that students from culturally and linguistically diverse backgrounds have been exposed to different experiences and environments than majority students. Though the particular influences of experiential and environmental differences are not clear, it is clear that differences must be taken into consideration when testing intelligence. Accounting for differences involves use of comprehensive intelligence testing strategies that consider cultural and language diversity.

Although some call for eliminating intelligence testing entirely, this would have few advantages and would have many disadvantages. The reality is that compared with subjective assessment, norm-referenced testing reduces bias and discrimination. Rather than eliminating intelligence tests, efforts are continuing to make sure that intelligence tests are valid for use with all students. Much progress has been made in giving and appropriately interpreting intelligence tests with careful consideration of the student's background and experiences. However, even more needs to be done to ensure fairness for all.

groups (Gregory, 2004). For this reason, test developers are continuing to develop ways of eliminating bias in intelligence testing. The classic response to the problem of partiality is the System of Multicultural Pluralistic Assessment, or SOMPA, developed by Mercer and Lewis (1978). SOMPA attempts to adjust for bias using several strategies. The system (explained in greater detail later in this chapter) consists of a complete program, including assessment of language and cultural factors through the use of sociocultural scales, health history inventories, and specialized norms for Black, Hispanic, and White children. SOMPA and other similar systems illustrate one response to solving the persistent problem of bias in assessment.

Those who question efforts to create culture-fair tests argue that an intelligence test is unfair only if it fails to predict academic success. They contend that intelligence tests effectively predict school success by identifying those with the requisite verbal skills and abstract reasoning ability. However, the issue of bias in testing is more than pedagogical because millions of students receive intelligence tests each year, and educational placement depends, in large part, on their performance on these tests. Further information about the issue of fairness in intelligence testing appears in the accompanying Multicultural Considerations feature.

Reflection
Do you think intelligence tests should be eliminated? Explain.

To check your comprehension of chapter contents, go to the *Teaching and Learning* module in Chapter 7 of the Companion Website, *www.prenhall.com/venn.*

☑ Check Your Comprehension

Intelligence testing represents a complicated and controversial area of assessing students with special needs. Although intelligence generally refers to the ability to learn based on experience, many complex definitions exist for the term. Likewise, psychologists have created different types of intelligence tests, most of which measure intelligence by using a combination of verbal language, motor performance, and visual reasoning items, although verbal items predominate. Controversies surrounding intelligence testing include questions about the role of intelligence testing in special education and concerns about the predictive validity of such tests. However, the greatest controversy centers on bias in the intelligence test scores of students from minority groups. Psychologists and special educators continue to develop procedures to reduce bias.

The two major categories of intelligence tests are individually administered tests of general intelligence and specialized measures of intellectual ability. Intelligence tests for children consist of samples of behavior. The general tests sample the widest variety of behaviors. The specialized tests use more restrictive behavior samples. Specialized tests exist for groups of students and for special populations, including infants, toddlers, preschoolers, and students with severe handicaps. However, evaluators rely on these tests only in situations that preclude use of more general measures.

Individually Administered Tests of General Ability

Measuring intelligence using general ability tests is a primary application of psychology with students who have special needs. Psychologists have developed a number of instruments for measuring general ability as well as highly specialized measures for special populations. Evaluators give individually administered intelligence tests to only one student at a time, and individual tests exist for all age groups. Most individual tests contain subtests for measuring different abilities, including verbal skills, motor performance, and visual reasoning skills. This enables the assessment team to gauge specific intellectual abilities and overall intelligence. Because examiners present test items orally or with pictures, students need not read, and most individually administered tests require limited written responses. The foremost general intelligence test is the Wechsler Intelligence Scale for Children, Fourth Edition. Comprehensive reviews of this and other widely used tests follow.

Wechsler Intelligence Scale for Children, Fourth Edition

The Wechsler Intelligence Scale for Children, Fourth Edition (WISC—IV) (Wechsler, 2003) has excellent technical qualities, well-designed administration and scoring procedures, and many additional features. Designed for students from age 6 through 16, the assessment is available in different editions, including an integrated version and a Spanish version. One version, the WISC—IV Integrated, features an extended group of 16 subtests to complement the core WISC—IV components. The additional process subtests help in diagnosing suspected processing problems or in obtaining additional information about performance in specific domains. The WISC—IV Spanish is a translation and adaptation of the instrument for evaluating Spanish-speaking, limited English proficient (LEP), and other bilingual students and Spanish-speaking individuals who have immigrated to the United States. A WISC—IV summary appears in Test Review.

The WISC—IV is one of a group of Wechsler intelligence tests spanning all ages. Other tests include the Wechsler Preschool and Primary Scale of Intelligence, Third Edition (WPPSI-III) (Wechsler, 2002) for preschool children, and the Wechsler Adult

---

╭─ **TEST REVIEW** ─╮

Wechsler Intelligence Scale for Children, Fourth Edition

Type of Test:	Norm referenced, individually administered
Purpose:	A general measure of intellectual ability
Content Areas:	Four indexes: verbal comprehension, perceptual reasoning, working memory, and processing speed
Administration Time:	Approximately 75 minutes
Age Levels:	6 to 16 years
Suitable for:	Students with mild, moderate, and severe disabilities, including learning disabilities, behavior disorders, mental retardation, visual impairments (verbal index), hearing impairments (perceptual, memory, and processing indexes), and physical handicaps (verbal index)
Scores:	Full-scale IQ scores, 4 factor-based index scores, and scaled scores for each the 10 core and 5 supplemental subtests
In Short:	The well-designed WISC-IV has superior technical characteristics. The improvements in this edition make it an outstanding assessment instrument.

Intelligence Scale, Third Edition (WAIS-III) (Wechsler, 1997) for adults from 16 years through retirement. The newest instrument in the Wechsler group is the Wechsler Abbreviated Scale of Intelligence (WASI) (Wechsler, 1999). The WASI is for individuals from ages 6 to 89 years.

WISC-IV General Description   The WISC IV assesses global intelligence using a variety of tasks. The familiar verbal and performance subtests from the WISC-III were renamed the verbal comprehension index and the perceptual reasoning index in the new edition. The WISC-IV now estimates overall learning potential and relative strengths and weaknesses using four indicators rather than two.

The four WISC-IV indexes are derived from 10 core and 5 supplemental subtests. The indexes are: verbal comprehension, perceptual reasoning, working memory, and processing speed. Scores from each index, based on the 10 core subtests only, combine to create a student's total score or full-scale IQ (FSIQ). The indexes and their subtests are as follows:

Verbal Comprehension Index (VCI):

1. Similarities

2. Vocabulary

3. Comprehension

4. Information (Supplemental)

5. Word Reasoning (Supplemental)

Perceptual Reasoning Index (PRI):

1. Block Design

2. Picture Concepts

3. Matrix Reasoning

4. Picture Completion (Supplemental)

Working Memory Index (WMI):

1. Digit Span

2. Letter-Number Sequencing

3. Arithmetic (Supplemental)

Processing Speed Index (PSI):

1. Coding

2. Symbol Search

3. Cancellation (Supplemental)

WISC-IV Materials   WISC-IV materials include administration and technical manuals, record forms, response booklets, scoring and report writing software on CD, and a training CD.

WISC-IV Administration   The WISC-IV takes about 75 minutes to give, depending on the response speed of the student. Certified evaluators administer the test following standardized procedures. Administration involves alternating the presentation of subtests in a specified order. This alternating procedure makes taking the test more interesting. Specific training and certification are required for evaluators, and test use is limited to psychologists and diagnosticians who have met these conditions.

WISC-IV Scoring   The WISC-IV yields IQs for the full scale and the four indexes. These scores have a mean of 100 and a standard deviation of 15. The evaluator summarizes the testing results on a form that includes identifying information, overall IQs, and graphs that profile the results. Scoring may also include use of a supplementary computer software report program that analyzes results and generates an interpretive report.

WISC-IV Interpretation   The full-scale WISC-IV IQ indicates a student's general intellectual ability, whereas IQ scores from the four indexes provide a profile of intelligence. Performance on the verbal comprehension index depends on a student's ability to orally answer questions presented verbally. In contrast, the perceptual reasoning, working memory, and processing speed indexes measure the ability to quickly perform nonverbal tasks using visual and fine motor skills. Discrepancies of more than 12 IQ points between the verbal and performance scales may have diagnostic implications. A difference of this magnitude represents a significant discrepancy between performance and verbal ability. Identifying discrepancies helps the evaluator interpret student performance when notable differences exist between functioning levels in performance and verbal ability. Possible reasons for discrepancies include interest or learning styles (e.g., a student with strong verbal skills but weak performance skills), cognitive styles, disabilities, sensory deficits, and information processing deficits (e.g., strengths or weaknesses in auditory or visual processing skills).

WISC-IV Technical Characteristics   As might be expected from the premier test of its kind, the WISC-IV exhibits outstanding technical characteristics in all areas. The norms are excellent, the validity is well established, and the reliability is superior. Split-half reliability coefficients range from .80 to .90 for the individual verbal subscales and from .69 to .87 for the individual performance subscales. The reliability coefficient for the full-scale IQ was much higher at .97. As with almost all tests of this type, the reliability coefficients of the subscale scores fall below those of the full-scale IQ scores. For this reason, the accuracy of interpretations based on subscale scores is limited. Validity research conducted with the WISC-IV included a correlation study with the WISC-III. The correlation for the full-scale IQ was .89, the correlations for the verbal-based scores were .87, and the correlations for performance-based scores were .74. Other WISC-IV validity studies included factor analysis research and intercorrelations among the subtests and the scales. The test developers obtained normative data by using a stratified sampling plan to ensure the selection of a representative sample group. The group consisted of 2,200 students. Sampling variables included age, gender, race, geographic region, and parent education level.

WISC-IV Critical Reviews   Critical reviews (Maller, 2005; Thompson, 2005) were favorable, citing high-quality administration and scoring procedures and excellent standardization. Both reviewers indicated that the WISC-IV is likely to remain the premier individually administered intelligence test. Weaknesses include insufficient evidence about item and test bias and a few technical deficiencies related to sample sizes and statistical procedures used to establish validity. Despite these criticisms, the reviewers concluded that the WISC-IV was carefully developed with excellent attention to detail, and it represents an improvement over the earlier version of the instrument.

WISC-IV Summary   The WISC-IV, which conceptualizes intelligence as a global ability, assesses student ability through a series of verbal and manipulative tasks. The WISC-IV represents an important diagnostic tool for assessing educational potential and evaluating disabilities. Examiners rely on the test extensively to assist in the process of identifying students with special needs.

Stanford–Binet Intelligence Scale, Fifth Edition

Binet and Simon published the original version of the Stanford–Binet Intelligence Scale in 1905. Designed to identify students in French schools who could not benefit from instruction, psychologists brought it to the United States soon after initial publication. In the United States, the scales were revised and published again in 1916 as the Stanford–Binet Intelligence Scale. Later revisions were published in 1937 and in 1960. The 1960 edition introduced use of the deviation IQ rather than a ratio IQ, and this significant improvement increased the accuracy and precision of the test scores. The norms for the 1960 scale were revised and published as the Stanford–Binet Intelligence Scale, Fourth Edition (SB4) in 1986, although the test items, administration, and scoring procedures remained similar to the 1960 edition. The new fifth edition of the Stanford–Binet Intelligence Scales (SB5) (Roid, 2003) is a valuable update to this well-established instrument. A version of the Stanford–Binet for young children is also available. The Stanford–Binet Intelligence Scales for Early Childhood, Fifth Edition (Early SB5) (Roid, 2005) includes the subtests from the SB5 along with a test observation checklist and a software-generated parent report. The Early SB5 is suitable for use with young children ages 2.0 to 7.3 years.

TEST REVIEW

Stanford-Binet Intelligence Scales, Fifth Edition

Type of Test:	Norm referenced, individually administered
Purpose:	A general measure of intellectual ability
Content Areas:	Five cognitive ability factors: fluid reasoning, knowledge, quantitative reasoning, visual-spatial processing, and working memory
Administration Time:	Approximately 1 hour
Age Levels:	2 to 89 years
Suitable for:	Students with mild, moderate, and severe disabilities, including learning disabilities, behavior disorders, and mental retardation
Scores:	A full-scale IQ, verbal and nonverbal IQs, composite indexes for the five factors, and an abbreviated IQ
In Short:	As was the original IQ test, the Sanford–Binet is historically significant. The well-designed and widely used SB5 is the most recent edition of this classic instrument.

SB5 General Description   The SB5 measures the general intellectual ability of individuals from between the ages of 2 to 85+ years using five cognitive ability factors: fluid reasoning, knowledge, quantitative reasoning, visual-spatial processing, and working memory. A summary of the SB5 appears in Test Review.

SB5 Materials   SB5 materials include four item books, a guide for administering and scoring, a technical manual, a record booklet, scissors, paper, a child card, and manipulative materials packaged in a briefcase.

SB5 Administration   The test takes about an hour to administer to a young child, but the administration time may be longer with an adolescent or adult. Because evaluators must obtain specific training and certification, use of the SB5 is limited to psychologists, diagnosticians, and other professionals who have received this training.

SB5 Scoring   Available SB5 scores include a full-scale IQ that combines all 10 subtests, verbal and nonverbal IQs based on the five verbal and five nonverbal subtests, and composite indexes for the five factors. All of these standard scores have means of 100 and standard deviations of 15. Subtest scores with a mean of 10, a standard deviation of 3, and a range of 1 to 19 are also available. Scoring options include an abbreviated battery IQ score derived from the two scores of the subtests.

SB5 Interpretation   The full-scale SB5 IQ score indicates overall intellectual performance whereas the five factor scores and the verbal and nonverbal IQs provide a profile of intellectual development across domains. Interpretation options include use of special composite subtest scores to assist in identifying students who are gifted, slow learners, and learning disabled. SB5 scoring and interpretation procedures also include use of change-sensitive scores that provide a way to compare changes in individual scores over time. This is especially helpful in evaluating extreme performance levels. These examples illustrate the variety of available SB5 interpretation options.

SB5 Technical Characteristics The norms were based on results from 4,800 individuals matched with the 2000 U.S. Census data. Development procedures included bias reviews of all items for the variables of gender, ethnicity, culture, religion, region, and socioeconomic status. Additionally, the SB5 was co-normed with the Bender-Gestalt Visual-Motor Gestalt Test, 2nd Edition. The reliability coefficients for the full-scale, nonverbal, and verbal IQ scores range from .95 to .98. Reliabilities for the factor indexes range from .90 to .92. For the 10 subtests, reliabilities range from .84 to .89. Concurrent and criterion validity data was obtained using several other intelligence and achievement tests. The SB5 provides very good overall technical qualities.

SB5 Critical Reviews Critical reviews (Johnson, 2005; Kush, 2005) describe the SB5 as well developed and technically accurate with a helpful new structure that includes measurement of working memory and additional emphasis on assessing nonverbal performance skills. According to the reviewers, the instrument does display some technical deficiencies related to stability with young children and students with low intellectual capabilities. It could also benefit from more evidence of construct validity. However, these are relatively minor weaknesses and the SB5 is still one of the most outstanding intelligence tests for use with children and adults.

SB5 Summary As the original intelligence test, it is difficult to overstate the historical effect of the Stanford-Binet Intelligence Scale on the major institutions in Western society. One outgrowth of this pioneering assessment tool has been the reliance on such tests by all of the major institutions, including business, industry, the military, and education. The initial Binet Intelligence Scale demonstrated, for the first time, a procedure for accurately and effectively measuring intellectual ability. Acceptance of the Stanford–Binet and other intelligence tests led to widespread use of other types of tests, such as achievement and aptitude tests.

Other Individually Administered Tests of General Ability

Woodcock–Johnson III Complete Battery The Woodcock–Johnson III (WJ III) Complete Battery (Woodcock, McGrew, & Mather, 2001) is a comprehensive diagnostic system for measuring general intelligence, specific cognitive abilities, scholastic aptitude, oral language, and achievement. The WJ III includes two batteries: the Tests of Cognitive Ability and the Tests of Achievement. The cognitive and the achievement tests both use the same norms, and this makes an ideal evaluation system for accurately diagnosing ability/achievement discrepancies.

Both tests are organized into a standard battery and an extended battery. This enables evaluators to utilize the supplemental tests in a flexible manner, depending on the needs of the student and time constraints. Giving the standard batteries usually takes less than 1 hour, but giving the extended batteries may take several hours and require more than one sitting.

No other test provides as many scores and profiles as the WJ III. These include cluster scores for cognitive factors, cluster scores, scholastic aptitudes, individual test scores, and discrepancy scores. Because the two WJ III tests are co-normed, the instrument is suited for identifying students with significant discrepancies between learning ability and academic achievement. Such comparisons are a necessary step in the process of making classification and placement decisions for students with specific learning disabilities.

Batería III Woodcock-Muñoz The Batería III Woodcock-Muñoz (Woodcock, Muñoz-Sandoval, McGrew, Mather, & Schrank, 2004) is the Spanish adaption and translation of the WJ III. The Batería III measures the cognitive abilities and achievement levels of

Spanish-speaking students using tests adapted from the WJ III, and Spanish performance is equated to similar performance levels on the English test. Like the WJ III, the instrument provides several options for brief as well as comprehensive assessment, and it includes a computer scoring program. The Batería III allows access to all the tests and interpretative options of the WJ III for Spanish-dominant individuals.

Kaufman Assessment Battery for Children, Second Edition The Kaufman Assessment Battery for Children, Second Edition (KABC-II) (Kaufman & Kaufman, 2004) is a well-designed intelligence test that reflects contemporary concerns for nondiscriminatory assessment, provides specific procedures for use with students with disabilities, and helps identify preferred learning styles. Encompassing an age range of 3 through 18 years, the KABC-II contains five scales: simultaneous, sequential, planning, learning, and knowledge. It takes about an hour to administer the KABC-II, and the instrument yields age-based standard scores, age equivalents, and percentile ranks for global intelligence and for the specific abilities measured by each scale. The KABC-II is attractively packaged with test items that appeal to and interest children. The subtests were designed to minimize verbal instructions and responses. This produces results with less influence due to language. The test items also contain a minimum of cultural content, so children from diverse backgrounds are assessed as fairly as possible. The KABC-II is co-normed with the Kaufman Test of Educational Achievement, Second Edition (KTEA II). This allows for in-depth ability/achievement comparisons.

Differential Ability Scales The Differential Ability Scales (DAS) (Elliott, 1990) contain 17 cognitive subtests and 3 achievement subtests for measuring the intelligence of children from 2 years 6 months to 17 years 11 months. The DAS features attractive, colorful manipulative materials for young children and interesting activities to hold the attention of older children. DAS results include a general conceptual ability score and cluster scores, including verbal and nonverbal ability for preschoolers and verbal reasoning, nonverbal reasoning, and spatial ability for school children. The DAS yields a nonverbal composite score for students who are language impaired or who are English language learners. The DAS norm sample included 3,475 children, stratified by age, sex, race/ethnicity, parent education, geographic region, and educational preschool enrollment. The sample included children who were exceptional. The DAS norm development process included analysis of the performance of large samples of African American and Hispanic children to identify and eliminate biased items.

☑ Check Your Comprehension

Assessment with individually administered tests of general intelligence is an integral step in identifying, classifying, and placing students with special needs. Although professionals may choose from a number of instruments, the WISC-IV remains the most widely used test. Other widely used measures include the SB5, the WJ III, and the KABC-II.

Because virtually all students in special education programs are tested with a general measure of intelligence, teachers should be familiar with these tests, their content, and their interpretation. In addition to the general intelligence tests, specialized tests are available for screening individuals and groups, for very young students, and for students with unique disabling conditions.

Specialized Measures of Intelligence

The specialized measures of intelligence include group intelligence tests; tests for students who have sensory impairments such as deafness and blindness, physical impairments, and severe mental retardation; and tests for very young children. Although the individually administered, general tests of intelligence are used whenever possible, evaluators sometimes use one or more of the specialized intelligence tests to meet the individual needs of one or a group of students.

Screening Tests

The screening tests of intellectual ability are for both individual and group administration. The screening tests are widely used for a number of purposes, including testing students referred for possible placement in gifted and talented programs. Students who "pass" a screening test for gifted placement always need follow-up assessment with an individually administered, general measure of intellectual ability to make an eligibility decision.

The advantages of the screening tests include the ability to assess students quickly and inexpensively. Because of this, the screening tests remain popular in education, business, industry, and the military. Like all screening tests, the specialized intelligence tests exhibit several limitations. First, the multiple-choice format limits the range and variety of questions. Second, most screening tests require students to "bubble in" their responses to multiple-choice questions on a machine-scored answer sheet. This pencil-on-paper format requires good reading skills, sophisticated test-taking knowledge, and sufficient fine motor dexterity. For this reason, screening tests are not suitable for students with special needs who have reading problems. For these students, a low score may reflect reading problems rather than low intelligence. Likewise, students with visual-perception problems, who have difficulty filling in computer-scored answer sheets and who often skip items, may receive low scores on a screening test due to visual-processing deficits and poor test-taking skills rather than intellectual deficiencies. Because of these limitations, schools restrict the use of screening tests to specific situations, and assessment teams avoid making major educational decisions based on screening results. Descriptions of representative screening tests follow.

Cognitive Abilities Test   The Cognitive Abilities Test (CogAT) (Lohman & Hagen, 2001) assesses the reasoning and problem-solving abilities of students from kindergarten through the 12th grade. Consisting of subtests that measure verbal, quantitative, and nonverbal (spatial) abilities, the CogAT takes approximately 90 minutes to complete and produces verbal, quantitative, nonverbal, and composite scores.

CogAT Nonverbal Battery, Edición en Español   The CogAT Nonverbal Battery, Edici´n en Español (Thorndike & Hagen, 1997) is an abilities test for Spanish-speaking students in grades kindergarten through 12. This test assesses students' abilities in reasoning and problem solving using spatial (nonverbal) symbols.

Naglieri Nonverbal Ability Test—Individual Administration   The *Naglieri Nonverbal Ability Test—Individual Administration* (NNATI–Individual Administration) (Naglieri, 2001) is a screening test for estimating the ability of students who do not speak English as their first language. The test measures visual reasoning ability using four types of items: pattern completion, serial reasoning, reasoning by analogy, and spatial visualization. These visual reasoning items, often referred to as progressive matrices, are less biased against minority students, hearing-impaired students, and students with impaired color vision than the language-based items on most ability tests. The NNAT1–Individual Administration does not require students to read, write, or speak; instead, they simply point to the answers they feel are correct.

Otis-Lennon School Ability Test   Perhaps the most widely used group intelligence test, the Otis–Lennon School Ability Test (OLSAT) (Otis & Lennon, 2002) consists of five subtests for estimating the intelligence of children from grades 1 through 12. The subtests are verbal comprehension, verbal reasoning, pictorial reasoning, figural reasoning, and quantitative reasoning. The OLSAT was standardized with the Stanford Achievement Test Series (Stanford 8) and administered with the Metropolitan Achievement Tests, Seventh Edition (MAT7). Giving the OLSAT with the Stanford 8 or the MAT7 yields an achievement/ability comparison index (AAC) that describes student ability in relation to the achievement of other students with the same measured ability.

Slosson Intelligence Test, Revised   The Slosson Intelligence Test, Revised (SIT-3) (Slosson, Nicholson & Hibpshman, 2002) is a measure of the cognitive ability of children from age 4 through adulthood. Designed for evaluating the mental ability of individuals who are learning disabled, mentally retarded, blind, or orthopedically disabled, the SIT-R provides a quick estimate of general verbal cognitive ability.

Test of Cognitive Skills, Second Edition   The Test of Cognitive Skills, Second Edition (TCS/2) (CBT/McGraw-Hill, 1992) contains four subtests: sequences, analogies, memory, and verbal reasoning. The TCS/2 measures the learning ability of students from grades 2 through 12 and takes approximately 50 minutes to administer. Scores are available for each subtest, and the combined scores yield an overall score called a Cognitive Skills Index (CSI). TCS/2 scores may also be used with scores from the Comprehensive Tests of Basic Skills (CTBS) or the California Achievement Test to predict achievement in later grades.

Wechsler Abbreviated Scale of Intelligence   The Wechsler Abbreviated Scale of Intelligence (WASI) (Wechsler, 1999) is a screening test for use in education, research, and clinical settings. The Wechsler Abbreviated produces verbal, performance, and full-scale IQ scores. Designed for children and adults from 6 to 89 years of age, the Wechsler Abbreviated can be given in four-subtest and two-subtest forms. The four-subtest form takes about 30 minutes to give, and it yields full-scale verbal and performance IQ scores. The two-subtest form takes about 15 minutes to give, and it yields only the full-scale IQ score. Useful for screening for possible exceptionalities such as mental retardation and gifted, the Wechsler Abbreviated is also helpful for reevaluating those who have previously had a complete evaluation. Other uses include estimating IQ scores with large samples of students, identifying students who may need comprehensive testing, estimating IQ scores for vocational, rehabilitation, and psychiatric purposes, and estimating IQ scores for research studies. As with all screening tests, care should be taken to avoid replacing diagnostic assessment of intelligence using a comprehensive test with the Wechsler Abbreviated.

Tests for Students with Unique Disabilities

The specialized intelligence tests are for students with severe language deficits, sensory impairments such as deafness and blindness, physical impairments, and severe mental retardation. Students with these disabilities have unique needs and characteristics that call for specialized assessment. By taking these unique characteristics into account, evaluators avoid errors in testing, difficulties in interpretation, and other inaccuracies in the assessment process. In most cases, special student characteristics do not prevent using a general test of intelligence, such as the WISC-IV. However, in some situations, unusual test-taking behaviors and learning styles preclude general tests. When this occurs, evaluators turn to one of several specialized intelligence tests to reduce errors and avoid discrimination.

The characteristics displayed by students with special needs vary depending on the specific disability. For example, tests that require motor performance, such as copying block designs, may be inappropriate for students with certain physical disabilities. Likewise, tests that emphasize verbal language skills may not be appropriate for students with hearing impairments. In a similar way, students with visual-perception impairments may not perform up to their ability level on tests that require visual-reasoning ability. Students with culturally different backgrounds also must be considered in intelligence testing because failure to consider their needs, experiences, and response styles may bias testing results. Although use of specialized intelligence tests is appropriately limited, they are valuable tools for situations in which students cannot be properly assessed using traditional instruments and methods. Descriptions of representative specialized tests follow.

Comprehensive Test of Nonverbal Intelligence   The Comprehensive Test of Nonverbal Intelligence (CTONI) (Hammill, Pearson, & Wiederholt, 1996) measures six different types of nonverbal reasoning abilities. No oral responses, reading, writing, or object manipulation are required. The CTONI is especially appropriate for use with individuals who are bilingual, speak a language other than English, or are socially/economically disadvantaged, deaf, language disordered, motor impaired, or neurologically impaired. Suitable for students ages 6 through 18, the CTONI is individually administered in less than 60 minutes. The raw scores of each subtest are translated into percentiles, age equivalents, and standard scores. Three composite scores are also provided: a nonverbal intelligence quotient, a pictorial nonverbal intelligence quotient, and a geometric nonverbal intelligence quotient. Standardized on a population of more than 2,000 students from 23 states, the CTONI exhibits adequate reliability and limited evidence regarding validity. The CTONI is also available in a computer-administered version, as described in the Technology Focus box.

Test of Nonverbal Intelligence, Third Edition   The Test of Nonverbal Intelligence, Third Edition (TONI-3) (Brown, Shervenou, & Johnsen, 1997) measures nonverbal intelligence and visual-reasoning ability. Useful with students who have limited language skills in reading, writing, speech, or listening, the age range of the TONI-3 is 5 to 85 years. Consisting of sets of abstract figures and drawings, the TONI-3 takes about 15 minutes to give. The evaluator may pantomime the simple instructions, if necessary, and the student responds by selecting the missing element from the sets of drawings, which test visual-matching ability and ability to comprehend visual analogies and progressions. The test is completely nonverbal and mostly motor free, requiring only a point, nod, or symbolic gesture to indicate response choices.

Evaluators may report TONI-3 results using an age-based standard score (M = 100, SD = 15) or a percentile rank. Two forms of the test provide a convenient method for retesting. Standardized on a sample of over 3,000 individuals, the TONI-3 exhibits adequate reliability. However, the manual presents limited information regarding validity.

Particularly useful with students who have limited English proficiency, speech and language problems, or physical impairments, the TONI-3 is a specialized instrument for measuring nonverbal problem-solving ability. Although restricted in scope, the TONI-3 represents a promising alternative to general intelligence testing in situations that require specialized instruments.

Reflection
While you were in school, did you take tests on the computer? Describe your reaction to this testing format.
What do you see as the benefits and the limitations of computer-based testing?

 To answer this reflection online, go to the *Teaching and Learning* module on the Companion Website at *www.prenhall.com/venn.*

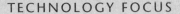

TECHNOLOGY FOCUS
Computer Administered Intelligence Testing

Computers are being used more frequently for all types of assessment, including intelligence testing. For example, virtually all intelligence tests now provide software programs that convert raw scores into standard scores and generate reports. In addition, one company has developed an innovative, interactive, multimedia intelligence test that students take entirely on a computer. The Comprehensive Test of Non-verbal Intelligence—Computer Administered (CTONI-CA) (Hammill, Pearson, & Wiederholt, 1997) uses the computer to give all the instructions to the student being tested in a clear, pleasant human voice. The student responds to questions by pointing the mouse and clicking the answer. The CTONI-CA automatically gives items until a ceiling is reached, and then the other subtests are given one by one. Students take the CTONI-CA at their own pace. When the testing is completed, the computer generates a report that can be viewed on the screen or printed, and the computer saves the report in a standard data format. Computer-based tests like the CTONI-CA offer many potential benefits, including saving time through automatic test administration, eliminating common scoring errors, and generating reports.

System of Multipluralistic Assessment   The System of Multicultural Pluralistic Assessment (SOMPA) (Mercer & Lewis, 1978) is significant because it made such a dramatic contribution to reducing racial and cultural bias in intelligence testing. Unlike traditional intelligence tests, the SOMPA is a comprehensive system that contains nine different measures for evaluating the intellectual abilities, perceptual-motor abilities, and adaptive behavior skills of students between the ages of 5 and 11 years. The SOMPA estimates learning potential by considering sociocultural and health factors as an integral part of the assessment process. By including evaluation of language and cultural differences in assessing intellectual performance, the SOMPA attempts to minimize racial and cultural bias in classifying and placing students in special education.

The SOMPA consists of two major components (parent interview materials and student assessment materials) and requires administration by a team of certified professionals. A trained social worker gives the parent interview to the student's primary caregiver in the home in about an hour. The parent interview includes three measures: (1) an adaptive behavior inventory, (2) a sociocultural scale, and (3) a health history inventory. A psychologist or diagnostician gives the student assessment in a school setting in about 2 hours. Materials in the student assessment component include measurement of physical dexterity, weight by height, visual acuity, auditory acuity, visual-motor skills, and intellectual ability (the latter determined by the Wechsler Intelligence Scale for Children or the Wechsler Preschool and Primary Scale of Intelligence).

In addition to using IQ scores in the conventional manner, the SOMPA scoring system accounts for social and cultural background variations by transforming WISC-R scores into a standard score referred to as estimated learning potential (ELP). The ELP represents ability level in comparison with students with similar backgrounds and avoids reliance on a traditional IQ score. Use of an ELP score rather than an IQ score is consistent with the views of Jane Mercer, one of the authors of the SOMPA, who advocates eliminating traditional IQ testing altogether because it tends to discriminate against certain students. However, other experts contend that ELP scores may not predict school performance as well as IQ scores. Furthermore, Sattler (2001) argues against using the SOMPA for classification and placement because of the inadequate validity of the ELP score and the lack of national norms. Although the SOMPA provides norms for Black, Hispanic, and White students, the norms were developed in California and therefore may not represent all students in other states.

Despite these criticisms, the SOMPA introduced many innovations that encourage reliance on culturally sensitive measures of behavior to support or modify classification decisions made during assessment. Although not widely used today, many of the features of the SOMPA have been incorporated into more contemporary measures, resulting in significant reductions in the number of students, especially minority students, who are clinically diagnosed as retarded but are not considered retarded in their home or community.

Universal Nonverbal Intelligence Test   One of the newest specialized intelligence tests, the Universal Nonverbal Intelligence Test (UNIT) (Bracken & McCallum, 1997) is a language-free test that requires no receptive or expressive language from the examiner or the examinee. According to McCallum and Bracken, tests like the UNIT are needed because of the increasing number of non-English-speaking or limited-English-proficient (LEP) students in the schools. Tests like the UNIT are also needed for children with hearing impairments or receptive and expressive language disabilities. Children with these impairments and those with limited English proficiency are unfairly disadvantaged when assessed by means of spoken language.

The UNIT, which is designed for use with children from age 5 through 17, contains six subtests in two major categories: memory and reasoning. The three memory subtests are object memory, spatial memory, and symbolic memory. The three reasoning subtests are cube design, mazes, and analogic reasoning. Completing the UNIT requires approximately 45 minutes; it may also be given in short form by administering only two or four subtests. The short-form versions require only 15 or 30 minutes to give and may have limited usefulness as gross screening measures. Available UNIT scores include a full-scale score, a memory quotient, a reasoning quotient, a symbolic quotient, and a nonsymbolic quotient. Individual subtest scores can also be obtained for each of the six subtests.

Standardized on a national sample, the initial reliability and validity data indicate that the UNIT displays adequate technical qualities and thus has the potential to become a valuable test in situations that require administration of a nonverbal intelligence test.

Tests for Infants, Toddlers, and Preschoolers

Infants, toddlers, and preschoolers represent a special population with unique characteristics, especially in the areas of language and communication. In general, specialized tests for this group of children estimate learning potential based on a relatively narrow sample of behavior, and unfortunately, some of these tests show limited reliability and validity. Because the behavior of very young children is less predictable and changes more rapidly than that of older students, measuring the intellectual development of infants, toddlers, and preschoolers is more difficult. For this reason, infant tests should be viewed as useful measures of development for predicting cognitive ability rather than as traditional measures of intelligence. Despite these limitations, tests of this type play an important role in identifying and serving very young students with special needs. Reviews of representative intelligence tests for infants, toddlers, and preschoolers follow.

Bayley Scales of Infant Development, Second Edition The most carefully designed and widely administered infant developmental scales are the Bayley Scales of Infant Development, Second Edition (BSID-II) (Bayley, 1993). Designed to measure the behavior of infants from 1 month to 30 months, the BSID-II includes a mental scale, a motor scale, and a behavior rating scale. The mental scale measures sensory and perceptual skills, vocalizations, memory, problem solving, and early verbal communication. The motor scale measures gross and fine motor skills. The behavior scale is a rating scale completed by a primary caregiver. The mental and motor scales take about 45 minutes to give, and each produces a standard score with a mean of 100 and a standard deviation of 16. Standardized using a national sample of over 1,000 infants, the Bayley Scales exhibit good technical characteristics. Split-half reliabilities for the mental scale range from .81 to .93 and for the motor scale from .68 to .92. Evidence supporting the construct validity of the test is available from numerous research studies with a variety of groups of infants. The Bayley Scales of Infant Development, Second Edition are tools for early identification of infants with disabilities and have separate mental and motor tests to pinpoint individual needs.

Bayley Infant Neurodevelopmental Screener A complementary product to the BSID-II is the Bayley Infant Neurodevelopmental Screener (BINS) (Aylward, 1995), which was developed for use by developmental pediatricians, pediatric nurse practitioners, occupational and physical therapists, and school psychologists who screen infants from 3 to 24 months. The BINS consists of items that assess basic neurological development, auditory and visual reception, cognitive process, and social development. Standardized on 600 infants, the sample represents infants from Neonatal Intensive Care Unit follow-up clinics who were born prematurely or asphyxiated at birth or who have experienced intraventricular hemorrhage, apnea, patent ductus arteriosus, or seizures. The BINS takes 5 to 10 minutes to give and a few more minutes to score. The individual items are scored as optimal or nonoptimal. Optimal items are summed, and the total score is determined relative to the cutoff score to determine an infant's risk classification.

Wechsler Preschool and Primary Scale of Intelligence, Third Edition The Wechsler Preschool and Primary Scale of Intelligence, Third Edition (WPPSI-III) (Wechsler, 2002) is for preschoolers from ages 2.6 through 7.3 years. One of the most widely used tests for measuring the intelligence of young children, the WPPSI-III contains 15 subtests and takes about 60 minutes to give. According to Coalson and Zhu (2001), this newest version provides updated normative data, increasing age-appropriateness and user-friendliness, and improved psychometric properties. The age-appropriateness and user-friendliness improvements include simplified, intuitive instructions to the child, less emphasis on speed performance, and the addition of more play-like tasks. The WPPSI-III also includes teaching and practice items for all subtests and less restricted use of queries and prompts.

☑ Check Your Comprehension

Specialized intelligence tests and intelligence tests for infants, toddlers, and preschoolers further illustrate the diversity that exists in the measurement of cognitive ability. Unlike general tests of intelligence, which rely primarily on verbal language skills, the specialized tests often depend on measurement of motor performance, visual reasoning ability, and receptive language skills to predict learning potential. The availability of so many tests provides a range of options in selecting appropriate measures for meeting the unique needs of students in special education.

The wide variety of specialized tests confirms the complexity of the concept of intelligence and also illustrates the diversity of opinion among test developers regarding methods for measuring cognitive ability. Representing attempts to make intelligence testing as fair as possible for students with unique learning characteristics and disabilities, these specialized tests provide viable alternatives, when used in appropriate situations, to the standard tests.

Guidelines for Teachers in Using Intelligence Test Results

Knowledge of intelligence tests is useless without considering the practical consequences of such testing. Because teachers provide direct services to students on a daily basis, they tend to be especially sensitive to the functional aspects of testing. The following applied, pragmatic considerations serve as guidelines for teachers to follow in using results from intelligence tests.

- When reporting an intelligence test score, always name the test and specify the date of testing as part of the reporting process. This is important because each test measures intelligence somewhat differently (e.g., an IQ of 68 on one test equals an IQ of 70 on another), and test scores more than 3 years old may not be as accurate as a current score.
- Although professionals should avoid making major educational decisions on the basis of test scores alone, the general procedure for interpreting intelligence test scores with a mean of 100 and a standard deviation of 15 is as follows:
Scores in the 85 to 115 range fall within 1 standard deviation from the mean (100 +/− 15) and reflect average intelligence.
Scores in the 115 to 130 range are 2 standard deviations above the mean and reflect above-average intelligence.
Scores of approximately 130 and above are more than 2 standard deviations above the mean and indicate superior intellectual ability.
Scores from 70 to 85 are 2 standard deviations below the mean and fall into the slow-learning category.
Very low IQs (below approximately 70 IQ points, or more than 2 standard deviations below the mean) indicate significant intellectual deficiency.
- Although intelligence and creativity are positively correlated, distinct differences also exist between the two traits. For this reason, teachers should avoid making assumptions about a student's creativity based on intelligence test results. In fact, because creativity is such a dynamic and divergent characteristic, evaluators rely on completely separate tests to measure it.
- Though the intelligence of individuals tends to remain stable throughout life, it can change over time. The specific factors that cause changes in intelligence are far from clear, but most experts agree that significant variations occur most frequently among those with extremely low or high levels of mental ability.
- Intelligence tests are excellent predictors of success in school, but they are poor predictors of other behaviors such as vocational success and personal or social satisfaction.
- Professionals must avoid judging intelligence test results in isolation. Instead they should consider intelligence test results along with other relevant assessment data,

including achievement, family history, motivation, adaptive behavior, and socio-cultural background.

- Intelligence tests play a key role in classifying and placing students in special education. However, most intelligence tests provide little information that directly translates into specific instructional objectives. Therefore, most teachers rely on estimates of intellectual ability as a guide in establishing overall educational goals rather than for identifying specific intervention needs.

Summary

Assessing intelligence, the process of measuring the learning ability of students, is a complex component of assessment in special education. Questions concerning the proper use of intelligence testing account for much of the complexity, but even the definition of intelligence itself is a topic of debate. Some contend that intelligence is a global ability, whereas others define it as a set of specific aptitudes. The diverse array of available intelligence tests further contributes to the complex nature of the subject. A summary chart listing the intelligence tests reviewed in this chapter appears in Table 7–1. Intelligence tests include the widely used general measures of intellectual ability, such as the WISC-IV, and a number of specialized instruments.

Table 7–1 Review of Intelligence Tests

Name	Type	Suitable for	Brief Description	Purpose
Batería III Woodcock-Muñoz	Comprehensive, individually administered general measure of intellectual ability and academic achievement	Individuals from age 2 through retirement	Spanish adaption and translation of the Woodcock-Johnson III (WJ III) Complete Battery	To measure the cognitive abilities and achievement levels of Spanish-speaking students
Bayley Infant Neurodevelopmental Screener (BINS)	Infant screening test	Infants from 3 to 24 months	Assesses basic neurological development, auditory and visual reception, verbal and motor expression, and cognitive processes	To screen infants and to obtain an estimate of the infant's risk classification
Bayley Scales of Infant Development, Second Edition (BSID-II)	Infant intelligence test	Infants from 1 to 42 months	Includes a mental scale, a motor scale, and a behavior rating scale	To identify children who have a cognitive or motor delay and to help develop intervention plans

(continued)

Table 7–1 *continued*

Name	Type	Suitable for	Brief Description	Purpose
Cognitive Abilities Test (CogAT)	Group-administered screening test	Students from kindergarten through 12th grade	Assesses reasoning and problem-solving abilities using verbal, quantitative and nonverbal subtests	To estimate potential for school success
CogAT Nonverbal Battery, Edición en Español	Nonverbal screening test	K–12 students who speak Spanish	Assesses reasoning and problem solving using spatial (nonverbal) symbols	To measure the intellectual abilities of Spanish-speaking students
Comprehensive Test of Nonverbal Intelligence (CTONI)	Nonverbal test	Students from age 6 to 18 years of age	Measures six different types of nonverbal reasoning abilities	To estimate the nonverbal intelligence of children who are from diverse cultural or linguistic backgrounds or who have disabilities
Comprehensive Test of Nonverbal Intelligence—Computer Administered (CTONI-CA)	Nonverbal test	Students from 6 to 18 years of age	Measures six different types of nonverbal reasoning abilities	To estimate nonverbal intelligence using a computer-administered test
Differential Ability Scales (DAS)	Individually administered, comprehensive test battery	Children and youth from 2 years 6 months to 17 years 11 months	Contains 17 cognitive subtests and 3 achievement subtests	To measure the general intellectual ability of children
Kaufman Assessment Battery for Children, Second Edition (KABC-II)	Comprehensive, individually administered, test battery	Children from 3 to 18 years	A general measure of intellectual ability and academic achievement with five subtests: simultaneous, sequential, planning, learning, and knowledge	To identify learning ability and achievement with specific procedures for use with students who have disabilities and for identifying preferred learning styles

Name	Type	Suitable for	Brief Description	Purpose
Multiple Intelligences Survey	Informal, criterion-referenced checklist	Students in grades 4–12	Includes nine sections measuring naturalist, musical, logical, existential, interpersonal, kinesthetic verbal, intrapersonal, and visual strengths	To informally measure multiple intelligences
Naglieri Nonverbal Ability Test—Individual Administration (NNATI – Individual Administration)	Nonverbal screening test	Children and youth from 5 to 17 years of age	Measures visual reasoning ability using four types of items: pattern completion, serial reasoning, reasoning by analogy, spatial visualization	To identify students who do not speak English as their first language and who may require further diagnostic testing
Otis-Lennon School Ability Test (OLSAT)	Group-administered screening test	Students from 1st through 12th grade	Consists of five subtests: verbal comprehension, verbal reasoning, pictorial reasoning, figural reasoning, and quantitative reasoning	To estimate potential for school success
Slosson Intelligence Test, Revised (SIT-R)	Screening test of verbal intelligence	Individuals from age 4 to adulthood	Contains six subtests: general information, similarities and differences, vocabulary, comprehension, arithmetic, and auditory memory	Designed for use as a quick estimate of general verbal cognitive ability

(continued)

Table 7–1 *continued*

Name	Type	Suitable for	Brief Description	Purpose
Stanford-Binet Intelligence Scales, Fifth Edition (SB5)	Comprehensive, individually administered test battery	Children and youth from 2 to 85+ years	Assesses five cognitive ability factors: fluid reasoning, knowledge, quantitative reasoning, visual-spatial processing, and working memory	To identify overall learning ability
Stanford-Binet Intelligence Scales for Early Childhood, Fifth Edition (Early SB5)	Comprehensive, individually administered test battery	Young children ages 2.0 to 7.3 years	Includes the subtests from the SB5 along with a test observation checklist and a software generated-parent report	To measure the general intelligence of young children
System of Multicultural Pluralistic Intelligence (SOMPA)	A system for estimating learning potential by considering sociocultural and health factors as an integral part of the testing process	Children between the ages of 5 and 11	Includes parent interview materials, student assessment materials, and procedures for evaluating language and cultural differences	Attempts to minimize racial and cultural bias in classifying and placing students in special education
Teele Inventory for Multiple Intelligences (TIMI)	An informal, criterion-referenced inventory	Students in grades 4 to 12	Includes an intelligence inventory, answer sheets, and a teacher's guide	To help teachers put multiple intelligences theory into action in their classrooms by identifying their students' strengths and talents
Test of Nonverbal Intelligence, Third Edition (TONI-3)	Specialized screening test for measuring nonverbal problem-solving ability	Individuals from 5 to 85 years of age	Measures nonverbal intelligence and visual-reasoning ability	For students with limited language skills in reading, writing, and speech, including students who have limited English proficiency, speech and language problems, or physical impairments

Name	Type	Suitable for	Brief Description	Purpose
Test of Cognitive Skills, Second Edition (TCS/2)	Group-administered screening test	Students in 2nd to12th grade	Contains four subtests: sequences, analogies, memory, and verbal reasoning	To estimate potential for school success
Wechsler Abbreviated Scale of Intelligence (WASI)	Screening test of general intelligence	Individuals from 6 to 89 years of age	Produces verbal, performance, and full-scale IQ scores	Useful for screening in a variety of situations requiring estimates of IQ scores
Wechsler Adult Intelligence Scale—Third Edition (WAIS-III)	Comprehensive, individually administered general test battery	Adults from 16 years to retirement	Contains two scales, verbal and performance, which can be given separately or together	To assess general learning ability
*Wechsler Intelligence Scale for Children—Fourth Edition (WISC IV)	Comprehensive, individually administered general test	Children from 6 to 16 years	A general measure of intellectual ability with four indexes: verbal comprehension, perceptual reasoning, working memory, and processing speed	To identify the global learning ability of children
Wechsler Preschool and Primary Scale of Intelligence —Third Edition (WPPSI-III)	Comprehensive, individually administered test battery	Children from 2.6 years to 7.3 years of age	Contains a verbal scale and a performance scale	To measure the intellectual abilities in young children; to classify and place young children with disabilities in special education
Woodcock-Johnson III Complete Battery (WJ-III)	Comprehensive, individually administered general measure of intellectual ability and academic achievement	Individuals from age 2 to retirement	Broad cognitive ability, academic achievement, and a variety of subtest and individual test scores	A valuable tool for making placement decisions and planning individual programs

(continued)

Table 7–1 *continued*

Name	Type	Suitable for	Brief Description	Purpose
Universal Nonverbal Intelligence Test (UNIT)	Language-free test that requires no receptive or expressive language	Children and youth from 5 to 19 years of age	A specialized measure of intelligence with subtests for memory and reasoning	Designed for non-English-speaking or LEP students and also for children with hearing impairments or receptive and expressive language disabilities

* Tests marked with an asterisk are featured in this chapter.

Although this variety adds to the intricacy of the subject, it also provides a range of options to choose from in selecting a test to meet the needs of the individual student.

In addition to the complex nature of the subject, controversy surrounds intelligence testing and the use of IQ scores. For special educators the debate encompasses several problems, including limited predictive validity, inaccuracy of IQ scores at the extremes, and bias against culturally and linguistically different students. As a result of these issues, some critics advocate the elimination of intelligence testing altogether. However, most experts support continued use of intelligence testing and promote continued efforts to improve assessment procedures and to reduce concerns about inequality and imprecision.

Because virtually all students in special education are given one or more intelligence tests, it is imperative for teachers to be familiar with the tests and understand the implications of the test results. Special education teachers equipped with this knowledge can better serve their students by helping to ensure accuracy and fairness in the use of intelligence tests.

 To check your comprehension of the chapter contents, go to the *Guided Review* and *Quiz* modules in Chapter 7 of the Companion Website, *www.prenhall.com/venn*.

Meeting Performance Standards and Preparing for Licensure Exams

The CEC Standards and PRAXIS™ material listed here connect with significant content in Chapter 7. The information in the parentheses identifies where to find the particular standard in the CEC Standards and the content reference in the PRAXIS™ material.

CEC Standards for Beginning Special Education Teachers

- Issues in definition and identification of individuals with exceptional learning needs, including those from culturally and linguistically diverse backgrounds (CC1K5)
- Issues, assurances, and due process rights related to assessment, eligibility, and placement within a continuum of services (CC1K6)
- Basic terminology used in assessment (CC8K1)
- Screening, prereferral, referral, and classification procedures (CC8K3)

- Interpret information from formal and informal assessments (CC8S5)
- Use assessment information in making eligibility, program, and placement decisions for individuals with exceptional learning needs, including those from culturally and/or linguistically diverse backgrounds (CC8S6)

PRAXIS™ Education of Exceptional Students: Core Content Knowledge

- Characteristics of students with disabilities including the influence of cognitive factors; affective and social-adaptive factors, including cultural, linguistic, gender, and socioeconomic factors; genetic, medical, motor, sensory, and chronological age factors (0353 I)
- Assessment including use of assessment for screening, diagnosis, placement, and the making of instructional decisions; for example: how to select and conduct nondiscriminatory and appropriate assessments and how to interpret standardized and specialized assessment results; procedures and test materials, both formal and informal, typically used for prereferral, screening, referral, classification, placement, and ongoing program monitoring (0353 III)

chapter 8

Developmental Assessment

Objectives

After reading this chapter, you will be prepared to do the following:

- Use developmental assessment with young children who have special needs.
- Apply the questions teachers ask in using the developmental approach in practical situations.
- Use curriculum-based developmental assessment procedures.
- Give developmental screening tests to identify children who are potentially at risk and need follow-up assessment.
- Administer diagnostic scales and developmental assessment systems
- Give readiness tests.
- Use specialized developmental tests for infants, toddlers, and preschoolers.

Overview

Developmental assessment, an increasingly important topic in special education, is the process of measuring and evaluating the growth and progress of children from infancy through the primary grades. Teachers of young children with disabilities need in-depth knowledge of developmental assessment. For other special educators, understanding developmental assessment is part of a comprehensive knowledge base in testing and evaluation.

This chapter assists you in learning the essential concepts and techniques of developmental assessment as it applies to young children with special needs. To achieve this goal, you consider the questions teachers ask about the developmental approach and examine the principles of developmental assessment. In addition, you investigate four types of developmental assessment instruments: screening tests, diagnostic scales, readiness tests, and specialized measures. Accompanying each type of instrument is a definition of the category, a description of representative evaluation tools, and a discussion of practical applications for special education teachers. At the conclusion of the chapter, you consider the current trends and issues in developmental assessment and review the developmental tests used most often by preschool teachers.

Defining and Describing Developmental Assessment

When Trisha Tisdale began her first year as a teacher of preschoolers with disabilities in a small rural school district she had several questions about developmental assessment. How could she use developmental screening tests to decide what to do and where to begin instructional

intervention with her new students? Which developmental assessment and intervention system should she use for IEPs, planning the curriculum, and measuring student progress? Should she use specialized developmental scales with children who have severe, multiple disabilities? Would she use any of the developmental readiness tests to determine the preparedness of her children for academic instruction? Ms. Tisdale decided to make an appointment with the coordinator for preschool programs to begin to develop answers to these questions.

In this chapter, you discover answers to Ms. Tisdale's questions about developmental assessment. You also learn about other ways teachers use developmental assessment in intervention programs for young children with special needs.

Defining Developmental Assessment

Developmental assessment is a specialized type of assessment for measuring the performance of young children, especially infants, toddlers, and preschoolers from birth to approximately 6 years of age. By utilizing predictable patterns that children follow as they grow, developmental assessment helps determine whether a child is following the normal sequence of skill acquisition at expected age levels. For example, the **developmental milestones** (critical skills in early childhood development), such as walking, saying one or two words, and toilet training, all occur at about the same age for most children. Children normally learn to walk and to say one or two words at about 1 year of age, and most children are toilet trained by age 2. Surprisingly, this similarity in development occurs across cultures and social classes for children up to approximately 6 years of age. For this reason, most developmental tests assess behavior within the age range of birth through 6 years. However, some instruments measure behavior beyond the 6-year-old level, and a few tools extend even into adulthood. In addition, specialized developmental scales evaluate behavior in narrow age ranges such as 4 to 6 years of age or birth to 3 years of age.

Experts in assessment of young children have given developmental tests a special name: **developmental scales**. Developmental scales are specialized checklists of behavior arranged by skill area in chronological order. Most developmental scales measure performance in several specific skill areas, often called **developmental**

learning areas. The curriculum in most educational intervention programs for infants, toddlers, and preschoolers includes these learning areas. The traditional developmental learning areas consist of the following:

- Fine motor (small muscle) skills
- Gross motor (large muscle) skills
- Communication and language development
- Social development
- Cognitive functioning
- Self-help skills

Specialized developmental scales evaluate behavior in additional learning areas such as sensorimotor skills and reflexive behaviors for infants and toddlers, and for preschool children, preacademic or readiness skills necessary for success in the first grade.

Using Developmental Assessment

In programs for young children, teachers use developmental scales as part of the diagnostic-prescriptive process. The diagnostic component encompasses administering a developmental scale to determine current levels of performance and, more important, to identify specific skills the child has learned, has not learned, and needs to learn next. The prescriptive component uses diagnostic information to develop a prescription or individual plan specifying appropriate goals for the child. The teacher then translates the objectives into learning activities and lessons for everyday use. Reassessment to measure progress over time occurs after implementing the individual prescription or intervention plan.

Comparing the results of the first assessment with the follow-up assessment provides an estimate of developmental growth. Revision of the child's individual program follows retesting. The revision process uses the reassessment data to establish new priorities for intervention, which become new or modified objectives in the individual plan. Such developmental assessment, however, should not take place in isolation but should occur as part of the overall intervention program that is consistent with best-practice guidelines and legal mandates, including the Individuals with Disabilities Education Act (IDEA).

Provisions for Infants and Toddlers in IDEA

The Individuals with Disabilities Education Act (IDEA) mandates a free, appropriate public education for 3- to 5-year-old children with disabilities and encourages early intervention programs for infants and toddlers under 3 years of age and their families. A key provision of the law requires the development of a special individual education plan (IEP) for each child. IDEA recognizes the importance of parents by replacing the IEP requirement with an **individual family service plan (IFSP)** requirement for infants and toddlers (birth through 3 years). Similar in content to the IEP, the guidelines for the IFSP include specific requirements for parental participation and additional regulations for assessing the child and the family.

Under IDEA, each child under 3 years must receive a multidisciplinary evaluation, which includes assessment of family needs. Like the IEP, the IFSP addresses the present levels of performance as well as goals and criteria for determining attainment of objectives. However, the family service plan assesses performance in the following areas:

- Physical development
- Cognitive development

- Language and speech development
- Psychosocial development
- Self-help skills

The law requires a statement of a family's strengths and needs related to their child and mandates a justification of the extent, if any, to which services will not be provided in a natural environment.

From this description, you can see the important role of assessment in planning programs for all children with disabilities. Furthermore, IDEA mandates use of a diagnostic-prescriptive approach to assessment and intervention by requiring the following:

- Identification of present levels of performance (diagnosis)
- Development of an intervention program based on goals (prescription)
- Follow-up evaluation to determine attainment of objectives (diagnosis)
- Revision of objectives (update of the prescription)

This legislation also calls for nondiscriminatory assessment procedures. To ensure nondiscriminatory testing, evaluation materials must be provided in the child's native language or other appropriate communication mode. In addition, the tests given to children with impaired sensory, manual, or speaking skills should accurately reflect the child's ability level rather than the child's impaired skills. This means that tests must be carefully selected to avoid discrimination. Obviously, for teachers to meet all of these legal mandates by themselves is difficult if not impossible. Therefore, teachers serve as members of a team that includes other professionals and parents. Further information about nondiscriminatory assessment including considerations regarding sociocultural influences appears in the accompanying Multicultural Considerations feature.

MULTICULTURAL CONSIDERATIONS

Sociocultural Influences

When assessing young children, we should be aware of and sensitive to the many sociocultural differences that may influence a child's performance. The following practical guidelines, developed by McAffee and Leong (1997), are especially suited to assessing young children. The basic principle is to assume that there will be sociocultural differences in children's actions, behaviors, and responses and then to account for these differences in the assessment process. A second important guideline is to involve parents, the community, and language, cultural, and social specialists in the assessment process. We should also be sure to use a variety of assessment approaches that allow children to demonstrate their full potential. This may involve rephrasing, restating, or recasting assessment tasks in ways that might be familiar and understandable to a child. It may also include changing assessment settings to ones that are more familiar to the child. When we do this, we are better able to assess the child's interests and activities by linking them to their homes and communities.

Think of ways you would change the testing environment for a 2-year-old from another country.

To answer this reflection online, go to the *Multicultural Considerations* module on the Companion Website at *www.prenhall.com/venn*.

The Team Approach

Because no single professional possesses all the knowledge and skills necessary to comprehensively assess a student, the team approach to developmental diagnosis enables professionals to combine efforts with parents to obtain the best possible assessment data for meeting the needs of the child and the family. The team approach relies on the expertise of professionals from various disciplines as well as on the family. Assessment teams often consist of several professionals, including teachers, home intervention specialists, therapists, diagnosticians, and social workers. Although several team approaches exist, the typical process involves having each team member assess the student in the team member's area of expertise. For example, the teacher may assess social skills, the occupational therapist might evaluate self-help skills, the physical therapist usually appraises gross motor skills, and the speech and language pathologist may measure performance in language and communication. Parents participate in the assessment activities as appropriate, and after completing the assessment, the team members identify and discuss priorities for intervention. In a staff meeting, the participants establish a set of intervention goals for the child and the family. Focus 8–1 discusses an innovative approach that relies on a simultaneous evaluation arrangement called arena assessment.

Questions Teachers Ask About the Developmental Approach

Use of developmental scales involves answering the following four questions:

1. What is normal development?

2. Is the child following the normal developmental pattern?

3. If not, why are delays in development occurring?

4. What can be done about the developmental delays?

F OCUS 8-1

Arena Assessment

Arena assessment is an innovative approach to team evaluation using a team of professionals from various disciplines who simultaneously evaluate a child in the same setting. By conducting the evaluation together, the team makes decisions based on a collective sample of behavior, and they have opportunities to talk with each other about those decisions. Because the team works together, they see all aspects of the child's development rather than separate sensory, motor, intellectual, language, and social domains. This approach has advantages for everyone: the child, the family, and the professionals. Arena assessment avoids the problem of having to schedule separate evaluation sessions, and this makes the process shorter. The parents or primary caregivers have to provide information only once instead of answering similar questions in separate sessions with individual professionals. A key advantage for professionals is immediate access to the skills and knowledge of their colleagues. This helps the team make unified assessment decisions regarding what is best for the child and the family (McLean & Crais, 1996).

What Is Normal Development?

Normal development refers to the typical patterns of skill acquisition that children follow as they grow, develop, and learn. Child development specialists have found that this pattern is remarkably similar among children. These well-documented patterns constitute the standard of behavior for measuring the developmental progress of individual children.

Is the Child Following the Normal Developmental Pattern?

Although most children follow a predictable developmental pattern, some progress much faster than average, and others exhibit significant developmental delays in one or more learning areas. Developmental diagnosis uses assessment procedures to identify patterns of individual development, which include determining the extent and nature of any deviations from normal development, identifying strengths and weaknesses within and across learning areas, and detecting splinter skills or gaps in development. **Splinter skills** are behaviors developed in isolation from related skills, such as learning to write the letters of the alphabet without understanding the meaning of the letters. **Gaps in development** are deficits in major skill areas that impede the development of higher-level skills. For example, problems with the basic locomotion skill of walking may block the development of higher-level locomotion skills such as running, jumping, skipping, and hopping.

Why Are Delays in Development Occurring?

If evaluators identify the presence of significant variations from normal development, they should determine the reasons for the variability. Reasons for deviation from normal development may include physical or sensory problems, such as a visual impairment that prevents a child from performing a particular skill, behavioral problems, cognitive delays, or a lack of experience and exposure. Identifying these reasons is vital in deciding the best possible approach to intervention.

What Can Be Done About the Developmental Delays?

After identifying specific delays and the reasons for those delays, the developmental approach to intervention involves creating an intervention program to help a child learn the skills or behaviors that occur next in the normal sequence. For example, a child who demonstrates the ability to copy a vertical and a horizontal line with a crayon should next learn to copy a circle and a cross. Likewise, after children learn single words, they are ready to begin saying two- and three-word sentences. The extent to which teachers follow the normal developmental sequence in intervention depends on several factors, including the severity of the delays, the reasons for and the extent of the developmental delays, and the child's age. In general, the developmental approach works best with young children. Older students often require a functional or practical skills approach to meet their needs. Functional skills are practical life skills associated with independence in daily living activities.

Principles of Developmental Assessment

The developmental assessment principles that follow are guidelines for professionals in using the developmental approach to assess the behavior and performance of young children. Originally described by Banus (1971) in a textbook for occupational therapists, these principles include the following:

- Children follow a predictable sequence as they develop.
- Lower developmental skills precede higher developmental skills.
- Higher skills usually begin to emerge before lower skills drop out.
- Developmental progress depends in part on maturation.
- Teachable moments exist for children as they grow.
- Children with disabilities may skip stages of development.
- Children with severe handicaps may develop abnormal patterns of development.

Predictable Sequence of Development

Children follow a predictable pattern as they grow. For this reason, test writers arrange the items on developmental scales according to this sequence. Teachers rely on this predictable sequence when they use developmental scales as curriculum guides for designing intervention programs and arranging learning activities.

Lower Skills Precede Higher Skills

Because skills develop in a predictable pattern, lower skills must precede higher skills. For example, scribbling (a lower skill) is a prerequisite for learning to draw the basic geometric shapes (a higher skill). Likewise, learning the meanings of words receptively represents a lower skill that is necessary for learning the higher-level skill of saying words expressively. Teachers rely on developmental scales, their knowledge of child development, and their experience with children to determine if a child has learned the prerequisite skills needed to begin learning higher-level skills.

Emergence of Higher Skills

In concert with the lower-to-higher skills concept is the principle that lower skills need not drop out completely before higher skills begin to emerge. Many teachers and parents have experienced a classic illustration of this principle with children who crawl and creep while simultaneously learning to walk. With nondisabled children, higher-level skills like walking seem to emerge naturally. However, with young children who have disabilities, higher-level skills may not emerge without intervention. Special educators rely on their professional judgment and experience to decide when to introduce higher-level skills, and intervention largely depends on the needs and interests of the particular child.

Maturation

Developmental progress depends in part on maturation of the nervous system as well as psychological maturation. For this reason, teachers should not expect performance of a skill until the child demonstrates the necessary physical and psychological maturation levels for learning that particular skill.

Teachable Moments

The principle of the **teachable moment** refers to the optimal time during which a child is physically, psychologically, and emotionally ready to learn a particular skill. Other terms for this phenomenon include the *critical period* and the *critical moment*. Developmental assessment helps professionals identify critical moments by determining mastered, emerging, and unlearned skills. When a teacher attempts to introduce a new skill before the critical moment, it may be difficult if not impossible for the child to learn the skill. Likewise, when teachers introduce a skill after the critical period, acquisition becomes increasingly difficult. For example, an infant reaches the critical moment for learning the eating skill of chewing at an early age (approximately 6 months). It is difficult (and dangerous due to the risk of choking on food) to introduce chewing before this age. If a child skips the chewing stage, it may become increasingly difficult to learn the skill at older ages.

Skipping Developmental Stages

Children with disabilities often skip stages of development. This may lead to gaps in development and splinter skills. A gap in development is a delay or slowdown in the development of a particular skill or set of skills. A splinter skill is a skill learned in isolation from related skills. Teachers use developmental tests to identify gaps and splinter skills in need of remedial programming.

Abnormal Patterns of Development

Children with severe disabilities often fail to follow the normal sequence of development and may even develop abnormal patterns due to the severity of their disabilities. For example, children with severe physical impairments frequently retain reflexive movements that normal infants integrate into higher-level movement patterns in the first few months of life. When children retain reflexive movement patterns, they may have difficulty learning to move, communicate, or perform self-help skills. For example, in the self-help skill area of eating, some children develop abnormal gag and bite reflexes due to physical impairments. These abnormal movement patterns often impair the ability to learn how to chew food and to develop normal speech.

Why Do We Use Developmental Assessment?

The following narrative illustrates how a diagnostic teacher used developmental assessment to evaluate the learning needs of J.J.

J.J., small, disheveled, and withdrawn, sat alone in a corner of the diagnostic classroom and did nothing: he did not participate, play, or even misbehave. In the meantime, he continued to fail the developmental milestones for his age group.

Curious about this unusual young child, the diagnostic teacher who was to administer a developmental test checked his records. The developmental screening test results from the Developmental Indicators for the Assessment of Learning, Third Edition (DIAL-3) identified potential delays in development, and the social history report indicated that J.J.'s mother had died when he was an infant and that his grandmother was raising him.

When the diagnostic teacher began testing J.J. with the Battelle Developmental Inventory, Second Edition (BDI-II), he withdrew and after several failed attempts, the teacher had to reschedule the testing for another day. During the next testing session, J.J. began withdrawing again. However, to avoid repeating the earlier failure, the diagnostic teacher tried popcorn and other tangible rewards for effort. Finally, J.J. began to interact, and the diagnostic teacher completed the testing successfully. For J.J. it was a positive experience. For the diagnostic teacher, it illustrated the necessity of modifying testing procedures to meet the needs of the individual student.

Afterward, the assessment team relied on the evaluation results provided by the diagnostic teacher to support the conclusion that although J.J. displayed some serious developmental lags, he performed many behaviors representative of his chronological age when given additional reinforcement.

After spending several weeks in the diagnostic classroom, J.J. returned to his regular preschool program (with some extra help from the staff). At age 5, J.J. was retested with the BDI-II. The results showed remarkable progress, and J.J. enrolled in a regular kindergarten program.

This vignette illustrates the use of developmental assessment instruments and procedures with young children who have special needs. The purpose of developmental screening using instruments such as the DIAL-3 is to identify young children with potential developmental delays. We also use screening to suggest what to do with new students and where to begin instruction while awaiting comprehensive developmental diagnosis. We use developmental diagnosis to identify, classify, and place infants, toddlers, and preschoolers. We also use developmental diagnosis in programming and curriculum development, including writing IEPs and developing intervention programs. The Battelle Developmental Inventory (BDI) is a developmental scale often used in developmental diagnosis to identify children with disabilities, to aid in curriculum and program development, and to measure developmental progress. A summary of the use of developmental assessment appears in Focus 8–2.

☑ Check Your Comprehension

Developmental assessment measures and evaluates the growth and progress of young children. An understanding of its purpose, use, and principles helps build a comprehensive knowledge base in this increasingly important area. This information, coupled with insight into legal mandates and programming implications, serves as the basis for considering the various types of developmental instruments used in special education. Teachers use developmental assessment as a component in the diagnostic-prescriptive process.

*F*OCUS 8-2

Why Do We Use Developmental Assessment?

- To screen young children for potential developmental and learning problems
- To assist in the process of diagnosing the disabilities of children with learning problems
- To assess the readiness skills of young children with special needs
- To obtain data and information for writing individual plans and developing interventions
- To measure the developmental progress of young children with special needs

Developmental Assessment Instruments

Like all assessment, developmental assessment includes a variety of different instruments. Each instrument has a different goal and produces specific assessment results. Developmental assessment instruments include screening tests, diagnostic scales, readiness tests, and specialized tests. Although overlap exists among instruments, each fulfills a different purpose. Developmental screening tests produce thumbnail sketches of overall development. In contrast, developmental scales furnish in-depth information about strengths, weaknesses, and gaps in development. Most readiness tests help determine whether a student is ready for the typical first-grade curriculum. The readiness tests focus on preacademic skills and concepts. Finally, specialized tests include scales and procedures for assessing children with unique needs, including infants and children with severe and profound disabilities. In most situations, developmental assessment begins with screening.

Developmental Screening

Developmental screening helps identify the general performance levels of young children from birth to approximately 6 years of age. Screening alerts parents and professionals to children who may have a developmental delay or learning disability. In addition, teachers often rely on developmental screening to develop initial programming goals with new students. When professionals conduct developmental screening, they use concise, abbreviated tests and evaluation procedures that provide an overall picture of functioning. Although developmental screening is an efficient way to identify children with possible delays, professionals must avoid using screening to label children or diagnose developmental disabilities. Screening focuses on one question: Does a potential learning or behavior problem exist that requires further attention?

Limited Predictive Validity of Developmental Screening Tests

Compared with diagnostic assessment, developmental screening tests and procedures exhibit limited predictive validity. This is due to the short length of screening tests coupled with the instability and the rapidly changing behavior of young children. As a result, evaluators must interpret results from developmental screening cautiously. Although screening provides useful information regarding possible levels of performance, professionals should treat screening results as estimates rather than exact or precise measures.

Guidelines for Developmental Screening

Screening guidelines are available from a variety of sources including the Committee on Children and Disabilities (2001) and the Illinois Association for Supervision and Curriculum Development (1990). These guidelines include practical considerations for meeting the needs of young children, such as:

- Rely on play as a key part of all screening activities.
- Conduct interactions with the child in a positive manner.
- Emphasize hands-on activities rather than paper-and-pencil tasks.
- Provide parents with written information about the purpose and limitations of screening.
- Allow parents to stay with their child during screening.

- Include a parent interview as part of the screening.
- Give parents immediate feedback about the results of the screening.
- Involve parents as active members of the screening team.
- Ensure that all evaluators have experience with the children being screened.
- Certify that all screeners are specifically trained, sensitive to sociocultural issues, and knowledgeable about the limitations of screening instruments.
- Follow developmental screening with formal audiological testing and vision screening.

Reflection
Why is there an emphasis on parent participation in the screening process?

To answer this reflection online, go to the *Teaching and Learning* module on the Companion Website at *www.prenhall.com/venn.*

Although these guidelines pertain to the screening process with young children, they are applicable to assessment activities in general. The emphasis on parent participation highlights the key role of the family in the assessment process.

Who Uses Developmental Screening?

Many professionals use developmental screening with young children. Special education teachers rely on screening tests when they conduct initial observations and form first impressions of new students. Teachers screen new students to identify levels of performance and determine the special needs and interests of the child and the family. Intervention specialists, who serve infants and toddlers in home-based programs, employ similar screening techniques as they begin working with children and their families. Specialists, such as speech and language pathologists, occupational therapists, and physical therapists, also depend on screening to identify children who may need therapy services.

A different use of screening involves conducting group screening at day-care centers and preschool kindergarten programs to identify children who are potentially at risk. Medical professionals, including pediatricians, nurses, and medical social workers, also employ developmental screening to identify children who may need to be referred for diagnostic assessment. Psychologists and educational diagnosticians also rely on screening tests as one of the initial steps in the assessment process.

Representative Developmental Screening Tests

Two representative developmental screening tests in widespread use are the Developmental Indicators for the Assessment of Learning, Third Edition (DIAL-3) and the Denver II. The DIAL-3, which is designed for use in group and individual settings, represents one of the leading tests of its type. Originally published in 1954, the Denver II was one of the first developmental screening tests and is still used today by many professionals.

Developmental Indicators for the Assessment of Learning, Third Edition

The Developmental Indicators for the Assessment of Learning, Third Edition (DIAL-3) (Mardell-Czudnowski & Goldenberg, 1998) assesses learning in motor development, conceptual development, language skills, self-help skills, and social development. Designed for individual administration by a single evaluator or group administration by a team of professionals and paraprofessionals, it requires 30 to 45 minutes to give. The DIAL-3 (summarized in the Test Review box) identifies children who need a complete diagnostic evaluation and is easy to use, with well-designed administration procedures and many supplemental features.

TEST REVIEW

Developmental Indicators for the Assessment of Learning, Third Edition

Type of Test:	Norm-referenced, group or individually administered
Purpose:	A screening test of developmental learning
Content Areas:	Motor development, concept development, language skills, self-help skills, and social development
Administration Time:	30 to 45 minutes
Age Levels:	3 to 6 years
Suitable for:	Identifying students with potential delays who need further evaluation
Scores:	The Dial-3 provides standard deviation and percentile cutoff points for total and subtest scores. Percentile ranks and standard scores are also provided.
In Short:	The well-designed DIAL-3 is a global screener appropriate for individual administration by a single evaluator or group administration by a team of professionals and paraprofessionals.

Screening teams frequently give the DIAL-3 to all of the children in a particular site such as a day-care center, a preschool progam, a group of kindergarten classes, or a Head Start program. Children scoring below the cutoff level are referred for a complete developmental evaluation as a follow-up to the screening process. In addition, the DIAL-3 is useful for assessing children on an individual basis.

DIAL-3 Materials   The DIAL-3 kit consists of a large canvas carrying bag that contains a manual, score sheets, parent questionnaires, manipulatives, dials, operator's handbooks in English and Spanish, and a training packet. The well-designed materials appeal to young children, making it easy to conduct assessment in a playlike atmosphere. Optional materials include a training video, a computer-assisted scoring program, and scannable software for exporting data. Further information about the computer scoring software appears in Technology Focus box.

DIAL-3 Administration and Scoring   When given to a group of children at a pre-arranged screening site, administration begins with a warm-up period for the children. After the children feel comfortable, they are guided through different testing stations. A play area serves as a waiting station. The DIAL-3 provides standard deviation and percentile cutoff points by chronological age at 2-month intervals for total and subtest scores in motor, concepts, language, self-help, and social areas. Percentile ranks and standard scores are also provided. A sample from the DIAL-3 showing decisions for the five screening areas and the DIAL-3 total recorded on the score summary for Ray (chronological age 4 to 8) appears in Figure 8–1. An example of the overall screening decision recorded on the front of Ray's record form appears in Figure 8–2.

DIAL-3 Technical Characteristics   Standardized on a sample of 1,560 English-speaking and 650 Spanish-speaking children, the DIAL-3 exhibits adequate technical qualities for use as a screening measure. The test developers conducted

TECHNOLOGY FOCUS
Computer Scoring Software

Available DIAL-3 software includes a Computer ASSIST for DIAL-3 program that enables fast, convenient, and accurate scoring along with the ability to print a complete scoring report and a report for parents. The report includes identifying information, a score summary, a narrative account of the screening results, and recommendations. The DIAL-3 also includes a scannable form for exporting data in a format usable by statistical and database programs for further analysis.

School districts are increasingly relying on software like this. For example, schools in Wichita, Kansas use the DIAL-3 to screen kindergarten children in the fall and the spring (American Guidance Service, 2001). In 1999–2000, the district screened 4,000 students to identify their overall developmental level, to identify students with potential developmental delays, and to measure progress. The school district used scannable forms that enabled developing customized reports and moving the testing data into a database for further analysis. In the 2000–2001 year, the district expanded this successful screening program to include prekindergarten children.

Figure 8–1   DIAL-3 Score summary for Ray (Ages 4 to 8)

Score Summary

Area	Scaled Score Total	Other	Decision — Potential delay	Decision — OK
Motor	7		X	
Concepts	13			X
Language	12			X
DIAL-3 Total	32			X

Area	Raw Score Total	Other	Decision — Potential delay	Decision — OK
Self-Help Development	19			X
Social Development	23			X

Use cutoffs found in Appendix E in the manual.
Cutoffs chosen:

- ☐ 16 percent (1.0 *SD*)
- ☐ 10 percent (1.3 *SD*)
- ☒ 7 percent (1.5 *SD*)
- ☐ 5 percent (1.7 *SD*)
- ☐ 2 percent (2.0 *SD*)

Sumario de puntaje

Area	Puntaje total compensado	Otro	Decisión — Retraso potencial	Decisión — OK
Motora	7		X	
Conceptos	13			X
Lenguaje	12			X
Total del DIAL-3	32			X

Area	Puntaje base ajustado	Otro	Decisión — Retraso potencial	Decisión — OK
Desarrollo de autosuficiencia	21			X
Desarrollo social	25			X

Use los valores indicados en el apéndice E del manual.
Valores elegidos:

- ☐ 16 por ciento (1.0 *SD*)
- ☐ 10 por ciento (1.3 *SD*)
- ☒ 7 por ciento (1.5 *SD*)
- ☐ 5 por ciento (1.7 *SD*)
- ☐ 2 por ciento (2.0 *SD*)

Source: From C. D. Mardell-Czudnowski & D. S. Goldenberg, 1998. *Developmental Indicators for the Assessment of Learning, Third Edition* (*DIAL-3*). Circle Pines, MN: American Guidance Service. Reprinted with permission of American Guidance Service, Inc.

Figure 8–2   Overall DIAL-3 screening decision for Ray (Ages 4 to 8)

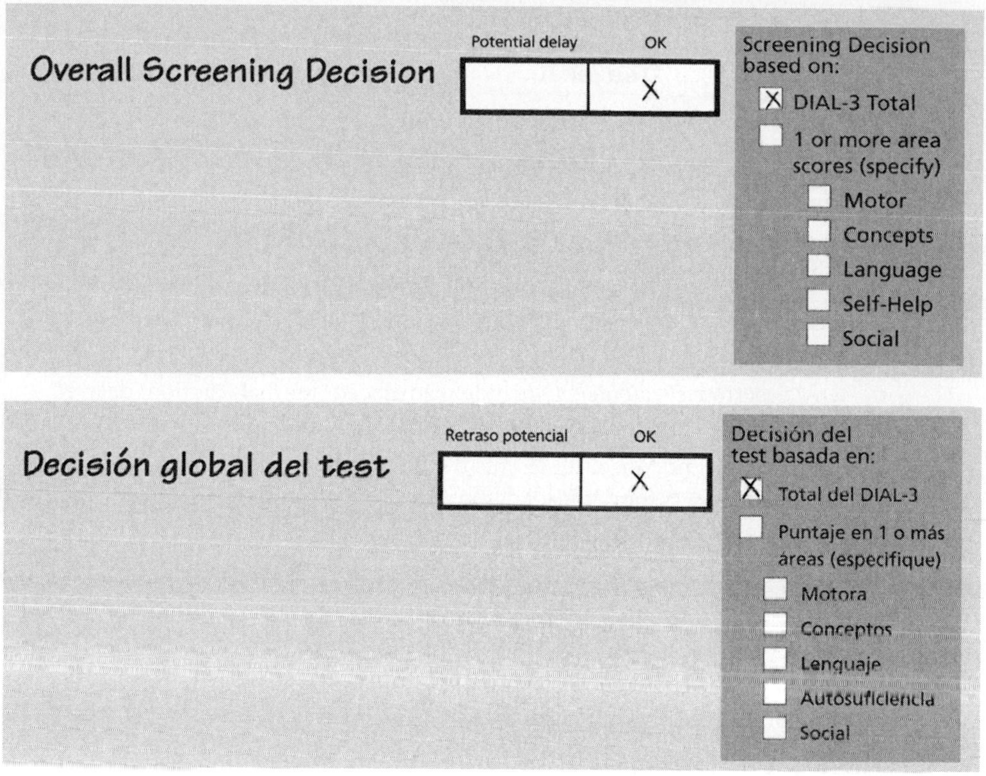

appropriate reliability and validity studies as part of the revision process, and additional studies using the DIAL and the DIAL-R have been conducted during the past two decades, providing further evidence of validity.

DIAL-3 Summary   The primary purpose of the DIAL-3, which is useful in a variety of settings, is to identify children with potential delays who need further evaluation. The instrument can be given to individuals or groups of children. The test kit includes well-designed materials for training an assessment team, making the DIAL-3 an excellent instrument for personnel preparation, especially in assessment courses that emphasize early intervention.

Denver II

The Denver II (Frankenburg et al., 1990) is an individually administered screening test for children from birth to 6 years of age. The Denver II evaluates developmental learning in personal-social, fine motor adaptive, language, and gross motor skills; see the Test Review box for a test summary. The authors initially designed the test for health care providers to screen young children in hospital settings, but professionals in many disciplines, including special educators, also use the instrument.

Denver II Materials   The well-designed Denver II test materials include a one-page score sheet and a brief manual. The Denver II features a compact test kit and

TEST REVIEW

Denver II

Type of Test:	Norm referenced, individually administered
Purpose:	A screening test of developmental learning
Content Areas:	Personal-social, fine motor adaptive, gross motor, and language skills
Administration Time:	20 to 30 minutes
Age Levels:	Birth to 6 years
Suitable for:	Identifying students with potential developmental delays who need further evaluation
Scores:	Uses descriptive statements, including advanced, normal, caution, delayed, and untestable, rather than number scores
In Short:	The Denver II no longer represents the best of the available developmental screening tests. Strong consideration should be given to using other screening instruments.

easy-to-follow scoring procedures. After an examiner becomes familiar with the test items, the brief manual is not needed to give the test.

Denver II Administration and Scoring   Administering the Denver II takes 20 to 30 minutes. As with the DIAL-3, the evaluator uses descriptive statements to interpret performance on individual items. The Denver II descriptions include advanced, normal, caution, and delayed. The evaluator, who has the option of scoring some items on the basis of a report from a parent or another primary caregiver, interprets overall performance by summarizing a child's performance on individual items and each subtest. The Denver II suggests that evaluators consider using the term *untestable* to interpret the performance of a child who refuses to perform most of the items. Unfortunately, some evaluators have relied on terms such as *untestable* to unfairly label children for whom appropriate assessment procedures were not available. Furthermore, labeling a child "untestable" using results from a brief screening test violates contemporary legal, ethical, and professional standards because a child's performance during a 20-minute testing session may not represent typical ability or overall behavior. Most special educators believe that the inability to test a particular child results from the lack of suitable testing procedures and that no child is untestable even though some children may be difficult to test.

Denver II Technical Characteristics   Test developers standardized the Denver II with a sample of more than 2,000 children from Colorado. Unfortunately, establishing norms with a sample group from only one state limits the representativeness of those norms. Despite this weakness, data on the Denver II indicate that the instrument exhibits appropriate validity and reliability.

Denver II Summary   Although the Denver II is substantially improved in comparison to the earlier edition of the test, the instrument no longer represents the best of the available screening tests for use in educational settings. In most situations, strong consideration should be given to selecting other screening instruments.

Snapshots of Other Developmental Screening Tests

In addition to the DIAL-3 and the Denver II, a number of other tests are useful in screening the developmental progress of young children. Snapshots of several of these tests follow.

AGS Early Screening Profiles The AGS Early Screening Profiles (ESP) (Harrison et al., 1990) measures performance in cognitive/language, motor, and self-help/social skills, and surveys the child's articulation, home environment, health history, and behavior. Designed to provide practical information to help make accurate screening decisions, the norm-referenced ESP is for children from 2 through 6 years of age and can be administered individually or to groups of children using a format in which children move from station to station. The entire instrument takes about 45 minutes to administer and offers two levels of scoring. Level I scores, which can be obtained quickly, consist of three descriptive statements—above average, average, or below average—for the three subtests. Level II scores include standard scores, normal curve equivalents, percentiles, stanines, and age equivalents for the three subtests and the total test. Level II scores also include descriptive statements of above average, average, or below average for the three subtests and the total test. The ESP was standardized on more than 1,000 children, and the manual provides considerable evidence regarding the reliability and validity of the instrument.

Brigance Screens The Brigance Screens are a series of four developmental screening tests: the Brigance Infant and Toddler Screen (Brigance, 2002) for ages birth to 23 months, Brigance Early Preschool Screen-II (Brigance, 2005a) for ages 2 and $2^{1}/_{2}$, the Brigance Preschool Screen-II (Brigance, 2005c) for ages 3 and 4, and the Brigance K&1 Screen-II (Brigance, 2005b) for kindergarten and first grade. All four Brigance instruments are available in English and Spanish versions. The tests yield an overall score with a total of 100 possible points. The manual recommends referring children who score below 60 points for further testing. The Brigance Screens instruments are criterion-referenced, and the manuals fail to provide reliability or validity information. For this reason, care should be taken to avoid using the instruments in making referral decisions. The instruments are most useful as brief curriculum guides for teachers to use with new children. Teachers can use Brigance Screens information to obtain ideas of what to do and where to begin while awaiting more comprehensive assessment.

FirstSTEP: Screening Test for Evaluating Preschoolers FirstSTEP: Screening Test for Evaluating Preschoolers (Miller, 1993) is an individually administered, norm-referenced screening test for children from 2 years 9 months, to 6 years 2 months and is designed to identify preschool children who are at risk for developmental delays in the five areas mandated by IDEA: cognition, communication, motor, social-emotional, and adaptive behavior. FirstSTEP also provides an optional parent/teacher scale that adds information about the child's typical behavior at home and at school to the behavior observed during screening. FirstSTEP takes about 15 minutes to administer.

Early Screening Inventory, Revised The Early Screening Inventory, Revised (ESI–R) (Meisels, Marsden, Wiske, & Henderson, 1997) is a norm-referenced, individually administered, developmental screening instrument for children from 3 to 6 years of age. The purpose of the ESI-R is to help identify young children who are at high risk for school failure and who may need special services. It takes about 15 to 20 minutes to give the ESI-R. The ESI-R includes a preschool version (ESI–P) and a kindergarten version (ESI–K). A complete Spanish version is available. The inventory assesses development in visual-motor/adaptive, language and cognition, and gross motor skills.

☑ Check Your Comprehension

Screening is a major category of developmental assessment that includes an assortment of tools. The diversity of available instruments allows professionals from a number of disciplines to use developmental screening as an important step in identifying children with potential disabilities who need further assessment. As with all assessment, the selection of a particular instrument depends on the needs of the individual child and the purpose of the screening.

Diagnostic Scales of Developmental Skills

Unlike screening tests, which provide an overview of developmental learning, diagnostic scales of developmental skills produce a comprehensive, in-depth evaluation of performance. Special educators require such diagnostic information to identify young children who require special education services, to place young children into appropriate programs, to develop individual plans, to develop intervention objectives, and to measure progress. To meet these diverse requirements, professionals may select from a variety of diagnostic scales. The following reviews of three representative tests illustrate the characteristics of diagnostic scales of developmental skills. The reviews cover several of the foremost instruments, including the Learning Accomplishment Profile, Third Edition, the Battelle Developmental Inventory, Second Edition, and the Brigance Diagnostic Inventory of Early Development-II.

Learning Accomplishment Profile, Third Edition

The Learning Accomplishment Profile, Third Edition (LAP-3) (Hardin, Eisner-Feinburg, & Weeks, 2005) measures the development of children from 26 to 72 months

---

TEST REVIEW

Learning Accomplishment Profile, Third Edition

Type of Test:	Criterion-referenced, individually administered
Purpose:	A diagnostic test of developmental learning
Content Areas:	Cognitive, fine motor and prewriting, personal social, language and literacy, gross motor, and self-help skills
Administration Time:	3 to 4 hours
Age Levels:	36 to 72 months
Suitable for:	Students with mild and moderate developmental delays
Scores:	Percentile ranks, standard deviation scores by age for subscales, and developmental age scores
In Short:	The LAP-3 is one of the leading diagnostic tests of developmental skills. It is useful as a diagnostic tool and programming guide.

of age. A summary of the LAP-3 appears in the Test Review box. The instrument is useful as both a diagnostic test and a curriculum guide.

The LAP-3 is an effective diagnostic tool for determining whether a student displays age-appropriate developmental skills. It generates detailed information about preacademic skill development in writing, counting, reading, naming, and comprehension. These are skills preschoolers must master to succeed in kindergarten and early first grade. Diagnosticians and teachers also rely on the test to specify skills in need of remediation and to establish priorities for intervention based on the student's individual profile of strengths, weaknesses, and gaps in development.

As a curriculum guide, the LAP-3 provides teachers with a checklist of specifically defined developmental skills useful for creating lessons and identifying goals for group learning activities. Supplemental materials for use with any child assessed with the LAP-3 simplify individual program development by providing written objectives and detailed learning activities. By adopting the LAP-3 as the curriculum guide for a program, teachers ensure coverage of the important content areas in the preschool curriculum. Furthermore, the LAP-3 evaluates program quality and monitors the progress of individuals and groups.

LAP-3 Materials   The bright, attractive LAP-3 kit includes test administration materials for each item. The kit also contains score sheets, a loose-leaf easel book with procedures for giving the test and scoring the items, a technical manual, and an examiner's manual. The LAP-3 provides software for scoring using personal digital assistants (PDAs), CDs, or the Internet.

LAP-3 Administration and Scoring   The LAP-3 developers conveniently designed the test for individual administration by dividing it into skills and subskills that can be given in intervals corresponding to a child's attention span. Because of the variability in performance levels among children and the broad range of skills covered by the test, establishing a firm limit on the administration time is difficult. However, it takes at least several hours to complete, and for this reason evaluators should give it in short periods over time rather than in one sitting. Professionals with training in assessment, experience with young children, and a thorough knowledge of the LAP-3 qualify to administer the instrument.

The evaluator plots developmental age scores on a well designed scoring summary and profile graph form. This scoring procedure provides a norm-referenced framework for evaluating individual performance, differentiating between emerging and mastered skills, and developing a precise individual plan for intervention.

LAP-3 Technical Characteristics   Development of the LAP-3 included research to examine the reliability and validity of the instrument. Three sets of analyses were conducted: criterion validity, test-retest reliability, and interrater reliability. The results indicated the LAP-3 is appropriate for assessing the developmental progress of young children.

LAP-3 Summary   The LAP-3 enables complete diagnostic evaluation as a foundation for developing individual intervention programs for preschool students. Supplementary evaluation and curriculum materials complement the LAP-3. These include instructional activities keyed to the test items and planning guides for developing preschool curricula.

TEST REVIEW

Battelle Developmental Inventory, Second Edition

Type of Test:	Norm referenced, individually administered
Purpose:	A diagnostic test of developmental learning
Content Areas:	Personal-social, adaptive, motor, communication, and cognitive skills
Administration Time:	Complete BDI-2: 1–2 hours, Screening Test: 10–30 minutes
Age Levels:	Birth to 7 years
Suitable for:	Students with mild, moderate, and severe disabilities
Scores:	Standard scores, percentile ranks, and age equivalents
In Short:	A comprehensive developmental assessment instrument, the BDI-2 is useful for screening, diagnosis, and program development.

Battelle Developmental Inventory, Second Edition

The norm-referenced *Battelle Developmental Inventory, Second Edition* (BDI-2) (Newborg, 2005) is a screening test and a comprehensive diagnostic scale for children from infancy to 7 years of age. The BDI-2 is useful for identifying children with disabilities, screening for school readiness, developing objectives and remediation activities, and conducting program evaluation for accountability. The domains measured by the BDI-2 include personal-social, adaptive, motor, communication, and cognition. The test may be used by a team of professionals, and separate testing booklets for each domain facilitate independent administration of subtests. The inventory is available in a Spanish version for screening, diagnosing, and evaluating early childhood development of non-English-proficient children. A summary of the BDI-2 appears in the Test Review box.

BDI-2 Materials   The well-designed BDI-2 materials include a manual, scoring books, and supplemental materials including child-friendly manipulatives for all ages.

BDI-2 Administration and Scoring   The screening test takes about 30 minutes to give, and the complete BDI-2 takes 1 to 2 hours to administer, depending on the age and performance level of the child. The BDI-2 has three administration options: structured, direct observation, or interview. It also has a three-point scoring system that enables measurement of both emerging and fully developed skills. In reporting results, evaluators may select from standard scores, percentile ranks, and age equivalents. Results can be scored on a computer, a palm-based PDA, by hand, or using a Web-based option.

BDI-2 Technical Characteristics   Normative data were obtained from more than 2,500 children. Bias reviews were conducted on all items to reduce gender and ethnicity concerns. Item desirability information from examiners was also considered in the selection of the final items.

BDI-2 Summary   One of the most comprehensive developmental systems, the BDI-2 expedites screening, diagnosis, and program development for children up to 7 years of age. The BDI-2 norms enable use of the instrument in making placement and staffing decisions.

Brigance Inventory of Early Development, II

The Brigance Inventory of Early Development, II (IED-II) (Brigance, 2004) is a criterion-referenced scale for children from birth to 7 years of age consisting of 11 sections as follows:

Comprehensive Skills Sequences

1. Preambulatory motor

2. Gross motor

3. Fine motor

4. Self-help

5. Speech and language

6. General knowledge and comprehension

7. Social-emotional

Early Academic Skills Sections

1. Readiness

2. Basic reading skills

3. Manuscript writing

4. Basic math

The IED-II is designed for teachers as an assessment instrument for identifying present levels of performance and measuring progress and as an instructional guide with written objectives for developing intervention programs. A summary of the IED II appears in the Test Review box.

IED-II Materials   The IED II materials consist of a large plastic folder holding the manual, the scales, and a package of student record booklets. Optional materials include a class record booklet, testing accessories, scoring software, goals and objectives writing software, and the IED-II on CD.

IED-II Administration and Scoring   The IED-II features flexible administration procedures so that teachers can give all or parts of the inventory depending on the needs of the student and the purpose of testing. Teachers may select only the relevant parts of the test for use with their students. The scoring procedures are also flexible and can be accomplished through parent interview, observations, or formal testing. Although the IED-II provides approximate age-level scores, the inventory is best when used to provide a detailed record of skills that a child can and cannot perform. Teachers can use this as a guide for developing IEPs and for measuring progress on specific skills over time.

IED-II Technical Characteristics   Although the IED-II displays excellent face validity and good content validity, it exhibits other technical inadequacies. Unfortunately, little data are available to support the reliability or validity of the scores derived from the instrument. For this reason, the IED-II is best when used as an informal checklist of skills and an excellent curriculum guide rather than as a formal assessment tool.

TEST REVIEW

Brigance Inventory of Early Development, II

Type of Test:	Criterion-referenced, individually administered
Purpose:	A diagnostic test of developmental learning
Content Areas:	Eleven major skills areas in the developmental curriculum
Administration Time:	Varies depending on use
Age Levels:	Birth to 7 years
Suitable for:	Students with mild and moderate disabilities
Scores:	Provides a detailed record of skill attainment rather than traditional scores
In Short:	Despite technical weaknesses, the IED-II has several outstanding features, including comprehensive coverage of a wide range of developmental skills and flexible administration procedures that encourage modification of assessment to meet individual student needs.

IED-II Summary   Despite technical weaknesses, the IED-II includes several outstanding features that explain its popularity in special education. The test provides comprehensive coverage of a wide range of developmental skills accurately reflecting the curriculum content in many preschool programs. This enables use of the inventory with children across a range of functioning levels. In addition, the flexible administration procedures encourage modification of assessment to meet individual student needs and the needs of the program. Furthermore, many teachers find the behavioral objectives provided for each item on the test ideally suited for developing IEPs.

Snapshots of Other Diagnostic Tests of Developmental Skills

Although the LAP-D Standardized Assessment, the Battelle Developmental Inventory, and the Inventory of Early Development represent three of the most frequently used developmental scales, special educators may select from among many other instruments to obtain a test that fits the needs of their students. Brief reviews of several of these tools follow.

Carolina Curriculum   The curriculum-based Carolina Curriculum products include the Carolina Curriculum for Infants and Toddlers with Special Needs, Second Edition (Johnson-Martin, Jens, Attermeier, & Hecker, 1991) and the Carolina Curriculum for Preschoolers with Special Needs (Johnson-Martin, Attermeier, & Hecker, 1990). These tools provide intervention strategies and assessment information for children from birth through 5 years of age. These curricula cover cognition, communication, social adaption, fine motor skills, and gross motor skills. The infant and toddler curriculum, which includes 24 curriculum sequences in a checklist format, is designed for children between the developmental ages of birth to 24 months. The preschool curriculum, which includes 25 skills sequences, is for children between the developmental ages of 2 and 5 years. Each curriculum includes an assessment log that graphically charts a child's ongoing progress. Teachers may complete these assessments using observation and direct testing with corresponding program areas for intervention.

Developmental Observation Checklist System   The Developmental Observation Checklist System (DOCS) (Hresko, Miguel, Sherbenour, & Burton, 1994) includes components for measuring general development, adjustment behavior, parent stress, and parent support. The general development component measures language, motor, social, and cognitive skills. The DOCS is designed for children from birth through 6 years of age and can be completed by parents or caregivers based on their observation of the child's daily behaviors. Standardized on more than 1,400 children, available DOCS scores include quotients, NCEs, age equivalents, and percentiles.

Gesell Developmental Schedules   The Gesell Developmental Schedules (revised by Knobloch & Pasamanick in 1974 and by Knobloch, Sterens, & Malone in 1980) are the original developmental scales that were first published in 1940. The Gesell Developmental Schedules describe the developmental progress of children from ages 4 weeks to 6 years in gross motor, fine motor, communication, personal-social, and adaptive behavior. Gesell designed the schedules for use as criterion-based measures of child progress rather than as a tool for identifying children with disabilities.

Mullen Scales of Early Learning: AGS Edition   The Mullen Scales of Early Learning: AGS Edition (Mullen, 1995) assess the language, motor, and perceptual abilities of children from birth to 5 years 8 months of age. The Mullen Scales include subtests in gross motor, visual reception, fine motor, expressive language, and receptive language. Administration times for the Mullen Scales are about 15 minutes with 1-year-old infants, about 30 minutes with 3-year-old toddlers, and about 60 minutes with 5-year-old preschoolers. Available scores for this norm-referenced measure include t-scores, percentile ranks, age equivalents for each scale, and standard scores and percentile ranks for the total test. The Mullen Scales of Early Learning include attractive test materials and optional computer scoring software that provides scoring information and furnishes a narrative report. An optional intervention report lists a number of suggestions for developmentally appropriate tasks from the *You and Your Small Wonder* books by Merle Karnes. Teachers can use these suggestions to develop learning games and to plan intervention activities.

✔ Check Your Comprehension

Diagnostic assessment with individually administered developmental scales is a key component in the process of providing individualized programs for preschool children receiving special education services. Diagnosticians employ developmental scales in the process of classifying and placing young children into appropriate special education programs and services. Special education teachers, on the other hand, rely on developmental scales to develop intervention programs and to measure student progress. Professionals may select from an array of available instruments to ensure that they match the assessment instrument to the needs of the child and the family.

Developmental Readiness Tests

The readiness tests are a special category of developmental assessment for measuring children's knowledge of the basic skills necessary for success in the beginning years of school. Whereas the more general developmental scales often measure behavior from birth through 6 years of age, the readiness tests usually measure the behavior of children from age 4 through 7 years. Most teachers consider readiness to include the following skills and knowledge:

- General information about oneself and the immediate environment
- The self-help skills of basic toileting, dressing, eating, and hygiene
- Fine motor skills consisting of manipulation, drawing, and manual dexterity
- The relational concepts of space, time, and quantity, including the categorizing and sequencing abilities necessary for success in beginning academics
- The gross motor skills of locomotion, catching and throwing, moving balance, and stationary balance
- Language development, including receptive, expressive, and speech skills
- Handwriting skills up to the level of drawing with crayons and using a primary pencil
- Reading readiness skills such as sound discrimination, sound-letter correspondence, knowledge of letters, and knowledge of words
- Number readiness skills associated with recognizing and printing numbers, counting, numerical sequencing, and knowledge of equivalent sets
- The social skills of constructive play, interactive play, and following instructions
- Classroom behavior skills necessary to play cooperatively with peers, follow directions, complete assignments independently, and participate in classroom activities

Teachers find that children with these skills tend to be successful in the beginning school years whereas children without these skills may struggle in first grade or even fail altogether. Preschool teachers use assessment information about a child's skill development to determine school readiness and to plan instruction. However, evaluation of children's readiness skills should consist of more than testing because the behavior of preschool children varies a great deal from day to day. For this reason, teachers should use other assessment information in the evaluation process, including direct observation, informal assessment, teacher judgment, parent needs, family background, and other relevant information.

Representative Readiness Tests

Two representative instruments, the Boehm Test of Basic Concepts—Revised and the Basic School Skills Inventory, Third Edition, illustrate the kinds of behaviors measured by readiness tests.

Boehm Test of Basic Concepts, Third Edition

The Boehm Test of Basic Concepts, Third Edition (Boehm-3) (Boehm, 2000) is a norm-referenced, group-administered instrument for measuring whether students understand verbal instructions well enough for success in the primary grades. A summary of the Boehm-3 appears in the Test Review box.

The Boehm-3 measures 50 basic concepts relevant to today's early childhood curriculum. Boehm-3 identifies areas of concern and validates suspected or observed problems in concept acquisition. The Boehm-3 may be given in the classroom, and it includes English and Spanish instructions along with two parallel forms that enable pre-and posttesting. The Boehm-3 is designed for children in kindergarten through grade 2. The test items, grouped into categories of space, time, and quantity, incorporate the concepts of following directions, understanding sequences of events, completing worksheets and tests, and performing problem-solving activities.

TEST REVIEW

Boehm Test of Basic Concepts, Third Edition

Type of Test:	Norm-referenced, group administered
Purpose:	To determine if a student understands verbal instructions well enough for success in the primary grades
Content Areas:	Measures 50 important concepts including more-less, first-last, and same-different
Administration Time:	40 minutes
Age Levels:	Kindergarten to grade 2
Suitable for:	Students who are at risk for school failure and may need further diagnostic assessment to determine if they have learning problems
Scores:	A class record form provides information about the performance of each child and the entire class, including the number and percent of children answering each item correctly, the percentile rank of each child, and the average raw score.
In Short:	Teachers can use Boehm–3 results to identify students who should be referred for further testing and to assist in designing both individual remediation and group instruction.

A version of the Boehm-3 for even younger children is also available. The Boehm-3 Preschool (Boehm, 2001) is for early identification of basic concept deficiencies. Designed for children from 3 to 5 years of age or for older children with identified language difficulties, the Boehm-3 Preschool is useful in preschool screening programs for identifying weaknesses in basic concept comprehension. It takes only 10 to 15 minutes to give and score the instrument.

Boehm-3 Materials   Boehm-3 materials include a manual, two alternate forms, and an applications booklet that measures skill in using concepts in combination, in sequences, and in making comparisons.

Boehm-3 Administration and Scoring   Designed for group administration, the Boehm-3 takes about 40 minutes to give. The evaluator records the results on a class record form that provides information about the performance of each child and the entire class, including the number and percent of children answering each item correctly, the percentile rank of each child, and the average raw score. An optional error-analysis scoring procedure and a parent-teacher conference report provide additional interpretive data.

Boehm-3 Technical Characteristics   The Boehm-3 developers created norms from a national sample of children tested at the beginning and end of the school year. The developers also conducted a variety of reliability and validity studies with the test and completed research on the use of the test with special populations, including children with visual impairments, hearing impairments, learning disabilities, and mild mental retardation.

Boehm-3 Summary Teachers can use the Boehm-3 results for both individual remediation and group instruction and for identifying children with potential learning problems that may need further assessment. The test authors recommend individualized instruction when the overall class performs well but some children score below average. They suggest group instruction when most of the children in the class score below average. Instruction should focus on items missed or omitted on the test, and after targeting specific concepts for instruction, teachers should present each concept in a regular sequence.

Basic School Skills Inventory, Third Edition

The Basic School Skills Inventory, Third Edition (BSSI-3) (Hammill, Leigh, Pearson, & Maddox, 1998) is a norm-referenced screening test that identifies children ages 4 through 6 who are at risk for school failure, who need more in-depth assessment, and who should be referred for additional study. The instrument assesses the skills necessary for success in beginning school. Unlike the Boehm-3, which measures the underlying concepts necessary for school success, the BSSI-3 emphasizes tasks the child is asked to perform in the classroom (see the Test Review box for a summary of the BSSI-3). The six BSSI-3 subtests include daily living skills, spoken language, reading readiness, writing readiness, math readiness, and classroom behavior.

BSSI-3 Materials The BSSI-3 materials include a teacher's manual, a picture book used with the inventory, and a pad of score sheets.

BSSI-3 Administration and Scoring The test authors designed the BSSI-3 for teachers and others who see a child in the classroom on a regular basis. For this reason, it may not be appropriate for use by psychologists, counselors, and parents unless they have systematically observed the child in the classroom setting.

BSSI-3 Technical Characteristics The authors standardized the BSSI-3 using a national sample of young children. In a review of the instrument, Bradley-Johnson (1999) concluded that the BSSI-3 is a unique and useful measure of the school skills of young children. The instrument displays adequate reliability and validity.

TEST REVIEW

Basic School Skills Inventory, Third Edition

Type of Test:	Norm-referenced, individually administered screening test
Purpose:	To locate children who are at risk for school failure, who need more in-depth assessment, and who should be referred for additional study
Content Areas:	Daily living skills, spoken language, reading readiness, writing readiness, math readiness, and classroom behavior
Administration Time:	10 minutes
Age Levels:	4 to 6 years
Suitable for:	Students who are at risk for school failure
Scores:	Standard scores, percentiles, and age and grade equivalents for each scale
In Short:	The BSSI-3 assesses the skills necessary for success in beginning school.

BSSI-3 Summary   The BSSI-3, a classroom-based assessment tool for teachers of preacademic children, is appropriate for children from 4 through 6 years of age. Teachers also find it suitable for older children who function in this developmental age range. The BSSI-3 provides a quick teacher rating scale of early readiness skills.

Snapshots of Other Readiness Tests

Brief reviews of several other readiness tests that teachers of preacademic children have found to be useful follow. In addition to these specialized readiness tests, many teachers find that general developmental scales such as the DIAL-3 and the LAP-D Standardized Assessment contain features that make them useful for readiness testing.

Daberon Screening for School Readiness Test, Second Edition   The Daberon Screening for School Readiness Test, Second Edition (DABERON-2) (Danzer, Gerber, Zyons, & Voress, 1991) is a norm-referenced, group-administered measure of school readiness in children ages 4 through 6. The DABERON-2 includes subtests for measuring body parts, color and number concepts, gross motor development, categorization, and other developmental abilities that relate to early academic success. The individually administered DABERON-2 takes 20 to 40 minutes to give and score and can help identify children at risk for school failure. Teachers can use the instrument to identify instructional objectives and develop IEPs. The test includes a classroom summary form, a report on readiness, a summary of performance, and practical suggestions for parents.

Early School Assessment   The Early School Assessment (ESA) (CTB/McGraw Hill, 1990) is a norm-referenced group test that measures the language, visual, auditory, mathematical, and memory skills of children from prekindergarten through second grade. The purpose of the instrument is to assess the prereading and premath skills that are prerequisite to formal learning. The ESA includes two test levels, hand and machine scoring options, and optional practice books for children. The test takes six separate sessions of up to 30 minutes each to administer. The test results provide valuable information for appropriate instructional planning. A conference form is available for explaining results to parents.

Metropolitan Readiness Tests, Sixth Edition   The norm-referenced Metropolitan Readiness Tests, Sixth Edition (MRT-6) (Nurss, 1995) uses a colorful easel format for individualized administration. The MRT-6 assesses literacy development in children from 4 through 7 years of age. The MRT-6 assesses skills in visual discrimination, beginning consonants, sound-letter correspondence, story comprehension, and quantitative concepts and reasoning. The MRT-6 is a comprehensive diagnostic tool that takes up to 85 minutes in four sittings to administer. It yields standard scores, percentile ranks, and stanines, and includes a conference report that explains the purpose of the MRT-6 and displays the results in a convenient format for teachers to use when conferring with parents.

☑ Check Your Comprehension

Readiness tests, which measure the skills necessary for academic success in the primary grades, represent a special category of developmental assessment tools. Teachers may select from a variety of readiness tests to obtain a tool suited to the needs of their particular students. These include both group- and individually administered scales.

Specialized Developmental Assessment

Some young children with disabilities display unique needs and characteristics that call for the use of specialized developmental assessment procedures. Such children include those with severe to profound intellectual impairment, severe language and communication deficits, sensory impairments, physical disabilities, severe emotional disturbance, and autism.

Students with the most severe of these disabilities may depend on others or on specialized medical equipment to maintain life functions such as breathing, eating, digestion, elimination, and circulation. In other cases, performance may be limited by inappropriate behaviors such as stereotypy (e.g., light flicking or rocking) or self-injury (e.g., head banging or hand biting). In addition, communication levels may range from little more than subtle physical movements to verbal and gestural abilities. All of these situations preclude the use of traditional developmental assessment tools and require evaluators to turn to a number of specialized developmental tests and assessment procedures. Unfortunately, a single source explaining developmental assessment for students with severe disabilities does not exist. For this reason, evaluators need to consult a variety of resources and work with a team of professionals from an array of disciplines. The team approach helps to ensure consideration of all aspects of a child's needs in the assessment process.

Unique Areas of Assessment for Students with Severe Disabilities

When assessing students with severe disabilities, evaluators must consider unique learning areas and specialized areas of assessment (Best, Heller, & Bigge, 2005; Florida Department of Education, 1986; Venn & Dykes, 1987). The unique areas of assessment include the following:

- Primary method of communication
- Sensory input and intactness of motor processes
- Medical stability
- Fatigue
- Maladaptive behaviors

Primary Method of Communication   Although some students with severe disabilities have normal speech, others present various speech, language, and communication deficits. At the more severe levels, the speech of some children may be unintelligible to all but the primary caregivers. In other cases, children may not speak at all but may communicate by nonverbal or nonvocal means, including sign language, gestures, or various body movements and vocalizations. In most situations, evaluators and teachers should collaborate with a speech, language, and communication therapist to identify and evaluate the primary response mode. After identifying the primary response mode, assessment procedures should be tailored to the individual communication skills of the child.

Sensory Input and Intactness of Motor Processes   Sensory input and intactness of motor processes refers to how well the child sees, hears, moves about, and performs fine motor manipulation and drawing tasks. Evaluators should assess these characteristics prior to general assessment. Because evaluators may need to use specialized assessment techniques and instruments to assess sensory and motor function, they often collaborate with specialists such as neurodevelopmental therapists, physical therapists, occupational therapists, vision teachers, or audiologists.

Medical Stability   Some medically fragile students require frequent medical care, including hospitalization. With these students, determining health and medical stability is an important consideration in the assessment process. In these cases, the participation of medical specialists as an integral part of the assessment team may be necessary.

Fatigue   Fatigue refers to stamina and attention during the assessment process. Some children with severe disabilities tire and lose concentration quickly. This may be influenced by medication, which may lower attention levels or make the student irritable or hypersensitive. Because fatigue represents a common problem with young children, the evaluator should consider this characteristic carefully as part of the assessment process. If the child lacks stamina or is inattentive, assessment may take longer to complete than if the child exhibits good stamina and is attentive.

Maladaptive Behaviors   Maladaptive behaviors exhibited by young children with severe disabilities include self-stimulation (e.g., light flicking), self-abuse (e.g., head banging), extreme noncompliance and task resistance, and other inappropriate behaviors that may interfere with the assessment process. Assessing maladaptive behavior is often necessary with young children who have severe disabilities.

Characteristics of Assessment Instruments for Students with Severe Disabilities

In addition to evaluating student characteristics, evaluators should look for several key characteristics of the assessment instruments themselves as part of the test selection process (Dykes & Erin, 1999; Venn & Dykes, 1987). These characteristics include the following:

- Adaptable response modes
- Flexible administration procedures
- Provisions for giving partial credit
- A wide sample of behaviors
- Procedures for developing a positive intervention plan

   The goal is to select instruments that minimize the student's impairments and maximize the student's ability to respond. This strategy produces the best possible assessment information for developing a positive intervention plan.

Adaptable Response Modes   Adapting the response mode refers to modifying a test item to match the child's unique patterns of responding. For nonverbal children, verbal test items need to be modified to allow response modes such as sign language or pointing to symbols on a communication board. For children with physical impairments, the response mode for test items that require motor responses can often be modified through the use of switches or other augmentative communication aids. Likewise, modifying assessment materials by substituting a motivating stimulus for a nonmotivating one improves the chances for student success. For example, toys that produce sound, have knobs to turn, buttons to push, and attractive visuals should be substituted for dull, uninteresting toys. The goal is to maintain the child's attention with sound, motion, color, and novelty.

Flexible Administration Procedures Although structured tests with specific administration procedures are necessary in certain situations, teachers generally prefer more flexible measures when they assess students prior to developing intervention programs. Flexible tests allow evaluators to modify the assessment to meet the unique needs and response styles of individual students. Some tests provide specific guidelines for adapting administration procedures and test items. For example, the Developmental Activities Screening Inventory-II (reviewed later in this chapter) includes instructions for adapting the instrument when testing children who are blind or nonverbal.

Provisions for Giving Partial Credit Partial credit refers to scoring that provides recognition for completing part of a task. Partial credit scoring goes beyond simple pass-fail scoring by furnishing more than two scoring criteria. Some developmental tests for special populations provide three scoring criteria: pass, which indicates independence on a particular skill; emerging, which denotes significant progress toward independence; and fail, which signifies little or no acquisition of a skill.

For example, a child may not walk independently (pass), but this skill may be emerging. With pass-fail scoring the child would fail this item. With three scoring criteria the child would receive partial credit (emerging) as an interim score between pass and fail. Some scales for special populations include more than three scoring criteria, and this enables measurement of small increments of progress in children. For example, the Developmental Assessment for Students with Severe Disabilities (Dykes & Erin, 1999) includes a "task resistive" scoring category, which refers to situations in which a child goes beyond failing an item by refusing to even attempt a task. Using a scoring system with this criterion makes it possible to show improvement when a child begins to cooperate in learning a task.

A Wide Sample of Behaviors The best instruments for children with severe disabilities have numerous test items that sample a wide range of behaviors. Instruments with a small number of items fail to provide an adequate sample for making accurate assessment decisions. In fact, children with severe disabilities usually fail so many items on short tests that the results show what the children cannot do rather than what they can do. In contrast, instruments with many items sample an array of behaviors, thus providing opportunities to discover emerging skills and behaviors that children can successfully perform. For this reason, teachers and evaluators prefer tests with a wide sample of behaviors.

Procedures for Developing a Positive Intervention Plan Rather than relying on testing to confirm low levels of performance and the lack of functional skills, evaluators should use instruments that provide a means to develop a positive intervention plan. Developmental scales that include extensive information on intervention and programming make it easier to achieve this goal. Likewise, scales that contain the features just described make it easier to generate a functional and practical plan for meeting the individual and often unique learning needs of students with severe and multiple disabilities.

Specialized Developmental Assessment Instruments

The specialized instruments reviewed next are tools for evaluating the developmental progress of young children with severe, profound, and multiple disabilities. Although similar in content to conventional developmental scales, each of these tests contains unique features that make them appropriate for specialized use.

Developmental Activities Screening Inventory

The Developmental Activities Screening Inventory-II (DASI-II) (Fewell & Langley, 1984) is a curriculum-based measure of cognitive development from a Piagetian perspective. This informal, criterion-referenced scale covers an age range of birth to 5 years and is designed for use by teachers, diagnosticians, and psychologists. Skills measured by the 67 DASI-II items include means-ends relationships, cause-effect memory, seriation, and reasoning. These neurological and cognitive skills are essential for young children as they grow and develop language and reasoning ability. DASI-II materials include learning activities for teaching the specific skills evaluated by the test and samples of intervention programs based on DASI-II test results. The test can be given either verbally or visually, and each test item includes adaptation for use with children who are visually impaired. These features make the DASI-II ideal for children with severe, profound, and multiple disabilities. In some situations, psychologists and diagnosticians find it helpful to give the DASI-II to nonverbal children as a supplemental test that complements data obtained from conventional intelligence testing with instruments such as the performance subtest of the WISC-III.

Developmental Assessment for Students with Severe Disabilities

The Developmental Assessment for Students with Severe Disabilities (DASH-2) (Dykes & Erin, 1999) offers concise information about individuals who are functioning between birth and age 6 to 11 developmentally. It consists of five subtests measuring performance in language, sensory-motor skills, activities of daily living, basic academic skills, and social-emotional skills. DASH-2 is sensitive to small changes in skill performance. It identifies these skills as task resistive, needing full assistance, needing partial assistance, needing minimal assistance, or an independent performance.

Hawaii Early Learning Profile

The Hawaii Early Learning Profile (HELP) assessment materials also measure Piagetian concept development using curriculum-based, criterion-referenced developmental scales. The Piagetian domains on the profile include developmental test items for cognitive concepts such as:

- Object permanence: The child looks for the hidden toy.
- Imitation skills: The child claps hands in imitation.
- Means-ends relationships: The child pushes the button to see the toy car go.
- Spatial concepts: The child builds with blocks.
- Cause-effect relationships: The child gives the complicated toy to an adult to make it go.

In addition to assessing these cognitive skills, the HELP system includes all of the major subtests in the developmental curriculum as well as a complete description of goals and learning activities for each of the 685 items. HELP products include a HELP Checklist 0–3 (Furuno, 1995a) and HELP Charts 0–3 (Furuno, 1994). The Checklist and the Charts are available in English and Spanish versions. Most practitioners consider the HELP materials to be especially applicable to students with severe and profound disabilities because they contain a large combination of developmental items.

HELP for Preschoolers Assessment & Curriculum Guide

The HELP for Preschoolers Assessment & Curriculum Guide (Furuno, 1995b) is a curriculum-based, criterion-referenced assessment tool and a set of instructional activities for young children from 3 to 6 years of age. HELP for Preschoolers measures performance in six developmental areas and includes a total of 622 items. For each item there is a definition, a description of needed materials for assessment, a list of assessment procedures, a discussion of possible accommodations, and instructional activities.

Vulpé Assessment Battery, Revised Edition

The Vulpé Assessment Battery, Revised Edition (VAB-R) (Vulpé, 1994) is a comprehensive developmental scale that measures the performance of children from birth through 8 years of age. Designed as a curriculum-based, criterion-referenced tool for individual administration, the Vulpé Assessment Battery provides detailed evaluation of performance in six domains: gross motor, fine motor, language, cognitive processes, adaptive behavior, and activities of daily living. In addition, the VAB-R includes measures of learning in areas typically not covered on developmental scales, such as organizational skills, basic senses and functions, developmental reflexes, and motor planning. The VAB-R uses a graduated scoring system approach for charting progress that is ideal for assessing low functional levels. It is one of the most curriculum-like instruments available.

The VAB-R is both an assessment instrument and a curriculum guide for evaluating the "whole"child in relation to the environment and to central nervous system function. As a result, the VAB-R is appropriate for use by a wide range of professionals, including special educators, occupational therapists, physical therapists, psychologists, diagnosticians, and home intervention specialists. It also lends itself to use by an assessment team made up of professionals from these disciplines. Because of the comprehensive nature of the battery, it is especially appropriate for young children who have severe, profound, and multiple disabilities. Vulpé wrote the scales based on extensive experience as an occupational therapist, and this professional orientation produced an instrument that is especially sensitive to the neurological and sensory-motor development of young children.

☑ Check Your Comprehension

Like the readiness tests, these developmental scales represent a specialized type of assessment designed to meet the unique needs of preschool students with severe and profound disabilities. Because they respond to the characteristics of these children, the content of these tests centers less on preacademic skills and more on language, cognitive, and motor skills. The tests in this group also include more flexible administration procedures to meet the needs of children with sensory, motor, neurological, and intellectual deficits.

Infant Assessment

Infant and toddler intervention specialists must reach out to a variety of sources to provide accurate and effective assessment. In addition, several differences exist between traditional assessment models and those designed for infants and toddlers. These differences include team approaches that emphasize the family unit, a focus on home-based assessment in natural settings rather than at a center or school-based testing, and direct participation by professionals from health-related disciplines, including physical and occupational therapy. Because of these variations from traditional evaluation, the steps in the assessment process differ somewhat from those of conventional testing. The steps include the following:

- Obtaining case history information through questionnaires and direct interviews in the home environment
- Conducting developmental screening in the home setting
- Completing comprehensive assessment in the natural environment, using appropriate instruments
- Interpreting results
- Discussing the results with the parents and other professionals

The Case History

Even in the best circumstances, it is difficult to test very young children because they have fewer behaviors and a more restricted range of behaviors than older children, and their behavior changes quickly due to rapid growth and development. For this reason, a complete case history is one of the best sources of information about infants and toddlers and their families. Evaluators may obtain such information from questionnaires or direct interviews, and this is a necessary step prior to testing a child. Evaluators should include the specific information outlined in Table 8–1 in a comprehensive case history (National Dissemination Center for Children with Disabilities, 2005; Rossetti, 1990).

Table 8–1 A Comprehensive Case History

Area-Specific Information
      Biographical information
      Date of birth
      Description of the problem
Medical History
      Significant medical problems before, during, and soon after birth
      Current medical treatments and medications
Developmental History
      Description of developmental milestones
      Areas of delay
      Recent developmental changes
      Results from developmental tests
Educational History
      Description of educational interventions
      Parents' view of educational needs and views from other
      family members or caretakers
Social History
      Description of siblings
      Interactions with parents and siblings
Behavior Problems

Developmental Assessment with Infants and Toddlers

After obtaining case history information, an evaluator or an evaluation team collects developmental assessment data. Developmental assessment with infants and toddlers, including developmental screening, represents a dynamic process in which the evaluator obtains samples of behaviors by observing in unstructured play settings. The evaluator also measures performance in more structured, test-like situations. Observing and measuring the behavior of infants and toddlers provides an estimation of a child's developmental level and gives better assessment information than testing in the traditional manner. This process yields information about developmental functioning across several domains of assessment, including the following:

- Language and communication
- Fine motor development
- Gross motor development
- Social development
- Reflex development
- Organizational behavior and cognitive processes
- Sensory skills
- Family assessment
- Environmental influences

Representative Assessment Instruments for Infants and Toddlers

Two representative assessment instruments for infants and toddlers are the Birth to Three Assessment and Intervention System and the Early Learning Accomplishment Profile.

Birth to Three Assessment and Intervention System, Second Edition   The Birth to Three Assessment and Intervention System, Second Edition (BTAIS-2) (Ammer & Bangs, 2000) is an integrated system for screening, assessing, and intervening with infants and very young children. The system consists of a Screening Test of Developmental Abilities for identifying children with potential developmental delays, a Comprehensive Test of Developmental Abilities for pinpointing specific skills that need intervention and for developing individual plans, and a Manual for Teaching Developmental Abilities that provides activities and tasks to help develop parent-centered programs for young children. The Screening Test has 85 items and the Comprehensive Test has 240 items. Both tests measure skills in language comprehension, language expression, nonverbal thinking, social/personal development, and motor development. The norm-referenced Screening Test takes about 15 minutes to give. The criterion-referenced Comprehensive Test is untimed. Parent involvement, parent training, and home instruction are key features of the Birth to Three intervention program. The well-organized and easy-to-follow Birth to Three System is best when used with infants and toddlers who have mild disabilities. Although the norms for the screening test display some weaknesses, the other technical aspects of the system are more than adequate. When used as a criterion-referenced tool, Birth to Three provides a complete developmental system that includes test results plus an intervention guide for developing individual programs for children and their families.

Early Learning Accomplishment Profile   The Early Learning Accomplishment Profile (E-LAP) (Glover, Preminger, & SanFord, 1988), a criterion-referenced test, assesses the overall development of children from birth to 36 months. The developmental subtests on the E-LAP include the following:

- Gross motor
- Fine motor
- Cognitive
- Language
- Self-help skills
- Social-emotional skill areas

Because subtests measuring skills such as sensory intactness and neurological status are not included on the E-LAP, it is best for very young children who have mild and moderate disabilities. The E-LAP results include a detailed profile of strengths and weaknesses across the six subtest areas, and the materials include a set of 380 early learning activity cards. These sequenced cards contain learning activities and teaching techniques keyed to the E-LAP test items. Each card includes a written objective as well as suggestions for helping a child learn a particular skill. Those who rely on the Learning Accomplishment Profile-Revised (LAP-R) (which has an age range of 3 to 6 years) may find that the E-LAP is an excellent supplement for children who function at or below the 3-year-old age level.

☑ Check Your Comprehension

Assessing infants and toddlers is a specialized type of developmental appraisal. With the growth of early intervention programs, this type of assessment has become increasingly important. The process of assessing infants and toddlers emphasizes the family unit, home-based natural settings, and a team approach that includes active participation of medical and other health professionals.

Summary

Developmental assessment encompasses appraisal techniques for use with children from infancy through the early primary grades. Recent refinements in developmental testing reflect several of the most important trends in assessment. One of these refinements, evaluating family needs in new ways, serves as an integral part of the developmental assessment process. Evaluating family needs goes beyond considering the parents to also including siblings and extended family members. Refinements in the use of the team approach, such as having the parents serve as key team members, represent another important consideration. Recognition that early assessment and intervention may either reduce the severity of or, in some cases, prevent a disability altogether is also a significant factor. Because of the importance of developmental assessment, preschool teachers and infant intervention specialists should be thoroughly familiar with the procedures and instruments. A review of the developmental scales referenced in this chapter appears in Table 8–2. For other special educators, understanding developmental assessment is one component in building a comprehensive knowledge base in appraisal. This knowledge helps teachers ensure that children receive appropriate assessment designed to fit their unique needs.

To check your comprehension of the chapter contents, go to the *Guided Review* and *Quiz* modules in Chapter 8 of the Companion Website, *www.prenhall.com/venn*.

Table 8–2 Review of Developmental Tests

Name	Type	Suitable for	Brief Description	Purpose
AGS Early Screening Profiles (ESP)	Norm-referenced, screening test	Children from 2 to 6 years of age	Uses multiple domains, settings, and sources to measure cognitive, language, motor, self-help, and social skills; also surveys the child's articulation, home environment, health history, and test behavior	To provide practical information for making accurate screening decisions
*Basic School Skills Inventory (3rd ed.) (BSSI-3)	Norm-referenced, individually administered readiness test	Children from 4 to 6 years of age	Measures daily living skills, spoken language, reading, writing, mathematics, and classroom behavior	To locate children who are at high risk for school failure, who need more in-depth assessment, and who should be referred for additional testing
*Battelle Developmental Inventory, Second Edition (BDI-2)	Norm-referenced, individually administered screening test and diagnostic scale	Children from birth to 7 years of age	Measures performance in personal, social, adaptive, motor, communication, and cognitive skills	To screen children for potential disabilities; to classify and place young children into appropriate special education programs; to develop IEPs and intervention programs; and to measure progress
Birth to Three Assessment & Intervention System, Second Edition (BTAIS-2)	Norm-referenced screening test, a criterion-	Children from birth to 3 years of age	Subtests include language comprehension, language expression,	To screen children at high risk for developmental delay, to obtain

Name	Type	Suitable for	Brief Description	Purpose
	referenced diagnostic scale, and a treatment guide		nonverbal thinking, social/personal development, and motor development	a diagnostic assessment, and to develop a classroom and home-based intervention system
Boehm-3 Preschool (Boehm, 2001)	Norm-referenced, individually administered, readiness test	Children from 3 to 5 years of age or older children with identified difficulties	Helps with early identification of children with basic concept deficiencies	Useful for preschool screening programs to identify weaknesses in basic concept comprehension
*Boehm Test of Basic Concepts, Third Edition (Boehm-3)	Norm-referenced readiness test, group administered	Children from K–2	Incorporates 50 important concepts such as more-less, first-last, same-different, following directions, understanding sequences, and problem solving	To measure a child's knowledge of the basic understanding necessary for success in the beginning years of school
Brigance Early Preschool Screen-II (Screen II)	Criterion-referenced, individually administered developmental screening test	Children from 2 to 2$^1/_2$ years of age	Measures fine motor skills, gross motor skills, general and knowledge, speech language, and preacademic/academic skills	To measure children's basic skills in the major developmental learning areas
Brigance Infant and Toddler Screen (Infant Toddler Screen)	Criterion-referenced, individually administered developmental screening test	Infants and toddlers from birth to age 2	Measures fine motor and gross motor skills, receptive and expressive language, self-help and social-emotional skills	To quickly screen infants and toddlers
Brigance Inventory of Early Development-II	Criterion-referenced,	Children from birth	Measures 11 major skills areas in the	A diagnostic test of

(continued)

Table 8–2 *continued*

Name	Type	Suitable for	Brief Description	Purpose
(IED-II)	individually administered	to 7 years of age	developmental curriculum	developmental learning that provides a detailed record of skill attainment
Brigance K & 1 Screen-II (K & 1 Screen II)	Criterion-referenced, individually administered developmental screening test	Children in kindergarten and grade 1	Measures general knowledge and comprehension, speech and language, gross motor, and fine motor skills, preacademic/ academic skills, social-emotional skills, self-help skill, reading, and manuscript writing	To quickly screen kindergarten and first-grade students
Brigance Preschool Screen-II (Preschool Screen II)	Criterion-referenced, individually administered	Preschoolers who are 3 and 4 years old	Measures general knowledge and comprehension, speech and language, gross motor and fine motor skills, preacademic/ academic skills, social-emotional skills, and self-help skills	To measure children's basic skills in the major developmental learning areas
Carolina Curriculum For Infants and Toddlers with Special Needs, Second Edition (Caroline Curriculum)	Criterion-referenced, individually administered curriculum guide and diagnostic checklist	Infants and toddlers from birth to 24 months of age	Covers cognition, communication, social adaption, fine motor skills, and gross motor skills	Provides intervention strategies and assessment information: includes an assessment log for charting the child's ongoing progress
Carolina Curriculum for Preschoolers with Special Needs	Criterion-referenced curriculum guide and	Preschoolers from 2 to 5 years of age	Covers cognition, communication, social adaption, fine motor skills,	Provides intervention strategies and assessment

Name	Type	Suitable for	Brief Description	Purpose
	diagnostic checklist		and gross motor skills	information includes an assessment log for charting the child' ongoing progress
Daberon Screening for School Readiness Test, Second Edition (DABERON-2)	Norm-referenced, group administered screening level readiness test	Preschoolers from 4 to 6 years of age	Samples knowledge of body parts, color and number concepts, gross motor development, categorization, and other developmental abilities related to early academic success	To identify children at risk for school failure, to help develop instructional objectives, and to assist in writing IEPs
*Denver II	Norm-referenced, individually administered screening test	Children from birth to 6 years of age	Measures developmental progress in personal-social, fine motor, adaptive, gross motor, and language skills	To screen young children with potential developmental delays
Developmental Activities Screening Inventory (DASI-II)	Criterion-referenced, individually administered screening test	Children from birth to 5 years of age	Measures cognitive development from a Piagetian perspective; can be given verbally or nonverbally; includes learning activities for teaching the specific skills evaluated by the test	To measure the cognitive development of young children with severe and multiple disabilities
Developmental Assessment for Students with Severe Disabilities (DASH-2)	Criterion-referenced, individually administered diagnostic scale	Children from birth to 6 years of age and older students children	Measures a wide sample of behaviors in all of the major learning areas, offers flexible administration procedures,	To measure the developmental progress of children with severe, profound, and multiple

(continued)

Table 8–2 *continued*

Name	Type	Suitable for	Brief Description	Purpose
		with severe disabilities	includes extensive provisions for giving partial credit	disabilities
*Developmental Indicators for the Assessment of Learning—Third Edition (DIAL-3)	Norm-referenced, group or individually administered screening test	Preschoolers from 2 to 6 years of age	Measures developmental progress in motor development, concept development, and language skills	To identify young children with potential development delays
Developmental Observation Checklist System (DOCS)	Norm-referenced, individually administered observation checklist	Children from birth through 6 years of age	Measures general development, adjustment behavior, parent stress, and parent support; the general development section includes language, motor, social, and cognitive	To measure child development based on parents' or caregivers' observation of the child's daily behaviors
Early Learning Accomplishment Profile (E-LAP)	Criterion-referenced, individually administered diagnostic scale	Infants and toddlers from birth to 3 years of age	Evaluate gross motor, fine motor, cognitive language, self-help, and developing IEP objectives and social-emotional skills	To assess overall development and to assist in intervention activities
Early School Assessment (ESA)	Norm-referenced, group test	Students from pre-K through grade 2	Measures language, visual, auditory, mathematical, and memory skills of children from prekindergarten through second grade	To assess the prereading and premath skills that are prerequisite to formal learning
Early Screening Inventory—Revised. (ESI-R)	Norm-referenced individually administered developmental	Children from 3 to 6 years of age	Assesses development in visual-motor/adaptive, language and	To help identify young children who are at high risk for school failure and who

Name	Type	Suitable for	Brief Description	Purpose
	screening instrument		cognition, and gross motor skills	may need special services
Gesell Developmental Schedules	Criterion-referenced, individually administered diagnostic scale	Young children from 4 weeks to 6 years of age	Measures gross motor, fine motor, communication, personal-social, and adaptive behavior	Gesell designed the schedules for use as criterion-based measures of child progress
FirstSTEP: Screening Test for Evaluating Preschoolers	Norm-referenced, individually administered screening test	Children from 2 years, 9 months to 6 years, 2 months of age	Evaluates development in the five areas mandated by IDEA: cognition, communication, motor, social-emotional, and adaptive behavior; also provides an optional parent/teacher scale to add information, about the child's typical behavior at home and at school	To identify preschool children who are at risk for developmental delays
HELP Charts 0–3	Curriculum-based, criterion-referenced, individually administered diagnostic scale	Infants and toddlers from birth to 3 years of age	Includes all of the major subtests in the developmental curriculum as well as a complete description of goals, objectives, and learning	Especially useful with young children who have severe and profound disabilities because it contains activities for each item on the test
HELP for Preschoolers Assessment and Curriculum Guide	Curriculum-based, criterion-referenced, individually administered diagnostic scale	Children from 3 to 6 years of age	Includes all of the major subtests in the developmental curriculum as well as a complete description of goals, objectives, and learning	Especially useful with young children who have severe and profound disabilities because it contains activities for each numerous test

(*continued*)

Table 8–2 *continued*

Name	Type	Suitable for	Brief Description	Purpose
*Learning Accomplishment Profile—Third Edition (LAP-3)	Criterion-referenced, individually administered diagnostic scale	Children from 36 to 72 months of age	Measures cognitive fine motor and pre social, language and writing, personal literacy, gross motor, and self-help skills	To assess overall development, to develop intervention programs, and to measure progress
Metropolitan Readiness Tests (MRT 6)	Norm-referenced, group or individually	Children from 4 to 7 years of age administered	Assesses visual discrimination, beginning consonants, sound-letter readiness test	To assess literacy development in prekindergarten and kindergarten children correspondence, story comprehension (using a big book), and quantitative concepts and reasoning
Mullen Scales of Early Learning: AGS Edition	Norm-referenced, individually administered diagnostic scale	Children from birth to 5 years, 8 months of age	Provides assessment of language, motor, and perceptual abilities with subtests in gross motor, visual reception, fine motor, expressive language, and receptive language	To develop and plan school-and home-based early intervention programs for young children with developmental disabilities
Vulpé Assessment Battery—Revised (VAB-R)	Criterion-referenced, individually administered diagnostic scale	Children from birth to 8 years of age	Measure performance in the developmental learning areas and in organizational skills, the environment, basic sense and functions, reflexes, muscle strength, motor planning, and balance	To assess the developmental progress of young children with severe, profound, and multiple disabilities

* Tests marked with an asterisk are featured in this chapter.

Meeting Performance Standards and Preparing for Licensure Exams

After reading this chapter, you should be able to demonstrate the following CEC Standards and PRAXIS™ test knowledge and skills. The information in parentheses identifies where to find the particular CEC standard and PRAXIS™ content reference.

CEC Standards for Beginning Special Education Teachers

- Typical and atypical human growth and development (CC2K1)
- Family systems and the role of families in supporting development (CC2K4)
- Develop and implement comprehensive, longitudinal individualized programs in collaboration with team members (CC7S2)
- Involve the individual and family in setting instructional goals and monitoring progress (CC7S3)
- Screening, prereferral, referral, and classification procedures (CC8K3)
- Use and limitations of assessment instruments (CC8K4)
- Administer nonbiased formal and informal assessments (CC8S2)
- Use technology to conduct assessments (CC8S3)
- Develop or modify individualized assessment strategies (CC8S4)
- Interpret information from formal and informal assessments (CC8S5)
- Develop or modify individualized assessment strategies (CC8S9)

PRAXIS™ Education of Exceptional Students: Core Content Knowledge

- Human development and behavior as related to students with disabilities, including social and emotional development and behavior, language development and behavior, cognition, and physical development, including motor and sensory (0353 I)
- Assessment, including use of assessment for screening, diagnosis, placement, and the making of instructional decisions, for example: how to select and conduct nondiscriminatory and appropriate assessments; how to interpret standardized and specialized assessment results; procedures and test materials, both formal and informal, typically used for prereferral, screening, referral, classification, placement, and ongoing program monitoring (0353 III)

chapter 9

Assessing Motor Proficiency, Perception, and Learning Styles

Objectives

After reading this chapter, you will be prepared to do the following:

- Define motor proficiency, perception, and perceptual-motor ability.
- Apply guidelines for assessing motor proficiency, perception, and perceptual-motor development.
- Describe the skills measured by perception and perceptual-motor development tests.
- Use representative tests of perception and perceptual-motor development.
- Assess the learning styles and modalities preferences of students with special needs.
- Assess the motor proficiency of students with special needs.
- Discuss the role of evaluating motor proficiency, perception, and learning styles in the overall process of assessing students with special needs.

Overview

In this chapter you investigate the concepts and techniques associated with assessing motor proficiency, perception, and learning styles. You begin your study by considering key terms, significant concepts, and important issues associated with assessment in these domains. Next, you review practical, applied guidelines for assessing motor skill development and perceptual-processing ability. Finally, you examine the tests and evaluation procedures for identifying performance levels and developing intervention programs. As you review each test and evaluation technique, you consider its purpose and use, materials, administration procedures, scoring and interpretation process, and technical characteristics.

Introduction to Assessing Motor Proficiency and Perception

The following two accounts introduce assessing motor proficiency and perception from the perspective of teachers of students with disabilities who want to learn more about using these evaluations. The deficits described in these accounts, a fine motor delay, and a visual-processing problem, are typical of the motor and perceptual difficulties of young children with special needs.

When two children with cerebral palsy joined Mrs. Fuller's special education class, she immediately began to ask questions about how to help them develop their motor proficiency. Because she had limited experience with students who had severe motor disabilities, she wondered what was meant by the terms fine motor skills and gross motor skills that appeared in reports in the children's cumulative folders. She was unfamiliar with the motor proficiency test that the diagnostician used to assess the children's motor development. She knew that she must first obtain some basic information about cerebral palsy and assessing motor development. She then could ask how to best develop intervention programs for her new students and implement their IEP objectives. This would also help measure the progress of the students in fine motor and gross motor development.

During preplanning, Mrs. Jones was transferred to a new class for young children with learning disabilities. Included in her class were several children with severe visual- and auditory-perception problems. For example, two 6-year-old children had difficulty copying and printing certain letters correctly. Their problems included consistent reversal and occasional rotation of letters such as p, b, and d. The children also exhibited difficulty learning basic reading skills. Mrs. Jones observed that the children had poor memory for visual information but good memory for auditory information. Fortunately, Mrs. Jones had formal coursework and field experience with young children with perceptual difficulties as part of her teacher education degree program. Because of her experience, Mrs. Jones knew the answers to several questions about where to begin and what to do, including the following: What are the most common perceptual problems of young children with learning disabilities? Are there specialized tests for assessing children with perceptual problems? How important is observational assessment in identifying and developing intervention programs? What is the best way to develop IEP goals? How should she measure progress in remediating the perceptual problems of her students?

These two scenarios highlight many of the questions teachers have about assessing students with motor and perceptual deficits. In this chapter we discover answers to these questions and investigate other aspects of the processes and procedures associated with evaluating motor proficiency and perception.

Defining Motor Proficiency and Perception

Assessing **motor proficiency** involves evaluating the efficiency of movements controlled by the body's muscles. The two major types of motor activity are fine and gross motor movement. **Fine motor** addresses movement and response speed controlled by the small muscles of the body and includes hand and finger dexterity, drawing, and manipulation of small objects. **Gross motor**, on the other hand, refers to movement controlled by the large muscles of the body, including those that regulate walking, throwing, catching, and balancing.

Perception is the process of comprehending information received by the senses. Assessing perception involves measuring the processing of information from the senses, especially visual and auditory information. In other words, perception is concerned with sensory input. In contrast, motor proficiency refers to movement output.

Perceptual-motor integration is the process of coordinating sensory information with corresponding body movements. Coordinating perceptual input with motor output includes visual-motor, auditory-motor, and tactile-motor skills. For example, **visual-motor processing** refers to coordinating sensory information from the eyes with corresponding movements such as eye-hand coordination and visual-motor control. Likewise, **auditory-motor processing** refers to coordinating sensory information from the ears with fine and gross motor body movements. When evaluating perception, perceptual-motor integration, and motor proficiency, evaluators follow certain guidelines to ensure accuracy in the assessment.

Guidelines for Assessing Motor Proficiency and Perception

The following guidelines for assessing motor proficiency and perception ensure accurate administration of assessments and appropriate interpretation of results. These guidelines include the following:

- Screen for vision or hearing impairment.
- Exercise caution with students who have physical or sensory impairments.
- Assess older students carefully.
- Determine the need for training.
- Carefully observe behavior.

Screen for Vision or Hearing Impairment   Prior to assessment, evaluators should rule out vision or hearing impairment as a cause of motor delays because sensory disabilities such as poor visual acuity or hearing loss can affect the results of evaluations and lead to misinterpretation of results. Evaluators may screen for vision or hearing deficits in several ways as appropriate to the individual situation and the needs of the student. Screening steps may include reviewing cumulative records for information about visual and hearing status, observing a student directly, or interviewing a teacher who is familiar with a student. If the screening process indicates a potential problem, the student should be referred to a specialist for evaluation. In some cases a teacher may observe sensory difficulties not detected during the screening. For example, if a teacher observes changes in visual or hearing functioning or recognizes an unusual visual or auditory behavior, the teacher should refer the student to a specialist. The referral should include a description of possible impairment and observed changes in behavior.

Exercise Caution with Students Who Have Physical or Sensory Impairments
Because students with severe physical or sensory impairments may not be able to perform certain test items, evaluators should use perceptual and motor tests cautiously. For example, seeing complex drawings on visual-motor tests may be impossible for

a student with a severe visual impairment. Likewise, a student with a hearing loss may be incapable of responding to auditory items on tests of auditory discrimination. In cases of severe physical or sensory impairment, specialized perceptual and motor tests and clinical evaluation procedures are necessary. In all cases, caution is needed when giving tests to students with physical and sensory disabilities because of the possible limitations of the results.

Assess Older Students Carefully   Most perceptual and motor tests are for young children (e.g., preschoolers and elementary students) rather than older students. With older students, the focus of instruction shifts to academic, social, and career skills rather than basic perceptual-processing and motor skills. As a result, the age range of tests should be checked before using them with older students.

Determine the Need for Training   Though many of the tasks associated with perceptual and motor tests are relatively culture- and language-free, some students may require and benefit from training prior to assessment. The accompanying Multicultural Considerations feature discusses the need for training among students with limited English proficiency and with students from deprived backgrounds.

Carefully Observe Behavior   Tests cannot replace the diagnostic information insightful teachers gather from daily observation of and contact with students. For this reason, careful observation is a key element in identifying needs and establishing intervention programs for students with perceptual processing and motor development problems. If the results of testing fail to confirm observations, the results should be carefully reviewed for accuracy.

 MULTICULTURAL CONSIDERATIONS

Assessing Students from Deprived Backgrounds

Students from deprived backgrounds and students with limited English proficiency may need experience with and exposure to perceptual and motor tasks prior to assessment. Providing training ensures accuracy and fairness in assessment. The training usually takes the form of extended practice with examples of the behaviors measured by perceptual and motor tests. For example, if an assessment requires building with 1-inch cubes, throwing and catching bean bags, and performing dynamic balance movements such as standing on one leg and walking a balance beam, the student should practice activities like these. Likewise, if a visual-motor perception test requires copying complex geometric drawings, care should be taken to make sure that the child has been exposed to similar tasks before testing. The practice training should include correcting errors and reinforcing appropriate responses to ensure that inexperience does not mitigate assessment results. However, evaluators must avoid training and practicing with actual test items.

Give an example of how students may have difficulty doing a task because of their background.

 To answer this reflection online, go to the *Multicultural Considerations* module on the Companion Website at *www.prenhall.com/venn*.

☑ Check Your Comprehension

Understanding the terminology is a necessary first step in building a knowledge base of assessment techniques in these specialized domains. Perception refers to processing information received by the senses; motor proficiency concerns movements controlled by the muscles; and perceptual-motor performance is the process of integrating information received by the senses with corresponding body movements. Perceptual-motor processes include visual-motor, auditory-motor, and tactile-motor performance. When assessing student ability in these domains, guidelines ensure the collection of accurate and effective information.

Assessing Motor Proficiency

Motor development plays a central role in the process of interacting with the environment, especially in the lives of children. In fact, much of the learning that takes place with young children is directly related to movement skills and motor performance, particularly in the first few years of life when control of the environment occurs primarily through sensory-motor actions. Specialists view motor activity as the vehicle children first use to interact with and comprehend the environment. As motor skills increase, a child's environment also expands. Furthermore, rather than occurring in isolation, motor development takes place in concert with perceptual, cognitive, and affective growth. Likewise, deficits in motor skill development hinder important learning experiences related to exploration, play, cognition, and socialization. For this reason, students who manifest difficulties in motor development require assessment to identify specific deficits and to develop instructional intervention programs designed to improve movement skills.

Why Do We Assess Motor Proficiency?

We assess motor proficiency for several reasons. First, we use screening tests to obtain a brief survey of overall motor proficiency and to identify children with potential motor disabilities. Second, we use comprehensive motor tests to obtain diagnostic evaluations that provide us with information regarding strengths, weaknesses, and gaps in gross and fine motor development. We also use comprehensive tests as curriculum guides, to assist in writing IEPs, and to develop age-appropriate intervention programs and activities. Finally, we assess motor proficiency to measure student progress and evaluate program effectiveness. A summary of the reasons for assessing motor proficiency appears in Focus 9–1.

The following account gives a practical example of why we assess the motor development of young children with special needs. In this scenario, a special education teacher relies on assessment to help a child with a fine motor skill deficit. The specific deficit is poor eye-hand coordination and delayed manual dexterity, a common motor impairment in children with special needs.

Ray, a 5-year-old student in a preschool class for children with learning disabilities, seemed to have significant deficits in fine motor development but appeared to function within the expected range in gross motor skill performance. Concerned about the nature and extent of Ray's fine motor problems, the teacher gave him the fine motor section of the Peabody Developmental Motor Scales, Second Edition *to diagnose specific strengths, weaknesses,*

FOCUS 9-1

Why Do We Assess Motor Proficiency?

- To screen children for possible deficits in motor proficiency
- To diagnose specific strengths, weaknesses, and gaps in fine and gross motor skills
- To assist in writing IEPs
- To help develop intervention programs and learning activities
- To measure student progress
- To evaluate the effectiveness of intervention programs

and gaps in fine motor development. The results revealed problems with eye-hand coordination and manual dexterity. More specifically, Ray had difficulty copying geometric shapes, building with blocks, and cutting with scissors. The results also showed that his performance was within expected limits for his age group on the fine motor tasks of grasping and hand use. After interpreting the assessment results, the teacher used the Peabody Motor Activities Program to write an IEP goal in fine motor development and prepare specific learning activities to help remediate Ray's deficits. Six months later, the teacher readministered the fine motor scale to measure his progress and gauge the effectiveness of the intervention program. The assessment results indicated that Ray had made good progress in fine motor skill development.

Representative Motor Proficiency Tests

The two most widely used measures of motor proficiency are the Peabody Developmental Motor Scales, Second Edition and the Bruininks–Oseretsky Test of Motor Proficiency, Second Edition. Comprehensive reviews of these instruments and brief reviews of other available motor tests follow.

Peabody Developmental Motor Scales, Second Edition

The Peabody Developmental Motor Scales, Second Edition (PDMS-2) (Folio & Fewell, 2000) is a comprehensive assessment tool and curriculum guide for children from birth to 5 years of age. The individually administered, norm-referenced developmental scales were designed to identify fine and gross motor skill development and develop age-appropriate intervention activities. Designed as a diagnostic instrument and instructional tool, the PDMS-2 is also valuable as a parent guide for developing home programs. The instrument is useful to special education teachers, physical therapists, occupational therapists, and adaptive physical education teachers who need a standardized diagnostic tool to assess motor proficiency and recommend intervention activities. This early childhood motor development instrument contains six subtests: reflexes, stationary, locomotion, object manipulation, grasping, and visual-motor integration. An illustrated guide to administering and scoring provides detailed descriptions of each item. A summary of the PDMS-2 appears in the Test Review box.

The Peabody Motor Activities Program (P-MAP), included in the complete kit, is the instruction/treatment program of the PDMS-2. P-MAP units facilitate the child's development in specific skill areas. Use of the scales with the activity program produces a complete system for combining diagnostic testing with instructional programming.

TEST REVIEW

Peabody Developmental Motor Scales, Second Edition

Type of Test:	A norm-referenced, individually administered developmental scale and curriculum guide
Purpose:	To assess motor proficiency and develop intervention programs
Content Areas:	Gross motor and fine motor development
Administration Time:	Approximately 1 hour
Age Levels:	Birth through 5 years
Suitable for:	Students with motor impairment, including those with severe disabilities, sensory impairments, and mild delays
Scores:	Age equivalents, percentiles, standard scores for overall motor, fine and gross motor development, and for each skill cluster
In Short:	The well-designed PDMS-2 produces detailed assessment data for identifying present levels of motor performance, developing intervention programs, and measuring student progress.

PDMS-2 Materials   The PDMS-2 kit includes a test manual, a picture book, profile/summary forms, and examiner record books along with all materials needed to give the test except for a few pieces of large equipment such as a balance beam for measuring dynamic balance.

PDMS-2 Administration and Scoring   Designed for individual administration, the PDMS-2 produces several standardized scores, including age equivalents, percentiles, and a standard score called a developmental motor quotient. Evaluators may obtain these scores for overall motor development, total fine and gross motor development, and each skill cluster. The PDMS-2 relies on three criteria for scoring each item rather than the usual pass-fail scoring. This three-point system has the advantage of including an "emerging" category that helps to identify developing skills and measure the progress of students who acquire new skills at a slow rate. The manual provides specific guidelines for interpreting test results by providing detailed case studies that illustrate use of the instrument to diagnose motor proficiency, write IEPs, and develop instructional programs.

PDMS-2 Technical Qualities   The PDMS-2 normative sample included 2,003 children from 46 states. Characteristics of the normative sample relative to geography, gender, race, and other critical variables matched U.S. Bureau of Census data. The normative information was stratified by age, and studies supporting the absence of gender and racial bias were conducted. Reliability coefficients were computed for subgroups of the normative sample (e.g., individuals with motor disabilities, African Americans, Hispanic Americans, females, and males) as well as for the entire normative sample. Validity studies were conducted with special attention to the validity of the test for subgroups as well as for the general population. Each item was evaluated using both conventional item analyses to choose "good" statistical items and the new differential item functioning analyses to find biased items.

PDMS-2 Summary   The PDMS-2 is an excellent tool for assessing the motor development of young children. In addition to providing developmental scales and accompanying activities specifically designed for children with motor problems, the PDMS-2 features an enhanced scoring system and a large number of items from which to choose. Appropriate for use with children who have severe disabilities, including sensory impairments, the PDMS-2 also works well with children who display mild delays in motor development. The PDMS-2 provides detailed assessment data for identifying present levels of motor performance, developing intervention programs, and measuring student progress.

Bruininks–Oseretsky Test of Motor Proficiency, Second Edition

The norm-referenced, individually administered Bruininks–Oseretsky Test of Motor Proficiency, Second Edition (BOT-2) (Bruininks & Bruininks, 2005) measures the fine and gross motor skills of children from 4 through 21 years of age. The test includes a short form for obtaining a brief survey of general motor proficiency and a complete battery for obtaining a diagnostic evaluation of specific strengths, weaknesses, and gaps in motor development (see the Test Review for a summary). Designed for use by adaptive physical education teachers, physical and occupational therapists, school psychologists, and special education teachers, the eight BOT-2 subtests measure the following:

* Fine Motor Precision (e.g., cutting out a circle, connecting dots)
* Fine Motor Integration (e.g., copying a star, copying a square)
* Manual Dexterity (e.g., transferring pennies, sorting cards, stringing blocks)
* Bilateral Coordination (e.g., tapping foot and finger, jumping jacks)
* Balance (e.g., walking forward on a line, standing on one leg on a balance beam)
* Running Speed and Agility (e.g., shuttle run, one-legged hop)
* Upper-Limb Coordination (e.g., throwing a ball at a target, catching a tossed ball)
* Strength (e.g., standing long jump, sit-ups)

⬤ TEST REVIEW ⬤

Bruininks–Oseretsky Test of Motor Proficiency, Second Edition

Type of Test:	Norm-referenced and individually administered
Purpose:	A diagnostic test of motor development
Content Areas:	Gross motor and fine motor development
Administration Time:	About an hour for the complete battery and 20 minutes for the screening test
Age Levels:	4 to 21 years
Suitable for:	Students with deficits in motor development associated with mild, moderate, and severe disabilities, including specific learning disabilities and mental retardation
Scores:	Age-based standard scores, percentiles, stanines, and age equivalents
In Short:	The BOT-2 is the premier instrument for measuring gross and fine motor skill development.

BOT-2 Materials The BOT-2 is contained in a large metal briefcase. Materials in the case include a test manual, an administration easel, scoring forms, examinee booklets, a scoring transparency, a balance beam, and other manipulative items.

BOT-2 Administration and Scoring The complete battery takes about an hour to administer and the short form takes about 20 minutes. Before giving the BOT-2, the examiner determines the arm and leg preference of the student because many subtest items require performance with the preferred limb. The test items are administered as game-like tasks designed to capture and hold students' attention. The examiner times a few of the items, such as response speed and upper limb speed and dexterity, with a stopwatch, but most items are not timed. For the complete battery, the examiner gives all eight subtests. For the short form, the examiner gives only selected items from among the subtests. The manual includes clear, easy-to-follow directions for presenting each item and scoring student performance.

The test produces age-equivalent scores for each of the eight subtests as well as for the composite scores. Available test scores also include standard scores, percentiles, and stanines for the gross and fine motor composites, the overall battery, and the short form.

BOT-2 Technical Qualities Technical information about the BOT-2, a revision of the original instrument, was not available when this book was printed. However, the first edition displayed adequate reliability and validity, and the new version should also have appropriate technical characteristics for use as a norm-referenced tool.

BOT-2 Summary The BOT-2 provides examiners with an instrument for obtaining either a brief overview of motor development, using the short form, or a complete picture of motor proficiency, using the complete battery. Consisting of enjoyable game-like tasks, this test format encourages students to perform at their best.

Other Tests of Motor Development

Brief descriptions of other available tests for measuring the motor development of children with special needs follow.

Movement Assessment Battery for Children The Movement Assessment Battery for Children (Movement ABC) (Henderson & Sugden, 1992) includes an assessment instrument and a program-planning guide for children. The battery includes a screening checklist; a comprehensive assessment tool that measures manual dexterity, ball skills, and static and dynamic balance; and a resource guide that offers practical remediation activities and ongoing programs, including case studies. Designed for children from 4 through 12 years of age, the Movement ABC takes about 30 minutes to administer. Although the Movement ABC provides norm-referenced percentiles by age group, the instrument is primarily designed as a criterion-referenced tool for identifying and correcting the movement difficulties of children with motor skills disabilities.

Test of Gross Motor Development The Test of Gross Motor Development (TGMD2) (Ulrich, 2000) measures the gross motor skills of children from 3 through 10 years of age. The TGMD2 identifies children who are significantly behind their peers in gross motor development, assists in developing instructional programs, monitors progress, and evaluates treatment. The TGMD2 takes about 20 minutes to administer, and it is made up of 12 skills (6 for each subtest). The locomotor subtest measures running, galloping, hopping, leaping, horizontal jumping, and sliding.

The object control subtest measures striking a stationary ball, stationary dribbling, kicking, catching, overhand throwing, and underhand rolling. Results from TGMD2 testing may be reported using percentiles, standard scores, or a composite quotient that expresses total gross motor developmental performance.

Multiple-Skill Tests with Motor Development Subtests In addition to the single-skill tests of motor development just reviewed, multiple-skill tests that include subtests for measuring motor skill development are useful for assessing motor proficiency. Among the available multiple-skill tests are the LAP-D Standardized Assessment, the Revised Brigance Diagnostic Inventory of Early Development, the Battelle Developmental Inventory, Second Edition, and the Hawaii Early Learning Profile. Although not as detailed as the single-skill instruments, the multiple-skill tests are often appropriate for measuring motor skill development when in-depth information is not required.

☑ Check Your Comprehension

Assessing motor proficiency involves determining levels of performance in both fine motor and gross motor development. Fine motor refers to small muscle movements such as hand and finger dexterity. Gross motor refers to large muscle movements such as walking and running. When students with special needs require in-depth diagnostic assessment, professionals use specialized tests such as the Peabody Developmental Motor Scales, Second Edition. Alternatively, many multiple-skill tests with motor subtests are useful for assessing motor proficiency. Regardless of the specific assessment approach, resulting information and data should help to identify specific motor problems and design appropriate remediation activities.

Assessing Perception and Perceptual-Motor Skills

Tests and measurements of perception and perceptual-motor skills assess levels of perceptual performance and identify deficits in perceptual skill development. Most often designed to assess specific perceptual or perceptual-motor skills, available instruments measure visual, auditory, and tactile perception as well as visual-motor and auditory-motor processing ability.

Why Do We Assess Perception and Perceptual-Motor Skills?

For students with perceptual and perceptual-motor deficits, assessing the extent and nature of those deficits is an essential step in the intervention and remediation process. A list of the reasons for assessing perception and perceptual-motor skills appears in Focus 9–2. In the initial stages assessment involves screening to identify students with potential perceptual and perceptual-motor deficits. Comprehensive assessment, which follows screening for students identified with a potential problem, helps to diagnose the exact nature and extent of the deficits. Most students have specific problems in particular perceptual-processing domains rather than generalized problems in all perceptual-processing domains. The most common problems include visual-processing deficits that result in poor visual-motor integration and weaknesses in visual perception. These difficulties are significant because good visual perception is a basic process necessary for interacting with the environment. Intact visual-processing ability is also important for learning basic academic skills such as handwriting and reading.

FOCUS 9 - 2

Why Do We Assess Perception?

- To screen for possible perception and perceptual-motor deficits
- To obtain diagnostic data and information regarding specific perception and perceptual-motor deficits
- To assist in developing IEPs and specific intervention activities
- To monitor the effectiveness of intervention programs for remediating perception and perceptual-motor deficits

The following practical, applied account illustrates why we assess perception and perceptual-motor skills. In this scenario a teacher uses assessment to help a child with an auditory-perception problem. The auditory-perception problem described in this account is one of the most common perception deficits in children.

Rossi, a quiet 6-year-old student of average intelligence, had difficulty remembering directions, especially when the teacher gave two or more directions at once. She also had trouble remembering details in long stories read aloud, and she had problems repeating nursery rhymes. Her teacher observed that Rossi displayed good memory for visual information but poor memory for auditory information. To identify the nature and extent of the problem, the teacher referred Rossi for assessment by a specialist. As part of the assessment, an audiologist screened Rossi's hearing to rule out an acuity problem as a causal factor. The audiologist failed to find any significant deficits. However, when a diagnostician gave Rossi a test of auditory perception, the results indicated that she performed significantly below average in auditory memory. Her specific problems included deficits in recognition memory and memory for content and sequence. As a result of the testing, the specialist recommended some remedial intervention activities for Rossi. The teacher implemented the activities in the classroom and made sure to present class information using both visual and the auditory modalities to accommodate Rossi's learning deficit and those of other children in the class with similar difficulties.

Questions About the Perceptual-Motor Approach

Although experts agree about the general nature of perception and perceptual-motor development, they disagree about the effectiveness of tests and intervention techniques. Theorists suggest that perceptual-motor deficits cause academic failure and that remediation improves academic performance. Unfortunately, a lack of evidence exists to support this contention. Critics point out that the perceptual-motor tests are often technically inadequate, and they question the effectiveness of the resulting intervention programs. In particular, many experts question the value of assessment and intervention with older students, who need to focus on academic and functional skills rather than basic processing skills. Despite these concerns, measuring perceptual-motor performance is one component in comprehensive assessment, especially with young children who have neurological deficits. With certain students, identifying perceptual and perceptual-motor deficits and developing appropriate intervention programs to remediate these deficits is part of a complete intervention program.

Reflection
Describe a visual/auditory intervention and discuss how to use this intervention to help a student.

To answer this reflection online, go to the *Teaching and Learning* module on the Companion Website at *www.prenhall.com/venn.*

Representative Perception and Perceptual-Motor Tests

The following reviews of tests of perception and perceptual-motor development include a detailed discussion of the Beery VMI, Fifth Editon along with brief descriptions of other available measures.

Beery VMI, Fifth Edition

The *Beery VMI, Fifth Edition* (Beery, Buktenica, & Beery, 2004) assesses the ability of children from 2 through 18 years of age to integrate visual perception with fine motor coordination. The Beery VMI test items, which are arranged in order of increasing difficulty, consist of geometric figures that children look at and then copy. A summary of the Beery VMI appears in the Test Review box. The Beery VMI provides supplemental visual perception and motor coordination tests, which use the same stimulus forms as the Short and Full Format tests. The supplemental tests are useful when results indicate the need for additional diagnostic information. The instrument was developed for use by preschool teachers, primary teachers, teachers of students with disabilities, and diagnosticians. The purpose of the Beery VMI is to prevent learning and behavioral problems through early screening and identification.

Beery VMI Materials   Beery VMI test materials include a student response booklet, an examiner's manual, and packages of short and long forms, visual test booklets, and motor test booklets.

Beery VMI Administration and Scoring   The Beery VMI takes about 15 minutes to administer and score, using a pass-fail criterion for each geometric design. The short form is best for assessing the visual-motor-integration of children from 2 to 8 years of age. The long form, designed for children from 2 to 18 years of age, can

---

TEST REVIEW

Beery VMI, Fifth Edition

Type of Test:	Norm-referenced screening test
Purpose:	To assess proficiency in integrating visual perception with fine motor coordination
Content Area:	Visual-motor integration
Administration Time:	10 to 15 minutes
Age Levels:	Long form: 2 to 18 years; short form: 2 to 8 years
Suitable for:	Students with visual perception and fine motor coordination difficulties
Scores:	Percentiles and standard scores
In Short:	The Beery VMI is a useful screening test of visual-motor skills. Beery VMI test items include various drawing and visual discrimination tasks such as drawing within lines, making geometric patterns, and identifying shapes.

also be used with adults who have visual-motor-integration deficits. Results are reported as percentiles and standard scores. A profile comparison of the results is also available.

Beery VMI Technical Qualities   The Beery VMI was standardized on a national sample of 2,512 individuals age 2 to 18 years. The manual provides information to support the reliability and validity of the test along with descriptions of research studies using the instrument. The Beery VMI exhibits satisfactory reliability and normative data, especially in comparison with similar tests of perceptual-motor ability.

Beery VMI Summary   The Beery VMI, a norm-referenced measure of visual-motor proficiency, has value when diagnosticians and teachers use it as a screening test or as one tool in an assessment battery. However, the test, consisting of geometric designs, measures a restricted sample of visual-motor ability, and for this reason it should be used together with other assessment data and information rather than in isolation.

Other Tests of Perception and Perceptual-Motor Skills

Tests of perception and perceptual-motor skills are often used with students who have special needs. Brief descriptions of some of the available perceptual tests follow.

Auditory Discrimination Test, Second Edition   The Auditory Discrimination Test, Second Edition (ADT) (Wepman & Reynolds, 1987) is a screening test for identifying the ability to recognize fine differences between the phonemes used in English speech that are necessary for reading. The ADT consists of 40 pairs of words that the examiner reads to the child. The child then indicates either vocally or with gestures whether the word pairs are the same or different. The norm-referenced ADT takes only about 15 minutes to give and to score. The ADT is a quick screening test of auditory discrimination ability for children from 4 to 8 years of age.

Detroit Tests of Learning Aptitude-4   The Detroit Tests of Learning Aptitude-4 (DTLA-4) (Hammill, 1998) are comprehensive, individually administered, norm-referenced diagnostic measures of psychological aptitudes and perceptual-processing abilities in four domains: linguistic, cognitive, attention, and motor. Designed for use with students from age 6 through 17 years, the DTLA-4 subtests include word opposites, design sequences, sentence imitation, reversed letters, story construction, design reproduction, basic information, symbolic relations, word sequences, and story sequences. DTLA-4 scores include standard scores, percentile ranks, age equivalents, and composite scores. Testing time for the DTLA-4 varies from 1 to 2 hours.

Detroit Tests of Learning Aptitude—Primary, Second Edition   The Detroit Tests of Learning Aptitude—Primary, Second Edition (DTLA–P-2) (Hammill & Bryant, 1991) are a modification of the DTLA-4 intended for children from age 3 through 9 years. The DTLA–P-2 measures abilities and deficiencies in three domains: language, attention, and motor. DTLA–P-2 subtests include articulation, conceptual matching, design reproduction, digit sequences, draw-a-person, letter sequences, motor directions, object sequences, oral directions, picture fragments, picture identification, sentence imitation, and symbolic relations. Administration time for the DTLA–P-2 is about 45 minutes, and available scores include standard scores, percentile ranks, age equivalents, composite scores, a total score, and a general mental ability score.

Developmental Test of Visual Perception: Second Edition   The individually administered, norm-referenced Developmental Test of Visual Perception: Second Edition (DTVP-2) (Hammill, Pearson, & Voress, 1993) is a comprehensive diagnostic instrument for assessing the visual-processing skills of children from ages 4 to 10 years. The test includes the following eight subtests:

Skill	Description
Eye-Hand Coordination	Drawing straight, curved, and diagonal lines within increasingly difficult boundaries
Copying	Copying increasingly complex figures from model drawings
Spatial Relations	Reproducing model patterns by connecting dots on a blank grid of dots
Position in Space	Discriminating and matching various figures in rotated and reversed positions
Figure-Ground	Finding geometric shapes hidden within a complex background of other shapes and forms
Visual Closure	Viewing geometric figures and selecting matching figures from a series of figures that all have missing parts
Visual-Motor Speed	Drawing special marks in geometric designs on a page filled with various designs
Form Constancy	Identifying geometric shapes displayed in different sizes, shadings, and positions

The DTVP-2 is a useful tool for identifying the presence and degree of visual-perception problems in children and measuring the effectiveness of intervention programs.

Kent Visual Perception Test   The Kent Visual Perception Test (KVPT) (Melamed, 1996) measures visual-perceptual skills using three perceptual-processing tasks: discrimination, memory, and copying (construction). The test may be given to children ages 5 through 11. The KVPT features a model of perceptual processing to assist in interpretation and also includes suggestions and examples of the best ways to use the test in school and in clinical and neuropsychological evaluations. KVPT norms were based on the performance of 741 children. The test takes about 30 minutes to administer and yields standard scores and percentile ranks for the total score and error analysis. The error-analysis procedure describes in detail a child's specific perceptual deficits.

Motor-Free Visual Perception Test, Third Edition   The Motor-Free Visual Perception Test (MVPT-3)(Colarusso & Hammill, 2002) is a screening test for measuring the visual perception of individuals between the ages of 4 and 85. Because it measures visual perception without reliance on motor skills, the MVPT-3 is especially useful with children who may have learning, cognitive, motor, or physical disabilities. Tasks include matching, figure-ground, closure, visual memory, and form discrimination. Stimuli are line drawings. Answers are presented in multiple-choice format, and responses may be given verbally or by pointing. The test plates may be individually administered and scored in about 15 minutes.

Test of Auditory-Perceptual Skills, Revised   The Test of Auditory-Perceptual Skills, Revised (TAPS-R) (Gardner, 1997) is a norm-referenced test of children's ability to perceive auditory information and is designed for use in diagnosing children from age 4 to 13 who have auditory difficulties, auditory modality deficits, and language problems that could underlie learning problems. The test takes about 25 minutes to give and score and contains subtests measuring auditory number memory, auditory sentence memory, auditory word memory, auditory interpretation of directions, auditory word discrimination, and auditory processing. The test also includes a hyperactive rating scale that may help determine the effects of a child's behavior on the test results as well as in the classroom. Available TAPS-R scores include standard scores, scaled scores, stanines, and percentiles.

Test of Auditory-Perceptual Skills: Upper Level   The Test of Auditory-Perceptual Skills: Upper Level (TAPS:UL) (Gardner, 1994) is designed for children ages 12 to 18. Like the TAPS-R, the TAPS:UL assesses auditory-perceptual skills for diagnosing children and teenagers who have auditory-perceptual difficulties, imperceptions of auditory processing, or language-related learning problems.

Full Range Test of Visual-Motor Integration   The Full Range Test of Visual-Motor Integration (FRTVMI) (Hammill, Pearson, Voress, & Reynolds, 2005) is a screening test of the visual-motor abilities of individuals ages 4 to 94. The test involves copying a series of increasingly complex geometric figures. It can be given individually and to groups. The test is scored by rating each item as either 0, 1, 2, or 3, which makes it possible to easily identify potentially severe as well as potentially superior copying skills.

Wide Range Assessment of Visual Motor Abilities   The Wide Range Assessment of Visual Motor Abilities (WRAVMA) (Adams & Sheslow, 1995) is a norm-referenced measure of the visual-motor skills of children and adolescents 3 to 17 years of age. WRAVMA includes subtests that measure visual-motor integration (evaluated using a drawing test), visual-spatial relations (evaluated using a matching test), and fine motor (evaluated using a pegboard test). It takes about 15 to 30 minutes to administer the WRAVMA. Available test scores include scaled scores, standard scores, age equivalents, and percentiles.

Check Your Comprehension

Assessing perception and perceptual-motor ability involves observing and measuring the way students process and respond to sensory information. Perception and perceptual-motor skills include visual and auditory perception as well as visual-motor and auditory-motor proficiency. Because of questions about the reliability and validity of assessment instruments in these domains, special educators should use tests carefully with full knowledge of their limits and imperfections.

Assessing Learning Styles

Learning styles are the primary or preferred ways for learning new or difficult information. Learning styles refer to the ways learners prefer to take in and process information. According to Felder (n.d.), the different ways include: by seeing and hearing, by reflecting and acting, by reasoning logically and intuitively, by analyzing and visualizing, and by working in groups and individually. Preferred teaching methods also vary. Some teachers prefer to lecture; others demonstrate or lead by self-discovery; some focus on principles and others on applications; some emphasize facts and others understanding. Learning styles also include the visual, auditory, and **kinesthetic** (a combination of feeling, balance, and motion) sensory modalities. Although students can learn through a variety of styles and modalities, most usually display learning style preferences. For example, many students prefer the visual mode. However, the auditory and tactile modes also play an important role in learning.

Observing Learning Styles and Modality Preferences

Assessing learning styles and modality preferences involves the use of tests but more often entails careful observation by trained teachers to identify strengths and weaknesses in daily behavior. Knowledgeable teachers usually identify preferred approaches by associating behaviors with learning styles. Although no one relies exclusively on one style or modality, most students display distinct preferences. For example, visual learners learn best by seeing and watching. In contrast, auditory learners prefer to listen. Tactile learners learn best during direct participation. An excerpt from an informal checklist for assessing modality strengths, adapted from an observation system developed by Milone (1981), appears in Figure 9–1. Teachers may use this checklist as a curriculum-based assessment tool for identifying the modality strengths of their students. After noting which of these behaviors a student typically displays in the classroom, teachers can then develop appropriate intervention activities.

Connecting Learning Style and Modality Assessment with Instruction

According to Milone (1981), the central element of assessment and instruction is identifying and teaching to students' learning strengths. Milone points out that because students display various modality strengths and learning preferences, instruction should include activities that draw on a variety of styles and modalities. For example, students who prefer the auditory modality may learn spelling best when they hear and say the letters aloud. On the other hand, strong visual learners may prefer to learn by seeing the words and creating mental pictures of them. Students who prefer the kinesthetic modality may learn best when they write the words on paper or on the chalkboard. Some students learn best in groups whereas others prefer individual assignments. However, lessons incorporating activities that tap an array of learning styles respond to the strengths of all students regardless of their preferences.

Reflection
What do you think your learning style is? What helps you most?

 To answer this reflection online, go to the *Teaching and Learning* module on the Companion Website at *www.prenhall.com/venn*.

Learning Style Inventories

Descriptions of several available inventories for assessing learning styles follow, beginning with the Canfield Learning Styles Inventory, one of many Web-based inventories available on the Internet. More information about Web-based modality and learning styles assessment appears in the Technology Focus box.

Canfield Learning Styles Inventory

The Canfield Learning Styles Inventory (Canfield, 2001) is an assessment tool for helping students and teachers understand learning preferences. This Web-based inventory is a screening test consisting of 30 multiple-choice items. The Canfield Inventory divides learning styles into levels of independence, working with others, content (numeric, qualitative, inanimate), and mode (listening, reading, iconic, direct experience). Inventory results are reported in percentiles.

Index of Learning Styles Questionnaire

The Web-based Index of Learning Styles Questionnaire (ILS) (Soloman & Felder, 2004) assesses preferences on four learning style dimensions: active/reflective, sensing/intuitive, visual/verbal, and sequential/global. The ILS is a screening instrument with 44 items. The ILS produces a graphical report with scores that indicate a balance, a moderate preference, or a strong preference in each dimension. The ILS Web site

Figure 9–1 Observable characteristics of modality strengths.

Date: _____ Student: _____
Observer: _____ School and Class: _____
Directions: The observer should know the student well. Complete the checklist by placing a checkmark after each behavior the student exhibits on a consistent basis. The relative number of checks in each modality provides an indication of modality strengths.

Behavior	Visual	✓	Authority	✓	Kinesthetic	✓
Learning style	Learns best by looking		Learns best by hearing		Learns best through direct experience	
	Likes to watch demonstrations		Likes verbal directions		Likes hands-on involvement	
Reading	Likes word pictures, descriptions, and illustrations		Likes drama, dialogue, and plays		Likes action stories	
	Learns from photographs, diagrams, graphs, and charts		May move lips or whisper when reading		May not enjoy reading	
Memory	Remembers by writing things down and drawing		Remembers best by saying things		Remembers what happened and who did what	
	Good memory for faces		Good memory for names		Good memory of events	
Distractibility	May notice visual distractions and extra motion		May notice excessive noise and sounds		Difficulty concentrating on visual information	
	May not notice sounds (e.g., a noisy class)		May not notice visual distractions and extra motion		Difficulty concentrating on auditory information	
Behavior during inactive periods	States into space or watches something		Talks with others		Restless, squirmy	
	Doodles or draws		Talks to self or hums		Wants to move around	

Behavior	Visual	✓	Authority	✓	Kinesthetic	✓
Communication	Tends to be quiet		Enjoys talking		Uses gestures and movement when talking	
	May become impatient when listening		Likes hearing others talk		Loses interest in long conversations	
Artistic interests	Prefers visual arts		Prefers music		Prefers sculpture and hands-on exhibits	
	Likes details and components		Likes work as a whole		May show little interest in art	
Physical appearance	Neat and orderly		May mix and match clothes		May look ruffled due to activity	
	May not vary appearance		May vary appearance		May appear disheveled	
Behavior in new settings	Looks around and watches		Talks about setting and environment		Moves about the environment	
	Examines details		Discusses setting and how it feels		Touches, feels, and handles	
Total number of checks	Visual characteristics		Auditory characteristics		Kinesthetic characteristics	

TECHNOLOGY FOCUS
Learning Style Assessments on the Internet

Numerous learning style inventories are available on the Internet. These include the Canfield Learning Styles Inventory and the Index of Learning Styles Questionnaire. Students complete these inventories on the Internet and they receive almost instantaneous results. Web-based inventories also provide interpretive information for teachers and students. The results, the interpretive information, and the inventories themselves may be printed for future reference.

Many Web-based inventories are free for individual users but have fees when used with groups. The fee-based services include the ability to submit and obtain results for groups as well as individuals. Computer-based assessments provide a way of assessing the learning and modality preferences that complements careful observation and is an option to traditional pencil-on-paper inventories.

provides useful information for interpreting results, including a description of each dimension and suggested learning strategies. The ILS is available at no cost to students and faculty at educational institutions who wish to use it for noncommercial purposes. A printed version of the ILS is available on the Internet for downloading.

Learning Styles Inventory—Version III

The Learning Styles Inventory—Version III (LSI III) (Renzulli, Smith, & Rizza, 2002) is a self-scoring instrument with 56 items designed to measure students' attitudes toward seven modes of instruction. A class set includes 30 student instruments, one teacher instrument, and one classroom summary sheet. Two versions of the inventory are available: one for elementary classes and the other for middle school classes.

✓ Check Your Comprehension

Assessing learning styles and modalities involves observing and measuring student preferences for learning new or difficult information. Most experts recognize the importance of assessing learning styles in education, and teachers find that many students display a preference for visual learning. Although teachers usually rely on direct observation of student behavior rather than testing to identify preferred learning modalities, they may also select from several available inventories to assess learning modality preferences. These inventories are best utilized when teachers use them as informal, criterion-based tools.

Summary

The process of assessing motor proficiency, perceptual ability, and learning styles includes a diverse collection of specific tests and techniques. A summary of the instruments reviewed in this chapter appears in Table 9–1. This collection encompasses measures of fine and gross motor development, perceptual ability, perceptual-motor performance, learning styles, and sensory learning modalities. These tests and procedures identify levels of performance as well as strengths, weaknesses, and gaps in development. Teachers use these results to write IEPs and to develop appropriate instructional objectives for students with processing deficits and motor delays. Although evaluating motor proficiency, perception, and learning styles is an essential step in identifying the learning needs of certain students, many pitfalls exist, including misconceptions about the meaning of perception and learning styles, questions about the validity of many available tests and observation procedures, and misuse of results. Fortunately, guidelines for avoiding these hazards exist, and by following them, professionals ensure accurate and effective assessment.

Despite the challenges associated with assessing motor proficiency, perception, and learning styles, those who serve students with disabilities should be well versed in the available tests and procedures and their appropriateness in given situations. For teachers of students with disabilities, understanding assessment in these domains is part of a complete knowledge base in appraisal techniques. This knowledge helps equip professionals with the necessary competencies to respond to the individual needs of students with motor skill and perceptual deficits.

To check your comprehension of the chapter contents, go to the *Guided Review and Quiz* modules in Chapter 9 of the Companion Website, *http://www.prenhall.com/venn*.

Table 9–1 Review of Perception, Learning Styles, and Motor Proficiency Assessments

Name of Test	Type of Test	Suitable for	Brief Description of Test	Purpose of Administering Test
Auditory Discrimination Test, Second Edition (ADT)	Norm-referenced, individually administered screening test	Children from 4 to 8 years of age	Consists of 40 pairs of words for assessing the ability to recognize fine differences between phonemes	To assess auditory discrimination ability
*Berry VMI, Fifth Edition	Norm-referenced screening test	Students from 2 to 18 years of age	Includes a variety of drawing and visual discrimination tasks such as drawing within the lines, making geometric patterns, and identifying shapes	To assess proficiency in integrating visual perception with fine motor coordination
*Bruininks-Oseretsky Test of Motor Proficiency, Second Edition (BOT-2)	Norm-referenced, individually administered diagnostic test including a short from and a complete battery	Students from 4 to 21 years of age	Measures fine and gross motor skills including fine manual control, gross manual control, body control, and strength and agility	To obtain a brief overview of motor development using the short complete picture of motor proficiency using the complete battery
Canfield Learning Styles Inventory	Criterion-referenced, Web-based screening test inventory results are reported in percentiles	Students with at least functional-level reading skills	Contains 30 multiple-choice items that measure level of independence, working with others, content (numeric, qualitative, inanimate), and mode (listening, reading, iconic, direct experience)	To help students and teachers understand learning preferences

(continued)

Table 9–1 *continued*

Name of Test	Type of Test	Suitable for	Brief Description of Test	Purpose of Administering Test
Detroit Tests of Learning Aptitude—4 (DTLA-4)	Norm-referenced, individually administered diagnostic test	Students from 6 to 17 years of age	Measures skills in four domains: linguistic, cognitive attention, and motor	To assess psychological aptitudes and perceptual processing abilities
Detroit Tests of Learning Aptitude—Primary, Second Edition (DTLA-P-2)	Norm-referenced, individually administered diagnostic test	Students from 3 to 9 years of age	Includes 13 subtests	To measure abilities and deficiencies in three domains: language, articulation, and motor
Developmental Test of Visual Perception: Second Edition (DTVP-2)	Norm-referenced diagnostic test	Students from 4 to 10 years of age	Measures eye-hand coordination, spatial relations, position-in-space, figure-ground, visual closure, visual-motor speed, and form constancy	To assess visual processing skills, identity the presence and degree of visual perception problems, and measure the effectiveness of intervention programs
Full Range Test of Visual Motor Integration (FRTVMI)	Norm-referenced, individually or group-administered screening test	Individuals from 4 to 17 years of age	Asks individuals to copy an increasingly difficult series designs	Assesses the ability to accurately relate visual stimuli to motor responses
Index of Learning Styles Questionnaire (ILS)	Criterion-referenced, Web-based, individually administered screening instrument	Students with good reading ability	Contains 44 items for assessing preferences on four learning style dimensions: active/reflective, sensing/intuitive visual/verbal, and sequential/global	To screen for learning style preferences and to develop instructional strategies
Kent Visual Perception Test (KVPT)	Norm-referenced diagnostic test	Students from 5 to 11 years of age	Measures three perceptual processing tasks: discrimination, memory, and copying (construction)	To assess the visual perception skills of children

Name of Test	Type of Test	Suitable for	Brief Description of Test	Purpose of Administering Test
Learning Styles Inventory, Version III (LSI III)	Criterion-referenced, individually or group-administered screening instrument	Elementary and middle school students	A self-scoring instrument with 56 items. Two versions of the inventory are available: one for elementary classes and the other for middle school classes.	Designed to measure students' attitudes toward seven modes of instruction
Motor-Free Visual Perception Test, Third Edition (MVPT-3)	Norm-referenced, individuallly administered screening test	Individuals from 4 to 85 years of age	Tasks include matching, figure-ground, closure, visual memory, and form discrimination	Designed to assess visual perception without reliance on an individual's motor skills
Movement Assessment Battery for Children (Movement ABC)	Criterion-referenced assessment instrument and programming guide	Children between the ages of 4 and 12	Measures manual dexterity, ball skills, and static and dynamic balance	To help identify and correct the movement difficulties of children with motor disabilities
*Peabody Developmental Motor Scales, Second Edition (PDMS-2)	Norm-referenced, individually administered diagnostic scale and curriculum guide	Children from birth to 5 years of age	Gross motor subtests include reflexes, balance, nonlocomotor, locomotor, and receipt and propulsion; fine motor subtests include grasping, hand use, eye-hand coordination, and manual dexterity	To obtain detailed assessment data for identifying present levels of motor performance, developing intervention programs, and measuring student progress
Test of Auditory-Perceptual Skills, Revised (TAPS-R)	Norm-referenced individually administered	4 to 13 years of age	Measures auditory number memory, auditory sentence memory, auditory word memory, auditory interpretation of directions,	To measure children's ability to perceive auditory information and diagnose children with

(continued)

237

Table 9–1 *continued*

Name of Test	Type of Test	Suitable for	Brief Description of Test	Purpose of Administering Test
			auditory word discrimination, and auditory processing	auditory difficulties
Test of Auditory-Perceptual Skills: Upper Level (TAPS: UL)	Norm-referenced, individually administered	12 to 18 years of age	Measures auditory number memory, auditory sentence memory, auditory word memory, auditory interpretation of directions, auditory word discrimination, and auditory processing	To assess the auditory perceptual skills of older children with difficulties in auditory processing and language
Test of Gross Motor Development (TGMD2)	Norm-referenced, individually administered diagnostic test	3 to 10 years of age	Measures locomotor skills and object control skills	To identify children who are significantly behind their peers in gross motor development, to assist in developing instructional programs, to monitor progress, and to evaluate treatment
Wide Range Assessment of Visual Motor Abilities (WRAVMA)	Norm-referenced, individually administered screening test	3 to 17 years of age	Measures visual-motor integration (evaluated using a drawing test), visual-spatial relations (evaluator using a matching test), and fine-motor (evaluated using a pegboard test)	To assess the visual-motor skills of children and adolescents

*Tests marked with an asterisk are featured in this chapter.

Meeting Performance Standards and Preparing for Licensure Exams

After reading this chapter, you should be able to demonstrate the following CEC Standards and PRAXIS™ test knowledge and skills. The information in parentheses identifies where to find the particular CEC standard and PRAXIS™ content reference.

CEC Standards for Beginning Special Education Teachers

- Specialized terminology used in the assessment of individuals with disabilities (GC8K1)
- Procedures for early identification of young children who may be at risk for disabilities (GC8K4)
- Use exceptionality-specific assessment instruments with individuals with disabilities (GC8S2)
- Select, adapt, and modify assessments to accommodate the unique abilities and needs of individuals with disabilities (GC8S3)

PRAXIS™ Education of Exceptional Students: Core Content Knowledge

- Assessment, including use of assessment for screening, diagnosis, placement, and the making of instructional decisions, for example: how to select and conduct nondiscriminatory and appropriate assessments, and how to interpret standardized and specialized assessment results (0353 III)
- Assessment, including procedures and test materials, both formal and informal, typically used for prereferral, screening, referral, classification, placement, and ongoing program monitoring (0353 III)
- How to select, construct, conduct, and modify nondiscriminatory, developmentally and chronologically age-appropriate informal assessments, including teacher-made tests, curriculum-based assessment, and alternatives to norm-referenced testing, including observations (0353 III)

chapter 10

Language and Bilingual Assessment

Objectives

After reading this chapter, you will be prepared to do the following:

- Describe the purpose of language assessment.
- Discuss current trends in language assessment.
- Describe the structural components of language.
- Link language assessment with classroom instruction.
- Assess phonemes, morphemes, and syntax.
- Assess semantics and pragmatics.
- Use comprehensive measures for assessing language.
- Assess students from culturally and linguistically diverse backgrounds.

Overview

Assessing language involves measuring receptive and expressive communication skills, including listening and speaking. In this chapter, you have the opportunity to study the curriculum-based evaluation procedures and the tests for assessing these skills. To achieve this goal you review the definition of language and the behaviors measured by language assessment procedures and tests. You also investigate the use of language assessment with students who have special needs, and you explore links between language assessment and instruction. After this introduction, you examine curriculum-based language assessment procedures and language tests. As you review each procedure and test, you consider the purpose of the assessment, the administration and scoring procedures, and the practical applications in the classroom. At the conclusion of the chapter, you consider procedures for assessing students from culturally and linguistically diverse backgrounds, an increasingly important topic due to the growing numbers of bilingual students in school.

The Importance of Language Assessment

Although Ms. Kaye studied language assessment in her teacher education classes, she had not worked in this area since graduating. Because she has several children in her class with severe language disabilities, she is considering language assessment for the first time. Before beginning she asks herself these questions: How much of what she studied in college about language assessment is applicable to the students in her class? Will language assessment

make a difference in the teaching and learning process with her students? After Ms. Kaye does some research, talks with colleagues, and consults with a speech pathologist, she decides to try language assessment. Her goal is to help diagnose specific skills in need of remediation and to document student learning. She decides to try the test recommended by another teacher and by the speech pathologist with the students in her class who have severe language delays.

In broad terms, **language** refers to any means used to receive or send messages. More specifically, language is the use of organized voice sounds and written symbols to communicate thoughts and feelings. Language occurs at expressive, receptive, and inner levels of communication. **Expressive language** involves sending messages and translating thoughts, ideas, and signals into vocal or motor expression (the latter includes writing, sign language, and other nonvocal forms of communication). **Receptive language** consists of receiving input with the senses (usually the ears) and giving meaning to the sensory input. **Inner language** is the use of language in thinking, planning, and cognition. Often referred to as thought within oneself, inner language is a necessary developmental building block for receptive and expressive language.

Development and use of language begins in infancy and continues throughout life. For infants the development of early communication skills provides the groundwork for later acquisition of symbolic language and serves as the basis for social and cognitive growth. For toddlers and preschoolers, language development includes learning an extensive range and variety of receptive and expressive language skills that develop in concert with cognitive, motor, and social skills. For school-age children, language is both the foundation for academic learning and the basis for organizing thought itself. For adults, language is an integral part of daily living at home, at work, and in the community. Thus, language is essential in all aspects of life.

Many students with disabilities exhibit significant language deficits. In fact, language problems are the single most common disability among school-age children. These problems may occur in both receptive (understanding messages) and expressive (sending messages) language. Speech difficulties, in the form of articulation disorders, represent by far the most common language deficits in children. Some students who use nonstandard English or English as a second language also have language deficits. Specific language problems are associated with certain disabilities.

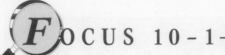

For example, students with hearing disabilities typically manifest severe speech and language deficits based on the type, severity, and age of onset of deafness. Likewise, some physical disabilities such as cerebral palsy cause characteristic speech problems. Students with mental retardation may exhibit general delays in developing language skills. The extent of the delays depends upon the severity of retardation. Because they represent one of the most common learning problems, teachers of students with special needs must understand language deficits, use assessment strategies for specific language problems, and develop and implement remedial intervention programs. Additional information about assessing speech and language disorders appears in Focus 10–1.

Considerations in Language Assessment

The considerations described in the following list clarify the meaning and use of language assessment with students who have disabilities.

- Many tests rely on language-based items. For example, most individually administered intelligence tests contain entire language-based subtests. Likewise, most tests of social and academic skills rely heavily on language ability. When assessing students with language disabilities using language-based tests, language deficits rather than lack of content knowledge may depress test results.
- Most language tests and assessment procedures measure the development and skills of young children. Fewer measures assess the language proficiency of adolescents and adults.
- Overton (2006) considers remediation of language disorders a shared responsibility among speech clinicians and teachers. Speech clinicians have primary

responsibility for diagnosing and guiding efforts to remediate speech disorders (e.g., articulation, voice, and fluency problems). However, clinicians should work together with teachers to diagnose problems and design intervention goals to improve a student's receptive, expressive, and written language skills. When clinicians and teachers use a team approach, they are better able to respond to the needs of their students.

- Interpreting assessment results includes considering language development in relation to general learning ability, academic achievement, and social skills.
- Students with learning disabilities frequently exhibit specific language deficits, including problems with word meanings, memory, and ability to generalize.
- A student's lack of motivation and inappropriate behavior may significantly depress language performance. Outgoing students may hide language deficiencies behind disruptive behavior whereas withdrawn students may simply refuse to display language skills up to their level of ability.
- In current practice, language assessment receives less emphasis than does assessment of academic skills. Although many factors contribute to this lack of emphasis, more attention should be devoted to assessment and intervention in this important domain.

The Structural Components of Language

Language consists of both receptive and expressive elements. *Receptive language* (listening) decodes the meaning of messages, including written ones. *Expressive language* (speech) translates ideas into vocal or motor expression, including sign language and writing. In addition to these receptive and expressive elements, language consists of five structural components.

Phonology

Phonology is the of study phonemes, the smallest units of sound in spoken language. American English includes 44 speech sounds or phonemes. Phonemes have no meaning by themselves but contribute to word meaning. For example, the word *boy* includes three phonemes: *b*, *o*, and *y*.

Morphology

Morphology is the study of morphemes, the smallest meaningful units of language. For example, the word *boy* has one morpheme, but the plural form of the word (*boys*) has two morphemes because *s* is a separate language unit.

Syntax

Syntax is the way morphemes or words go together to form phrases and meaningful sentences. For example, the sentence "I am going to the store" is syntactically correct, but the sentence "I going store" is incorrect. Morphemes and syntax are the two components of grammar.

Semantics

Semantics involves understanding and expressing word meanings and relationships, including vocabulary, synonyms, antonyms, word categories, ambiguities, and absurdities. For example, word relationships include the associations that exist between words such as *8:45* and a *quarter to nine*, and between *house* and *home*.

Table 10–1 Structural Components of Language

Component	Receptive Language	Expressive Language
Phonology	Discriminating speech sounds	Articulating speech sounds
Morphology and syntax	Understanding grammatical structure of language	Using grammar in words and sentences
Semantics and pragmatics	Understanding word meanings and contextual language cues	Using word meanings and using language in context

Pragmatics

Pragmatics is the use of language in context, especially during social interaction. The essence of pragmatics is the process of sharing intents, which occurs in a wide variety of settings and contexts, including those involving two people, small groups, and large groups. For example, the verbal sharing of intents includes intimate communication such as whispering in someone's ear as well as highly formal communication such as being introduced at a presidential reception. Pragmatics involves a rule system consisting of the setting, the characteristics of the participants, the topic, and the purpose of the interaction.

Assessing language involves measuring receptive and expressive skills in these structural components. A description of the receptive and expressive aspects of the structural components of language appears in Table 10–1.

Why Do We Assess Language?

Language problems are the single most common disability among school-age children. For this reason, teachers of students with special needs must have a thorough grounding in the techniques associated with language assessment and intervention. Language assessment is a necessary element of screening children with potential language disabilities who may need further assessment to determine whether they qualify for and would benefit from special education services. Language assessment is also essential in classifying and placing children with language deficits. In the classroom, teachers use language assessment to help develop IEPs, to plan instructional programs, and to develop specific learning activities for individual children and groups of children. Finally, measuring children's progress in language development also requires the use of language assessment. A summary

F OCUS 10 - 2

Why Do We Assess Language?

- To screen children who may have language deficits
- To identify, classify, and place children with language deficits
- To help develop IEPs, plan instructional programs, and develop specific language interventions
- To measure the progress of children with language deficits

of the reasons for assessing the language of students with special needs appears in Focus 10–2.

The following account illustrates one way in which language assessment helps diagnose the language problems of a child, develop remedial intervention activities, and measure the progress of a child with a language deficit.

Jeffrey was 10 years old and in the fourth grade when the child-study team recommended him for a comprehensive language evaluation. Although he had not received speech or language therapy or other special assistance in the primary grades, the team suspected language problems as the cause of his academic difficulties, including his failing grades in school. Jeffrey's teachers, puzzled by his lack of academic progress, described his classroom performance as "weak," "inconsistent," and "confused." As part of the assessment, a speech and language pathologist gave Jeffrey several formal tests of language ability and obtained a spontaneous language sample for later analysis. The results revealed Jeffrey's most serious difficulty as understanding word meanings. A second difficulty concerned word knowledge and word-finding skills. As a result of the assessment, the child-study team identified Jeffrey's language disability and arranged for him to begin receiving language therapy. The language therapist tried several intervention approaches to improve Jeffrey's word-finding skills, including word-finding strategies and self-cueing techniques. These approaches helped Jeffrey improve his speed and accuracy in word finding. The therapist also monitored the carryover effects of the direct intervention on Jeffrey's oral and silent reading, reading comprehension, and writing performance in the classroom. As part of the monitoring process, the therapist consulted with the classroom teacher on a regular basis. After a year of intervention, Jeffrey posted gains of about 3 years in understanding word meanings, word knowledge, and word-finding skills.

Jeffrey, now in junior high school, receives assistance with schoolwork from a professional tutor rather than a language therapist. His parents are committed to helping their son in the future by providing him with learning aids (such as tape recorders and computers) that he will need in high school and college.

This account, based on a case study by Wiig and Semel (1984), illustrates the importance of assessment in identifying language problems and developing intervention programs. In Jeffrey's case, professionals relied on assessment to diagnose specific deficits and used the results to develop an individualized intervention plan and monitor progress.

Curriculum-Based Language Assessment

Although norm-referenced tests are valuable in instruction, curriculum-based assessment provides the most direct link between assessment and classroom instruction. Some of the most useful curriculum-based assessment techniques include:

- Collecting spontaneous language samples in real-life settings
- Analyzing the mean length of utterances (MLUs)
- Conducting developmental sentence analysis
- Interviewing the child and the parents
- Completing criterion-referenced checklists of specific language behaviors
- Observing the child's language in natural settings such as the classroom, the home, or with peers

☑ Check Your Comprehension

Assessing language involves measuring receptive and expressive communication skills, including listening and speaking. The most common language deficits among school-age children are associated with expressive and receptive language problems, which may correlate with any of the five structural components of language: phonemes, morphemes, syntax, semantics, and pragmatics. Although norm-referenced tests are valuable in the instructional process, informal, curriculum-based assessment provides the most direct link between assessment and intervention.

Assessing the Sounds of Language: Phonology

Reflection
Do you think it is harder/easier for new parents to detect language problems? Explain.

To answer this reflection online, go to the *Teaching and Learning* module on the Companion Website at *www.prenhall.com/venn.*

Assessing phonemes involves evaluating the use of speech sounds both receptively and expressively. All spoken languages consist of basic sounds or phonemes. The expressive elements of oral language begin with these basic speech sounds. However, for children with disabilities development of phonemes often occurs later than usual. Articulation disorders, the most common of all speech disorders, occur when a student fails to produce phonemes appropriately. Phonological assessment includes evaluating the ability to discriminate between speech sounds when listening and to articulate these sounds when speaking. Reviews of two representative tests of phonology, the Goldman-Fristoe Test of Articulation, Second Edition and the Goldman-Fristoe-Woodcock Test of Auditory Discrimination, follow.

Goldman-Fristoe Test of Articulation, Second Edition

The Goldman-Fristoe Test of Articulation, Second Edition (GFTA-2) (Goldman & Fristoe, 2000) provides a structured method for evaluating an important element of speech: articulation of consonant sounds. Designed for children and youths from age 2 through 21, the test includes a sounds-in-words subtest to measure articulation of speech sounds, a sounds-in-sentences subtest to evaluate sound production in connected speech, and a stimulability subtest to gauge the ability to correct misarticulated sounds when given a model of correct production. Goldman and Fristoe designed the GFTA-2 for speech pathologists to use before beginning therapy and for audiologists and special educators to use as a diagnostic tool. A summary of the GFTA-2 appears in the Test Review box.

GFTA-2 Materials   GFTA-2 materials include an easel booklet, a manual, a package of 25 response forms, and a supplemental developmental norms booklet. The materials are contained in a canvas carry bag. Optional materials include a scoring assist software program.

GFTA-2 Administration and Scoring   The GFTA-2 takes approximately 15 minutes to administer. The sounds-in-words subtest uses pictures that prompt articulation of speech sounds in the initial, medial, and final positions. The sounds-in-sentences subtest contains two stories read while a student looks at pictures illustrating the key words in the story. The student then tells the story to the evaluator while looking at the pictures. The evaluator scores the student's skill at articulating the key words in the story. The stimulability subtest measures the ability to correct misarticulated sounds after the evaluator models the correct sound production.

TEST REVIEW

Goldman-Fristoe Test of Articulation, Second Edition

Type of Test:	Norm- and criterion-referenced, individually administered
Purpose:	To diagnose articulation problems
Content Areas:	Sounds in words (normed), sounds in sentences, and stimulability
Administration Time:	Approximately 15 minutes
Age Levels:	2 to 21 years
Suitable for:	Students with articulation impairments or as a tool for identifying such students
Scores:	Item analysis of specific articulation errors
In Short:	The GFTA-2 provides a structured tool for identifying errors in articulation, including positions in which errors occur, types of frequently occurring errors, error patterns as complexity increases, and errors in voicing.

Available scores include age-based standard scores, percentiles, and test-age equivalents. There are two levels of scoring dependent on the qualifications of the examiner. In level 1, sound production is judged only for presence of error. A speech-language pathology assistant may complete this scoring. In level 2, sound production is judged for presence and type of error. Only trained speech-language pathologists should complete level 2.

Evaluators may enhance GFTA-2 assessment by using the instrument together with the Khan-Lewis Phonological Analysis, Second Edition (KLPA-2) (Khan & Lewis, 2002). The KLPA-2 makes use of the 53 target words elicited by the GFTA-2 sounds-in-words subtest. To use the norm-referenced KLPA-2, evaluators first administer the GFTA-2 and then transfer the responses to the KLPA-2 analysis form that lists the most common sound changes when words are mispronounced. Then evaluators use the sound change booklet to identify the phonological processes used. The last step is to prepare a phonological summary and progress report that includes intervention activities for parents and remediation goals and objectives for IEPs.

GFTA-2 Technical Characteristics   The GFTA-2 displays very good technical characteristics. The normative sample included 2,350 children and youths from age 2 through 21 who were tested at over 300 sites nationwide. Reliability studies produced median reliability coefficients ranging from .94 to .98 and interrater percentages ranging from 90 to 93. Validity studies included measures of content and construct validity.

GFTA-2 Summary   The GFTA-2 provides speech and language pathologists with a standardized tool for identifying errors in articulating the consonant sounds of Standard American English. It includes measures of single-word and conversational-speech production both spontaneously and after modeling.

╭─── **TEST REVIEW** ───╮

Goldman-Fristoe-Woodcock Test of Auditory Discrimination

Type of Test:	Norm-referenced and individually administered
Purpose:	A screening test of auditory discrimination
Content Areas:	Auditory discrimination under noisy and quiet conditions
Administration Time:	Approximately 20 minutes
Age Levels:	4 years to adult
Suitable for:	Students with auditory discrimination deficits, including those with speech and learning disabilities, mental retardation, and hearing impairments
Scores:	Standard scores, percentiles, and error pattern analysis of specific discrimination errors
In Short:	The GFW is a well-designed screening test with good technical characteristics.

Goldman-Fristoe-Woodcock Test of Auditory Discrimination

The Goldman-Fristoe-Woodcock Test of Auditory Discrimination (GFW) (Goldman, Fristoe, & Woodcock, 1976), an individually administered screening test, measures the ability to differentiate between speech sounds in quiet and noisy situations. The authors designed the GFW for speech, language, and hearing clinicians, and they also recommend it for use by audiologists, diagnosticians, reading specialists, and special educators. The GFW assesses the auditory discrimination ability of children from 4 years of age through adulthood. A summary of the GFW appears in the Test Review box.

GFW Materials   Goldman-Fristoe-Woodcock test materials include an easel-kit of stimulus pictures, a manual, an audiocassette, and a scoring sheet.

GFW Administration and Scoring   Requiring about 20 minutes to administer, the GFW uses a cassette recorder to play a 7½-minute tape that contains the two subtests. The manual provides clear directions for administering, scoring, and interpreting results, including a discussion of problems associated with testing discrimination ability and suggestions for auditory training techniques to remediate discrimination deficits. The GFW provides both standard scores and percentiles, and it includes an error pattern analysis procedure to identify specific types of listening errors for developing intervention objectives.

GFW Technical Characteristics   Standardized on a sample group of individuals from ages 3 to 84, the GFW exhibits satisfactory reliability and validity. In addition to comparing norms for the general population, evaluators may compare a child's listening ability to that of subjects from nine clinical samples, including groups with learning deficits, mental retardation, hearing impairments, and speech disabilities.

GFW Summary　　The Goldman-Fristoe-Woodcock Test of Auditory Discrimination provides a rapid and easy method for identifying performance levels in auditory discrimination. The instrument has value as a screening test with students who display difficulty in listening.

☑ Check Your Comprehension

Assessing phonology, the sounds of language known as phonemes, involves measuring student proficiency in the use of speech sounds. Representative tests of phonology include the Goldman-Fristoe Test of Articulation, Second Edition and the Goldman-Fristoe-Woodcock Test of Auditory Discrimination. Designed primarily for use by speech clinicians, special educators also rely on these instruments to identify learning needs and develop instructional objectives for students with language problems.

Assessing Units of Meaning (Morphology) and Phrases and Sentences (Syntax)

Morphemes, the smallest units of meaning in language, may be either free or bound. Free morphemes, meaningful when they stand alone, include words such as *run, slow,* and *teach.* Bound morphemes, meaningful only when attached to a free morpheme, include units such as *-ly* in *slowly* and the *-er* in *teacher.* Syntax, the way in which words combine to form phrases and sentences, follows a set of grammatical rules. Assessing syntax involves measuring the ability to understand the meaning of sentences and to form sentences that follow the grammatical rules. The Test for Auditory Comprehension of Language, Third Edition is a representative test of morphology and syntax. A review of this instrument follows along with a description of informal measures of morphology and syntax.

Test for Auditory Comprehension of Language, Third Edition

The Test for Auditory Comprehension of Language, Third Edition (TACL-3) (Carrow-Woolfolk, 1999) is an individually administered, norm-referenced test for assessing the language comprehension of children from 3 through 9 years of age. The TACL-3 assesses auditory comprehension of language in three categories: vocabulary (literal meaning of words), morphology (grammatical morphemes), and syntax (meaning from sentences). The author developed the TACL-3 to identify children with language deficits, to measure school readiness, to plan instructional programs, and to monitor student progress. A summary of the TACL-3 appears in the Test Review box.

TACL-3 Materials　　TACL-3 materials include an examiner's manual, a test booklet containing line drawings, and a profile/examiner record booklet.

TACL-3 Administration and Scoring　　Consisting of 142 items, the TACL-3 presents a page containing three line drawings, and an evaluator reads a word or sentence that corresponds to one of the drawings. The child responds by pointing to the drawing that shows the correct meaning of the word or sentence. The TACL-3 requires no oral response. The TACL-3 vocabulary items measure receptive understanding of various words and word relations such as "riding a little bicycle."

TEST REVIEW

Test for Auditory Comprehension of Language, Third Edition

Type of Test:	Norm-referenced, individually administered
Purpose:	Assesses auditory comprehension ability
Content Areas:	Vocabulary, morphology, and syntax
Administration Time:	25 minutes
Age Levels:	3 to 9 years
Suitable for:	Students with mild and moderate disabilities, including speech and learning disabilities, emotional disturbance, mental retardation, and physical impairments
Scores:	Percentile ranks, standard scores, and age equivalents
In Short:	A well-designed picture test for assessing receptive language abilities

Morphological items assess receptive grammatical ability by using prepositions, nouns, and verbs. Syntactical items assess understanding of the meaning of sentences that use passive and active voices and direct and indirect objects. TACL-3 scores include percentile ranks and age equivalents. In addition, evaluators may convert percentile ranks into standard scores. The test takes about 25 minutes to administer.

TACL-3 Technical Characteristics Standardized with a group of more than 1,100 children, the sample was designed to represent demographic characteristics of the national population. The normative information was stratified by age relative to gender, race, ethnicity, and disability. Studies to identify gender, racial, disability, or ethnic bias were conducted and appropriate modifications were made. Reliability coefficients were computed for subgroups of the normative sample (e.g., individuals with speech disabilities, African Americans, European Americans, Hispanic Americans, females) as well as for the entire normative group. Validity studies were conducted to provide evidence that the test is valid for a wide variety of subgroups as well as for the general population. The test items were evaluated using both conventional item analyses to choose "good" items, and differential analyses to find and eliminate potentially biased items.

TACL-3 Summary An individually administered, norm-referenced picture test of language ability, the Test of Auditory Comprehension of Language, Second Edition measures the receptive vocabulary, morphology, and syntax abilities of students between 3 and 9 years of age. The TACL-R demonstrates adequate technical qualities for use as a norm-referenced tool.

Informal Measures for Assessing Morphology and Syntax

Informal measures of morphology and syntax include assessing mean length of utterance and developmental sentence analysis. These curriculum-based approaches assess spontaneous language, which is the candid, unrehearsed verbal expression as it occurs in natural real-life situations.

Assessing Spontaneous Language   Assessing **spontaneous language** involves recording speech samples for later transcription and analysis. Spontaneous language sampling has distinct advantages over formal testing, including:

- Placing fewer controls on the student than structured language tests
- Obtaining phrases and sentences in spontaneous speech not observed during formal testing
- Observing language during interactions with others in natural settings
- Evaluating the words and sentences a student knows well enough to use in everyday language

Limitations of spontaneous language sampling include the sample size. In typical situations, a spontaneous speech sample contains 50 to 100 utterances. Because this is a relatively small sample, situational variables such as the topic of conversation, the task at hand, the age of the student, and the elicitation procedures can negatively affect the quality of the samples. Larger samples consisting of 300 to 800 utterances reduce these negative influences. However, it is not always feasible to collect and analyze large samples. Therefore typical language samples tend to be less than ideal in size and usually focus on analysis of specific spontaneous measures of language.

Mean Length of Utterance   The **mean length of utterance (MLU)** assessment measures the ability to form words, phrases, and sentences. Based on a procedure originally developed by Brown (1973), MLU analysis is ideal for measuring the language level of young children. The MLU assessment procedure involves recording and later analyzing a spontaneous speech sample containing a minimum of 50 consecutive utterances. The evaluator elicits a speech sample by using stimuli such as story pictures or toys and asking open-ended questions such as "What can you tell me about this?" After transcribing the speech sample from the tape, the evaluator calculates an MLU by counting the number of morphemes produced and dividing the total by the number of utterances. For example, a toddler who says "Get ball" (2 morphemes), "Mama" (1 morpheme), "Dog woof" (2 morphemes), and "Dog" (1 morpheme) produces an MLU of 1.5 morphemes (6 ÷ 4 = 1.5), where 6 is the number of morphemes produced and 4 is the number of utterances. MLU analysis is a helpful technique, but it is time consuming. Brown (1973) suggests using MLUs with utterances that have a maximum of four morphemes. This means that MLUs work best with young children and students with severe language delays.

Developmental Sentence Analysis   **Developmental sentence analysis**, originally developed by Lee (1974), involves collecting and analyzing a speech sample to measure the ability to spontaneously produce words and sentences. Unlike the MLU procedure, which simply counts the average length of utterances, developmental sentence analysis involves examination of eight grammatical categories that represent syntactic ability:

1. Indefinite pronouns and noun modifiers

2. Personal pronouns

3. Main verbs

4. Secondary verbs

5. Negatives

6. Conjunctions

7. Interrogative reversals

8. Wh- questions

The administration procedure is similar to the MLU method. An evaluator records and later transcribes a natural language sample using an informal interview format with pictures or other appropriate stimuli to elicit responses. Scoring the sample requires 50 consecutive sentences and produces a quantitative score called a developmental sentence score (DSS). Lee (1974) defines a complete sentence as any utterance containing a noun and verb in a subject-predicate relationship such as "Mama bye-bye." The evaluator assigns a point value (from 1 to 8) to each word in the sample, with developmentally advanced words receiving higher point values. For example, third-person pronouns (2 points) receive more points than first- or second-person pronouns (1 point), and plurals receive the highest pronoun point values (3 points). The evaluator calculates a developmental sentence score by totaling the number points given to the words in the sample and dividing the total by the number of sentences (50). Finally, the evaluator converts the raw score into an age-based percentile rank that shows where the score falls in relation to the 10th, 25th, 50th, and 75th percentiles.

Developmental sentence analysis is a norm-referenced procedure designed for children from 2 through 6 years of age. The author based the norms on a sample of 200 children from middle-class homes in four states. Unfortunately, this restricted sample limits the usefulness of the norms. In addition, limited reliability and no validity data exist to support the technical adequacy of the procedure. For this reason, evaluators should rely on developmental sentence analysis as an informal technique. Special educators and speech clinicians may use results from developmental sentence analysis to generate intervention objectives that respond directly to a child's expressive language strengths and weaknesses. Developmental sentence analysis is valuable as a measure of performance levels in expressive language as well as an instructional guide.

Computer-Based Sentence Analysis Programs   Computer-based programs assist with a variety of language analysis procedures, including morphological and syntax analysis. Descriptions of two available programs appear in the Technology Focus box.

Language Sampling, Analysis, and Training: A Handbook, Third Edition   The Language Sampling, Analysis, and Training: A Handbook, Third Edition (LSAT-3) (Tyack & Venable, 1998) includes a variety of criterion-referenced language-sampling procedures along with detailed information about measuring and reporting progress. The handbook provides useful information on multicultural issues. LSAT-3 was designed for speech-language pathologists, speech-language pathology students and professors, and special education teachers. LSAT-3 offers valuable information applicable both to direct instruction in oral language and reading comprehension and to collaboration with classroom teachers. The goal of the handbook is to provide information for planning and monitoring spoken language remediation and also for pinpointing and remediating specific reading comprehension problems.

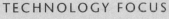

TECHNOLOGY FOCUS

Computer-Based Language Analysis Programs

Computerized Profiling (CP) (Long, 2002) offers several programs to help learn and carry out a broad range of language analysis procedures. The CP programs are freeware, which means they can be downloaded and used without restriction. CP is useful for analyzing both language samples transcribed orthographically and phonological samples transcribed phonetically. Available procedures offer the ability to analyze semantics, grammar, phonology, pragmatics, and narrative.

Systematic Analysis of Language Transcripts (SALT) (Miller, 2001) transcribes language samples, calculates a variety of standard measures, and compares results with age-matched peers. To transcribe language samples, transcripts are typed into a customized editor. The SALT program contains built-in help screens with information on using the editor and entering transcripts following the SALT transcript-entry conventions. It identifies errors in transcript format, and positions you at the point of each error in the transcript. After the transcript is entered, the program provides a variety of standard analyses, including measures of syntax such as MLU in words and morphemes, morphology, fluency and rate, and discourse. The program also offers the ability to compare results with age-matched peers.

☑ Check Your Comprehension

Both formal tests and informal clinical evaluation procedures are available to assess morphology and syntax. Though the various techniques differ in design and purpose, the goal of all of the assessments is to help identify language deficits and design appropriate intervention procedures. Because of the complexity of language, speech and language pathologists usually conduct the assessment. These specialists then work together with teachers of students with disabilities to implement appropriate remediation programs. Regardless of the specific approach, the assessment should help place students appropriately, identify specific language problems, and design appropriate IEPs.

Assessing Semantics and Pragmatics

Assessing semantics involves measuring receptive and expressive vocabulary skills as well as the ability to define words, categorize words, identify synonyms and antonyms, and comprehend absurdity or ambiguity. Vocabulary is the most frequently measured element of semantics. Vocabulary assessment instruments include the widely used Peabody Picture Vocabulary Test, Third Edition (PPVT-III), of which a detailed review follows.

Instruments for measuring other aspects of semantics as well as devices for measuring pragmatics are not as readily available. However, professionals may select from among a few commercial devices, including several informal inventories for assessing use of word relationships and the contextual use of language. Pragmatics, the use of language in context, refers to understanding the structure of different forms of communication. Pragmatic rules include the following:

- Routines for taking turns in conversations
- Use of formal versus informal conversations among supervisors, family, and peers
- Appropriate use of verbal humor in social situations

Available tests of pragmatics include the Test of Pragmatic Language (TOPL) and the Test of Pragmatic Skills.

Peabody Picture Vocabulary Test, Third Edition

Receptive language vocabulary, the ability to understand word meanings, is an important semantic language skill. Although a number of tests include receptive language vocabulary subtests, one test, the Peabody Picture Vocabulary Test, Third Edition (PPVT-III) (Dunn & Dunn, 1997), measures this aspect of language in isolation. Perhaps the most widely used language test with students who have special needs, the PPVT-III is a norm-referenced screening test of receptive (hearing) vocabulary. Designed for individuals from age 2½ years to adulthood, the PPVT-III does not require reading or writing ability and is used in schools and clinics to screen children at all levels of ability. Each PPVT-III item consists of four simple line drawings on a page. The test is given by having the child select a drawing (from among the four choices) that best represents the meaning of each word presented orally. Because a student can select the drawing by naming the number of the drawing (1 through 4) or pointing to it, the PPVT-III is suitable for use with children who are nonverbal or nonvocal. A summary of the PPVT-III appears in the Test Review box.

TEST REVIEW

Peabody Picture Vocabulary Test, Third Edition

Type of Test:	Norm-referenced, individually administered screening test
Purpose:	To assess receptive language vocabulary
Content Areas:	Receptive (hearing) vocabulary
Administration Time:	Approximately 20 minutes
Age Levels:	2.5 years to adulthood
Suitable for:	Students with mild, moderate, and severe disabilities, including learning and physical disabilities, emotional disturbance, and mental retardation
Scores:	Standard score equivalents, percentiles, stanines, and age equivalents
In Short:	The PPVT-III is a well-written, easy-to-use test for estimating receptive language vocabulary with excellent technical characteristics.

A Spanish version of the test, the TVIP: Test de Vocabulario en Imágenes Peabody (Dunn, Lugo, Padilla, & Dunn, 1986), is available for assessing the receptive vocabulary of Spanish-speaking children and adolescents from 2½ to 18 years of age. The TVIP is designed for evaluating the language development of Spanish-speaking preschool children, screening Spanish-speaking children entering kindergarten or first grade, determining more effective language instruction for bilingual children, and evaluating the Spanish vocabulary of older students. Based on the Peabody Picture Vocabulary Test, Revised, the TVIP contains 125 translated items to assess the vocabulary of Spanish-speaking and bilingual students. The manual is available in English and Spanish, and norms are available for both combined and separate Mexican and Puerto Rican standardization samples.

PPVT-III Materials   PPVT-III materials consist of separate, easel-type booklets for form A and form B, both containing 204 plates with four line drawings on each plate. The PPVT-III also includes a well-written and thorough test manual.

PPVT-III Administration and Scoring   The well-designed PPVT-III administration procedures make it easy for evaluators to give and score the test in 20 minutes or less. A sample test plate from the PPVT-III administration booklet appears in Figure 10–1. Evaluators may report PPVT-III results using standard scores, percentiles, stanines, or age equivalents.

In the past, professionals relied on the PPVT as more than a screening measure of receptive language vocabulary. Because it yields a standard score with a mean of

Figure 10–1   Sample test plate from the Peabody Picture Vocabulary Test, Third Edition

Training Plate D

Source: From L. M. Dunn & L. M. Dunn, 1997, *Peabody Picture Vocabulary Test, Third Edition.* Circle Pines, MN: American Guidance Service. Reprinted with permission of Lloyd and Leola Dunn.

100 and a standard deviation of 15, some evaluators employed earlier versions of the PPVT as a picture test of intelligence. Others used it as a more general measure of language development. However, the PPVT-III is a screening test rather than a diagnostic tool. As a screening test, it estimates only present levels of performance in receptive vocabulary and does not replace comprehensive diagnostic evaluation. For this reason, one should use the PPVT-III for screening purposes or as a single instrument in a battery of assessments that make up a comprehensive diagnostic evaluation. The PPVT-III was co-normed with the Expressive Vocabulary Test (EVT), which is reviewed later in this chapter. Because the EVT measures expressive vocabulary and word retrieval, pairing it with the PPVT-III produces diagnostic information.

PPVT-III Technical Characteristics   Standardized on a national sample of children and adults from 2½ to 90 years of age, the PPVT-III norms were based on U.S. Census figures for gender, race/ethnicity, region, and education level. A variety of studies of the split-half, alternate-form, and test-retest reliability have established the consistency of PPVT-III scores. Likewise, the effectiveness of the instrument has been clearly demonstrated through numerous content, construct, and concurrent validity studies. Furthermore, many researchers use the PPVT-III as a criterion measure in various independent scientific studies that provide further evidence to support the excellent technical qualities of the tool.

PPVT-III Summary   The PPVT-III is a well-designed, easy-to-use tool for estimating an important component of oral language: receptive language vocabulary. In addition to displaying excellent technical characteristics, the outstanding design of the PPVT-III makes it easy to administer, score, and interpret. A wide range of professionals, including special educators, school and clinical psychologists, educational diagnosticians, counselors, and speech and language pathologists, use the PPVT-III with children and adults at all levels of ability.

Other Tests of Semantics and Pragmatics

A range of tests and informal assessment procedures is available to evaluate the semantic and pragmatic skills of children with special needs. Brief reviews of many of these measures follow.

Boehm Test of Basic Concepts, Third Edition   The Boehm Test of Basic Concepts, Third Edition (Boehm-3) (Boehm, 2000) assesses the receptive vocabulary development of students from kindergarten through grade 2. Designed for group administration in a classroom setting, this norm-referenced test evaluates mastery of the basic concepts essential for understanding the verbal instructions necessary for early school achievement. The Boehm-3 contains 50 items that measure understanding in three major context categories: space, quantity, and time. A preschool version of the test, the Boehm III—Preschool (Boehm, 2001) includes 26 easier concepts and is appropriate for children from 3 to 5 years of age.

Comprehensive Receptive and Expressive Vocabulary Test, Second Edition   The Comprehensive Receptive and Expressive Vocabulary Test, Second Edition (CREVT-2) (Wallace & Hammill, 2002) is a norm-referenced, individually administered test designed to identify students who are significantly below their peers in oral vocabulary proficiency. Designed for children and adults from 4 through 89 years of age, the CREVT-2 has an expressive and a receptive subtest and two equivalent forms. It takes about 30 minutes to administer the instrument.

Expressive One-Word Picture Vocabulary Test, 2000 Edition The Expressive One-Word Picture Vocabulary Test, 2000 Edition (EOWPVT) (Brownell, 2000a) is an individually administered, norm-referenced test. Standardized for use with children and youths ages 2 through 18 years, 11 months, the EOWPVT was co-normed with the Receptive One-Word Picture Vocabulary Test, 2000 Edition (ROWPVT) so that meaningful comparisons can be made between expressive and receptive language. Total time for administration and scoring of the instrument is about 20 minutes.

Expressive Vocabulary Test The Expressive Vocabulary Test (EVT) (Williams, 1997) is a norm-referenced, individually administered measure of expressive vocabulary and word retrieval for Standard American English. Designed for children and adults from 2½ to 85-plus years of age, the EVT takes about 25 minutes to give. Co-normed with the PPVT-III, the EVT features two types of items: labeling and synonyms. The student responds to each item with a one-word answer. All items are presented with pictures. Some of the test items include instructions to help the student perform well on later items. Other test items include prompts that the evaluator can give when a student gives a close or related response. Like the PPVT-III, the test requires no reading or writing skills. Available scores include standard scores, percentile ranks, stanines, and age equivalents.

Listening Comprehension Scale and Oral Expression Scale The Listening Comprehension Scale and the Oral Expression Scale are two scales within the Oral and Written Language Scales (OWLS) (Carrow-Woolfolk, 1995). The scales are norm-referenced, individually administered tests of the receptive and expressive language of children and young adults from 3 through 21 years of age. A review of the third component of the OWLS, the Written Expression Scale, appears in Chapter 17. The Listening Comprehension Scale measures receptive language and consists of three examples and 111 items. The evaluator reads the verbal stimulus, and the child responds by selecting one of four pictures. The Listening Comprehension Scale takes about 15 minutes to administer. The Oral Expression Scale measures the understanding and use of spoken language and consists of two examples and 96 items. The evaluator reads a verbal stimulus and shows a picture or pictures, and the student responds orally by answering a question, completing a sentence, or generating one or more sentences. The Oral Comprehension Scale takes about 25 minutes to administer. The scales provide a variety of clinical and school-based applications for measuring language knowledge and processing skills in children and adolescents. These applications include identifying children with language deficits, designing language intervention tasks, and monitoring growth in language skills.

Receptive One-Word Picture Vocabulary Test, 2000 Edition The norm-referenced, individually administered Receptive One-Word Picture Vocabulary Test, 2000 Edition (ROWPVT) (Brownell, 2000b) assesses the receptive hearing vocabulary of children from 2 through 18 years of age. Designed as a companion test to the Expressive One-Word Vocabulary Test, 2000 Edition, the ROWPVT takes about 20 minutes to administer.

Test of Pragmatic Language The norm-referenced, individually administered Test of Pragmatic Language (TOPL) (Phelps-Terasaki & Phelps-Gunn, 1992) measures social language skills using 44 items. Administration of the TOPL involves showing a picture and offering a verbal stimulus to elicit a response to the social context situation presented. The TOPL takes about 45 minutes to administer and is suitable for students from ages 5 to 13. The test measures six core subcomponents of pragmatic language: physical setting, audience, topic, purpose (speech acts), visual-gestural cues, and abstraction.

Test of Pragmatic Skills   The Test of Pragmatic Skills (Shulman, 1986), a criterion-referenced, individually administered instrument, enables analysis of expressive language as it occurs in structured play interactions. For example, in one of the play sessions the evaluator and the student use puppets to talk about television programs. The evaluator leads the student through each of four play sessions based on a written script. Designed for children from age 3 through 8, the test measures 10 different communicative intents:

1. Requesting information

2. Requesting action

3. Rejecting or denying

4. Naming or labeling

5. Answering or responding

6. Informing

7. Reasoning

8. Summoning or calling

9. Greeting

10. Closing conversation

Reflection
Why would measuring pragmatics be difficult? Give examples.

To answer this reflection online, go to the *Teaching and Learning* module on the Companion Website at *www.prenhall.com/venn*.

☑ Check Your Comprehension

Assessing semantics involves measuring a student's ability to understand and express word meanings and relationships. Devices for measuring receptive vocabulary include the widely used PPVT-III. Measures of other aspects of semantics, as well as devices for measuring pragmatics, the usage of language in context, are not as readily available.

Comprehensive Measures of Language

In addition to the instruments for assessing specific structural components of language, there are a variety of comprehensive measures of language. Rather than focusing on a single construct, these measures contain separate subtests for evaluating different structural components of language. Three representative comprehensive language tests are the Test of Language Development—Primary, Third Edition, the Test of Language Development—Intermediate, Third Edition, and the Test of Adolescent and Adult Language—3. Detailed reviews of these tests follow along with brief reviews of other available comprehensive language tests.

Test of Language Development—Primary, Third Edition

The Test of Language Development—Primary, Third Edition (TOLD-P: 3) (Newcomer & Hammill, 1997) is a comprehensive, norm-referenced, individually administered test of spoken language. Designed for children from 4 through 8 years of age, the TOLD-P:3 helps to identify language disorders and isolate particular types of language deficits in need of remediation. A summary of the TOLD-P:3 appears in the Test Review box.

TEST REVIEW

Test of Language Development—Primary, Third Edition

Type of Test:	Norm-referenced, individually administered
Purpose:	Comprehensive diagnostic assessment of language abilities
Content Areas:	Picture, relational and oral vocabulary, grammatical understanding and completion, sentence imitation, word discrimination, phonemic analysis, and word articulation (see Table 10–2)
Administration Time:	Approximately 1 hour
Age Levels:	4 to 8 years
Suitable for:	Students with mild and moderate disabilities, including speech and language impairments, learning disabilities, emotional disturbance, and mild mental retardation
Scores:	Standard scores, percentiles, and age equivalents
In Short:	This well-written diagnostic test of language ability helps to identify students with language disorders, isolate particular types of disorders, and develop individual intervention programs.

TOLD-P:3 Materials The TOLD-P:3 test kit contains an examiner's manual, a picture book, and a package of 25 profile/record forms in a small cardboard storage box. Computer software for scoring the TOLD-P:3 is available as an optional item.

TOLD-P:3 Administration and Scoring Designed for individual administration, the TOLD-P:3 takes about an hour to administer and score. Results can be reported as standard scores, percentiles, or age equivalents. Combining scores from different subtests provides scores for overall spoken language, listening, speaking, semantics, and syntax. A summary of the language skills evaluated by the TOLD-P:3 appears in Table 10–2. The scoresheet includes a profile for visual presentation of results, which is useful for gauging strengths and weaknesses in various language ability areas.

TOLD-P:3 Technical Characteristics Standardized with a group of more than 1,000 students from 30 states, the TOLD-P:3 sample included children from diverse ethnic, language, and socioeconomic backgrounds. Standardization followed a well-designed testing plan to ensure representation of the national population. The developers estimated the reliability of TOLD-P:3 scores based on coefficient alpha and test-retest methods and used several procedures to establish validity, including relating the test's content to children's actual language, correlating subtests with other commonly used tests, and studying the relationship of TOLD-P:3 scores to age, IQ, and achievement. These reliability and validity measures provide initial evidence to support the consistency and effectiveness of TOLD-P:3 scores. Overall, the test exhibits adequate technical characteristics for use as a norm-referenced instrument.

TOLD-P:3 Summary The primary version of the Test of Language Development, Third Edition is a norm-referenced, individually administered test for identifying children with language problems and pinpointing specific types of deficiencies. The TOLD-P:3 displays adequate technical characteristics for use in classification and

Table 10–2   Language Skills Evaluated by TOLD-P:3 Subtests

Structural Subtest	Specific Skill	Component
Picture vocabulary	Understanding words	Semantics
Relational vocabulary	Mediating vocabulary	Semantics
Oral vocabulary	Defining words	Semantics
Grammatic understanding	Understanding sentence meaning	Syntax
Grammatic completion	Understanding sentence formation	Syntax
Sentence imitation	Repeating sentences	Syntax
Word discrimination	Noticing sound differences	Phonics
Phonemic analysis	Segmenting words into smaller units	Phonics
Word articulation	Saying words correctly	Phonics

instructional programming. The instrument is well-written and easy to administer and score. These positive qualities account for the popularity of the TOLD-P:3 among speech clinicians and special educators.

Test of Language Development—Intermediate, Third Edition

The Test of Language Development—Intermediate, Third Edition (TOLD-I:3) (Hammill & Newcomer, 1997) is a comprehensive, norm-referenced, individually administered test of spoken language for children from 8 through 12 years of age. A summary of the TOLD-I:3 appears in Test Review Box.

TEST REVIEW

Test of Language Development—Intermediate, Third Edition

Type of Test:	Norm-referenced, individually administered
Purpose:	Comprehensive diagnostic assessment of language abilities
Content Areas:	Sentence combining, picture vocabulary, word ordering, generals, spoken language skills, grammatic comprehension, and malapropisms (see Table 10–3)
Administration Time:	Approximately 1 hour
Age Levels:	8 to 12 years
Suitable for:	Students with mild and moderate disabilities, including speech and language impairments, learning disabilities, emotional disturbance, and mild mental retardation
Scores:	Standard scores, percentiles, and age-equivalent scores
In Short:	This well-written diagnostic test of language ability is useful for identifying students with language disorders, isolating particular types of disorders, and using the results to develop intervention programs.

Table 10–3   TOLD I:3 Subtests

Structural Subtest	Specific Skill	Component
Sentence combining	Constructing sentences	Syntax
Picture vocabulary	Understanding word relationships	Semantics
Word ordering	Making sentences	Syntax
Generals	Understanding abstract words	Semantics
Grammatic comprehension	Understanding grammar in comprehension sentences	Syntax
Malapropisms	Correcting ridiculous sentences	Semantics

TOLD-I:3 Materials   The TOLD-I:3 kit includes an examiner's manual, a picture book, and 25 profile/examiner record forms. An optional computer scoring system helps to score the TOLD-I:3 and generates a multipage report.

TOLD-I:3 Administration and Scoring   Designed for individual administration, the TOLD-I:3 takes about an hour to administer and score. Results can be reported as standard scores, percentiles, or age equivalents. The scoresheet includes a profile for visual presentation of results and for illustrating individual strengths and deficiencies in basic language abilities. A listing of the TOLD-I:3 subtests appears in Table 10–3.

TOLD-I:3 Technical Characteristics   The TOLD-I:3 was standardized using a sample group of more than 700 children from 19 states. Test reliability was investigated using coefficient alpha and test-retest methodology. The manual provides evidence to support the content, concurrent, and construct validity of the TOLD-I:3. Overall, the test exhibits adequate technical characteristics for use as a norm-referenced instrument.

TOLD-I:3 Summary   The intermediate version of the Test of Language Development, Third Edition is a norm-referenced, individually administered test for identifying children with language problems and pinpointing individual strengths and deficiencies in basic language abilities. The well-written, easy-to-administer TOLD-I:3 is one of the most popular tests of spoken language.

Test of Adolescent and Adult Language, Third Edition

The Test of Adolescent and Adult Language, Third Edition (TOAL-3) (Hammill, Brown, Larsen, & Wiederholt, 1994) is a norm-referenced measure of the receptive and expressive language abilities of students from age 12 through 24 years. One of only a few instruments specifically designed for adolescents, this test includes items that identify performance levels and determine the deficits of students with language delays. The TOAL-3 is a comprehensive measure of language abilities, evaluating semantic and syntactical ability in listening, speaking, reading, and writing. A summary of the TOAL-3 appears in Test Review Box.

TOAL-3 Materials   Test kit materials include an examiner's manual, 10 test booklets, 50 answer booklets, and 50 summary/profile sheets. Optional scoring software is available.

TOAL-3 Administration and Scoring   It takes from 1 to 3 hours to administer the TOAL-3. Giving the test involves using a variety of administration procedures.

TEST REVIEW

Test of Adolescent and Adult Language, Third Edition

Type of Test:	Norm-referenced, individually administered
Purpose:	An individually administered diagnostic test of language development
Content Areas:	Vocabulary and grammar listening, speaking, reading, and writing
Administration Time:	1 to 3 hours
Age Levels:	12 to 24 years
Suitable for:	Students with mild and moderate disabilities, including speech and language impairments,
Scores:	A total language standard score and standard scores in 10 areas: listening, speaking, reading, writing, spoken language, written language, vocabulary, grammar, receptive language, and expressive language.
In Short:	Designed for junior high and high school students, the TOAL-3 is a comprehensive diagnostic test that measures both expressive and receptive language abilities.

For example, the test employs a picture vocabulary format to measure listening vocabulary. Several subtests involve reading a series of words or sentences and having the student select from the stimulus words or sentences. In the writing vocabulary subtest, the adolescent reads a word and then writes a sentence using the word. The TOAL-3 provides a total language standard score and standard scores in 10 composite areas: listening, speaking, reading, writing, spoken language, written language, vocabulary, grammar, receptive language, and expressive language.

TOAL-3 Technical Characteristics The developers derived the TOAL-3 test scores from the performance of a sample of more than 3,000 people from 22 states and 3 Canadian provinces. Although the sample size is more than adequate, the developers failed to provide details about the sampling plan and the method of subject selection. This lack of information makes it difficult to determine the adequacy of the standardization plan. The test manual presents information on three types of reliability (internal consistency, test-retest, and interscorer), with most coefficients falling in the .80 to .90 range, indicating scores with satisfactory accuracy. The manual also provides data to support the content, criterion-related, and construct validity of the instrument. A description of the effectiveness of the test items and subtests provides an indication of content validity. Several studies compare the test to other language tests. The construct validity of the TOAL-3 rests primarily on data from a study showing that scores from the instrument discriminate between students with known language disabilities and those without language problems. Overall, the test presents mediocre evidence of validity.

TOAL-3 Summary One of only a few tests designed specifically for junior high and high school students, the TOAL-3 provides a norm-referenced measure of several important dimensions of language. This comprehensive diagnostic test evaluates semantic and syntactical ability in the areas of listening, speaking, reading, and writing.

Other Comprehensive Language Development Tests

In addition to the tests just reviewed, brief reviews of some of the other available comprehensive tests of language development follow. These include tests for very young children as well as tests for older children and adolescents.

Bankson Language Test, Second Edition   The Bankson Language Test, Second Edition (BLT-2) (Bankson, 1990) is a norm-referenced, individually administered test of children's psycholinguistic skills. The BLT-2 is organized into three categories that assess (1) semantic knowledge, including body parts, nouns, verbs, categories, functions, prepositions, and opposites; (2) morphological/syntactical rules, including pronouns, verb usage/verb tense, plurals, comparatives/superlatives, negations, and questions; and (3) pragmatics, including ritualizing, informing, controlling, and imagining. Designed for children from 3 through 6 years of age, the BLT-2 results may be reported as standard scores or percentiles. The BLT-2 includes a long form for diagnostic purposes and a 20-item short form for use in screening.

Clinical Evaluation of Language Fundamentals, Fourth Edition (CELF-4)   The norm-referenced, individually administered Clinical Evaluation of Language Fundamentals, Fourth Edition (CELF-4) (Semel, Wiig, & Secord, 2003) measures the language skills of children and youths from 5 through 21 years of age. The CELF-4 measures receptive and expressive language skills in morphology, syntax, semantics, and memory. The CELF-4 takes about 45 minutes to administer and score and produces standard scores, percentile ranks, stanines, and normal curve equivalents. Designed to identify and diagnose language deficits and to measure child progress in developing language skills, the CELF-4 has very good technical qualities. Related CELF assessment materials include the CELF-3—Spanish Edition (Semel, Wiig, & Secord, 1997) the CELF-3—Screening Test (Semel, Wiig, & Secord, 1996a), the CELF-3—Observational Rating Scales (Semel, Wiig, & Secord, 1996b), and the CELF-Preschool (Wiig, Secord, & Semel, 1992).

Test of Early Language Development, Third Edition   The Test of Early Language Development, Third Edition (TELD-3) (Hresko, Reid, & Hammil, 1999) is a norm-referenced, individually administered test of the language development of children from age 2 through 7. The TELD-3 includes subtests measuring expressive and receptive language and provides two equivalent forms with results reported as standard scores, percentiles, NCEs, or age equivalents. The TELD-3 identifies spoken language disorders and isolates particular types of spoken language deficits.

Utah Test of Language Development, Fourth Edition   The norm-referenced, individually administered Utah Test of Language Development, Fourth Edition (UTLD-3) (Mecham, 2003) measures the expressive and receptive language skills of children from 3 through 9 years of age. The UTLD-3 takes about 45 minutes to administer and yields subtest scores in language comprehension and language expression as well as an overall total language score.

☑ Check Your Comprehension

These comprehensive tests represent a major language assessment category. Instead of focusing on a single component, they include separate subtests for evaluating the different structural components of language. These instruments are useful for identifying students with language disorders and isolating specific disorders. Comprehensive tests also provide an overview of language function across domains and identify strengths, weaknesses, and gaps in skill development. The results of comprehensive testing help in developing instructional objectives that respond to the individual needs of students with language delays and disorders.

Assessing Students Who Are Culturally and Linguistically Diverse

The number of students from diverse cultures is predicted to increase to 24 million, or 37% of the school-age population, by the year 2010. The term **culturally and linguistically diverse (CLD)** refers to students from minority cultures who know and use two languages. Although students speak many different languages, a majority of CLD students speak Spanish as their native language and acquire English as a second language. Unfortunately, many CLD students, especially those with disabilities, exhibit limited English proficiency. **Limited English proficiency (LEP)** refers to CLD students who display inadequate skills in understanding and speaking the English language. One of the most pressing challenges associated with educating students from culturally and linguistically diverse experiences is accurate assessment of disabilities.

According to experts (Farr & Trumbull, 1997; Hakuta & Beatty, 2000), current tests and assessment procedures fail to adequately assess the needs of students with limited English proficiency. One of the central problems is the lack of standards and guidelines for deciding the readiness for testing in English. Another concern is the validity of current options for testing students in their native language. These options include translating tests into the native language, using interpreters, using tests with norms in the primary language, and relying on bilingual psychologists to administer tests.

In addition to these options, evaluators often rely on other practical procedures to ensure that they have all the information needed to make the best possible assessment decisions. These procedures include gathering detailed information about a student's school history, medical and health status, and family background. Incorporating background data helps evaluators respond to individual student needs. To ensure that they have sufficient information for discussing all relevant aspects of a student's language, evaluators often expand the assessment protocol in other ways as well. For example, assessment may include evaluation of language proficiency in both the first language and in English. In addition, the evaluator may use informal assessment procedures such as spontaneous language sampling. The Basic Inventory of Natural Language (Herbert, 1983) is an example of an assessment system for obtaining spontaneous language samples in Spanish and 31 other languages. Designed for students from kindergarten through the 12th grade, the inventory scores a language sample in the areas of fluency, complexity, and average sentence length.

Best-practice guidelines recommend that schools conduct their own language proficiency assessments. Frequently used tests for such assessment include the Test de Vocabulario en Imágenes Peabody (TVIP), the Peabody Picture Vocabulary Test—III, the Dos Amigos Verbal Language Scales (Critchlow, 1996), and the Batería III Woodcock-Muñoz (Woodcock, Muñoz-Sandoval, McGrew, Mather, & Schrank, 2004). In addition to using formal tests, evaluators should also use curriculum-based methods to obtain a comprehensive profile of a child's language proficiency. These methods include collecting spontaneous language samples and conducting student interviews. Other commonly used methods include observing the student and conducting a parent interview. Though some school districts rely on language proficiency information from outside sources, the validity of this information is often questionable. Therefore, experts suggest avoiding outside sources in most situations, especially when the information is more than 6 months old.

Although many procedures are in place, more needs to be done to solve the complex issues surrounding assessment of students with limited English proficiency who receive special education services. Specialists in bilingual education, special educators, and researchers are continuing to provide improved assessments, and they are developing additional insights into ways of better using currently available options. A list of assessment strategies for students from culturally and linguistically diverse experiences appears in the accompanying Multicultural Considerations feature.

Assessing Students with Severe Communication Disorders

Some students have severe communication disorders due to disabilities such as physical impairments, severe mental retardation, developmental disabilities, or severe forms of autism. For example, students with severe cerebral palsy may be nonvocal (unable to speak due to a motor disability). Similarly, some students with severe or profound mental retardation may be nonverbal (unable to speak due to an intellectual deficit). Some students who are nonvocal use aided communication systems such as

 MULTICULTURAL CONSIDERATIONS

Strategies for Students Who Are Culturally and Linguistically Diverse

Screening Strategies

- Evaluate proficiency in the native language and in English.
- Refer for special education assessment only after the student has adjusted to the new culture.
- Look for indicators of language problems beyond language acquisition.

Comprehensive Assessment Strategies

- Avoid relying on outside sources of information regarding language proficiency.
- Use current language assessment data (no more than 6 months old).
- Obtain and use both formal and informal assessment information.

Give examples of how you could use one of the screening strategies.
Give examples of how you could use one of the comprehensive assessment strategies.

 To answer this reflection online, go to the *Multicultural Considerations* module on the Companion Website at *www.prenhall.com/venn*.

FOCUS 10–3

Assessing Students with Severe Communication Disorders

Assessment Pinpoint	Assessment Question
Ecological assessment	What language, communication, and interaction occurs in the student's daily environment?
Assessing met and unmet needs	What types of communication does the student presently use?
Appraisal of future needs	What communication system will the student need in the future?
Team assessment	Which communication system will best meet current and future needs?
Progress monitoring	How well is the student learning to use the communication system?
Data collection	Is the system helping to meet communication needs?

communication boards (with pictures or words) or synthesized speech voice output devices. Likewise, students who are nonvocal may also use unaided communication systems including gestures or sign language to communicate. Specialized assessment strategies are needed that are sensitive to these communication disorders. A description of assessment strategies for students with severe communication disorders appears in Focus 10–3.

Communication systems for students who are nonvocal or nonverbal fall into two major categories. Aided systems require the use of some sort of device such as a communication board (with pictures, symbols, or words), a communication notebook, or a digitized speech device. Speak Easy and DynaMyte are two representative digitized speech devices. Speak Easy allows for up to 12 recorded messages accessed through touch or switch. DynaMyte allows a greater number of messages to be preprogrammed as well as real-time creation through on-screen keyboards (letter or picture). It also allows the creation of multiple pages by separating message screens into categories (i.e., food, school, home, clothing). Unaided systems are those in which the child uses only hand or body motions (e.g., gestures, sign language, or fingerspelling) to communicate.

The primary assessment question with students who are nonvocal or nonverbal focuses on selecting the appropriate assistive-technology communication devices. Further, the Individuals with Disabilities Education Act requires functional evaluation in selecting, acquiring, and using assistive-technology devices. The functional evaluation process should include several components.

One of the essential first steps is an ecological evaluation of communication needs. **Ecological assessment** should produce information about communication needs at home, at school, and in other environments. The next step is to identify the ways the student currently meets communication needs and determine unmet communication needs. This may lead to setting priorities for communication. The assessment and selection of a specific communication system should be addressed by a team that includes the child (when possible), the parents, a speech and language pathologist, an occupational therapist, a teacher, and other participants as necessary.

The team should consider a number of factors including chronological age, imitative ability, motor control, cognitive level of functioning, and desire to communicate. In the process of selecting a communication system, the team should also consider options for meeting future communication needs. Once the team has selected a communication system, progress in learning to use the system should be monitored, and instructional planning should include regular data collection to verify the effectiveness of the chosen system (Cohen & Spenciner, 2002).

Summary

Assessing language is a complex process, due in part to the intricate structure of language, which consists of the following components:

- Phonemes: language sounds
- Morphemes: the smallest meaningful language units
- Syntax: word formation in phrases and sentences
- Semantics: word meanings and relationships
- Pragmatics: language usage in context

The wide range and variety of tools for assessing language further contributes to the depth of the subject (see Table 10–4). The many choices include comprehensive diagnostic tests measuring more than one structural language component, single-skill tests for evaluating individual aspects of language, and curriculum-based procedures such as language sampling for measuring language as it occurs in natural settings.

Language is an integral part of daily life at home, in school, and in the community. In addition, it is the foundation of academic learning and, many experts believe, serves as the basis of intellectual development. Because deficits in language and poor language skills severely limit a student's potential for success, teachers of students with special needs must have a working knowledge of available assessment procedures and tests. This knowledge, coupled with hands-on experience, helps in making placement and intervention decisions that respond to the often unique needs of students with language deficits.

To check your comprehension of the chapter contents, go to the *Guided Review* and *Quiz* modules in Chapter 10 of the Companion Website, *www.prenhall.com/venn*.

Meeting Performance Standards and Preparing for Licensure Exams

After reading this chapter, you should be able to demonstrate the following CEC Standards and PRAXIS™ test knowledge and skills. The information in parentheses identifies where to find the particular CEC standard and PRAXIS™ content reference.

CEC Standards for Beginning Special Education Teachers

- Issues in definition and identification of individuals with exceptional learning needs, including those from culturally and linguistically diverse backgrounds (CC1K5)

Table 10–4 Review of Language Assessments

Name	Type	Suitable for	Brief Description	Purpose
Bankson Language Test, Second Edition (BLT-2)	Norm-referenced, individually administered	Children from 3 to 6 years of age	Organized into three general categories: semantic knowledge, morphological/syntactical rules, pragmatics	To measure children's psycholinguistic abilities
Batería III Woodcock-Muñoz	Norm-referenced, individually administered	Individuals from 2 to 90+ years of age	The parallel Spanish version of the Woodcock-Johnson III	To assess cognitive abilities and achievement levels in Spanish-speaking children and adults
Batería Woodcock de Proficiencia en el Idioma	Norm-referenced, individually administered	Individuals from 3 to retirement	Measures oral language, reading, and written language. All subtests taken directly from the Woodcock-Johnson Psycho-Educational Battery. A revised version, Batería Woodcock-Muñoz-Revisada, is available	To assess cognitive abilities and achievement levels in Spanish-speaking children and adults
Boehm Test of Basic Concepts—Third Edition (BTBC-3)	Norm-referenced, group or individual administration	Students from kindergarten through grade 2	Contains 50 concepts for measuring understanding in three major context categories: space (e.g., top, next to, and through), quantity (e.g., first, most, and part), and time (e.g., starting, after, and before)	To evaluate mastery of the basic concepts necessary for understanding the verbal instructions necessary for early school achievement
Boehm-3—Preschool	Norm-referenced, group or individual administration	Children from 3 to 5 years of age	A preschool version of the Boehm Test of Basic Concepts that measures 26 basic concepts	To evaluate mastery of the basic concepts necessary for understanding the verbal instructions necessary for early school achievement
CELF-3—Spanish Edition	Norm-referenced, individually administered	Students from 6 to 21 years of age	Measures receptive and expressive skills in morphology, syntax, semantics, and memory	To diagnose language disorders of students who speak Spanish
CELF-3—Screening Test	Norm-referenced, individually administered	Students from 6 to 21 years of age	Items parallel CELF-3 items representing the most discriminating tasks for identifying language disorders	To quickly identify students who may be at risk for language disorders

Name	Type	Suitable for	Brief Description	Purpose
CELF-3— Observational Rating Scales	Criterion-referenced, individually administered	Students from 6 to 21 years of age	Three parallel Rating Scale Forms (Teacher's Form, Parent's Form, and Student's Form) each contain 40 statements that describe problems in listening, speaking, reading, and writing	To obtain descriptive indicators of students' language performance in class and at home
CELF—Preschool	Norm-referenced, individually administered	Children 3 to 6 years of age	Includes subtests for measuring expressive and receptive language skills	To comprehensively assess language skills
Clinical Evaluation of Language Fundamentals— Fourth Edition (CLEF-4)	Norm-referenced, individually administered	Children and youth from 5 to 21 years of age	Measures receptive and expressive language skills in morphology, syntax, semantics and memory using four core subtests along with supplementary subtests	To identify and diagnose language deficits and to measure the child's progress in developing language skills
Comprehensive Receptive and Expressive Vocabulary Test, Second Edition (CREVT-2)	Norm-referenced, individually administered	Individuals from 4 to 89 years of age	Includes an expressive and a receptive subtest and two equivalent forms	To identify children who are significantly below their peers in oral vocabulary proficiency
Computerized Profiling (CP)	Criterion-referenced, individually administered	Preschool and school-age children	Several programs to help learn and carry out a broad range of language analysis procedures to analyze semantics, grammar, phonology, pragmatics, and narrative	Useful for analyzing both language samples transcribed orthographically and phonological samples transcribed phonetically
Dos Amigos Verbal Language Scales	Norm-referenced, individually administered screening test	School-age children	Consists of two separate scales, English and Spanish, each of which contains a list of 85 stimulus words and their opposites, arranged in ascending order of difficulty	To reveal the comparative development of a child's English and Spanish and to identify the child's dominant language
Expressive One-Word Picture Vocabulary Test—2000 Edition (EOWPVT)	Norm-referenced, individually administered screening test	Children and youth from 2 to 18 years of age	Consists of 100 black-and-white line drawings of common objects and collections of objects	To measure the verbal expression of language by having children make word-picture associations

(continued)

Table 10–4 *continued*

Name	Type	Suitable for	Brief Description	Purpose
Expressive Vocabulary Test (EVT)	Norm-referenced, individually administered screening test	Individuals from 22 to 85-plus years of age	Includes two types of items, labeling and synonyms; items are presented with pictures and the child responds to each item with a one-word answer	To measure expressive vocabulary and word retrieval for Standard American English
*Goldman-Fristoe Test of Articulation, Second Editon (GFTA-2)	Norm-referenced, individually administered	Children and youth from 2 to 21 years of age	Contains subtests for measuring articulation of speech sounds, sound production in connected speech, and the ability to correct misarticulated sounds when given a model of correct production	For speech pathologists to use as a diagnostic tool before beginning therapy
*Goldman-Fristoe-Woodcock Test of Auditory Discrimination (GFW)	Norm-referenced, individually administered screening test	Individuals from 4 years of age through adulthood	Contains three parts: a training procedure, a quiet subtest, and a noise subtest	To measure the ability to differentiate between speech sounds in quiet and noisy situations
Khan-Lewis Phonological Analysis, Second Edition (KLPA-2)	Norm-referenced, individually administered	Children and youth from 2 to 21 years of age	Makes use of the 53 target words elicited by GFTA-2 sounds-in-words subtest to provide further diagnostic information	Designed as a companion tool to the Goldman-Fristoe Test of Articulation—Second Edition (GFTA-2) to obtain in-depth analysis of overall phonological process usage
Language Sampling, Analysis, and Training: A Handbook, Third Edition (LSAT-3)	Criterion-referenced, individually administered	Young children from 2 to 12 years of age	A handbook that includes a variety of criterion-referenced language sampling procedures along with detailed information about measuring and reporting progress	To provide information for planning and monitoring spoken language remediation and also for pinpointing and remediating specific reading comprehension problems

Name	Type	Suitable for	Brief Description	Purpose
Listening Comprehension Scale and Oral Expression Scale	Norm-referenced individually, administered	Individuals 3 to 21 years of age	The Listening Comprehension Scale measures receptive language and consists of three examples and 111 items; the Oral Expression Scale measures the understanding and use of spoken language and it consists of two examples and 96 items	To measure language knowledge and processing skills in children and adolescents
*Peabody Picture Vocabulary Test, Third Edition (PPVT-III)	Norm-referenced, individually administered screening test	Individuals from 2.5 years through adulthood	Contains 204 items; each item consists of four simple line drawings on a page; the child selects a drawing (from among the four choices) that best represents the meaning of each word presented orally	To assess receptive language (hearing) vocabulary
Receptive One-Word Picture Vocabulary Test—2000 Edition (ROWPVT)	Norm-referenced, Individually administered screening test	Children and youth from 2 to 18 years of age	Designed as a companion test to the Expressive One-Word Vocabulary Test— Revised	To assess receptive hearing vocabulary
Systematic Analysis of Language Transcripts (SALT)	Criterion-referenced, individually administered, computer-based	Preschool and school-age children	Transcribes language samples, calculates a variety of standard measures, and compares results with age-matched peers	To provide a variety of standard analyses including measures of syntax such as MLU in words and morphemes, morphology, fluency and rate, and discourse
*Test of Adolescent and Adult Language, Third Edition (TOAL-3)	Norm-referenced, individually administered, comprehensive test	Students from 12 to 24 years of age	A comprehensive measure of language abilities, evaluating semantic and syntactical ability in listening, speaking, reading, and writing	To identify performance levels in receptive and expressive language and to determine the deficits of students with language delays

(continued)

Table 10–4 *continued*

Name	Type	Suitable for	Brief Description	Purpose
*Test for Auditory Comprehension of Language, Third Edition (TACL-3)	Individually administered, norm-referenced, comprehensive test	Children from 3 to 9 years of age	Measures auditory comprehension of language in three categories: vocabulary (literal meaning of words), morphology (grammatical morphemes), and syntax (meaning from sentences)	To identify children with language deficits, measure school readiness, plan instructional programs, and monitor student progress
Test of Early Language Development, Second Edition (TELD-3)	Norm-referenced, individually administered	Children from 2 to 7 years of age	Provides two equivalent forms with results reported as standard scores, percentiles, NCEs, or age equivalents	To identify spoken language disorders and to isolate particular types of spoken language deficits
*Test of Language Development—Intermediate, Third Edition (TOLD-I:3)	Norm-referenced, individually administered	Children from 8 to 12 years of age	Contains six subtests: sentence combining, picture vocabulary, word ordering, generals, and grammatic comprehension	To identify spoken language disorders and to isolate particular types of spoken language deficits
*Test of Language Development—Primary, Third Edition (TOLD-P:3)	Norm-referenced, individually administered	Children from 4 to 8 years of age	Contains nine subtests: picture vocabulary, relational vocabulary, oral vocabulary, grammatic understanding, grammatic completion, sentence imitation, word discrimination, phonemic analysis, and word articulation	To identify spoken language disorders and to isolate particular types of spoken language deficits
Test of Pragmatic Language (TOPL)	Norm-referenced, individually administered	Students from 5 to 13 years of age	Measures six core sub-components of pragmatic language: physical setting, audience, topic, purpose (speech acts), visual-gestural cues, and abstraction	To assess social language skills
Test of Pragmatic Skills	Criterion referenced, individually administered	Children from 3 to 8 years of age	Measures 10 different communicative intents: requesting information, requesting action, rejection or denial, naming or labeling, answering or responding, informing, reasoning, summoning or calling, greeting, and closing conversation	To analyze expressive language as it occurs in the context of structured play Interactions

Name	Type	Suitable for	Brief Description	Purpose
TVIP: Test de Vocaulario en Imágenes Peabody	Norm-referenced, individually administered	Children and youth from 22 to 18 years of age	Based on the Peabody Picture Vocabulary Test—Revised, the TVIP contains 125 translated items to assess the receptive vocabulary of Spanish-speaking and bilingual students	Designed to evaluate the receptive vocabulary development of Spanish-speaking children and youth
Utah Test of Language Development, Fourth Edition (UTLD-4)	Norm-referenced, individually administered	Children from 3 to 9 years of age	Includes a language comprehension subtest and a language expression subtest	To measure expressive and receptive language skills

^Tests marked with an asterisk are featured in this chapter.

- Differing ways of learning of individuals with exceptional learning needs including those from culturally diverse backgrounds and strategies for addressing these differences (CC3K5)
- Characteristics of one's own culture and use of language and the ways in which these can differ from other cultures and uses of languages (CC6K2)
- Augmentative and assistive communication strategies (CC6K4)
- Impact of language development and listening comprehension on academic and nonacademic learning of individuals with disabilities (GC6K1)
- Plan instruction on the use of alternative and augmentative communication systems (GC6S5)
- Use assessment information in making eligibility, program, and placement decisions for individuals with exceptional learning needs, including those from culturally and/or linguistically diverse backgrounds (CC8S6)

PRAXIS™ Education of Exceptional Students: Core Content Knowledge

- Curriculum and instruction and their implementation across the continuum of educational placements, including instructional format and components; for example, ESL and limited English proficiency, and language and literacy acquisition (0353 III)
- Technology for teaching and learning in special education settings, for example, integrating assistive technology into the classroom; computer-assisted instruction; augmentative and alternative communication; adaptive access for microcomputers (0353 III)
- Assessment, including use of assessment for screening, diagnosis, placement, and the making of instructional decisions; for example, how to select and conduct nondiscriminatory and appropriate assessment, and how to interpret standardized and specialized assessment results (0353 III)
- Assessment including procedures and test materials, both formal and informal, typically used for prereferral, screening, referral, classification, placement, and ongoing program monitoring (0353 III)
- How to select, construct, conduct, and modify nondiscriminatory, developmentally and chronologically age-appropriate informal assessments, including teacher-made tests, curriculum-based assessment, and alternatives to norm-referenced testing, including observations (0353 III)

chapter 11

Assessing Behavior

Objectives

After reading this chapter, you will be prepared to do the following:

- Understand the principles of assessing behavior.
- Understand the behaviors measured by behavior rating scales and checklists.
- Use behavior rating scales and checklists.
- Conduct direct observations.
- Implement behavioral recording systems to assess student conduct and inappropriate behavior.
- Understand the emotions that self-concept inventories measure.
- Use self-concept inventories.
- Use tests to evaluate student attitudes and interests.
- Use tests and rating scales to assess attention deficit hyperactivity disorder.

Overview

Assessing behavior encompasses several important dimensions of conduct and personality as well as self-concept, attitudes, and interests. Techniques and tests for assessing behavior help identify behavior problems, and assessment results help develop intervention programs and measure student progress. In this chapter, you learn the essential concepts and techniques associated with assessing behavior. To achieve this goal, you review the principles that guide the assessment of behavior, and you examine evaluation instruments, curriculum-based procedures, and tests used in the assessment process, including the following:

- Behavior rating scales
- Direct observation
- Self-concept measures
- Methods for assessing school attitudes and interests
- Measures of attention deficit hyperactivity disorder (ADHD)

Throughout the chapter, we consider current trends and issues in measuring and evaluating behavior as related to assessing students with special needs.

The Importance of Assessing Behavior

The following account illustrates the use of assessment to identify and place a student with a severe behavior disorder.

David displayed extreme difficulty controlling his behavior in the regular classroom and the special education resource room. He became easily upset and was often verbally and sometimes physically aggressive. When doing classwork, David usually began a task and then quickly became distracted. When prompted to return to work, he often demonstrated his anger by tearing up his papers. He seemed unaware of the consequences of his conduct.

David's disturbing behaviors prompted his teachers to inquire about placing David in a program for children with severe emotional disturbance. The teachers discovered that the process involved gathering quite a bit of assessment data. For example, the coordinator of the staffing team asked David's teachers to complete behavior rating scales and document attempted interventions designed to control his aggressive behavior. In addition, the teachers arranged for the school counselor to conduct two observations of David's behavior in the classroom. Furthermore, the staffing coordinator arranged for a psychologist to conduct a clinical interview with David. Finally, the staffing team used the results from these assessments, along with other relevant information, to recommend placing David in a program for students with severe emotional disturbance.

Special educators often serve students who, like David, display severe disruptive behaviors. Unfortunately, these problems, if ignored, not only interfere with the educational progress of the individual student but also often impede the performance of the entire class. Therefore, teachers must intervene to manage student misbehavior and disruptions. One of the essential components in the intervention process is assessment.

Assessing behavior involves using several types of measurement and evaluation procedures. In the classroom, teachers usually rely on practical, applied procedures such as observation of student behavior. However, when professionals conduct assessment to determine eligibility and make placement decisions, they use more formal evaluation procedures. *Student behavior* is a broad term that encompasses a range of nonacademic behaviors. For this reason, assessing behavior includes

MULTICULTURAL CONSIDERATIONS

Functional Assessment with Students from Culturally Diverse Backgrounds

The number of minority children in the United States is increasing dramatically, with Hispanic children making up the fastest-growing group. Unfortunately, data suggest that African-American and Hispanic students tend to be overrepresented in special education programs whereas Asian students tend to be underrepresented. Data also suggest minority children tend to be overreferred for possible behavior problems.

Several factors may contribute to these problems. First, children from culturally diverse backgrounds may have language differences that influence how others perceive and interact with them. These differences may be interpreted as behavior problems. Second, educators may have preconceived biases toward culturally different children that may ultimately lead to referral and placement in special education programs for children with behavior problems. Consequently, children from culturally different groups are at risk for misidentification because of higher referral rates.

These factors all point to the need for assessment practices designed to reduce the overreferral of minority children and minimize test bias. Functional assessment is one approach that may help because it involves directly evaluating student behavior and performance under existing teaching conditions, altering instructional practices to improve student performance, and monitoring student performance on a continuous basis. Because functional assessment is direct and continuous, it minimizes bias due to cultural differences.

Specific functional assessment procedures include conducting interviews, using rating scales, collecting direct observation data, and using functional analysis. Functional analysis is a specialized element of functional assessment involving direct manipulation of antecedent and consequent variables identified during interviews and observations. For example, a student may be observed in a series of classroom activities, some of which include significant task demands and some of which do not. If the student displays more frequent inappropriate behavior during demanding activities, the teacher can modify the task demands to see whether this reduces inappropriate behavior and thus eliminates the need for a referral.

Much more needs to be done to reduce referrals and minimize bias in testing. One way to respond to this challenge is to develop greater awareness of the potential for using functional assessment with children from culturally diverse backgrounds who display behavior problems.

Explain why you think Africa-American and Hispanic students are more likely to be referred to special education than Asian students.

To answer this reflection online, go to the *Multicultural Considerations* module on the Companion Website at www.prenhall.com/venn.

evaluating social-emotional development, student self-concept and attitudes, and behavior outside the classroom. A thorough assessment, then, includes the school, the family, the neighborhood, and the community. In other words, the best assessment incorporates all elements that influence behavior and social-emotional development. Teachers also use **functional assessment,** a specialized type of behavior assessment. Functional assessment is especially useful with students from culturally diverse backgrounds and experiences. Information about using functional assessment to minimize cultural bias appears in the accompanying Multicultural Considerations feature.

As you can see, assessing behavior consists of more than dealing with conduct disorders. In fact, it includes procedures for making a range of decisions about behavior associated with the affective domain, which refers to opinions, attitudes, and behaviors derived from emotions rather than from thought. Obviously, measuring affective behavior is more subjective than measuring academic skills such as math achievement or physical ability such as running speed and throwing accuracy. One of the reasons for this subjectivity is that behavior occurs within the context of complex interaction patterns among student, teacher, and peers. Furthermore, behavior disorders involve personal and emotional feelings and values about acceptable limits for behavior. Deciding whether a particular behavior falls beyond acceptable limits is not as clear-cut as grading a math worksheet or a spelling test. Behavior involves social, emotional, family, and community factors that make precise measurement difficult. For this reason, the procedures for assessing behavior differ in form and content from the procedures for assessing cognitive indicators. Fortunately, principles are available for professionals to follow as guides to assessing behavior.

Behavior Assessment Principles

Most measures of behavior are not tests in the traditional sense. Instead, they are structured methods for recording observations of behavior. These include behavior rating scales, behavior observation procedures, and self-concept inventories. The following principles include important considerations about using these assessment procedures.

- Assessing behavior is a dynamic process requiring competent observers who make subjective decisions about attitudes and conduct. For example, teachers complete behavior rating scales based on professional judgment and experience coupled with their knowledge of a student's typical conduct in the classroom. Likewise, when using direct observation to measure student misbehavior, teachers rely on training, experience, and professional judgment to select appropriate target behaviors and measurement procedures.
- Behavior observation procedures require the assessor to apply specific and often technical measurement procedures. Accurate and effective use of these procedures often involves specialized training.
- In addition to using rating scales and direct observation, a variety of other sources are helpful when assessing student behavior. These include formal and informal communication with parents, peers, teachers, and students; review of school records that detail social and educational history; and the influence of social, emotional, family, and community factors.

Reflection
Do you think family structure could influence student behavior? Explain your answer.

 To answer this reflection online, go to the *Teaching and Learning* module on the Companion Website at *www.prenhall.com/venn*.

Why Do We Assess the Behavior of Students with Special Needs?

As teachers, we are well prepared to monitor and assess students, and student behavior is always one of our primary concerns. We assess behavior in a number of ways and for a variety reasons, including to screen for possible problems and to help identify students with behavior disorders. Sometimes our assessment is informal, and we just generally keep an eye on things to make sure that the classroom is orderly, anticipate difficult situations, and keep track of how things are going. During our general observations, we may notice important behaviors or events that require attention: Juan is upset and agitated, Felicia is asleep, or two students are yelling at each other right outside the classroom door. In educational settings with students who have behavior disorders, we may look for very specific behaviors such as signs of impending verbal or physical aggression, appropriate social behavior we should reinforce, or students who need our attention to stay on task. We use the information gained from our observations to make assessment decisions about student behavior, especially as it affects academic performance. Focus 11–1 summarizes the reasons for assessing the behavior of students with special needs.

☑ Check Your Comprehension

Teachers must often intervene to manage student misbehavior, and assessment is one of the essential tools of effective behavior, intervention. A variety of procedures help with assessment of problem behaviors, including rating scales, behavioral observations, and self-concept inventories. When assessing student behavior, following established principles helps to ensure accurate information. Assessing student behavior is important in screening, diagnosing, intervening, and measuring progress.

Behavior Rating Scales

Behavior rating scales evaluate the conduct of students who exhibit inappropriate behavior. Behavior rating scales consist of written questionnaires containing lists of behaviors. Raters complete the questionnaires by assigning a rating (often using a scale of 1 to 5) to each item on the list. Raters are usually teachers, parents, or other primary caregivers who are familiar with a student's typical conduct. Available rating scales include instruments designed specifically for evaluating student behavior in school programs, for measuring student behavior at home and in the community, and

$\mathcal{F}$OCUS 11 - 1

Why Do We Assess Behavior?

- To screen for possible emotional disturbance or behavior disorders
- To diagnose students with emotional disturbance or behavior disorders
- To develop plans for managing behavior and improving academic performance
- To measure the effectiveness of intervention programs

for assessing student behavior in specialized treatment programs such as residential centers and psychiatric hospitals.

Because they consist of checklists of behaviors rated by an evaluator, most scales take only 20 minutes or so to complete. The checklist format is easy to administer and score. However, behavior scales use an indirect, pencil-on-paper type of measurement using ratings from informants such as teachers and parents. Because of the potential for bias in ratings by informants, results from rating scales may not always match the actual behavior of the student. In addition, most rating scales and checklists are general screening measures that provide an overview of behavior problems rather than in-depth diagnostic information. For these reasons, most professionals rely on rating scales for screening and initial identification of student behavior problems rather than for developing instructional objectives. Two representative behavior rating scales are the Devereux Behavior Rating Scale—School Form and the Social Skills Rating System. Detailed reviews of these instruments appear in the following sections. This is followed by brief reviews of other available instruments.

Devereux Behavior Rating Scale—School Form

The norm-referenced, individually administered Devereux Behavior Rating Scale—School Form (Naglieri, LeBuffe, & Pfeiffer, 1993) is a checklist for identifying behaviors that may indicate severe emotional disturbance in children and adolescents. The 40-item Devereux School Form is also useful for obtaining an ongoing record of classroom behavior, measuring behavior change, facilitating communication among professionals and parents, and conducting educational research. The Devereux School Form is designed for students ages 5 to 18 to measure behaviors that, according to experienced teachers, interfere with academic functioning and achievement. The four subscales measure the areas addressed in the federal definition of serious emotional disturbance: interpersonal problems, inappropriate behaviors and feelings, depression, and physical symptoms and fears. A summary of the Devereux Behavior Rating Scale—School Form appears in the Test Review box.

Devereux School Form Materials   Devereux School Form materials include a manual and separate scoring forms for children ages 5 to 12 and for adolescents ages 13 to 18.

Devereux School Form Administration and Scoring   Teachers, psychologists, guidance counselors, and other assessment professionals can use the Devereux School Form. The informants who rate the items include teachers who have observed a student in a classroom setting, parents, or primary caregivers. Teacher raters need observation time before rating a student's behavior. The length of time depends on the class size and the amount of time the student spends with a teacher. The actual rating with the scales takes only 5 to 10 minutes. The scale is scored by recording the rating for each item on a profile form. Available scores include a total scale score, subscale scores, and problem item scores for identifying specific problem behaviors for treatment. The subscale scores can help in IEP and intervention program development.

Devereux School Form Technical Characteristics   The developers standardized the Devereux School Form with a national sample of more than 3,000 cases. The standardization study produced separate norms for males and females, and for parent and teacher raters.

╭─────────────────╮
│ **TEST REVIEW** │
╰─────────────────╯

Devereux Behavior Rating Scale—School Form

Type of Test:	Norm-referenced, individually administered
Purpose:	To identify behaviors that may indicate severe emotional disturbance
Content Areas:	Interpersonal problems, inappropriate behaviors and feelings, depression, and physical symptoms and fears
Administration Time:	5 to 10 minutes
Age Levels:	5 to 18 years
Suitable for:	Students who exhibit severe behavior problems
Scores:	Total scale score and subscale scores
In Short:	A useful instrument for identifying problem behaviors and measuring behavior change

Devereux School Form Summary The Devereux Behavior Rating Scale—School Form is a questionnaire for rating problem behaviors and is useful for identifying students with severe emotional disturbance, comparing results across informants (i.e., teachers and parents), identifying problem behaviors in the classroom, providing an ongoing record of behavior, measuring behavior change, and providing a means for communication among professionals and parents.

Social Skills Rating System

The Social Skills Rating System (SSRS) (Gresham & Elliot, 1990) consists of a standardized series of questionnaires measuring the frequency and importance of behaviors that affect performance at home and in school. Designed for use with students from age 3 to 18, the SSRS includes rating forms that are completed by the teacher, the parents, and the child. The authors developed the SSRS to assist in planning intervention programs for students with behavior disorders, learning disabilities, or mild mental retardation, or with any student who exhibits social or behavior problems. A summary of the SSRS appears in the Test Review box.

The SSRS measures behavior in three domains:

1. Social skills
   a. Cooperation
   b. Assertion
   c. Responsibility
   d. Self-control

2. Problem behaviors
   a. Externalizing problems
   b. Internalizing problems
   c. Hyperactivity

3. Academic competence
   a. Reading and mathematics
   b. Motivation

```
┌─────────────────────────────────────────────────────────────────────────────┐
│                        ╭─────────────────────────╮                            │
│                        │      TEST REVIEW         │                            │
│                        ╰─────────────────────────╯                            │
│                                                                               │
│                         Social Skills Rating System                           │
│                                                                               │
│   Type of Test:              Norm-referenced, individually administered       │
│   Purpose:                   Diagnostic rating of social skills and problem   │
│                              behaviors                                         │
│   Content Areas:             Social skills, problem behaviors, and academic   │
│                              competence                                        │
│   Administration Time:       Approximately 60 to 90 minutes to complete all   │
│                              scales                                            │
│   Age Levels:                3 to 18 years                                    │
│   Suitable for:              Students with behavior disorders, learning       │
│                              disabilities, mild mental retardation, or any     │
│                              student who exhibits social or behavior problems  │
│   Scores:                    Behavior levels, standard scores, and percentiles │
│   In Short:                  The well-designed SSRS uses a multiple-rater     │
│                              system (teacher, parent, and student) to assess   │
│                              social skills and provide data for developing     │
│                              behavior intervention programs.                   │
│                                                                               │
└─────────────────────────────────────────────────────────────────────────────┘
```

c. Parental support

d. General cognitive functioning

SSRS Materials SSRS materials consist of a test manual, three rating forms (teacher, parent, and student versions), and an assessment and intervention planning record. The teacher and parent rating forms are available for three levels: preschool, kindergarten through grade 6, and grades 7 through 12. The student self-rating form is available at two levels: grades 3 through 6 and grades 7 through 12. The assessment and intervention planning form provides a system for summarizing all information obtained from the raters and identifying problem areas in need of intervention. Optional materials include computerized scoring and reporting software that provides behavioral objectives and suggestions for intervention. The software offers eight different report options for analysis of social behavior that include an intervention narrative and a behavioral objective report. Teachers may also use the *Social Skills Intervention Guide* (Elliot & Gresham, 1991) to link intervention strategies directly with SSRS assessment. The guide includes 43 lessons with skills grouped around cooperation, assertion, responsibility, empathy, and self-control.

SSRS Administration and Scoring Rather than a test given to a child by an evaluator, the SSRS is a set of rating scales completed by the child, the teacher, and the parent to measure social skill development. It takes 10 to 25 minutes for respondents to complete their scale and about 5 minutes for the evaluator (usually a teacher or parent) to score each scale. The SSRS relies on a three-point rating system (0 for never, 1 for sometimes, and 2 for very often) for all scales except the academic competence scale, which uses a five-point system. Scoring involves converting the raw scores from each questionnaire into standard scores, percentiles, and behavior levels. The manual includes detailed illustrations and sample cases that explain the scoring process and the procedures for identifying strengths and weaknesses. The evaluator interprets student performance based on norm-group comparisons and individual score patterns. The manual also provides sample profiles and a list of assessment questions to aid in the interpretation of results.

SSRS Technical Characteristics   The SSRS was standardized with a national sample of more than 4,000 students, including students from racial and ethnic minority groups and students with disabilities. The manual reports average internal consistency coefficients ranging from .90 to .95 for the three major content areas and average coefficients for the individual subtests from .51 to .92. Average test-retest reliability coefficients of teacher and parent ratings were in the .80s, and student rating coefficients were .68. The manual also includes extensive information describing the content and concurrent validity of the SSRS. Overall, the SSRS exhibits good technical characteristics.

SSRS Summary   The Social Skills Rating System is a well-designed instrument for assessing the social skill development of students from 3 to 18 years of age. It uses a multiple-rater system (teacher, parent, and student) to provide data for assessing children with problem behaviors and for developing IEPs and intervention programs. The SSRS evaluates a broad range of behaviors that affect teacher-student relationships, peer acceptance, and academic performance. The three rating forms—teacher, parent, and student—give a comprehensive picture across school, home, and community settings.

Other Behavior Rating Scales

The use of behavior rating scales is widely accepted in special education and related disciplines. Brief descriptions of other available behavior rating scales follow.

Adjustment Scales for Children and Adolescents   The norm-referenced, individually administered Adjustment Scales for Children and Adolescents (ASCA) (McDermott, 1993) provides comprehensive assessment of behavior problems, psychopathology, and styles of healthy adjustment. Designed for children ages 5 to 17, the ASCA takes about 20 minutes to administer. The ASCA contains 97 problem behavior pinpoints and 26 positive behavior indicators, each presented in one of 29 specific situations involving authority, peers, smaller or weaker youths, recreation, learning, or confrontation. The specific behavior syndromes assessed by the ASCA are the following:

- Attention-deficit hyperactive
- Solitary aggressive (provocative)
- Solitary aggressive (impulsive)
- Oppositional defiant
- Diffident avoidant
- Delinquent
- Lethargic

Standardized on a sample of 1,400 children, the ASCA provides separate forms designed specifically for male and female children and produces two composite overall adjustment scores and percentiles for the eight behavior syndromes just listed.

Behavior Assessment System for Children, Second Edition   The norm-referenced, individually administered Behavior Assessment System for Children, Second Edition (BASC-2) (Reynolds & Kamphaus, 2004) is a set of instruments for evaluating the behaviors, thoughts, and emotions of children and adolescents from 2 through 21 years of age. The three core instruments in the system are a teacher rating scale, a parent rating scale, and a self-report of personality. The system also includes a tool for collecting a structured developmental history, a procedure for directly observing a student's behavior in the classroom, and scales measuring functional communication, activities of daily living, attention problems, and hyperactivity. The system gives a comprehensive picture of the student by providing teacher, parent, and child self-report ratings of behavior along with data from directly observed classroom behavior and information from a developmental history. The BASC-2 measures numerous aspects of behavior and personality, including positive, adaptive behaviors as well as negative, problematic dimensions. It also provides assessment data linked to ADD and ADHD. The parent rating scale measures adaptive and problem behavior in community and home settings. The teacher rating scale measures adaptive and problem behavior in the school setting. The self-report personality measure assesses children's thoughts and feelings about themselves and their environment. Optional BASC-2 materials include software to assist with scoring and developing reports.

Behavior and Emotional Rating Scale, Second Edition   The norm-referenced, individually administered Behavior and Emotional Rating Scale, Second Edition (BERS-2) (Epstein, 2004) helps measure the personal strengths of students from 5 through 18 years of age. Designed for use in schools, mental health clinics, and child welfare agencies, the BERS-2 measures the behavior from three perspectives: the child (Youth Rating Scale), parent (Parent Rating Scale), and teacher or other professional (Teacher Rating Scale). All of the BERS-2 scales were normed on children without disabilities, and the Teacher Rating Scale was normed on children with emotional and behavioral disorders. The BERS-2 is useful in evaluating children as part of the preferral process and in placing children in specialized services. It can also help in evaluating the outcomes of services.

Behavior Rating Profile-2   The Behavior Rating Profile-2 (BRP-2) (Brown & Hammill, 1990) is a norm-referenced measure for obtaining information about a student's behavior in a variety of settings. Designed for students from 6 to 18 years of age, the profile consists of scales completed by the student, the parent, and the teacher. Completed by the student's classmates, a **sociogram** measures social acceptance and peer popularity by having students rate each of their classmates in a nonobtrusive manner. Sociograms analyze the group structure in a classroom and identify the popularity of individual students. The BRP-2 uses an ecological approach that measures differences in ratings among teachers, parents, and classmates. Ecological assessment considers both student and environmental characteristics (such as the classroom setting, the community, and the family situation) in the evaluation process. In ecological assessment, the evaluator analyzes student behavior within the context of the environment, setting, or situation in which the behavior occurs.

Child Behavior Checklist for Ages 6–18   The Child Behavior Checklist for Ages 6–18 (CBCL/6–18) (Achenbach, 2001) is a norm-referenced instrument for recording children's competencies and problems as reported by their parents or parent surrogates. The CBCL/6–18 items obtain parents' reports of the amount and quality of their child's participation in sports, hobbies, games, activities, jobs and chores, and friendships; how well the child gets along with others and plays and works alone; and school functioning. The items are scored on a three-step response scale. The CBCL/6–18 also includes a teacher report form and a youth self-report form. Instruments such as the CBCL/6–18 are useful as one component of many in a comprehensive assessment of behavior. Other components include teacher observations, standardized tests, and physical assessment and direct assessment of the student.

For children too young for the CBCL/6–18, the Child Behavior Checklist/$1\frac{1}{2}$–5) (CBCL/$1\frac{1}{2}$–5) (Achenbach, 2002) is available. These instruments for multi-informant child and young adult assessment are supported with normative data, and they have been used in more than 4,000 studies from 50 countries. These instruments are useful in diverse situations, including schools and mental health, medical, forensic, residential treatment, training, public health, child and family services, and research settings.

Comprehensive Behavior Rating Scale for Children   The Comprehensive Behavior Rating Scale for Children (CBRSC) (Neeper, Lehey, & Frick, 1990) is a norm-referenced, individually administered measure of children's classroom behavior. Designed for students from 6 to 14 years of age, the scale addresses cognitive as well as emotional and behavioral dimensions. The 70-item scale takes 10 to 15 minutes to complete and provides t-scores and percentiles for the total sample, for gender, and for ages. The CBRSC includes nine subscales: inattention/disorganization, reading problems, cognitive deficits, oppositional-conduct disorder, motor hyperactivity, anxiety, sluggish tempo, social competence, and daydreaming. The CBRSC provides useful information for diagnosis and for developing intervention plans for children having school problems.

Draw a Person: Screening Procedure for Emotional Disturbance   The Draw a Person: Screening Procedure for Emotional Disturbance (DAP:SPED) (Naglieri, McNeish, & Achilles, 1991) is a norm-referenced screening test that helps identify children and adolescents with potential emotional problems that require further evaluation. Designed for use with individuals or groups of children from 6 to 17 years of age, the DAP:SPED rates drawings of a man, a woman, and the self. Normed on a sample of 2,260 children, the DAP:SPED was developed using the extensive literature on human figure drawing. The DAP:SPED is easy to administer and fast to score.

☑ Check Your Comprehension

A variety of behavior rating scales and checklists are available for evaluating student conduct. Designed to provide an overall measure of general levels of student behavior, most scales take only a few minutes to rate and score. The scales are helpful for screening and identification of students with behavior problems as well as for measuring student progress over time. Available scales and inventories include instruments designed for use in schools, at home, and in specialized treatment centers.

Direct Observation

Unlike rating scales that measure student behavior indirectly, **direct observation** is firsthand recording of actual behavior as it occurs. Direct observation is the preferred procedure for in-depth assessment of problem behaviors. Trained teachers or paraprofessionals conduct direct observation by recording student actions, using specific techniques to ensure accurate measurement. Direct observation is excellent for assessing student conduct as well as cognitive behaviors, including academic achievement. Unlike rating scales that provide screening information, observations provide in-depth diagnostic data and information for developing intervention programs and for documenting changes in behavior. In most situations, direct observation is the assessment procedure of first choice for measuring inappropriate behavior such as acting out, noncompliance, aggressive behavior, **stereotypy,** and self-injurious behavior. This practical, applied type of measurement provides authentic assessment data for realistically defining the intensity of a problem, developing intervention programs that respond directly to a specific problem, and evaluating genuine student progress. Direct observation, however, is not a single type of procedure; rather, it includes a spectrum of both informal and formal techniques.

Informal Observation

Informal observation involves gathering information about behavior in a casual, unsystematic manner. Teachers usually document informal observations by writing descriptions of specific events after they occur. This documentation is usually a brief log of incidents. Sometimes, however, informal documentation consists of subjective impressions about the causes of and solutions to a behavior problem. Subjective assessment may also involve estimating the frequency or duration of a behavior without any supporting data. Because it is unstructured, informal observation may produce unsatisfactory results. Overton (2006) describes several of the problems with informal observation. They include the following:

- Inaccuracies due to observation of unrepresentative behaviors
- Unreliability because observers rely on personal definitions of behavior rather than precise or stable definitions
- Bias resulting from the subjective nature of most unsystematic observations
- Difficulty in independently verifying subjective information

Because of inadequacies, experts usually recommend using more formal, systematic observation procedures. An explanation of the formal observation process follows.

The Observation Process

The process of conducting formal, systematic observation includes the following:

- Identifying an observable target behavior
- Selecting a procedure for measuring the target behavior, including setting up a data collection system
- Observing the target behavior and collecting data
- Recording the results on a graph
- Interpreting and applying the results

These steps help to ensure the collection of accurate observations. One of the keys to success is selecting an appropriate measurement procedure. The most common procedures include anecdotal recording, event recording, duration recording, partial interval recording, and momentary time sampling.

Anecdotal Recording

Anecdotal recording is especially helpful in understanding why a behavior occurs. Overton (2006) defines anecdotal recording as systematic observation of behavior in which the observer writes down the behaviors and interactions that occur during a specific time interval. Typical time intervals include an academic period such as a math class or a nonacademic time such as lunch or recess. With anecdotal recording, observers write down their observations during specified periods and document the event that precedes the behavior (the antecedent) and the event that follows the behavior (the consequence). Observers record their observations on a recording form. Before the actual recording begins, however, the observer selects one or more

Figure 11–1 Anecdotal recording form

Student _____	Date _____
Observer _____	Setting _____
Observation Starting Time _____	Ending Time _____
Total Observation Time _____	
Antecedent _____	Behavior _____	Consequence _____
(who, what, where, when)	(includes estimated frequency and/or duration)	(what occured next?)

target behaviors to observe and plans the observation sessions. In most situations, the observer needs to obtain at least two or three separate samples of behavior to provide enough information for making accurate decisions. A sample anecdotal recording form appears in Figure 11–1.

Compared with other forms of direct observation, anecdotal recording displays several advantages. It allows for documenting the antecedents, the behavior itself, and the consequences. The procedure also enables analysis of the sequence of events as they occur within the context of surrounding events. This is especially helpful during the beginning stages of behavior management. Anecdotal recording helps select the most important behaviors to target for intervention and points out other relevant aspects of the setting in which the behavior occurs. Although anecdotal recording does not produce quantitative data suitable for graphing, it is appropriate for documenting the extent and nature of one or more problem behaviors.

Event Recording

In contrast to anecdotal recording, **event recording** has the advantage of providing quantitative data. Event recording involves counting the number of occurrences of a target behavior during a specified time. To employ event recording successfully, the observer must identify the beginning and end of each occurrence of a target behavior; like all forms of behavior assessment, this method requires use of a recording form (see Figure 11–2). Many types of recording forms are available for event recording. Additional recording form examples appear in Figure 11–3. Event recording is best for documenting discrete behaviors of short duration, such as the number of aggressive acts during the school day or the frequency of talking out during a 50-minute class period. It is a poor measure of nondiscrete behaviors of relatively long duration, such as temper tantrums. To record behaviors of long duration as accurately as possible, special educators rely on another form of behavioral assessment: duration recording.

Duration Recording

Certain behaviors are relatively continuous and do not occur as discrete events. These include temper tantrums, crying, sustained conversation, and stereotypy, as well as behaviors such as off-task and out-of-seat. One way to accurately measure sustained behaviors is through **duration recording,** which records the total time that a target behavior occurs during a given time. To obtain accurate duration-recording data, the observer usually uses a stopwatch to measure the total time a student spends engaged in a target behavior during a set time. A sample form for conducting duration recording appears in Figure 11–4.

Figure 11–2 Event recording form

Time	Monday	Tuesday	Wednesday	Thursday	Friday
8:30–9:30					
9:30–10:30					
10:30–11:30					
Total					

Student _____   Date _____
Observer _____   Setting _____
Target Behavior _____

Figure 11–3 Other event recording forms

Student _____   Observer _____
Observation Setting _____
Observation Dates _____

Day	M	T	W	Th	F	Total
Completed work tasks						
Cleaned work station						

Target Behavior _____
Observer   _____
Setting   _____
Date   _____

Student	AM Break	Lunch Break	PM Break

Partial Interval Recording

Although it is possible to use duration recording to measure behaviors such as on-task and off-task accurately, observers often prefer to use another form of behavioral observation—**partial interval recording**—because it enables measurement of more than one target behavior during each observation period (e.g., off-task, talking-out,

Figure 11–4 Duration recording data collection form

Student _____   Date _____

Observer _____   Setting _____

Target Behavior _____

Observation Time _____

Occurrence	Occurrence Duration		Occurrence	Occurrence Duration
1			6	
2			7	
3			8	
4			9	
5			10	

Total Duration Time _____

Comments _____

and out-of-seat). Partial interval recording involves dividing time periods into brief intervals (e.g., a 1-minute period into 10-second intervals, or a 10-minute period into 1-minute intervals) and observing whether a target behavior occurs during the interval. A sample partial-interval recording form appears in Figure 11–5. Unfortunately, partial interval recording requires observation throughout each interval, which makes the technique difficult for teachers to use in the classroom. As a result, teachers often employ an alternative recording method—momentary time sampling—because it does not require continuous observation.

Momentary Time Sampling

Because it does not require continuous observation, **momentary time sampling** is the preferred option for teachers and other observers who must record behavior while they are involved in other activities. Momentary time sampling involves recording the occurrence or nonoccurrence of one or more target behaviors at the end of a specified period (e.g., at the end of every 5 minutes or at the end of every minute). Recording whether a student is off-task at the end of every 5 minutes during a 50-minute class period, for example, produces a sample indicating the percentage of time in which the target behavior occurred. If a student were off-task during 6 of 12 time samples, the behavior occurred in 50% of the samples during that particular period. Collecting momentary time samples daily for a week or two provides a reliable estimate of the amount of time a student spends in off-task behavior. An example of a momentary time sampling recording form appears in Figure 11–6.

Reporting Methods

Observers may report results using several different methods. The goal is to summarize results accurately in a manner that best describes student behavior. Often simple methods such as reporting the number of times a problem behavior occurs (e.g., the

Figure 11–5 Partial-interval data recording form

Student _____   Date _____
Observer _____
Target Behavior _____

Setting _____
Starting Time _____   Ending Time _____   Total Time _____

Minutes	Seconds	Data		Minutes	Seconds	Data
1	20			6	20	
2	20			7	20	
3	20			8	20	
4	20			9	20	
5	20			10	20	

Key × = occurrence, — = nonoccurrence
Observation Summary
# of occurrences _____ % of occurrences _____
# of nonoccurrences _____ % of nonoccurrences _____

Figure 11–6 Momentary time-sampling data collection form

Student _____   Date _____
Observer _____
Target Behavior _____
Setting _____

Time Interval	Occurrence	Nonoccurrence
10:10		
10:10		
10:20		
10:30		
10:40		
10:50		

Observation Summary
# of occurrences _____ % of occurrence _____
# of nonoccurrences _____ % of nonoccurrences _____

Figure 11–7 Graphs of behavioral observation data

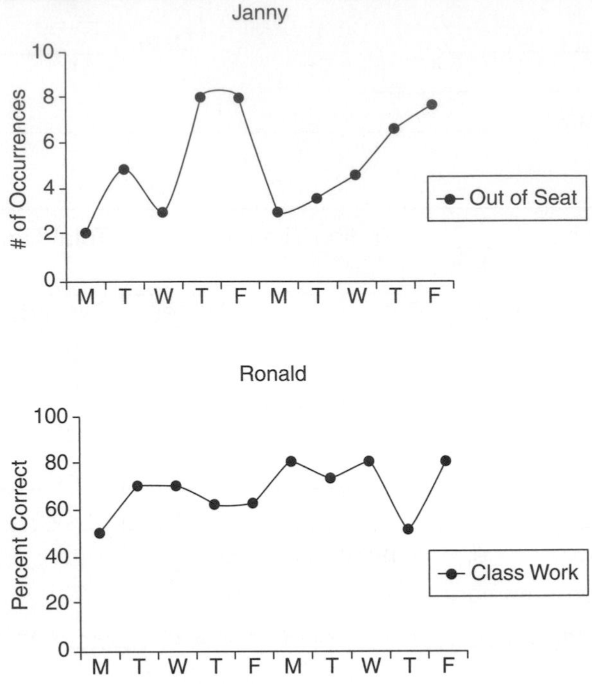

number of talk-outs in a class period) or documenting the percentage of time that a behavior occurs (e.g., percentage of off-task behavior during a class period) are best. However, the most common reporting technique relies on graphs to display the results. Graphing involves plotting results, usually on a line or bar chart. Because graphs visually illustrate behavior, they help measure progress and facilitate decision making. Two sample graphs appear in Figure 11–7.

☑ Check Your Comprehension

Direct observation is firsthand observation and objective recording of actual student behavior as it occurs. Direct observation procedures include relatively simple techniques such as anecdotal, event, and duration recording, and more complex partial-interval recording and momentary time-sampling approaches. Regardless of the specific technique, however, the goal is to employ observation to identify the extent of a problem, to help establish intervention programs, and to measure progress. Observers most often summarize results using graphs that visually illustrate results.

Assessing Self-Concept

Self-concept, also referred to as self-esteem, is a personality characteristic that defines how students feel about themselves in various life situations (Bracken, 1995). Self-concept is an important dimension of personality and behavior because it correlates with many factors associated with school performance, including achievement,

| **TEST REVIEW** | | |

Piers-Harris Children's Self-Concept Scale, Second Edition

Type of Test:	Norm-referenced, individually or group administered
Purpose:	To assesses self-concept
Content Areas:	Physical appearance and attributes, intellectual and school status, happiness and satisfaction, freedom from anxiety, behavioral adjustment, and popularity
Administration Time:	15 to 20 minutes
Age Levels:	7 to 18 years
Suitable for:	Assessing the self-concept of students with mild and moderate disabilities, including attention deficit disorders, learning disabilities, and emotional disturbance
Scores:	Percentiles, stanines, and t-scores
In Short:	Although it exhibits the technical problems common among tests of this type, the Piers-Harris is a well-designed screening instrument useful for identifying students with self-concept problems.

ethnic and cultural background, and social development. However, measuring self-concept presents problems because of the low reliability and validity of the tests. For this reason, when assessing self-concept, evaluators should use multiple sources of assessment information. Information sources include interviews with students, parents, and professionals; formal and informal interactions with students; and direct observation of student behavior. Following is a review of a representative self-concept inventory, the Piers-Harris Children's Self-Concept Scale, Second Edition, along with brief descriptions of other available self-concept measures.

Piers-Harris Children's Self-Concept Scale, Second Edition

The Piers-Harris Children's Self-Concept Scale, Second Edition (Piers, Harris, & Herzberg, 2002) is norm-referenced scale designed to measure the way students feel about themselves. Consisting of 60 questions that students answer about themselves, the scale measures the self-concept of students from 7 to 18 years of age. Evaluators can use the scale to identify students with special needs, to aid in individual assessment, and to do research. The developers arranged the items on the scale in six subtest areas: physical appearance and attributes, intellectual and school status, happiness and satisfaction, freedom from anxiety, behavioral adjustment, and popularity. A summary of the Piers-Harris Children's Self-Concept Scale, Second Edition appears in the Test Review box.

Piers-Harris Scale Materials   Piers-Harris Scale materials include a four-page scoring booklet, a test manual, and a scoring key for hand-scoring student responses on the booklet. Computerized administration and scoring with groups of students requires other materials, including scannable answer sheets. A Spanish Test Booklet is available for children who read Spanish only.

Piers-Harris Scale Administration and Scoring   Administration involves having students respond, with either a yes or a no, to 60 statements such as "I am smart," "I forget what I learn," and "I have a pleasant face." The test is suitable for individual or group administration and is administered in one of three ways: having students circle their responses in a four-page booklet, having students complete a scannable answer sheet, or having students use a microcomputer program. The Piers-Harris Scale requires a third-grade reading level; however, the evaluator may read the test items out loud to students with reading skills below the third-grade level. Although professionals or paraprofessionals with training on the Pier-Harris Scale may administer the instrument, only professionals with training in assessment should interpret the results. The evaluator scores student responses to indicate both general and specific self-concept in behavior, intellectual and school status, physical appearance and attributes, anxiety, popularity, and happiness and satisfaction.

Piers-Harris Scale Technical Characteristics   The instrument was normed on a group of 1,387 students from school districts throughout the United States. Like all measures of self-concept, a number of problems affect the validity of the Piers-Harris Scale. The manual includes information concerning several validity issues related to assessing self-concept. **Faking,** a common validity problem with tests of this type, refers to attempts by students to distort the test results in a positive direction. Although it is acceptable and normal for students to display a certain amount of faking during the testing, students who respond positively to all items are usually fabricating answers, or faking. The Piers-Harris procedure to control for faking is to interpret total scores that deviate more than 1.5 standard deviation units in a positive direction as abnormal. The Piers-Harris design controls for acquiescence (the tendency to respond positively to all items) and negative response bias (the tendency to respond negatively) by balancing the number of positively and negatively worded statements. To guard against problems due to random responses, the Piers-Harris scoring procedure includes an inconsistency index. Finally, some children from different ethnic and cultural backgrounds respond in diverse ways to test items measuring aspects of personality such as self-concept. To help control for this validity problem, the manual includes guidelines for giving the Piers-Harris Scale to students from diverse backgrounds.

Piers-Harris Scale Summary   The Piers-Harris Children's Self-Concept Scale, Second Edition is a questionnaire for measuring students' feelings about themselves. The Piers-Harris is most useful as a screening instrument or as one test in a comprehensive diagnostic assessment battery given to an individual student. Although the instrument is well designed, it exhibits the validity and reliability problems common among tests of this type.

Other Self-Concept Measures

Measures of self-concept are widely used for assessing students' feelings about themselves. Brief descriptions of some of the other available measures of this aspect of personality and behavior follow.

Culture-Free Self-Esteem Inventories, Third Edition   The Culture-Free Self-Esteem Inventories, Third Edition (CFSEI-3) (Battle, 2002) assess the self-esteem of students from age 6 through 18. The CFSEI-3 includes forms for primary, intermediate, and adolescent students. Suitable for individual and group administration, the instrument is a self-report measure that can be administered and scored in about 20 minutes.

Multidimensional Self-Concept Scale   The Multidimensional Self-Concept Scale (MSCS) (Bracken, 1992) is a norm-referenced instrument for assessing global self-concept and six context-dependent self-concept domains: social, competence, affect, academic, family, and physical. Each domain can be assessed independently by giving any of the six 25-item scales. Giving all six scales produces a 150-item assessment of global self-concept. The complete MSCS can be given to individuals or groups in about 20 minutes. The instrument was normed on a national sample of 2,501 adolescents between the ages of 9 and 19.

Self-Esteem Index   The Self-Esteem Index (SEI) (Brown & Alexander, 1990) is a norm-referenced measure of the way children and adolescents ages 7 through 18 perceive and value themselves. The SEI can be given to individuals or groups in about 30 minutes. The self-report format has children read the SEI items and classify each one using a scale with always true, usually true, usually false, and always false. The four SEI scales are academic competence, family acceptance, peer popularity, and personal security.

Student Self-Concept Scale   The Student Self-Concept Scale (SSCS) (Gresham, Elliott, & Evans-Fernandez, 1993) is an individually or group administered measure of self-concept for students in grades 3 through 12. The SSCS takes about 20 to 30 minutes to give, and it includes separate elementary and secondary male and female norms. The SSCS has students rate items on three dimensions: self-confidence, importance, and outcome confidence. This 72-item self-report measure of self-concept documents the perceived confidence and importance of specific behaviors influencing the development of students' self-concepts.

Teacher-Made Self-Concept Scales   Teachers may develop their own self-concept scales to assess students' feelings about themselves. A sample teacher-made scale appears in Figure 11–8. According to Wallace, Larsen, and Elksnin (1992), teacher-developed measures have reliability and validity levels comparable to those associated with widely used standardized tests of children's self-concepts. The informal self-concept test in Figure 11–8 uses a scoring system in which yes responses receive 1 point and no responses receive no points. The test uses reverse scoring for items 4, 7, and 15.

Check Your Comprehension

Assessing self-concept involves the use of scales and other less formal assessment procedures. Although promising tests and techniques exist, most instruments suffer from less than adequate reliability and validity. As a result, assessment of self-concept should include interviews with students and observation of student behavior to validate test results.

Assessing Attention Deficit Hyperactivity Disorder

Students with special needs often exhibit behaviors that are bothersome or irritating and trigger negative responses from others. When these behaviors are severe, they may indicate disorders of attention and activity. Commonly known as attention deficit disorder (ADD) or attention deficit hyperactivity disorder (ADHD), these disorders are characterized by severe and chronic problems in regulating attention and activity. Although the terms ADD and ADHD are sometimes used interchangeably, ADHD refers to both attention and activity problems.

Reflection
Why do you think self-concept and student behavior is so difficult to assess? Give examples to support your answer.

 To answer this reflection online, go to the *Teaching and Learning* module on the Companion Website at *www.prenhall.com/venn.*

Figure 11–8 A teacher-made self-concept scale

| Name _____ | | Date _____ |
| Class _____ | | Teacher _____ |

Item	Yes	No
1. I like myself.		
2. I am pretty.		
3. I am usually happy.		
4. I am a poor reader.		
5. I like school.		
6. I have many friends.		
7. I am ugly.		
8. My parents like me.		
9. My teachers like me.		
10. I am popular.		
11. I am smart.		
12. I like staying home from school.		
13. I like to please my teachers.		
14. I enjoy helping others.		
15. I wish I were someone else.		

Assessment of ADHD focuses on obtaining data and information to help devise plans for managing classroom behavior and instruction. Although parents or others may notice ADHD characteristics before a child enters school, the seriousness of the problem emerges when students face the demands of the classroom. In the classroom, ADHD may become unbearable due to extreme attention and activity problems coupled with poor academic performance (Kaufmann, 2005).

The primary ADHD assessment methods are direct observation and rating scales. Direct observation in various school settings (for example, the classroom, playground, cafeteria, and the hallways) and daily records of academic performance are critical aspects of assessment. Rating scales help organize and quantify a student's academic and social behavior. Rating scales also help identify specific behaviors that need remediation and measure the effectiveness of intervention programs. Both objective records from direct observation and subjective judgments from rating scales are important in managing ADHD (Kaufmann, 2005). Information about direct observation appeared earlier in this chapter. Information about rating scales for assessing ADHD follows.

Rating Scales for Assessing ADHD

Rating scales and similar measures help identify and diagnose ADHD, assist in developing plans for managing the behavior of children with ADHD, and help monitor changes in behavior. These tools include screening-level assessments and comprehensive instruments for conducting diagnostic evaluation. Brief reviews of representative rating scales follow.

Attention-Deficit/Hyperactivity Disorder Test The norm-referenced, individually administered Attention-Deficit/Hyperactivity Disorder Test (ADHDT) (Gilliam, 1995) is a screening instrument to assist in identifying and evaluating attention deficit disorders in students ages 3 to 23. Designed for use in schools and clinics, teachers, parents, and others who are knowledgeable about the student may complete the rating scale. The 36 items on the ADHDT are based on the diagnostic criteria for attention-deficit hyperactivity disorder found in the fourth edition of the *Diagnostic and Statistical Manual of Mental Disorders* (DSM-IV) (American Psychiatric Association, 1994). The three ADHDT subtests represent the key symptoms necessary in the identification of ADHD: hyperactivity, impulsivity, and inattention. The ADHDT was normed using a sample of more than 1,200 people who were diagnosed with attention deficit disorders. Separate norms are available for males and females.

ADHD Symptom Checklist The ADHD Symptom Checklist (ADHD-SC4) (Gadow & Sprafkin, 1997) is a 50-item rating scale completed by parents and teachers. The ADHD-SC4 is designed to assess the effectiveness of interventions with children and adolescents who have ADHD and Oppositional Defiant Disorder (ODD). The ADHD-SC4 checklist contains the symptoms of these disorders along with a Peer Conflict Scale (to assess peer aggression) and a Stimulant Side Effects Checklist (to monitor medication). The ADHD-SC4 is a norm-referenced screening and treatment-monitoring instrument that takes about 5 minutes to complete. The norms for the instrument rely on a sample of 2,175 teachers and 1,844 parents based on Child Symptom Inventories completed for children ages 3 to 18 years.

BASC Monitor for ADHD The BASC Monitor for ADHD (Reynolds & Kamphaus, 1998) is a system for treatment planning and evaluation for children with ADHD. The BASC Monitor was developed from the Behavior Assessment System for Children, which was reviewed earlier in this chapter. The Monitor includes a teacher rating scale with 45 items that measures attention problems, hyperactivity, internalizing problems, and adaptive skills. The Monitor also includes a parent rating scale that measures the same behaviors with a few different items. Additional Monitor components include an observation system for timed and untimed classroom observation along with software for scoring, graphing, and analyzing behavior ratings, observation data, and other measures or variables throughout intervention. The BASC Monitor is appropriate for use with students from 4 through 18 years of age. The instrument helps measure whether the behaviors of students with ADHD change as a result of intervention. The teacher and parent rating scales may be used repeatedly with the same student. The software stores ratings, observations, behavior plans, and other information over time and prints tables and graphs to illustrate behavior changes.

Brown Attention-Deficit Disorder Scales The criterion-referenced, individually administered Brown Attention-Deficit Disorder Scales (Brown ADD Scales) (Brown, 1996) provide a way to quickly screen for indications of ADD in adolescents and adults. Consisting of 40 self-report items, the Brown ADD Scales can be administered in 20 to 40 minutes. One form of the Brown ADD Scales is for adolescents age 12 to 18, and the other is for adults. Results from the scales indicate whether a student would benefit from a full evaluation for the disorder. The Brown ADD Scales identify the following clusters often associated with ADD:

- Activating and organizing to work
- Sustaining attention and concentration

- Sustaining energy and effort
- Managing affective interference
- Utilizing working memory and accessing recall

Although screening for ADD using a tool like the Brown ADD Scales is an important first step in the assessment process, a full evaluation is required to diagnose ADD. The Brown ADD Scales include a form for conducting a full evaluation that meets the diagnostic criteria for ADD. The Brown ADD Diagnostic Form gives a set of procedures, tools, and worksheets to use in this process. Like the Brown ADD Scales, there are two diagnostic forms, one for adolescents and one for adults. The Brown ADD Diagnostic Forms include the following items:

- Protocol and record form for conducting a semistructured clinical interview
- Scoring summary
- Mulitrater evaluation form for complete DSM-IV ADHD criteria
- Worksheet for analysis of IQ subtest data relevant to ADD
- Screener for co-morbid disorders
- IQ test summary form
- Overall diagnostic summary form

The Brown ADD Scales and the included Brown ADD Diagnostic Form are useful for assessing attention-deficit disorders in adolescents and adults.

Children's Attention & Adjustment Survey   The norm-referenced, individually administered Children's Attention & Adjustment Survey (CAAS) (Lambert & Sandoval, 1990) helps screen for specific behavior problems related to hyperactivity and attention problems. The CAAS includes four scales: inattentiveness, impulsivity, hyperactivity, and conduct problems/aggressiveness. The CAAS uses two forms: a home form, which is completed by the parent or primary caregiver, and a school form, which the teacher completes. Designed for children ages 5 to 13, the CAAS takes about 10 to 15 minutes per form to administer. Test results include a standard score and a percentile for each scale.

The Conners' Scales   The Conners' Scales include a series of instruments for assessing ADHD and related disorders. One of the instruments in the series is the Conners' Rating Scales, Revised (CRS-R) (Conners, 1997a). The CRS-R is norm-referenced and individually administered. CRS-R components include a parent rating scale, a teacher rating scale, and a student self-report form. The CRS-R includes a short and a long form for screening students who are at risk for ADHD and may need further diagnostic evaluation. Norms are available for students aged 3 to 17. The CRS-R scales correspond with symptoms used in the DSM-IV as criteria for ADHD. A hyperactivity index is also included in the long form of the parent and teacher rating scales.

Another instrument in the series is the Conners' ADHD/DSM-IV Scales (CADS) (Conners, 1997b). This screening measure helps identify students from ages 3 to 17 who are at risk for ADHD. The CADS includes a parent rating, a teacher rating, and an adolescent self-report. Administration time is 10 minutes. The CADS is available in English and Spanish.

Conners has also developed instruments for assessing adults with ADHD, including the Conners' Adult ADHD Diagnostic Interview for DSM-IV (CAADID) (Conners, Epstein, & Johnson, 2001), the Conners' Adult ADHD History Form (Conners, 1994), and the Conners' Adult ADHD Rating Scales (CAARS) (Conners, Erhardt, & Sparrow, 1997). Information about these instruments appears in summary Table 11–1 at the end of the chapter. In addition to these tools, Conners has developed computer-based

TECHNOLOGY FOCUS
Computer-Based Assessment of ADHD

Computer-based assessment instruments are becoming more common each year. Conners has developed two computer-based assessments for use in identifying students who may have attention problems including ADHD. These two instruments are also useful for measuring the effectiveness of intervention programs. The instruments are the *Connors' Continuous Performance Test II (CPT II) Computer Program for Windows* (Conners, 2000) and the *Conners' Continuous Performance Test for Windows: Kiddie Version (K-CPT)* (Conners, 2000). The CPT II is for students six years and older who are suspected of having attention problems. The CPT II also helps measure the effectiveness of intervention programs. The *CPT II* administers the protocol directly using the computer screen and keyboard or mouse. The student takes the test by pressing the spacebar or mouse button following presentation of specific letters on the computer screen. A standard mode of presentation controls the number of trials, target letters presented, and intervals between the presentation of the letters. It takes 14 minutes to administer, and the results can be accessed immediately. Test results are compared with population norms and a reference group of individuals diagnosed with ADHD. Results include graphs of reaction time, number of errors, risk taking, sensitivity, and number of target hits. The K-CPT is similar to the CPT II but is designed for use with young children ages 4–5 years.

programs for assessing students suspected of having attention problems. Information about these computerized assessments appears in the Technology Focus box.

Test of Variables of Attention   The Test of Variables of Attention (TOVA) (Greenberg, 1993) is a norm-referenced, individually administered test for screening children and adults for attention deficit disorder (ADD). Designed for individuals from age 4 to retirement, the TOVA is a computer-based test that consists of game-like tasks. The test, which is taken on a computer, requires the student to press a micro switch whenever a "correct" stimulus is presented during a $22^{1}/_{2}$-minute continuous visual performance test. The computer records the student's reactions for analysis and interpretation. Measured variables include omission errors (inattention), commission errors (impulsivity), reaction time, variability, postcommission reaction time, and anticipatory and multiple responses. The TOVA is useful in the school as a screening tool and should be used in conjunction with classroom behavior rating. It may be used to measure attention in individuals with neurological injuries and disorders as one tool in a comprehensive assessment battery. It can also identify responses to medication, determine optimal medication dosage, and monitor dosages by gauging reaction to medication over time. The instrument takes 25 to 30 minutes to administer.

Scales for Diagnosing Attention Deficit/Hyperactivity Disorder   The Scales for Diagnosing Attention Deficit/Hyperactivity Disorder (SCALES) (Ryser & McConnell, 2002) identifies and evaluates attention deficit hyperactivity disorder in children ages 5 through 18. The SCALES consist of two forms; one for the home and the other for school. The SCALES are modeled after the ADHD guidelines in the

Diagnostic and Statistical Manual of Mental Disorders, Fourth Edition—Text Revision (DSM-IV-TR) (American Psychiatric Association, 1994). The SCALES include evaluation using normative benchmarks or DSM-IV-TR criteria. The instrument evaluates the behavior using subtests that measure inattention, hyperactivity, and impulsivity. The SCALES were standardized using more than 3,000 children with norms for those not identified with or not suspected of having ADHD and those already diagnosed with ADHD.

Computer-Based Assessment of ADHD

Conners developed two computer-based tests for identifying students who may have attention problems, including ADHD, and for measuring the effectiveness of intervention programs. The tests are the Conners' Continuous Performance Test II (CPT II)—Computer Program for Windows (Conners, 2000a) and the Conners' Continuous Performance Test for Windows: Kiddie Version (K-CPT) (Conners, 2000b). The CPT II is for students 6 years and older who are suspected of having attention problems. The CPT II also helps measure the effectiveness of intervention programs. The CPT II administers the protocol directly using the computer screen and keyboard or mouse. The student takes the test by pressing the spacebar or mouse button following presentation of specific letters on the computer screen. A standard mode of presentation controls the number of trials, target letters presented, and intervals between the presentation of the letters. It takes 14 minutes to administer, and the results can be accessed immediately. Test results are compared with population norms and a reference group of individuals diagnosed with ADHD. Results include graphs of reaction time, number of errors, risk taking, sensitivity, and number of target hits. The K-CPT is similar to the CPT II but is designed for use with young children ages 4 to 5.

☑ Check Your Comprehension

Teachers assess ADHD to develop plans to manage behavior and academic performance. To achieve this goal teachers rely on both subjective and objective measures. Subjective measures include behavior rating scales and other tests that provide reliable data regarding the nature and severity of attention and activity disorders. The objective measures include a variety of direct observation techniques that help pinpoint problem behaviors and measure the effectiveness of interventions.

Summary

Behavior assessment relies on a wide range of measurement techniques and assessment instruments. A summary of these tools appears in Table 11–1. In instructional settings, teachers most often use practical, applied assessment procedures such as direct observation. When assessing for student eligibility for services and making placement decisions, professionals rely on formal, norm-referenced instruments. Behavior assessment focuses on measuring student conduct and misconduct; it also encompasses appraisal of other affective behaviors, including self-concept, attitudes, and interests.

Those who serve students with disabilities should be well versed in the available procedures for assessing behavior. Behavior assessment greatly affects the potential for success of students with disabilities. For this reason, it is imperative to understand

Table 11-1 Review of Behavior Assessment Instruments

Name	Type	Suitable for	Brief Description	Purpose
ADHD Symptom Checklist (ADHD SC4)	Norm-referenced, individually administered rating scales	Children and youth from 3 to 18 years of age	A 50-item rating scale completed by parents and teachers	To screen for ADHD and assess intervention effectiveness
Adjustment Scales for Children and Adolescents (ASCA)	Norm-referenced, individually administered behavior rating scales	Students from 5 to 17 years of age	Measures the following behavior syndromes: attention deficit hyperactive, solitary aggressive (provocative), solitary aggressive (impulsive), oppositional defiant, diffident, avoidant, delinquent, and lethargic	To assess behavior problems, psychopathology, and styles of healthy adjustment
Attention-Deficit/Hyperactivity Disorder Test (ADHDT)	Norm-referenced, individually administered screening test	Children and youth from 3 to 23 years of age	Three subtests represent the key symptoms necessary in the identification of ADHD: hyperactivity, impulsivity, and inattention	To assist in identifying and evaluating attention deficit disorders
Behavior Assessment System for Children, Second Edition (BASC-2)	Norm-referenced, individually administrated assessment system	Children and youth from 2 to 21 years of age	Includes teacher and parent rating scales; a self-report of personality; a tool for collecting a developmental history; a procedure for directory observing behavior; and scales measuring communication, activities of daily living, attention problems, and hyperactivity	A set of instruments for evaluating the behaviors, thoughts, and emotions of children and adolescents
BASC Monitor for ADHD	Norm-referenced, individually administrated rating scales	Students from 4 to 18 years of age	Contains teacher and parent rating scales, an observation system, and accompanying software	To assist in treatment planning and student evaluation

(continued)

Table 11–1 *continued*

Name	Type	Suitable for	Brief Description	Purpose
Behavior and Emotional Rating Scales Second edition (BERS-2)	Norm-referenced, individually administrated behavior rating scale	Students from 5 to 18 years of age	Contains 52 items for measuring five aspects of a child's strength: interpersonal strength, involvement with family, intrapersonal strength, school functioning, and affective strength	To evaluate children as part of the prereferral process and the process of placing children in specialized services; also helpful in developing IEP goals and objectives and in creating intervention programs
Behavior Rating Profile-2 (BRP-2)	Norm-referenced, individually administrated behavior rating scale	Students from 6 to 18 years of age	Includes scales completed by the student, the parent, and the teacher, and a sociogram completed by the student's classmates	To obtain information about a student's behavior in a variety of settings
Brown Attention-Deficit Disorder Scales (Brown ADD Scales)	Criterion-referenced, individually administrated screening level, self-report scale	Individuals from 12 years to adult	Identifies the following clusters often associated with ADD: activating and organizing to work, sustaining attention and concentration, sustaining energy and effort, managing affective interference, and utilizing working memory and accessing recall	To quickly screen for indications of ADD in adolescents and adults
Child Behavior Checklist for Ages 6–18 (CBCL/6-18)	Norm-referenced, individually administrated behavior checklist	Separate checklists for three age groups: 4–5, 6–11, and 12–16 years	A checklist completed by an evaluator during an interview with a parent or primary caregiver	To measure behavior problems
Child Behavior Checklist for Ages 1½–5 parent (CBCL/1½–5)	Norm-referenced, individually administered behavior checklist	Young children from 1½ to 5 years of age	A checklist completed by an evaluator during an interview with a parent or primary caregiver	An adaptation of the original Child Behavior Checklist for very young children

Name	Type	Suitable for	Brief Description	Purpose
Children's Attention & Adjustment Survey (CAAS)	Norm-referenced, individually administered screening test	Children from ages 5 to 13	Includes four scales: inattentiveness, impulsivity, hyperactivity, and conduct problems/aggressiveness	To screen for specific behavior problems related to hyperactivity and attention problems
Conners' Adult ADHD History Form	Criterion-referenced screening form	Adults 18 years or older	May be mailed and completed before the first visit or answered at the initial consultation	Designed for adults suspected of having ADHD
Conners' ADHD/DSM TV Scales (CADS)	Norm-referenced, individually administered screening test	Ages 3 to 17 years	Includes a parent rating, a teacher rating, and an adolescent self-report	A screening test using the DSM-IV for children at risk for ADHD
Conners' Adult ADHD Diagnostic Interview for DSM IV (CAADID)	An individually administered diagnostic interview	Adults 18 years and older	The CADDID is divided into two parts, administered separately, with each part requiring about 90 minutes to complete	A two-part structured interview that aids diagnosing ADHD in adults
Conners' Adult ADHD Rating Scales (CAARS)	Norm-referenced, individually administered rating scales	Adults 18 years and older	Includes self-report and observer ratings that provide a multiple informant assessment of adult symptoms and behaviors	A multidimensional adult ADHD assessment instrument
Conners' Continuous Performance Test II (CPT II)—Computer Program for Windows	Norm-referenced, individually administered screening test	Individuals 6 years and older	Presents specific letters on the computer screen that the students select by pressing the spacebar or clicking a mouse	To assess students suspected of having attention problems
Conners' Continuous Performance Test Computer Program for Windows: Kiddie Version	Norm-referenced, individually administered screening test	Preschoolers ages 4 and 5	Presents specific letters on the computer screen that the students selects by pressing the spacebar or clicking a mouse	To assess young children suspected of having attention problems

(continued)

Table 11–1 *continued*

Name	Type	Suitable for	Brief Description	Purpose
Conners' Rating Scales, Revised	Norm-referenced, individually administrated rating scales		Includes a parent rating scale, a teacher rating scale, a student self-report form, and a hyperactivity index	To screen students who are at risk for ADHD and may need further diagnostic evaluation
Comprehensive Behavior Rating Scale for Children (CBRSC)	Norm-referenced, individually administrated rating scale	Children from 6 to 14 years of age	Includes nine subscales: inattention/disorganization, reading problems, cognitive deficits, oppositional-conduct disorder, motor hyperactivity, anxiety, sluggish tempo, social competence, and daydreaming	Provides useful information for diagnosis and for developing intervention plans for children having school problems
Culture-Free Self-Esteem Inventories Third Edition (CFSEI-3)	Norm-referenced, individually or group-administrated self-report scale	Students 6 to 18 years of age	Evaluates children's self-esteem in five domains: general, peers, school, parents, and lie (defensiveness); measures adult self-esteem using four scales: general, social, personal, and lie	To assess the self-esteem of children and adults
*Devereux Behavior Rating Scale — School Form	Norm-referenced, individually administrated rating scale	Students 5 to 18 years of age	Interpersonal problems inappropriate behaviors and feelings, depression, and physical symptoms and fears	To identify behaviors that may indicate severe emotional disturbance, to help in developing intervention programs, and to measure behavior change
Draw A Person: Screening Procedure for Emotional Disturbance (DAP:SPED)	Norm-referenced screening test for individual or group administration	Students 6 to 17 years of age	Contains items for rating the drawings of a man, a women, and the self	To help identity children and adolescents with potential emotional problems that require further evaluation

Name	Type	Suitable for	Brief Description	Purpose
Multidimensional Self-Concept Scale (MSCS)	Norm-referenced, rating scale for individual or group administration	Students 9 to 19 years of age	Measures social, competence, affect, academic, family, and physical	To assess global self-concept and six content-dependent self-concept domains
*Piers-Harris Children's Self-Concept Scale, Second Edition	Norm-referenced, individually administered self-report scale	Students 7 to 18 years of age	Contains 80 questions that students answer about themselves, which are arranged in six subtest areas: physical appearance and attributes, intellectual and school status, happiness and satisfaction, freedom from anxiety, behavioral adjustment, and popularity	To measure the way students feel about themselves
Scales for Diagnosing Attention Deficit-Hyperactivity Disorder (SCALES)	Norm-referenced, individually administered rating scale	Students 5 to 18 years of age	Includes a school form and a home form	To identify and evaluate students with ADHD
Self-Esteem Index (SEI)	Norm-referenced, individually or group-administered self-report scale	Students 7 to 18 years of age	Measures academic competence, family acceptance, peer popularity, and personal security	To measure the way children and adolescents perceive and value themselves
*Social Skills Rating System (SSRS)	Norm-referenced, individually administered rating scale	Students 3 to 18 years of age	Measures social skills, problem behaviors, and academic competence using a multiple-rater system (teacher, parent, and child)	To assess social skills and to provide data and information for developing behavior intervention programs
Student Self-Concept Scale (SSCS)	Norm-referenced, individually or group-administered self-concept inventory	Students in grades 3 through 12	Measures self-confidence, importance, and outcome confidence	To assess perceived confidence and behaviors that influence the development of self-concept

(continued)

Table 11–1 *continued*

Name	Type	Suitable for	Brief Description	Purpose
Test of Variables of Attention (TOVA)	Norm-referenced, individually administered, computerized screening test	Individuals age 4 to retirement	Measured variables include omission errors (inattention), commission errors (impulsivity), reaction time, variability, post commission reaction time, and anticipatory and multiple responses	Useful in the school as a screening tool; should be used together with classroom behavior rating

*Tests marked with an asterisk are featured in this chapter.

behavior assessment, select appropriate measurement procedures, and conduct assessment accurately. Assessing behavior is an essential tool for providing the best possible educational services to students with special needs.

 To check your comprehension of the chapter contents, go to the *Guided Review* and *Quiz* modules in Chapter 11 of the Companion Website, *www.prenhall.com/venn.*

Meeting Performance Standards and Preparing for Licensure Exams

After reading this chapter, you should be able to demonstrate the following CEC Standards and PRAXIS™ test knowledge and skills. The information in parentheses identifies where to find the particular CEC standard and PRAXIS™ content reference.

CEC Standards for Beginning Special Education Teachers

- Use procedures to increase the individual's self-awareness, self-management, self-control, self-reliance, and self-esteem (CC4S5)
- Use functional assessments to develop intervention plans (CC7S4)
- Make responsive adjustments to instruction based on continual observations (CC7S13)
- Implement procedures for assessing and reporting both appropriate and problematic social behaviors of individuals with disabilities (GC8S1)

PRAXIS™ Education of Exceptional Students: Core Content Knowledge

- Assessment including use of assessment for screening, diagnosis, placement, and the making of instructional decisions; for example: how to select and conduct nondiscriminatory and appropriate assessments; how to interpret standardized and specialized assessment results; procedures and test materials, both formal and informal, typically used for prereferral, screening, referral, classification, placement, and ongoing program monitoring (0353 III)
- Assessment, including how to select, construct, conduct, and modify nondiscriminatory, developmentally and chronologically age-appropriate informal assessments, including teacher-made tests, curriculum-based assessment, and alternatives to norm-referenced testing (including observations, anecdotal records, self-evaluation questionnaires and interviews) (0353 III)

- Structuring and managing the learning environment, including classroom management techniques; for example, behavioral analysis (identification and definition of antecedents, target behavior, and consequent events); behavioral interventions; functional analysis; and data gathering procedures (such as anecdotal data, frequency methods, and interval methods) (0353 III)

chapter 12

Assessing Adaptive Behavior

Objectives

After reading this chapter, you will be prepared to do the following:

- Define adaptive behavior.
- Describe the range of behaviors measured by adaptive behavior scales.
- Describe the role of the informant in assessing adaptive behavior.
- Describe the uses of adaptive behavior scales with students who have special needs.
- Use adaptive behavior scales and inventories with children and youth who have special needs.

Overview

Adaptive behavior is the ability to adjust to personal and social demands in the environment. Assessing adaptive behavior involves measuring the conceptual, social, and practical skills that people use in their everyday lives. In this chapter, you will develop an understanding of the procedures for assessing adaptive behavior. To achieve this goal you review the meaning of the term and consider the types of behaviors measured by adaptive behavior scales. You investigate the use of adaptive behavior scales and analyze the issues surrounding their use. After this introduction, you examine the range of instruments for assessing adaptive behavior, including the most frequently used individually administered scales and inventories. As you review each scale, you consider the purpose and use of the instrument, the test materials, the administration and scoring procedures, and the technical characteristics.

Assessing Adaptive Behavior

Perhaps the best way to introduce assessment of adaptive behavior is through the eyes of a beginning teacher of students with mental retardation.

When asked by the school psychologist to rate the adaptive behavior of one of his students, Mr. Davis had many questions. Mr. Davis remembered studying adaptive behavior in school, but he had never actually used an adaptive behavior scale. The psychologist explained that rating scales, rather than tests, were used to assess adaptive behavior. This prompted Mr. Davis to ask the psychologist questions. What behavior does a teacher rate? How accurate is my rating of adaptive behavior? And what is the difference between adaptive behavior and intelligence? The psychologist understood Mr. Davis's concerns and patiently explained adaptive behavior and its assessment.

In this chapter, you will discover the answers to these assessment questions. You will also investigate other aspects of assessing the adaptive behavior of students with special needs, beginning with a definition of adaptive behavior and a description of its assessment.

Defining Adaptive Behavior

Adaptive behavior is the collection of conceptual, social, and practical skills that people have learned so they can function in their everyday lives. Significant limitations in adaptive behavior impact a person's daily life and affect the ability to respond to a particular situation or to the environment (American Association on Mental Retardation, 2002, p. 1). Assessing adaptive behavior involves the use of scales that sample behaviors related to conceptual, social, and practical skills. Because the behaviors related to these skills change as one ages, adaptive behavior scales include a range of items for measuring skill development at different age levels. For example, with young children, practical skills include self-help activities such as dressing, eating, hygiene, and toileting. With older children, however, practical skills encompasses a wide range of daily living activities, such as selecting and caring for appropriate clothing and eating independently in cafeterias and restaurants. Social skills include behaviors such as trustworthiness, commitment, appropriate socialization, proper interpersonal interaction, and self-direction. For young children, the behaviors associated with social skills include complying with parents, getting along with siblings, and playing constructively. For older children, social skill behaviors include taking care of personal items, making friends at school, and completing schoolwork.

Measuring Adaptive Behavior Indirectly

Adaptive behavior scales use a distinctive type of indirect measurement that focuses on performance over time rather than one-time performance on a test. Unlike standardized tests given during a testing session, adaptive behavior scales rely on information from an informant who is familiar with the student. The informant is usually a teacher or parent who knows the student's typical performance in real-life settings. With adaptive behavior, the ability to perform a particular skill is insufficient if the student fails to use the skill as needed. For example, a student may have the ability to manage money but may not do so on a regular basis. In this case, the student's adaptive behavior is insufficient.

Evaluators must rely on indirect measurement to assess adaptive behavior because, in most instances, they are unable to observe directly the typical behavior of a student in real-life settings. An evaluator would need an extended period to directly assess behaviors such as eating in restaurants, hygiene skills, social interaction patterns, and mobility skills in the home, the school, and the community. Therefore, in place of direct observation, evaluators rely on the observations of an informant who knows a student well.

The Role of the Informant in Assessing Adaptive Behavior

One of the keys to successful use of adaptive behavior scales is the **informant**, who provides the information required to rate the items on a scale. The informant may be a teacher, parent, grandparent, teacher aide, or another primary caregiver. Because the informant is so important in the process of assessing adaptive behavior, the evaluator must judge the accuracy of an informant's responses (Sattler, 2001). Most informants provide reliable information, and the best informants give highly accurate, balanced, and clear information. Credible informants make it easy to rate precisely. However, some informants give biased or distorted answers. When evaluators have serious doubts about the validity of a set of responses, they must gather additional information by interviewing another informant, which enables an evaluator to compare responses for consistency. Sattler suggested that discrepancies among respondents result from the following:

- Student behavior that varies in different settings
- Unreliable informant information
- Differences in informant interpretation of student behavior
- Differences in informant familiarity with a student
- Biased or prejudiced informant attitudes

The use of multiple sources provides a better profile of adaptive behavior, and for this reason, evaluators should attempt to conduct more than one interview whenever possible. For example, teachers can provide information from observations of student behavior in an educational setting. Parents, on the other hand, can supply information about at-home behaviors such as sleeping, leisure activities, and eating. Additional information about the role of the informant appears in Focus 12–1.

Controversial Aspects of Measuring Adaptive Behavior

Controversial aspects of measuring adaptive behavior (Beirne-Smith, Patton, & Kim, 2006) include arguments about the concept of adaptive behavior and debate over the more practical concerns of measuring adaptive behavior. The conceptual argument centers on disagreement over the specific definition of adaptive behavior. This disagreement occurs because the concept includes many different behaviors across a wide age span (infancy to retirement). Practical concerns include questions about the reliability of informant data, and racial and ethnic bias.

In an attempt to control for possible sources of bias, Mercer and Lewis (1977) developed a comprehensive system of multipluralistic assessment designed to minimize bias against students from minority groups. This system consists of a complete

FOCUS 12-1

The Role of the Informant in Assessing Adaptive Behavior

- The informant is usually a teacher or parent who knows the child's typical performance in real-life settings.
- Teachers can provide information from observations of child behavior in an educational setting.
- Parents can supply information about at-home behaviors such as sleeping, leisure-time activities, and eating.
- The evaluator must judge the accuracy of an informant's responses.
- More than one informant should be interviewed whenever possible.
- When evaluators doubt the validity of a set of responses, they must gather additional information by interviewing another informant.

program that is especially sensitive to language and cultural factors. The system contains valuable features, including sociocultural scales, health history inventories, and norms for Black, Hispanic, and White children. Rather than emphasizing a student's intelligence test score, the system emphasizes comprehensive evaluation of adaptive behavior. Evaluators measure adaptive behavior with a unique inventory, the Adaptive Behavior Inventory for Children (1977), which is a component of the System of Multicultural Pluralistic Assessment (Mercer & Lewis, 1978). This inventory includes measures of student role performance in the family, the community, and the peer group; the nonacademic aspects of school; and the earner or consumer role. The system of multipluralistic assessment is one response to the persistent problem of bias in evaluation. Other specialists (Overton, 2006, Reschly, 1982) have also pointed to the use of adaptive behavior measurement as one way to promote nonbiased assessment of students from culturally and linguistically diverse experiences. Additional information about this important topic appears in the accompanying Multicultural Considerations feature.

Why Do We Assess Adaptive Behavior?

We assess the adaptive behavior of students with special needs for several reasons. Adaptive behavior scales produce an accurate measure of a student's ability to adjust to the personal and social demands in the environment and to changes in these demands. In fact, the most significant characteristic of students with deficits in adaptive behavior is the difficulty they have in adjusting to changes in the environment. For example, the Vineland Social Maturity Scales, Second Edition measures functional communication skills, practical daily living skills, and applied socialization skills. Students with deficits in adaptive behavior have difficulty learning these skills, especially in new situations. For this reason, we use norm-referenced adaptive behavior scales, along with other assessment information, to identify students with disabilities, determine eligibility for special education services, and make placement decisions.

Assessing adaptive behavior is especially important in diagnosing mental retardation, which is defined as subaverage intellectual functioning that exists concurrently with significant deficits in adaptive behavior. Special educators also use data from adaptive behavior scales to help write IEPs and develop intervention programs, often for students with severe and multiple disabilities who require intensive instruction in personal, social, and occupational skill development. Specialized adaptive behavior

MULTICULTURAL CONSIDERATIONS

Promoting Nonbiased Assessment

Recent developments in research, legislation, and litigation have emphasized issues of bias in assessment, adaptive behavior, and sociocultural background as key considerations in identifying students with disabilities. Of particular concern are issues associated with assessing students from minority and economically disadvantaged backgrounds. These students are often overrepresented in programs for students who are mildly mentally retarded (MacMillan & Reschly, 1998). Evidence exists (Overton, 2006; Reschly, 1982) that supports the need for further emphasis on assessing adaptive behavior as one way to enhance fairness. Adaptive behavior assessment is a helpful tool in reducing bias because it measures important behaviors that should be considered along with intelligence and achievement in the eligibility determination process. A major change occurred with the passage of the original IDEA legislation (P.L. 94–142). This legislation gave a more prominent role to assessing adaptive behavior in identifying and classifying students as mildly mentally retarded. Even more needs to be done to develop procedures for using adaptive behavior and sociocultural background as ways to find solutions to issues of fairness. The goal is to promote assessment practices that lead to fairness in assessment for all students, including students from minority and disadvantaged backgrounds.

What bias could show up when assessing a student's adaptive behavior? Explain.

 To answer this reflection online, go to the *Multicultural Considerations* module on the Companion Website at *www.prenhall.com/venn*.

scales are available for students with specific disabilities, including learning disabilities, profound mental retardation, and trainable mental retardation. Finally, assessment of adaptive behavior continues over time to measure student progress in adjusting to changes in the environment and learning new adaptive behavior skills.

The following vignette describes how a staffing team used results from an adaptive behavior assessment to help make a difficult placement decision.

Jimmy was a streetwise child with a history of defiant, aggressive, and disobedient behavior. Because of poor academic skills, immature social behavior, and small stature, Jimmy's school retained him in a primary, self-contained classroom (grades 1 and 2) for students with mild and moderate mental retardation instead of promoting him into a classroom for students his age (grades 3, 4, and 5). However, when he reached age 10, the school moved him to the class for older students. At first, Jimmy appeared motivated and cooperative, but he made little academic progress. As the year progressed, he became frustrated and often refused to participate in class activities and complete assigned work. He also began to behave aggressively by threatening peers and disrupting class.

Because of these problems, Jimmy's teacher met with a staffing team to discuss possible placement in a different program. When the staffing team decided to reevaluate him, the teacher completed the classroom edition of the Vineland Adaptive Behavior Scales, Second Edition. Jimmy received an overall standard score of 60 on the Vineland Scales, with a subtest score of 64 on the social domain. In contrast, he received a standard score of 40 on an

FOCUS 12-2

Why Do We Assess Adaptive Behavior?

- To measure the ability to adjust to the environment and to changes in the environment
- To assist in diagnosing mental retardation
- To identify students with disabilities, determine eligibility for services, and make placement decisions
- To help write IEPs and develop intervention programs, often for students with severe and multiple disabilities who require intensive instruction in personal, social, and occupational skill development
- To measure progress in adjusting to the environment and in learning adaptive behavior skills

intelligence test (the WISC-IV). Although the intelligence test score may have qualified him for placement in a program for students with severe retardation, the staffing team recommended keeping Jimmy in his present placement because of his relatively high adaptive behavior (as measured by the Vineland Scales) and his good verbal skills. However, the team agreed to continue to monitor his progress and asked his teacher to complete a follow up adaptive behavior evaluation before the end of the school year.

This true story illustrates one important use of adaptive behavior scales. A summary of reasons for assessing adaptive behavior appears in Focus 12–2.

☑ Check Your Comprehension

Adaptive behaviors are the conceptual, social, and practical skills that students must learn to function in everyday life. These behaviors focus on the practical knowledge needed to live independently as an adult, including daily living skills, vocational skills, social skills, applied academic skills, and community survival skills. Adaptive behavior scales rely on indirect measurement because of the difficulty in directly observing typical daily living behaviors in real-life settings. One of the keys to successful use of adaptive behavior scales is obtaining reliable information from informants.

Adaptive Behavior Scales

A professional, such as a teacher who knows the student well or a psychologist who interviews a parent or other primary caregiver, completes the adaptive behavior scales. These scales measure performance with a checklist of items arranged by age in a developmental sequence. Comprehensive reviews of representative scales of adaptive behavior are given next, followed by brief reviews of other available instruments.

Vineland Adaptive Behavior Scales, Second Edition

The Vineland Adaptive Behavior Scales, Second Edition (Vineland II) (Sparrow, Cicchetti, & Balla, 2005), one of the most widely used instruments, measures communication, daily living skills, socialization, and motor skills with an optional maladaptive behavior subscale for evaluating inappropriate behaviors.

Reflection
What was the importance of the adaptive behavior scale in this scenario? Explain.

To answer this reflection online, go to the *Teaching* and *Learning* module on the Companion Website at *www.prenhall.com/venn*.

There are four separate versions of the scales: a survey interview form, a parent/caregiver rating form, an expanded interview form, and a teacher rating form. The survey interview form is a screening instrument, and it is given to a parent or caregiver in a semistructured interview format. This interview uses open-ended questions to promote rapport between the interviewer and respondent. The parent/caregiver rating form has the same content as the survey interview but uses a rating scale format. This approach is necessary when time or access is limited. The expanded interview form is a comprehensive diagnostic instrument, and like the survey form, it uses the semistructured interview format. This version of the Vineland II is appropriate for use in developing educational programs. The teacher rating form uses a questionnaire format to assess the adaptive behavior of a student in the classroom and school setting. Similar to the previous Vineland Classroom Edition, this form uses a questionnaire format completed by the teacher.

The age range of the survey, parent/caregiver, and expanded forms is birth through 90 years. The classroom edition measures the adaptive behavior of students from 3 through 21 years of age. The norm-referenced, standardized Vineland II scales are useful in identifying and classifying students with mental retardation, developmental delays, autism spectrum disorder, ADHD, posttraumatic brain injury, and hearing impairment. The expanded form of Vineland II is also useful for obtaining evaluation data for programming and intervention purposes. A summary of the Vineland II appears in the Test Review box.

Vineland II Materials   Vineland II materials include manuals and scoring booklets for each form. Optional materials include an audiocassette tape of a model interview process, a report to the parents, and a Spanish edition of the survey form. Evaluators may also obtain optional computer software for scoring and developing profiles.

TEST REVIEW

Vineland II

Type of Test:	Norm-referenced, individually administered
Purpose:	Assesses personal and social skills
Content Areas:	Communication, daily living skills, socialization, and motor skills
Administration Time:	20 to 60 minutes to give the survey, parent/caregiver, and teacher rating forms; 60 to 90 minutes to give the expanded form
Age Levels:	Survey, parent/caregiver, and expanded forms: Birth to 90 years; teacher rating form: 3 to 21 years
Suitable for:	Students with mild, moderate, and severe disabilities, including mental retardation, autism spectrum disorder, and ADHD
Scores:	Standard scores, percentile ranks, adaptive levels, and age equivalents
In Short:	The Vineland II helps to identify and place students with disabilities and obtain evaluation data for developing intervention programs.

Vineland II Administration and Scoring   Evaluators give the Vineland II in the form of a general interview rather than as an item-by-item questioning procedure. The interviewer establishes rapport with the child's parent, teacher, or other primary caregiver (who knows the child well) as the respondent and introduces the Vineland II before starting the interview. The interviewer begins by having the respondent discuss the behavior related to specific subtests in a general way. If the respondent does not provide enough information during the general discussion, the interviewer then uses probing questions to obtain information for scoring specific items and may need further probes to score some items. For example, the interviewer may say, "Give me some examples of how John uses the telephone." If the respondent fails to provide sufficient information to score each item relating to telephone skills, the interviewer probes for further information.

The survey, parent/caregiver, and teacher rating forms take 20 to 60 minutes to give. The expanded form takes from 60 to 90 minutes to give. Scoring the Vineland II takes 10 to 15 minutes. Vineland II test users should have a doctorate in psychology or be a certified or licensed school psychologist or social worker. The Vineland II uses three criteria for scoring each item. The Vineland II manuals provide detailed information for interpreting results, including sample case studies. The evaluator begins the interpretation process by identifying a student's general level of functioning in adaptive behavior. Next, the evaluator analyzes the subtest scores and then compares results with scores from supplementary norm groups. Finally, the evaluator interprets results from the maladaptive behavior subtest.

Evaluators then use more specific interpretation procedures, which are based on the reasons for giving the Vineland II. For example, if these scales are to diagnose mental retardation, interpretation focuses more on the standardized test scores. If given to provide information for planning an individual program, interpretation focuses on the content in the subtests. When interpreting results from the expanded form, the Vineland II provides program planning profiles in the scoring booklet.

Vineland II Technical Characteristics   The Vineland II was standardized using a national sample of more than 2,000 individuals who were carefully selected to represent the characteristics of the population. The Vineland II development procedures included both reliability and validity studies to establish the consistency and effectiveness of the scores. The revision of the Scales included extending the age range, adding new content, and updating existing content. This improved the utility of the instrument and made it even more valuable as a tool for assessing students with a variety of disabilities.

Vineland II Summary   The Vineland Adaptive Behavior Scales, Second Edition assesses personal and social skills in communication, daily living activities, socialization, and motor proficiency and includes an optional maladaptive behavior scale. The Vineland II versions include survey, parent/caregiver, and expanded forms for individuals from birth through 90 years of age; and a teacher rating form for students from 3 through 21 years of age. These norm-referenced, standardized tools are useful for identifying students with mental retardation and other disabilities, and obtaining evaluation data for planning intervention programs.

AAMR Adaptive Behavior Scales—School, Second Edition

The AAMR (American Association on Mental Retardation) Adaptive Behavior Scales—School, Second Edition (ABS-S:2) (Lambert, Nhira, & Leland, 1993) measures the adaptive behavior of children and youth from 3 through 18 years of age.

TEST REVIEW

AAMR Adaptive Behavior Scales—School, Second Edition

Type of Test:	Norm-referenced, individually administered
Purpose:	Assesses social competence with emphasis on independence in daily living and social skill development
Content Areas:	Personal independence and social maladaption
Administration Time:	30 to 45 minutes
Age Levels:	3 to 18 years
Suitable for:	Students being evaluated for mental retardation, autism, and behavior disorders
Scores:	Standard scores and percentiles
In Short:	The ABS-S:2 is a comprehensive measure of adaptive behavior that provides considerable diagnostic and instructional information.

Designed to assess the current functioning of students who are being evaluated for evidence of mental retardation, the ABS-S:2 also helps to assess the adaptive behavior of children with autism. A summary of the ABS-S:2 appears in the Test Review box. A residential and community edition, the AAMR Adaptive Behavior Scales—Residential and Community, Second Edition (ABS-RC:2) (Nihira, Leland, & Lambert, 1993) is also available. The ABS-RC:2 measures the behavior of adults from 18 through 80-plus years of age.

The school version of the scale is divided into two parts. Part One measures personal independence in nine behavior domains:

Independent functioning	Prevocational/vocational activity
Physical development	Self-direction
Economic activity	Responsibility
Language development	Socialization
Numbers and time	

Part Two evaluates maladaptive behaviors in seven domains:

Social behavior	Self-abusive behavior
Conformity	Social engagement
Trustworthiness	Disturbing interpersonal behavior
Stereotyped and hyperactive behavior	

ABS-S:2 Materials   ABS-S:2 materials include an evaluator's manual, a package of 25 examination booklets, a package of 25 profile/summary forms, and an optional software scoring and report system.

ABS-S:2 Administration and Scoring   It takes 30 to 45 minutes to give the ABS-S:2, and evaluators may administer it by either a first-person or third-party approach. With the first-person method, the evaluator has a professional, such as a teacher who knows the student well, rate the behaviors on the scale. With the third-party approach, the evaluator completes the scale by interviewing a parent or primary care-giver familiar with the student. Available ABS-S:2 scores include standard scores and percentiles.

ABS-S:2 Technical Characteristics   The ABS-S:2 norm sample consisted of more than 2,000 children and youth with developmental disabilities and more than 1,000 students without disabilities. Children from 31 states were included in the norm group. Several studies were conducted to measure the reliability and validity of the ABS-S:2 scores, and the results indicated that the ABS-S:2 scores were consistent and effective.

ABS-S:2 Summary   The AAMR Adaptive Behavior Scales—School, Second Edition is a comprehensive measure of adaptive behavior that provides useful information for making diagnostic and instructional decisions.

Other Adaptive Behavior Scales

Reviews of other available adaptive behavior scales follow. These include norm- and criterion-referenced tools for measuring the adaptive behavior of children and adults.

Adaptive Behavior Inventory   The Adaptive Behavior Inventory (ABI) (Brown & Leigh, 1986) is a norm-referenced measure of adaptive behavior. Designed for use by classroom teachers and other professionals who know a student well, the inventory consists of subtests that measure self-care, communication, social, aca-demic, and occupational skills. The ABI includes two forms: a short form contain-ing 50 items and a long form consisting of 150 items. The ABI consists of a test manual, a scoresheet for the short form, and a profile and scoresheet for the long form. The ABI takes about 25 minutes to complete and consists of rating each of the items on the scale. The ABI produces the following scores: standard scores, standard errors of measurement, and percentile ranks. These scores are available for each subtest and for the total test. The evaluator can compare individual results to intelligence scores from a sample of nondisabled students or from a sample of students with mental retardation. The evaluator may also compile a brief profile of results as part of the scoring procedure. The developers standardized the ABI with two samples of students, including a group of 1,296 students without disabilities and a separate group of 1,076 students with mental retardation. The manual de-scribes the characteristics of these students but fails to adequately delineate the procedures used to select the students for each sample, which limits the validity of the ABI norms. The manual provides data concerning the internal consistency, test-retest reliability, and concurrent validity of the instrument, which provides an ini-tial indication that ABI scores are consistent and effective. The technical characteristics of the ABI appear adequate.

Assessment of Adaptive Areas   The Assessment of Adaptive Areas (AAA) (Bryant, Taylor, & Rivera, 1996) is a tool for regrouping the items from Part One of the AAMR Adaptive Behavior Scales—Residential and Community: Second Edition and the AAMR Adaptive Behavior Scales—School: Second Edition. The regrouping produces scores for the 10 adaptive areas in the newest AAMR definition of mental retardation (American Association on Mental Retardation, 2002). This definition requires that a student must have a deficit in at least two of the following 10 adaptive skill areas: communication, self-care, home living, social skills, community use, self-direction, health and safety, functional academics, leisure, and work. In order to obtain AAA scores, it is necessary to give Part One of the AAMR ABS-RC:2 or the AAMR ABS-S:2. The AAA then reconfigures those scores to fit the AAMR definition. The process involves placing the ABSRC:2 or ABSS:2 response form next to the AAA response form and transferring the scores to the AAA form. The AAA scoring system produces standard scores (M 5 10, SD 5 3) and percentiles for each of the 10 adaptive skill areas.

Adaptive Behavior Assessment System, Second Edition   The Adaptive Behavior Assessment System, Second Edition (ABAS-II) (Harrison & Oakland, 2003) is a norm-referenced measure of the adaptive behavior of individuals from 0 to 89 years of age. The ABAS includes 5 forms: a parent form, birth–5; a parent form, 5–21; a teacher/day care form, 2–5; a teacher form, 5–21; and an adult form, 16-89. It takes 15–20 minutes for respondents to complete a form. The ABAS-II is compliant with the American Association of Mental Retardation (AAMR) guidelines for evaluating adaptive behavior in the general areas of conceptual, social, and practical skills, and it evaluates the 10 adaptive skill areas specified in the Diagnostic and Statistical Manual (DSM-IV) published by the American Psychiatric Association.

Adaptive Behavior Evaluation Scale, Revised   The norm-referenced, individually administered Adaptive Behavior Evaluation Scale, Revised (ABES-R) is a screening instrument for measuring the adaptive behavior of students from 5 through 18 years of age. The ABES-R includes a Home Version (McCarney, 1995a) and a School Version (1995b). Both versions are identical except for a few minor rewordings. The difference is that the school version respondents are teachers rather than parents. The ABES-R takes about 20 minutes to complete and includes 104 items. The ABES-R items measure the 10 adaptive areas of communication skills, self-care, home living, social skills, community use, self-direction, health and safety, functional academics, leisure, and work skills.

Checklist of Adaptive Living Skills (CALS) and Adaptive Living Skills Curriculum The Checklist of Adaptive Living Skills (CALS) (Morreau & Bruininks, 1991) is a comprehensive, criterion-referenced checklist of specific daily living skills. The Adaptive Living Skills Curriculum (ALSC) (Bruininks, Morreau, Gilman, & Anderson, 1991) is a comprehensive curriculum designed to facilitate instruction of specific skills needed in daily living, including those related to personal care, home living, and school, work, leisure, and community participation. These two curriculum-based tools combine to make a connected assessment and intervention package for programs that include instruction in adaptive living skill development. The CALS and the ALSC are linked to the Scales of Independent Behavior, Revised (SIB-R) and the Inventory for Client and Agency Planning (ICAP). These linkages combine to produce a comprehensive assessment, instruction, and progress measuring system.

The CALS and ALSC include more than 800 specific skills in 24 modules within four domains: personal living skills, home living skills, community living skills, and employment skills. For each CALS skill there is a corresponding ALSC instructional unit. The skills cover development from early childhood to adulthood. CALS is a planning tool for deciding instructional needs, developing individual training objectives, and recording progress. The ALSC instructional units focus on real-life skills necessary to live as successfully and independently as possible in natural community settings.

Inventory for Client and Agency Planning   The Inventory for Client and Agency Planning (ICAP) (Bruininks, Hill, Weatherman, & Woodcock, 1986) is a norm-referenced assessment instrument for assessing adaptive and maladaptive behavior. The ICAP is useful for making eligibility decisions, planning intervention services, evaluating and reporting client progress, or evaluating service programs. The ICAP measures adaptive and maladaptive behavior, and it produces an overall measure that is helpful in predicting the intensity of service required by individual clients.

Responsibility and Independence Scale for Adolescents   The Responsibility and Independence Scale for Adolescents (RISA) (Salvia, Neisworth, & Schmidt, 1990) measures the adaptive behavior of youth from 12 through 19 years of age. The RISA, a norm-referenced, individually administered scale, assesses adaptive behaviors related to social expectations, responsibility, and independence. The 136 items on the scale are organized into nine functional areas: self-management, social maturity, social communication, domestic skills, money management, citizenship, personal organization, transportation skills, and career skills. The RISA is given using a standardized interview format to a respondent who is familiar with the adolescent. Most adaptive behavior scales focus on low-level skills. In contrast, the RISA measures higher-level skills, so the scale would be appropriate for use with juvenile offenders, teenagers with mild disabilities, and teenagers without disabilities.

Scales of Independent Behavior-Revised   The norm-referenced, individually administered Scales of Independent Behavior—Revised (SIB-R) (Bruininks, Woodcock, Weatherman, & Hill, 1996) provides a comprehensive assessment of adaptive and maladaptive behavior. Designed for individuals from infancy to retirement, the full SIB-R scales take about an hour to administer. The short form and the early development form take only about 20 minutes to give. A special version of the SIB-R Short Form for use with individuals who have visual impairments is available. The SIB-R Short Form for the Visually Impaired (Knowlton et al., 1997) contains 40 items and is a suitable screening test of adaptive behavior. The full SIB-R includes 14 adaptive behavior subtests and 8 problem behavior subtests. Supplemental SIB-R materials include a scoring and reporting software program as described in the Technology Focus box.

TECHNOLOGY FOCUS
SIB-R Scoring and Reporting Software

The SIB-R Scoring and Reporting Program computer software for the Scales of Independent Behavior— Revised is available in Windows or Macintosh formats. After entering identifying information and raw scores for all subscales administered, the program computes available scores and produces a narrative, interpretive report. In addition, the program produces parent letters in English and Spanish. The program features include the ability to:

- Generate all scores and an interpretive, narrative report
- Produce a full report, a summary report, or a table of scores only
- Create parent letters in English and Spanish
- Export easily to a word-processing program for editing
- Print from the program or a word-processing program
- Work with the SIB-R Full Scale, Short Form, or Early Development Form

☑ Check Your Comprehension

When students require assessment in adaptive behavior, evaluators may select from among a variety of scales and inventories. Because the various instruments differ in design and purpose, it is important to select the appropriate tool on the basis of individual student requirements and the purpose for the assessment. However, laws and professional standards require that evaluators use norm-referenced scales for making identification and classification decisions. In contrast, most teachers prefer to use less formal, more flexible scales for making curriculum-based instructional decisions.

Summary

Adaptive behavior is the ability to adjust to the personal and social demands in the environment, especially to changes in the environment. Adaptive behavior scales provide assessment information about student performance in personal self-sufficiency, independence in the community, and personal-social responsibility. A summary of the adaptive behavior assessment instruments reviewed in this chapter appears in Table 12–1. Adaptive behavior focuses on assessing typical performance in real-life settings rather than on ability to perform in a testing situation. For this reason, adaptive behavior scales consist of checklists of items arranged by age. Informants usually provide the information necessary for measuring adaptive behavior, and whenever possible, evaluators should use more than one informant to obtain a comprehensive picture of behavior as it occurs in different settings.

Table 12–1 Review of Adaptive Behavior Scales

Name of Test	Type of Test	Suitable for	Brief Description	Purpose
*AAMR Adaptive Behavior Scales—School, Second Edition (ABS-S:2)	Norm-referenced, individually administered comprehensive scale	Children and Youth 3 to18 years of age	Includes subscales for measuring personal independence and social maladaption	To assess social competence with emphasis on independence in daily living and social skill development, to assess children who are being evaluated for evidence of mental retardation, to assess the adaptive behavior of children with autism, and identify children with behavior disorders who require special education services from those who can be served in regular education
AAMR Adaptive Behavior Scales— Residential and Community, Second Edition (ABS-RC:2)	Norm-referenced, individually administered comprehensive scale	Adults from 18 to 80+ years of age	A residential and community edition for adults with mental retardation	To assess social competence with emphasis on independence in daily living and social skill development

Name of Test	Type of Test	Suitable for	Brief Description	Purpose
Adaptive Behavior Evaluation Scale, Revised (ABES-R)	Norm-referenced, individually administered screening instrument	Children and youth 5 to18 years of age	Measures the 10 adaptive skill areas of communication skills, self-care home living, social skills, community use, self-direction, health and safety, functional academics, leisure, and work skills identified by the American Association on Mental Retardation (AAMR)	To measure the adaptive behavior of children with mental retardation
Adaptive Behavior Assessment System, Second Edition (ABAS-II)	Norm-referenced, individually administered, scale	0 to 89 years of age	Includes 5 forms: a parent form, birth 5; a parent form, 5–21; a teacher/day care form, 2–5; a teacher form, 5–21; and an adult form, 16–89	To assess adaptive skills functioning for the purpose of assessing how and individual is responding to daily demands, developing intervention goals, and evaluating the capability of adults to live independently version can be completed by the individuals being assessed if they have adequate reading comprehension. The forms are written at a fifth-grade reading level. It takes about 15 minutes for respondents to complete a form.
Adaptive Behavior Inventory (ABI)	Norm-referenced, individually administered; includes a screening form and a compre-hensive form	Children and youth 5 to18 years of age	Self-care communication, social, academic, and occupational skills	Provides a functional assessment of adaptive behavior
Assessment of Adaptive Areas (AAA)	A tool for regrouping the items on the AAMR Adaptive Behavior Scales	3 to 80+ years of age	Assess communication skills, self-care, home living, social skills, community use, self-direction,	Designed for regrouping the items from Part One of the AAMR Adaptive Behavior Scales—Residential and Community: Second Edition and the AAMR Adaptive Behavior Scales—

(continued)

Table 12–1 *continued*

Name of Test	Type of Test	Suitable for	Brief Description	Purpose
			health and safety, functional academics, leisure, and work skills	School: Second Edition to obtain scores matching the 10 adaptive areas in the newest AAMR definition of mental retardation (American Association on Mental Retardation, 2002)
Checklist of Adaptive Living Skills (CALS)	Comprehensive, criterion-referenced checklist	School-age students	Measures specific daily living skills including those related to personal care, home living, and school, work, leisure, and community participation	Linked to the SIB-R and ICAP to produce a comprehensive assessment, instruction, and progress-measuring system
Inventory for Client and Agency Planning (ICAP)	Norm-referenced assessment instrument	Clients in adult service and support programs	Measures adaptive and maladaptive behavior and produces an overall measure helpful in predicting the intensity of service required by individual clients	Useful for making eligibility decisions, planning intervention services, evaluating and report client progress, and evaluating service programs
Responsibility and Independence Scale for Adolescents (RISA)	Norm-referenced, individually administered comprehensive scale	12 to 19 years of age	Includes 136 items for assessing adaptive behavior in 9 functional areas: self-management, social maturity, social communication, domestic skills, money management, citizenship, personal organization, transportation skills career	To assess the adaptive behavior associated with social expectations, responsibility, and independence
Scales of Independent Behavior—Revised (SIB-R)	Norm-referenced, individually administered; includes a	Individuals from infancy though retirement	Includes 14 adaptive behavior subscales and 8 problem behavior scales	Comprehensive assessment of adaptive and maladaptive behavior

Name of Test	Type of Test	Suitable for	Brief Description	Purpose
	screening form and a comprehensive form			
SIB-R Short Form for the Visually Impaired	Norm-referenced, individually administered screening instrument	Individuals from infancy through retirement	Contains 40 items and is suitable for use as a screening test of adaptive behavior	A special version of the SIB-R Short Form for use with individuals who have visual impairments
*Vineland Adaptive Behavior Scales, Second Edition (Vineland II)	Norm-referenced, individually administered; includes survey, parent/caregiver, teacher, and expanded forms	Infants, children, and youth birth to 19 years; teacher form 3 to 21 years	Includes subscales for measuring communication, daily living skills, socialization, motor skills, and an optional subscale for assessing maladaptive behavior	To assist in identifying and placing students with mild, moderate, and severe disabilities, including mental retardation, autism spectrum disorder, and ADHD to obtain evaluation data for programming and intervention purposes

*Tests marked with an asterisk are featured in this chapter.

Norm-referenced adaptive behavior scales are used along with other tests and assessment information to identify students with disabilities, determine eligibility for services, and make classification decisions. Because mental retardation is defined in part as resulting from deficits in adaptive behavior, assessing adaptive behavior is a major element in identifying students with mental retardation. Adaptive behavior scales are also useful in formulating instructional programs focusing on personal, social, and occupational skill development.

To check your comprehension of the chapter contents, go to the *Guided Review* and *Quiz* modules in Chapter 12 of the Companion Website, *www.prenhall.com/venn*.

Meeting Performance Standards and Preparing for Licensure Exams

After reading this chapter, you should be able to demonstrate the following CEC Standards and PRAXIS™ test knowledge and skills. The information in parentheses identifies where to find the particular CEC standard and PRAXIS™ content reference.

CEC Standards for Beginning Special Education Teachers

- Use and limitations of assessment instruments (CC8K4)
- Use technology to conduct assessments (CC8S3)
- Develop or modify individualized assessment strategies (CC8S4)

- Interpret information from formal and informal assessments (CC8S5)
- Evaluate instruction and monitor progress of individuals with exceptional learning needs (CC8S8)
- Specialized terminology used in the assessment of individuals with disabilities (GC8K1)
- Use exceptionality-specific assessment instruments with individuals with disabilities (GC8S2)

PRAXIS™ Education of Exceptional Students: Core Content Knowledge

- Assessment, including use of assessment for screening, diagnosis, placement, and the making of instructional decisions; for example, how to select and conduct nondiscriminatory and appropriate assessments; how to interpret standardized and specialized assessment results (0353 III)

chapter 13

Career and Vocational Assessment

Objectives

After reading this chapter, you will be prepared to do the following:

- Define career and vocational assessment.
- Discuss the four stages of career education.
- Use assessment data in planning transition services.
- Administer and interpret vocational interest inventories.
- Assess prevocational and employability skills.
- Use work samples to assess career and vocational skills.
- Conduct situational and on-the-job assessment procedures.
- Use task analysis to assess career and vocational skills.

Overview

Assessing career and vocational skills involves measuring and evaluating work-related behaviors as well as competencies in social interaction, functional academics, and activities of daily living. Teachers of adolescents with disabilities need in-depth knowledge of the procedures of career and vocational assessment. Other teachers need an understanding of the basics of career and vocational evaluation. This chapter assists you in learning the essential concepts and techniques of career and vocational assessment. To achieve this goal, you will consider the meaning of the terms and investigate various curriculum-based assessments and formal tests for assessing career and vocational skills, including the following:

- Written tests
- Work samples
- Situational and on-the-job assessment
- Task analysis

For each type of assessment, you examine the definition of the category, representative evaluation procedures and tests, and practical applications. Throughout the chapter, you focus on why teachers assess the career and vocational skills of students with disabilities and how they utilize this type of assessment in instructional programs.

Introducing Career and Vocational Assessment

The following narrative illustrates how to begin career and vocational assessment and shows the value of assessment in this domain.

When Barry Schwartz started developing a vocational and career skills curriculum for his students with disabilities, he went to his program coordinator for information about where to begin. The coordinator suggested beginning by assessing the career and vocational skills of the students to see what skills the students needed to develop. First, Barry needed to know the most appropriate assessment to use. The coordinator showed him what was available and helped select an assessment. After studying the instrument, Barry administered it to his students and used the results to develop transition services and learning activities for each student.

Defining Career and Vocational Assessment

Career assessment encompasses evaluation of a broad range of practical life skills that are part of living and working as an adult. Career skills include social behaviors, functional academics, and daily living activities necessary for success on the job and in the community. Students usually begin learning career-related competencies in the elementary grades. Unlike the broad range of career skills, **vocational assessment** has a more specific connotation. It refers to the particular skills necessary for success in specific jobs, professions, or trades. Because vocational skills are limited to particular job skills, students usually begin to learn vocational skills in high school.

Stages of Career Development

The traditional model for explaining the role of career education in preparing students with the wide variety of practical skills necessary for success in postschool

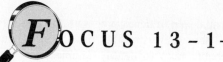

FOCUS 13-1

Assessment in the Stages of Career Education

Stage of Career Education	Assessment Questions
Career Awareness	Does the student have an understanding of the meaning of work and knowledge of a variety of jobs?
Career Exploration	What are the student's job interests and aptitudes?
Career Preparation	What are the student's specific job goals? What skills does the student need to reach these goals?
Placement and Follow-Up	What are the student's transition issues and needs? What are the student's future goals? Which agencies will participate in reaching these goals?

activities includes four stages: career awareness, career exploration, career preparation, and placement and follow-up (see Focus 13–1). In the elementary grades, career education focuses on career awareness. During this stage, students learn the value of working, and they develop the academic and social skills necessary for career success. Assessment of career awareness includes measuring and evaluating students' knowledge of various jobs and their understanding of the meaning of work. In the middle grades, the focus of career education shifts to career exploration, and students begin to experience particular types of work. Assessment in this stage involves measuring student interests and aptitudes for specific jobs, occupations, and professions. In high school, the emphasis changes to career preparation, during which students select a specific job as a career goal and begin to learn the skills necessary for success in that job. This stage emphasizes vocational assessment and training. In the final stage, placement and follow-up, educators coordinate their efforts with other agencies to ensure that students make a successful transition from education to the adult world of living and working in the community. Assessment involves identifying transition issues and needs, establishing future goals, and identifying the agencies that will participate in reaching these goals.

Transition Services

The Individuals with Disabilities Education Improvement Act (IDEA 2004) (Department of Education, 2005, p. 118) defines **transition services** as a coordinated set of activities for a child with a disability that (a) is designed to be a results-oriented process that is focused on improving the academic and functional achievement of the child with a disability to facilitate the child's movement from school to postschool activities, including postsecondary education, vocational education, integrated employment (including supported employment), continuing and adult education, adult services, independent living, or community participation; (b) is based on the individual child's needs, taking into account the child's strengths, preferences, and interests. IDEA requires the inclusion of a statement describing needed transition services in the IEPs of all students, beginning at age 14 years and annually thereafter. The statement must include a description of interagency responsibilities or linkages necessary to ensure a successful transition. Assessment is an essential step in developing appropriate statements. The assessment process requires collaboration with other professionals from agencies and institutions (e.g., vocational rehabilitation) to identify suitable postschool services and develop linkages so that students can access those services.

The addition of transition services to the IEPs of older students points out the current emphasis on functional assessment in career and vocational evaluation. **Functional assessment** evaluates student performance in real-life, natural settings to identify proficiency in performing practical, applied skills (Sitlington & Clark, 2006). For high school students, this means assessing performance at home, at school, on the job, and in the community. According to Sitlington and Clark, functional assessment not only recognizes the importance of academics and specific job competencies but also includes daily living, personal-social development, and community-based skills as equally important learning domains. One of the ways to conduct functional assessment is to use instruments such as the Transition Planning Inventory and the Transition-to-Work Inventory.

Transition Planning Inventory

The Transition Planning Inventory (TPI) (Clark & Patton, 1997) is a criterion-referenced, individually administered instrument for identifying and planning for the transition needs of students with disabilities. The TPI kit includes an administration and resource guide and packages of 25 profile and assessment recommendation forms, school forms, home forms, and student forms. The administration and resource guide includes a planning notes form, which is the key assessment and individualized planning document, and a list of more than 600 transition goals correlated to each planning statement. The recommended procedure for using the TPI includes the following:

- Having students, parents/guardians, and school-based personnel complete the appropriate inventory form
- Collecting the completed forms and profiling the results on the profile form
- Conducting a meeting to discuss the student's transition needs
- Completing the planning notes form at the meeting that specifies additional assessment (if needed), IEP goals that need to be written, linkage activities with postschool agencies, and services that will be required after graduation

Transition Behavior Scale, Second Edition

The Transition Behavior Scale, Second Edition (TBS-2) (McCarney & Anderson, 2000) includes school and self-report versions. The school version was standardized on 2,624 students from 20 states. The TBS-2 subtests measure student behavior in three areas: work related, interpersonal relations, and social/community expectations. The TBS-2 provides norms for male and female students 12 through 18 years of age. It takes about 15 minutes to complete the TBS-2. A companion Transition Behavior Scale IEP and Intervention Manual includes IEP goals, objectives, and interventions for all 62 items on the scale.

Transition-to-Work Inventory, Second Edition

The Transition-to-Work Inventory, Second Edition (Liptak, 2004) is a criterion-referenced, individually administered instrument for identifying suitable jobs and determining work activities and working environments requiring accommodation or redesign. Although most career assessment inventories use past work experience and

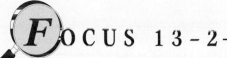

Why Do We Assess Career and Vocational Skills?

- To identify instructional needs in skill areas required for successful personal development and employment
- To evaluate what the student knows and can do
- To identify occupational interests, aptitudes, strengths, and weaknesses

educational attainment as key factors in identifying job options for the future, the Transition-to-Work Inventory is suitable for students with little or no work experience and with limited ability to identify job options and make the transition to employment. The Transition-to-Work Inventory assesses interest in a wide variety of activities by having test takers review and rate 84 nonwork activities. The ratings connect with 14 major career interest areas.

Why Do We Assess Career and Vocational Skills?

With the current emphasis on transition planning, educators are placing more attention on assessing career and vocational skills, especially with teenagers who have special needs (see Focus 13–2). In the case of career and vocational skills, teachers conduct assessment to help identify the instructional needs of students in skill areas required for successful personal development and employment. The goal is to utilize efficient, comprehensive, and accurate assessments that respond to the specific needs of the students. Teachers do this to evaluate what the student knows and can do and to identify interests, aptitudes, strengths, and weaknesses. Assessment in community-based settings is an important part of evaluating these skills. The most effective assessments, especially during the transition phase, include the participation of the student, parents, and service providers who will be involved in the transition process.

The following true story illustrates how assessment of vocational and career skills meets the needs of a student with a severe disability.

When Nancy, a student with a severe disability, was a senior in high school, the school began a supported employment program (a specialized type of job training and placement service) for the graduating students. When she enrolled in the program, her job coach gave Nancy a picture interest inventory and interviewed her parents and teachers to identify her vocational interests. Later, the job coach matched Nancy's interests and aptitudes with a job opening as a kitchen helper in a nursing home. As part of the process of placing Nancy in this job, the job coach provided intensive, one-on-one, on-the-job training that included the use of task analytic assessment to help Nancy learn the most difficult jobs in the kitchen. The job coach also arranged for the kitchen supervisor to provide weekly evaluations of Nancy's performance. Gradually, as Nancy learned to complete her job tasks more independently, the job coach decreased the level of supervision. After weeks of intensive training and months of follow-along training, Nancy learned to perform all aspects of her job without assistance from the job coach. At this point, the job coach stopped helping her directly but continued to provide follow-up services as necessary. These included periodic evaluations to ensure that she continued to work at acceptable performance levels. When Nancy graduated from high school, the nursing home hired her as a permanent, full-time employee. The nursing home was so pleased with Nancy's work and with the supported employment program that they hired another student with a severe disability to work in grounds maintenance.

The next narrative, based on a case study by Hasazi and Cobb (1988), chronicles the use of vocational and career assessment to help meet the needs of a student with a learning disability.

During the summer before he entered 11th grade, Robert, a student with a learning disability, enrolled in a career exploration class at a regional vocational center. To assess his vocational interests and aptitudes, the vocational teacher used work samples based on actual jobs that provided simulated experience with various types of work. Robert performed especially well on the printing tasks work sample associated with work in commercial print shops. In fact, he enjoyed the printing experience so much that in the fall he enrolled in a printing program at the regional center. At his individualized education plan (IEP) meeting at the end of his junior year, Robert and his parents decided that a printing career was an appropriate goal. The IEP team developed a transition plan that included work experience in a local print shop during his senior year. When he began his work placement during the spring semester, the work experience specialist from the school accompanied him to the work site. The specialist conducted on-the-job assessment to monitor his work daily for the first week and then gradually decreased the monitoring visits to once a week.

Upon graduation, a placement specialist from the state vocational rehabilitation agency placed Robert in a job with a local printing company. The work experience specialist from the school provided him with a follow-up evaluation 6 months after graduation to assess his employment status and coordinate appropriate referrals if necessary.

These vignettes illustrate the role of assessment in providing career and vocational services to students with disabilities. Another important consideration in all assessment including appraisal in this domain is evaluating students from diverse backgrounds, including English language learners. Some of the important considerations in multicultural assessment appear in the accompanying Multicultural Considerations feature.

☑ Check Your Comprehension

Career assessment is a broad term that includes vocational competencies as well as social behaviors, functional academics, and daily living skills. *Vocational assessment* is a specific term that refers to measuring and evaluating student accomplishment of the competencies necessary for success in particular jobs, professions, or trades. Assessing and teaching career skills begins in the elementary grades and continues in later grades. However, in the later grades (especially high school) the emphasis shifts to preparing students with specific vocational skills. IDEA requires that the IEPs for students who are 16 years and older include a statement describing needed transition services. Furthermore, the IEP writing team must update the transition statement each year as part of the annual IEP-writing process. In order to assess student needs for transition services appropriately, links with the agencies that provide postschool services must be established and maintained.

MULTICULTURAL CONSIDERATIONS

Diversity in Career and Vocational Assessment

The process of vocational and career assessment with students from diverse backgrounds involves much more than testing. Aptitude, achievement, language, cultural background, opportunity, and experience are important factors in appraisal. In addition, Drummond and Jones (2006) recommend considering the following cultural and diversity factors in vocational and career assessment:

- Socioeconomic class, which may affect the pattern of scores on some career and vocational tests, especially interest tests, should be considered in the assessment process. In particular, scores for upper- and middle-class students may be more predictive than scores for lower-class students.
- Many career and vocational assessments, especially interest inventories, focus on the professions rather than skilled and semi-skilled jobs. Therefore, exercise caution when assessing students who may be more suited for skilled and semi-skilled jobs.
- Societal expectations and cultural traditions may be more important than interest in determining vocational selection. Gender bias in particular is a major concern and needs to be considered when selecting instruments and interpreting profiles.
- Because some vocational and career assessments require advanced reading skills, care should be taken to match the student's reading level with the test.

Explain why scores for upper- and middle-class students may be predictable.

To answer this reflection online, go to the *Multicultural Considerations* module on the Companion Website at **www.prenhall.com/venn**.

Assessing Career and Vocational Interests

Relatively inexpensive and easy-to-administer **written tests** are widely used to assess career and vocational interests. A primary advantage of written tests is that evaluators can administer and score them efficiently in short time periods. Like all assessment procedures, however, written tests have certain limitations. The major drawback is that, in some cases, written test results differ from assessment results derived from observation of actual student performance in real work situations. Because of the inherent weaknesses of pencil-on-paper testing, written test results should not be the sole criterion for making career and vocational placement decisions.

Interest Assessment Techniques

Several techniques are useful in measuring interest. Drummond and jones (2006) describe four methods:

1. Expressed interests—What students say about their interests during interviews and conversations

2. Manifest interests—What students are observed doing

3. Testing—What students know about different careers and jobs

4. Inventories—How students respond to the items on interest inventories

These ways of measuring interests illustrate the need to check the validity of test or inventory results by asking students about their interests and activities, by inquiring about their preferences, and by finding out what students like and dislike. The process of identifying student interests involves much more than testing. Often, aptitude and achievement data helps in the decision-making process. Factors such as opportunity and experience are also important.

Vocational Interest Inventories

Vocational interest inventories are specialized tests for assessing the job and career preferences of individuals and groups of students. Teachers use vocational interest inventories to assist in developing career awareness and career exploration activities based on the student's job interests. Similarly, vocational evaluators use interest inventories as a component in comprehensive assessment of work potential. In addition, job placement specialists often rely on interest inventories to identify potential for success in specific jobs, trades, or professions. Reviews of the Reading Free Vocational Interest Inventory and the Wide Range Interest and Opinion Test follow, along with snapshots of other available inventories.

Reading Free Vocational Interest Inventory:2

The Reading Free Vocational Interest Inventory:2 (R-FVII:2) (Becker, 2001) is a picture test of vocational interests. Evaluators administer the inventory by having students choose a preferred activity from 55 sets of three pictures. Becker designed this norm-referenced, individually or group-administered test for students with intellectual and learning disabilities who display limited reading ability or language problems. R-FVII:2 results are useful for vocational planning and placement and as a guide

---

TEST REVIEW

Reading Free Vocational Interest Inventory: 2

Type of Test:	Norm-referenced
Purpose:	A group screening test of vocational interests
Content Areas:	11 vocational interest areas
Administration Time:	20 minutes
Age Levels:	Age 13 and above
Suitable for:	Students and adults with disabilities who display limited reading ability or language impairment
Scores:	Percentile ranks, t-scores, and cluster scores
In Short:	The Reading Free Vocational Interest Inventory: 2 is a useful screening measure for students with limited reading ability.

for developing instructional objectives and activities. A summary of the Reading Free Vocational Interest Inventory:2 appears in the Test Review box.

The inventory contains the following 11 interest areas:

Animal care
Automotive
Building trades
Clerical
Food service
Horticulture
Housekeeping
Laundry service
Materials handling
Patient care
Personal service

The R-FVII:2 clusters are:

Mechanical
Outdoor
Mechanical/Outdoor
Clerical/Personal care
Food service/Handling operations

R-FVII:2 Materials   Inventory materials include a manual, a test booklet containing 55 test plates, a scoresheet, and a student profile graph. Each booklet has two detachable pages that provide a record of interest and cluster scores that can be used as a permanent record of an individual's vocational likes and dislikes.

R-FVII:2 Administration and Scoring   The inventory is quick and easy to administer and score. Evaluators administer the inventory by presenting the series of 55 test plates (each containing three line drawings) to students, who circle the drawing they like best from each plate. Administration takes about 20 minutes, and scoring involves converting raw scores into t-scores, percentiles, and cluster scores. Evaluators also complete a student profile form that shows vocational interests across 11 job areas. However, because it is a group screening test, the results lack sufficient detail for identifying specific interests.

R-FVII:2 Technical Characteristics   The R-FVII:2 was standardized using a sample of 15,564 individuals. The sample was drawn from 29 different states and completed in 1998. The manual reports both reliability and validity data to support the use of the instrument as a norm-referenced tool.

R-FVII:2 Summary   The Reading Free Vocational Interest Inventory:2, a picture test of vocational interests, is a norm-referenced group screening test. The author developed the test specifically for students with mental retardation and learning disabilities. The inventory is best used as a screening measure rather than as a diagnostic tool.

Other Available Interest Inventories

Brief reviews of other available interest inventories follow. These inventories include group-administered instruments and online inventories. Information about online inventories appears in the Technology Focus box.

TECHNOLOGY FOCUS
Online Interest Inventories

With the growth of Internet-based career resources, a variety of online career interest quizzes are now available. Online assessment has the advantage of providing instantaneous, dynamic career interest results. Several online interest inventories are available for measuring vocational interests, including the Jackson Vocational Interest Survey (JVIS) and the Self-Directed Search. Descriptions of these instruments appear in this chapter. For current information about other online inventories, type in the key words "online vocational interest inventories" using a search engine such as Google and follow the links.

Career Interest Profiler   The Career Interest Profiler (CIP) (Bakker & Macnab, 2004) was developed to measure self-reported interests and relate them to work and career options. Most students complete the 180 CIP items in approximately 20 to 30 minutes. Designed for people who are 14 years of age or older, the CIP scales reflect interests in six areas: realistic, investigative, artistic, social, enterprising, and conventional. CIP results include a career interest profile report showing scores on six interest scales, an analysis of the two top career interests, descriptions of 20 to 40 occupations related to key interest areas, and career planning exercises.

Jackson Vocational Interest Survey   The norm-referenced, individually administered Jackson Vocational Interest Survey (JVIS) (Jackson, 1999) consists of 289 items. The JVIS is a comprehensive diagnostic tool that can be administered in hard copy, stand-alone Windows-based PC, or via the Internet. The results are divided into 34 basic interest scales, comprised of 26 work roles and 8 work styles. The same items can also be scored to produce 10 occupational themes that are an expansion of Holland's six occupational personality types. The JVIS, available in English, French, and Spanish, requires a seventh-grade reading level and takes about an hour to administer.

Occupational Aptitude Survey and Interest Schedule, Third Edition   The norm-referenced Occupational Aptitude Survey and Interest Schedule, Third Edition (OASIS-3) (Parker, 2001) can be given individually or to groups of up to 10 students. Teachers, counselors, and other professionals can administer the OASIS-3 in about 45 minutes to students in grades 8 through 12 or adults. The aptitude survey measures general ability, verbal aptitude, numerical aptitude, spatial aptitude, perceptual aptitude, and manual dexterity. The 240 items on the interest schedule measure 12 interest areas related to occupations, including artistic, scientific, nature, protective, mechanical, industrial, business detail, selling, accommodating, humanitarian, leading-influencing, and physical performing. An optional OASIS-3 interpretation workbook is available to help students understand their scores and identify what they should consider in career planning. This self-administered workbook matches aptitudes and interests with more than 250 jobs.

Self-Directed Search   The Self-Directed Search (SDS) (Holland, 1994) is one of the most widely used interest inventories. Current revisions are available in traditional pencil-on-paper versions and in an online version. The SDS helps students and adults with career exploration and career planning. Based upon the Holland theory that people are most satisfied and successful when their careers match their personalities, the SDS categorizes people in six personality types: Realistic, Investigative, Artistic, Social, Enterprising, or Conventional. The SDS is a self-administered inventory that takes about 45 minutes to complete. The SDS asks questions about aspirations, activities, competencies, occupations, and self-estimates. SDS results enable individuals to choose careers and fields of study that best match their self-reported skills and interests. SDS results can help students understand more about themselves and how their skills and interests relate to career choices.

Strong Interest Inventory   The Strong Interest Inventory, Revised (SII) (Strong, Campbell, & Hanson, 2004) is available in several versions including a standard edition, a college edition, a high school edition, and an online edition. The SII theoretical foundation is that individuals are more satisfied and productive when they work in jobs or at tasks that they find interesting and when they work with people whose interests are similar to their own. The SII includes 30 basic interest scales, with a new focus on technology, finance and investing, marketing, and entrepreneurship. The instrument covers six general occupational themes, identifying investigative thinkers to enterprising persuaders. The inventory uses a five-point answer format to measure individual preferences for more than 120 jobs. The SII takes about 25 minutes to complete and the results include a personalized report identifying career choices based on interests and additional related occupations with brief job descriptions. The SII is useful for helping students make career choices and choose education and training. The SII requires an eighth-grade reading level.

Wide Range Interest and Occupation Test, Second Edition   Like the Reading Free Vocational Interest Inventory:2, the Wide Range Interest and Occupation Test, Second Edition (WRIOT2) (Glutting & Wilkinson, 2003) is a picture test measuring vocational interests with a series of line drawings showing people in various work-related situations. The WRIOT2 contains 238 full-color pictures. Students decide whether they like, dislike, or are undecided about each job depicted. The WRIOT2 does not require reading or language understanding. WRIOT2 results graph a student's strength in 17 occupational, 16 interest, and 6 Holland type areas. The WRIOT2 can be given on the computer using a CD or manually administered using a picture book.

Check Your Comprehension

Many inventories are available to assess career and job interests. These include the Reading Free Vocational Interest Inventory, Revised and more traditional inventories such as the Self-Directed Search. The process of assessing student interests involves more than inventory assessment. Data and information from inventories should be validated by asking students about their interests, observing students, and testing student knowledge of jobs and occupations. Though inventories provide useful data and information in an efficient manner, the assessment process involves considering multiple factors. These factors include achievement, aptitude, opportunity, and experience.

Reflection
Explain what you would consider to be important when helping students make career choices.

 To answer this reflection online, go to the *Teaching and Learning* module on the Companion Website at *www.prenhall.com/venn*.

Assessing Prevocational and Employability Skills

Students need to acquire certain prevocational and employability skills to ensure success on the job and in the community. **Prevocational skills** are the personal, social, and applied academic skills necessary for success on any job. Likewise, **employability skills** are generic skills important to qualify for entry-level jobs in the workplace regardless of the particular occupation or profession. Tests of prevocational and employability skills help to identify student performance levels, and the results serve as guides for developing instructional objectives. Reviews of several representative tests of prevocational and employability skills appear in the following sections.

Brigance Inventories

Two Brigance Inventories are helpful in assessing prevocational and employability skills: the Brigance Diagnostic Life Skills Inventory and the Brigance Employability Skills Inventory.

Brigance Diagnostic Life Skills Inventory The Brigance Diagnostic Life Skills Inventory (Brigance, 1994) is a criterion-referenced tool for assessing listening, speaking, reading, writing, comprehending, and computing skills in nine life skills areas: speaking and listening, functional writing, words on common signs and warning labels, telephone skills, money and finance, food, clothing, health, and travel and transportation. The inventory, designed for use as both an assessment tool and a curriculum guide, provides sequenced activities for instructional programs that focus on teaching functional life skills. The Life Skills Inventory is useful in secondary special education, vocational education, English Speakers of Other Languages (ESOL) programs, and adult education programs. Inventory materials include a learner record book that provides for ongoing record-keeping and a program record book that tracks up to 15 students. Goals and objectives software for writing IEPs is available as an optional item.

Brigance Employability Skills Inventory The Brigance Employability Skills Inventory (Brigance, 1995) is a criterion-referenced tool for assessing basic skills and employability skills in the context of job-seeking or employment situations. The content includes measures of career awareness and self-understanding, reading skills, speaking and listening, job-seeking skills and knowledge, preemployment writing, and math skills and concepts. The skills assessed by the instrument range in difficulty level from grade 3 to high school.

Life Centered Career Education, Revised Edition

The Life Centered Career Education, Revised Edition (LCCE) (Brolin, 2004) is a curriculum guide and assessment tool for life skills and transition education. It organizes life skills competencies into subcompetencies, objectives, and supporting activities for school and community. Available LCCE assessment tools include a student competency rating scale, a knowledge battery, and a performance battery.

☑ Check Your Comprehension

Many assessment instruments and curriculum guides are available for assessing and teaching vocational interests, prevocational skills, employability skills, and related career behaviors. Written tests, which are relatively inexpensive and easy to give, enable evaluators to complete administration and scoring efficiently in short time periods. However, written tests have limited ability to predict performance in actual vocational and career situations. For this reason, written tests are best used together with other, more direct assessment procedures such as work samples and situational assessments.

Work Sample Evaluation

In response to the many deficiencies of written testing, vocational evaluation specialists developed the work sample approach for assessing vocational and career skills (Rotatori, 1990). **Work samples** are tasks, materials, tools, and equipment taken from real jobs or job clusters and used to measure vocational interest and potential. Because they are based on actual jobs, work samples provide students with simulated experiences of various types of work. Special educators later adapted the original work sample approach for use in school-based programs. This practical, hands-on approach enables professionals to evaluate student job interests and occupational aptitudes by performance on a variety of work samples rather than by answers to questions on written tests. With most work samples, evaluators use production rates as the criterion for judging performance. Production rates are the number of units produced in a specific time period or the speed of task completion. Standardized work sample systems provide norms based on the average production rates of typical workers in competitive employment. During work sample assessment, the evaluator compares a student's production rate to the average production rate of the workers in the norm sample group.

Valpar Component Work Sample System

The Valpar Component Work Sample System (Brandon, Balton, Rup, & Raslter, n.d.) contains 24 work samples designed for use by individuals from age 14 through adulthood. Because it takes about 8 hours to administer all 24 samples, an evaluator may select particular samples from the complete set, depending on the needs of the individual student. Valpar work samples include the following:

1. Small tools

2. Size discrimination

3. Numerical sorting

4. Upper extremity range of motion

5. Whole body range of motion

6. Tri-level measurement

7. Eye-hand-foot coordination

8. Electronic soldering and inspection

9. Clerical comprehension

10. Independent problem solving

11. Multi-level sorting

12. Simulated assembly

13. Money handling

14. Integrated peer performance

15. Electrical circuitry and print reading

16. Drafting

17. Prevocational readiness battery

18. Conceptual understanding

19. Dynamic physical capacities

20. Physical capacities and mobility

21. Mechanical assembly/alignment

22. Mechanical reasoning

23. Fine finger dexterity

24. Independent perceptual screening

Each self-contained sample contains all necessary materials. Students complete some of the small samples at a desk or on a table. Other samples take up a large amount of space and require a separate workstation or work area.

Teacher-Made Work Samples

Instead of using commercial work samples such as the VALPAR, many teachers develop their own work samples. Teacher-made work samples give students hands-on experience with tasks associated with real jobs; they are usually inexpensive, and teachers can individualize them to meet the particular interests of students. Examples of typical work samples include the following:

- Simple assembly tasks such as packaging and parts assembly
- Clerical tasks such as collating, folding, and stapling
- Maintenance and sanitation jobs such as janitorial and laundry services
- Jobs associated with running small businesses, such as a school supply store or the making and selling of craft items

☑ Check Your Comprehension

The work sample approach provides assessment data not available from written tests. Work samples include commercially available systems and teacher-made job tasks. Although work samples are valuable assessment and teaching tools, they only simulate real work environments. As a result, they measure a restricted sample of the behaviors necessary for success on actual jobs. For this reason, career and vocational assessment also includes situational and on-the-job assessment procedures to obtain evaluation data that are as realistic as possible.

Situational and On-the-Job Assessment

Situational assessment is not a single procedure. Instead, it includes a variety of techniques for assessing student performance in functional settings. Situational assessment is the use of systematic observation to evaluate work- and career-related performance on the job or in real or simulated environments such as vocational training settings, simulated workstations, job tryouts in the community, and other community-based settings. Specialists in vocational rehabilitation initially developed situational assessment as a tool for evaluating student performance in structured vocational settings such as work evaluation centers and sheltered workshops (Gaylord-Ross, 1988). In these settings, situational assessment consists of a 20- to 30-day evaluation of performance on actual jobs. During this period, the evaluator assesses specific work skills and work-related behaviors. Specific work skills include the amount of training needed to learn new tasks, production rates, and accuracy of work performed. Work-related behaviors include social skills, tolerance, and motivation.

In recent years, special educators and other professionals have adapted traditional situational assessment for use in measuring and evaluating student vocational and career-related skills in many different work and community-based settings (Bigge & Stump, 1999; Wehman, 2005). Situational assessment is ideal for use in community-based instructional programs that occur "on location" at the workplace or in other places such as the shopping mall, bus stop, grocery store, post office, drugstore, public library, and park.

Advantages and Disadvantages of Situational Assessment

In comparison with other assessment techniques, situational assessment offers both advantages and disadvantages. Sitlington and Clark (2006) describe the following benefits and drawbacks. The beneficial aspects include the following:

- Assessing students in real-life settings rather than in artificial testing situations
- Assessing students when they are engaged in real jobs and participating in real community-based activities
- Avoiding the worry and fear produced by formal testing
- Providing authentic information about student performance (what students actually do instead of what they can do)
- Improving instructional planning by producing genuine assessment results that relate more directly to the curriculum

Drawbacks include the following:

- Problems with generalizing results obtained in one situation to other situations
- Validity that depends on the use of accurate and appropriate data collection procedures
- Difficulty in controlling bias resulting from evaluator errors in observing, recording, and interpreting behavior

On-the-Job Assessment

On-the-job assessment is a specific type of situational evaluation for measuring vocational behavior in actual work settings. Although even the experts have difficulty separating various types of on-the-job assessment, most distinguish between on-the-job tryouts and job-site evaluations. On-the-job tryouts place students in jobs for experience. In contrast, placement specialists use job-site evaluations for assessing the performance of individuals on actual competitive jobs. Gaylord-Ross (1988) described the typical characteristics of on-the-job tryouts as situations in which the following occur:

- Students are not paid
- Job placement is for training students
- Job placement is for experience rather than employment
- The student is an addition to the workforce, not a replacement
- Both the employer and education personnel assess student performance

Hursh and Kerns (1988) described the usual characteristics of job-site evaluation as consisting of the following:

- Placement in an actual competitive job in the community
- Employer supervision of the student
- Provision of additional training, supervision, and evaluation to ensure that the student performs the job in a satisfactory manner

Regardless of the specific type of job placement in the community, on-the-job assessment has the potential of providing a realistic evaluation of student performance by enabling the evaluator to determine whether a student can perform successfully in the workplace.

Situational and On-the-Job Assessment Evaluation Procedures

When special educators conduct situational and on-the-job assessment, they rely on more than one evaluation procedure. In some situations they may use written tests, usually in the form of checklists and scales, to evaluate student behavior and measure student performance. In other situations they may use behavioral observation techniques. Special educators also rely on task analysis, an instructional method and assessment procedure that is an ideal situational assessment tool. Often special educators use a combination of evaluation procedures rather than relying exclusively on one method. Brief descriptions of procedures for using written tests and behavioral observations in situational assessment appear in the following sections, followed by a more detailed discussion of task analysis.

Written Tests   For special educators, written tests, usually rating scales and checklists, are valuable tools for assessing student performance on the job, in the community, and in other career-oriented instructional settings. Often teachers working by themselves or as part of a professional team develop their own rating scales and checklists for specific situations. For example, if students are frequently placed in a particular business or specific setting in the community, then the best assessment tool may be a checklist of skills or rating scale of behaviors that the teacher develops for that situation. When teachers develop their own instrument, they can include items that are unique to each situation, thus helping to ensure that the instrument reflects a student's particular learning needs.

Direct Observation The direct observation techniques for assessing student behavior described in Chapter 11 are also useful for assessing student performance on the job and in the community. For example, anecdotal recording helps analyze problem behaviors or skill deficiencies within the context of surrounding events. Anecdotal recording also helps isolate relevant aspects of the situation or setting that may influence the problem behaviors. Therefore, when teachers need to identify why a student is experiencing difficulty in a specific work- or community-based situation, they often use anecdotal recording procedures. Partial-interval recording and momentary time-sampling procedures are also useful as situational assessment tools. Direct observation provides task-specific assessment data for helping students learn especially difficult jobs.

Task Analysis Task analysis is a valuable curriculum-based assessment procedure and a useful instructional technique. Business and industry originated the term to describe the process of breaking down a job into its component parts. In business and industry, task analysis enables worker specialization and increases production efficiency, especially in assembly-line work (Sailor & Guess, 1983). Gold (1975) first introduced an adapted version of task analysis for training students with severe disabilities. Gold defined task analysis as breaking down a difficult task into small steps to enable the learner to learn the task more easily. More recently, Mercer and Mercer (2005) described task analysis as dividing a learning project into parts to determine needed skills, especially those that are prerequisites for performing the complete project. The analysis process helps students learn demanding vocational and career-related tasks more quickly and easily. Task analysis is also useful in teaching academic skills and a variety of life management skills, including self-help skills and activities of daily living.

Developing a Task Analysis. Developing a task analysis involves the following steps:

- Analyze the content of a task to identify the separate steps.
- Evaluate the process of a task to determine appropriate teaching strategies.
- Prepare a data collection form to measure student progress.
- Begin instruction.
- Revise the task analysis on the basis of progress data (as necessary).

Using Task Analysis to Measure and Report Progress. Teachers may report the results of task analysis in several ways. The goal is to summarize results accurately in a manner that best describes student performance. Simply reporting the number of steps in a task a student has mastered (e.g., 9 of 10 steps performed correctly) is an efficient way to communicate results. However, when teachers need a more formal report of progress, they often use graphs to illustrate student performance. Teachers graph the results of task analysis by taking assessment information from a data collection form and plotting it on a line or bar chart. Graphs visually illustrate behavior and this helps assess student performance and facilitates communicating assessment information with others. One type of data collection system enables the display of student performance data as a graph on the form itself, an

Reflection
Think of a complex skill that would lend itself to task analysis. How would you go about developing a tasks analysis for this skill?

 To answer this reflection online, go to the *Teaching and Learning* module on the Companion Website at *www.prenhall.com/venn.*

Figure 13–1 Task analysis data collection form and graph

Data Collection Form

Task: Photopying
Student: Jason
Teacher: Ms. Jones

Dates

Steps	4/21	4/22	4/25	4/27	4/28	4/29	5/1	5/2	5/3	5/8	5/9	5/10
	15	15	15	15	15	15	15	15	15	15	15	15
	14	14	14	14	14	14	14	14	14	14	14	14
	13	13	13	13	13	13	13	13	13	13	13	13
	12	12	12	12	12	12	12	12	12	12	12	12
	11	11	11	11	11	11	11	11	11	11	11	11
10. Take copies back	10	10	10	10	10	10	10	10	10	10	10	10
9. Remove copies	9	9	9	9	9	9	9	9	9	9	9	9
8. Repeat 3–7 for each page	8	8	8	8	8	8	8	8	8	8	8	8
7. Remove original	7	7	7	7	7	7	7	7	7	7	7	7
6. Start machine	6	6	6	6	6	6	6	6	6	6	6	6
5. Set quantity	5	5	5	5	5	5	5	5	5	5	5	5
4. Align paper	4	4	4	4	4	4	4	4	4	4	4	4
3. Place paper	3	3	3	3	3	3	3	3	3	3	3	3
2. Go to machine	2	2	2	2	2	2	2	2	2	2	2	2
1. Get originals	1	1	1	1	1	1	1	1	1	1	1	1

Notes and Comments _____

_____

example of which appears in Figure 13–1. This form lists the steps in the task from last to first. Each time a student performs a step correctly, the teacher draws a line through the number on the data sheet that represents that step. After each trial, the teacher circles the number that shows the total number of steps completed correctly. After a series of trials, the teacher connects the circles to form a line graph showing student performance across multiple trials. Many task analysis procedures and data collection forms are available for use with students who have special needs. In addition, teachers and schools often develop their own variations of task analysis. Examples of two other task analysis data collection forms appear in Figure 13–2.

Figure 13–2   Other task analysis data collection forms

Task Analysis Data Sheet

Name of Task _Operating Paper Cutter_

Student: _Julie_

Teacher: _Jim Wilson_

Description _____

_____

Criterion _4/4 correct trials_

Scoring Code

3 – Without Assistance
2 – Verbal Help
1 – Modeling/Demonstration
0 – Physical Assistance

Date

Step	5-1	5-2	5-3	5-7	5-8	5-9						
1. _Pick paper_	2	3	3	3	3	3						
2. _Place paper_	2	2	2	2	2	3						
3. _Raise cutting arm_	1	1	3	3	3	3						
4. _Slide paper to mark_	0	1	2	2	2	3						
5. _Hold paper_	0	1	2	2	3	3						
6. _Lower cutting arm_	0	0	2	2	3	3						
7. _Remove and place paper_	1	1	2	2	3	3						
8.												
9.												
10.												
11.												
12.												
13.												
14.												
15.												

Comments _____

_____

(continued)

☑ Check Your Comprehension

Situational assessment techniques include checklists, observations, and task analysis. Situational assessment is useful on the job, in the community, or at home because it evaluates students in authentic activities in functional environments. However, as with all forms of assessment, careful planning and skillful use of situational assessment provides the best possible assessment data and information for decision making.

Figure 13–2 *continued*

		Get materials	Wet surface	Apply cleaner	Rub with rag	Rinse surface	Rinse rag	Put materials away								Trial Time
Trials	**Date**															

Task Analysis Data Collection Form

Name of Task *Clean Classroom Sink*

Student *Larry*   School   *Pinewood Elementary*

Teacher *Donna Jones*   criterion   *3/3 correct trials*

Description *steps for cleaning classroom sink*

Trials	Date	Get materials	Wet surface	Apply cleaner	Rub with rag	Rinse surface	Rinse rag	Put materials away								Trial Time
1	4/19	+	−	−	+	−	−	−								14 min.
2	4/20	+	−	−	+	−	−	+								14 min.
3	4/21	+	+	−	+	−	−	+								12 min.
4	4/22	+	+	+	+	−	−	+								11 min.
5	4/23	+	+	+	+	−	+	+								10 min.
6	4/27	+	+	+	+	−	−	+								11 min.
7	7/28	+	+	+	+	−	+	+								10 min.
8	4/29	+	+	+	+	−	+	−								11 min.
9	4/30	+	+	+	+	+	+	+								8 min.
10																
11																
12																
13																
14																
15																

Notes _____

Summary

Assessing career and vocational skills involves measuring and evaluating work skills as well as competencies in social interaction, functional academics, and daily living activities. More specifically, career assessment encompasses evaluation of the practical life skills needed for postschool success. Vocational assessment, a more restrictive term, refers to the appraisal of skills required for particular jobs. Numerous appraisal procedures and tests are used to assess career and vocational performance (see Table 13–1). These include written tests, work samples, situational and on-the-job assessment techniques, and task analysis.

Table 13–1 Review of Career and Vocational Assessment Instruments

Name	Type	Suitable for	Brief Description	Purpose
Brigance Diagnostic Life Skills Inventory	Criterion-referenced, individually administered life skills inventory	High school students through adulthood	Measures nine life skills areas: speaking and listening, functional writing, words on common signs and warning labels, telephone skills, money and finance, food, clothing, health, and travel and transportation	Designed for use as both an assessment tool and a curriculum guide with sequenced activities for instructional programs that teach functional life skills
Brigance Employability Skills Inventory	Criterion-referenced, individually administered inventory	Students from grade 3 through high school	Includes measures of career awareness and self-understanding, reading skills, speaking and listening, job-seeking skills and knowledge, preemployment writing, and math skills and concepts	For assessing basic skills and employability skills in the context of job-seeking or employment situations
Career Interest Profiler (CIP)	Criterion-referenced interest inventory	Students who are 14 years of age or older	A 180-item questionnaire measuring interests in six areas: realistic, investigative, artistic, social, enterprising, and conventional	To measure self-reported interests and relate them to work and career options
Jackson Vocational Interest Survey (JVIS)	Norm-referenced, individually administered, comprehensive diagnostic tool	Students who are reading at a 7th-grade level or above	Consists of 289 items and is available in hard copy, stand-alone Windows-based PC, or via the Internet	To assess vocational interests and preferences
Life Centered Career Education, Revised Edition (LCCE)	Criterion-referenced, individually administered, Curriculum-based assessment instrument	High school students, especially with students in educable mentally handicapped and learning disabilities programs	Includes a competency rating scale, a knowledge battery, and a performance battery	To measure the career education knowledge and skills of students with disabilities, provides a foundation for life skills and transition education

(continued)

Table 13–1 *continued*

Name	Type	Suitable for	Brief Description	Purpose
Occupational Aptitude Survey and Interest Schedule, Third Edition	Criterion-referenced, individually or group-administered to up to 10 students	Grades 8 to 12	Contains an aptitude survey measuring general ability, verbal aptitude, numerical aptitude, spatial aptitude, perceptual aptitude, and manual dexterity and an interest schedule measuring 12 interest areas related to occupations, including artistic, scientific, nature, protective, mechanical, industrial, business detail, selling, accommodating, humanitarian, leading-influencing, and physical performing	To assess occupational aptitudes and vocational interests
*Reading Free Vocational Interest Inventory—2 (R-FVII-2)	Norm-referenced, group-administered screening test of vocational interest	Students who are 13 years of age and older	A picture test of vocational interests administered by having students choose a preferred activity from 55 sets of 3 pictures	Vocational planning and placement, and as a guide for developing instructional objectives and activities
Self-Directed Search (SDS)	Self-administered inventory available in hard copy, online, or computer-based versions	Middle school students through adults	Asks questions about aspirations, activities, competencies, occupations and self-estimates and categorizes people in six personality types: Realistic, Investigative, Artistic, Social, Enterprising, or Conventional	To help students and adults with career exploration and career planning

Name	Type	Suitable for	Brief Description	Purpose
Strong Interest Inventory, Revised (SII)	Versions include a standard edition, a college edition, a high school edition, and an online edition	High school students and adults who read at an eighth grade level or higher	Measures interests in a wide range of occupations, occupational activities, hobbies, leisure activities, and types of people	To help students make career choices and choose education and training
Transition Behavior Scale, Second Edition (TBS-2)	Norm-referenced, individually administered	Teenagers with disabilities	Measures students behavior in three areas: work-related, interpersonal relations, and social/community expectations	To help students make the transition into employment in the community
Transition Planning Inventory (TPI)	Criterion-referenced, individually administered, assessment, and transition planning curriculum guide	Teenagers with disabilities who need an ITP	Includes an administration and resource guide and packages of 25 profile and assessment recommendation forms, school forms, home forms, and student forms. The administration and resource guide includes a planning notes form, which is the key assessment and individualized planning document, and a list of more than 600 transition goals correlated to each planning statement.	To identify and plan for the transition needs of students with disabilities
Transition-to-Work Inventory, Second Edition	Criterion-referenced, individually administered instrument	Individuals with little or no work experience	Contains 84 nonwork activities and connects to 14 major career interest areas	To identify the jobs most suitable for individuals with differing abilities and determining which work activities and working environments require accommodation or redesign

(continued)

Table 13–1 *continued*

Name	Type	Suitable for	Brief Description	Purpose
Valpar Component Work Sample System	Criterion-referenced, individually administered work samples	14 years through adulthood	Contains 24 work samples	To evaluate job interests and occupational aptitudes using work-like tasks administered under specific instructions
Wide Range Interest and Occupation Test, Second Edition (WRIOT2)	Norm-referenced, individually administered screening test	Students from age 5 to adult	A picture test of vocational interests consisting of a series of line drawings that show people in various work-related situations	To measure work interests for use in career and vocational planning, including counseling, employee selection, and coordinating instruction with student interests

*Tests marked with an asterisk are featured in this chapter.

Because of the importance of career and vocational assessment with older students, high school teachers should be thoroughly familiar with the available tests. For other teachers of students with special needs, understanding career and vocational assessment is one part of a complete knowledge base of appraisal techniques in special education. This knowledge helps teachers ensure that when students leave school, they are well prepared to make a successful transition into the adult world of living and working in the community.

To check your comprehension of the chapter contents, go to the *Guided Review and Quiz* modules in Chapter 13 of the Companion Website, *www.prenhall.com/venn*.

Meeting Performance Standards and Preparing for Licensure Exams

After reading this chapter, you should be able to demonstrate the following CEC Standards and PRAXIS™ test knowledge and skills. The information in parentheses identifies where to find the particular CEC standard and PRAXIS™ content reference.

CEC Standards for Beginning Special Education Teachers

- Use and limitations of assessment instruments (CC8K4)
- Administer nonbiased formal and informal assessments (CC8S2)
- Use technology to conduct assessments (CC8S3)
- Develop or modify individualized assessment strategies (CC8S4)
- Interpret information from formal and informal assessments (CC8S5)
- Evaluate instruction and monitor progress of individuals with exceptional learning needs (CC8S8)
- Develop or modify individualized assessment strategies (CC8S9)
- Specialized terminology used in the assessment of individuals with disabilities (GC8K1)

- Select, adapt and modify assessments to accommodate the unique abilities and needs of individuals with disabilities (GC8S3)

PRAXIS™ Education of Exceptional Students: Core Content Knowledge
- The influence of (an) exceptional condition(s) throughout an individual's life span (0353 I)
- Federal laws and legal issues related to special education, including Public Law 94–142, Public Law 105–17 (IDEA '97), and Section 504—Americans with Disabilities Act (ADA) (0353 II)
- The school's connections with the families, prospective and actual employers, and communities of students with disabilities, for example, interagency agreements and the cooperative nature of the transition planning process (0353 II)
- Historical movements/trends affecting the connections between special education and the larger society, for example, application of technology and transition (0353 II)
- Background knowledge, including placement and program issues such as transition of students into and within special education placements; community-based training; postschool transitions (0353 III)
- Assessment, including use of assessment for screening, diagnosis, placement, and the making of instructional decisions, for example, how to select, construct, conduct, and modify nondiscriminatory, developmentally and chronologically age-appropriate informal assessments, including teacher-made tests, curriculum-based assessment, and alternatives to norm-referenced testing (including observations, anecdotal records, error analysis, miscue analysis, self-evaluation questionnaires and interviews, journals and learning logs, and portfolio assessment) (0353 III)

part IV

Assessing Academic Achievement

chapter 14

Assessing Academic Achievement
Curriculum-Based and Norm-Referenced Strategies

Objectives

After reading this chapter, you will be prepared to

- Assess the academic achievement of students with special needs, including students from culturally and linguistically diverse backgrounds.
- Compare curriculum-based assessment and norm-referenced testing of academic achievement.
- Conduct curriculum-based assessment of academic achievement.
- Use norm-referenced tests to assess academic achievement.

Overview

Measuring academic learning is a central aspect of teaching students with learning problems. Academic achievement is student performance after instruction, and it includes reading, mathematics, written expression, and scholastic subjects such as science and history. In this chapter, you will have the opportunity to develop your knowledge and skills in this critical area of assessment. To realize this goal you will learn the definition of achievement assessment and the types of behaviors measured by achievement tests. You will consider the use of achievement tests and measures to meet student needs, and you will investigate current issues surrounding the assessment of achievement. After this introduction, you will examine assessment procedures and achievement tests, including the most widely used curriculum-based strategies and norm-referenced tests. As you learn each assessment method, you will consider the purpose and use of the assessment, the administration and scoring procedures, and the technical characteristics.

Introduction to Assessing Academic Achievement

Ms. Wan received excellent training in assessment when she earned her degree in teacher education. Her training included assessment experiences in methods courses, field experiences, and internship. Now that she is a first-year teacher, she is very interested in trying out what she learned. She wonders how to apply her knowledge and skills in her inclusion class team-teaching situation, and she asks herself several questions. What specific curriculum-based assessments would be best for her students? What, if any, norm-referenced tests should she use? How can she best link assessment with IEPs?

After participating in some inservice training at her school on improving literacy, she worked with her co-teacher in implementing a program using running records, a curriculum-based assessment procedure, to measure the oral reading performance of the students in the class. Ms. Wan found that the running records provided useful diagnostic information for gauging the reading progress of her students. Ms. Wan also decided to use a norm-referenced test, the Peabody Individual Achievement Test—Revised/Normative Update (PIAT-R/NU) to assess the overall performance of her students. To find out for herself what norm-referenced achievement testing could do, she gave the PIAT-R/NU reading subtests to two of her students with reading difficulties. Finally, she made plans to use the results from these assessments in the process of revising the IEPs of her students at the end of the year.

Defining and Describing the Assessment of Academic Achievement

Achievement tests measure student learning in the academic subjects that make up the regular school curriculum. These academic areas subdivide into particular skill clusters. For example, reading includes word identification, word attack, word comprehension, passage comprehension, and oral reading skills.

Teachers use a diverse array of tools, techniques, and strategies to assess student achievement. In fact, academic achievement contains a wider range and variety of tests and evaluation procedures than any other domain; furthermore, the age range of achievement testing begins at kindergarten and extends through high school into college and adulthood. The tools used to measure achievement include informal, curriculum-based strategies and more formal group and individual tests. Although overlap occurs among these appraisal methods, each type has distinct characteristics and optimal uses. Given the wide assortment of procedures and tests to choose from, the teacher selects particular techniques or instruments based on student needs, the curriculum, and the purpose for the evaluation. Regardless of the strategy or test, teachers need to consider several factors when they conduct assessment, including the influence of cultural and linguistic diversity on the performance of individual students. Information about the influence of acculturation on the assessment of achievement appears in the accompanying Multicultural Considerations feature.

 MULTICULTURAL CONSIDERATIONS

Acculturation and Achievement

Acculturation is a cultural change process in individuals that occurs when two cultures meet. Acculturation leads individuals to adopt elements of another culture, including values, languages, and social behaviors. The acculturation process includes different phases, and acculturation in individuals depends on several variables. One of the most important variables is stress. Acculturation is stressful for students and their families, and stress may be especially acute for students with significant learning problems. When assessing the academic achievement of students from diverse cultural and linguistic backgrounds, it is important to consider the acculturation process. This includes making an allowance for the phases of acculturation and taking into account how well a student is dealing with the stresses of acculturation. Students who are in the early phases of acculturation and who are experiencing significant acculturation stress will need more assessment accommodations and modifications than students who are in later and less stressful acculturation phases. The following interview questions, developed by Sattler (2001), are useful in determining a student's degree of acculturation. As written, these questions are best suited for older students.

1. In what language do you usually talk with your mother? Your father? Your brothers and sisters? Your grandparents?
2. When you talk with your friends, what language do you use?
3. In what language are the television programs you watch? The music you listen to?
4. When you think, read, and write, what language do you use?
5. What cultural or ethnic holidays and traditions do you celebrate?
6. What culture do you identify with most closely?

1. What acculturation stress do you think a teenager might experience, compared to a younger student?
2. Considering the questions developed by Sattler, what overview of the student do you think these questions would provide?

 To answer this reflection online, go to the *Multicultural Considerations* module on the Companion Web site at **www.prenhall.com/venn**.

Table 14–1 Why Do We Assess Achievement?

- To screen students who may have deficits in achievement
- To identify, classify, and place students with disabilities
- To determine present levels of academic performance
- To develop IEPs
- To plan instructional programs and develop intervention activities
- To evaluate student progress
- To monitor program effectiveness

Why Do We Assess Achievement?

We assess achievement to determine present levels of educational performance and identify strengths and weaknesses in academic skills for developing the best possible instructional program for each student. Measurement of achievement occurs in all phases of the assessment process, including screening, determining eligibility, IEP development, instructional intervention, student progress evaluation, and program effectiveness monitoring. Though these steps in the assessment process are not always distinctly separated, different tests and techniques exist for each function. When screening students, for example, we depend on specially developed screening instruments, including group achievement tests, designed to facilitate initial identification of those who may have problems in one or more academic learning areas. A listing of several of the most frequently used academic screening tests appears in this chapter. Determining eligibility, on the other hand, relies on formal, norm-referenced diagnostic achievement tests. This chapter includes reviews of several of these individually administered, diagnostic tests. A major element in the process of determining eligibility for special education services involves interpreting the results from these tests. The staffing team uses the achievement test results, along with other test scores and evaluation information, to make a placement decision. When staffing teams identify students with learning problems who qualify for special education services, they work together as a team with the parents to develop an initial IEP. The team uses the diagnostic assessment data and information gathered during the identification process as a guide for developing the goals and learning objectives in the initial IEP. Although teachers often use norm-referenced tests in instructional planning and intervention with students, they rely more often on less formal, curriculum-based assessment techniques. With curriculum-based assessment, the teacher selects from a series of assessment strategies that lead directly to the development of instructional objectives. For example, many teachers use checklists of skills to identify and record achievement and track student progress. Likewise, special education teachers and educational diagnosticians select from a variety of both formal and informal appraisal techniques for evaluating student progress and monitoring program effectiveness. A summary of the reasons for assessing the achievement of students with learning problems appears in Table 14–1.

☑ Check Your Comprehension

Assessing achievement involves evaluating the academic performance of students in subjects such as reading, writing, and mathematics. Teachers may select from a wide range and variety of strategies to assess achievement. In some cases, especially in classroom instruction, assessing achievement relies on informal curriculum-based techniques that help identify appropriate instructional objectives for individuals and groups of students. In other situations, particularly in staffing situations, optimal assessment entails giving norm-referenced tests. Many times, however, the best possible assessment relies on data and information from both curriculum-based assessment and norm-referenced testing.

Curriculum-Based Assessment of Academic Achievement

Curriculum-based assessment (CBA) of academic achievement is both an instructional approach and a collection of strategies. The main idea of the CBA instructional approach is the more we know as teachers about what and how our students are learning, the better we can meet learning needs by planning appropriate instructional activities and accurately measuring student progress. CBA incorporates a vast array of techniques. Many but not all CBA strategies consist of quick, easy, and accurate evaluation activities that produce useful feedback about the teaching-learning process and about how well the students are progressing in the curriculum. Thus, CBA helps teachers measure student progress in learning the skills and objectives in the curriculum, plan appropriate instructional activities, and respond directly to student learning needs.

As described earlier in Chapter 1, curriculum-based assessment is an evaluation approach with a direct relationship to the student's curriculum. This direct link is achieved by using repeated measures from the student's curriculum to evaluate instructional effectiveness and guide instructional changes. For example, teachers often use student performance on homework assignments, classwork, and teacher-made tests to make curriculum-based assessment decisions. The result is more effective teaching methods and improved student achievement.

Curriculum-Based Strategies

A discussion of many CBA strategies follows. For each strategy, there is a brief description along with information about where additional details and examples appear in the book. This list provides an overall view of the wide range and variety of available CBA strategies. Most teachers use some combination of the following strategies, but few if any teachers use them all. The specific strategies that teachers employ depend on student needs, program goals, and the teacher's instructional style. Most teachers avoid using only one or two CBA strategies. Instead, they prefer to rely on several strategies to obtain broad-based measurement data and information for making assessment decisions.

Authentic Tasks   **Authentic tasks** are genuine activities that occur in a real-life context. Examples include shopping, banking, measuring a ballpark, designing a home, or building a bridge or tower. The process of using authentic tasks for assessment involves collecting appropriate data and/or information on student performance with a tool such as a checklist of skills, a written record of an observation, or some other suitable measure that documents competency in completing the task or tasks. Teachers use authentic tasks to ensure transfer and generalization of skills learned in the classroom into the real world.

Charts   Behavior charts are perhaps the most commonly used type of chart, but teachers routinely use many other charts to measure progress, including charts documenting the number of books read during a particular point in time, the specific math skills learned by each student in a class, and the achievement of benchmarks in standards-based educational programs.

Checklists   Various types and formats of checklists help to identify and record achievement levels and track student progress. Most checklists are simply lists of skills or behaviors arranged in a format that enables recording of student progress in demonstrating the competencies associated with each item. Teachers may score checklists with rubric levels (e.g., 1, 2, 3, and 4), letter grades, numerical values, or simple yes/no notation. Chapter 15 includes detailed information about checklists, including sample checklists for measuring oral reading, silent reading, and reading comprehension skills.

Conferences   Conferences are meetings held for educational purposes such as discussing learning needs, reviewing progress, and establishing learning goals. Peers, teachers, parents, and others who know the student may participate in conferences designed to discuss and assess learning. Student conferences are a key element in portfolio assessment. Detailed portfolio conference strategies appear in Chapter 18.

Differentiated Assessment   Differentiated assessment (Staub, 2004) is a strategy for adapting teacher-made tests. The strategy involves creating tests that teachers adapt to meet the individual learning needs of students. When applied to a test with 15 questions, for example, teachers create questions in three groups of five using Bloom's taxonomy. The first five items should be relatively easy factual-level questions. The next five questions should be more difficult, mostly at the factual and application levels. The last group should contain the most difficult items at the highest taxonomy levels: evaluation, analysis, and synthesis. A test like this can be used for differentiated or adaptive assessment by arranging for students to take the test at any one of the three difficulty levels depending on how comfortable they feel with the material. Grading can be adjusted depending on the level of difficulty. Students who answer only the first five items at the easiest level may earn a grade of "C" if they correctly answer all five questions. Students who opt to answer all 15 items may receive an "A" if they correctly answer all the questions. Differentiated assessment is one way to include all students in classroom testing without putting too much pressure on those who are not quite ready to answer the most difficult questions. This type of test also takes some pressure off teachers by giving them a strategy to develop one test that meets diverse learning needs.

Error Analysis   Teachers routinely use **error analysis** procedures to assess student performance in reading, mathematics, spelling, and writing. Error analysis refers to a number of strategies for systematically evaluating student mistakes and determining the reasons for the mistakes. In mathematics, for example, teachers use error pattern analysis that involves gathering work samples, identifying the error patterns, and developing intervention strategies from the results of the analysis. Additional information about error pattern analysis appears in Chapter 16. Miscue analysis is a similar process that teachers use to analyze reading mistakes. A description of how to conduct miscue analysis appears in Chapter 15.

Games   Games provide excellent opportunities for simulations and small- and large-group assessment. For example, teachers may use scores from academic games to assess student comprehension of specific ideas, theories, facts, or competencies.

Interviews   Teachers use many different types of interviews in the process of assessing student achievement. Interview formats range from highly structured to unstructured. Highly structured interviews rely on preset questions and recording of responses in a set manner. Unstructured interviews involve free-flowing conversations with topics discussed as they emerge. Interviewers may talk with students individually or in groups about preferences, learning styles, interests, goals, and interactions with others. Interviews may be single conferences or a series of conferences. Additional information about interviews appears in Chapter 16 as part of the discussion of - error pattern analysis in mathematics and in Chapter 18 in the description of portfolio conferences.

Observations   Observations of behavior and academic performance are keys to success in the assessment process. Observations are components in virtually all initial, annual, and reevaluation procedures. Because observations are so widely used, they encompass many forms and types. Observers may obtain valid data using several direct observation methods. Chapter 11 provides detailed information about specific types of direct observation. Observers may also collect anecdotal information by keeping written records of their observations of student achievement collected over time. Teacher observations generally consist of a series of ongoing, firsthand observations of student performance.

Portfolios   Portfolios are collections of student work showing progress and achievements. **Portfolio assessment** relies on authentic samples of genuine student work to evaluate performance. Portfolio assessment includes student participation in selecting the content, specific criteria for judging the content, and evidence of student self-reflection. Comprehensive information about portfolio assessment appears in Chapter 18.

Presentations   Individual and group presentations provide a way for students to demonstrate the skills used in the completion of an activity or the acquisition of curricular outcomes/expectations. Examples of presentations include skits, lectures, lab presentations, debates, and multimedia shows. Teachers use a variety of strategies to assess presentations. In some cases, teachers simply observe the presentation and give verbal feedback. Sometimes teachers write informal comments in the form of notes or more formal narrative feedback in the form of several written paragraphs. Teachers may also develop rating scales or checklists to grade presentations.

Rubrics   Rubrics provide guidelines for measuring achievement by describing learning outcomes, establishing clear performance criteria, and providing a rating scale or checklist for holistically evaluating performance. Rubrics list descriptors that serve as examples so that teachers and students know what characteristics or elements to look for in a work and how to place that work on a scale. Rubrics are best for overall evaluation of student performance, especially writing samples, problem-solving activities, and other tasks with varying levels of performance rather than right or wrong responses.

Running Records   Running records are tools for coding and analyzing reading behaviors. Taking running records involves sitting alongside students as they read an unfamiliar passage that is on their reading level. Running records use a set of generally accepted codes to record and number each oral reading miscue. One of the most important steps in taking running records is to look over the results to see what the student has done and then develop a brief summary of where the student is as a reader. Detailed information about running records is available in Chapter 15.

Self-Assessment   Self-assessment involves having students evaluate their own learning progress and learning goals. Self-assessment is an element of reflective teaching and learning in which learners have the opportunity to analyze their own progress. Self-evaluation is often difficult for students, especially for students with learning problems. Therefore, teachers need to model and guide students in small steps as they learn to become reflective learners.

Task Analysis   Task analysis involves breaking complex learning tasks into small steps to enable the learner to learn the tasks. Task analytic assessment consists of tracking progress in learning each step in the task and recording the progress with a chart or form. Chapter 13 contains detailed information and practical examples that show how to use task analysis as a CBA strategy.

TECHNOLOGY FOCUS
Test-Generation Software

Test-generation software programs enable teachers to type in questions, scoring criteria, test format information, and other test specifications using relatively simple, menu-driven computer software. Teachers can revise, review, modify, update, and print out the resulting tests. These software programs allow for mixing multiple-choice, short-answer, true-false, and other types of questions by selecting those that apply to them manually or having the computer randomly select them. For example, Schoolhouse Technologies offers several Windows-based software tools for creating instructional worksheets, activities, and tests for a wide range of student levels and abilities. Its products include Schoolhouse Test 2 (Schoolhouse Techologies, n.d.), a software program for developing quizzes, tests, and exams using a variety of questions types. Schoolhouse Test is easy to use and has several attractive features, including an interface that shows what the test will look like when it is printed and a answer key system that makes grading quick and accurate.

Although test-generation programs such as these have many attractive features, they also display limitations related to test security and student supervision, especially with computer-based test administration. In addition, many teachers lack access to the suitable computer hardware and software necessary to use these programs. Finally, flexibility limitations imposed by computer-based test-generation programs may make it difficult to adapt tests for learners with special needs.

Tests, Exams, and Quizzes Tests, exams, and quizzes are very helpful tools for measuring student achievement and performance. Teachers use many forms and varieties of class tests, exams, and quizzes. Specific information showing how to modify teacher-made tests to meet the needs of learners with disabilities appears in Chapter 3. Many teachers are now using computer software to generate classroom tests and other classroom-based assessments. Examples of available programs appear in the Technology Focus box.

Written Records Written records provide objective, narrative accounts of student performances, strengths, needs, progress, and negative/positive behaviors. Teachers routinely maintain many written records ranging from informal notes to formal reports.

Classroom Assessment Techniques

Classroom Assessment Techniques (CATs) are a specific type of CBA (Angelo, 1998) that help teachers determine what their students think about a class and how well they are learning class material. Unlike the CBA strategies discussed in the previous section, CATs focus on evaluating the effectiveness of the curriculum rather than evaluating student progress. CATs help teachers understand student learning with the goal of improving instruction rather than tracking the performance of an individual student or a group of students. For each of the following CATs, there is a definition of the procedure, an explanation of how to analyze the results, and an estimate of the time requirements to prepare, conduct, and analyze the technique.

Using CATs involves selecting a technique that provides helpful feedback for improving instruction. Make sure to select techniques consistent with your teaching style and easy to implement in your class. Next, explain the CAT to your students and conduct the assessment in class. After class, review and analyze the results and decide what changes in instruction, if any, to make based on the results of the assessment. Finally, let the students know what you learned from the CAT and how you will use the information.

Chain Notes   Chain notes involve arranging for students to pass around an envelope on which the teacher has written one question about the class, such as "What activity did you enjoy the most in this class?" Students spend a moment responding to the question and then place their responses in the envelope. Analysis involves reading and categorizing student responses. By discussing the responses with students, teachers can facilitate better teaching and learning. This strategy has low preparation, in-class, and analysis time requirements.

Exam Evaluations   Select a type of test that you are likely to give more than once or that has a significant impact on student performance. Create a few questions that evaluate the quality of the test. Add these questions to the exam or administer a separate, follow-up evaluation. Try to distinguish student comments that address the fairness of your grading from those that address the fairness of the test as an assessment instrument. Respond to the general ideas represented by student comments. The time requirements for preparing exam evaluations are medium. The in-class and analysis time requirements are low.

Minute Papers and 2-Minute Reflections   During the last few minutes of the class period, have students respond to two or three of the following questions on a half-sheet of paper: What is the most important point you learned today? What point remains least clear to you? What was the lesson about? What did you learn from this lesson? What did you find out about how you learn? The purpose is to elicit information and reflections from students' comprehension of information from a particular class. Review the responses and, during the next class, emphasize the issues illuminated by your students. Minute papers and 2-minute reflections have low time requirements in preparation, in class, and in analysis.

Student-Generated Test Questions   Have students write test questions and model answers for specified topics in a format consistent with course exams. This provides students the opportunities to evaluate the course topics, reflect on what they understand, and review the course material. Make a rough tally of the questions your students propose and the topics that they cover. Evaluate the questions and use the good ones as prompts for discussion. Consider revising the questions for use on an upcoming exam. The preparation time for this procedure is low, but the in-class and analysis time is high. Therefore, writing test questions may be a homework assignment.

Connecting Assessment with Instruction

Linking assessment with instruction is a key element of effective teaching, and CBA strategies connect assessment with instruction in ways that lead to positive learning outcomes for students. CBA promotes connections by helping teachers determine student progress in the curriculum. With most CBA strategies, teachers develop the assessment directly from curriculum materials. This creates a direct link with instruction and assessment. In addition to using CBA strategies, teachers also rely on commercially published, criterion-referenced tools such as the Comprehensive Inventory of Basic

Companion Website Resources

Curriculum-Based Assessment Strategies and Classroom Assessment Techniques

The Companion Website (www.prenhall.com/venn) describes additional curriculum-based assessment strategies including contracts, curriculum-based measurement, field trips, questionnaires, scales, simulations, student journals, and student profiles. Additional CATs on the Companion Web site include Application Cards, Directed Translation, Memory Cells, and Quick Summaries.

Skills, Revised, the Monitoring Basic Skills Progress (Fuchs, Hamlett, & Fuchs, n.d.), and the norm-referenced tests discussed later in this chapter. Commercial instruments like these can be useful tools for measuring student performance by using externally validated achievement standards.

Monitoring Basic Skills Progress   Monitoring Basic Skills Progress (MBSP) (Fuchs, Hamlett, & Kuchs, n.d.) is a curriculum-based computer program for automatically monitoring student progress in reading, math computation, and math concepts and applications. The computer provides students with immediate feedback on their progress, and provides teachers with individual and classwide reports to help them plan more effective instruction. Students complete the MBSP at the computer, and the computer automatically administers and scores the tests, giving students immediate feedback.

Comprehensive Inventory of Basic Skills, Revised   The Comprehensive Inventory of Basic Skills, Revised (CIBS-R) (Brigance, 1999) is a criterion referenced measure of academic achievement for students from kindergarten through grade 9. The widely used CIBS-R is actually a special type of CBA instrument with some of the features of the norm-referenced tests explained later in this chapter. For example, like the norm-referenced tests, the CIBS-R contains a fixed, standardized set of questions. However, like CBAs, Brigance developed the instrument for use without norms. Designed for use in elementary and middle schools, the CIBS-R is a valuable resource for programs emphasizing individualized instruction. The CIBS-R is especially helpful in programs serving students with special needs, especially in IEP development and program planning. The CIBS-R assesses specific areas of educational need, helps in the development of performance goals, provides indicators of progress on specific skills, and facilitates reporting to staff and parents. Teachers select assessments from the CIBS-R according to individual student needs. CIBS-R results are in terms of skills mastered or not mastered. Each skill section begins with systematic instruction on how to administer assessments, record performance, and develop instruction goals and objectives/IEPs. With the CIBS-R, as with most curriculum-based assessments, the teacher may give the complete assessment or parts of the instrument as needed. This flexibility allows the CIBS-R to serve as a curriculum guide that produces instructional objectives rather than a traditional test that produces scores. Instead of test score results, the CIBS-R provides assessment information that translates directly into remediation activities for individuals and small groups of students. A listing of the CIBS-R subtests appears in Table 14–2.

Giving and scoring the CIBS-R is informal and flexible, and the instrument can be adapted to accommodate different situations and needs. Giving the complete assessment takes at least several hours, and for this reason most teachers use only the relevant parts of the instrument.

Table 14–2 Comprehensive Inventory of Basic Skills, Revised Subtests

Readiness	Numbers
Speech listening	Number facts
Word recognition	Computation of whole numbers
Oral reading	Fractions/mixed numbers
Reading comprehension	Decimals
Word analysis	Percents
Functional word recognition	Time
Spelling	Money
Writing	Measurement/geometry
Graphs and maps	

The CIBS-R displays excellent face validity and measures important skills. As a result, it is appropriate for use as an informal, criterion-referenced tool. The CIBS-R is actually a set of "item pools" arranged in an informal checklist of skills with directories of teaching activities. This makes it a valuable curriculum-planning device, especially for identifying appropriate instructional intervention activities. Unfortunately, the CIBS-R has poor norms, making it unsuitable for use as a formal, norm-referenced test. The inadequate norms are a serious technical weakness and, for this reason, evaluators should avoid using scores from the norm-referenced subtests for identification and placement (Cizek, 2001; McLellan, 2001).

☑ Check Your Comprehension

As you can see from the many strategies included in this chapter, CBA is flexible, creative, thoughtful, and full of variety. CBA strategies are useful for assessing academic achievement in many different types of instructional settings, including general education classrooms. Many CBA strategies are quick and easy to implement, and they yield accurate evaluation results with useful feedback about the teaching-learning process and about student progress in the curriculum. Strategies for measuring student progress, assigning grades, and evaluating the effectiveness of the curriculum are all part of CBA. For these reasons, most teachers rely heavily on curriculum-based assessment to help plan appropriate instructional activities, respond directly to student learning needs, and connect assessment with instruction.

Norm-Referenced Assessment of Academic Achievement

Norm-referenced achievement testing plays an important role in educating students with special needs; consequently, there are hundreds of available tests. Some tests are survey batteries that provide a general overview of academic performance. Other tests provide more comprehensive, diagnostic information. Some of the tests are for groups of students and others are designed for individual students. All norm-referenced achievement tests have certain common characteristics, including a fixed set of test items measuring a clearly defined domain, specific directions for standardized administration and scoring, and norms developed from representative groups of students. The standardized administration and scoring procedures, along with the test norms, produce test scores allowing comparison of performance among individuals and groups. Although norm-referenced achievement tests have common characteristics, wide variability exists in the design and quality of these tests. Most, but not all, norm-referenced achievement tests are carefully developed and have excellent measurement qualities. For example, the Peabody Individual Achievement Test, Revised/Normative Update exhibits excellent design characteristics and outstanding technical properties. In contrast, the Wide Range Achievement Test, Expanded Edition has questionable technical qualities and weak content. These examples show that selecting norm-referenced achievement tests from among the many tests available requires study of the test content and material. In some situations, a group test of achievement best fulfills the purpose for the assessment. In other situations, an individually administered achievement test may provide the most useful evaluation information.

Norm-referenced achievement tests include group tests, multiple-skill tests, and single-skill tests. **Group achievement tests,** given to groups of students, are brief screening measures that provide an overview of achievement rather than specific diagnostic information. In contrast, most **multiple-skill achievement tests** are given individually and usually contain several subtests for measuring student proficiency across academic subjects. For example, most multiple-skill tests, such as the Wechsler Individual Achievement Test, Second Edition, include reading, mathematics, spelling, and writing subtests. Psychologists and educational diagnosticians use multiple-skill tests in the classification and placement process; teachers use them in classrooms as well. In later chapters, you will examine the **single-skill achievement tests** that provide in-depth data and information about student performance in single domains such as reading or mathematics and contain subtests for evaluating specific skills in those domains. For example, the single-skill tests of mathematics achievement, such as the KeyMath Diagnostic Test of Arithmetic, typically include subtests for assessing content, operations, and applications. As you can see, the great variety of assessment demands an understanding of decision making across many different academic subjects. However, the goal of all achievement assessment remains the same: to obtain information designed to meet the individual and often unique academic learning needs of students.

Group Tests

Group tests differ in format and content from individual tests because students take them all together at one time rather than individually. Often referred to as survey batteries, most group tests are brief screening instruments that give an overview of achievement. Group tests usually include subtests measuring the basic skills of reading, language, mathematics, and study skills. Study skills include library and reference skills and reading maps, graphs, and tables. In addition, some tests include content-oriented subtests for evaluating listening comprehension, science, and social studies. A few group tests also include written expression subtests that require students to write a brief essay. However, most schools test basic skills only because the content-oriented subtests become outdated quickly and may not match with the objectives in the local school curriculum (Linn & Miller, 2005).

High schools use group achievement tests less frequently because the wide range of classes and the variability in content make it hard to identify a common core of skills suitable for group testing. For this reason, most high school tests measure the same basic skills of reading, mathematics, language, and study skills as the elementary tests. This provides continuous measurement of these same skills across all grade levels in kindergarten through high school (Linn & Miller, 2005).

Group testing administration procedures often cause difficulties for diverse and at-risk students and students with learning problems for several reasons (McLoughlin &

Lewis, 2005). Group tests require reading ability, even when assessing skills other than reading. Thus, the test scores of students with reading problems may reflect reading skill deficits rather than lack of specific content knowledge. Students write their answers usually on separate, bubble-in answer sheets. This response mode is less than optimal for students with writing difficulties. Group administration requires students to work independently, self-monitor their behavior, and attend to test-taking tasks. Students with learning and behavior problems often fail to demonstrate these requisite behaviors. Because of these difficulties, students with disabilities frequently take tests with one or more accommodations such as extended testing time, additional rest breaks, separate testing locations, a test reader, or a recorder/writer of answers.

Almost all group tests use a multiple-choice format and are machine scored. In contrast, the individually administered tests, reviewed later in this chapter, sample a greater range of behaviors, and evaluators may score them by hand rather than by machine. When developers write test questions for group tests, they limit the items to content that fits on machine-scored, multiple-choice response sheets. This format makes most group tests screening-level instruments that identify the average of the group. In contrast, individual diagnostic tests provide in-depth information that translates into instructional objectives. Despite their limitations, group tests are widely used, especially to measure student achievement for accountability purposes. When group achievement tests are given near the end of the school year, they are often called high-stakes tests because the results carry significant consequences for students, schools, and educators. In fact, the stakes in high-stakes testing have been increasing over the years as educators and politicians have learned how to use the results to increase accountability for schools and students. Above-average school scores on the high-stakes test may bring public praise, but low scores definitely bring public embarrassment. For individual students, low scores may result in grade retention or denial of a high school diploma.

The most widely used group achievement survey batteries, listed by publisher (Web addresses for these publishers are available on the Companion Web site), include the following:

CTB McGraw-Hill

TerraNova, Second Edition (2000) (The TerraNova test series includes the California Achievement Tests and the Comprehensive Test of Basic Skills.)

Riverside Publishing

Iowa Tests of Basic Skills (ITBS) (Hoover, Dunbar, & Frisbie, 2001)
Iowa Tests of Educational Development (ITED) (Forsyth, Ansley, Feldt, & Alnot, 2001)

Harcourt Brace Educational Measurement

Stanford Achievement Test Series, Tenth Edition (Stanford 10) (2003)
Metropolitan Achievement Tests, Eighth Edition (2000)

Although the group tests provide valuable data and information for a variety of purposes, limitations reduce their effectiveness with students who have learning and behavior problems. The limitations are primarily associated with the format and administration procedures of group testing. Due to these limitations, educators and psychologists often use individual achievement tests more suited to the needs of students with disabilities.

Individual Achievement Tests

Individual, norm-referenced, multiple-skill achievement tests provide overall evaluation of performance across the major academic skills in the school curriculum. These tests are popular for several reasons, including the following:

- Coordination among subtests such as reading, math, and spelling
- Reduction of errors due to common administration and scoring across subtests
- Cost savings by using one test to assess achievement in multiple subjects
- Time savings by using one test to evaluate achievement in all subject areas
- Comparison of performance across subject areas with common norms (Kubiszyn & Borich, 2005)

Although individual, multiple-skill achievement tests exhibit many advantages over other tests, they also display certain disadvantages, including the following:

- Low reliabilities among subtests, reducing the validity of comparisons across subject areas
- Emphasis on broad coverage of many subject areas rather than in-depth coverage of one or more areas
- Limitations on the amount of specific diagnostic information available (Kubiszyn & Borich, 2005)

However, the advantages of multiple skill tests outweigh the disadvantages. Therefore, teachers, diagnosticians, and psychologists frequently use them to determine the overall achievement levels of students. From among the large number of available multiple-skill test batteries, teachers and diagnosticians rely on several tests most often. Reviews of each of these widely used instruments follow, beginning with the Peabody Individual Achievement Test—Revised/Normative Update.

Peabody Individual Achievement Test— Revised/Normative Update

The Peabody Individual Achievement Test—Revised/Normative Update (PIAT-R/NU) (Markwardt, 1998) assesses a wide range of academic ability across all major subjects of the school curriculum. Special educators frequently rely on this test, which is norm-referenced and individually administered, to provide a clear overview of scholastic achievement. A summary of the PIAT-R/NU appears in the Test Review box.

PIAT-R/NU Materials   The PIAT-R/NU materials include four test plate booklets, a manual, a test record, and a written expression booklet. The test plate booklets are in easel-kit fashion, providing a convenient and motivating way to present the test items. Scoring the PIAT-R/NU is much easier with the optional software that converts raw scores into derived scores and provides subtest comparisons. The software has a report option that includes a score summary report, profiles for standard scores and grade and age equivalents, and a personalized narrative report.

PIAT-R/NU Administration and Scoring   The PIAT-R/NU is designed for individual administration to students from kindergarten through high school, and it takes about 60 minutes to administer. The PIAT-R/NU produces a total test score, a total reading score, and scores for each subtest. These scores include age- and grade-based standard scores, age- and grade-equivalent scores, percentiles, normal curve equivalents, and

```
┌─────────────────────────────────────────────────────────┐
│                    TEST REVIEW                           │
```

Peabody Individual Achievement Test—Revised/Normative Update

Type of Test:	Norm-referenced
Purpose:	A diagnostic test of academic achievement
Subtests:	General information, reading recognition, reading comprehension, mathematics, spelling, and written expression
Administration Time:	Approximately 60 minutes
Age Levels:	Grades K through 12
Suitable for:	Students with mild and moderate disabilities, including learning disabilities, behavior disorders, educable mental retardation, sensory impairments, and physical disabilities
Scores:	Age- and grade-based standard scores, age- and grade-equivalent scores, percentiles, normal curve equivalents, and stanines
In Short:	The well-designed PIAT-R/NU is an excellent tool for measuring academic performance in the major subjects of the school curriculum.

stanines. The score sheet includes a profile for visual presentation of results. A sample PIAT-R/NU scoring form and scoring profile appear in Figure 14–1.

The manual provides a clear description of administration, scoring, and interpretation procedures, including a special form for reporting results to parents. The manual indicates that the evaluator may send the report form to parents if a meeting is not possible. In most situations, sending a technical report to parents instead of meeting directly with them is ill advised. The PIAT-R/NU manual suggests using the instrument for both screening and comprehensive diagnostic programming.

PIAT-R/NU Technical Characteristics Following a well-designed testing plan to ensure representation of the national population, the most recent version of the PIAT-R/NU incorporates a 1998 normative update based on a sample of over 3,000 people. The PIAT-R/NU developers used several methods of estimating the reliability of the scores, including split-half, test-retest, and item-response theory. Using a variety of reliability measures provides evidence from different perspectives to support the consistency of PIAT-R/NU scores. In terms of validity, the manual provides extensive evidence pertaining to the content, criterion-related, and construct validity of the test. Reviewers (Cross, 2001; Fager, 2001) concluded that the PIAT-R/NU is carefully designed and well constructed, with more than adequate technical and psychometric properties. The updated norms provide even further evidence of the high quality of this test.

Kaufman Test of Educational Achievement, Second Edition: KTEA-II

The Kaufman Test of Educational Achievement, Second Edition (KTEA-II) by Kaufman and Kaufman (2004) is both a screening test and a comprehensive diagnostic test of student achievement. The KTEA-II measures the academic performance of

Figure 14–1 Sample forms from the PIAT-R/NU

Norms Used: ☑ Updated ☐ Original

Grade Placement 2.9
Chronological Age 7-9

	RAW SCORES ①	DERIVED SCORES: ☐ Grade Equivalents ☑ Age Equivalents (Table G.1 or G.3) ②	Standard Scores ☐ Grade (G.2) ☑ Age (G.4) F W S (circle one) ③	Percentile Ranks (Table G.5) ④
	68 % confidence	68 % confidence	68 % confidence[3]	68 % confidence
General Information Raw Score *SEM* Values by Confidence Level — Grade / Age: K-7 / 5-13: 68% (3), 90% 5, 95% 6; 8-12 / 14-18+: 68% 2, 90% 3, 95% 4	60 (−SEM) · 63 · 66 (+SEM)	10-5 (−SEM) · 10-9 · 11-1 (+SEM)	127 (−SEM) · 131 · 135 (+SEM)	96 (−SEM) · 98 · 99 (+SEM)
Reading Recognition Raw Score *SEM* Values by Confidence Level — Grade / Age: K-12 / 5-18+: 68% (2), 90% 3, 95% 4	37 (−SEM) · 39 · 41 (+SEM)	8-0 (−SEM) · 8-2 · 8-2 (+SEM)	102 (−SEM) · 104 · 106 (+SEM)	55 (−SEM) · 61 · 66 (+SEM)
Reading Comprehension Raw Score *SEM* Values by Confidence Level — Grade / Age: / 5-6: 68% 4, 90% 7, 95% 8; K-12 / 7-18+: 68% (3), 90% 5, 95% 6	43 (−SEM) · 46 · 49 (+SEM)	8-2 (−SEM) · 8-5 · 8-7 (+SEM)	105 (−SEM) · 108 · 111 (−SEM)	63 (−SEM) · 70 · 77 (+SEM)
TOTAL READING[1] Raw Score *SEM* Values by Confidence Level — Grade / Age: 1-12 / 5-15: 68% (4), 90% 7, 95% 8; K / 16-18+: 68% 3, 90% 5, 95% 6	81 (−SEM) · 85 · 89 (+SEM)	8-1 (−SEM) · 8-3 · 8-4 (+SEM)	103 (−SEM) · 105 · 107 (+SEM)	58 (−SEM) · 63 · 68 (+SEM)
Mathematics Raw Score *SEM* Values by Confidence Level — Grade / Age: K-4 / 5-9: 68% (2), 90% 3, 95% 4; 5-12 / 10-18+: 68% 3, 90% 5, 95% 6	34 (−SEM) · 36 · 38 (+SEM)	8-8 (−SEM) · 8-10 · 9-0 (+SEM)	107 (−SEM) · 111 · 115 (+SEM)	68 (−SEM) · 77 · 84 (+SEM)
Spelling Raw Score *SEM* Values by Confidence Level — Grade / Age: K-6 / 5-17: 68% (2), 90% 3, 95% 4; 7-12 / 18+: 68% 3, 90% 5, 95% 6	33 (−SEM) · 35 · 37 (+SEM)	7-4 (−SEM) · 7-6 · 7-8 (+SEM)	92 (−SEM) · 95 · 98 (+SEM)	30 (−SEM) · 37 · 45 (+SEM)
TOTAL TEST[2] Raw Score *SEM* Values by Confidence Level — Grade / Age: K-8 / 5-14: 68% (6), 90% 10, 95% 12; 9-12 / 15-18+: 68% 5, 90% 8, 95% 10	213 (−SEM) · 219 · 225 (+SEM)	8-6 (−SEM) · 8-7 · 8-8 (+SEM)	106 (−SEM) · 108 · 110 (+SEM)	66 (−SEM) · 70 · 75 (+SEM)

[1] The Total Reading composite raw score is the sum of the Reading Recognition and Reading Comprehension subtest raw scores.
[2] The Total Test composite raw score is the sum of the General Information, Reading Recognition, Reading Comprehension, Mathematics, and Spelling subtest raw scores. Do not include the total Reading Composite raw score.
[3] Values to be used in the standard score confidence intervals are given in Appendix H of the manual.

Written Expression
☐ Level I
☑ Level II, Prompt (A) B (circle one)

Raw Score 28
Grade-based Stanine 5 ⑤
(Levels I and II) (*Table G.6 or G.7*)
Developmental Scaled Score 5 ⑥
(Level II only) (*Table G.8*)

WRITTEN LANGUAGE COMPOSITE
Spelling Raw Score 35 → 3 Scaled Score
Written Expression Raw Score 28 → 5 Scaled Score
(*Table I.1 or I.7*)
3 + 5
Scaled Score Sum 8

Standard Score
☐ Grade (*Table I.2 or I.8*)
F W S (circle one)
☑ Age (*Table I.3 or I.9*)
68 % confidence (*I.4 or I.10*)
92 (−SEM) · 95 · 98 (+SEM)

Percentile Rank
30 (−SEM) · 37 · 45 (+SEM)
(*Table G.5*)

Source: From *Peabody Individual Achievement Test—Revised/Normative Update (PIAT-R/NU)*, by F.C. Markwardt, 1998, Circle Pines, MN: American Guidance Service. Reprinted with permission of American Guidance Service, Inc.

(*continued*)

Figure 14–1 *continued*

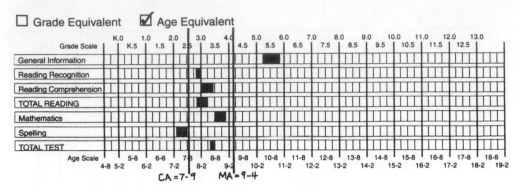

CA = 7-9   MA = 9-4

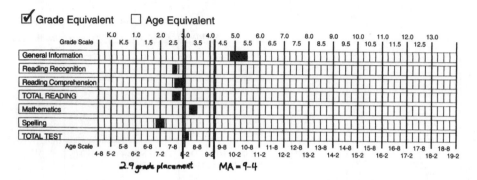

2.9 grade placement   MA = 9-4

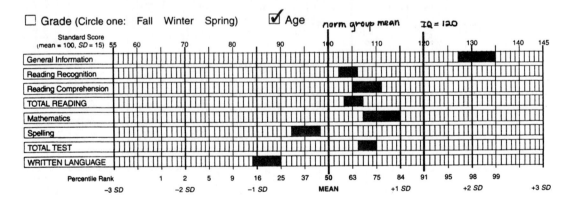

students from age 4H through adulthood using one of two forms. The brief form is a short screening test, and the comprehensive form is a complete battery for measuring achievement across all of the basic scholastic subjects. A summary of the KTEA-II appears in the Test Review box.

KTEA-II Materials   The Comprehensive Form Kit materials include 2 easel administration booklets, a manual, a norms book, 25 record forms, 25 student response booklets, 25 error analysis booklets, 2 each of 3 written expression booklets, all necessary stimulus materials, an administration CD, a puppet, and a tote bag. The KTEA-II Comprehensive Form can be scored by hand or with the optional computer scoring program. The computer scoring program quickly converts raw scores into derived scores, and it provides a student performance summary, subtest comparisons, achievement/ability

---

TEST REVIEW

Kaufman Test of Educational Achievement, Second Edition (KTEA-II)

Type of Test:	Norm-referenced
Purpose:	Screening and diagnosis of academic achievement
Subtests:	Reading decoding, reading comprehension, spelling, mathematics computation, and mathematics applications
Administration Time:	Approximately 1 hour for the comprehensive form and 30 minutes for the brief form
Age Levels:	Grades K through 12
Suitable for:	Students with mild and moderate disabilities, including learning disabilities, behavior disorders, educable mental retardation, sensory impairments, and physical disabilities
Scores:	Standard scores, age equivalents, grade equivalents, percentiles, stanines, and normal curve equivalents
In Short:	The well-designed KTEA-II provides a complete system for measuring academic achievement.

---

comparisons, error analysis for the standard subtests, and instructional suggestions for developing IEP goals by matching scores with intervention strategies.

KTEA-II Administration and Scoring   The KTEA-II Comprehensive Form takes about an hour to give, and the Brief Form takes about 30 minutes. Although the administration and scoring process is complex, it is well organized. Available KTEA-II scores include age- and grade-based standard scores (M = 100, SD = 15), age and grade equivalents, percentile ranks, normal curve equivalents (NCEs), and stanines. The KTEA-II offers two forms allowing measurement of progress and response to instruction, thus facilitating adjustment of intervention based on performance. The instrument also features enhanced error analysis for better remediation.

KTEA-II Technical Characteristics   The developers updated the norms for the KTEA-II with a group of more than 3,000 students. This normative update followed a well-designed development plan, resulting in norms that represent students from across the nation. The manual reports very good split-half and test-retest measures of reliability and presents both construct and concurrent validity data to demonstrate the effectiveness of the KTEA-II as an assessment instrument. The authors used a multistage approach to obtain construct validity data and correlated the KTEA-II with other tests. In summary, the KTEA-II displays very good technical qualities.

Wechsler Individual Achievement Test, Second Edition

The Wechsler Individual Achievement Test, Second Edition (WIAT-II) (Wechsler, 2001a) is a comprehensive diagnostic test of academic achievement. The WIAT-II is for individuals from age 4 through adulthood, and it includes norms for 2-year and 4-year college students. A brief version of the instrument, the Wechsler Individual Achievement Test, Second Edition, Abbreviated (WIAT-II-A) (Wechsler, 2001b) is available for obtaining a quick overview of skill development. The developers empirically linked the WIAT-II with a group of instruments that assist in assessment and intervention planning. These instruments include the Wechsler Intelligence Scale for Children, Fourth Edition (Wechsler, 2003), the Wechsler Preschool and Primary Scale of Intelligence, Third Edition (Wechsler, 2002), and the Wechsler Adult Intelligence Scale, Third Edition (Wechsler, 1997). The WIAT-II links with a new diagnostic tool, the Process Assessment of the Learner (PAL): Test Battery for Reading and Writing (Berninger, 2000). These linkages enable technically sound comparisons across the evaluation process. As a result, psychologists and special educators can make meaningful comparisons between achievement and ability that produce well-grounded curriculum and intervention decisions. The WIAT-II is useful for achievement skills assessment, learning disability diagnosis, special education placement, curriculum planning, and clinical appraisal. A summary of the WIAT-II appears in the Test Review box.

WIAT-II Materials   The complete WIAT-II kit includes two stimulus books, a package of 25 record forms, a package of 25 response booklets, and an examiner's manual and adult norms booklet all contained in a carrying bag. The WIAT-II developers designed the test materials to make administration as easy as possible and to hold the interest of children. The easel-type test booklets are easy to manage, and they contain colorful drawings and illustrations. An optional WIAT-II scoring software program has an automatic norms look-up feature and provides a basic report for exporting to a word processor for expansion.

WIAT-II Administration and Scoring   It takes about 50 minutes to administer the entire WIAT-II battery to young children and about 75 minutes to give to adolescents

---

TEST REVIEW

Wechsler Individual Achievement Test, Second Edition

Type of Test:	Norm-referenced
Purpose:	To comprehensively assess achievement for making diagnostic, placement, intervention, and curriculum programming decisions
Subtests:	Oral language, listening comprehension, written expression, spelling, pseudoword decoding, word reading, reading comprehension, numerical operations, and mathematics reasoning
Administration:	50 minutes for young children; 75 minutes for adolescents and adults
Age Levels:	4 years through adults, including norms for college students
Suitable for:	Obtaining achievement information to guide learning disability diagnosis, special education placement, curriculum planning, and clinical appraisal
Scores:	Age-and grade-based standard scores and composite score information; percentile ranks, stanines, NCEs, and age and grade equivalents
In Short:	The well-designed WIAT-II provides a rich and reliable source of information about achievement skills.

and adults. Evaluators can administer the entire battery or selected subtests for a more focused assessment. Designed for individual administration, the manual provides a clear description of administration, scoring, and interpretation procedures. The WIAT-II yields a variety of score results, including age- and grade-based standard scores and composite score information, percentile ranks, stanines, NCEs, and age and grade equivalents.

WIAT-II Technical Characteristics   Wechsler standardized the WIAT-II using a large representative sample that included individuals with learning disabilities, ADD, language-learning disabilities, mental handicaps, emotional disturbance, hearing impairment, and those who were gifted and talented. Fall, winter, and spring norms enable measurement of progress over the school year. The WIAT-II test manual provides solid evidence to support the reliability and validity of the WIAT-II as a diagnostic test of achievement for assessing academic difficulties.

Other Achievement Tests

Brief reviews of other representative achievement tests are given next, followed by a listing of other widely used achievement tests. These include screening instruments and diagnostic tests for children, youths, and adults.

Diagnostic Achievement Battery, Third Edition   The Diagnostic Achievement Battery, Third Edition (DAB3) (Newcomer, 2001) uses 14 short subtests to determine a child's strengths and weaknesses across several areas of achievement. Scores from these subtests combine to form eight composites. The DAB3 includes a supplemental manual enabling the examiner to probe student responses on the standardized test. The purpose of probing is to identify the thinking processes and problem-solving strategies that result in both correct and incorrect responses.

Diagnostic Achievement Test for Adolescents, Second Edition   The Diagnostic Achievement Test for Adolescents, Second Edition (DATA-2) (Newcomer & Bryant, 1993) measures the spoken language ability and academic achievement levels of students in grades 7 through 12. The DATA-2 subtests measure receptive vocabulary, receptive grammar, expressive grammar, expressive vocabulary, word identification, reading comprehension, math calculations, math problem solving, spelling, and writing composition. Three supplemental subtests measure science, social studies, and reference skills.

Hammill Multiability Achievement Test   The Hammill Multiability Achievement Test (HAMAT) (Hammill, Hresko, Ammer, Cronin, & Quinby, 1998) provides subtests in reading, writing, mathematics, and facts. HAMAT test scores include percentiles, standard scores, and age and grade equivalents. The test was normed on 2,901 students residing in 30 states. The developers linked (co-normed) the HAMAT with the Hammill Multiability Intelligence Test (HAMIT) (Hammill, Bryant, & Pearson, 1998). This allows examiners to compute discrepancy scores.

Scholastic Abilities Test for Adults   The Scholastic Abilities Test for Adults (SATA) (Bryant, Patton, & Dunn, 1991) is a norm-referenced screening test of academic achievement. Designed to measure the scholastic abilities of adults from 16 through 70 years of age, the SATA norms were developed from a sample of more than 1,000 people in 17 states. It measures aptitude and achievement and enables an aptitude-achievement discrepancy analysis for identifying adults who may have learning disabilities.

Tests of Achievement and Proficiency   The Tests of Achievement and Proficiency (TAP) (Scannell, Haugh, Loyd, & Risinger, 1996) instrument provides comprehensive and objective measures of students' progress in a high school curriculum. TAP is an individual diagnostic test with subtests for measuring skills in vocabulary, reading comprehension, written expression, math concepts, problem solving, math computation (optional), social studies, science, and information processing.

Woodcock-Johnson III Tests of Achievement   The Woodcock-Johnson III Tests of Achievement (WJ III ACH) (Woodcock, McGrew, & Mather, 2001a) is a comprehensive set of tests for measuring oral language and academic achievement. Designed for individuals from 2 to 90 years in kindergarten through graduate school, the WJ III ACH takes approximately 65 minutes to administer. WJ III ACH subtests include letter-word identification, reading fluency, passage comprehension, calculation, math fluency, applied problems, spelling, writing fluency, and writing sample. The Woodcock-Johnson III (WJ III), a revision of the widely used WJ-R, consists of two distinct, co-normed batteries: the WJ III Tests of Achievement (WJ III ACH) and the WJ III Tests of Cognitive Abilities (WJ III COG) (Woodcock, McGrew, & Mather, 2001b). Together these batteries comprise a wide age-range, comprehensive system for measuring general intellectual ability, specific cognitive abilities, scholastic aptitude, oral language, and achievement. Normative data are based on a single sample that was administered on both the cognitive and the achievement tests. This feature creates a diagnostic system for evaluating domain-specific skills with related cognitive abilities as well as traditional ability/achievement discrepancies. A complete review of the WJ III appears in Chapter 7.

Wide Range Achievement Test—Expanded Edition   The Wide Range Achievement Test—Expanded Edition (WRAT-EXPANDED) (Robertson, 2002) is an individual or group-administered screening test of academic achievement for kindergarten through adulthood. Although quick and easy to administer, the WRAT-EXPANDED suffers from questionable norms and other inferior technical qualities. Inadequate test content coupled with a lack of sufficient items to identify deficits in learning makes the WRAT-EXPANDED useful only as a rough screening measure. For this reason, evaluators should use the test cautiously, if at all.

With the increasing numbers of students whose primary language is Spanish, a critical need exists for achievement tests in Spanish. In response to this need, test publishers have developed a number of achievement tests specifically for students who speak Spanish. The Multicultural Considerations Focus box describes two representative tests.

☑ Check Your Comprehension

Individual achievement tests represent a major element of assessment in special education. Evaluators test virtually all students with mild or moderate disabilities by using at least one of these instruments; furthermore, diagnosticians and teachers repeatedly measure the achievement of some students with these tests. Fortunately, special educators may select from a variety of well-designed, individual achievement tests to conduct these evaluations. Although these multiple-skill tests serve many purposes, they fail to meet all of the assessment needs of students with mild and moderate disabilities. In some situations, students require more in-depth diagnostic evaluation. When this need occurs, special educators often prefer to use a single-skill achievement test or assessment procedure. Information about single-skill tests and procedures appears in Chapters 15, 16, 17.

MULTICULTURAL CONSIDERATIONS

Achievement Tests in Spanish

The shifting United States demographics have increased the need for assessing students with limited English proficiency, especially students for whom Spanish is the primary language. As a result, test publishers have developed achievement tests specifically for students who speak Spanish. Benefits include evaluating students' achievement levels in their native language and seeing students' progress relative to English-speaking peers. Available Spanish-language achievement tests include the Aprenda: La Prueba de Logros en Español, Segunda Edición (Aprenda 2) (1997) and the TerraNova SUPERA (1997). The Aprenda 2 is a norm-referenced achievement test specifically designed and created in Spanish to meet the needs of students who speak Spanish. Aprenda 2 assesses students in kindergarten through grade 12. Aprenda 2 subtests include reading, mathematics, language, and listening, with optional tests in writing and English. The instrument features optional open-ended assessments, performance standards, original reading and listening selections, an optional English subtest, and a companion nonverbal ability test. The Stanford Achievement Test Series, Ninth Edition (Stanford 9) is the comparable English-language achievement test for the Aprenda 2. The developers designed the norm-referenced TerraNova SUPERA specifically for native Spanish speakers. TerraNova SUPERA features include original literature with engaging artwork and themes and everyday contexts to measure reading, language arts, and mathematics. SUPERA subtests include reading, language arts, and mathematics.

1. In your view, how important is it to measure students' achievement levels in their native language? Why?

2. Most major publishing companies have equivalent Spanish-language versions of their major group achievement tests. Do you think this is helpful in instructional intervention with Spanish-speaking students who have special needs? Explain your answer.

3. Should students be tested in both their native language and in English?

To answer this reflection online, go to the *Multicultural Considerations* module on the Companion Web site at **www.prenhall.com/venn**.

Summary

Assessing achievement, the process of evaluating student learning through instruction, represents one of the most diverse elements of assessment in special education. Scholastic achievement encompasses appraisal techniques for students from kindergarten through adulthood and includes three major strands: reading, mathematics, and written language. These strands contain a wide range of skills across extended age levels, which accounts for much of the diversity in achievement testing. Another factor, the large assortment of tests and procedures for measuring achievement, also contributes to the diversity in achievement testing (see Table 14–3).

In addition to diversity, another notable aspect of achievement is its importance in schools where academics receive the highest priority, sometimes to the exclusion of other vital educational programs and services. At the same time, most students

Table 14–3 Review of Achievement Tests

Name	Type	Suitable for	Brief Description	Purpose
Aprenda: La Prueba de Logros en Español, Segunda Edición (Aprenda 2)	Screening test	Grades K–12	Specifically designed and created in Spanish to meet the needs of students who speak Spanish	To obtain present levels of performance in reading, mathematics, language, and listening with optional tests in writing and English
Comprehensive Inventory of Basic Skills—Revised (CIBS-R)	Individual diagnostic curriculum guide	Grades K–9	A criterion-referenced checklist of academic skills	To provide comprehensive content and curriculum features not available in traditional tests
Diagnostic Achievement Battery-3 (DAB3)	Individual screening test	Ages 6–14	Measures total achievement, listening, speaking, reading, writing, and mathematics	To obtain a general idea of overall achievement
Diagnostic Achievement Test for Adolescents, Second Edition (DATA-2)	Individual diagnostic test	Grades 7–12	Measures a variety of skills in vocabulary reading, math, writing, science, and social studies	To assess the achievement levels of adolescents in basic scholastic skills and in content areas
Hammill Multiability Achievement Test (HAMAT)	Group screening test	Ages 7–17	Measures skills in reading, writing, mathematics, and facts	To provide a quick, timely assessment of student ability that reflects the content of today's school curriculum
Iowa Tests of Basic Skills (ITBS)	Group screening test	Grades K–9	Measures reading, language, and mathematics	To assess student progress in the basic academic skills
Iowa Tests of Educational Development (ITED)	Group screening test	Grades 9–12	Measures vocabulary, ability to interpret literary materials,	To assess intellectual skills representing the long-term goals

Name	Type	Suitable for	Brief Description	Purpose
			correctness and appropriateness of expression, ability to do quantitative thinking, analysis of social studies materials, analysis of science materials, and use of sources of information	of secondary education, particulary critical-thinking skills of analysis and evaluation
*Kaufman Test of Educational Achievement, Second Edition (KTEA II)	Individual screening and diagnostic test	Grades K–12	Measures reading decoding, reading comprehension, spelling, mathematics computation, and mathematics applications	To provide a complete system for measuring academic achievement
Metropolitan Achievement Tests, Eighth Edition	Group screening test	Grades K–12	Measures achievement in basic skill areas of reading, math, and language	To assess the basic academic skills in the school curriculum
Monitoring Basic Skills Progress (MBSP)	Curriculum-based computer program	Grades K–6	Measures student progress in reading and mathematics	To automatically conduct curriculum based measurement and monitor student progress
*Peabody Individual Achievement Test—Revised/ Normative Update (PIAT-R/NU)	Individual screening test	Grades K–12	Measures general information, reading recognition, reading comprehension, mathematics, spelling, and written expression	To conduct wide-range screening of academic achievement in the major subjects of the school curriculum
Scholastic Abilities Test for Adults (SATA)	Individual screening test	Ages 6–70	Includes measures of aptitude and achievement	To measure the scholastic abilities of adults and help identify adults who may have learning disabilities

(continued)

Table 14–3 *continued*

Name	Type	Suitable for	Brief Description	Purpose
Stanford Achievement Test Series, Tenth Edition (SAT10)	Group screening test	Grades K–12	Includes the Stanford Early School Achievement Test (SESAT), the Stanford Achievement Test Series (SAT), and the Stanford Test of Academic Skills (TASK)	To assess basic academic skills
Tests of Achievement and Proficiency (TAP)	Individual diagnostic test	Grades 9–12	Subtests in vocabulary, reading comprehension, written expression, math concepts, problem solving, math computation (optional), social studies, science, and information processing	To provide a comprehensive and objective measure of students' progress in high school
TerraNova, Second Edition	A series of group screening tests	Grades K–12	A series of tests including the TerraNova Comprehensive Achievement Test (CAT) and the TerraNova Comprehensive Test of Basic Skills (CTBS)	To provide a wide range of content and assessment options in a modular architecture that makes it easy for school districts to meet specific educational standards, goals, and reporting requirements
TerraNova SUPERA	Group test	Grades K–12	Reading, language arts, and mathematics subtests feature original literature with engaging artwork, themes, and everyday contexts	Designed with native Spanish speakers in mind

Name	Type	Suitable for	Brief Description	Purpose
*Wechsler Individual Achievement Test, Second Edition	Individual diagnostic test	Ages 4–adults with norms for College Students	Includes measures of oral language, listening comprehension, written expression, spelling, pseudoword decoding, word reading, reading comprehension, numerical operations, and mathematics reasoning	To obtain information about an individual's academic skills to guide appropriate intervention, learning disability diagnosis, special education placement, curriculum planning, and clinical appraisal
Wechsler Individual Achievement Test, Second Edition, Abbreviated (WIAT-II-A)	Screening test	Ages 4–adults	Subtests in spelling, word reading, and numerical operations	To quickly identify skill deficits in spelling, reading, and math
Wide Range Achievement Test—Expanded Edition (WRAT EXPANDED)	Individual screening test	Kindergarten—adulthood	Measures reading recognition, arithmetic, and spelling	To screen the academic achievement of children and youth
Woodcock-Johnson III Tests of Achievement (WJ III ACH)	Individual diagnostic test	Ages 2–adulthood	Includes measures of letter-word identification, reading fluency, passage comprehension, calculation, math fluency, applied problems, spelling, and writing fluency	A comprehensive set of tests for assessing oral language and academic achievement with a wide age-range of individuals

*Tests marked with asterisks are featured in this chapter.

with special needs encounter significant difficulties in learning academic subjects. Because of the diverse nature and importance of academic achievement, special educators need a working knowledge of available tests so that they can select appropriate tools and conduct skillful evaluations. This knowledge, coupled with hands-on experience, helps teachers and other professionals make the best possible assessment decisions that respond to the academic needs of their students.

Special educators require a variety of measures because generic assessment models fail to meet unique academic needs and learning styles. Therefore, a blend of tools and techniques, including curriculum-based assessments and norm-referenced tests, provide data for educational decision making. This chapter provides an overview of curriculum-based assessment strategies along with reviews of multiple-skill tests. The following three chapters provide in-depth coverage of specific types of curriculum-based assessment and single-skill tests for evaluating student achievement in reading, mathematics, and written expression.

 Chapter review and application activities appear on the Companion Web site at *www.prenhall.com/venn*. The activities include multiple-choice review questions and essay questions in a self-assessment format with feedback.

Meeting Performance Standards and Preparing for Licensure Exams

After reading this chapter, you should be able to demonstrate the following CEC Standards and PRAXIS™ test knowledge and skills. The information in parentheses identifies where to find the particular CEC standard and PRAXIS™ content reference.

CEC Standards for Beginning Special Education Teachers

- Use and limitations of assessment instruments (CC8K4)
- Administer nonbiased formal and informal assessments (CC8S2)
- Use technology to conduct assessments (CC8S3)
- Interpret information from formal and informal assessments (CC8S5)
- Use assessment information in making eligibility, program, and placement decisions for individuals with exceptional learning needs, including those from culturally and/or linguistically diverse backgrounds (CC8S6)
- Evaluate instruction and monitor progress of individuals with exceptional learning needs (CC8S8)
- Develop or modify individualized assessment strategies (CC8S9)
- Create and maintain records (CC8S10)

PRAXIS™ Education of Exceptional Students: Core Content Knowledge

- Assessment, including use of assessment for screening, diagnosis, placement, and the making of instructional decisions, for example, how to select and conduct nondiscriminatory and appropriate assessments; how to interpret standardized and specialized assessment results (0353 III)
- Assessment, including procedures and test materials, both formal and informal, typically used for prereferral, screening, referral, classification, placement, and ongoing program monitoring (0353 III)
- Assessment, including how to select, construct, conduct, and modify nondiscriminatory, developmentally and chronologically age-appropriate informal assessments, including teacher-made tests, curriculum-based assessment, and alternatives to norm-referenced testing (including observations, anecdotal records, error analysis, miscue analysis, self-evaluation questionnaires and interviews, journals and learning logs, and portfolio assessment) (0353 III)

chapter 15

Assessing Reading Achievement

Objectives

After reading this chapter, you will be prepared to do the following:

- Define reading achievement.
- Use clinical observation to assess reading performance.
- Develop diagnostic checklists to assess oral reading, silent reading, and reading comprehension.
- Conduct miscue analysis to evaluate reading performance.
- Use cloze procedures to evaluate reading performance.
- Gather running records to evaluate reading performance.
- Use informal reading inventories.
- Construct teacher-made informal reading inventories.
- Use norm-referenced reading tests.

Overview

In this chapter, you will investigate curriculum-based measurement procedures and tests for assessing reading achievement. Reading, a complex process of understanding printed or written material, requires many skills and perceptual processes. Teachers, parents, and students place a high value on learning to read, and it represents the most important academic skill in the school curriculum. During the early grades, students with reading deficits experience difficulty because most of the curriculum focuses on emerging literacy and other language-based skills. In the later grades, poor readers have problems because mastery of most subjects requires well-developed reading skills. Because it is such an important skill, more measurements and tests are available to assess literacy skills than any other academic subject. This chapter enables you to develop your knowledge and skills of assessment in this key scholastic domain. Your study of literacy assessment includes review of curriculum-based assessment procedures, informal reading inventories, and norm-referenced reading tests. As you review these assessments, you will consider the purpose, administration, scoring, and interpretation of each instrument or procedure. You will also consider the diagnostic uses, educational implications, and practical applications of each assessment.

The Importance of Assessing Reading

The following narrative illustrates one of the many reasons for assessing the reading achievement of students with special needs.

Timmy, a bright, outgoing, husky 10-year-old, worked at many of his school assignments with enthusiasm but often became frustrated with reading tasks. As a result, he sometimes misbehaved in class. Timmy's teacher thought he was an intelligent student who just didn't try hard enough, especially in reading, and she was frustrated with Timmy's misbehavior. The baffled and discouraged teacher decided to refer Timmy to the child-study team, who assigned a diagnostician to give Timmy an individually administered diagnostic test of achievement. The results indicated that he performed much lower in reading than in math and general information. More specifically, the results suggested a particular weakness in reading recognition. When the child-study team reviewed the results with the teacher, she realized that Timmy's poor performance in class may have been due to a reading problem rather than lack of effort.

The child-study team recommended further assessment, and the teacher worked with the diagnostician to identify the specific nature of the problem so that they could provide special assistance for Timmy. The special assistance included use of an assessment procedure called miscue analysis, which pinpointed Timmy's problems in reading recognition. In Timmy's case the miscue analysis revealed a consistent pattern of visual closure errors in which Timmy seemed to see only parts of some words rather than whole words. The problem was particularly evident with compound words such as birthday, something, and baseball. When the teacher gave Timmy special help with syllables and whole words, his reading recognition skills began to improve.

Definition of Reading

Composed of many complex skills, reading involves understanding the meaning of printed or written material. Reading readiness, for example, encompasses prerequisite skills such as letter and shape recognition, left-to-right sequencing, and top-to-bottom progression. Beyond the readiness level, further reading skills include the following:

- Reading recognition, a word-attack skill involving correctly pronouncing words aloud
- Reading comprehension, a skill consisting of understanding and attaching meaning to written material
- Silent reading, which is characterized by lack of speech or sound and relies on special skills assessed separately from the other types of reading

Scholastic success as well as success in most vocational settings requires reading proficiency; therefore, it is unfortunate that so many students exhibit deficits in this area. In fact, experts consider reading difficulties to be the most common academic learning problem. For this reason, special educators should possess a thorough understanding of methods for assessing and teaching literacy. The accompanying Multicultural Considerations feature discusses the importance of early intervention in addressing reading problems.

MULTICULTURAL CONSIDERATIONS

Reading Assessment with At-Risk Learners

A growing body of evidence suggests that reading problems are preventable for the vast majority of students who encounter difficulty in learning to read if these students receive extra support in the form of an early intervention program (Pikulski, 1998). The term *early intervention* refers to early school intervention programs designed to prevent problems in literacy from developing rather than trying to correct problems after the fact. Most such programs focus on at-risk children, including students who are English language learners, and several of these programs have proven effective when compared to conventional compensatory reading programs. A number of factors seem characteristic of successful intervention programs, including an emphasis on reading for meaning, intensive intervention instruction on a frequent and regular basis, a small pupil-to-teacher ratio, fast-paced instruction, and assessment that is meaningful, practical, efficient, and ongoing.

The most common form of practical assessment in successful early intervention programs is evaluation of oral reading performance using passages that have been part of instruction. Experts use various terms such as *running records, miscue analysis,* and *oral reading checks* to describe the process of measuring student progress in oral reading. Regardless of the specific type of ongoing oral reading assessment system, evidence suggests that this type of curriculum-based assessment is an important element in successful early intervention programs, including programs for students from culturally and linguistically diverse backgrounds.

Give examples of cultural behaviors that would hinder development of reading skills in young preschool children.

To answer this reflection online, go to the *Multicultural Considerations* module on the Companion Website at *www.prenhall.com/venn.*

FOCUS 15-1

Why Do We Assess Reading?

- To screen students who may have deficits in reading
- To identify and place students with reading disabilities
- To plan reading instruction and intervention programs
- To identify present levels of reading performance
- To develop IEP goals in reading
- To assess student progress in reading
- To monitor the effectiveness of reading programs

Why Do We Assess Reading Achievement?

Special educators assess the reading achievement of children with special needs for several reasons. The overall goal of reading assessment is to inform the teaching and learning process. More specifically, reading assessment helps screen students who may have deficits in reading, identify and place students with reading disabilities, plan reading instruction and intervention programs, identify present levels of reading performance, develop IEP goals and objectives in reading, assess student progress in reading, and monitor the effectiveness of reading programs (see Focus 15–1). Different CBA techniques and reading tests exist for each of these purposes. Screening students with potential reading problems is an essential first step in the assessment process, and specially developed screening tests exist for this purpose. In contrast, identification and placement of students with reading disabilities relies on individually administered, norm-referenced reading tests. Although teachers sometimes use norm-referenced tests in instructional planning and intervention with students, most rely primarily on less formal, curriculum-based reading assessment techniques. Teachers select particular curriculum-based assessments from a series of strategies that are directly linked with instructional intervention.

☑ Check Your Comprehension

Reading, a complex process involving many skills, is the most important academic subject in the elementary school curriculum, and in later grades most subjects require well-developed reading skills. Therefore, it is unfortunate that reading difficulties are such a common academic learning problem. Because it is so complex and important, test developers have created more tests for assessing literacy than any other academic skill. When teachers assess reading, they should consider the needs of students from diverse backgrounds and students who are at risk for failure. Teachers should give particular attention to the best ways of using curriculum-based strategies for assessing reading.

Curriculum-Based Reading Assessment

Teachers and diagnosticians use many informal, curriculum-based assessment strategies to measure reading performance and develop instructional objectives and activities. With curriculum-based assessment, teachers use student work such as in-class reading assignments, class papers, homework, and class tests to evaluate reading skill and development. Curriculum-based assessment also allows teachers to conduct evaluation as part of the ongoing learning activities in the classroom. This links assessment directly with the curriculum and helps to make evaluation an integral part of the teaching and learning process.

The use of technology is becoming more widespread in all areas of education, including in reading assessment. Teachers are continually finding new and innovative ways to employ both old and new technology to help them assess the reading progress of their students. A list of helpful technology tools for assessing reading, including some great gadgets, appears in the Technology Focus box.

Like all appraisal procedures, curriculum-based reading assessment has drawbacks. One problem is conducting assessment in ways that produce reliable and valid results. In actual operation, many curriculum-based procedures, especially the observational techniques, lack the precision necessary to accurately measure the complexities associated with reading. This occurs in part because reading is an interactive process, and it is difficult to isolate individual skills. Reading comprehension, for example, must be inferred because it is an internal process that cannot be directly observed. Furthermore, different approaches to teaching reading require somewhat different assessment procedures. The challenge is to refine curriculum-based assessment in ways that overcome these limitations.

Despite difficulties, curriculum-based assessment has many advantages. The primary advantage is the ability to evaluate student performance in direct relation to the curriculum. This allows the teacher to make educational decisions based on actual reading behavior. Teachers have a special interest in this type of assessment because it connects evaluation with instruction in ways that inform the teaching and learning process. Specific curriculum based techniques discussed in this chapter include clinical observation, diagnostic checklists, miscue analysis, cloze procedures, and running records.

TECHNOLOGY FOCUS
Great Gadgets for Reading Assessment

Recording reading progress using old and new technology can be efficient and effective. The challenge is to recognize significant learning events that need documentation and identify appropriate technology that can help in the assessment process. Because technology can also complicate things, teachers should carefully select suitable technology tools. The best technology gadgets help free teachers up to focus on the students. Buckleitner (2001) suggested the following handy gadgets for record-keeping, listed from low- to high-tech.

Sticky Notes

Sticky notes do not need batteries, and they provide a great way to document key learning events over the course of a day. Teachers can stick them directly on a student's paper, a classroom newsletter, or a note going home to attract attention to something specific. For example, a teacher can write something positive to parents about their children on sticky notes and then place the sticky notes on the students' cubbies on Friday afternoons for parents to see at pick-up time.

Tape Recorders

Teachers can use small, portable voice recorders that easily fit in a pocket to keep notes on student learning, including first attempts at reading, singing,

> **Great Gadgets for Reading Assessment (continued)**
>
> counting, or telling a story. For students who are learning English as a second language, a recorder is a great device for tracking emerging reading abilities over time. This can be accomplished by having students describe the same picture or read the same passage at different points in the year.
>
> **Photocopiers**
>
> Photocopiers have many assessment uses, including making quick copies of a student paper for portfolios that document reading progress. Teachers can also use a photocopier to enlarge small sections of student writing samples for display.
>
> **Scanners**
>
> Scanners work like photocopiers, except the images appear on a computer monitor. Teachers can e-mail student work to parents, send it home on a computer disk, post it on a Web page, or print it. Students enjoy seeing their work being scanned and older students can scan their own work. Scanners also enable development of electronic portfolios.
>
> **Software**
>
> More and more teachers, schools, and school districts are using software programs to help students build reading skills and to help teachers measure learning. For example, Merit Software offers programs in reading fundamentals, reading comprehension, and ESL grammar. Renaissance Learning offers a series of reading programs, including Accelerated Reader, STAR Reading, and STAR Early Literacy, that combine technology with professional development to help improve student test scores and build critical-thinking skills. The Learning Company sells the widely used Edmark Reading program software for students with severe disabilities. Widely used reading software is also available from Knowledge Adventure and The Learning Village. Computer-based reading programs keep records of student skill development so that teachers can check progress at any time, print out reports, and conduct other assessment tasks.

Clinical Observation

Observing students, often called **clinical observation**, involves directly and systematically observing students in different reading situations. Observation gives teachers an impression of students' reading abilities, their awareness of books, and their social development. Teachers sometimes write notes from impressions formed during observations to provide evidence of progress. Although observation is part of all types of informal and formal assessment, it is essential in specific situations. For example, observation is the best way to assess behaviors such as student motivation and attention, two important factors in reading success. When used as an assessment procedure, teachers should observe student reading performance over a period of time and in different situations, including oral reading, silent reading, casual reading, small-group instruction, and class testing. Specific observation techniques include observation at a distance and close-in observation.

Observation at a distance involves periodically taking 5 minutes or so to watch students. The teacher should explain the process to the students, so they know to avoid interrupting during this brief time. When observing reading activities such as sustained silent reading, the teacher can answer questions such as: Do the students select appropriate books? How many students actually read? How long do the students read?

Close-in observation involves individual students. Questions the teacher can answer include: Does the student show interest in the reading material? What reading strategies does the student appear to be using? Which reading activities seem to be easy and difficult for the student? What does the student do after finishing the reading material? (Booth, Swartz, & Zola, 1994).

Teachers can record their observations in a variety of formats, including simply writing down their observations on notepaper or in a notebook or constructing a checklist of reading behaviors. Teachers can place completed checklists in student folders or portfolios and update them with additional observations to show progress over time. Observation is rarely a one-time event. Instead, observations should occur throughout the year. Although this requires planning, it avoids the situation in which teachers realize that they have no observational assessment data with which to provide an accurate picture of student progress.

One way to obtain observational information over time is to record observations of one or two students per day or to conduct observations during part of one day a week or one week a month. During these periods, the teacher concentrates on observation while the students continue their normal activities. Mercer and Mercer (2005, p. 300) provide a set of questions that teachers should keep in mind when observing student reading performance. These questions appear in Focus 15–2.

Teachers can use clinical observation by itself, but most combine their observations with other types of assessment. For example, teachers can combine their observations with norm-referenced test results and data from teacher made checklists of reading behavior. These three sources of assessment data, when used together, provide a comprehensive picture of student progress and achievement in reading.

Diagnostic Checklists

When teachers want to systematically record observations, they often use diagnostic checklists, which pinpoint behaviors in chart format, making it easy to document

FOCUS 15-2

Questions Teachers Should Ask When Observing Reading Performance

1. What is the student's attitude toward reading?
2. What specific reading interest does the student have?
3. Is the student making progress in reading?
4. What strengths and weaknesses in reading does the student exhibit?
5. During oral reading, does the student read word by word or with fluency?
6. What kinds of errors does the student make consistently?
7. What word analysis skills does the student use?
8. Does the student use context clues to recognize words?
9. Does the student have good sight vocabulary?
10. Does the student appear to pay attention to the meaning of the material when reading?

performance and keep notes. Teachers use diagnostic checklists to assess many different reading behaviors, but checklists are especially useful for gathering information about student reading style. Checklists produce a permanent record, and they can be designed to record multiple observations, to provide space for making brief written comments about specific behaviors, and to write notes about the student and the assessment. Checklists with blank rows also give room for adding other significant behaviors that the teacher may notice during observation or instruction. Although teachers need not document all observations by recording student behavior on a checklist or other data form, such records produce a permanent account useful for identifying present levels of performance, making referrals, determining possible intervention activities, and measuring progress. Checklists are especially helpful in evaluating oral reading.

Oral Reading

When teachers use diagnostic checklists to assess oral reading style, they should look for specific behaviors. A diagnostic checklist of oral reading style that lists these behaviors (Smith, Finn, & Dowdy, 1983; Zigmond, Vallecorsa, & Siverman, 1983) appears in Figure 15–1.

Figure 15–1 Diagnostic checklist of oral reading

| Student _____ | | | | Teacher _____ |
| Grade Level of Passage _____ | | | | Date _____ |

Oral Reading Behavior	Observations			Comments
	1	2	3	
1. Reads expressively				
2. Reads clearly with good pronunciation				
3. Reads at an appropriate rate				
4. Reads for meaning				
5. Observes punctuation				
6. Not easily frustrated				
7. Attempts unfamiliar words				
8. Uses morphological skills				
9. Uses context clues				
10. Displays good comprehension				
11. Other notable behaviors (specify)				

Notes _____

_____

_____

Figure 15–2 Diagnostic checklist of silent reading

| Student _____ | Teacher _____ |
| Grade Level of Passage _____ | Date _____ |

Silent Reading Behavior	Observations			Comments
	1	2	3	
1. Points to individual words				
2. Runs a finger under each line				
3. Runs a finger down the page				
4. Whispers words				
5. Says words aloud				
6. Moves head while reading				
7. Holds book too close				
8. Holds book too far away				
9. Reads too slowly				
10. Reads too quickly				
11. Other notable behaviors (specify)				

Notes _____

_____

_____

Silent Reading

Hargrove and Poteet (1984) identified the 10 behaviors in the silent reading checklist shown in Figure 15–2. Silent reading is assessed by observing a student reading suitable passages. Teachers should have the student read several passages at various levels of difficulty to detect whether any problem behaviors occur with passages that are more difficult.

Reading Comprehension

Reading comprehension occurs at several levels, including the following:

Factual:	recognizing and recalling facts, including the main idea
Organizational:	classifying, categorizing, and summarizing
Inferential:	interpreting and predicting
Evaluation:	judging (e.g., reality, appropriateness)
Analysis:	questioning, identifying feelings, and expressing opinions

The process of evaluating reading comprehension includes several steps, beginning with selecting appropriate reading passages and preparing a set of comprehension

Figure 15–3   Diagnostic checklist of reading comprehension

Student _____				Teacher _____

Grade Level of Passage _____   Date _____

Reading Comprehension Level	Observations			Comments
	1	2	3	
1. Answers factual questions about the passage				
2. Classifies, categorizes, and summarizes the passage				
3. Makes inferences and predictions based on the passage				
4. Answers valuative questions about the passage				
5. Critically analyzes the passage				
6. Other notable behaviors (specify)				

Notes _____
_____
_____

questions based on the selections. After the student reads the selected passages, the teacher asks questions that gauge comprehension at each level. Finally, the teacher analyzes the answers to identify the student's comprehension level and develop instructional objectives. Error rates of 25% or more indicate student frustration and difficulty in understanding the meaning of a passage. When this occurs, the evaluator should select an easier passage and repeat the procedure to establish the student's instructional level for reading comprehension, which is defined as missing less than 25% of a set of comprehension questions. The diagnostic checklist of reading comprehension (Luftig, 1989) shown in Figure 15–3 includes space for up to three observations about each observed behavior.

Miscue Analysis

One of the most widely used curriculum-based assessment procedures is **miscue analysis**. Also called *error analysis*, the technique involves systematically measuring and evaluating student mistakes and using the results to plan remediation. The technique is helpful in determining error patterns as well as chronic errors and is best when used to assess oral reading skills. Subjects such as mathematics, spelling, and written expression also lend themselves to miscue analysis.

With oral reading, teachers use the procedure to measure and evaluate common student mistakes. Typical oral reading errors include the following:

1. Mispronunciations: "gran" instead of "grain"
2. Omissions: "reading is process" instead of "reading is a process"
3. Insertions: "on a the table" instead of "on the table"
4. Repetitions: "What, what's the matter?" instead of "What's the matter?"

Miscue analysis reveals whether a student makes one or more of these mistakes in oral reading persistently or in a random fashion. Identifying patterns leads directly to developing intervention goals and activities.

The miscue analysis process begins with identifying a suitable group of reading passages. Appropriate passages may be selected from class textbooks and reading materials of interest to a student. The passages should be at or near the student's current reading level. Next, as the student reads, the teacher records the errors on a copy of the passage. The teacher then analyzes the performance to identify the patterns of errors and chronic errors. Finally, the teacher summarizes the results, providing a basis for developing instructional objectives and intervention activities. For example, in Figure 15–4, Pamela's oral reading sample reveals a consistent error in omitting word endings. Specifically, Pamela omitted endings such as -*ed*, -*ing*, and -*a* in oral reading. The sample passage contains 55 words, and Pamela made 6 errors. This calculates into an error rate of approximately 11% (6/55 = 11%). Error rates of 10% and higher indicate that the passage is too difficult and frustrating for the student. When this happens, the evaluator should repeat the analysis procedure with an easier passage to establish the student's instructional level, which is reading with at least 95% accuracy. In the sample passage, the student needs assistance with ending sounds and units. The teacher may attempt one of several interventions to help with this problem, including visual discrimination exercises focusing on recognizing whole words and special instruction to help Pamela build skills with syllables and whole words.

Running Records

Like miscue analysis, running records assess text reading. Teachers use running records to guide teaching, assess text difficulty, and capture progress (Clay, 2000). Running records give teachers a way to analyze reading "on the run," so to speak. The analysis provides insights or "windows" into the reading process by pointing to the meaning, structural, and visual cues students use when reading. Teachers can use running records with text in any language. The basic steps in taking, scoring, and analyzing running records (Rug, 2001) follow.

Figure 15–4   Sample miscue analysis

kitty   *Susan*
A big, gray kit<u>ten</u> named Susan<u>a</u> ran away from her mother.

play
She found a ball. She play<u>ed</u> with it. A big dog came

run   *want*
run<u>ning</u> by. She was afraid and want<u>ed</u> to go home, but she did not know the way. Her mother had been looking for her.

Susan
When she found Susan<u>a</u>, she took her home.

How to Take Running Records

1. Have a student read a passage from a book to you.

2. As the student reads, use a record form like the sample record form in Figure 15–7 or a blank sheet of paper to mark the reading behavior and record miscues.

3. If the student stops during reading, allow the student enough time to read the word or phrase before supplying it. At the same time, do not wait so long that the student loses the meaning of the story while trying to solve the unknown word.

4. Use a structured system to record words read correctly, substitutions, omissions, and deletions.

5. Take note of self-corrections, which indicate the reader is monitoring comprehension.

6. Note hesitations, repetitions, and other reading behaviors that may not affect accuracy but provide information about the strategies the reader is using.

How to Score Running Records   Score substitutions, insertions, omissions, and teacher-told responses as errors, but do not score repetitions as errors. Score corrected responses as self-corrections and avoid penalizing attempts that result in a correct response. Score multiple unsuccessful attempts at a word as one error only. Score each word omitted as an error. If the reader omits a page, deduct the number of words on the page from the total word count. If the reader repeatedly makes an error with a proper noun, count this as an error the first time only. All other incorrect responses count as errors each time. Do not count pronunciation differences as reading errors unless accompanied by incorrect locating responses.

To obtain a percentage of accuracy score, divide the number of words read correctly by the total number of words and multiply by 100. The percentage of accuracy data indicates the level of difficulty of the selected text for the reader: easy, instructional, or difficult. Use the following levels: Independent Reading Level—over 95% accuracy, Instructional Reading Level—90 to 95% accuracy, and Frustration Level—below 90% accuracy.

How to Check Cue Usage   For each miscue, try to determine whether the reader used cues from the meaning (semantics), the structure of the language (syntax), the visual information contained in the print (graphophonics), or a combination of these. The most common reading miscue is substituting another word for the one that is in the text. Other miscues include omissions, insertions, or repetitions. Understanding miscues in the reading process requires knowledge of cueing systems. When students use meaning cues, they apply background knowledge and the context of the sentence or passage to identify words. When students use visual cues, they apply what they know about letter-sound correspondences to decode words. When students use structural cues, they apply knowledge about how language goes together to identify words.

For self-corrections, try to analyze what led the reader to make the error and what cueing system the reader used to correct it. Finally, review the cues used to find out which cue or cues the reader used most often. The goal is for the reader to use all cue sources together in order to decode accurately.

How to Check Comprehension   Because the procedure focuses on test reading skills rather than on comprehension skills, some teachers choose to conduct a comprehension check as part of the process. One way to accomplish this is to simply have the reader retell the story. Retelling provides an indication of what the reader knows about the story structure, the sequencing, the most important information, and the story details. Asking comprehension questions is a faster way to check comprehension. The questions should include factual and inferential questions.

Samples of running record recording and scoring forms from the Center for the Education and Study of Diverse Populations (2001) appear in Figures 15–5, 15–6, and 15–7. The sample in Figure 15–5 illustrates the process of taking running records. Figure 15–6 gives examples of some of the notations used in a running records system. A sample analysis form appears in Figure 15–7.

Cloze Procedures

The **cloze procedures** are informal tests of word prediction abilities for measuring comprehension skills and the way students use cues to identify words. Like miscue

Figure 15–5   Sample running record

Text	Student's Oral Reading	Running Record
The cow hid in the garden.	The cow hid in the grass.	✔✔✔✔✔ grass / garden
The dog hid in the shed.	The dog hid in the shop.	✔✔✔✔✔ shop / shed
The duck hid in the closet.	The duck hid in the closet.	✔✔✔✔✔✔
The pig hid under the bed.	The pig hid uh, uh.. the bed, under the bed.	✔✔✔ uh..uh - SC ✔✔ / under

Figure 15–6   Running records notation system

Notations	Descriptions of the Notations
✔✔✔✔✔✔	Accurate reading
✔✔ girl / Lady	Substitution: The student substituted the word; the actual text appears on the bottom.
✔✔ was - / Was	Self-Correction (SC): The student read the word incorrectly but then self-corrected the word.
✔✔ n-n..ne / Name	A - Appeal: The student asked for help. / T - Told: The teacher gave the word.
✔✔ ~ / man	Omission or Skip: The student completely skipped the word.
SC ⟵ R / ✔✔ man ✔✔✔ / moon	Self-Correction (SC) and Repeat (R): The student goes back and rereads a phrase or a sentence for clarity.
✔✔ the ✔✔ / ~	Insertion: The student inserts a word that is not there.

Figure 15-7 Sample running record analysis form

Identifying Information

Name: _Dixon Graves_   Date: _February 18_   Grade: _Third_

School: _Mayport Elementary_

Recorder: _Margaret Cody_   Book Title: _Ramona Quimby_   Reading Level: _Age 8_
(Third-Grade Level)

Page #	Running Record	# of Es	# of SCs	Error Analysis*	Self-Correction Analysis*
37	X X X X X X X X Mrs. Quimby said <u>said Mrs. Quimby</u>	II		MSV MSV	
	X X X X X X X X				
	X forget/forgot X X X X X X X	I		<u>M</u> S V	
	X X X X X				
	X X X X X X X X				
	X X X X X X X				
	ex..expl.. / exasperation X X X X X X	I		M S <u>V</u>	
	X X X X X X				
	X X ho.../horrid X X X X I				
38	X X X X X X X X				
	X X X X X X now/know X X X	I	1	M S <u>V</u>	<u>M</u> S <u>V</u>
	X X X X X X X X X				
	X X X X X X				
	bring/being X X X X X X X	I	1	M S <u>V</u>	<u>M</u> S <u>V</u>
	hard/harder X X X	I		M S <u>V</u>	
	accepted/expected X X X X X X X X X X X	I		M S <u>V</u>	

Results Summary

*M: Meaning, S: Structure, V: Visual

Running Words (RW): _127_   Errors (E): _2_   Error Rate (ER): _1 : 16_

Self-Corrections (SC): _2_   Self-Correction Rate (SCR): _2 : 4_   Accuracy (ACC): _94%_

Observations: _Dixon read with good comprehension. His initial attempts were overly dependent on syntax and visual clues._

Next Learning Steps: _Given his accuracy rate of 94%, Dixon appears ready for more difficult text._

analysis, the cloze procedures enable teachers to determine a student's reading level using a textbook or some other readily available reading material. The most common procedure, visual cloze (Bormuth, 1968), involves selecting a brief passage (about 250 words) and altering it by deleting every fifth word of the text, leaving the first and last sentences intact. The student reads the altered passage aloud and orally fills in the blanks. When a student correctly completes between 44% and 57% of the missing words, the text is considered appropriate for instruction. When a student supplies less than 44% of the words, the passage is too difficult. Likewise, when a student furnishes more than 57% of the words, the passage is too easy for use in reading instruction. Take, for example, the following passage:

"Dodger was a big brown dog with long ears and a short tail. Dodger loved to play in the yard but sometimes he would go under the fence and run away."

This would become

"Dodger was a big _____ dog with long ears _____ a short tail. Dodger _____ to play in the _____ but sometimes he would _____ under the fence and _____ away."

In this example, the passage occurs at the instructional level for students who correctly supply three of the six missing words. Auditory cloze is a related cloze procedure in which the student inserts the correct word to complete sentences spoken by the evaluator. Appropriate for use with young children, auditory cloze serves as a good beginning task because it does not require reading ability.

Teachers often modify cloze procedures to provide additional assessment of word prediction abilities. One of the modifications, visual cloze with alternatives, involves having the student select the correct word from two choices (e.g., "Dodger ran after the _____ [mall/ball]"). With visual cloze, the student may complete the blank with any word. In contrast, visual cloze with alternatives relies more heavily on the ability to read the sentence as well as the alternatives. Another modification, cloze with initial grapheme, consists of giving the student the initial grapheme of the missing word ("The cat ran up the t_____ [tree]"). This modification is more difficult than traditional cloze because it limits the range of appropriate answers to words that match the initial grapheme.

A number of computer software programs are available to assist teachers in designing and constructing cloze assessments and instructional exercises. These include the Cloze Test, Cloze Wizard, and Cloze Pro. A variety of cloze formats are available with these programs, including cloze reading passages with or without word lists, cloze passages with extra words, cloze with alternate words, cloze punctuation, cloze scramble, and cloze meanings.

✓ Check Your Comprehension

When teachers conduct curriculum-based assessment, a type of informal, authentic evaluation, they use regular classroom materials and instructional activities to evaluate reading performance. Curriculum-based techniques include use of clinical observations, diagnostic checklists, miscue analysis, and cloze procedures. Because it leads directly to developing instructional objectives, this type of assessment is of special interest to teachers. Like all appraisal procedures, curriculum-based assessment of reading has drawbacks related to producing reliable and valid results. The challenge is to refine curriculum-based assessment in ways that overcome these limitations. Despite the difficulties, curriculum-based assessment has many advantages, including the ability to evaluate student performance in direct relation to the curriculum. This direct relationship allows the teacher to make educational decisions based on actual reading behavior. Additional curriculum-based assessment procedures for evaluating reading appear in

Reflection
Which CBA appeals to you? Why?

 To answer this reflection online, go to the *Teaching and Learning* module on the Companion Web site at *www.Prenhall.com/venn*.

Chapter 18, which discusses portfolio assessment, and in Chapter 3, which focuses on assessment in inclusive settings.

Informal Reading Inventories

Diagnosing a reading disability is best accomplished with standardized tests such as those described at the end of this chapter. When planning intervention, however, most teachers prefer to use **informal reading inventories**. Teachers find that assessment information from informal reading inventories translates more directly into daily instruction than do scores from standardized tests. Most informal inventories contain graded word lists for testing word recognition ability and graded reading passages for evaluating oral reading, silent reading, and comprehension. Teachers may select from among many commercially available informal reading inventories. Descriptions of three representative informal reading inventories follow. Teachers may locate additional informal reading inventories by conducting a search with the ETS Test File at http://ericae.net/testcol.htm using the search term "reading inventories." Some teachers prefer to develop their own assessments. For this reason, a systematic description of how to construct teacher-made informal reading inventories also follows.

Analytical Reading Inventory, Seventh Edition

The Analytical Reading Inventory, Seventh Edition (Woods & Moe, 2003), with accompanying audiotape, is a comprehensive K–12 informal reading inventory that includes narrative and expository passages. The text contains everything future teachers, inservice teachers, reading specialists, and psychometrists need to administer a thorough, one-on-one analysis of the reading strategies. The authors designed the instrument for use with all students in gifted through remedial classes at the elementary, middle, and high school levels. Extensive field testing and years of classroom use have made teachers confident that the results obtained through the inventory are both valid and reliable. The inventory renders accurate information about each student's level of instruction, strategies to recognize words and comprehend text, and oral and silent reading performance.

Basic Reading Inventory

The Basic Reading Inventory: Pre-Primer Through Grade Twelve & Early Literacy Assessments, Ninth Edition (Johns, 2005) consists of six individually administered informal reading tests. Each book includes a multimedia CD with video clips demonstrating administration of the inventory. Scoring sheets on the CD can be printed as needed. The graded passages on each test include an informal miscue analysis tally system. A Spanish version is available for grades K–4.

English-Español Reading Inventory for the Classroom

This informal reading inventory (Flynt & Cooter, 1999) has been adapted to meet the strong demand for K–12 teachers to assess Spanish-speaking students in their native tongue. Because it can assess a student's reading competency in Spanish as well as English, this inventory is particularly valuable considering the influx of English as a second language (ESL) students and Spanish-speaking students in the public schools. Taking a constructivist approach, the authors combine both traditional and holistic methods to determine a student's reading level. This pragmatic, well-designed inventory can be used in undergraduate/graduate courses dealing with reading remediation, in public schools with Latino populations, and in ESL teacher training programs.

Teacher-Made Reading Inventories

Teachers often assess student reading levels by developing their own informal reading inventories using graded materials from the classroom (Bond, Tinker, Wasson, & Wasson, 1989; Harris & Sipay, 1985; Mercer & Mercer, 2005). Teacher-made informal reading inventories have the advantage of reflecting the reading material used in the classroom, thus providing a direct link between evaluation and instruction.

Informal reading inventories identify three different reading levels: independent, instructional, and frustration. At the independent level, students read by themselves with accuracy rates of 98–100% in word recognition and 90–100% in answering comprehension questions. When reading material at the independent level, students are self-reliant and can read for enjoyment. Library books and seatwork instructions should be at the independent level. The instructional level refers to reading that students can accomplish with teacher assistance. At this level, students recognize 95% of the words and comprehend at least 75% of the material. Reading instruction in the classroom should be geared to this level. The frustration level refers to material that is too difficult for the student to read. At the frustration level, recognition of words is 90% or below, and comprehension falls below 50%. In teaching situations, teachers should avoid asking students to read at the frustration level.

Constructing informal reading inventories involves preparing passages of increasing difficulty, usually from a basal reading series. The specific steps appear in Focus 15–3. Because programs and materials differ significantly, teachers may modify these procedures depending on the reading program they use with their students. Although developing an inventory takes time and effort, teacher-made reading inventories have the advantage of connecting assessment with the instructional emphasis, vocabulary content, and level of difficulty in the instructional program.

☑ Check Your Comprehension

Informal reading inventories include graded word lists and graded reading passages. These inventories provide valuable assessment information for planning interventions with students who have reading disabilities. Most inventories measure word recognition ability, oral reading, silent reading, and comprehension at three levels: independent, instructional, and frustration. Teachers may select from among many commercially available reading inventories or may develop their own teacher-constructed inventories using graded materials from the classroom.

Reflection
How could informal reading inventories help teachers throughout the school year? Explain.

 To answer this reflection online, go to the *Teaching and Learning* module on the Companion Website at *www.prenhall.com/venn*.

Norm-Referenced Reading Tests

Formal assessment of reading skills with standardized instruments relies on a number of norm-referenced screening and diagnostic tests. These include the multiple-skill tests reviewed in the previous chapter as well as a variety of single-skill tools. Both the multiple- and single-skill measures are available at the screening and diagnostic levels of assessment; however, the single-skill diagnostic instruments provide the most in-depth assessment information. For this reason, special educators, diagnosticians, psychologists, reading specialists, and other professionals often use single-skill diagnostic tests when they need detailed information to identify specific reading problems, develop instructional objectives, and create intervention activities. Because they produce standardized scores, norm-referenced reading tests are also useful in classifying and placing students in reading programs and special education programs.

FOCUS 15-3

How to Construct an Informal Reading Inventory

The steps in developing a teacher-made inventory are these:

1. With primary children, select passages of about 50 words for each grade level of difficulty to be assessed. With secondary students, each passage should be 150–200 words in length.
2. Limit the selection of passages to a specific range (e.g., five levels: two levels below the student's grade level, one at the grade level, and two levels above).
3. To determine a student's independent reading level, assessment should begin below the student's grade level. The teacher needs two copies of each passage. As the student reads aloud from one copy, the teacher records errors on the other copy and then asks three to five comprehension questions about the passage.
4. Record the percentage of words read accurately in each passage (divide the number of words read accurately by the number of words in the passage) and the percentage of comprehension questions answered correctly (divide the number of correct answers by the number of questions).
5. After establishing the student's independent level, the assessment continues with the student reading increasingly difficult graded passages to determine an instructional level and a frustration level. Stop testing as soon as a frustration level is established.
6. Teachers may modify these procedures to assess specific skills such as word attack, oral reading, and comprehension ability.

Useful linkages exist between norm-referenced test results and informal, curriculum-based reading assessment. In fact, rather than being in conflict, the two types of assessment actually complement each other. For example, many teachers and most child-study teams use formal testing along with curriculum-based assessment when making staffing and placement decisions. In other words, curriculum-based and norm-referenced assessment work well together by providing a complete picture of a student's present level of performance, strengths, weaknesses, and gaps in skill development. In addition, teachers can use curriculum-based assessment data and information to support scores obtained from standardized, norm-referenced tests. The following in-depth reviews of three representative norm-referenced reading tests illustrate the range and variety of formal assessment instruments.

Test of Early Reading Ability, Third Edition

The Test of Early Reading Ability, Third Edition (TERA3) (Reid, Hresko, & Hammill, 2001) is a screening test for young children ages 3 years 6 months through 8 years 6 months. Rather than assessing children's readiness, the TERA3 assesses their mastery of early developmental reading skills. The three TERA3 subtests measure alphabet knowledge and uses, conventions of print, and the construction of meaning from print. A TERA3 summary appears in the Test Review box.

TERA3 Materials   The TERA3 is available as separate items or in kit form. The complete kit includes a manual, an administration/picture book, and profile/examiner

TEST REVIEW

Test of Early Reading Ability, Third Edition

Type of Test:	Norm-referenced
Purpose:	Screening early reading ability
Content Areas:	Alphabet, conventions, and meaning
Administration Time:	20 to 30 minutes
Age Levels:	3 years 6 months through 8 years 6 months
Suitable for:	Students with mild and moderate disabilities, including learning disabilities, behavior disorders, educable mental retardation, physical impairments, and hearing impairments
Scores:	Standard scores, percentile ranks, and NCEs
In Short:	TERA3 is useful for measuring the emerging reading ability of young children.

scoring sheets for Form A and Form B. The TERA3 uses logos and labels from such national companies as McDonald's and Kraft, and these logos are provided in the test kit. The logos make the TERA3 colorful and meaningful. All pictures are in color to present a more appealing look to children.

TERA3 Administration and Scoring   It takes 20 to 30 minutes to give the TERA3. Evaluators can report performance using standard scores, percentiles, normal curve equivalents, or age and grade equivalents.

TERA3 Technical Characteristics   The TERA3 includes normative data from a sample of 875 children stratified by age relative to geography, gender, race, residence, and ethnicity. Test development research includes studies that provide evidence of the absence of gender, racial, disability, and ethnic bias. Reliability coefficients for subgroups of the normative sample (e.g., African Americans, Hispanic Americans, females) as well as for the entire normative sample are consistently high. Validity studies included special attention to the effectiveness of the test for a wide variety of groups as well as for a general population. This edition of the instrument includes new items to make the test more reliable and valid for the upper and lower ages covered by the test. The technical characteristics make the instrument appropriate for use as a screening test.

TERA3 Summary   The Test of Early Reading Ability, Third Edition is a screening test for identifying young children from 3 years 6 months to 8 years 6 months of age who may be at risk for reading difficulties. Consisting of three subtests, the TERA3 includes two alternate forms for testing and retesting and is notable because it assesses mastery of early developing reading skills.

Woodcock Reading Mastery Tests, Revised, Normative Update

Foremost among the diagnostic reading tests is the Woodcock Reading Mastery Tests, Revised (WRMT-R/NU) (Woodcock, 1998). The WRMT-R/NU, a major revision of the original Woodcock Reading Tests (Woodcock, 1973), is a diagnostic tool for assessing students from kindergarten through college and into adulthood. Woodcock designed the tests for educational diagnosticians, reading specialists, and teachers. A summary of the WRMT-R/NU appears in the Test Review box.

The WRMT-R/NU is available in two different forms. Form H contains four reading achievement subtests and is the shorter version. Form G, the complete battery, includes the four reading achievement subtests plus three readiness subtests as follows:

Reading achievement subtests

   Word identification
   Word attack
   Word comprehension (antonyms, synonyms, analogies)
   Passage comprehension

Readiness subtests

   Visual-auditory learning
   Letter identification
   Supplementary letter checklist

WRMT-R/NU Materials   WRMT-R/NU materials include Form G and Form H test books, Form G and Form H test record forms, sample summary record forms, a pronunciation guide cassette, a sample report to parents, an examiner's manual, and a storage box. The WRMT-R/NU also offers an optional computer software program with test scores and profiles, an aptitude-achievement discrepancy analysis report, and a narrative report. The discrepancy analysis report facilitates the identification

---

TEST REVIEW

Woodcock Reading Mastery Tests, Revised, Normative Update

Type of Test:	Norm-referenced and individually administered
Purpose:	To diagnose reading achievement
Content Areas:	Visual-auditory learning, letter identification, word identification, word attack, and word and passage comprehension
Administration Time:	10 to 30 minutes per subtest
Age Levels:	5 years to retirement
Suitable for:	Students with mild disabilities, including learning disabilities, behavior disorders, sensory impairments, and physical disabilities
Scores:	Age and grade percentile ranks, standard scores, normal curve equivalents, and age and grade equivalents
In Short:	The WRMT-R/NU is a well-designed, single-skill diagnostic test with features usually not available in multiple-skill tests, including an error analysis procedure and five interpretive profiles.

of students with specific reading disabilities by comparing aptitude (measured with an intelligence test) to reading achievement (measured by the WRMT-R/NU).

WRMT-R/NU Administration and Scoring　The manual provides a thorough description of the complex administration, scoring, and interpretation procedures. It takes from 10 to 30 minutes to administer each subtest. The subtests combine to form the following clusters: readiness, basic skills, reading comprehension, total reading (full scale), and total reading (short scale for a quick 15-minute screening).

For each of these clusters, derived scores include age- and grade-based percentile ranks, standard scores, normal curve equivalents (NCEs), age equivalents, and grade equivalents. In addition, the test provides advanced scoring and interpretation procedures such as relative performance index scores, an instructional level profile, and a percentile rank profile.

The complexity of WRMT-R/NU scoring makes the time needed to prepare a student's scores much longer than with other tests. Cohen and Cohen (1994) indicated that the first-time evaluator needs about an hour to score the WRMT-R/NU; experienced evaluators need about 30 minutes. Optional computer software, the WRMT-R/NU Automated System for Scoring and Interpreting Standardized Tests (ASSIST), greatly reduces scoring time.

WRMT-R/NU Technical Characteristics　The developers updated the WRMT-R/NU norms in 1998 using a national sampling of over 3,000 people. These new norms provide accurate score comparisons for reading decoding and reading comprehension with the other achievement batteries with which it was co-normed: K-TEA/NU, KeyMath-R/NU, and PIAT-R/NU. The co-norms give added flexibility by providing the ability to substitute a subtest from a different battery if a subtest is spoiled or to obtain additional diagnostic information.

Reviewers (Crocker, 2001; Murray-Ward, 2001) praised the clarity of the new norms but criticized the representativeness and relevance of the updated normative sample. According to these reviewers, using the same norm-study participants to co-norm the test with other tests introduced technical issues. As a result, users should use the results with caution and avoid overinterpreting the subtest scores.

In a comprehensive review of the WRMT-R, Cohen and Cohen (1994) described the many advanced diagnostic features of the test that in some ways make the instrument more complicated and time consuming to administer, score, and interpret than most tests. However, because it was designed for prescriptive remediation rather than for simple screening, these critics concluded that the clinical value of the instrument takes precedence over concerns about administration and scoring convenience.

Despite these criticisms, the WRMT-R/NU displays very good overall technical qualities. The WRMT-R/NU followed a detailed and precise standardization plan that ensured development of representative norms. The WRMT-R/NU has very good reliability, and numerous studies support the content and concurrent validity of the test. Overall, the WRMT-R/NU has excellent technical qualities.

WRMT-R/NU Summary　The WRMT-R/NU is an excellent diagnostic tool for making placement decisions and creating instructional objectives and remedial intervention activities. The WRMT-R/NU includes advanced diagnostic features such as an error analysis for identifying specific strengths and weaknesses and five interpretive profiles that enable examiners to interpret test scores in a variety of ways. The WRMT-R/NU also measures reading vocabulary in four areas: general, science-mathematics, social studies, and humanities. These features illustrate the benefits derived from a well-designed, single-skill diagnostic test like the WRMT-R/NU.

Test of Reading Comprehension, Third Edition

The Test of Reading Comprehension, Third Edition (TORC3) (Brown, Hammill, & Wiederholt, 1995) is the most recent revision of the TORC, originally published in 1978 and revised in 1986. Reading teachers, special educators, and diagnosticians use the TORC3 as a screening tool for measuring the silent reading comprehension of individuals and groups of students from age 7 through 17. A summary of the TORC3 appears in the Test Review box. The test includes eight subtests grouped into general reading comprehension and diagnostic supplements. The general reading comprehension core includes four subtests: general vocabulary, syntactic similarities, paragraph reading, and sentence sequencing. Four diagnostic supplements provide a more comprehensive evaluation of various comprehension abilities. The supplements include measures of content area vocabulary in mathematics, social studies, and science, and a measure of the understanding of written directions commonly found in schoolwork.

TORC3 Materials   The complete TORC3 kit, which is packaged in a storage box, includes an examiner's manual, answer sheets, subtest forms, profile/examiner record forms, and student booklets.

TORC3 Administration and Scoring   It takes about 30 minutes to test with the TORC3. It can be given to individuals or to groups of students. The evaluator can administer individual subtests or all eight subtests depending on the needs of the student and reasons for testing. Available TORC3 scores include standard scores, percentiles, a composite reading comprehension quotient, grade equivalents, and age equivalents.

TORC3 Technical Characteristics   The TORC3 was developed using a sample of 1,962 students from 19 states. The test manual reports information about the sample relative to geographic region, gender, residence, race, ethnicity, and disabling condition. The TORC3 manual also discusses studies showing the absence of gender and racial bias and research to support the reliability and validity of the instrument, which includes investigations of test-retest reliability, criterion-related validity, and content validity.

TEST REVIEW

Test of Reading Comprehension, Third Edition

Type of Test:	Norm-referenced
Purpose:	A screening test of silent reading comprehension
Content Areas:	General vocabulary, syntactic similarities, paragraph reading, sentence sequencing, and understanding written directions
Administration Time:	Approximately 30 minutes
Age Levels:	7 through 17
Suitable for:	Students with mild and moderate disabilities.
Scores:	Standard scores, percentiles, age scores, and grade scores
In Short:	The TORC3 is a useful screening tool for reading teachers, special educators, and diagnosticians to assess reading comprehension.

TORC3 Summary   The Test of Reading Comprehension, Third Edition assesses the silent reading comprehension ability of students from ages 7 to 17. Consisting of eight subtests, the TORC3 is suitable for use with individuals and groups.

Other Norm-Referenced Reading Tests

Many other norm-referenced reading tests are available and widely used. Brief reviews of five of these tools follow.

Diagnostic Assessments of Reading with Trial Teaching Strategies   The Diagnostic Assessments of Reading with Trial Teaching Strategies (DARTTS) (Roswell & Chall, 1992) links reading assessment and reading instruction using a two-component, integrated program designed for reading teachers, classroom teachers, special education and Title I teachers, and other professionals charged with helping students read better. The Diagnostic Assessment of Reading (DAR) component provides individual diagnostic information in essential areas of reading and language: word recognition, word analysis, oral reading, silent reading comprehension, spelling, and word meaning. The Trial Teaching Strategies (TTS) component identifies how each student learns best through microteaching sessions.

Dynamic Indicators of Basic Early Literacy Skills, Sixth Edition   The Dynamic Indicators of Basic Early Literacy Skills, Sixth Edition (DIBELS) (Good & Kaminski, 2003) are a set of standardized, individually administered measures of early literacy development. DIBELS consists of brief (1-minute) fluency measures to regularly assess the development of prereading and early reading skills of students from kindergarten through third grade. The authors recommend giving these individually administered, benchmark assessments to all students in a class three times per year and to at-risk students on a weekly basis to monitor and track individual progress. The DIBELS produces seven fluency scores for measuring initial sounds, letter naming, phoneme segmentation, nonsense words, oral reading, oral retelling, and word use.

Gray Oral Reading Tests, Fourth Edition   The Gray Oral Reading Tests, Fourth Edition (GORT4) (Wiederholt & Bryant, 2001) measures oral reading skills of students from ages 6 through 18 using two parallel forms, each containing 14 developmentally sequenced reading passages with five comprehension questions. Available scores include a fluency score derived from the reader's performance rate (timed in seconds taken to read each passage) and accuracy (number of deviations from print made in each passage) and an oral reading comprehension score. It takes about 30 minutes to administer the test. Designed to identify students who are significantly behind in reading proficiency and who may benefit from interventions, the GORT4 also helps to pinpoint reading strengths and weaknesses and to document student progress in reading.

Stanford Diagnostic Reading Test, Fourth Edition   The Stanford Diagnostic Reading Test, Fourth Edition (Karlsen & Gardner, 1995) is a group-administered test that provides teachers with information about students' reading processes and strategies. SDRT4 includes recreational, textual, and functional reading material. SDRT4 subtests include phonetic analysis, vocabulary, comprehension, and scanning along with three optional informal assessment instruments: a reading strategies survey, a reading questionnaire, and a story retelling test.

Test of Word Reading Efficiency   The Test of Word Reading Efficiency (TOWRE) (Torgesen, Wagner, & Rashotte, 1999) is a nationally normed, individually administered measure of word reading accuracy and fluency for students from ages 6 through 24. This brief screening test measures the ability to accurately recognize familiar words as whole units or "sight words" and the ability to "sound out" words quickly.

Check Your Comprehension

Norm-referenced reading tests are useful in identifying specific reading prob- lems, developing instructional objectives, creating intervention activities, measuring progress, and making staffing and placement decisions. Available norm-referenced instruments include screening tests and comprehensive diagnostic tools. The screening tests provide an overview of reading perfor- mance; the diagnostic instruments provide detailed assessment information.

Summary

Reading consists of complex behaviors necessary to recognize and comprehend written words and passages. Reading recognition involves translating the printed word into spoken counterparts, and reading comprehension involves understanding written con- tent. With students who may have reading problems, assessment begins with screening followed by more formal diagnostic evaluation if necessary. Formal evaluation most of- ten involves use of norm-referenced, single-skill testing. In the classroom, teachers most often use curriculum-based assessment and informal reading inventories. Curriculum- based reading assessments include clinical observation, diagnostic checklists, miscue analysis, cloze, and running records. Informal reading inventories include commercial and teacher-made instruments. Though the curriculum-based measures provide the most direct link between assessment and instruction, all types of reading assessment, including norm-referenced tests, are useful in meeting the needs of students with read- ing problems. In all cases, the evaluator should select the test or assessment procedure that best meets the individual needs of the student (see Table 15-1).

 To check your comprehension of the chapter contents, go to the *Guided Review and Quiz* modules in Chapter 15 of the Companion *Website, www.prenhall.com/venn.*

Table 15–1 Review of Reading Tests

Name	Type	Suitable for	Brief Description	Purpose
Analytical Reading Inventory, Sixth Edition (2003)	Criterion- referenced, individually administered informal reading inventory	Students in grades K–12	Includes narrative and expository passages that measure silent reading, listening, and comprehension	To obtain information about appropriate levels of instruction and oral and silent reading performance
Basic Reading Inventory: Pre- Primer Through Grade Twelve & Early Literacy Assessments, Ninth Edition	Criterion- referenced, individually administered informal reading tests	Pre-primary through grade 12 students	Includes a set of six reading inventories, instruction on how to use reading inventories in the classroom, and multimedia support materials	To assess the reading performance of students using a variety of reading inventories

Name	Type	Suitable for	Brief Description	Purpose
Diagnostic Assessments of Reading with Trial Teaching Strategies (DARTTS)	Individually administered, norm-referenced diagnostic reading test	Individuals from 6 to adult	Measures word recognition, word analysis, oral reading, silent reading comprehension, spelling, and word meaning	To assess reading achievement and discover appropriate methods and materials to enhance learning
The Dynamic Indicators of Basic Early Literacy Skills, Sixth Edition (DIBELS)	Norm-referenced, individually administered screening test	Students in grades K–3	Produces seven fluency scores for measuring: initial sounds, letter naming, phoneme segmentation, nonsense words, oral reading, oral retelling, and word use	Consists of brief (1-minute) fluency measures to regularly assess the development of prereading and early reading skills
English-Espanol Reading Inventory for the Classroom	Criterion-referenced, individually administered informal reading inventory	Students in grades K–12	Consists of graded passages to determine a student's reading level	To assess a student's reading competency in Spanish as well as English
Gray Oral Reading, Tests, Fourth Edition (GORT4)	Norm-referenced, individually administered oral reading test	Students, from 6–18 years of age	Contains 14 developmentally sequenced reading passages with 5 comprehension questions for each passage	To identify students who are significantly behind in reading proficiency and who may benefit from interventions
Stanford Diagnostic Reading Test, Fourth Edition (SDRT 4)	Norm-referenced, group-administered reading test	Students in grades 1.5–13	Includes recreational, textual, and functional reading material with subtests measuring phonetic analysis, vocabulary, comprehension, and scanning along with optional informal measures of reading strategies, reading attitudes, and story retelling skills	To provide teachers with information about students' reading processes and strategies
*Test of Early Reading Ability— Third Edition (TERA3)	Norm-referenced, individually administered screening test	Children from 3–6 through 8–6 years of age	Measures knowledge of the alphabet and its uses, the conventions of print, and the construction of meaning from print	To assess the reading ability of young children

(continued)

Table 15-1 *continued*

Name	Type	Suitable for	Brief Description	Purpose
*Test of Reading, Comprehension Third Edition (TORC3)	Norm-referenced, individually or group-administered screening test	Students from 7 to 17 years of age	Includes eight subtests grouped into general reading comprehension and diagnostic supplements	To measure the silent reading comprehension of individuals and groups of students
Test of Word Reading Efficiency (TOWRE)	Norm-referenced, individually administered screening test	Individuals from 6 to 24 years of age	Contains sight word efficiency (SWE) and phonetic decoding efficiency (PDE) subtests	To monitor the the ability to accurately recognize familiar words as whole units or "sight words" and the ability to "sound out" words quickly
*Woodcock Reading Mastery Test—Revised (WRMT-R/NU)	Individually administered, norm-referenced diagnostic test	Individuals from 5 years of age retirement	Measures visual-auditory through learning, letter identification, word identification, word attack, and word and passage comprehension	To comprehensively diagnose reading achievement

*Tests with an asterisk are featured in this chapter.

Meeting Performance Standards and Preparing for Licensure Exams

After reading this chapter, you should be able to demonstrate the following CEC Standards and PRAXIS™ test knowledge and skills. The information in parentheses identifies where to find the particular CEC standard and PRAXIS™ content reference.

CEC Standards for Beginning Special Education Teachers

- Implement systematic instruction in teaching reading comprehension and monitoring strategies (GC4S14)
- Use and limitations of assessment instruments (CC8K4)
- Administer nonbiased formal and informal assessments (CC8S2)
- Use technology to conduct assessments (CC8S3)
- Develop or modify individualized assessment strategies (CC8S4)
- Interpret information from formal and informal assessments (CC8S5)
- Evaluate instruction and monitor progress of individuals with exceptional learning needs (CC8S8)
- Develop or modify individualized assessment strategies (CC8S9)
- Create and maintain records (CC8S10)
- Specialized terminology used in the assessment of individuals with disabilities (GC8K1)
- Select, adapt and modify assessments to accommodate the unique abilities and needs of individuals with disabilities (GC8S3)

PRAXIS™ Education of Exceptional Students: Core Content Knowledge

- Assessment, including use of assessment for screening, diagnosis, placement, and the making of instructional decisions; for example, how to select and conduct nondiscriminatory and appropriate assessments; how to interpret standardized and specialized assessment results (0353 III)
- Assessment, including procedures and test materials, both formal and informal, typically used for prereferral, screening, referral, classification, placement, and ongoing program monitoring (0353 III)
- Assessment, including how to select, construct, conduct, and modify nondiscriminatory, developmentally and chronologically age-appropriate informal assessments, including teacher-made tests, curriculum-based assessment, and alternatives to norm-referenced testing (including observations, anecdotal records, error analysis, miscue analysis, self-evaluation questionnaires and interviews, journals and learning logs, and portfolio assessment) (0353 III)

chapter 16

Assessing Mathematics Achievement

Objectives

After reading this chapter, you will be prepared to do the following:

- Describe the skills measured by mathematics tests.
- Demonstrate use of mathematics tests.
- Use curriculum-based procedures for assessing mathematics.
- Conduct error pattern analysis.
- Give diagnostic interviews.
- Use performance measurement.
- Conduct performance rate assessment.
- Administer and score norm-referenced mathematics tests.

Overview

In this chapter, you will investigate the assessment of student achievement in mathematics. Your investigation includes review of curriculum-based assessment procedures and norm-referenced tests. You will learn that most teachers prefer curriculum-based assessment because it is more selective and pinpoints skills that require remediation. Your study of curriculum-based measurement will include detailed review of procedures such as error pattern analysis, diagnostic interviews, and performance measurement. Careful use of these assessment procedures links assessment with instruction and helps teachers identify exactly what students need to know. You will also discover that norm-referenced tests are helpful for identifying overall math achievement levels and for determining the scope and sequence in mathematics instruction. Your study of formal instruments includes in-depth review of the KeyMath Revised: A Diagnostic Inventory of Essential Mathematics, specifically designed for use with students having difficulty in mathematics.

The Importance of Assessing Mathematics

The following narrative illustrates some of the questions teachers have about assessing mathematics and mentions some widely used curriculum-based assessment techniques and math tests.

Ms. White teaches students with mild and moderate disabilities. She has never assessed mathematics before, but because she will be teaching middle school math next year, she is wondering what type of math assessment to use with her class. Her questions about math assessment include these: What are the different kinds of assessment procedures and tests? What math assessments are specifically designed for students with special needs? Why should she use math assessment? Can math assessment really help, or will it take away valuable instructional time? Will math assessment improve the teaching and learning process?

Ms. White consults with some other teachers and does some reading. She discovers error pattern analysis and other curriculum-based assessment techniques that help link assessment with classroom instruction. She also learns about a norm-referenced math test, the KeyMath Revised: A Diagnostic Inventory of Essential Mathematics, developed specifically for students with learning problems in mathematics. She decides to try the error pattern analysis procedure and the KeyMath to discover if these assessments will help her meet the instructional needs of her students.

Defining Mathematics Assessment

Mathematics, the ability to understand numerical patterns, groupings, and correlations, is a basic subject in the academic curriculum. Although it does not permeate the school curriculum like reading does, many students with disabilities encounter difficulty in mathematics. Developing math skills is a cumulative process in that students must master lower skills before learning higher-level skills. For this reason, students in the early grades who fail to learn basic math skills also experience problems in later grades with higher-level math and applied math. In addition to becoming increasingly difficult, mathematics includes numerous concepts and skills. As a result, many students with special needs require diagnostic assessment and intensive remedial instruction in mathematics.

Behaviors Measured by Mathematics Tests

Assessing student proficiency in mathematics involves measuring numerous concepts and skills. Connolly (1998) grouped mathematics skills as follows:

- Content including numeration, fractions, algebra, and geometry
- Operations consisting of counting, computation, and reasoning
- Applications such as measurement, problem solving, money, and time

Because of the complex, abstract nature of mathematics, many students with learning problems require repeated practice and comprehensive instruction to master even basic math operations. The need for intensive instruction limits the ultimate achievement level of many students, especially in math content. In addition, some students, particularly those with severe disabilities, need more of a functional mathematics curriculum that emphasizes practical applications such as measurement, money, and time skills. Students from linguistically and culturally diverse backgrounds should receive special consideration in math assessment. Tips for assessing the math skills of students from language-minority backgrounds appear in the accompanying Multicultural Considerations feature.

Because students who leave school without adequate math skills often find it difficult to succeed in vocations and survive in daily life, teachers need techniques to assess and remediate math deficiencies. Like most academic areas, appraisal in mathematics includes both informal and formal techniques. Informal, curriculum-based assessment, such as error pattern analysis and performance rate scoring, relies on evaluation of student performance on class assignments and other easily available work samples. In contrast, formal assessment relies on student performance on standardized, norm-referenced tests.

Why Do We Assess Mathematics Achievement?

We assess mathematics achievement to screen, identify, and place students, to plan instruction and intervention, to develop IEPs, to evaluate progress, and to monitor program effectiveness (see Focus 16–1). Although some overlap occurs among these purposes, specialized math tests and assessment techniques are available for each function. For example, screening tests identify students who may have such severe problems in mathematics that further assessment is needed to determine whether a disability exists. Likewise, comprehensive, norm-referenced diagnostic tests identify students with math disabilities and help place them in appropriate programs. Although teachers use norm-referenced tests for instructional planning purposes, they rely more often on less formal, curriculum-based assessment techniques. These include a variety of appraisal strategies, all of which link assessment with classroom instruction. This chapter includes extensive information about the use of curriculum-based mathematics assessment. Other reasons for assessing mathematics are to evaluate student progress and monitor program effectiveness, for which both formal and informal appraisal techniques are useful.

The following case study, based on a vignette by Gable and Coben (1990), illustrates why teachers use informal, curriculum-based assessment in their classrooms to assess the performance of students who are experiencing severe problems learning specific math skills.

MULTICULTURAL CONSIDERATIONS

Math Assessment with English Language Learners

Teachers should consider a variety of factors when assessing the mathematics performance of students with disabilities who are English language learners (Raborn, 1995). These factors include the student's learning characteristics and cultural and linguistic backgrounds. As in all multicultural situations, teachers should be aware of these influences, and they should provide appropriate modifications and accommodations as necessary to obtain the best possible appraisal of ability. The following strategies and considerations help in assessment.

- Some students may have high math ability and yet not be able to communicate their ability due to lack of English proficiency or lack of communication skills in either language. Therefore, math ability should be appraised based on cognitive ability and not assumed based on proficiency in English or because of a disability that affects communication skills.
- Assessment should include all areas of mathematics. This concern is especially relevant for students with learning disabilities, whose strengths may lie in areas of mathematics other than computation.
- Integrate teacher observation into the appraisal process by considering how the learner responds to new or novel demands in math, what algorithms the student uses, how the student interprets mathematical questions, and how the student relates to quantifiable material and mathematical stimuli in the environment.
- Make sure to consider linguistic factors during mathematics assessment and instruction. Math vocabulary is precise but not always familiar. Special problems exist for students with disabilities who are concurrently learning English.
- Students from language-minority backgrounds may have difficulty following the algorithms taught in the American schools. This is because South American or Asian countries, for example, have different algorithms. For this reason, it is more important to determine if students know how to obtain the correct answer and if they can explain the procedure, rather than how well the algorithms used match those in American schools.
- Remember that individual needs and strengths vary with all students, including English language learners.

Lack of reading skills can make life difficult for people with disabilities; however, lack of adequate math skills can hurt individuals also. Can you give some examples of daily life tasks for which math skills are needed?

To answer this reflection online, go to the *Multicultural Considerations* module on the Companion Website at www.prenhall.com/venn.

OCUS 16-1

Why Do We Assess Mathematics Achievement?

- To screen children
- To determine eligibility for special services
- To diagnose math disabilities
- To identify overall math achievement levels
- To compare math achievement levels among children
- To determine the scope and sequence in mathematics instruction
- To identify strengths, weaknesses, and gaps in development
- To help create appropriate objectives and remedial activities
- To assist in developing IEPs
- To assess progress in meeting IEP goals
- To discover what the student knows and does not know in mathematics
- To determine areas in need of remediation
- To understand how much a student has learned as a result of instruction
- To measure student progress over time
- To evaluate the effectiveness of instructional programs in mathematics

Although most students in Debbie Kaye's class were experiencing some difficulty learning subtraction with regrouping, Horace was failing miserably. In response to the problem, Debbie gathered a sample of math papers Horace had completed in class and prepared an informal diagnostic test with 20 subtraction problems. After giving Horace the diagnostic test over a 2-day period, Debbie analyzed the results by categorizing the errors on a chart. The chart revealed that Horace made five mistakes on the diagnostic test, four of which involved regrouping and one of which was a random error. Debbie also noticed that all of the regrouping errors involved problems with zeros in the minuend. After confirming this error pattern by examining the other work samples, she conducted a diagnostic interview with Horace. On the basis of these curriculum-based assessment procedures, Debbie concluded that Horace knew the basic addition and subtraction facts and could handle most three- and four-digit subtractions, except those with zeros in the minuend. When faced with zeros, Horace tended to lose track of the process and make mistakes. Debbie's solution was to simplify the column labels and then use modeling with specific feedback to teach Horace the simplified regrouping process.

Though some educators may consider math a universal subject, factors related to language, culture, and cognition must be considered in math assessment. Careful consideration of these factors will yield valuable assessment data and information that teachers can use to help students with diverse learning characteristics be successful in math.

☑ Check Your Comprehension

Many students with learning problems require diagnostic assessment and intensive remedial instruction in mathematics. Assessing mathematics achievement involves measuring numerous concepts and skills using informal, curriculum-based assessment and formal, norm-referenced testing. We assess the math achievement of students with learning problems to screen, identify, and place students, to plan instruction and intervention for them, to develop IEPs, to evaluate student progress, and to monitor program effectiveness.

Curriculum-Based Assessment of Mathematics Performance

Teachers frequently use curriculum-based assessment techniques to evaluate mathematics performance. Because it provides a direct link with instruction, curriculum-based assessment is ideal for developing objectives and learning activities. Widely used curriculum-based procedures include performance measurement, performance rate scoring, and error pattern analysis. Error pattern analysis is especially suitable for developing remedial intervention for students who are struggling in math.

Error Pattern Analysis of Mathematics Skills

Error pattern analysis fits mathematics well because students perform most math assignments with pencil and paper. This produces a written record, making it easy to systematically evaluate mistakes and determine the reasons for the errors. This analysis yields information that teachers need to plan remedial intervention programs. Various models for analyzing math errors exist. Ashlock (2006), for example, identified four common math errors:

- Wrong operations involving attempts to respond by performing an operation other than the one required to solve the problem.
- Obvious computational errors in which the student applies the correct operation but makes basic number fact errors.
- Defective algorithms in which the student attempts to use the correct operation but makes errors other than number fact errors in carrying through the necessary steps.
- Random responses with no obvious connection to the problem.

Defective algorithm techniques account for the largest number of errors among all students. Among low-achieving students, however, random responses were the most commonly occurring error. Ashlock presented an expanded classification system with eight common error types:

- Basic fact error
- Defective algorithm
- Grouping error
- Inappropriate inversion
- Incorrect operation
- Incomplete algorithm
- Identity error
- Zero error

Although various experts employ slightly different error categories, the process of placing common mistakes into logical groupings is the essential error pattern analysis element in mathematics. Gable and Coben (1990) described the following common error patterns in mathematics:

1. Incorrect operations in which students complete problems but use the wrong operation, such as subtracting rather than adding.

Problems		Explanation
52	87	The student used the wrong operation.
+43	+37	
09	50	

2. Computation mistakes in which students use the correct operation but fail to recall a basic math fact.

	Problems		Explanation

Problems   *Explanation*

  8   9   The student failed to recall a basic math fact.
×6 ×7
45 56

3. Incorrect algorithms in which students follow the correct operation but use an incorrect or incomplete process to solve the problem.

Problem   *Explanation*

397   The student incorrectly regrouped the hundreds column.
− 58
239

4. Random responses in which students make random errors that fail to follow a specific pattern. Often such errors are due to sloppiness or inattention to the task. Teachers detect this chronic problem when mistakes occur on problems previously completed correctly.

Steps in Conducting Error Pattern Analysis   Error pattern analysis works best when teachers use it in a systematic manner. Gable and Coben (1990) recommend a four-stage error pattern analysis implementation procedure, a summary of which appears in Focus 16–2.

In the first stage, the teacher gathers representative samples of a student's work. The samples should reflect the curriculum content, include the math problems that the student is having difficulty with, and incorporate enough items to establish a clear pattern. Consistent data are obtained from repeated testing with at least three to five items from each subskill area. For example, in the vignette at the beginning of this chapter, Mrs. Kaye gathered sample math papers and prepared an informal diagnostic test with 20 subtraction problems that were given over a 2-day period. In this example, the samples were accurately collected with sufficient items to establish a clear pattern.

In stage two the teacher conducts the actual analysis by assessing the errors in the sample papers. This process goes beyond marking each problem as correct or incorrect because the teacher analyzes the incorrect problems to identify the pattern of errors. The teacher then records each error in the appropriate category on a chart and counts the number of errors in each category. The chart provides a permanent record of the analysis. A sample mathematics error analysis chart, adapted from a form

*F*OCUS 16-2

Four-Stage Error Pattern Analysis Procedure

- Gather representative samples of a student's work.
- Analyze the error patterns.
- Conduct a diagnostic interview.
- Record the results and develop an intervention strategy.

Figure 16–1   Error analysis chart

Student _____	Teacher _____
Date _____	Number of Math Problems Analyzed _____

Description of Math Problems Analyzed

_____

_____

Type of Error	Number of Errors	Remediation Strategies
Wrong operation		
Obvious computational error		
Defective algorithm		
Random response		
Other (specify)		
Other (specify)		

Notes

_____

_____

_____

_____

developed by Gable and Coben (1990), appears in Figure 16–1. The chart lists common errors, but teachers may add other categories as necessary.

Diagnostic Interviews   In stage three the teacher conducts a diagnostic interview with the student. **Diagnostic interviews** are a single conference or a series of conferences to help determine the reasons for the errors. Just prior to the interview, students should complete a few math problems that are of the type they are having difficulty with. During the interview the teacher has the student explain the steps used to solve each problem. Having the student talk through each problem gives the teacher insight into the way the student solves problems and the student's attitude toward mathematics. The interview should take place without time constraints or pressure, and the teacher should use nonjudgmental probing questions to gather as much information as possible.

Interviews are often the most valuable part of error analysis. The interview gives students the opportunity to share their thoughts and feelings about the math problems they were asked to complete. This gives the teacher vital information about the causes for mistakes and what might help reduce errors. Interviews also help teachers understand student perceptions of math and the cognitive processes that students use to solve math problems. For this to occur, the teacher must avoid conducting the interview like an oral examination, which means the teacher must avoid criticizing, correcting, and sharing opinions. Having students explain how they solve difficult math problems helps them develop awareness of their errors. It also alerts the teacher to students who lack the awareness or motivation necessary for improving their math skills (Smith, Finn, & Dowdy, 1993).

In stage four, the teacher records the error pattern analysis results and develops appropriate intervention strategies. Teachers may use charts such as the error analysis chart shown in Figure 16–1 to accomplish this. Keeping charts or other appropriate written records enables the teacher to document intervention attempts and show progress over time.

Practical Guidelines for Conducting Error Pattern Analysis   The following practical guidelines provide suggestions for conducting error pattern analysis and ensuring accurate and useful results (Ashlock, 2006; Gable & Hendrickson, 1990).

- When learning how to conduct error pattern analysis, start with one student and set a comfortable time period of about 2 weeks for completing the process.
- Error analysis is best with students who are experiencing severe difficulty learning essential math skills. It is usually not necessary to conduct error analysis with students who are making satisfactory progress in math.
- Analyze and chart student performance as soon as possible after collecting appropriate work samples.
- Diagnosis using error analysis is quite personal and requires student cooperation, especially during the interview. The teacher must be accepting of all student responses, including wrong answers. The student needs to know that all answers are acceptable.
- Separate data collection from teaching. Diagnostic evaluation and teaching are different procedures. Diagnosis involves collecting data for making intervention decisions. Teaching involves giving instruction, training, and guidance. In most situations, teachers should avoid making responses as right or wrong, instructing students, and correcting mistakes during diagnosis. Put another way, this means that teachers should refrain from direct instruction during the analysis process.
- Conduct multiple diagnoses by setting aside short periods of time for assessment during instruction. The idea is to give students time to reflect, and the teacher time to observe behavior, by asking them questions such as, "Can you try it another way?" or "Can you think of another way to solve that problem?"
- Watch for patterns to emerge from diagnostic and instructional activities. Rather than focusing on a single bit of diagnostic information for making intervention decisions, the goal of the analysis is to identify consistent patterns from multiple samples of a student's work. This type of analysis is really a problem-solving activity with the goal of finding a consistent pattern of errors that can be remediated as the student learns correct or more precise procedures.

Performance Measurement

Performance measurement is a widely used and practical means for assessing math skills. Teachers use performance measurement procedures with a variety of student work, including class math papers, homework assignments, and teacher-constructed tests. Salvia and Hughes (1990) identified percent correct and performance rate scoring as the most common and useful forms of performance measurement. Performance measurement involves calculating a percent correct score with untimed math work. The percent correct score is obtained by calculating the percentage of correctly completed problems divided by the total number of problems multiplied by 100. For example, a math paper with 15 correct answers out of 20 problems would receive a percent correct score of 75% ($15 \div 20 = .75 \times 100 = 75\%$). With percent correct scoring, the teacher should establish a student mastery level such as 80% or 90% or use a grading scale such as A (90–100), B (80–89), C (70–79), D (60–69), and F (59 and below). Like all assessment, performance measurement is best when used repeatedly over time to obtain an overall picture of student performance.

Performance Rate Scoring

Performance rate scoring is the use of timed probes or tests to measure the number of correct responses in a specified period. This approach is effective in producing long-term gains in math performance, especially in basic addition, subtraction, multiplication, and division. Performance rate is an ideal way to assess simple computations, multiplication facts, and other math skills that students should complete quickly and accurately. The teacher assesses student performance rates by giving timed math assignments and calculating the number of correct responses per minute. For instance, if a student correctly completes 40 math problems in a 5-minute period, the performance rate is 8 problems per minute. Teachers must establish criteria for acceptable performance rates, depending on the type of math assignment. With some assignments, such as simple addition or basic multiplication facts, teachers should expect high rates of performance and accuracy. With other assignments, such as long division or simple word problems, teachers should expect much lower rates of performance. For students who are struggling in math, teachers can use games and team competitions to introduce performance rate activities. For example, teachers can give appropriate rewards to students who finish their assigned math problems within a specified period of time. Alternatively, teachers can place students on teams and arrange for team competitions. The teams that finish within the specified time period receive extra points or rewards.

Other Curriculum-Based Assessment Procedures

Curriculum-based assessment of mathematics encompasses a wide range of methods, procedures, and techniques. In addition to the methods just described in detail, other ways in which teachers can obtain informal, curriculum-based assessment data designed to inform the teaching and learning process include the following:

- Teacher-made math tests
- Clinical observation with anecdotal recording
- Diagnostic checklists
- Interviews
- Conferences
- Student notebooks
- Student exhibitions
- Portfolios
- Student self-assessment
- Student reflections
- Computer software programs (see the Technology Focus box)

☑ Check Your Comprehension

Special education teachers may select from among several curriculum-based assessment techniques for evaluating the mathematics performance of their students. Because it links assessment directly with instruction, teachers find

TECHNOLOGY FOCUS

Classroom-Based Math Assessment Software

Teachers may select from a variety of classroom-based math assessment software programs. These include shareware, freeware, and commercial software for use in assessment and instruction. Shareware and freeware programs are available for downloading from the Internet.

Shareware is inexpensive software that you can try before purchasing. If you like it, you pay a nominal fee, usually from $5.00 to $10.00, for the full-featured program. Freeware is software that you can download and use without cost. Available math assessment shareware includes My Math Quiz Sheets, a program that produces worksheets, quizzes, and tests for mathematics classes. Programs like this one are available for downloading from the Internet through a number of different Web sites. To locate a download site, simply type the program name in a search engine such as Google. The search engine will locate the software for you.

Alan's Math is a downloadable freeware program that administers simple arithmetic tests to help students practice addition, subtraction, multiplication, and division. The program logs all questions and responses to a text file, along with user name, time, and performance statistics. Teachers may select the number of problems per test, turn sounds on or off, and set a variety of problem characteristics such as the largest answer for addition problems and the highest table for multiplication problems.

AssessMath! is a commercial program that gives teachers the ability to customize tests to meet individual student needs and respond to specific classroom teaching and learning goals. The program contains a database of over 1,000 mathematics tasks for grades K–8. AssessMath! offers tasks at multiple levels of difficulty, ranging from basic skills and computations to open-ended questions. For each problem, the program can report the grade level, mathematical content, difficulty level, item format, and time criteria. Once a teacher creates a test, the software can check the balance of content, skills, and levels of thinking represented to assure that an appropriate variety is included. AssessMath! is a tool for the individual teacher, but it can also serve as a shared resource within a single school or district.

that curriculum-based assessment is ideal for developing instructional objectives, preparing learning activities, and remediating deficits. Specific techniques include error pattern analysis, diagnostic interviews, performance measurement, and performance rate scoring.

Formal Assessment in Mathematics

In addition to informal, curriculum-based assessment, teachers also need knowledge of formal tests of mathematics achievement, such as the KeyMath-R/NU. Formal tests assist in the process of identifying present levels of performance for staffing, placement, and developing instructional objectives and intervention programs in mathematics.

The formal tests help teachers identify strengths, weaknesses, and gaps in development, and this leads to creating appropriate objectives and remedial activities. To obtain this diagnostic information, special educators may select from several formal math achievement tests, which include the multiple-skill tools (reviewed earlier in Chapter 14) as well as the single-skill instruments reviewed in this chapter.

The mathematics subtests included in most multiple-skill tests, though not covering as much detail as single-skill tests, provide a reliable measure of mathematics achievement that is often more than adequate for many diagnostic and instructional uses. When diagnosticians and teachers need even more detailed information about math achievement, however, they frequently use one of the single-skill mathematics tests. Foremost among these is the KeyMath-Revised/NU: A Diagnostic Inventory of Essential Mathematics—Normative Update.

KeyMath-Revised/NU: A Diagnostic Inventory of Essential Mathematics—Normative Update

The KeyMath-Revised/NU: A Diagnostic Inventory of Essential Mathematics—Normative Update (KeyMath-R/NU) (Connolly, 1998) is an individually administered, norm-referenced diagnostic test of math skills and concepts from kindergarten to grade 12. The KeyMath-R/NU is an updated version of the KeyMath Diagnostic Arithmetic Test (Connolly, 1988; Connolly, Nachtman, & Pritchett, 1976). The test, originally developed for students with mild disabilities, was later refined and expanded for all students who need comprehensive diagnostic assessment and remedial instruction in mathematics. The authors designed the KeyMath-R/NU for special education teachers, educational diagnosticians, and math specialists to use in identifying specific strengths and weaknesses and for planning instructional programs. A summary of the KeyMath-R/NU appears in the Test Review box.

Two parallel forms allow students to be retested without duplication. The test contains 13 subtests in three strands:

TEST REVIEW

KeyMath-Revised/NU

Type of Test:	Norm-referenced and individually administered
Purpose:	To diagnose mathematics achievement
Content Areas:	Basic concepts, operations, and applications
Administration Time:	Approximately 1 hour
Age Levels:	Kindergarten to grade 12
Suitable for:	Students with mild and moderate disabilities
Scores:	Standard scores, grade and age equivalents, percentiles, stanines, and NCEs for the total test and the three content areas
In Short:	The KeyMath-R/NU is useful for measuring performance levels and developing instructional objectives. It has excellent content, valuable supplemental features, and adequate technical characteristics.

Strand One: Basic Concepts
   Numeration
   Rational numbers
   Geometry
Strand Two: Operations
   Addition
   Subtraction
   Multiplication
   Division
Strand Three: Applications
   Measurement
   Time and money
   Estimation
   Interpreting data
   Problem solving
   Mental computation

KeyMath-R/NU Materials   The well-designed KeyMath-R/NU materials include easel kits for both Form A and Form B, test records for both forms, a manual, and a sample report to parents. Supplementary teaching materials and an available computer software scoring and interpretation program enhance the test's usefulness. The software automatically converts scores and connects them to the IEP and the KeyMath Teach and Practice (TAP) instructional intervention program. Software options include a score summary profile, a domain performance summary, a narrative report, item objectives, and TAP resources. The KeyMath-R/NU is an excellent example of a diagnostic test that includes many valuable instructional features, a summary of which appears in Focus 16–3. These features make it easy for teachers to connect assessment data derived from the KeyMath-R/NU with instructional intervention programs in the classroom.

KeyMath-R/NU Administration and Scoring.   The manual provides extensive information about administering, scoring, and interpreting the KeyMath-R/NU. The test, which takes approximately 1 hour to administer, produces a variety of scores, including standard scores (M = 100, SD = 15), grade and age equivalents, percentile ranks, stanines, and NCEs for the total test and the three strands. In addition, the test

FOCUS 16-3

Instructional Features of the KeyMath-R/NU

- Contains numerous test items for comprehensively measuring mathematics achievement
- Helps determine scope and sequence in mathematics instruction
- Provides a detailed measure of performance levels in mathematics
- Serves as an instructional guide
- Includes a software program that provides score conversions, a narrative report, and recommendations for intervention
- Provides supplemental materials including remedial activities, worksheets, drills, and games

provides scaled scores (M = 10, SD = 3), percentile ranks, stanines, and NCEs for each of the 13 subtests. Spring and fall norms enable precise assessment of student performance levels at the beginning and end of the school year. Furthermore, a score profile form, one of the strongest scoring features of the test, graphically summarizes results and facilitates visual interpretation of test data. By graphically illustrating strengths and weaknesses, the profile makes it easy to analyze area and subtest performance. A companion software program, KeyMath-R/NU Assist, expedites score conversion and provides a four- to five-page narrative report with student performance data and recommendations for programming. A sample scoring summary form from the KeyMath-R/NU appears in Figure 16–2.

KeyMath-R/NU Technical Characteristics Standardized with a group of more than 3,000 students, the KeyMath-R/NU normative update followed a well-designed development plan using a representative national sample. The KeyMath-R/NU exhibits adequate split-half and alternate-form reliability; however, like many similar tests, some subtest reliabilities fall below acceptable levels. Although the KeyMath-R/NU displays excellent content validity, it exhibits limited concurrent and construct validity. Despite these technical issues, Wollack (2001), in a comprehensive review of the test, concluded that the KeyMath-R/NU was one of the best tests for assessing math performance and providing useful diagnostic information. In an earlier review, Larsen and Williams (1994) indicated that the rich history of development, use, and study of

Figure 16–2 Scoring summary form from the KeyMath-R/NU

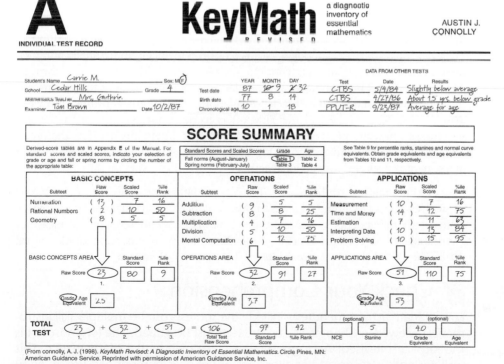

Source: From *KeyMath Revised: A Diagnostic Inventory of Essential Mathematics*, by A. J. Connolly, 1998, Circle Pines, MN: American Guidance Service. Reprinted with permission of American Guidance Service, Inc.

the KeyMath makes the test complete and thorough. Overall, the KeyMath-R/NU displays adequate technical qualities with many excellent measurement features.

KeyMath-R/NU Summary   Because it contains excellent content along with attractive supplemental features, the KeyMath-R/NU serves as an effective diagnostic tool for evaluating skills in mathematics. Larsen and Williams (1994) described the instrument as a great asset to educators who need to determine scope and sequence in mathematics instruction. The test organization makes the information especially accessible to teachers. Valuable as a measure of performance levels in mathematics and an instructional guide, teachers can use the KeyMath-R/NU together with the KeyMath Teach and Practice (TAP) (Connolly, 1985) materials. The TAP consists of remedial activities in basic concepts and includes worksheet activities, drills, and games.

Other Diagnostic Tests of Mathematics

In addition to the KeyMath-R/NU, teachers and evaluators may select from among other diagnostic math tests. The brief reviews of representative tests that follow provide an overview of the range and variety of commercially available instruments for measuring mathematics.

Stanford Diagnostic Mathematics Test, Fourth Edition   The Stanford Diagnostic Mathematics Test, Fourth Edition (SDMT 4) (Beatty, Madden, Gardner, & Karlsen, 1995) is a norm-referenced screening test for students from 1st through 12th grade. The purpose of the SDMT 4 is to identify the math achievement levels of groups of students. The test is divided into six levels, each of which includes multiple-choice and free-response items. Two forms of the test are available. The test results can be hand scored or machine scored locally. Central scoring and reporting services are also available from the publisher.

Test of Early Mathematics Ability—2   The Test of Early Mathematics Ability—2 (TEMA-2) (Ginsburg & Baroody, 1990) is a norm-referenced, individually administered measure of emerging math concepts. Designed for children from age 3 through age 8, the TEMA-2 measures concepts of relative magnitude, reading and writing numerals, counting skills, number facts, calculation, calculation algorithms, and base-10 concepts. The purpose of the TEMA-2 is to determine specific strengths and weaknesses, measure progress, evaluate programs, and guide instruction and remediation. The TEMA-2 takes 20 to 30 minutes to administer, and the materials include assessment probes and instructional activities.

Reflection
Why do you think most teachers would prefer CBAs in math rather than norm-referenced tests? Explain.

Test of Mathematical Abilities—2   The Test of Mathematical Abilities-2 (TOMA-2) (Brown, Cronin, & McEntire, 1994) is a norm-referenced, individually administered diagnostic test for students in grades 3 through 12. TOMA-2 subtests include measures of vocabulary, computation, general information, story problems, and attitude toward math. The TOMA-2 takes approximately 1 1/2 hours to administer.

 To answer this reflection online, go to the *Teaching and Learning* module on the Companion Website at *www.prenhall.com/venn.*

☑ Check Your Comprehension

Formal math achievement tests include the subtests on the multiple-skill instruments reviewed in Chapter 14 and the tests just described. The foremost test is the KeyMath Revised: A Diagnostic Inventory of Essential Mathematics. This well-designed instrument has a long history of development and use. In addition, it features a complete series of teaching and practice materials for use in conjunction with the test.

Summary

When students require in-depth, diagnostic evaluation in mathematics, special educators may select from among several multiple-skill and single-skill diagnostic tests as well as a variety of curriculum-based evaluation procedures (see Table 16–1). Because the various techniques differ in design and purpose, teachers should select an appropriate procedure on the basis of individual student needs and the purpose of the assessment. Although laws and professional standards mandate use of individually administered, norm-referenced tests for making placement decisions, most teachers prefer less formal procedures for making classroom-based instructional decisions. Regardless of the specific assessment approach, resulting data should help the teacher to place students appropriately, identify specific math problems, and design appropriate remediation activities.

To check your comprehension of the chapter contents, go to the *Guided Review* and *Quiz* modules in Chapter 16 of the Companion Website, www.prenhall.com/venn.

Table 16–1 Review of Mathematics Achievement Tests

Name of Test	Type of Test	Suitable for Children Who Are	Brief Description of Test	Purpose of Administering Test
*Keymath-Revised: A Diagnostic Inventory of Essential Mathematics—Narrative Update (KeyMath-R-NU)	Norm-referenced, Individually administered, diagnostic math test	Kindergarten–grade 9	Measures basic concepts, operations, and applications; includes excellent content and valuable supplemental features	To diagnose mathematics achievement, identify strengths and weaknesses, and develop instructional objectives
Stanford Diagnostic Mathematics Test—Fourth Edition (SDMT 4)	Norm-referenced, group-administered screening test	Grades 1–12	Provides six levels with multiple-choice and free-response items for each level	To identify the math achievement levels of groups of students
Test of Early Mathematics Ability—2 (TEMA-2)	Norm-referenced, individually administered	Ages 3–9	Measures concepts of relative magnitude, reading and writing numerals, counting skills, number facts calculation, calculational algorithms, and base-10 concepts	To determine specific strengths and weaknesses, measure progress, evaluate programs, and guide instruction and remediation

(continued)

Table 16–1 *continued*

Name of Test	Type of Test	Suitable for Children who Are	Brief Description of Test	Purpose of Administering Test
Test of Mathematical Abilities—2 (TOMA-2)	Norm-referenced, individually administered	Grades 3–12	Measures vocabulary, computation, general information, and story problems	To measure math performance in major skill areas in math as well as attitude, vocabulary, and general application of mathematics concepts in real life

*Tests marked with an asterisk are featured in this chapter.

Meeting Performance Standards and Preparing for Licensure Exams

After reading this chapter, you should be able to demonstrate the following CEC Standards and PRAXIS™ test knowledge and skills. The information in parentheses identifies where to find the particular CEC standard and PRAXIS™ content reference.

CEC Standards for Beginning Special Education Teachers

- Gather relevant background information (CC8S1)
- Administer nonbiased formal and informal assessments (CC8S2)
- Use technology to conduct assessments (CC8S3)
- Develop or modify individualized assessment strategies (CC8S4)
- Develop or modify individualized assessment strategies (CC8S9)
- Create and maintain records (CC8S10)

PRAXIS™ Education of Exceptional Students: Core Content Knowledge

- Assessment, including use of assessment for screening, diagnosis, placement, and the making of instructional decisions; for example, how to select and conduct nondiscriminatory and appropriate assessments; how to interpret standardized and specialized assessment results (0353 III)
- Assessment, including procedures and test materials, both formal and informal, typically used for prereferral, screening, referral, classification, placement, and ongoing program monitoring (0353 III)
- Assessment, including how to select, construct, conduct, and modify nondiscriminatory, developmentally and chronologically age-appropriate informal assessments, including teacher-made tests, curriculum-based assessment, and alternatives to norm-referenced testing (including observations, anecdotal records, error analysis, miscue analysis, self-evaluation questionnaires and interviews, journals and learning logs, and portfolio assessment) (0353 III)

chapter 17

Assessing Written Expression

Objectives

After reading this chapter, you will be prepared to do the following:

- Define the assessment of written language.
- Understand the subskills measured by tests of written language.
- Consider why we assess the written language of students with special needs.
- Develop curriculum-based procedures for assessing spelling.
- Conduct error pattern analysis of spelling.
- Develop curriculum-based procedures for assessing written expression.
- Assess written expression using the written language profile.
- Use norm-referenced tests for assessing written language.

Overview

In this chapter, you explore the knowledge base for assessing written language, beginning with the definition of written language and a description of the skills measured by written language tests. Following this introduction, you investigate curriculum-based assessment procedures for evaluating written language. These include an error analysis procedure for evaluating spelling skills and a written expression profile for assessing writing ability. You will discover how to use these informal assessment tools to guide the teaching and learning process and to ensure that relevant written expression tasks appear in the curriculum. Later in the chapter, you examine the most widely used, individually administered tests of written expression and spelling. As you learn about each test, you will consider the educational uses of the instrument, the administration and scoring procedures, and the technical qualities.

Assessing Written Language

The following anecdote, written by a teacher of students with learning disabilities, illustrates the way many students with special needs feel about writing. For many students, even a writing assignment that requires "just a few words" is an overwhelming task.

Student:	"How much do we have to write?"
Young:	"One well-developed paragraph ... about 100 to 150 words."
Student:	"I CAN'T WRITE THAT MUCH!!!!"
Young:	"Well, write for about 20 minutes."
Student:	"TWENTY MINUTES!!!!!"
Young:	"Well, then ... just try a few words." (Young, 1993, p. 3)

Because so many students with special needs have trouble like this with writing, it is imperative that teachers know how to assess written expression skills.

Defining Written Language

Written language is the expression of ideas and feelings in written form. Written language skills in the school curriculum include written expression, spelling, and handwriting. Of these, written expression is the most difficult to assess because of the subjectivity involved in measuring the intricacies of writing.

Because written expression is a complex form of communication, many students with disabilities have difficulty with it. Students without proficiency in written language lack a critical skill for academic success in school and for vocational success in the community. However, unlike the wealth of educationally useful procedures available to assess reading and mathematics, relatively few instructionally sound instruments exist for evaluating written language ability.

Teachers usually rely on curriculum-based assessment to evaluate written language. For this reason, this chapter focuses on the various types of curriculum-based assessment most applicable to instructional settings. The chapter also includes information about available norm-referenced tests for evaluating written language performance.

Why Do We Assess Written Language?

The primary reason for assessing written expression is to identify present levels of writing and spelling performance as the basis for designing intervention programs. Assessment provides the teacher with information about specific strengths and weaknesses as well as what each student knows and does not know about writing and spelling. Assessment also helps teachers understand the writing strategies the student knows and uses. This knowledge leads directly to the establishment of priorities for intervention in writing and spelling. Planning an instructional program in written

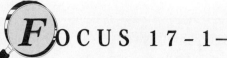

Why Do We Assess Written Language Skills?

- To identify current levels of performance in writing and spelling
- To determine specific student strengths and weaknesses in writing and spelling
- To identify what the student knows and does not know
- To understand the writing strategies a student knows and uses
- To identify priorities for writing skill development
- To plan a student's intervention program
- To help determine instructional approaches
- To monitor the instructional program
- To determine progress in meeting IEP goals

expression also includes deciding which particular instructional methods will be the most responsive to the often unique needs of individual students and groups of students. Finally, assessment of written expression helps teachers monitor the instructional program and determine student progress in meeting IEP goals. Focus 17–1 outlines the reasons for assessing written language skills.

Curriculum-Based Written Language Assessment

Curriculum-based assessment of written language is process-oriented and criterion-referenced. The best procedures are flexible, learner-centered strategies that relate directly to daily instruction. These include observations, informal inventories, and teacher-constructed tests. In contrast, norm-referenced testing of written expression is a product-oriented type of testing that centers on numerical outcomes, including scores and standardized results. Though both types of assessment are useful, most teachers prefer curriculum-based evaluation procedures such as the following:

- Using instructional probes
- Using grading rubrics
- Giving teacher-made tests
- Conducting error analysis
- Developing checklists
- Distributing questionnaires
- Conducting interviews
- Holding conferences
- Reviewing work samples
- Grading writing journals and notebooks
- Evaluating writing portfolios
- Giving oral feedback
- Giving written feedback
- Holding discussions with students and parents
- Video assessment to measure student ability and progress
- Online essay scoring (see the Technology Focus box)

TECHNOLOGY FOCUS
Online Essay Scoring

Online scoring allows students to submit essays using Web-based programs and receive nearly instantaneous feedback. Because online scoring is on the Internet, it extends learning beyond the classroom by enabling students to work independently at home, at the library, or in a computer lab. This is an example of how technology is changing teaching, learning, and evaluation.

Several online essay programs are available, including Holt Online Essay Scoring. Students use Holt Online Essay Scoring by entering their essays in response to the writing prompts provided on the Web site. A computer scoring system evaluates each essay and provides a holistic score and analytic feedback related to five writing traits: content and development, focus and organization, use of effective sentences, word choice and grammar, and usage and mechanics. The Holt Online Essay Scoring Web site offers a guided tour showing how it works and a free demo site where students can submit an essay based on one of two prompts.

Online essay scoring technology holds much promise for the future. What once sounded like science fiction is now a valid way to score writing samples. With the emergence of online learning, more educators should explore the efficacy of these types of programs.

Linking Assessment with Instruction

Teachers may select from a variety of available options for linking instruction in written language with assessment of written language. A list of these options appears on the following page. The list includes ideas for gathering assessment information that connects with daily lessons and strategies for giving feedback to students and parents in ways that occur as a regular part of classroom instruction. Additional strategies for assessing the writing skills of students from diverse backgrounds appear in the accompanying Multicultural Considerations feature.

Brainstorming

Brainstorming is a free-flowing, open-ended process of sharing ideas as a class or in small groups. Brainstorming helps students understand the different strategies they use to learn. Brainstorming sessions are best when the teacher begins with specific question prompts such as "What do you do when you do not understand a writing assignment?" "How do you decide when a paper you write is finished?"

Interviews

Interviews or questionnaires also help teachers assess learning strategies. In most situations, the teacher develops questions to elicit strategies for a particular writing topic or task. Prior to a unit on poetry, for example, the teacher might ask the following set of questions: "If your assignment for tomorrow were to write a poem in the style of Langston Hughes, what would you do first?" "Where would you find information?" "How would you decide what words to use?" "What would you do if you were stuck?"

MULTICULTURAL CONSIDERATIONS

Assessing Learning Strategies

In classrooms with learners from diverse backgrounds, the learning styles of the students may not match the expectations and routines of the school community. This is particularly true of learners from culturally different backgrounds who are at risk for school failure. Improving the writing and other academic skills of these students requires modeling and explicit instruction. Assessing learning strategies is one step toward designing the best possible instructional programs for these students. DiCerbo (2001) suggested using techniques such as brainstorming, interviews, journals, and think-alouds to assess and compare different learning strategies.

Give examples of how student's learning strategies are influenced by their culture.

To answer this reflection online, go to the *Multicultural Considerations* module on the Companion Website at **www.prenhall.com/venn**.

Journals

Asking students to write in their journals or to reflect silently on the question of how they learn provides an excellent starting point for discussion of learning strategies. Teachers may begin with specific prompts for class or homework such as "What steps do you take when you have to write a paper in your senior English class?" "What do you do differently when you write a paper in your science class?"

Think-Alouds and Think-Afters

A great deal of what students do to understand and complete a writing assignment occurs inside their heads. Think-alouds and think-afters put a voice to these thinking processes and model their use for students. Thus, thinking aloud while completing an assignment or thinking aloud after completing an assignment often helps to discover and compare learning strategies. For example, teachers often give feedback to students and model appropriate writing behavior when they verbalize the process of drafting a paper on a specific subject. Likewise, teachers often ask students to think aloud when they have difficulty with an assignment so that the teacher can provide suggestions.

The best learning occurs when teachers account for the fact that students arrive in classrooms with learning strategies influenced by their language and their culture. Teachers can gather important information about how their students learn by using techniques such as brainstorming, interviews, journals, think-alouds, and think-afters. Techniques like these help teachers identify and evaluate the particular learning strategies used by their students.

Observations

Observations are among the most frequently used curriculum-based procedures. Teacher observations of student behavior, also called classroom observations, help to identify the strategies students use to complete written language tasks as well as to determine the attention span and frustration level of students. Although informal and subjective, the observations of experienced teachers often yield vital assessment information for creating remediation programs and intervention activities. In some situations, teachers may benefit from observations conducted by others. Depending on the purpose and goal of the observation, parents, paraprofessionals, colleagues, specialists, and even volunteers can serve as observers. When teachers rely on other observers, they should ensure that the observer understands the purpose of the observation and follows established observation procedures.

Informal Inventories and Tests

Many informal inventories and tests are available, including teacher-constructed measures, commercial inventories, and instruments developed by local school systems and state education agencies. Teacher-made inventories and tests include classroom spelling quizzes to identify student mastery of instructional content, teacher-created checklists of written expression skills, and rubrics used to grade student work. The widely used Brigance Diagnostic Inventories (Brigance, 1999) is a set of commercially available inventories that offers several useful subtests for evaluating written language. Available Brigance subtests include spelling, grammar and mechanics, and reference skills for the elementary grades, and language arts and communication skills at the secondary level. Informal diagnostic tests like the Brigance Inventories serve as both classroom assessment tools and curriculum guides.

Curriculum-Based Spelling Assessment

Most of the time when teachers score spelling tests, they simply mark the incorrect words and assign a grade based on a percent correct score. This common grading practice is appropriate in many instructional situations; however, it fails to provide the kind of diagnostic information that teachers need with students who have severe spelling problems. Moreover, it can lead to inaccurate conclusions about the reasons for errors. When teachers need more detailed assessment information, they use more complex curriculum-based assessment procedures.

Comprehensive curriculum-based assessment of spelling involves identifying the overall level of spelling achievement, determining specific strengths and weaknesses, and evaluating spelling error patterns. To achieve this level of assessment, Ariel (1992) recommended the following informal procedure for testing of spelling ability. Teachers can use this informal procedure with individual students or an entire class.

1. Select 30 to 50 words based on an appropriate graded list.
2. Administer the spelling test.
3. Score the test and tabulate the results. If used with a class, note the lowest 20%.
4. Have the pupils define the words they misspelled. Omit unfamiliar words because they are not in the children's vocabulary.
5. Have the pupils spell any remaining words orally. Keep a record of the spelling, noting the syllabification, phonic use, and speech or hearing difficulties.
6. Compare the original spelling to note differences in oral and written responses.
7. Ask the children to study words missed (for about 10 minutes), and observe their methods of study.
8. Analyze errors and incorporate information from the data obtained from other sources.

9. Draw conclusions about the nature of the spelling problem. Plan educational strategies to overcome the difficulties.
10. Discuss the analysis and teaching plan with the pupil.
11. Provide for pupils to see progress. (p. 448)

Analyzing Spelling Errors

Diagnostic analysis of spelling errors provides the details necessary to develop accurate remediation activities. Steps in the error analysis process include collecting a sample of spelling errors, conducting a diagnostic interview with the student, classifying the errors, determining a corrective strategy, implementing the strategy, and monitoring student progress (Hendrickson & Gable, 1990).

Teachers may record the results of error analysis using a form like the sample spelling error analysis chart in Figure 17–1 This chart, developed from a list of typical student spelling errors by Ariel (1992), places the most common error types in categories and displays the results from analysis of the writing sample that appears in Figure 17–2.

Written Language Profile

Assessing written expression skills requires measurement of several elements. Raiser (1996) defined these elements as follows:

Fluency	The quantity of written output as measured by the number of words written in a specific period
Average Thought Unit	A measure of writing maturity and complexity based on syntax
Vocabulary Diversity	The originality, maturity, and variety of words used in writing
Structure	The mechanical aspects of writing, including capitalization, punctuation, and language usage
Organization	The coherence of a composition as evidenced by the quality of the narrative, the essay, or the story

The Written Language Profile developed by Raiser (1996) for assessing these written language components appears in Figure 17–3. Instructions for using the Written Language Profile appear in Figure 17–4. Teachers can use this curriculum-based assessment tool to guide teaching and learning. The Profile provides a way to carefully analyze written language abilities so that teachers can focus instructional time on teaching students what they need to know. The list of the 100 most common words that appears in Figure 17–5 is used in completing the Written Language Profile.

Because the Written Language Profile is an informal evaluation tool, teachers can use it in a flexible manner. In some situations, teachers may elect to use the complete Written Language Profile to obtain a comprehensive overview of student performance. Alternatively, teachers may select only parts of the Profile to obtain information about student performance in specific written expression skills.

Figure 17–1   Spelling error analysis chart

Student __Kenneth__   Teacher __Janelle Venn__   Date __9/22__

Description of the Spelling Sample ____A story written by Kenneth_____

Description of Spelling Problems Analyzed _____

Total Words _70_   Misspelled Words _22_   Percent of Correctly Spelled Words _68%_

Error Category	Error Type	# of Errors	Remediation Plan
Omission errors	Omission of a pronounced letter (e.g., "say" for "stay")	2	
	Omission of a silent letter (e.g., "ofen" for "often")		
	Omission of double letters (e.g., "super" for "supper")		
Substitution errors	Consonant sound confusion (e.g., *t* for *d*, *t* for *v*, *sh* for *ch*, *s* for *z*)	3	
	Vowel sound confusion	13	Focus on vowel sound/sight match in the most common 3-, 4-, 5- letter words from the Hillerich's list of 100 most frequently used words
	Phonetic substitution for a word (e.g., "obay" for "obey")		
	Word substitution ("gals" for "girls")		
Addition/insertion errors	Addition of unnecessary sounds and letters	3	
	Addition by doubling ("supper-vision" for "supervision")		
	Unnecessary addition of *ed*		
	Addition of unnecessary suffixes		
Confusion of digraphs	Such as "wead" for "weed"		
Phonetic spelling of nonphonetic words	Such as "sum" for "some"		
Confusion between homonyms	Words with similar pronunciation (e.g., "except" for "accept")		
Sequencing errors	One letter out of sequence (e.g., "barn" for "bran")	1	
Sound letter reversals	Such as "form" for "from"		

Notes _____

_____

Figure 17–2   Student writing sample for assessing written expression

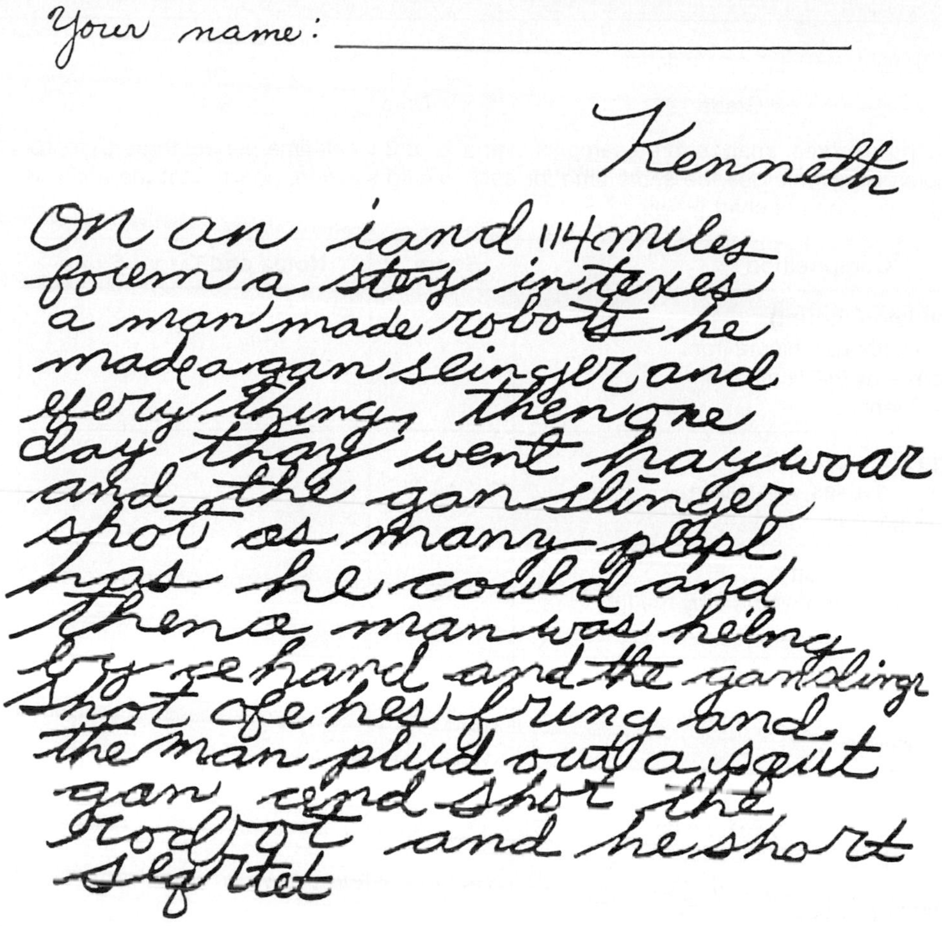

Your name: _____

Kenneth

On an iand 114 miles
foem a story in texes
a man made robot he
madeargan slinger and
eory thing then one
day thay went haywoar
and the gan slinger
shot es many plopl
ngs he could and
then a man was heing
by re hand and the gansling
shot of hes fring and
the man plud out a squt
gan and shot the
rodot and he short
sqrtet

On an island 114 miles from a city in Texas a man
made robots. He made a gun slinger and everything. Then
one day they went haywire and the gun slinger shot as many
people as he could and then a man was hanging by a hand and
the gun slinger shot off his finger and the man pulled out a
squirt gun and shot the robot and he short circuited.
Total words: 70   Misspelled: 22   Correctly spelled: 68%
Grade: 6   IQ: 97   Age: 13

Figure 17–3 Written Language Profile

Name _____   Teacher _____

Age _____   Grade _____   Date_____

To obtain the best scores, analyze three samples over a 2- to 3-week time period; three 5- to 10-minute samples work well. Use the same time for each writing session, and repeat the analysis midyear and at year end to chart growth.

Composition	Score	Notes and Target Skills
1. Fluency (word count) Sum of the words per minute from each sample ÷ by the number of samples = fluency		
2. Average Thought Unit Total words − garbles ÷ T-units = average thought unit		
3. Vocabulary Diversity Number of uncommon words ÷ by the total number of words = vocabulary diversity		
4. Organization: Narrative 1 − 5 rating scale (1 = lowest rating, 5 = highest rating)		
5. Organization: Story 1 − 5 rating scale (1 = lowest rating, 5 = highest rating)		
6. Organization: Essay 1 − 5 rating scale (1 = lowest rating, 5 = highest rating)		
7. Structure: Capitalization Count the total number of capitalization errors and note error patterns.		
8. Structure: Punctuation Count the number of punctuation errors and note error patterns.		
9. Structure: Language Usage Count the number of language usage errors and note error patterns.		

Comments _____

_____

_____

Figure 17–4   Instructions for the Written Language Profile

The Written Language Profile is an informal assessment of student abilities intended to guide instructional planning. Through careful analysis of written language abilities, teachers can spend instructional time teaching students exactly what they need to know. The profile will be most effective in classrooms where writing is taking place on a regular basis, preferably daily because effective writing requires frequent practice.

Collecting Samples

Collect three samples over a period of 2–3 weeks to get an accurate measure. Samples should be 75–100 words long; three 5- to 10-minute timed samples work well. Young writers and less experienced writers need longer time.

Profile Analysis Procedures

1. MEASURE FLUENCY

If you use periodic timed writings, you can measure fluency, which is the number of words written over time. With daily practice in 5- to 10-minute timed writings, you can expect the number of words to increase. It's easier to compute words per minute if you use the same time each day.

Have students count the words written each day, and write this number at the top of their papers before they turn them in. Then they can chart their own increases on their graphs (e.g., "Words I Wrote in 10 Minutes").

Procedure for Measuring Fluency

a. Count the total number of words (TW). Ignore punctuation and count all words that make sense. Exclude garbles that are incomplete words, conversational asides, false starts, redundancies, or words that do not make sense in context. Subtract garbles from total words (TW).
b. Ignore misspelled words. Try very hard to use context to decipher invented spellings before counting strange-looking words as garbles. With practice, you will become better at decoding unusual spellings.
c. Count names and number as one word (e.g., John Paul is one word; 114 is one word). Count compound words written separately as two words (e.g., *every thing* = two words).
d. Teach your students to routinely count the number of words they write and to put the number at the top of the front page of their papers.
e. Divide the TW by the time (in minutes) taken to complete the writing sample to obtain the number of words per minute (word count). For example, if a student writes 100 words in 10 minutes, then the words per minute is 10: 100(TW) ÷ 10 (minutes of writing) = 10 words per minute.

(continued)

FIGURE 17–4 *continued*

f. If you use more than one writing sample, add the number of words per minute from each sample and divide by the number of samples to obtain the average words per minute.

2. CALCULATE AVERAGE THOUGHT UNITS

Average thought units measure writing maturity and complexity based on the syntax of the piece. Syntax is the way words are put together in phrases, clauses, or sentences to make complete thoughts. The formula is:

$$\text{Total words} \div \text{T-units} = \text{Average Thought Units}$$

Procedure for Calculating Average Thought Units

a. Count the total number of words written using the procedure outlined in the procedure for fluency.
b. Count the number of T-units present. A T-unit is the shortest grammatically correct segment that makes a complete thought. When counting T-units, ignore punctuation (many of your students won't use it anyway) and ignore spelling. Do not count garbles, which are incomplete sentences, conversational asides, false starts, redundancies, and words that don't make sense. Try to decipher spelling before counting strangely spelled words as garbles. When in doubt because of handwriting errors, give credit. Ignore "ands" that connect complete thoughts but include "ands" in the Total Word count. For example, the following sentence contains 14 total words and three T-units. "The dog is big/and the cat is small/ and the rat is smaller/."
c. Divide the Total Words by the number of T-units present. The example contains 14 words and 3 T-units. Therefore, the Average Thought Unit is 4.6. Calculate this as follows: 14 (Total Words) ÷ 3 (T-units) = 4.6 (Average Thought Units)

Interpreting the Average Thought Unit Score

Longer T-units indicate more complex writing. As sentences become more complex, T-units grow very slowly. Expect less than one unit of growth each year. T-unit averages of fewer than 9 words indicate immature writing.

Use the following T-unit averages as benchmarks: 4th graders—8.6 words; 8th graders—11.5 words; 12th graders—14.4 words; 6th and 7th graders with learning disabilities—8.6 words. You may also develop your own benchmarks by analyzing a collection of writing samples from your students.

Teach your students to count T-units. They will learn to recognize complete thoughts and sentence fragments quicker this way than they will with a worksheet. It's also good practice with averaging and decimals; therefore, let them use calculators.

3. MEASURE VOCABULARY DIVERSITY

Vocabulary diversity is the variety of words used in written expression as measured by the percentage of diverse or uncommon words in a composition. Writing should become more original, mature, and diverse as students develop their written expression skills. The formula is:

Number of uncommon words (UW) ÷ Total Words = Vocabulary Diversity

Procedure for Calculating Vocabulary Diversity

a. Count all uncommon words. These are words not on the 100 Most Common Words list (Hillerich, 1978) that ppears in Figure 17–5. Count uncommon words used more than once each time they are used.
b. Count the total words in the writing sample.
c. Divide the number of uncommon words by the total words to obtain the vocabulary diversity (percentage of uncommon words).

Interpreting the Vocabulary Diversity Score

The 100 Most Common Words make up 60% of words that students use in writing in grades 2–6. Uncommon words make up 40% of words used. A score above 40% indicates higher writing development. Students can learn to do this analysis.

4. RATE THE ORGANIZATION: NARRATIVE

A narrative is the type of composition tht tells an event or a story. Rate the narrative quality of the sample by answering the following questions: Is the piece clearly focused? Is it logically sequenced? Does it have a definite beginning, middle, and end? Does it make sense? Use rating scale scoring with a range of 1 to 5 to obtain a narrative score. A rating of 1 indicates a poor narrative. A rating of 5 indicates a superior narrative.

5. RATE THE ORGANIZATION: STORY

A story is an account of a happening or group of happenings. Rate the quality of the story by answering the following questions: Are the characters well developed? Is the setting well developed? Does the story include a problem to solve? Does the story present a problem resolution? Use rating scale scoring with a range of 1 to 5 to obtain a story score. A rating of.1 indicates a poor story; a rating of 5 indicates a superior story.

6. RATE THE ORGANIZATION: ESSAY

An essay is a composition on a specific subject. Rate the quality of the essay by answering the following questions: Do the paragraphs contain

(continued)

FIGURE 17–4 *continued*

lead/topic sentences? Does the essay provide supporting details? Does the essay include a conclusion? Use rating scale scoring with a range of 1 to 5 to obtain an essay score. A rating of 1 indicates a poor essay; a rating of 5 indicates a superior essay.

7. MEASURE THE STRUCTURE: CAPITALIZATION

Identify capitalization errors including sentence beginnings, proper names, important words in titles, and abbreviations. Score capitalization by counting the number of capitalization errors, and look for patterns of errors.

8. MEASURE THE STRUCTURE: PUNCTUATION

Identify punctuation errors, including periods, question marks, exclamation points, commas, semicolons, and quotations (e.g., "I can go," said Tommy). Score punctuation by counting the number of punctuation errors, and look for patterns of errors.

9. MEASURE THE LANGUAGE USAGE

Identify language usage errors including subject and verb agreement, object agreement, verb tense consistency throughout the piece, appropriate pronoun usage, and other errors. Score language usage by counting the number of usage errors, and look for patterns of errors.

Source: From *Written Lanuage Profile* by L. Raiser, 1996, Unpublished Manuscript, University of North Florida, Jacksonville. Reprinted with permission.

Writing Sample and Completed Written Language Profile

Alisha, a fourth-grade student, wrote the following story about her grandmother in 15 minutes. The composition has been assessed using the Written Language Profile. The completed Profile appears in Figure 17–6.

My Grandmother

My grandmother is a strong black lady who marched with Dr. Martin Luther King back in the 60's. She was at that time pregnant with my father and have two young daughter at home. My grandmother spent time in jail for this march, but she never gave up her right to speech. My grandmother raises five children and worked an 8 hour job. She never let them go hunger or dirty and she was alway there to make sure they was on their best behavior. My grandmother is still alive and well. But she can not do the things she like to do for very long without getting try. Doing her time traveling with my grandfather in the navy my grandmother would travel with her children every where. I love you my grandmother very much.

Figure 17–5   100 most common words

The 100 most common words are found on most basic sight word lists; they are the words children and adults need most often in their writing. If your students know how to spell these 100 words, they will know 60% of all the words they need to know how to spell when writing about their own self-selected topics.

When students learn to spell these words, they will then need to worry only about the other 40% they need to spell in their writing. Students should keep this list, the Dolch sight word list, and their own personal list in their writing process folios for reference.

The words *I, and*, and *the* account for 11.8% of the most commonly used words. Add the words *a* and *to* and you have 18.2% of the word. Add *was, in, it, of, my*, and *you* for 26.1%. The following list of 100 words makes up 60% of all the words used by the children in Hillerich's study (1978). These words came from the free writing (unassigned writing) of regular education students in grades 2–6.

100 MOST COMMON WORDS IN ABC ORDER

a	for	mother	them
about	from	my	then
after	get	no	there
all	go	not	they
am	got	now	things
an	had	of	think
and	have	on	this
are	he	one	time
around	her	or	to
as	him	our	too
at	his	out	two
back	homo	over	up
be	house	people	us
because	I	put	very
but	if	not	was
by	in	now	we
came	into	said	well
can	is	saw	went
could	it	school	were
day	just	see	what
did	know	she	when
didn't	like	so	who
do	little	some	will
don't	man	that	with
down	me	the	would

☑ Check Your Comprehension

The curriculum-based strategies include observations, informal inventories, and teacher-constructed tests. Teachers routinely evaluate written language using informal procedures such as grading class writing assignments, giving weekly spelling tests, and completing informal checklists of written language skills. When teachers need even more detailed assessment information, they often rely on error analysis procedures. Error analysis, using representative samples of student work, can be highly useful in diagnosing

Figure 17–6 Completed Written Language Profile

Name Alisha		Teacher John Venn
Age 11	Grade 4th	Date 4/2

Composition	Score	Notes and Target Skills
1. Fluency (word count) Sum of the words per minute from each sample ÷ by the number of samples = fluency	9 wpm	Increase overall fluency
2. Average Thought Unit Total words − garbles ÷ T-units = average thought unit	8.5	None
3. Vocabulary Diversity Number of uncommon words ÷ by the total number of words = vocabulary diversity	32%	Increase overall diversity
4. Organization: Narrative 1 − 5 rating scale (1 = lowest rating, 5 = highest rating)	3	Focus the paragraph on one theme
5. Organization: Story 1 − 5 rating scale (1 = lowest rating, 5 = highest rating)	3	Develop the grandmother as a character
6. Organization: Essay 1 − 5 rating scale	3	Write a topic sentence that connects the paragraph
7. Structure: Capitalization Count the total number of capitalization errors and note error patterns.	0	I am pleased that you are doing so well with!
8. Structure: Punctuation Count the number of punctuation erros and note error patterns.	2	Be sure to put commas before coordinating conjunctions
9. Structure: Language Usage Count the number of language usage errors and note error patterns.	5	Work on subject verb agreement and verb tense

Comments _____

_____

_____

_____

spelling deficits. Likewise, teachers rely on various forms of analysis to evaluate written composition samples. These include measuring fluency, calculating average thought units, evaluating vocabulary diversity, rating organization, and identifying structural errors. The next chapter, which deals with portfolio assessment, also provides useful information regarding curriculum-based evaluation of written language. In fact, most of the procedures for portfolio assessment can be applied directly to the assessment of written language.

Formal Written Language Assessment

To obtain diagnostic information about student performance in written language, special educators may select from among several formal, norm-referenced tests. These tests include the multiple-skill tools reviewed in Chapter 14 and the single-skill instruments reviewed next.

Test of Written Language—3

The norm-referenced Test of Written Language—3 (TOWL-3) (Hammill & Larsen, 1996) evaluates the written expression skills for students from ages 7 though 17. Designed to pinpoint a student's current level of performance in written expression and identify types of writing errors, the test helps teachers develop instructional objectives and plan appropriate intervention activities. The TOWL-3 uses essay analysis and other evaluation techniques to measure both spontaneous and contrived written expression skills. A summary of the TOWL-3 appears in the Test Review box. The TOWL-3 includes the following subtests:

Spontaneous Formats

1. Contextual conventions: Measures capitalization, punctuation, and spelling
2. Contextual language: Measures vocabulary, syntax, and grammar
3. Story construction: Measures plot, character development, and general composition

Contrived Formats

4. Vocabulary: Measures word usage
5. Spelling: Measures ability to form letters into words
6. Style: Measures punctuation and capitalization
7. Logical sentences: Measures ability to write conceptually sound sentences
8. Sentence combining: Measures syntax

TEST REVIEW

Test of Written Language—3

Type of Test:	Norm-referenced and individually administered
Purpose:	To diagnose written expression
Content Areas:	Spontaneous and contrived expression
Administration Time:	30 to 45 minutes
Age Levels:	Grades 2 to 12
Suitable for:	Students with mild disabilities, including learning disabilities and behavior disorders
Scores:	Percentile ranks and standard scores for the total test and the two subtests
In Short:	The TOWL-3 is a helpful tool for evaluating the written language skills of individuals and groups. The test is useful for classification, placement, and classroom instruction.

TOWL-3 Materials   The TOWL-3 kit contains an examiner's manual, 25 student response booklets (Form A), 25 student response booklets (Form B), and 50 Profile/Story Scoring Forms. An optional computer scoring system is also available.

TOWL-3 Administration and Scoring   The TOWL-3 takes about 90 minutes to administer to individuals or to groups. Students complete the spontaneous expression subtests by writing essays based on stimulus pictures. For the contrived subtests, students respond to dictated stimulus words and sentences, correct illogical sentences, and combine simple sentences into complex ones. The derived scores include percentiles and standard scores for overall, contrived, and spontaneous writing as well as for each subtest.

TOWL-3 Technical Characteristics   The TOWL-3, which was standardized on a sample of more than 2,000 students living in 26 states, displays adequate reliability and validity for use as a diagnostic tool. The authors provide data to support the internal consistency, test-retest, and interscorer reliability of the TOWL-3. The reliability coefficients average in the .80s at most ages. The manual also includes descriptions of several validity studies conducted with the TOWL-3.

The TOWL-3 was designed to detect and eliminate as many sources of cultural, gender, and racial bias as possible. Steps taken to reduce bias included including targeted demographic groups (i.e., gender, race, social class, and disabled groups), reliability and validity for targeted groups, analysis of item bias, and avoiding time limits, which are thought to be biased against many groups.

TOWL-3 Summary   The TOWL-3, a norm-referenced measure of written language, is a widely used tool for assessing written language. The test meets the nationally recognized standards for assessing the presence of deficits in written language.

Written Expression Scale

The *Written Expression Scale* (WE) measures the written language of children and young adults from 5 to 21 years of age. The WE is one of three scales that make up the Oral and Written Language Scales (OWLS) (Carrow-Woolfolk, 1995). The other two scales, which were reviewed in Chapter 10, are the Listening Comprehension Scale (LCS) and the Oral Expression Scale (OES). The WE measures three writing skills: use of conventions, including letter formation, spelling, capitalization, and punctuation; use of linguistic forms, including modifiers, phrases, and sentence structure; and ability to communicate meaningfully, including appropriate content, coherence, unity, word choice, and details. A summary of the WE appears in the Test Review box.

WE Materials   The Written Expression Scale is available in a kit that includes a manual, a package of 25 record forms, a package of 25 student response booklets, and an administration card. A computer software scoring program, the Written Expression Assist for DOS, Macintosh, and Windows, is available separately. The software provides a score profile, a score narrative, and a descriptive analysis.

WE Administration and Scoring   It takes approximately 40 minutes to administer the WE to individuals or small groups. The evaluator asks the student to complete various writing tasks that are similar to writing activities found in a classroom. Some items have pictures or print, and others are presented orally. Students take the test by writing their responses directly in a response booklet. The test manual provides detailed scoring rules along with samples of actual responses. The scoring booklet

TEST REVIEW

Written Expression Scale

Type of Test:	Norm-referenced, administered individually or in small groups
Purpose:	To diagnose written language skills
Content Areas:	Use of conventions, linguistic forms, and ability to communicate meaningfully
Administration Time:	Approximately 40 minutes
Age Levels:	5 to 21 years
Suitable for:	Students with mild disabilities, including learning disabilities and behavior disorders
Scores:	Age- or grade-based standard scores, percentiles, NCEs, stanines, and age or grade equivalents
In Short:	The Written Expression Scale measures the writing skills of students from 5 to 21 years of age. The WE features a comprehensive sample of written language skills covering a wide age range.

includes abbreviated scoring rules for quick reference during item-by-item scoring. Evaluators can report WE results as age- or grade-based standard scores, percentiles, NCEs, stanines, and age or grade equivalents. The test also provides score comparison procedures for analyzing differences among scores and a score profile that gives a visual representation of performance.

WE Technical Characteristics   The WE was co-normed with the Listening Comprehension and Oral Expression Scales using a national standardization sample of 1,795 children and youth. The sample was stratified using the 1991 Current Population Survey data for the demographic variables of gender, race, ethnicity, region, and mother's level of education. The manual reports high internal consistency and test-retest reliability coefficients for the scales. Several validity investigations were conducted using the WE, including nine concurrent validity studies and eight clinical studies with 850 subjects.

WE Summary   Because it provides a detailed sampling of written language and covers a wide age span, the WE is valuable in clinical and school settings. The instrument is useful to clinicians, psychologists, and teachers who need accurate test scores and detailed diagnostic information about the written expression skills of students.

Other Tests of Written Language

Test of Written Spelling   The Test of Written Spelling (TWS-4) (Larsen, Hammill, & Moats, 1999) is a norm-referenced measure of the spelling proficiency of students from 1st through the 12th grade. Designed to pinpoint a student's current level of performance in spelling and identify types of spelling errors made by the student, the test helps the teacher develop instructional objectives and plan appropriate intervention activities. The TWS-4 is suitable for individual or group administration. It takes about 25 minutes to give the test.

Test of Written Expression   The Test of Written Expression (TOWE) (McGhee, Bryant, Larsen, & Rivera, 1995) is a norm-referenced tool for assessing the writing achievement of students from age 6 through 14. The instrument provides two separate assessment methods for measuring a comprehensive set of writing skills, including ideation, vocabulary, grammar, capitalization, punctuation, and spelling. The TOWE evaluates writing using two assessment procedures. One procedure involves administering 76 items that measure written expression ability, and the other involves having the student write a complete story from a story starter. The completed story provides a writing sample that can be used independently to obtain a norm-referenced assessment or as a component in a student's portfolio.

Test of Early Written Language, Second Edition   The norm-referenced Test of Early Written Language, Second Edition (TEWL-2) (Hresko, Herron, & Peak, 1996) evaluates the emerging written language skills of youngsters from age 3 through 11. The TEWL-2 measures skills that relate directly to the learning activities of young schoolchildren, including basic and contextual writing. It takes about 45 minutes to administer the TEWL-2.

Writing Process Test   The norm-referenced Writing Process Test (WPT) (Warden & Hutchinson, 1992) measures writing performance by having students plan, write, and revise an original composition. The WPT evaluates the written product and the writing process. Suitable for individuals and groups of students from grades 8 through 12, it usually takes about an hour to give the WPT.

Word Identification and Spelling Test   The Word Identification and Spelling Test (WIST) (Wilson & Felton, 2004) measures word identification, spelling, and sound-symbol knowledge using an elementary version (grades 2–5) and a secondary version (grades 6–12). The WIST helps identify students who are struggling with reading and spelling. Available WIST scores include percentiles, standard scores, and age and grade equivalents. The WIST includes three informal procedures for analyzing performance on: (a) the test items, (b) sound-symbol skills, and (c) errors peculiar to written words. Information from these analyses support the test performance interpretation and help formulate a literacy intervention plan.

☑ Check Your Comprehension

Tests of written language provide teachers, clinicians, and psychologists with standardized measures useful for identifying, diagnosing, and measuring written language skills. Some of these tests are survey instruments that assess a range of skills for identifying overall achievement. Other tests focus on specific skills such as spelling and emerging writing.

Summary

Written language assessment guides the process of helping students develop written expression skills. Several types of assessment procedures and instruments are available to achieve this goal (see Table 17–1). In instructional settings, teachers most often rely on curriculum-based measures of composition and spelling, including error

Table 17–1 Review of Written Language Tests

Test	Type	Suitable for	Brief Description	Purpose
Test of Early Written Language, Second Edition (TEWL-2)	Norm-referenced, individually administered	Young children from 3 to 11 years of age	Measures basic writing and contextual writing	To identify the emerging written language skills of young children
Test of Written Expression (TOWE)	Norm-referenced, administered individually or in small groups	Students from 6 to 14 years of age	Measures ideation, vocabulary, grammar, capitalization, punctuation, and spelling	To diagnose writing achievement
*Test of Written Language—3 (TOWL-3)	Norm-referenced, administered individually or in groups	Students who are 7 to 17 years of age	Measures spontaneous and contrived expression writing	To evaluate the performance of students with deficits
Test of Written Spelling (TWS-4)	Norm-referenced, suitable for individual or group administration	Students from grades 1 through 12	Measures spelling proficiency by assessing the ability to spell predictable and unpredictable words	To pinpoint a student's current level of performance in spelling and to identify types of spelling errors made by the student
Word Identification and Spelling Test (WIST)	Norm-referenced, Individually administered	Ages: 7.0 through 18.11	Measures word identification, spelling, and sound-symbol knowledge	Identifies students who are struggling with reading and spelling
*Written Expression Scale (WE): Oral and Written Language Scales (OWLS)	Norm-referenced, individually administered	Students from 5 to 21 years of age	Measures use of conventions, use of linguistic forms, and the ability to communicate meaningfully	To provide detailed diagnostic information about the written expression skills of students
Writing Process Test (WPT)	Norm-referenced	Individuals and groups of students from grades 8 through 12	Measures writing performance by having students plan, write, and revise an original composition	To evaluate the product and the process of writing

*Tests marked with an asterisk are featured in this chapter.

pattern analysis procedures, teacher observations, inventories, tests, and checklists, to measure student growth and development. Some of these criterion-referenced assessments, including error analysis, rely on student work samples. Assessment using actual student work samples helps link assessment with instruction. This linkage is especially useful in developing remediation programs for students with severe written language deficits. When teachers need formal norm-referenced assessment information, they may select from among several multiple-skill and single-skill tests that measure writing, spelling, and handwriting skills. These include screening tests as well as comprehensive diagnostic instruments. These norm-referenced tools yield vital assessment information for making identification, staffing, and placement decisions and for evaluating intervention programs.

 To check your comprehension of the chapter contents, go to the *Guided Review* and *Quiz* modules in Chapter 17 of the Companion Website www.prenhall.com/venn.

Meeting Performance Standards and Preparing for Licensure Exams

After reading this chapter, you should be able to demonstrate the following CEC Standards and PRAXIS™ test knowledge and skills. The information in parentheses identifies where to find the particular CEC standard and PRAXIS™ content reference.

CEC Standards for Beginning Special Education Teachers

- Use and limitations of assessment instruments (CC8K4)
- Administer nonbiased formal and informal assessments (CC8S2)
- Use technology to conduct assessments (CC8S3)
- Develop or modify individualized assessment strategies (CC8S4)
- Interpret information from formal and informal assessments (CC8S5)
- Use assessment information in making eligibility, program, and placement decisions for individuals with exceptional learning needs, including those from culturally and/or linguistically diverse backgrounds (CC8S6)
- Develop or modify individualized assessment strategies (CC8S9)
- Specialized terminology used in the assessment of individuals with disabilities (GC8K1)

PRAXIS™ Education of Exceptional Students: Core Content Knowledge

- Assessment, including use of assessment for screening, diagnosis, placement, and the making of instructional decisions; for example, how to select and conduct nondiscriminatory and appropriate assessments; how to interpret standardized and specialized assessment results (0353 III)
- Assessment, including procedures and test materials, both formal and informal, typically used for prereferral, screening, referral, classification, placement, and ongoing program monitoring (0353 III)
- Assessment, including how to select, construct, conduct, and modify nondiscriminatory, developmentally and chronologically age-appropriate informal assessments, including teacher-made tests, curriculum-based assessment, and alternatives to norm-referenced testing (including observations, anecdotal records, error analysis, miscue analysis, self-evaluation questionnaires and interviews, journals and learning logs, and portfolio assessment) (0353 III).

chapter 18

Portfolio Assessment

Objectives

After reading this chapter, you will be prepared to do the following:

- Describe advantages and disadvantages of portfolio assessment.
- Develop portfolio contents and materials.
- Create a portfolio management system.
- Ensure the reliability of portfolio assessments.
- Use holistic and analytical scoring rubrics.
- Use external and internal scoring protocols.
- Integrate student self-assessment in portfolio evaluation.
- Hold portfolio conferences.

Overview

In this chapter you investigate the processes for using student portfolios as assessment tools. Your study begins with a description of portfolios, which includes an explanation of the portfolio concept, an examination of the growing interest in portfolio assessment, a review of the advantages and disadvantages of portfolio assessment, and a discussion of portfolios for students with disabilities. Next you examine procedures for planning, building, and using portfolios in ways that ensure reliable appraisal of student performance. Later in the chapter, you examine specific portfolio assessment processes, including scoring systems and reporting procedures. Finally, you consider portfolio conferences that provide opportunities for review, reflective discussion, and student self-assessment.

Growing Interest in Portfolio Assessment

The following narrative shows the many questions teachers have about portfolios and also illustrates the growing interest in portfolios.

Mrs. Geneva is a teacher of students with learning disabilities. She has never used portfolios before, but because she has heard so much about portfolios lately, she wonders whether she could use portfolio assessment in her class. But first, she asks herself: What exactly are portfolios and what kind of assessments do they use? Are there different kinds of portfolios? Next, she asks: Why use portfolios? Is the use of portfolios in education a trendy phase that will quickly pass, or can portfolios really make a difference in learning and teaching? What can portfolio assessment do for me that other assessment methods don't? What about my students? What can portfolios do for them?

Mrs. Geneva does some research, consults with others, and decides to try portfolios because of their purported advantages such as increased sense of student ownership of work and documentation of improvement over the course of a year. She gets some helpful information from these resources on implementing portfolios. She doesn't know, though, how to tailor the portfolio for her students with learning disabilities. None of the articles she read mentioned this, and her colleagues have limited experience with portfolios for students with special needs. She wonders: Will her students' portfolios be different from those of "typical" students? How will portfolios meet instructional needs? What specifically can they do for students with disabilities that other assessment methods don't? Will her students be able to handle the paperwork and self-reflective activities involved in creating a portfolio? Whom does she talk with to find out? She decides to visit with the district's support staff and consult a special education teacher in another school who she has heard uses portfolios with success.

Portfolios in the Classroom

A portfolio literally is a flat, portable case for carrying documents, drawings, and similar materials. Artists, architects, photographers, and investors all use such carrying cases as holders for their valuable materials. The portfolio concept, as applied to education, is based on this idea. Artists' portfolios, for example, consist of carefully selected collections that show their finest paintings, photographs, or other works. Likewise, student portfolios should consist of carefully selected schoolwork representing the students' best work. Portfolios are not static compilations but dynamic collections that artists update periodically. Like an artist's portfolio, the contents of a student's portfolio are not fixed. Students may eliminate older samples of work when they update their collection with more recent accomplishments.

Defining Portfolios and Assessment

A **student portfolio** is a purposeful collection of student work and related material that depicts a student's activities, accomplishments, and achievements in one or more school subjects. Most portfolios include evidence of student reflection and self-evaluation, guidelines for selecting the portfolio contents, and criteria for judging the quality of the work. The goal is to help students assemble portfolios that illustrate their talents, represent their writing capabilities, and tell their stories of school achievement (Stiggins, 2005). **Portfolio assessment** is an ongoing process that captures the many activities and accomplishments associated with reflective teaching and learning that occur in portfolio-based instruction. By evaluating progress using a collection of authentic samples of student work, portfolio assessment provides an ongoing record of student performance and mastery of specific competencies (Vavrus, 1990).

Emphasis on Performance

Rather than emphasizing test scores to measure student progress, portfolio assessment focuses on evaluation of samples of a student's best work. Clearly, measuring student learning with portfolios is much different from traditional grading, in which teachers assign grades based on test scores and other assignments such as homework. Teachers then use the test scores and other grades to calculate a report card grade. Although this is an efficient method of evaluation, it may fail to provide details about student performance. In contrast, when teachers use portfolios, they are more concerned with maintaining the details and less concerned with efficiency. Although most portfolios focus assessment on the process of learning and the quality of the final portfolio product rather than on test scores, tests are a valid measure of student performance that can be included in portfolios. Though some portfolios avoid tests altogether, others routinely incorporate tests as a valuable assessment element (Stiggins, 2005).

Focus on Writing and Reading

Most student portfolios focus on writing and reading activities, although portfolios are useful in most subjects, including science and math. Having students collect writing samples is an established way to begin portfolio-based instruction. Assessment may include measurement of how much writing a student accomplishes and the stages through which written documents progress from the rough draft to the final product.

Likewise, having students develop reading portfolios is an excellent way to initiate portfolio-based instruction and assessment. Reading portfolios can consist of a list of readings that document how much a student has read and identify a student's particular interests. Such reading portfolios are more than a simple listing and should include elements such as annotations by students, book reports, vocabulary lists, and invented endings. Reading portfolios can also be much more complex. They may include peer feedback, teacher impressions, and self-reflections that allow students to discuss and react to reading materials. These portfolio elements can help students organize what they understand and feel, and demonstrate what they have learned through their readings. Having students prepare reading portfolios can also motivate and encourage them to pursue additional reading.

Types of Portfolios

Process and product portfolios represent the two major types of portfolios. A process portfolio documents the stages of learning and provides a progressive record of student growth. A product portfolio demonstrates mastery of a learning task or a set of learning objectives and contains only the best work. Cole, Ryan, Kick, and Mathies (1999) described process evaluation as the major and more dynamic type of portfolio. Teachers use process portfolios to help students identify learning goals, document progress over time, and demonstrate learning mastery. In addition to these two major types, there are many others, including celebration, showcase, language arts, and teacher-developed portfolios like the "Big Book" portfolio described later in this chapter.

Process Portfolios

Process portfolios may include a variety of materials such as unfinished work, journals, reflections, notes, independent work, conference reports, teacher evaluations, peer evaluations, self-evaluations, and even test results. However, rather than a random collection of work samples, the process portfolio should contain carefully selected materials that illustrate specific learnings.

In general, teachers prefer to use process portfolios because they are ideal for documenting the stages that students go through as they learn and progress. This type of portfolio is especially useful with students from diverse cultural and linguistic backgrounds. Information about using process portfolios with learners who are diverse appears in the accompanying Multicultural Considerations feature.

In the initial stages of process portfolio development, the teacher and the students identify the materials that will go into the portfolio, and the teacher helps the students specify their learning goals. Students with special learning needs may require extra assistance at this beginning stage. After this initial step, the portfolio begins to take shape. At this point students include interim evidence in their portfolios to demonstrate progress toward reaching their learning goals. For example, a process portfolio in the interim stages might contain an outline for a paper, a rough draft of the paper, and an edited second draft of the same manuscript with teacher comments and student reflections. Teachers may need to provide special support for struggling students during the interim stages. Support may include peer tutoring, assistance from a paraprofessional, or extra time with the teacher. Some struggling students may need assistance with self-reflections, which can be a difficult task for at-risk learners. All of this support helps students prepare for completing their portfolios with the final output as evidence of mastery.

Product Portfolios

Managing and producing a process portfolio takes time, and the notebook or storage container can be bulky. For this reason, teachers sometimes have students prepare a more concise portfolio called a product portfolio. **Product portfolios,** which are

MULTICULTURAL CONSIDERATIONS

Process Portfolios and Diverse Learners

Because process portfolios provide the teacher with detailed diagnostic information, they are especially responsive to the needs of learners from culturally and linguistically diverse backgrounds who have learning deficits. For example, when students with limited English proficiency prepare writing portfolios that include rough drafts, teachers can identify specific areas in need of remediation. If a student makes mistakes using articles or helping verbs, the teacher can quickly identify the error pattern and start remediation. Likewise, with students who use nonstandard English, teachers can use portfolio assessment to help identify error patterns and initiate appropriate interventions.

How do you think portfolio assessment could encourage students with limited English proficiency?

To answer this reflection online, go to the *Multicultural Considerations* module on the Companion Website at www.prenhall.com/venn.

used less often in the classroom, are shorter, more accessible documents. The materials in the portfolio should be final products illustrating success at the mastery level. Teachers and students may include summary statements that reflect the level of student learning. In some situations, teachers may have students transform their process portfolios into product portfolios. The most practical time for this transformation is at the completion of a program or the end of a school year. The school then keeps a copy of the product portfolio for future reference (Cole et al., 1999).

Celebration Portfolios

Although process and product portfolios represent two major types, there are many creative ways to develop portfolios. For example, Stiggins (2005) recommends **"celebration" portfolios**, which students can use as mementos of their favorite learning experiences and activities. Students are free to create these portfolios without teacher-prescribed requirements. The teacher asks students to select materials in response to the question, "What are your favorite class materials and activities, and why are they your favorites?"

This type of imaginative portfolio helps students learn to identify special work and develop understanding of the meaning of quality. Because students develop their own standards, the celebration portfolio helps them learn to make choices and reflect on their own strengths and interests. For this reason, the celebration portfolio is particularly useful with children with learning problems who suffer from poor self-esteem or fear of failure. Sharing their celebration portfolios with families and others gives students a way to communicate school successes.

Showcase Portfolios

Showcase portfolios display a student's best work (Linn & Miller, 2005). Showcase portfolios are like those used by professionals to illustrate their work. These portfolios require the highest-quality work from all students. However, achieving this level of quality takes time. This means that students must have opportunities to revise their work until it achieves appropriate standards of excellence. Many students will also need close monitoring, plentiful feedback, and models to follow. Showcase portfolios are ideal for use with student-led conferences. Information about student-led conferences appears later in the chapter.

A "Big Books" Portfolio Project

In the following narrative account of a "Big Books" portfolio project, Katherine Curtis, a teacher of students with special needs in Orange Park, Florida, discusses her concept of the benefits of portfolios. Katherine's Big Books activity contained elements of both process and product portfolios. The process elements were the sloppy, neat, and final copies of the story. The final products were the "Big Books" that the students prepared and presented to students in other classes.

This year I designed a "Big Book" portfolio activity for my fifth and sixth graders. This particular portfolio project gave my students an opportunity to use a variety of academic skills to create their Big Books. They developed written expression skills as they created their stories, which they accomplished by picking a topic and then writing sloppy copies, rough drafts (which I edited), and neat copies. They learned creative art skills by designing a picture for the cover of their Big Books. Presentation skills were also part of the project. The students practiced reading their books in class, and this prepared them for the final step of reading their stories to children in a kindergarten or first-grade class.

This portfolio activity also helped improve student self-esteem and confidence. I was pleased to observe my students gain self-assurance because of their hard work and determination. The portfolio helped meet many of my students' affective IEP goals. The activity was so successful that I plan to continue using it. The project showed me the many benefits of portfolio-based instruction.

Samples of student work from the Big Books project appear in Figure 18–1. The samples include a "sloppy copy," a rough draft (with the teacher's comments), and a

Figure 18–1 Amber's sloppy copy, rough draft, and neat copy for her Big Book story

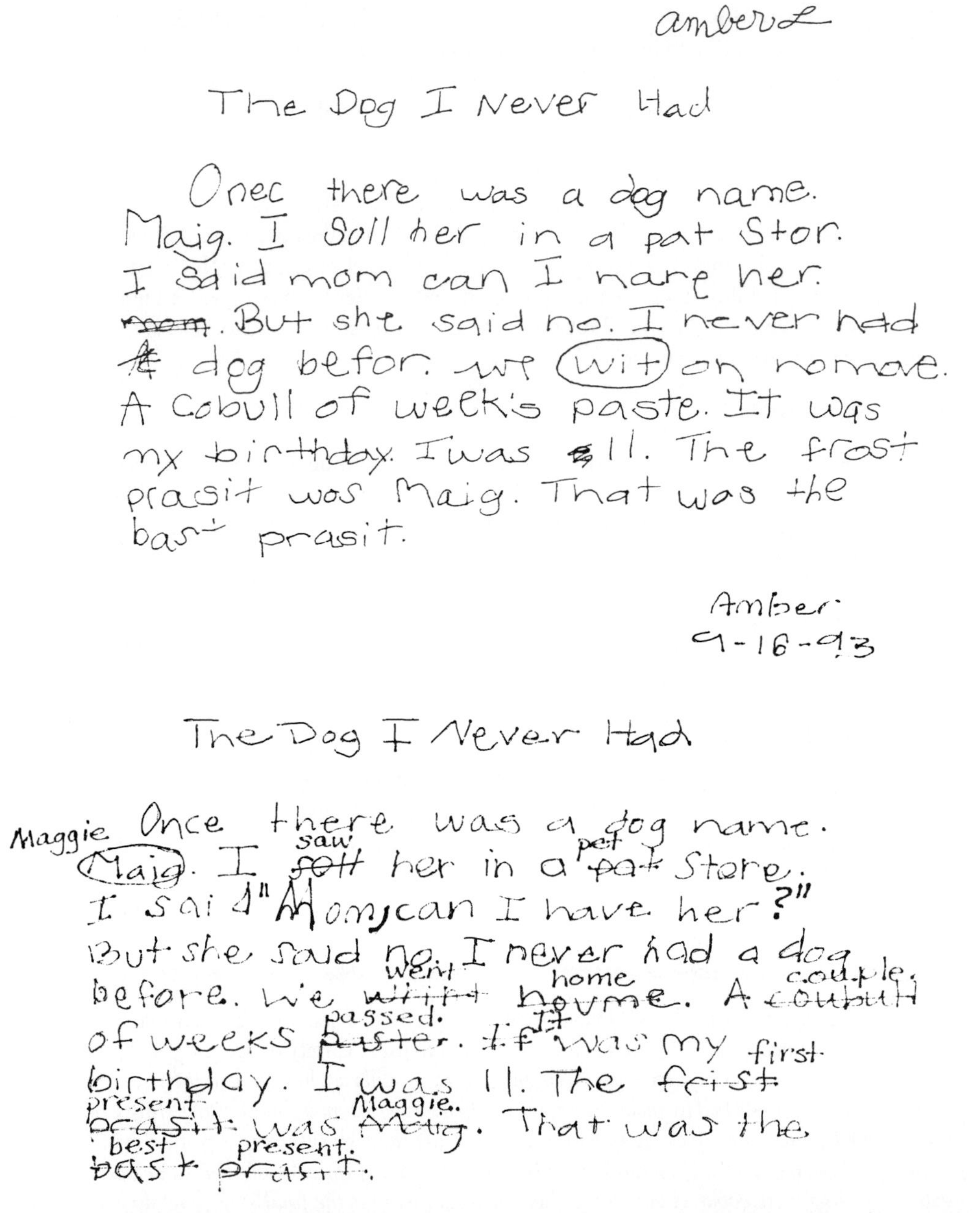
amberL

The Dog I Never Had

Onec there was a dog name. Maig. I Soll her in a pat Stor. I Said mom can I nare her. ~~mom~~. But she said no. I never had ~~A~~ dog befor. we (wit) on nomae. A Cobull of week's paste. It was my birthday. I was ~~8~~11. The frost prasit was Maig. That was the bast prasit.

Amber
9-16-93

The Dog I Never Had

Maggie Once there was a dog name. (Maig). I saw ~~soll~~ her in a pet ~~pat~~ Store. I said "Mom can I have her?" But she said no. I never had a dog before. We went ~~witt~~ home ~~houme~~. A couple ~~coubull~~ of weeks passed ~~paster~~. It ~~it~~ was my first birthday. I was 11. The first ~~frist~~ present ~~prasit~~ was Maggie ~~Maig~~. That was the best ~~bast~~ present ~~prasit~~.

Amber

The Dog I Never Had

Once there was a dog named Maggie. I saw her in a pet store. I said, "Mom, can I have her?" But she said no. I never had a dog before. We went home. A couple of weeks passed. It was my birthday. I was 11. The first present was Maggie. That was the best present.

neat copy of the Big Book story called "The Dog I Never Had," written by Amber, a student in the class.

Digital Portfolios

Digital portfolios use new technology such as graphics, video, and audio. Traditional portfolios are usually stored in folders, boxes, or three-ring binders, but digital portfolios can be stored on a computer, on removable media, or on the Internet. Students gain valuable computer skills while creating their own digital portfolios. More information about digital portfolios appears in the Technology Focus box.

TECHNOLOGY FOCUS
Digital Portfolios

Teachers and students have a wide array of digital design options for preparing, storing, and presenting portfolios. Possibilities range from basic word processing to totally digital portfolios, which are entire portfolios that students prepare and store on computers. Students may use multimedia presentation and graphic design software to prepare their digital portfolios.

For students with disabilities, teachers should consider a number of accessibility options including specialized hardware such as adapted keyboards and touch screens. Speech-to-text and text-to-speech software also help some students. Useful software adaptations are available for keyboard, display, and mouse functions. Students with written expression deficits may benefit from spell-checking, grammar, and text-to-speech programs.

Table 18–1 Digital Portfolio Scoring Rubric

Name _____   Date _____

Teacher _____   Class _____

Item	Try Again 5 points	Okay 10 points	On Target 15 points	First-Rate 17 points
Design	Poor, sloppy	Adequate, but could be neater	Attractive and colorful	Attractive, colorful, and creative
Mechanics	Many spelling, grammar, and other mechanical mistakes	Some mechanical errors	Minor mistakes	No errors
Links	Less than 3 links	4–5 links	6–7 links	More than 7 links
Sounds	Inappropriate or distracting	Adequate	High quality	Highest quality and original
Content	Low quality	Adequate	High quality	Highest quality
Reflections	Few reflections	Some reflections	Reflections with personal feelings	Descriptive, insightful reflections

Points

Overall Grade and Comments

_____

_____

_____

Reflection

Discuss what you see as the "pros" and "cons" of portfolio assessment.

  To answer this reflection online, go to the *Teaching and Learning* module on the Companion Website at *www.prenhall.com/venn.*

Rubrics provide an excellent way to evaluate digital portfolios. A sample rubric for assessing digital portfolios, adapted from Worchester (n.d.), appears in Table 18–1. Students should receive the rubric before beginning their digital portfolio project so that they are aware of the criteria ahead of time. A percentage score is calculated by adding the points earned in each category of the rubric.

✔ Check Your Comprehension

Widespread use of portfolios by teachers, schools, school systems, and entire states has made portfolio evaluation an increasingly important assessment topic. Portfolio assessment, which relies on samples of real student work, is a type of curriculum-based, authentic assessment that emphasizes systematic collection of work that demonstrates achievement and reflective learning. Students usually present their work in an organized, well-planned notebook or another appropriate container. The concept, based on artists' and architects' portfolios, uses samples of a student's best work to show mastery learning; however, many teachers also have students develop creative and individualized portfolios, such as celebration portfolios. Although most portfolios focus on written expression and related language arts activities, portfolios are also useful in other disciplines, including math and science.

Why Do We Use Portfolio Assessment?

Like all evaluation procedures, portfolio assessment has both advantages and disadvantages. Although the benefits of portfolio assessment typically outweigh the drawbacks, an understanding of the limitations helps us avoid potential pitfalls. Some teachers readily adapt to portfolio-based instruction because it fits easily into their teaching style. Regardless of individual teaching styles, the widespread interest in portfolios is due, in large part, to disillusionment with traditional teaching and testing practices. At the same time, many educators are enthusiastic about opportunities for reflective teaching and learning that allow students to actively participate in the learning process.

Although portfolio assessment is not new, it is coming into more widespread use as educators reexamine standards for student performance. Several factors account for the growing interest in portfolio assessment. One factor is the expanding use of whole language instruction. Like portfolio-based instruction, whole language instruction focuses on the language arts, especially written expression. A second factor is the movement toward assessment reform. Assessment reform is part of overall school restructuring, which emphasizes standards-based education. Finally, dissatisfaction with high-stakes testing has led many teachers to embrace portfolio assessment because it provides a more realistic and relevant alternative to traditional testing. Although most teachers are generally familiar with portfolios, they should carefully consider the advantages and disadvantages of portfolio assessment before implementing the system in their own classrooms.

Advantages of Portfolio Assessment

Portfolio-based assessment provides several distinct advantages. These include the following:

- Promoting student self-evaluation, reflection, and critical thinking
- Measuring performance based on genuine samples of student work
- Providing flexibility in measuring how students accomplish their learning goals
- Enabling teachers and students to share the responsibility for setting learning goals and for evaluating progress toward meeting those goals
- Giving students the opportunity to have extensive input into the learning process
- Facilitating cooperative learning activities, including peer evaluation and tutoring, cooperative learning groups, and peer conferencing
- Providing a process for structuring learning in stages
- Providing opportunities for students and teachers to discuss learning goals and the progress toward those goals in structured and unstructured conferences
- Enabling measurement of multiple dimensions of student progress

Disadvantages of Portfolio Assessment

Like all assessment procedures, portfolio assessment has certain disadvantages, which include the following:

- Requiring extra time to plan an assessment system and conduct the assessments
- Gathering all of the necessary data and work samples can make portfolios bulky and difficult to manage
- Developing a systematic and deliberate management system is difficult, but this step is necessary in order to make portfolios more than a random collection of student work

- Use of subjective evaluation procedures such as rating scales and professional judgment, which limits reliability
- Holding portfolio conferences is difficult, and the length of each conference may interfere with other instructional activities

Using Portfolios with Students Who Have Learning Problems

Because the contents of portfolios are flexible, they are particularly useful with students who have learning problems. This flexibility gives students opportunities to demonstrate achievement in a variety of creative ways. Flexibility is especially helpful with students who perform poorly on tests and traditional class assignments. Instead of taking tests, for example, students can demonstrate progress through drawings, audiotapes, videotapes, checklists of skills, or behavior charts. Second, portfolios help individualize learning activities, which lets teachers tailor assignments to the needs of each student. Next, portfolios enhance motivation by allowing students to focus their efforts on the areas of greatest interest to them. Fourth, portfolios promote mastery learning because students can be given the time and the practice necessary to become proficient at particular skills before they must move on to new skills; therefore, portfolios enable teachers to arrange the learning environment so that students begin at their level of achievement and progress at their own pace rather than at some externally imposed level and pace. Finally, for students with serious reading and written expression deficits, portfolios provide an ideal way to build reading and writing skills and develop the self-confidence necessary to learn new skills. A summary of the reasons for using portfolios appears in Table 18–2.

The following vignette is an account written by Susan Oliver, who describes how she successfully incorporated portfolios with her students who have severe and multiple disabilities.

Because portfolios are such a valuable instructional tool and a hot topic right now, I decided to begin using them with my students who have severe and multiple disabilities. Although I attended an excellent workshop on portfolios, and I talked with teachers who were using portfolios, I knew that my students needed flexibility in selecting their portfolio items. For example, instead of written essays and book reports, my students included lists of new vocabulary words (or signs) and their favorite stories and songs. Many of my students also included their best drawings or art projects, lists of favorite class activities, letters from parents, and checklists of recently learned functional skills. Perhaps the most individual item was in Timmy's portfolio. Timmy, who is autistic, decided to include two of his favorite pieces of wire sculpture. One of his favorite activities is to collect pieces of wire that he shapes into objects of interest. His portfolio included two wire sculptures that he had shaped into Chevrolet "bowtie" symbols that he sees on automobiles.

Table 18–2   Using Portfolios with Students Who Have Learning Problems

- Portfolio flexibility encourages students to demonstrate progress in creative ways.
- Portfolios encourage individualization in response to the special learning needs.
- Portfolio assessment enhances student motivation.
- Portfolios promote mastery learning.
- Portfolios help develop self-confidence.

As I reflect on my portfolio experience, I think that the most motivating part of the project for my students was when they shared their work with other adults in the school and with their parents. For me as the teacher, the portfolios were most useful as tools for communicating with parents; as a way to introduce students in a positive light to new teachers, therapists, paraprofessionals, and volunteers; as vehicles for documenting mastery of skills; and as tools for measuring progress in practical and interesting ways.

For these reasons, I plan to continue using portfolios, and I would not hesitate to recommend them to other teachers of students with severe, profound, and multiple disabilities.

At the same time, I did not realize how much effort and time it would take to set up and manage all of this. In the end, however, my efforts were worthwhile because my students really enjoyed and learned from the experience.

☑ Check Your Comprehension

Although portfolios offer several distinct advantages, the major benefit is promoting student self-evaluation and reflective teaching and learning. The major drawback concerns the extra time required to plan and conduct portfolio instruction and assessment. For students with learning problems, portfolios offer some attractive features, including flexibility, enhanced student motivation, and opportunities for students to develop proficiency by mastering targeted skills.

The Portfolio Assessment Process

The portfolio assessment process has three major steps. First, the teacher and the student need to clearly identify the portfolio contents, which may include samples of student work, reflections, teacher observations, and conference records. Second, the teacher should develop evaluation procedures for keeping track of the portfolio contents and for grading the portfolios. The evaluation procedures include the planning and record-keeping necessary to build portfolios that accurately measure student progress and achievement. Most portfolios include student self-management as part of the overall evaluation system. Third, the teacher needs to plan portfolio conferences, which are formal and informal meetings in which students review their work and discuss their progress. Because they encourage reflective teaching and learning, these conferences are an essential part of the portfolio assessment process.

Selecting Portfolio Contents

Selecting what should go into the portfolio is one of the first decisions in the process. Student portfolios may include a variety of elements that depend on many considerations, such as the grade level, the subject, the learning objectives, the student's IEP, and performance standards for the school and the class. Although the specific contents of a particular portfolio can vary, most portfolios contain several basic elements, and the best portfolios include a combination of student- and teacher-selected items.

Student ideas are important in the selection process because they portray learning from the student's point of view. The teacher, however, may require additional items to measure student progress and respond to particular benchmarks. Along with including student ideas, portfolios should connect with instructional goals. For students with disabilities, the collection of materials in the portfolio should relate to IEP objectives as well as standards for the grade level, the program, the school, and the district. Additionally, portfolios can be an excellent vehicle for showing multiple dimensions of student progress and learning. For example, process portfolios convey the steps by which work is accomplished along with the accomplished work itself. This provides details about the student's academic proficiencies and shows student growth and achievement. To achieve this, portfolios should include different types of data and materials (Wesson & King, 1996).

Portfolio Holders

Students should have the opportunity to provide input in selecting and designing their portfolio holder. Appropriate holders keep materials of different sizes, help organize these materials, and give a sense of responsibility and ownership. Paper file holders or briefcases with flaps, pockets, and attached bands or strings may be appropriate, but some teachers prefer cardboard or plastic file boxes. Because these holders are expensive, some teachers use cardboard boxes, flat-bottom shopping bags, or similar containers that students can decorate with many different kinds of materials, including cutouts, paints, markers, vinyl, logos, and construction paper. Portfolio holders should be durable, creative, low cost, functional, neat, and stylish (Miller, 2001). Porfolio holders need not be limited to traditional file folders, notebooks, or boxes. They can also include digital containers, as explained in the Technology Focus box.

Typical Portfolio Contents

A list of typical portfolio contents (Wesson & King, 1996) for elementary students with disabilities appears in Table 18–3. This list gives ideas about possible items that can go into portfolios. It is not an exhaustive list, and portfolios need not include all of these items. Some portfolios have specific contents; others have a wider range of content across several subjects in the curriculum.

In a survey to find out what teachers preferred in portfolios, Johns and Vanleirsburg (1991) asked the participants, who had all used portfolios, to indicate the items they would include in a literacy portfolio. Writing samples related to literacy experiences were rated as the most preferred item. Listings of materials read and samples of student work on important reading skills or strategies were also highly ranked by the teachers as items they would definitely or possibly include. Most teachers indicated they would also include student self-evaluation, checklists of relevant reading behaviors, and teacher observations and insights in their students' portfolios.

In some situations, the portfolio contents are prescribed by state or school-district standards. For example, Vermont's Portfolio Project (Abruscato, 1993) developed guidelines for writing portfolios that require six samples of student work, including the student's response to a formal writing assignment called the uniform writing assessment. Several states and many school districts have developed similar portfolio requirements. The Vermont guidelines require the following items:

- A table of contents
- A "best piece"
- A letter
- A poem, short story, play, or personal narrative
- A personal response to a cultural, media, or sports exhibit or event or to a book, current issue, math problem, or scientific phenomenon
- One prose piece from any curriculum area other than English or language arts (for fourth graders) and three prose pieces from any curriculum area other than English or language arts (for eighth graders)
- The piece produced in response to the uniform writing assessment as well as related outlines, drafts, and so on (Abruscato, 1993, p. 475)

Table 18–3 Portfolio Contents

Item	Example
Writing samples	Copies of writing samples, which may include rough drafts, revisions, and completed papers
Reading samples	A list of books read during the grading period that may include titles, authors, dates completed, and student appreciation ratings of the books
Reading journal	Excerpts from a reading response journal or reflections log
Conference records	Completed conference record forms
Handwriting samples	A sample of a student's best handwriting
Audiotapes	A tape of the student reading orally. The student may reread the same piece periodically to measure progress.
Photographs	Photos of student projects that show mastery of the material
Videotapes	Students working cooperatively on a language arts project such as a skit that shows understanding of a story
Parent reflections	Parent notes or observations that show student progress
Teacher reflections	Notes that the teacher makes during observations that document instructional decisions
Artwork	Drawings, paintings, or self-portraits that the student prepares as part of an assignment
Student reflections	A self-evaluation in narrative or rating-scale form that the student completes after finishing a major assignment
Checklist of skills	Skills the student needs to master, such as phonics rules, or writing conventions such as capitalization and punctuation
Charts and graphs	A self-evaluation chart of student behavior that shows improvement over time

An example of district-wide requirements comes from the Pittsburg Public School District, which implemented a portfolio process to evaluate student writing in grades 6 through 12 (Linn & Miller, 2005). The portfolio contents included four student-selected writing samples with drafts, the final version, and a written reflection.

Portfolio Evaluation Procedures

Teachers quickly form impressions of performance when they observe students' work on their portfolios, hold conferences, and review portfolios. As a result, teachers almost always know the effort that students put into their portfolios and the progress they are making. Teachers form these impressions regardless of whether they grade a portfolio; however, when teachers grade portfolios, they must support their evaluation with evidence that goes beyond their subjective impressions. The contents of the portfolio itself are the primary documents that provide this evidence. Portfolio contents should include a series of materials that teachers can use to evaluate what students have learned and how well they learned it.

Well-designed portfolios provide more evidence of achievement than poorly designed portfolios, and the best ones tell a story that clearly demonstrates student progress over time. Although portfolios are creative documents that might include a variety of measures, most incorporate the following essential measures: a tracking and evaluation system, criteria for evaluating the entire portfolio and its contents, evidence of student self-assessment, and evidence of portfolio conferences. One of the initial steps in this evaluation process is developing the management system.

Developing a Management System

Because portfolios may be arranged in many different ways, they may include a variety of materials. This variety requires successful portfolios to have an organizational focus and a management system. For example, reading items in a language portfolio could be placed in one section, while written expression materials appear in another section. Alternatively, portfolios may reflect thematic units or specific curriculum goals. Materials may appear in chronological order to show progress over time, or they may appear together with the same theme in response to specific goals. Regardless of the arrangement, teachers should develop a management system that enables them to keep records of the elements in the portfolio. One of the first steps is developing a tracking and evaluation procedure for monitoring overall student progress. An ideal way to accomplish this is with a portfolio contents checklist. Sample checklists appear in Figure 18–2 and Figure 18–3. The portfolio management checklist is for teachers, and the student portfolio checklist is for student use.

Figure 18–2 Teacher's portfolio management checklist

Teacher _Deirdre McDowell_   Date _first 9 Weeks_
Class _5th & 6th Grades_

Student Names

Contents	John	Tamara	Keisha	Kim	Mickely	Jan	Fio	Johnson								
Writing sample-rough draft																
Writing sample-revision																
Writing sample-final																
List of books read																
Reading response journal																
Conference records																

Marking Key   Notes
+   Complete
+/−   Needs improvement
−   Not complete

Figure 18–3   Student portfolio management checklist

| Student _Keisha_ | | Teacher _Ms. McDowell_ | | |
| Class _Fifth Grade_ | | | | |

Portfolio Item	Activity Log			
Writing sample-rough draft	9/22			
Writing sample-revisions	9/25	9/26		
Writing sample-final paper				
List of books read	9/16	9/24		
Reading response journal				
Conference record forms				
Picture for My Big Book		9/28		

Notes _____

_____

_____

Scoring Portfolios

Although portfolio assessment should include an overall management system, the evaluation process involves more than keeping a checklist. The specific scoring procedures depend on the type of portfolio and the reason for the assessment. It is possible for students to develop their own individualized portfolios, but this requires the teacher to develop separate scoring criteria for each one. Although valuable in some learning situations, this is usually difficult to implement in instructional settings with groups of students (Wolcott, 1993).

Most teachers set requirements for the number of items and the specific materials that go into the portfolios. This standardization provides criteria for accurately and effectively assessing portfolios and helps to develop a reliable scoring system that produces consistent results across students. Some educators oppose standardization of portfolios for scoring and grading purposes because they believe it limits the value of portfolios as individual learning tools; however, most educators support standardization of at least some aspects of the portfolio to facilitate evaluation (Wolcott, 1993). A compromise is to let students choose items for the portfolio with the teacher giving some criteria. For example, the teacher tells students they must complete all assignments but include in their portfolios only five in-class writings (of 10 that were assigned), two essays (of three written), and two collaborative writings (of four). This way the teacher gets a "standard" to grade, and students have some autonomy.

Rubrics

A **rubric** is a scoring tool with criteria for a piece of student work. For example, a rubric for an essay might tell students that their work will be judged on purpose, organization, details, voice, and mechanics (Andrade, 2001). Thorndike (2005) points out that scoring student performance usually takes one of two forms: fixed response or variable response. Fixed-response scoring involves matching answers to one or more correct responses, such as marking the questions on a multiple-choice test as either correct or incorrect. Variable-response scoring is more complicated. With variable-response scoring no one correct answer or set of answers exists. Instead, scoring relies on sets of criteria often referred to as rubrics, which are scoring criteria that describe an array of possible responses and specify the qualities or characteristics that occur at different levels of performance. Most portfolio assessment systems rely on rubrics such as the sample holistic and analytical portfolio scoring systems that appear later in this chapter. Likewise, teachers use rubrics whenever they create variable-response, curriculum-based scoring systems for grading student performance. The increasingly popular statewide assessment systems for measuring student performance in written expression, mathematics, and other academic skills are based on rubrics.

According to Thorndike (2005), the best rubrics for scoring provide clear criteria for evaluating student proficiency and performance that are keyed to educational objectives in the student's curriculum. Rubrics include various types of checklists, rating scales, and observation systems that teachers use to assess student products and performances. The best rubrics provide samples of student responses that illustrate student performance at below average, average, and above average levels. When scorers receive adequate training in using explicit scoring criteria, rubrics produce consistent and effective assessment data. On the other hand, incomplete scoring criteria used by poorly trained scorers usually produce unreliable results with inadequate validity.

Reliability Considerations

Because portfolio assessment is a type of informal, criterion-referenced measurement, scoring is subjective. In order to make the process as reliable as possible, teachers should develop rubrics that identify criteria and serve as standards, and then judge each portfolio in reference to these criteria and standards. The standards may be informal criteria presented in a teacher-made checklist or more formal competencies developed by a school system or a state department of education. Because these standards are subjective, teachers must exercise professional judgment when rating student performance. As with any system that involves professional judgment, reliability is always a central concern.

Developing and maintaining a reliable system can be a challenging task. For example, in the first year of Vermont's statewide portfolio assessment system, different teachers scored the same student portfolios quite differently. When experts studied the problem, they found that scoring differences reflected low reliability in the grading system rather than differences in the quality of student work. Recognizing the importance of this reliability problem, Vermont changed the rubrics to improve reliability. These changes included providing additional training for the teachers who served as scorers, eliminating the most-difficult-to-score items from the student portfolios, and modifying the scoring protocols by reducing the number of scoring dimensions. Vermont's struggle to improve reliability illustrates why many teachers and schools use multiple-choice tests (which are easier to make reliable) to measure

Figure 18–4 Portfolio scoring summary

Student _____ Teacher _____

Date _____ Grade _____ School _____

Rating: 1—Below Average,   2—Average,   3—Above Average,   4—Excellent

Pinpoint	Rating	Comments
Amount of writing (completes writing tasks, writes on a variety of topics, revises ideas)		
Quality of writing (neatness, organization, vocabulary, mechanics)		
Attitude toward writing (motivation, effort, determination)		

student achievement even though they do not capture critical details of important competencies (Murnane & Levy, 1996). This example also illustrates why portfolio assessment has limited use in the entitlement process of identifying children who qualify for special education services due to a disability.

In response to these reliability concerns, Vavrus (1990) suggested that the key to successful scoring is setting standards that relate to students' learning goals. This can be difficult for teachers who are implementing portfolios for the first time. To overcome startup problems, teachers should develop a scoring form listing the criteria they will use to grade the portfolio. A sample scoring form, based on a form developed by Farr and Tone (1998), appears in Figure 18–4. Beginning teachers may also wish to consult with more experienced teachers to obtain information about how they set standards to ensure reliability.

Another way to improve reliability is to develop an evaluation scale that lists a progression of performance standards with representative examples of work at each level of performance. The teacher can determine what students should demonstrate at each level and then describe what constitutes inadequate, satisfactory, and exemplary work. This is most easily accomplished after teachers have successfully used portfolios in classes and have the opportunity to collect samples of student work that can be used as examples. This process of describing characteristics at each level makes it possible to locate where a student's work toward a particular goal falls in terms of the set of standards (Vavrus, 1990).

Holistic and Analytical Scoring Protocols

Most teachers ensure accurate assessment by developing one scoring protocol for evaluating all student portfolios. The scoring protocol can be holistic or analytical.

Holistic scoring involves evaluating the portfolio in its entirety and giving a single overall score. **Analytical scoring** involves evaluating each piece separately and combining the individual scores to obtain an overall score. The question of whether teachers should use holistic or analytic scoring depends on several factors, including the purpose of the portfolio, the intended use of the final product, and the setting in which the students are developing their portfolios. Most teachers find that holistic scoring is preferable for evaluating large groups of portfolios. In contrast, analytical scoring tends to be better in small-group situations in which teachers and students have the time to focus on the process as well as the final product (Wolcott, 1993).

As with all evaluation procedures, strengths and weaknesses exist for each type of portfolio scoring (Spandel & Stiggins, 1997). The benefits of holistic assessment include the following:

- For many teachers, holistic scoring "feels right" because they can judge how well the parts work together.
- Holistic scoring is faster and less expensive than analytical scoring.
- Holistic scoring measures the quality and the coherence of the entire work, thus avoiding problems that arise when evaluating materials as isolated pieces.
- Holistic scoring may be easier for beginners to understand and learn than analytical scoring.

The possible drawbacks to holistic scoring include the following:

- Holistic scoring provides general information that lacks the specifics necessary to diagnose and pinpoint strengths and weaknesses.
- Holistic scoring has the potential for bias if a rater scores a portfolio in response to ideas, handwriting, or opinions rather than the work as a whole.
- Because holistic assessment yields an overall score, the ratings may not reflect relative strengths and particular deficits.

In contrast, analytical scoring has the following benefits:

- The relative strengths and weaknesses of particular materials can be determined with analytical scoring, which is especially important with students who have disabilities.
- Analytical scoring provides information for developing remediation programs, which is often needed for students with learning problems.
- Analytical scoring may also help students identify particular deficits that need improvement.

Possible problems with analytical scoring include the following:

- The extra time and expense associated with scoring each individual piece in a portfolio.
- The difficulty in defining specific criteria for each individual work in a collection.
- The possible frustration that new raters may experience because of the complexity associated with analytical scoring.

An example of a holistic scoring form appears in Figure 18–5, followed by an example of an analytical form in Figure 18–6. These sample forms, based on scoring sheets developed by Wolcott (1993), are most appropriate for use at the middle school and secondary level. Teachers at the elementary level should modify the individual

Figure 18–5 Holistic scoring form

Rating pinpoints	Excellent	Very Good	Good	Fair	Below Average	Poor
Quality of content		✓				
Organization			✓			
Style and grammar			✓			
Self-evaluation		✓				
Originality	✓					

Student _Eloysa_   Date _1/17/05_
Scorer _Ms. Chen_   Overall Score _Very Good B –_

Comments

Eloysa

I enjoyed your writing. It is lively and creative. However, you still

need to work on grammar. Overall, your portfolio shows progress.

items to make them more suitable for younger students. These sample forms can also be modified in other ways to meet individual needs.

Internal and External Scoring

Another scoring consideration involves internal and external scoring. **Internal scoring** relies on scorers who have direct contact with the portfolio authors; this includes teachers who score the portfolios of their own students. **External scoring** relies on scorers who have had no contact with the portfolio authors. In many situations teachers are responsible for grading their own students' portfolios without any input from external sources. Because teachers know their students so well, they may lack the objectivity of external scorers, and in some situations they might even be too critical of their own students. Further, when the teacher is the only scorer, no opportunity exists for checking interrater reliability. A practical solution is to agree to a "portfolio swap" with a teacher in another classroom. If the second teacher's opinion differs greatly from your own, you may want to revisit the student's portfolio and reconsider the grade. If the other teacher's evaluation is similar to yours, this will confirm the reliability of your assessment. Because reliability tends to increase with more than one scorer, external raters can help improve the consistency of portfolio grading. At the same time, however, using external scorers can increase scoring time (Wolcott, 1993).

Student Self-Assessment

Student self-assessment, an element that distinguishes portfolio assessment from traditional evaluation, is not one specific procedure; it includes various types of reflections and self-evaluations. Self-assessment involves having students review their entire portfolio, reflect on a series of revisions, compare two work samples to show growth in a specific topic, or self-evaluate a single work sample. An example of a self-reflection written by

Figure 18–6 Analytical scoring form

Scorer _Ms. Chen_   Student _Eloysa_   Date _1/17/05_

Pinpoint	Informal Essay	Formal Essay	Best Essay	Spontaneous Writing Sample #1	Spontaneous Writing Sample #2	Total Score
Clarity (Purpose and Thesis)	4	4	4	3	3	18
Organization	2	2	2	2	2	10
Quality of Content	4	4	4	3	4	19
Vocabulary	3	3	3	2	2	13
Sentence Style	2	3	3	1	1	10
Sentence Structure	2	2	3	1	1	9
Punctuation and Spelling	2	2	3	1	1	9
Originality	4	4	4	4	4	20
Self-assessment Skills (Reflections)	3	3	3	3	3	15
Overall Score	36 26	36 27	36 29	36 20	36 21	180 123

Rating Scale

Excellent	= 4
Very Good	= 3
Good	= 2
Fair	= 1
Poor	= 0
Highest Possible Score	= 180

Notes _Nice work Eloysa. Your strengths as a writer remain with your originality and ability to communicate clearly. Next quarter, let's concentrate on improving your writing on the sentence-level (punctuation, spelling, sentence style, and structure), especially spontaneous writing._

a student with special needs appears in Focus 18–1. Self-assessment options range from informal written statements, such as student comments in the margins, to more formal self-evaluations in which students respond to specific questions. For example, when reviewing a writing sample, students might consider the following questions:

What do I like best about this writing sample?
What was most important to me when I wrote this?
If I wrote this over again, what would I change?
Is this like my other writing? Why/Why not?
Has my writing changed since I wrote this? How?
Is this my best writing? Why/Why not?

Helping students develop their self-evaluation skills is an essential part of portfolio assessment. However, students are not automatically reflective, and teaching

FOCUS 18-1

A Student's Self-Reflection

"This piece is important because it is the first time I ever had characters talk to each other. You know with quotation marks. The other extremely important thing about this paper is that I actually wanted to do a revision. Two revisions. And I like the final copy. I've never done a revision on purpose before." (Hill & Ruptic, 1994, pp. 44–45)

self-assessment can be difficult. Of course, giving students experience with collecting their work and writing reactions to it will help. For this reason, it is important to give students enough time on a regular basis to reflect. This is accomplished when students have time to get out their portfolios, review what is in them, read everything, and, most important, think and write about what they have accomplished. In other words, portfolios should be part of regular instruction, not a separate activity. Even when teachers encourage reflection, most students need additional assistance. One way to do this is to circulate while students are working on their portfolios. Ask questions that encourage and promote reflection:

- "That's a great comment about how your writing has changed! When did you notice this change?"
- "What could you write about your drawing? That's good! Will you write that comment beneath your drawing?"
- "I didn't know that you liked to read comic books. Are you going to report them in your list of books read? What is it about them that makes them fun?"

Another way to help students learn self-assessment is by having them select two pieces, one that they like and one that they do not like. Students should read their selections and write comments such as why they liked or disliked each piece or what they noticed about themselves as writers. Other ideas include having students maintain reflective reading and writing logs. Examples of these appear in Figure 18–7 and Figure 18–8. Portfolio conferences also provide students with opportunities for self-evaluation. Through conferences, students may discuss their learning goals, evaluate their progress, and receive immediate feedback. More specific information about conferences appears in the next section of this chapter.

✓ Check Your Comprehension

Portfolios may include a variety of different materials depending on their intended use. In most situations, the school or the teacher requires certain basic materials in all student portfolios; teachers and students may include unique and creative elements as well. Moreover, some portfolios allow for students to include optional materials that reflect their particular learning goals and interests.

Successful portfolio assessment requires careful planning and record-keeping. Most teachers use portfolio content checklists as an essential element in a management

Figure 18–7   My writing log

Name	_Demetrius_

Name _____ _Demetrius_ _____

Grade _____ _5_ _____

Rating Guide   Best   ✓ ✓ ✓ ✓
               Very Good   ✓ ✓ ✓
               Good   ✓ ✓
               Poor   ✓

Date	Title	Rating Overall	Review
2/22	Thank-you letter	✓ ✓	This was okay.
3/2	Book report — President Kennedy	✓ ✓ ✓	This report was good.
3/13	Book report — Martin Luther King	✓ ✓ ✓ ✓	I liked this most.
3/14	Portfolio conference record	✓	I don't like this. I don't like the goals.

and tracking system. The checklists help the teacher monitor the progress of individual students and the entire class. More specific evaluation involves use of either holistic or analytical scoring protocols. With holistic scoring the scorer rates the entire portfolio using overall scoring; with analytical scoring the scorer rates each portfolio item separately.

Helping students develop self-evaluation skills is also an important part of portfolio assessment. Teachers should give students enough time on a regular basis to engage in reflective learning activities. This means that students should have structured time to think and write about what is in their portfolio.

Portfolio Conferences

Portfolio conferences, a key element in the portfolio assessment process, consist of meetings in which students review learning goals and discuss progress. Most conferences occur between individual students and their teacher. Conferences are important because they give students opportunities to consider their interests and assess their abilities. Conferences provide opportunities for reflective discussion, enable students to participate actively in the assessment process, and help teachers assess student progress (Bailey & Gusky, 2001; Benson & Barnett, 1999; Farr & Tone, 1998).

Figure 18–8 Reading log portfolio conferences

| Name | Jerrod | | |
| Teacher | Mr Johnson | | |

Date	Book	Rating		
March 10	Fire Engines	☺	☺(circled)	☹
March 19	Tommy's Dental Check	☺(circled)	☺	☹
March 20	Jack Sprat	☺	☺	☹(circled)
		☺	☺	☹
		☺	☺	☹
		☺	☺	☹
		☺	☺	☹
		☺	☺	☹

The portfolio conference process involves several steps. When teachers first introduce portfolios, they need to describe and discuss conferences. Initial conferences occur soon after the students begin to compile their portfolios. Prior to conferencing, students should write down their learning goals and evaluate their progress toward achieving those goals; students should bring this written information to the conference. Often the best way to accomplish this is to have students fill out a conference record form before the meeting (Farr & Tone, 1998). Some students may not have sufficient self-assessment skills to fill out a form before the meeting. In these cases, teachers may use the conferences as a way to provide students with individual coaching and tutoring to help them begin to develop reflection skills.

Examples of two conference record forms appear in Figure 18–9 and Figure 18–10. The first form (Figure 18–9) is divided into a Student Report section and a Teacher Comments section. In the report section, students list their learning goals and evaluate their progress toward meeting those goals. Students complete this section prior to meeting with the teacher. During the conference, the teacher and student use this form as the basis for discussion. At the end of the conference, teachers provide written feedback by filling out the comments section. The second sample form (Figure 18–10), adapted from Farr and Tone (1994) and Johnson and Rose (1997), is less formal. It simply provides a way for the teacher and the student to write down notes during the conference. Because this is completed during the conference, students need not prepare this form in advance. After the conference, students place the record form in their portfolio. This record form documents the conference and provides valuable evaluation information.

Figure 18–9 Portfolio conference report

| Name _Demi_   Date _____   Grading Period _____ |

Student Report

My learning goals _To get done with my big book dinosore story and read more books. I want to read my dinasour story to the other class._

Progress in meeting my goals _Okay. my dinasour picture is done. I need to get done with my story_

My new goals _I want to learn to write on the computer_

Teacher Comments

Notes on student's goals and progress _Your overall progress is good and you have a very good story idea. You need to update your student checklist and begin work on your reading response journal. Make sure to put this conference record form in your portfolio._

Figure 18–9 illustrates a typical form that teachers might use with middle school or high school students. Teachers can modify this basic form for use in other situations. For example, with students who are very young or unable to write, the teacher may conduct the conference as a personal interview by asking them a series of questions and making notes about their responses.

Scheduling Conference Time

Finding the time to schedule and hold conferences can be one of the most difficult challenges in portfolio implementation. Most individual portfolio conferences take about 15 minutes to conduct, and Farr and Tone (1998) recommend that teachers hold four portfolio conferences with each student during a typical academic year. For teachers with many students, 15 minutes of conferencing with each student four times a year takes a significant amount of time.

For this reason, finding the time to hold conferences is a concern. Finding conference time is especially difficult for teachers who rely primarily on direct instruction. In response to this problem, teachers may arrange time for conferencing by incorporating student-centered learning activities as part of the daily routine. For example, teachers can conference with students while the rest of the class works in cooperative learning groups, participates in sustained silent reading, engages in a portfolio work session, or completes individual class assignments. The goal is to make conferences a normal part of ongoing class activities rather than a separate

Figure 18–10 Conference notes

Name _Fabrice_	Date of Conference _March 23_

Teacher's Notes	Student's Notes

Fabrice,
 	
    I think your portfolio is very, very good. I really enjoyed your summer camp story and I hope you get to go to camp again this summer. I think when your Mom reads your story about how much you want to go it might help!
 	
           K. Eggen
	I just wrote my story about summer camp and how much I want to go. It would be a lot of fun and I hope my Mom lets me. I like this story the best because I really want to go.

Source: Adapted from *Portfolio and Performance Assessment: Helping Students Evaluate Their Progress as Readers and Writers,* by R. Farr and B. Tone, 1998, Orlando FL: Harcourt Brace; (2nd ed.) and *Portfolios: Clarifying, Constructing, and Enhancing,* by N. J. Johnson and L. M. Rose, 1997, Lancaster, PA: Technomic.

activity that interferes with instruction. When this is not possible, teachers may be able to obtain assistance from a teaching assistant, teacher aide, or parent volunteer to help with the class while the teacher meets with students (Farr & Tone, 1998).

Despite these potential solutions, the time problem is a legitimate concern in most instructional situations; consequently, teachers need to balance the benefits of conferences against the time it takes to hold them. In some situations, finding the time is so difficult that teachers employ alternatives to individual conferences.

Peer, Small-Group, and Student-Led Conferences

Alternatives to individual student teacher conferences include peer, small-group, and student-led conferences (Bailey & Gusky, 2001; Benson & Barnett, 1999; Farr & Tone, 1998). Peer conferences are meetings between two students to discuss portfolio goals, activities, and progress. Peer conferences are valuable in many instructional situations, especially with older students. In order for the conferences to be effective, the teacher should establish clear guidelines including time limits and activities. Peer conferences work best later in the school year after students have completed individual conferences with their teacher. Teachers can introduce peer conferencing by modeling an appropriate conference to the entire class.

Small-group conferences consist of meetings with three to five students. They may be organized around reading or writing groups or some other appropriate grouping. Small-group conferences give students opportunities to discuss their portfolios with peers. Although not as effective as individual conferences, small groups are especially useful if the teacher finds it difficult to find time for individual conferences. As with all

Figure 18–11   Peer conference review form summary

Peer Conference Review Form

Portfolio Owner _____

Portfolio Reviewer _____

Date of the Review _____

1. What do you think is really good about this portfolio? Why?

2. What do you think is the best piece in the portfolio? Why?

3. What is **one** thing the writer can do to make this portfolio better?

conferences, students should keep a brief written record describing their participation in each peer conference. A sample peer conference record form appears in Figure 18–11.

Student-led conferences address the issue of how to communicate with parents about the learning activities of their children (Bailey & Gusky, 2001). With this type of conference, students are given responsibility to share their progress with their parents in structured conferences. The teacher's role is to facilitate the conference. The students' role is to use their portfolios as a tool for describing their work to their parents. One of the most important benefits of this innovative approach is that students have the opportunity to actively evaluate and reflect upon their learning. Although preparing, conducting, and evaluating student-led conferences is time consuming, it pays significant benefits. These benefits include improved communication with parents and increased student self-reliance.

Reflection
How do you think parents would respond to student-led conferences? Explain.

 To answer this reflection online, go to the *Teaching and Learning* module on the Companion Website at *www.prenhall.com/venn.*

☑ Check Your Comprehension

Conferences are meetings with students to review learning goals and discuss progress. Teachers usually document conferences with some type of form that also provides valuable evaluation information. Because finding time to schedule and hold conferences is often difficult, teachers must balance the benefits of conferences against the time it takes to hold them. Alternatives to teacher-led conferences include peer, small-group, and student-led conferences.

Summary

Chapter 2 included a biographical sketch of special education teacher Brenna Bateh. This account described, in general terms, how Ms. Bateh incorporated assessment into her instruction. This biographical sketch described her experiment with a language arts portfolio activity to help her secondary students with disabilities develop more reflective learning strategies. In the following narrative we see how she incorporated process and product portfolios, holistic and analytical scoring, student self-management, and portfolio conferences into her instruction.

One of the high school classes that I teach regularly is basic English grammar. In order to pass the first 9-week term, my students must learn to write simple and compound sentences. I have always taught this class using a traditional approach with lectures, worksheets, home-work assignments, and class tests. Many students successfully learned to write sentences us-ing these methods, but many students also failed. For this reason, I decided to try a portfolio approach to see if this method would help more students acquire sentence-writing skills and become more reflective learners.

Because of my experience with portfolios, I knew that developing effective assessment pro-cedures was a key to success. Therefore, I wrote a couple of assessment forms, including a self-management checklist for my students, an analytical scoring form for detailed grading, and a holistic form for overall grading. [Copies of these assessments appear in Figures 18–12, 18–13, and 18–14.] I showed my students how to use the self-management checklist to keep up with their portfolio assignments. I then used the analytical form as my primary grading tool. I arranged for two external graders to score the final sentences written by my students. These graders used the holistic scoring form. The external graders were two of my faculty colleagues who volunteered to help. At the beginning of the term, I shared the forms with my students and showed them how we were going to use each form to evaluate their portfolios.

After using portfolios to teach sentence structure, my class experienced a higher level of understanding and higher grades at the end of the term. Using portfolios helped monitor lev-els of comprehension. By monitoring, I could intervene when a student needed special assis-tance. The use of external graders helped students gain confidence in their ability to express their thoughts to others and gave me valuable assessment information.

Figure 18–12   Student self-management checklist

Simple and Compound Sentences		
	Portfolio Item	Completion Date
Worksheets	Identifying the subject in simple sentences	
	Identifying the verb in simple sentences	
	Memorizing the seven coordinating conjunctions	
	Identifying the coordinating conjunction in compound sentences	
	Identifying the comma in compound sentences	
Sentences	5 simple sentences (practice #1)	
	10 simple sentences (practice #2)	
	10 simple sentences (final)	
	5 compound sentences (practice #1)	
	10 compound sentences (practice #2)	
	10 compound sentences (final)	
Assessments	Reflection #1	
	Reflection #2	
	Portfolio Conference Record #1	
	Portfoio Conference Record #2	

Figure 18–13 Analytical scoring form

Simple and Compound Sentences						
Name _____ Scorer _____ Date _____						
Pinpoint	Worksheets	Practice Sentences	Final Sentences	Reflections	Conferences	Total Score
Subjects						12
Verbs						12
Idea						12
Conjunction						12
Style and punctuation						12
All work completed						20
Self-assessment skills						16
Conference skills						8
Overall scores	24	24	24	8	8	88

Figure 18–14 Holistic scoring form

Simple and Compound Sentences					
Student _____ Scorer _____ Date _____ Overall Score _____					
Rating pinpoint	Excellent	Very Good	Average	Weak	Poor
Quality of content (subject, verb, conjunction, idea)					
Punctuation					
Style, neatness, creativity					

Like Ms. Bateh, many teachers are implementing portfolio-based instruction and assessment. In addition, programs, schools, and entire school systems are relying on portfolios as assessment tools to measure student performance and achievement. Although not new, portfolio assessment is being used more widely as educators question the effectiveness of traditional testing and implement standards for student performance.

Portfolio assessment is a type of curriculum-based, authentic evaluation that relies on samples of genuine student work to measure student progress. Student portfolios usually focus on written expression and related language arts activities, including reading. Most contain a similar set of basic contents, but teachers and students may include unique and creative elements as well.

Successful portfolio assessment requires careful planning and record-keeping. Most teachers develop a contents checklist that they use as a management tool for monitoring the progress of individual students and the entire class. Teachers also use holistic and analytical scoring protocols. Holistic scoring is generally preferred with large groups of portfolios, whereas analytical scoring is usually better in small-group situations that focus on the process as well as the final product. Portfolio conferences, for the purpose of discussing learning goals and measuring progress, are also part of the assessment process. They provide opportunities for reflective discussion and review, and this self-evaluation helps students focus their thoughts and carefully consider their portfolio. Portfolio assessment promotes reflective teaching and learning, encourages active student participation in assessment, and links evaluation with classroom activities. These benefits help make assessment meaningful and provide insights about the successes of students with disabilities. Portfolio assessment has a promising future as an innovative approach to measuring student performance.

To check your comprehension of the chapter contents, go to the *Guided Review* and *Quiz* modules in Chapter 18 of the Companion Website, www.prenhall.com/venn.

Meeting Performance Standards and Preparing for Licensure Exams

After reading this chapter, you should be able to demonstrate the following CEC Standards and PRAXIS™ test knowledge and skills. The information in parentheses identifies where to find the particular CEC standard and PRAXIS™ content reference.

CEC Standards for Beginning Special Education Teachers

- Use technology to conduct assessments (CC8S3)
- Develop or modify individualized assessment strategies (CC8S4)
- Interpret information from formal and informal assessments (CC8S5)
- Report assessment results to all stakeholders using effective communication skills (CC8S7)
- Evaluate instruction and monitor progress of individuals with exceptional learning needs (CC8S8)
- Develop or modify individualized assessment strategies (CC8S9)
- Create and maintain records (CC8S10)

PRAXIS™ Education of Exceptional Students: Core Content Knowledge

- Assessment, including use of assessment for screening, diagnosis, placement, and the making of instructional decisions; for example, how to select and conduct nondiscriminatory and appropriate assessments; how to interpret standardized and specialized assessment results (0353 III)
- Assessment, including how to select, construct, conduct, and modify nondiscriminatory, developmentally and chronologically age-appropriate informal assessments, including teacher-made tests, curriculum-based assessment, and alternatives to norm-referenced testing (including observations, anecdotal records, error analysis, miscue analysis, self-evaluation questionnaires and interviews, journals and learning logs, and portfolio assessment) (0353 III)

References

Abruscato, J. (1993). Early results and tentative implications from the Vermont Portfolio Project. *Phi Delta Kappan, 74,* 474–77.

Achenbach, T. M. (2001). *Child behavior checklist for ages 6–18.* Burlington, VT: ASEBA.

Achenbach, T. M. (2002). *Child behavior checklist 11/2–5.* Burlington, VT: ASEBA.

Adams, W., & Sheslow, D. (1995). *Wide range assessment of visual motor abilities.* Wilmington, DE: Wide Range.

Amaro, R. (1997). Hooked on real-time grades: Daily access to their scores on my IBM clones keeps kids motivated. *Electronic Learning, 16*(4), 62.

American Association on Mental Retardation. (2002). *Fact sheet.* Retrieved October 31, 2005, from http://www.aamr.org/Policies/mental_retardation.shtml.

American Educational Research Association. (1999). *Standards for educational and psychological testing.* Washington, DC: Author.

American Guidance Service. (2001, February). *Wichita schools "DIAL 3" for successful preschool screening.* Retrieved October 25, 2005, from http://www.speechandlanguage.com/article/wichita.asp.

American Guidance Service. (n.d.). *Interpretation problems of age and grade equivalents.* Retrieved January 30, 2002, from http://www.agsnet.com/assessments/age_grade.asp.

American Psychiatric Association. (1994). *Diagnostic and statistical manual of mental disorders* (4th ed.). Washington, DC: Author.

American Psychological Association. (1999). *Standards for educational and psychological testing.* Washington, DC: Author.

Ammer, J., & Bangs, T. (2000). *Birth to three assessment and intervention system* (2nd ed.). San Antonio, TX: Psychological Corp.

Andrade, H. G. (2001, April 18). The effects of instructional rubrics on learning to write. *Current Issues in Education* [On-line], *4*(4). Available at http://cie.ed.asu.edu/volume4number4.

Angelo, T. (1998). *Classroom assessment and research: An update on uses, approaches, and research findings: New directions for teaching and learning.* New York, NY: Jossey-Bass

Aprenda: La Prueba de Logros en Español, Segunda Edición. (1997). San Antonio, TX: Harcourt Brace Educational Measurement.

Ariel, A. (1992). *Education of children and adolescents with learning disabilities.* New York: Merrill/Macmillan.

Ashlock, R. B. (2006). *Error patterns in computation* (9th ed.). Upper Saddle River, NJ: Merrill/Prentice Hall.

Aylward, G. P. (1995). *Bayley infant neurodevelopmental screener.* San Antonio, TX: Psychological Corp.

Bailey, J. M., & Gusky, T. R. (2001). *Implementing student-led conferences.* Thousand Oaks, CA: Corwin Press.

Bakker, S., & Macnab, D. (2004). *Career interest profiler.* Edmonton, Alberta, CA: Psychometrics.

Bankson, N. W. (1990). *Bankson language test—2.* Austin, TX: PRO-ED.

Banus, B. S. (1971). *The developmental therapist: A prototype of the pediatric occupational therapist.* Thorofare, NJ: Charles B. Slack.

Battle, J. (2002). *Culture-free self-esteem inventories* (3rd ed.). Austin, TX: PRO-ED.

Bayley, N. (1993). *Bayley scales of infant development* (2nd ed.). San Antonio, TX: Psychological Corp.

Beatty, L. S., Madden, R., Gardner, E. F., & Karlsen, B. (1995). *Stanford diagnostic mathematics test* (4th ed.). San Antonio, TX: Psychological Corp.

Becker, R. L. (2001). *Reading free vocational interest inventory: 2.* Columbus, OH: Elbern.

Beery, K. E., Buktenica, N. A., & Beery, N. A. (2004). *Beery VMI,* (5th ed.). Austin, TX: PRO-ED.

Beirne-Smith, M., Patton, J. R., & Kim, S. (2006). *Mental retardation* (7th ed.). Upper Saddle River, NJ: Merrill/Prentice Hall.

Benson, B., & Barnett, S. (1999). *Student-led conferencing using showcase portfolios.* Thousand Oaks, CA: Corwin Press.

Berninger, V. W. (2000). *Process assessment of the learner: Test battery for reading and writing.* San Antonio, TX: The Psychological Corp.

Best, S., Heller, K., & Bigge, J. (2005). *Teaching individuals with physical, health, or multiple disabilities* (5th ed.). Upper Saddle River, NJ: Merrill/Prentice Hall.

Bielinski, J., Ysseldyke, J., Bolt, S., Friedebach, M., & Friedebach, J. (2001). Prevalence of accommodations for students with disabilities participating in a statewide testing program. *Assessment for Effective Intervention, 26*(2), 21–28.

Bigge, J., & Stump, C. S. (1999). *Curriculum, assessment, and instruction for students with disabilties.* Belmont, CA: Wadsworth.

Binet, A., & Simon, T. (1905). Méthodes nouvelles pur le diagnostic du niveau intéllectual des anormaux. *L'Annee Psychologique, 11,* 191–244.

Blankenship, C. (1985). Using curriculum-based assessment data to make instructional decisions. *Exceptional Children, 52,* 233–38.

Boehm, A. (2000). *Boehm test of basic concepts* (3rd ed.). San Antonio, TX: Psychological Corp.

Boehm, A. (2001). *Boehm-3 preschool.* San Antonio, TX: Psychological Corp.

Boehm, A. E. (2000). *Boehm test of basic concepts* (3rd ed.). San Antonio, TX: Psychological Corp.

Boehm, A. E. (2001). *Boehm-3 preschool.* San Antonio, TX: Psychological Corp.

Bond, G. L., Tinker, M. A., Wasson, B. A., & Wasson, J. B. (1989). *Reading difficulties: Their diagnosis and correction* (6th ed.). Upper Saddle River, NJ: Prentice Hall.

Booth, D., Swartz, L., & Zola, M. (1994). *Classroom voices: Language-based learning in the elementary school.* Toronto: Harcourt Brace, Canada.

Bormuth, J. R. (1968). The cloze readability procedure. *Elementary English, 45,* 429–36.

Bracken, B. A. (1992). *Multidimensional self-concept scale.* Austin, TX: PRO-ED.

Bracken, B. A. (1995). *Handbook of self-concept: Developmental, social, and clinical considerations.* New York: Wiley.

Bracken, B. A., & McCallum, R. S. (1997). *Universal nonverbal intelligence test.* Chicago: Riverside.

Bradley-Johnson, S. (1999). Review of the Basic School Skills Inventory, (3rd ed.). *Psychology in the Schools, 36,* 83–85.

Brandon, T., Balton, D., Rup, D., & Raslter, C. (n.d.). *Valpar component work sample system.* Tuscon, AZ: Valpar Corp.

Brigance, A. (1994). *Brigance diagnostic life skills inventory.* North Billerica, MA: Curriculum Associates.

Brigance, A. (1995). *Brigance employability skills inventory.* North Billerica, MA: Curriculum Associates.

Brigance, A. H. (1999). *Brigance comprehensive inventory of basic skills* (Rev. ed.). North Billerica, MA: Curriculum Associates.

Brigance, A. H. (2002). *Brigance infant and toddler screen.* North Billerica, MA: Curriculum Associates.

Brigance, A. H. (2004). *Brigance diagnostic inventory of early development-II.* North Billerica, MA: Curriculum Associates.

Brigance, A. H. (2005a). *Brigance early preschool screen-II.* North Billerica, MA: Curriculum Associates.

Brigance, A. H. (2005b). *Brigance K & 1 screen-II.* North Billerica, MA: Curriculum Associates.

Brigance, A. H. (2005c). *Brigance preschool screen-II.* North Billerica, MA: Curriculum Associates.

Brolin, D. E. (2004). *Life centered career education,* (Rev. ed.). Reston, VA: Council for Exceptional Children.

Brown, L. L., & Alexander, J. (1990). *Self-esteem index.* Austin, TX: PRO-ED.

Brown, L. L., & Hammill, D. D. (1990). *Behavior rating profile—2.* Austin, TX: PRO-ED.

Brown, L., & Leigh, J. E. (1986). *Adaptive behavior inventory.* Austin, TX: PRO-ED.

Brown, L., Shervenou, R. J., & Johnsen, S. K. (1997). *Test of nonverbal intelligence* (3rd ed.). Austin, TX: PRO-ED.

Brown, R. (1973). *A first language.* Cambridge, MA: Harvard University Press.

Brown, T. E. (1996). *Brown attention-deficit disorder scales.* San Antonio: TX: Psychological Corp.

Brown, V. L., Cronin, M. E., & McEntire, E. (1994). *Test of mathematical abilities* (2nd ed.). Austin, TX: PRO-ED.

Brown, V. L., Hammill, D. D., & Wiederholt, J. L. (1995). *Test of reading comprehension* (3rd ed.). Austin, TX: PRO-ED.

Brownell, R. (2000a). *Expressive one-word picture vocabulary test* (2000 ed.). Novato, CA: Academic Therapy.

Brownell, R. (2000b). *Receptive one-word picture vocabulary test* (2000 ed.). Novato, CA: Academic Therapy.

Bruininks, R. H., & Bruininks B. D. (2005). *Bruininks–Oseretsky test of motor proficiency,* (2nd ed.). Circle Pines, MN: American Guidance Service.

Bruininks, R. H., Hill, B. K., Weatherman, R. F., & Woodcock, R. (1986). *Inventory for client and agency planning.* Itasca, IL: Riverside.

Bruininks, R. H., Woodcock, R. W., Weatherman, R. E., & Hill, B. K. (1996). *Scales of independent behavior—revised.* Itasca, IL: Riverside.

Bruininks, R., Morreau, L. Gilman, C., & Anderson, J. (1991). *Adaptive living skills curriculum.* Itasca, IL: Riverside.

Bryant, B. R., Patton, J. R., & Dunn, C. (1991). *Scholastic abilities test for adults.* Austin, TX: PRO-ED.

Bryant, B., Taylor, R., & Rivera, D. (1996). *Assessment of adaptive areas.* Austin, TX: PRO-ED.

Buckleitner, W. (2001, October 17). *Great gadgets for assessment.* Retrieved October 18, 2005 from http://teacher.scholastic.com/professional/teachtech/greatgadget sassment.htm#author.

Burke, D. A., & Beech, M. (2000). *Developing quality individual educational plans: A guide for instructional personnel and families.* Tallahassee, FL: Florida Department of Education.

Bursuck, W., Polloway, E. A., Plante, L., Epstein, M. H., Jayanthi, M., & McConeghy, J. (1996). Report card grading and adaptations: A national survey of classroom practices. *Exceptional Children, 62,* 301–18.

Canfield, A. (2001). *Canfield learning styles inventory*. Retrieved October 11, 2005, from http://www.tecweb.org/styles/canfield1.html.

Carlson, H., Ellison, D., & Dietrich, J. (1988). *Servicing low achieving pupils and pupils with learning disabilities: A comparison of two approaches*. Duluth, MN: University of Minnesota, Duluth, and Duluth Public Schools. (ERIC Document Reproduction Service No. ED 283 341)

Carrow-Woolfolk, E. (1995). *Oral and written language scales: Manual for listening comprehension and oral expression*. Circle Pines, MN: American Guidance Service.

Carrow-Woolfolk, E. (1999). *Test for auditory comprehension of language* (3rd ed.). Austin, TX: PRO-ED.

Center for the Education and Study of Diverse Populations. (2001, November 8). *Using running records to assess reading*. Retrieved October, 2002 from http://www.cesdp.nmhu.edu/standards/primer/assess/run1.htm.

Chen, J., & Gardner, H. (1997). Alternative assessment from a multiple intelligences theoretical perspective. In D. P. Flanagan, J. L. Genshaft, & P. L. Harrison (Eds.), *Contemporary intellectual assessment: Theories, tests, and issues* (pp. 105–21). New York: The Guilford Press.

Cizek, G. J. (2001). Review of the Brigance Diagnostic Comprehensive Inventory of Basic Skills, Revised. In D. S. Plake & J. M. Impara (Eds.), *The fourteenth mental measurements yearbook* (pp. 172–175). Lincoln, NB: Buros Institute of Mental Measurements.

Clark, G. M., & Patton, J. R. (1997). *Transition planning inventory*. Austin, TX: PRO-ED.

Clay, M. (2000). *Running records for classroom teachers*. Westport, CT: Heinemann.

Coalson, D., & Zhu, J. (2001). Development of the WPPSI-III. *Assessment Focus Newsletter, 10*(2), 1–2.

Cohen, E. G. (1994). Restructuring the classroom: Conditions for productive small groups. *Review of Educational Research, 64*(1), 1–35.

Cohen, L. G., & Spenciner, L. J. (2002). *Assessment of young children*. New York: Longman.

Cohen, S. H., & Cohen, J. (1994). Review of the Woodcock Reading Mastery Tests, Revised. In D. J. Keyser and R. C. Sweetland (Eds.), *Test critiques* (Vol. X). Austin, TX: PRO-ED.

Colarusso, R. P., & Hammill, D. D. (2002). *Motor-free visual perception test,* Third edition. Austin, TX: PRO-ED.

Cole, D. J., Ryan, C. W., Kick, F., & Mathies, B. K. (1999). *Portfolios across the curriculum and beyond* (2nd ed.). Thousand Oaks, CA: Corwin Press.

Committee on Children and Disabilities, American Academy of Pediatrics. (2001). Developmental surveillance and screening for infants and young children. *Pediatrics 108*(1), 192–196.

Conners, C. K. (1994). *Conners' adult ADHD history form*. Toronto, ON: MHS.

Conners, C. K. (1997a). *Conners' rating scales—revised*. Toronto, ON: MHS.

Conners, C. K. (1997b). *Conners' ADHD/DSM-IV scales*. Toronto, ON: MHS.

Conners, C. K. (2000a). *Conners' continuous performance test II—computer program for Windows*. Toronto, ON: MHS.

Conners, C. K. (2000b). *Conners' continuous performance test for Windows: Kiddie version*. Toronto, ON: MHS.

Conners, C. K., Epstein, J., & Johnson, D. (2001). *Conners' adult ADHD diagnostic interview for DSM-IV*. Toronto, ON: MHS.

Conners, C. K., Erhardt, D., & Sparrow, E. (1997). *Conners' adult ADHD rating scales*. Toronto, ON: MHS.

Connolly, A. J. (1985). *KeyMath teach and practice*. Circle Pines, MN: American Guidance Service.

Connolly, A. J. (1988). *KeyMath revised: A diagnostic inventory of essential mathematics*. Circle Pines, MN: American Guidance Service.

Connolly, A. J. (1998). *KeyMath revised. A diagnostic inventory of essential mathematics* (Normative update). Circle Pines, MN: American Guidance Service.

Connolly, A. J. (1998). *KeyMath–Revised: A diagnostic inventory of essential mathematics*. Circle Pines, MN: American Guidance Service.

Connolly, A. J. (1998). *KeyMath: A diagnostic inventory of essential mathematics*. Circle Pines, MN: American Guidance Service.

Connolly, A., Nachtman, W., & Pritchett, E. (1976). *KeyMath diagnostic arithmetic test*. Circle Pines, MN: American Guidance Service.

Connolly, A., Natchman, W., & Pritchett, E. (1971). *KeyMath diagnostic arithmetic test*. Circle Pines, MN: American Guidance Service.

Critchlow, D. E. (1996). *Dos amigos verbal language scales*. Novato, CA: Academic Therapy.

Crocker, L. (2001). Review of the Woodcock Reading Mastery Test, Revised (1998 Normative Update). In B. S. Plake & J. M. Impara (Eds.), *The fourteenth mental measurements yearbook* (pp. 1370–1371). Lincoln, NB: Buros Institute of Mental Measurements.

Cross, L. H. (2001). Review of the Peabody Individual Achievement Test, Revised (1998 Normative update). In B. S. Plake & J. M. Impara (Eds.), *The fourteenth mental measurements yearbook* (pp. 904–906). Lincoln, NB: Buros Institute of Mental Measurements.

CTB McGraw-Hill. (2001). *How is the normal curve equivalent intended to be used?* Monterey, CA: Author. Retrieved February 5, 2002, from http://www.ctb.com/about_assessment/assess_faq/faq5.shtml.

CTB/McGraw Hill. (1990). *Early school assessment.* Monterey, CA: Author.

CTB/McGraw-Hill. (1992). *Test of cognitive skills* (2nd ed.). Monterey, CA: Author.

Danzer, V., Gerber, M. F., Lyons, T., & Voress, J. K. (1991). *Daberon screening for school readiness test* (2nd ed.). Austin, TX: PRO-ED.

Davis, W. E. (1989). The Regular Education Initiative debate: Its promises and problems. *Exceptional Children, 55,* 440–46.

Department of Education. (2005). *Individuals with Disabilities Education Improvement Act.* Washington, DC: Author.

DiCerbo, P. (2001). School skills. In *The classroom: A toolkit for effective instruction of English learners.* Retrieved January 22, 2002, from http://www.ncbe.gwu.edu/classroom/toolkit/skills.html.

Doll, E. (1935). A genetic scale of social maturity. *The American Journal of Orthopsychiatry, 5,* 180–188.

Drummond, R. J., & Jones, K. (2006). *Appraisal procedures for counselors and helping professionals* (6th ed.). Upper Saddle River, NJ: Merrill/Prentice Hall.

Dunn, L. M. (1959). *Peabody picture vocabulary test.* Circle Pines, MN: American Guidance Service.

Dunn, L. M., & Dunn, L. M. (1997). *Peabody picture vocabulary test* (3rd ed.). Circle Pines, MN: American Guidance Service.

Dunn, L. M., & Markwardt, F. C. (1970). *Peabody individual achievement test.* Circle Pines, MN: American Guidance Service.

Dunn, L. M., Lugo, D. E., Padilla, E. R., & Dunn, L. E. (1986). *TVIP: Test de vocabulario en imágenes Peabody.* Circle Pines, MN: American Guidance Service.

Dykes, M. K., & Erin, J. (1999). *Developmental assessment for students with severe disabilities.* Austin, TX: PRO-ED.

Educational Testing Service. (2004, December 3). *Information about testing accommodations.* Retrieved January 17, 2005, from http://www.ets.org/disability/info.html.

Elliot, S. N., & Gresham, F. M. (1991). *Social skills intervention guide.* Circle Pines, MN: American Guidance Service.

Elliott, C. (1990). *Differential ability scales.* San Antonio, TX: Psychological Corp.

Elliott, S. (2001). Including students with disabilities in assessments. *Council for Exceptional Children Today, 8*(3), 12.

Epstein, M. H. (2004). *Behavior and emotional rating scale* (2nd ed.). Austin, TX: PRO-ED.

Ezell D., & Klein, C. (2002). The portfolio assessment criteria checklist for teachers. *Florida Educational Leadership, 2*(2), 39.

Fager, J. J. (2001). Review of the Peabody Individual Achievement Test, Revised (1998 Normative update). In B. S. Plake & J. M. Impara (Eds.), *The fourteenth mental measurements yearbook* (pp. 906–908). Lincoln, NB: Buros Institute of Mental Measurements.

Farr, B., & Trumbull, E. (1997). *Assessment alternatives for diverse classrooms.* Norwood, MA: Christopher-Gordon.

Farr, R., & Tone, B. (1994). *Portfolio and performance assessment: Helping students evaluate their progress as readers and writers.* Orlando: Harcourt Brace.

Farr, R., & Tone, B. (1998). *Portfolio and performance assessment: Helping students evaluate their progress as readers and writers* (2nd ed.). Orlando, FL: Harcourt Brace.

Felder, R. M. (n.d.). *Learning styles.* Retrieved October 12, 2005, from http://www.ncsu.edu/felder-public/Learning_Styles.html

Fewell, R. R., & Langley, M. B. (1984). *Developmental activities screening inventory-II.* Austin, TX: PRO-ED.

Florida Department of Education. (1986). *Assessment: Educating the severely/profoundly handicapped.* Tallahassee, FL: Florida Department of Education.

Flynt, E. S., & Cooter, R. B. (1999). *English-Español reading inventory for the classroom.* Upper Saddle River, NJ: Merrill/Prentice Hall.

Folio, R. M., & Fewell, R. R. (2000). *Peabody developmental motor scales* (2nd ed.). Austin, TX: PRO-ED.

Forsyth, R. A., Ansley, T. N., Feldt, L. S., & Alnot, S. D. (2001). *Iowa tests of educational development.* Itasca, IL: Riverside.

Frankenburg, W., Dodds, J., Archers, P., Bresnick, B., Maschka, P., Edelman, N. (1990). *Denver developmental screening test-II.* Denver, CO: Denver Developmental Materials.

Fuchs, L., Hamlett, C., & Fuchs, D. (n.d.). *Monitoring basic skills progress.* Austin, TX: PRO-ED.

Furuno, S. (1994). *HELP charts 0–3.* Palo Alto, CA: VORT.

Furuno, S. (1995a). *HELP checklist 0–3.* Palo Alto, CA: VORT.

Furuno, S. (1995b). *HELP for preschoolers assessment and curriculum guide.* Palo Alto, CA: VORT.

Gable, R. A., & Coben, S. S. (1990). Errors in arithmetic. In R. A. Gable & J. M. Hendrickson (Eds.), *Assessing students with special needs: A sourcebook for analyzing and correcting errors in academics* (pp. 30–45). New York: Longman.

Gable, R. A., & Hendrickson, J. M. (1990). Making error analysis work. In R. A. Gable & J. M. Hendrickson (Eds.), *Assessing students with special needs: A sourcebook for analyzing and correcting errors in academics* (pp. 146–53). New York: Longman.

Gadow, K. D., & Sprafkin, J. (1997). *ADHD symptom checklist.* Stonybrook, NY: Checkmate Plus.

Gardner, H. (1983). *Frames of mind: The theory of multiple intelligences.* New York: BasicBooks.

Gardner, H. (1993). *Multiple intelligences: The theory in practice.* New York: BasicBooks.

Gardner, H. (2000). *Intelligence reframed: Multiple intelligences for the 21st century.* New York: BasicBooks.

Gardner, M. F. (1994). *Test of auditory-perceptual skills: Upper level.* Austin, TX: PRO-ED.

Gardner, M. F. (1997). *Test of auditory-perceptual skills* (Rev. ed.). Austin, TX: PRO-ED.

Gargiulo, R. M., & Kilgo, J. (2000). *Young children with special needs.* Albany, NY: Delmar.

Gaylord-Ross, R. (Ed.). (1988). *Vocational education of persons with handicaps.* Mountain View, CA: Mayfield.

Gesell, A. (1940). *Gesell developmental schedules.* Cheshire, CT: Nigel Cox.

Gesell, A., & Armatruda, C. S. (1941). *Developmental diagnosis.* New York: Hoeber.

Gilliam, J. (1995). *Attention-deficit/hyperactivity disorder test.* Austin, TX: PRO-ED.

Ginsburg, H. P., & Baroody, A. J. (1990). *Test of early mathematics ability—2.* Austin, TX: PRO-ED.

Glover, M. E., Preminger, J. L., & Sanford, A. R. (1988). *Early learning accomplishment profile.* Lewisville, NC: Kaplan School Supply Corp.

Glutting, J. J., & Wilkinson, G. (2003). *Wide range interest and occupation test,* (2nd ed.). Austin, TX: PRO-ED.

Gold, M. (1975). *Try another way training manual.* Champaign, IL: Research Press.

Goldman, R., & Fristoe, M. (2000). *Goldman-Fristoe test of articulation* (2nd ed.). Circle Pines, MN: American Guidance Service.

Goldman, R., Fristoe, M., & Woodcock, R. W. (1976). *Goldman-Fristoe-Woodcock test of auditory discrimination.* Circle Pines, MN: American Guidance Service.

Good, R. H. & Kaminski, R. A. (2003). *Dynamic indicators of basic early literacy skills,* (6th ed.), Longmont, CO: Sopris West.

Graham, M. A. (1992). *Evaluation and assessment of infants and toddlers: Participant guide.* Tallahassee, FL: Center for Prevention and Early Intervention Policy, FSU Institute of Science and Public Affairs.

Greenberg, L. (1993). *Test of variables of attention.* Circle Pines, MN: American Guidance Service.

Gregory, R. (2004). *Psychological testing: History, principles, and applications* (4th ed.). Boston: Allyn and Bacon.

Gresham, F. M., & Elliot, S. N. (1990). *Social skills rating system.* Circle Pines, MN: American Guidance Service.

Gresham, F. M., Elliott, S. N., & Evans-Fernandez, S. E. (1993). *Student self-concept scale.* Circle Pines, MN: American Guidance Service.

Gronlund, N. (1982). *Constructing achievement tests* (3rd ed.). Upper Saddle River, NJ: Prentice Hall.

Hakuta, K., & Beatty, A. (2000). *Testing English-language learners in U.S. schools: Report and workshop summary.* Washington, DC: National Academy Press

Hammill, D. D. (1998). *Detroit tests of learning aptitude—4.* Austin, TX: PRO-ED.

Hammill, D. D., & Bryant, B. R. (1991). *Detroit tests of learning aptitude—primary* (2nd ed.). Austin, TX: PRO-ED.

Hammill, D. D., & Larsen, S. C. (1996). *Test of written language—3.* Austin, TX: PRO-ED.

Hammill, D. D., & Newcomer, P. L. (1997). *Test of language development—intermediate* (3rd ed.). Austin, TX: PRO-ED.

Hammill, D. D., Brown, V. L., Larsen, S. C., & Wiederholt, J. L. (1994). *Test of adolescent and adult language—3.* Austin, TX: PRO-ED.

Hammill, D. D., Leigh, J. E., Pearson, N. A., & Maddox, T. (1998). *Basic school skills inventory* (3rd ed.). Austin, TX: PRO-ED.

Hammill, D. D., Pearson, N. A., & Voress, J. K. (1993). *Developmental test of visual perception* (2nd ed.). Austin, TX: PRO-ED.

Hammill, D. D., Pearson, N. A., & Wiederholt, J. L. (1996). *Comprehensive test of nonverbal intelligence.* Austin, TX: PRO-ED.

Hammill, D. D., Pearson, N. A., & Wiederholt, J. L. (1997). *Comprehensive test of nonverbal intelligence—computer administered.* Austin, TX: PRO-ED.

Hammill, D. D., Pearson, N. A., Voress, J. K., & Reynolds, C. R. (2005). *Full range test of visual-motor integration.* Austin, TX: PRO-ED.

Hammill, D., Bryant, B., & Pearson, N. (1998). *Hammill multiability intelligence test.* Austin, TX: PRO-ED.

Hammill, D., Hresko, W., Ammer, J., Cronin, M., & Quinby, S. (1998). *Hammill multiability achievement test.* Austin, TX: PRO-ED.

Hardin, R. J., Eisner-Feinburg, E. S., & Weeks, S. W. (2005). *Learning accomplishment profile,* (3rd ed.) Lewisville, NC: Kaplan Early Learning.

Hargrove, L. J., & Poteet, J. A. (1984). *Assessment in special education: The education evaluation.* Upper Saddle River, NJ: Prentice Hall.

Harris, A. J., & Sipay, E. R. (1985). *How to increase reading ability: A guide to developmental and remedial methods.* New York: Longman.

Harrison, P. L., Kaufman, A. S., Kaufman, N. L., Bruininks, P. H., Rynders, J., Ilmer, S., et al. (1990). *AGS early screening profiles.* Circle Pines, MN: American Guidance Service.

Harrison, P., & Oakland, T. (2003). *Adaptive behavior assessment system* (2nd ed.). San Antonio, TX: Psychological Corp.

Hasazi, S. B., & Cobb, R. B. (1988). Vocational education of persons with mild handicaps. In R. Gaylord-Ross (ed.), *Vocational education of persons with handicaps* (pp. 331–354). Mountain View, CA: Mayfield.

Henderson, S. H., & Sugden, D. A. (1992). *Movement assessment battery for children.* San Antonio, TX: Psychological Corp.

Hendrickson, M. J., & Gable, R. (1990). Errors in spelling. In R. A. Gable & J. M. Hendrickson (Eds.), *Assessing students with special needs: A sourcebook for analyzing and correcting errors in academics* (pp. 78–88). New York: Longman.

Herbert, C. H. (1983). *Basic inventory of natural language.* Monterey, CA: Publishers Test Service.

Herrnstein, R. J., & Murray, C. (1994). *The bell curve: Intelligence and class structure in American life.* New York: Free Press.

Hill, B. C., & Ruptic, C. (1994). *Practical aspects of authentic assessment: Putting the pieces together.* Norwood, MA: Christopher-Gordon.

Hillerich, R. L. (1978). *A writing vocabulary of elementary children.* (Eric Document Reproduction Service No. ED161084)

Holland, J. (1994). *Self-directed search.* Lutz, FL: Psychological Assessment Resources.

Hoover, H. D., Dunbar, S. B., & Frisbie, D. A. (2001). *Iowa tests of basic skills.* Itasca, IL: Riverside.

Hresko, W. P., Miguel, S. H., Sherbenour, R. J., & Burton, S. D. (1994). *The developmental observation checklist system.* Austin, TX: PRO-ED.

Hresko, W. P., Reid, D. K., & Hammill, D. D. (1999). *Test of early language development* (3rd ed.). Austin, TX: PRO-ED.

Hresko, W., Herron, S. R., & Peak, P. K. (1996). *Test of early written language* (2nd ed.). Austin, TX: PRO-ED.

Hursh, N. C., & Kerns, A. F. (1988). *Vocational evaluation in special education.* Boston: College Hill Press.

Illinois Association for Supervision and Curriculum Development. (1990, Spring). How does your screener stack up? *Assessment Information Exchange: American Guidance Service,* 7–11.

Individuals with Disabilities Education Act (October 30, 1990). *United States statutes at large* (Vol. 104, pp. 1103–1151). Washington, DC: U.S. Government Printing Office.

International Test Commission. (2000a). *Test adaptation guidelines.* Stockholm, Sweden: Author. Retrieved January 31, 2002, from http://www.intestcom.org/test_adaptation.htm.

International Test Commission. (2000b). *International guidelines for test use.* Stockholm, Sweden: Author. Retrieved January 31, 2002, from http://www.intestcom.org/itc_projects.htm.

Jackson, D. (1999). *Jackson vocational interest survey.* London, Ontario, Canada: Research Psychologists Press.

Johns, J. (2005). *The basic reading inventory: Pre-primer through grade twelve & early literacy assessment,* (9th ed.). Dubuque, IA: Kendall/Hunt.

Johns, J. L., & Vanleirsburg, P. (1991). How professionals view portfolio assessment. In C. B. Smith (Ed.), *Alternative assessment of performance in the language arts: What are we doing now? Where are we going?* (pp. 242–48). Bloomington, IN: Eric Clearinghouse on Reading and Communication Skills.

Johnson, D. W., Johnson, R. T., & Holubec, E. H. (1998). Assessment and evaluation. In *Supplemental text for foundations of cooperative learning* (Chapter 7). Jacksonville, FL: Workshop handout.

Johnson, J. (2005). Review of the Stanford-Binet Intelligence Scales, Fifth Edition. In R. A. Spies, & B. S. Plake (Eds.), *The sixteenth mental measurements yearbook.* Lincoln, NE: Buros Institute of Mental Measurements.

Johnson, N. J., & Rose, L. M. (1997). *Portfolios: Clarifying, constructing, and enhancing.* Lancaster, PA: Technomic.

Johnson-Martin, N. M., Attermeier, S. M., & Hecker, B. J. (1990) *The Carolina curriculum for preschoolers with special needs.* Baltimore: Paul H. Brookes.

Johnson-Martin, N. M., Jens, K. G., Attermeier, S. M., & Hecker, B. J. (1991). *The Carolina curriculum for infants and toddlers with special needs* (2nd ed.). Baltimore: Paul H. Brookes.

Karlsen, B., Gardner, E. F., (1995). *Stanford diagnostic reading test* (4th ed.). San Antonio: Harcourt Educational Measurement.

Kauffman, J. M. (1989). The Regular Education Initiative as Reagan-Bush education policy: A trickle-down theory of education of the hard-to-teach. *Journal of Special Education, 23,* 256–78.

Kaufman, A. A., & Kaufman, N. L. (2004). *Kaufman assessment battery for children,* (2nd ed.). Circle Pines, MN: American Guidance Service.

Kaufman, A. S., & Kaufman, N. L. (2004). *Kaufman test of educational achievement,* (2nd ed.). Circle Pines, MN: American Guidance Service.

Kaufmann, J. M. (2005). *Characteristics of emotional and behavioral disorders of children and youth* (8th ed.). Upper Saddle River, NJ: Merrill/Prentice Hall.

Khan, L., & Lewis, N. (2002). *Khan–Lewis phonological analysis* (2nd ed.). Circle Pines, MN: American Guidance Service.

Klein-Ezell, C., & Klein, D. (2005). Use of portfolio assessment with students with cognitive disabilities/mental retardation. *Assessment for Effective Intervention, 30*(4), 15–24.

Knobloch, H., & Pasamanick, B. (1974). *Gesell and Amatruda's developmental diagnosis: The evaluation and management of normal and abnormal neuropsychological development in infancy and early childhood* (3rd ed.). New York: Harper & Row.

Knobloch, H., Stevens, F., & Malone, A. F. (1980). *Manual of developmental diagnosis.* New York: Harper & Row.

Knowlton, M., Lee, I., Bruininks, R. H., Woodcock, R. W., Weatherman, R. E., & Hill, B. K. (1997). *SIB-R short form for the visually impaired.* Itasca, IL: Riverside.

Kubiszyn, T., & Borich, G. (2005). *Educational testing and measurement: Classroom application and practice* (7th ed.). New York: Wiley and Sons.

Kush, J. C. (2005). Review of the Stanford-Binet Intelligence Scales, Fifth Edition. In R. A. Spies, & B. S. Plake (Eds.), *The sixteenth mental measurements yearbook.* Lincoln, NE: Buros Institute of Mental Measurements.

Lambert, N. M., Nihira, K., & Leland, H. (1993). *AAMR adaptive behavior scales—school* (2nd ed.). Austin, TX: PRO-ED.

Lambert, N., & Sandoval, J. (1990). *Children's attention & adjustment survey.* Circle Pines, MN: American Guidance Service.

Larsen, J. A., & Williams, J. D. (1994). Review of the KeyMath, Revised. In D. Keyser & R. C. Sweetland (Eds.), *Test critiques* (Vol. X). Austin, TX: PRO-ED.

Larsen, S. C., & Hammill, D. D., & Moats, L. (1999). *Test of written spelling—4.* Austin, TX: PRO-ED.

Lee, L. L. (1974). *Developmental sentence analysis.* Evanston, IL: Northwestern University Press.

Linn, R. L., & Miller, M. D. (2005). *Measurement and assessment in teaching* (9th ed.). Upper Saddle River, NJ: Merrill/Prentice Hall.

Liptak, J. J. (2004). *Transition-to-work inventory* (2nd ed.) Indianapolis, IN: JIST Publishing.

Lohman, D., & Hagen, F. (2001). *Cognitive abilities test, form 6.* Itasca, IL: Riverside.

Long, S. (2002). *Computerized profiling.* Retrieved August 15, 2002, from http://www.computerizedprofiling.org/index.html.

Luftig, R. L. (1989). *Assessment of learners with special needs.* Boston: Allyn & Bacon.

Lyman, H. B. (1998). *Test scores and what they mean* (6th ed.). Upper Saddle River, NJ: Prentice Hall.

MacMillan, D. L., & Reschly, D. J. (1998). The disproportionate representation of African-Americans in special education: The case for greater specificity or reconsideration of the variables examined. *Journal of Special Education, 32,* 15–24.

Maller, S. J. (2005). Review of the Wechsler Intelligence Scale for Children, Fourth Edition. In R. A. Spies, & B. S. Plake (Eds.), *The sixteenth mental measurements yearbook.* Lincoln, NE: Buros Institute of Mental Measurements.

Mardell-Czudnowski, C. D., & Goldenberg, D. S. (1998). *Developmental indicators for the assessment of learning* (3rd ed.). Circle Pines, MN: American Guidance Service.

Markwardt, F. C. (1998). *Peabody individual achievement test, revised.* Circle Pines, MN: American Guidance Service.

Markwardt, F. C. (1998). *Peabody individual achievement test, revised/normative update.* Circle Pines, MN: American Guidance Service.

McAffee, O., & Leong, D. (1997). *Assessing and guiding young children's development and learning* (2nd ed.). Boston: Allyn & Bacon.

McCallum, R. S., & Bracken, B. A. (1997). The universal nonverbal intelligence test. In D. P. Flanagan, J. L. Genshaft, & P. L. Harrison (Eds.), *Contemporary intellectual assessment: Theories, tests, and issues* (pp. 268–80). New York: Guilford Press.

McCarney, S. B. (1995a). *Adaptive behavior evaluation scale: Home version, revised.* Columbia, MO: Hawthorne Educational Services.

McCarney, S. B. (1995b). *Adaptive behavior evaluation scale: School version, revised.* Columbia, MO: Hawthorne Educational Services.

McCarney, S. B., & Anderson, P. D. (2000). *Transition behavior scale* (2nd ed.). Columbia, MO: Hawthorne Educational Services

McDermott, P. (1993). *Adjustment scales for children and adolescents.* Philadelphia, PA: Edumetric and Clinical Science.

McGhee, R., Bryant, B., Larsen, S., & Rivera, D. (1995). *Test of written expression* Austin, TX: PRO-ED.

McKenzie, W. (1999). *Multiple intelligences survey.* Available online at http://surfaquarium.com/Miinvent.htm.

McLean, M., & Crais, E. R. (1996). Procedural considerations in assessing infants and preschoolers with disabilities. In M. McLean, D. B. Bailey, & M. Wolery (Eds.), *Assessing infants and preschoolers with special needs* (2nd ed., pp. 46–65) Upper Saddle River, NJ: Merrill/Prentice Hall.

McLellan, M. J. (2001). Review of the Brigance Diagnostic Comprehensive Inventory of Basic Skills, Revised. In B. S. Plake & J. M. Impara (Eds.), *The fourteenth mental measurements yearbook* (pp. 175–176) Lincoln, NB: Buros Institute of Mental Measurements.

McLoughlin, J. A., & Lewis, R. B. (2005). *Assessing students with special needs,* (6th ed.). Upper Saddle River, NJ: Merrill/Prentice Hall.

Mecham, M. J. (2003). *Utah test of language development* (4th ed.). Austin, TX: PRO-ED.

Meisels, S., Marsden, D., Wiske, M., Henderson, L. (1997). *Early screening inventory—revised.* San Antonio, TX: Psychological Corp.

Melamed, L. E. (1996). *Kent visual perception test.* Austin, TX: PRO-ED.

Mercer, C. D., & Mercer, A. R. (2005). *Teaching students with learning problems* (7th ed.). Upper Saddle River, NJ: Merrill/Prentice Hall.

Mercer, J. R., & Lewis, J. F. (1977). *Adaptive behavior inventory for children.* San Antonio, TX: Harcourt Brace Educational Measurement.

Mercer, J. R., & Lewis, J. F. (1978). *System of multicultural pluralistic assessment.* San Antonio, TX: Psychological Corp.

Mercer, J. R., & Lewis, J. F. (1978). *System of multicultural pluralistic assessment.* San Antonio: The Psychological Corp.

Metropolitan achievement tests (8th ed.). (2000). San Antonio, TX: Harcourt Educational Measurement.

Miller, J. F. (2001). *Systematic analysis of language transcripts.* Retrieved October 9, 2005, from http://www.languageanalysislab.com/.

Miller, L. J. (1993). *FirstSTEP: Screening test for evaluating preschoolers.* San Antonio, TX: Psychological Corp.

Miller, W. H. (2001). *Alternative assessment techniques for reading and writing.* Hoboken, NJ: Wiley.

Milone, M. N. (1981). *An introduction to modality-based instruction.* Columbus, OH: Zaner-Bloser.

Morreau, L., & Bruininks, R. (1991). *Checklist of adaptive living skills.* Itasca, IL: Riverside.

Mullen, E. M. (1995). *Mullen scales of early learning: AGS edition.* Circle Pines, MN: American Guidance Service.

Murnane, R. J., & Levy, F. L. (1996). *Teaching the new basic skills.* New York: The Free Press.

Murphy, K. R., & Davidshofer, C. O. (2005). *Psychological testing: Principles and applications* (6th ed.). Upper Saddle River, NJ: Prentice Hall.

Murphy, L. L., Impara, J. C., & Plake, B. S. (2002). *Tests in print VI.* Lincoln, NE: Buros Institute of Mental Measurements.

Murray-Ward, M. (2001). Review of the Woodcock Reading Mastery Test, Revised (1998 Normative Update). In B. S. Plake & J. M. Impara (Eds.), *The fourteenth mental measurements yearbook* (pp. 1371–1373). Lincoln, NB: Buros Institute of Mental Measurements.

Naglieri, J. (2001). *Naglieri nonverbal ability test—individual administration.* San Antonio, TX: Psychological Corp.

Naglieri, J. A., LeBuffe, P. A., & Pfeiffer, S. I. (1993). *Devereux behavior rating scale—School form.* San Antonio, TX: Psychological Corp.

Naglieri, J., McNeish, T., & Achilles, B. (1991). *Draw a person: Screening procedure for emotional disturbance.* Austin, TX: PRO-ED.

National Dissemination Center for Children with Disabilities. (2005). *Finding help for young children with disabilities: Parent guide 2.* Washington, DC: Author.

National Dissemination Center for Children. (2004). *IDEA reauthorization news.* Retrieved August 26, 2004, from http://www.nichcy.org/reauth/index.html.

Neeper, R., Lahey, B. B., & Frick, P. J. (1990). *Comprehensive behavior rating scale for children.* San Antonio, TX: Psychological Corp.

Newborg, J., (2005). *Battelle developmental inventory* (2nd ed.). Itasca, IL: Riverside.

Newcomer, P. (2001). *Diagnostic achievement battery* (3rd ed.). Austin, TX: PRO-ED.

Newcomer, P. L., & Hammill, D. D. (1997). *Test of language development—primary* (3rd ed.). Austin, TX: PRO-ED.

Newcomer, P., & Bryant, B. R. (1993). *Diagnostic achievement test for adolescents* (2nd ed.). Austin, TX: PRO-ED.

Nihira, K., Leland, H., & Lambert, N. M. (1993). *AAMR adaptive behavior scales—residential and community* (2nd ed.). Austin, TX: PRO-ED.

Nitko, A. J. (2004). *Educational assessment of students* (4th ed.). Upper Saddle River, NJ: Merrill/Prentice Hall.

Nurss, J. R. (1995). *Metropolitan readiness tests* (6th ed.). San Antonio, TX: Psychological Corp.

Otis, A. S., & Lennon, R. T. (2002). *Otis–Lennon school ability test* (8th ed.). San Antonio, TX: Psychological Corp.

Overton, T. (2006). *Assessing learners with special needs: An applied approach* (5th ed.). Upper Saddle River, NJ: Merrill/ Prentice Hall.

Parker, R. M. (2001). *Occupational aptitude survey and interest schedule* (3rd ed.). Austin, TX: PRO-ED.

Peterson, N. (1987). *Early intervention for handicapped and at-risk children.* Denver, CO: Love.

Phelps-Terasaki, D., & Phelps-Gunn, T. (1992). *Test of pragmatic language.* San Antonio, TX: The Psychological Corp.

Piers, E. V., Harris, D. B., Herzberg, D. S. (2002). *Piers-Harris children's self-concept scale* (2nd ed.). Los Angeles: Western Psychological Services.

Pikulski, J. J. (1998, January). *Preventing reading problems: Factors common to successful early intervention programs.* Retrieved October, 2002 from http://www.ncbe.gwu.edu/pathways/reading/index.html.

Pomplan, M. (1996). Cooperative groups: Alternative assessment for students with disabilities? *Journal of Special Education, 30,* 1–17.

Pomplan, M. (1997). When students with disabilities participate in cooperative groups. *Exceptional Children, 64,* 49–59.

Raborn, D. T. (1995). Mathematics for students with learning disabilities from language-minority backgrounds: Recommendations for teaching. *New York State Association for Bilingual Education Journal, 10,* 25–33. Retrieved December 17, 2001, from http://www.ldonline.org/ld_indepth/bilingual_ld/esl_ld_math.html.

Raiser, L. (1996). *Written language profile.* Unpublished manuscript. University of North Florida, Jacksonville.

Reid, D. K., Hresko, W. P., & Hammill, D. D. (2001). *Test of early reading ability* (3rd ed.). Austin, TX: PRO-ED.

Renzulli, J. S., Smith, L. H., & Rizza, M. G. (2002). *Learning styles inventory, version III*. Mansfield Center, CT: Creative Learning Press.

Reschly, D. (1982). Assessing mild mental retardation: The influence of adaptive behavior, sociocultural status, and prospects for nonbiased assessment. In C. R. Reynolds & T. B. Gutkin (Eds.), *The handbook of school psychology* (pp. 209–242). New York: Wiley.

Reynolds, C. R., &. Kamphaus, R. W. (1998). *BASC monitor for ADHD*. Circle Pines, MN: American Guidance Service.

Reynolds, C. R., & Kamphaus, R. W. (2004). *Behavior assessment system for children* (2nd ed.). Circle Pines, MN: American Guidance Service.

Robertson, G. J. (2002). *Wide range achievement rest, Expanded edition*. Wilmington, DE: Wide Range.

Rodgers, D. (1998). *KeyMath–revised ASSIST*. Circle Pines, MN: American Guidance Service.

Roid, G. (2003). *The Stanford-Binet intelligence scale* (5th ed.). Chicago: Riverside.

Roid, G. J. (2005). *Stanford-Binet intelligence scales for early childhood* (5th ed.). Chicago: Riverside.

Rossetti, L. M. (1990). *Infant-toddler assessment: An interdisciplinary approach*. Boston: Little, Brown.

Roswell, F. G., & Chall, J. S. (1992). *Diagnostic assessments of reading with trial teaching strategies*. Itasca, IL: Riverside.

Rotatori, A. F. (1990). *Comprehensive assessment in special education: Approaches, procedures, and concerns*. Springfield, IL: Charles C. Thomas.

Rug, L. (2001). *Running records*. Retrieved October 29, 2001 from http://24.72.1.100/lang/1998–99/running.htm.

Ryser, G., & McConnell, K. (2002). *Scales for diagnosing attention deficit/hyperactivity disorder*. Austin: PRO-ED.

Sailor, W., & Guess, D. (1983). *Severely handicapped students: An instructional design*. Boston: Houghton Mifflin.

Salend, S. & Duhaney. L. (2002). Grading students in inclusive settings. *Teaching Exceptional Children, 34*, 8–15.

Salend, S. (2005). *Creating inclusive classrooms: Effective and reflective practices* (5th ed.). Upper Saddle River, NJ: Merrill/Prentice Hall.

Salvia, J., & Ysseldyle, J. (2004). *Assessment in special and inclusive education* (9th ed.). Boston: Houghton Mifflin Company.

Salvia, J., & Hughes, C. (1990). *Curriculum-based assessment: Testing what is taught*. Upper Saddle River, NJ: Merrill/Prentice Hall.

Salvia, J., Neisworth, J., & Schmidt, M. (1990). *Responsibility and independence scale for adolescents*. Itasca, IL: Riverside.

Sattler, J. (2001). *Assessment of children: Cognitive applications,* (4th ed.). San Diego: Author.

Scannell, D. P., Haugh, O. M., Loyd, B. H., & Risinger, C. F. (1996). *Tests of achievement and proficiency*. Itasca, IL: Riverside.

Schmeiser, C. B., Geisinger, K. F., Johnson-Lewis, S., Roeber, E. D., & Schafer, W. D. (1995). *Code of professional responsibilities in educational measurement*. Washington, DC: National Council on Measurement in Education.

Schoolhouse Technologies. (n.d.). *Schoolhouse test 2*. Seattle, WA: Author.

Semel, E., Wiig, E. H., & Secord, W. (1996a). *CELF-3— Screening test*. San Antonio, TX: Psychological Corp.

Semel, E., Wiig, E. H., & Secord, W. (1996b). *CELF-3— Observational rating scales*. San Antonio, TX: Psychological Corp.

Semel, E., Wiig, E. H., & Secord, W. (1997). *CELF-3— Spanish edition*. San Antonio, TX: Psychological Corporation.

Semel, E., Wiig, E. H., & Secord, W. (2003). *Clinical evaluation of language fundamentals* (4th ed.). San Antonio, TX: Psychological Corp.

Shriner, J., & DeStefano, L. (2001). Participation in statewide assessments: Views of district-level personnel. *Assessment for Effective Intervention, 26*(2), 9–16.

Shulman, B. B. (1986). *Test of pragmatic skills* (Rev. ed.). Tucson, AZ: Communication Skill Builders.

Sitlington, P. L., & Clark, G. M. (2006). *Transition education and services for students with disabilities* (4th ed.). Boston: Allyn & Bacon.

Skinner, B. F. (1968). *The technology of teaching*. New York: Appleton Century Crofts.

Slosson, R. L., Nicholson, C. L., & Hibpshman, T. H. (2002). *Slosson intelligence test* (Rev. ed.). East Aurora, NY: Slosson Educational Publications.

Smith, T., Finn, D., & Dowdy, C. (1993). *Teaching students with mild disabilities*. Fort Worth, TX: Harcourt Brace Jovanovich.

Smith, T., Finn, D., & Dowdy, C. L. (1983). *Teaching students with mild disabilities*. Fort Worth, TX: Harcourt Brace Jovanovich.

Soloman, B. A., & Felder, R. M. (2004). *Index of learning styles questionnaire*. Retrieved October 12, 2005, from http://www.engr.ncsu.edu/learningstyles/ilsweb.html.

Spandel, V., & Stiggins, R. J. (1997). *Creating writers: Linking assessment and writing instruction* (Rev. ed.). White Plains: NY: Addison-Wesley Longman.

Sparrow, S. S., Balla, D. A., & Cicchetti, D. V. (1984). *Vineland adaptive behavior scales: Expanded form manual* (Interview ed.). Circle Pines, MN: American Guidance Service.

Sparrow, S. S., Cicchetti, D. V., & Balla, D. A. (2005). *Vineland adaptive behavior scales* (2nd ed.). Circle Pines, MN: American Guidance Service.

Spies, R. A., & Plake, B. S. (2005). *The sixteenth mental measurements yearbook*. Lincoln, NE: Buros Institute of Mental Measurements.

Stanford achievement test series, tenth edition. (2003). San Antonio, TX: Harcourt Educational Measurement.

Staub, J. (2004). *Differentiated assessment.* Los Angeles: Unpublished document.

Stiggins, R. J. (2005). *Student-involved classroom assessment for learning* (4th ed.). Upper Saddle River, NJ: Merrill/Prentice Hall.

Strong, E. K., Campbell, D. P., & Hanson, J. C. (2004). *Strong interest inventory, revised.* Stanford, CA: Stanford University Press.

Teele, S. (1997). *Teele inventory for multiple intelligences.* Redland, CA: Sue Teele and Associates.

TerraNova SUPERA. (1997). Monterey, CA: CTB/McGraw Hill.

TerraNova, second edition. (2000). Monterey, CA: CTB/McGraw Hill.

Thompson, B. (2005). Review of the Wechsler Intelligence Scale for Children, Fourth Edition. In R. A. Spies & B. S. Plake (Eds.), *The sixteenth mental measurements yearbook.* Lincoln, NE: Buros Institute of Mental Measurements.

Thompson, S., & Thurlow, M. (2001). Participation of students with disabilities in state assessment systems. *Assessment for Effective Intervention, 26*(2), 5–8.

Thorndike, R. L., & Hagen, E. (1997). *CogAT nonverbal battery, edición en Español.* Itasca, IL: Riverside.

Thorndike, R. M. (2005). *Measurement and evaluation in psychology and education* (7th ed.). Upper Saddle River, NJ: Merrill/Prentice Hall.

Thurlow, M. (2001). Message from the guest editor. *Assessment for Effective Intervention, 26*(6), 1–3.

Tiegerman-Farber, E., & Radziewicz, C. (1998). *Collaborative decision making: The pathway to inclusion.* Upper Saddle River, NJ: Merrill/Prentice Hall.

Torgesen, J., Wagner, R., & Rashotte C., (1999). *Test of word reading efficiency.* Austin, TX: PRO-ED.

Tyack, D., & Venable, G. P. (1998). *Language sampling, analysis, and training: A handbook* (3rd ed.). Austin: PRO-ED.

Ulrich, D. A. (2000). *Test of gross motor development.* Austin, TX: PRO-ED.

Vavrus, L. (1990). Put portfolios to the test. *Instructor.* August, 48–53.

Venn, J. J., & Dykes, M. K. (1987). Assessing the physically handicapped. In W. H. Berdine and S. A. Meyer (Eds.), *Assessment in special education* (pp. 278–308). Boston: Little, Brown.

Vulpé, S. (1994). *Vulpé assessment battery, revised.* East Aurora, NY: Slosson Educational Publications.

Wallace, G., & Hammill, D. D. (2002). *Comprehensive receptive and expressive vocabulary test* (2nd ed.). Austin, TX: PRO-ED.

Wallace, G., Larsen, S. C., & Elksnin, L. K. (1992). *Educational assessment of learning problems: Testing for teaching* (2nd ed.). Boston: Allyn & Bacon.

Warden, A. R., & Hutchinson, T. A. (1992). *Writing process test.* Austin, TX: PRO-ED.

Webb, N. M. (1995). Group collaboration in assessment: Multiple objectives, processes, and outcomes. *Educational Evaluation and Policy Analysis, 17,* 239–61.

Wechsler, D. (1991). *Wechsler intelligence scale for children* (3rd ed.). San Antonio: Psychological Corp.

Wechsler, D. (1997). *Wechsler adult intelligence scale* (3rd ed.). San Antonio: Psychological Corp.

Wechsler, D. (1999). *Wechsler abbreviated scale of intelligence.* San Antonio: Psychological Corp.

Wechsler, D. (2000). *Wechsler individual achievement test* (2nd ed.). San Antonio, TX: Psychological Corporation.

Wechsler, D. (2002). *Wechsler preschool and primary scale of intelligence,* (3rd ed.). San Antonio, TX: The Psychological Corp.

Wechsler, D. (2002). *Wechsler preschool and primary scale of intelligence.* San Antonio: Psychological Corp.

Wechsler, D. (2003). *Wechsler intelligence scale for children,* (4th ed.). San Antonio, TX: The Psychological Corp.

Wehman, P. (2005). *Life beyond the classroom: Transition strategies for youg people with disabilities* (4th ed.). Baltimore: Paul H. Brookes.

Weiss, D. J. (1985). Adaptive testing by computer. *Journal of Consulting and Clinical Psychology, 53*(6), 774–789.

Wepman, J. M., & Reynolds, W. M. (1987). *Auditory discrimination test* (2nd ed.). Los Angeles: Western Psychological Services.

Wesson, C. L., & King, R. P. (1996). Portfolio assessment and special education students. *Teaching Exceptional Children, 28,* 44–48.

Wiederholt, J. L., & Bryant, B. R. (2001). *Gray Oral reading tests* (4th ed.). Austin, TX: PRO-ED.

Wiig, E. H., & Semel, E. (1984). *Language assessment and intervention for the learning disabled* (2nd ed.). New York: Merrill/Macmillan.

Wiig, E. H., Secord, W., & Semel, E. (1992). *CELF—preschool.* San Antonio, TX: Psychological Corp.

Williams, K. T. (1997). *Expressive vocabulary test.* Circle Pines, MN: American Guidance Service.

Wilson, B. A., & Felton, R. (2004). *Word identification and spelling test.* Austin, TX: PRO-ED.

Wolcott, W. (1993). Addressing theoretical and practical issues of using portfolio assessment on a large scale in high school settings. In T. Vernetson (Ed.), *Florida Educational Research Bulletin on alternative/portfolio assessment* (pp. 123–32). Sanibel, FL: Florida Educational Research Council.

Wollack, J. A. (2001). Review of the KeyMath-Revised: A Diagnostic Inventory of Essential Mathematics (1998 Normative update). In B. S. Plake & J. C. Impara (Eds.), *The fourteenth mental measurements yearbook* (pp. 640–650). Lincoln, NB: Buros Institute of Mental Measurements.

Wood, J. W. (2006). *Adapting instruction to accommodate students in inclusive settings* (5th ed.). Upper Saddle River, NJ: Merrill/Prentice Hall.

Woodcock, R. (1973). *Woodcock reading mastery tests*. Circle Pines, MN: American Guidance Service.

Woodcock, R. (1998). *Woodcock reading mastery tests, revised edition, normative update*. Circle Pines, MN: American Guidance Service.

Woodcock, R. J., McGrew, K., & Mather, N. (2001). *Woodcock-Johnson III complete battery*. Itasca, IL: Riverside.

Woodcock, R. J., McGrew, K., & Mather, N. (2001a). *Woodcock–Johnson III tests of achievement*. Itasca, IL: Riverside.

Woodcock, R. J., McGrew, K., & Mather, N. (2001b). *Woodcock–Johnson III tests of cognitive abilities*. Itasca, IL: Riverside.

Woodcock, R. J., Muñoz-Sandoval, A. F., McGrew, K., Mather, N., & Schrank, F. (2004). *Batería III Woodcock-Muñoz*. Itasca, IL: Riverside.

Woodcock, R. W., Muñoz-Sandoval, A. F., McGrew, K. Nancy Mather, & N., Schrank, F. (2004). *Batería III woodcock-muñoz*. Itasca, IL: Riverside.

Woods, M. L., & Moe, A. J. (2003). *Analytical reading inventory* (7th ed.). Upper Saddle River, NJ: Merrill/Prentice Hall.

Worcester, T. (n.d.). *Assessment of electronic portfolios*. Retrieved October 17, 2005, from http://www.essdack.org/port/rubric.html

Young, G. M. (1993). Images. In K. Gill (Ed.), *Process and portfolios in writing instruction*. Urbana, IL: National Council of Teachers of English.

Zigmond, N., Vallecorsa, A., & Silverman, R. (1983). *Assessment for instructional planning in special education*. Upper Saddle River, NJ: Prentice Hall.

Glossary of Assessment Terms

Abnormal distribution   A pattern in which scores cluster at either the high or the low end rather than the middle or the average of a distribution. See also *skewed distribution*.

Achievement quotient   This is a specific type of age score that expresses the achievement levels of students.

Accommodations in testing   Modifications and adjustments in test administration that give students with special needs a fair opportunity to demonstrate their knowledge and skills.

Accountability   Documenting what students are learning and how well they are progressing in their learning.

Achievement tests   Most frequently used in educational settings, achievement tests measure learning in academic subjects such as reading, spelling, written expression, mathematics, and general information.

Acquiescence   The tendency to respond positively to all items on self-report inventories and other types of questionnaires.

Adaptive behavior   The ability to adapt to the environment, especially by developing independent personal and social behavior; acquiring functional, practical competence in communication, daily living, and social interaction; and adjusting to changes in the environment.

Affective domain   Opinions, attitudes, and behaviors derived from emotions and feelings rather than from thought.

Age score   A score that represents typical or average performance for individuals of a particular chronological age.

Alternate-form reliability   An estimate of accuracy that involves comparing scores from two forms of the same test.

Alternative assessment   A group of informal assessment techniques that emphasize open-ended, criterion-referenced evaluation that occurs as an integral part of instruction rather than a separate testing activity. See also *portfolio assessment* and *authentic assessment*.

Alternative grading   Procedures such as pass/fail grading, assigning multiple grades, grading for effort, portfolio grading, and IEP grading that teachers use in the classroom to meet the individual needs of students with special needs. See also *IEP grading*.

Analytical scoring   Evaluating each part of a portfolio or other student work separately and combining the individual scores to obtain an overall score. See also *holistic scoring*.

Anecdotal assessment information   Refers to procedures that evaluators follow when they include written notes and comments about students on scoring sheets and in written assessment reports.

Anecdotal recording   Systematic observation of behavior in which the observer writes down the behaviors and interactions that occur during a specific time interval.

Assessment   The process of using tests and other measures of student performance and behavior to make educational decisions. Assessment consists of an assortment of techniques for evaluating, estimating, appraising, and making conclusions about the behavior, performance, and learning of students.

Assessment environment   The setting, circumstances, and conditions surrounding an evaluation.

Assessment proficiency checklist (APC)   An informal tool that provides a practical, applied way to measure an evaluator's skill in administering and scoring an assessment instrument.

Auditory-motor processing   Refers to the process of coordinating sensory information from the ears with fine and gross motor body movements.

Authentic assessment An assessment approach that links evaluation and instruction by measuring student performance in direct relation to what has been taught in the curriculum. See also *alternative assessment, curriculum-based assessment*, and *portfolio assessment*.

Authentic tasks Genuine activities that occur in a real-life context such as shopping, banking, measuring a ballpark, designing a home, or building a bridge or tower.

Average thought unit A measure of writing maturity and complexity based on syntax.

Behavior rating scales Written questionnaires containing lists of behaviors that raters complete by assigning a rating (usually based on a scale of 1 to 5) to each item on the checklist. Raters are usually teachers, parents, or other primary caregivers who are familiar with a student's typical actions and conduct.

Behavior observation A procedure for directly observing behavior that involves recording student actions using specific techniques to ensure accurate measurement.

Bell-shaped curve The bell-shaped curve or bell curve is another name for a normal distribution because the shape of a normal distribution, when graphed, looks somewhat like a bell. See also *normal distribution*.

Career assessment Evaluating the broad range of practical life skills that are part of living and working as an adult, including the social behaviors, functional academics, and daily living activities necessary for success on the job and in the community.

Cash validity A superficial type of nontechnical validity that involves how well a test sells in the marketplace.

Celebration portfolios Portfolios that students use as mementos of their favorite learning experiences and activities.

Central tendency The measures of central tendency are statistics that describe typical, or representative, scores in a group of scores.

Child-study team A team of professionals who coordinate the screening activities associated with the referral process that leads to identifying students with disabilities. A team usually includes a school administrator, a counselor, regular teachers, and special education teachers.

Clinical observation A curriculum-based assessment technique that relies on direct observation of student behavior and systematic recording of observation findings. The technique is useful for obtaining diagnostic data concerning a student's actual performance in the classroom and other educational settings; practitioners often use checklists of behavior to record their observations and maintain a record of results.

Cloze procedures A group of curriculum-based assessment techniques that consists of informal tests of word-prediction abilities for measuring comprehension skills and the way students use cues to identify words. The most common cloze procedure, visual cloze, involves selecting a brief passage (about 250 words), altering it by deleting every fifth word of the text, and having a student read the altered passage aloud while filling in the blanks.

Community independence Refers to autonomy in the community, which, for young children, includes playing at school, at home, and in the yard with minimal supervision, and for teenagers and adults includes self-reliance in the community as related to work, recreation, and leisure activities.

Competency-based grading With this type of grading, students demonstrate attainment of required skills and receive grades based on their progress in reaching prespecified criterion levels of performance.

Computer adaptive testing A type of computer-based test administration that enables interaction between the test and the test taker.

Consequences of testing Term for a new validity consideration that involves documenting the validity of a test for use in improving classroom instruction and producing positive outcomes for students.

Construct validity A measure of effectiveness that refers to how well a test assesses a theoretical construct or attribute. Examples of constructs include traits such as intelligence, mathematical reasoning ability, receptive language vocabulary, and gross motor skill. Establishing construct validity entails a lengthy process of putting together scientific research data about the relationship between test performance and the theoretical construct measured by the test.

Content validity A measure of effectiveness that refers to how well a test covers a domain or learning area. The process of establishing content validity involves developing test specifications, writing test items, conducting field tests, reviewing and revising the test, and compiling the final test.

Contract grading   This grading process involves having the teacher and the student sign a contract that describes the work the student will complete to earn a specific letter grade of "A," "B," or "C" depending on the amount and quality of work.

Cooperative learning   Specialized assessment approaches that include peer editing, peer evaluation of class presentations, peer assessment, and group assessment.

Criterion-referenced assessment   Assessment that is closely related to instruction and that measures student knowledge on relatively small and discrete units.

Criterion-referenced score   A score that describes performance in relation to a functional level rather than the performance of others.

Criterion-related validity   A measure of effectiveness that involves analysis of the relationship between a test and other independent criteria. The two types of criterion-related validity are as follows: predictive validity, which entails measuring the effectiveness of a test in predicting future performance, and concurrent validity, which consists of correlating a test with a comparable test or other measure of proven validity.

Critical moment   The optimal time during which a child is physically, psychologically, and emotionally ready to learn a particular skill. Other terms for this phenomena include the *critical period* and the *teachable moment*. Developmental assessment helps professionals identify critical moments by determining mastered, emerging, and unlearned skills.

Critical period   See *critical moment*.

Culturally and linguistically diverse   Children from minority cultures who know and use two languages.

Culture fair   The fairness or equity of tests to all students regardless of cultural background. Cultural-fair tests attempt to provide equal opportunity for success by students of different cultures and life experiences. As a result, developers of culture-fair tests must limit test content to material that is common to all cultures or is unfamiliar to students from

a variety of different cultural backgrounds. See also *fairness in testing* and *nonbiased testing*.

Curriculum-based assessment (CBA)   An assessment approach that measures educational success based on student progress in the local school curriculum rather than in relation to scores on standardized, norm-referenced tests. Curriculum-based assessment involves using class tests, homework assignments, classwork, and teacher impressions (based on direct observation) to make assessment decisions. See also *authentic assessment*.

Deciles   A type of percentile that expresses percentile scores in 10 equal units, or tenths. See also *percentile score*.

Descriptive grading   This type of grading relies on descriptive comments that the teacher writes to explain the quality of a student's performance.

Developmental age   A type of age score designed to compare individual performance to the average performance of children of the same chronological age.

Developmental assessment   A specialized type of assessment for measuring the performance of young children, especially infants, toddlers, and preschoolers from birth to around 6 years of age. Developmental assessment provides, on the basis of the predictable patterns that children follow as they grow and develop, a means to determine whether a child is following the normal sequence of skill acquisition at expected age levels.

Developmental learning areas   The traditional developmental learning areas include fine motor, gross motor, communication and language, social, cognitive, and self-help skills.

Developmental milestones   Critical skills in early childhood development such as walking, saying one or two words, and toilet training.

Developmental quotient   This is a special type of age score that expresses the ability of young children from birth through 6 years of age.

Developmental scales   Specialized tests of the performance of young children that consist of scales or checklists of behavior arranged in chronological order.

Developmental screening   A special type of assessment for identifying the general performance levels of young children from birth to approximately 6 years of age. Screening alerts parents and professionals to children who may have a developmental delay or learning problem. In addition, teachers often rely on developmental screening to determine overall levels of functioning and to develop initial programming goals with new students.

Developmental sentence analysis An assessment procedure for collecting and analyzing a speech sample to measure the ability to spontaneously formulate and produce words and sentences. Developmental sentence analysis involves examination of eight grammatical categories that represent syntactic ability.

Deviation IQ A standard score that provides an index of general mental ability based on the deviation between a student's score and the average score for students in a norm group of the same age.

Diagnostic interviews One or a series of conferences with a student to determine the reasons for errors in academic work. During an interview a teacher has the student explain in a step-by-step manner the process used to solve each problem.

Diagnostic-prescriptive model A system of assessment that involves conducting an initial evaluation to identify present levels of performance (diagnosis), using the results to determine appropriate intervention objectives (prescription), and conducting periodic reevaluations to measure progress and revise the objectives.

Digital portfolios Digital portfolios use technology including graphics, video, and audio to prepare, store, and present portfolios.

Direct observation The process of assessing performance by listening to or watching a student over a period of time in a structured, systematic manner. Examples of direct observation include keeping progress graphs on students, counting incidents of misbehavior to establish a baseline for evaluating subsequent treatment, and using audio- or videotapes to measure change in behavior over time.

Distribution A procedure for grouping a large set of scores into a meaningful arrangement that visually summarizes and illustrates the relationship among the scores. The process involves organizing scores in rank order from highest to lowest, grouping them in intervals, and graphing them.

Duration recording A method for accurately measuring sustained behaviors by recording the total time that a target behavior occurs during a specified time period.

Ecological assessment An assessment technique that considers both student and environmental characteristics (such as the classroom setting, the community, and the family situation) in the evaluation process. In ecological assessment, the evaluator analyzes student behavior within the context of the environment, setting, or situation in which the behavior occurs.

Eligibility process This is a process for deciding the nature and severity of a learning problem and determining eligibility for special education services.

Employability skills The generic skills important to qualify for entry-level jobs in the workplace regardless of the particular occupation or profession.

Error pattern analysis A curriculum-based assessment procedure that involves systematically measuring student mistakes and using the results to plan a remedial program. The procedure is also called *error analysis* and *miscue analysis*. See also *miscue analysis*.

Event recording A behavioral assessment procedure that involves counting the number of occurrences of a target behavior during a specified period of time.

Expressive language Sending messages and translating thoughts, ideas, and signals into vocal expression or motor expression (the latter includes writing and sign language or other nonvocal forms of communication).

External bias The use of test results in an unfair manner.

External scoring Relies on scorers who have had no contact with the students. See also *internal scoring*.

Face validity A superficial type of nontechnical validity that involves quickly reviewing a test to determine whether it appears valid on the surface.

Fairness in testing Refers to equity of tests for all students regardless of race, ethnicity, language, gender, or cultural background. See also *culture-fair* and *nonbiased testing*.

Faking A common validity problem with self-report inventories caused by respondents who attempt to distort the test results in a positive direction.

Fine motor Addresses movement and response speed controlled by the small muscles of the body, including hand and finger dexterity, drawing, and manipulating small objects.

Fluency The quantity of output as measured by the total output in a specified time period, such as the number of words written in 20 minutes.

Full inclusion Participation of all students with disabilities, including those with severe and profound disabling conditions, in the general education classroom and in the general curriculum with full aids and support services.

Functional assessment Measuring and evaluating student performance in real-life, natural settings (e.g., at home, in school, on the job, and in the community) for the purpose of identifying proficiency in performing practical, applied skills.

Functional skills Practical life skills associated with the independence in daily living activities, employment, and participation in the community.

Gaps in development Major skill deficits that impede the development of higher-level skills. For example, problems with the basic locomotion skill of walking may block the development of higher-level locomotion skills such as running, jumping, skipping, and hopping. See also *splinter skills*.

Grade score A score that describes student performance according to scholastic grade levels. Other terms for grade score include *grade equivalent score, grade-referenced score,* and *grade placement score.*

Grading for effort Some teachers use grading for effort with students whose ability is so low that they have difficulty meeting even minimum performance standards.

Graphical report A reporting procedure that produces a profile or visual representation of performance. The procedure is especially useful for illustrating progress over time and for analyzing strengths and weaknesses across skills.

Gross motor Refers to movement controlled by the large muscles of the body, including those that regulate walking, throwing, catching, and balance.

Group achievement tests Tests given to groups of students at one time as brief screening measures to obtain an overview of achievement.

Group intelligence tests Tests designed to be given to more than one student at a time and often given to large groups as a screening measure for initial identification of those who may need comprehensive assessment of their intellectual ability.

Group assessment Given to groups of students rather than individuals, group assessments are usually brief screening instruments that give an overview of performance rather than specific diagnostic information.

Group celebrations Cooperative learning activities occurring after completion of assessment and grading that give students the opportunity to salute their success and reflect on how well they collaborated to achieve their learning goals.

High-stakes testing programs These programs involve giving tests to students in a school, school district, or an entire state for accountability purposes. Such programs are "high stakes" when the results are used to make significant decisions about students, teachers, and schools.

Holistic scoring Evaluating portfolios and other student materials in their entirety and giving a single overall score. See also *analytical scoring.*

IEP grading Grading that reflects student attainment of IEP goals in which the teacher measures progress and assigns grades using the evaluation criteria for each IEP objective.

Inclusion Participation of students with disabilities in the general education classroom and in the general curriculum, with appropriate aids and support services.

Individual education plan (IEP) A written document developed jointly by parents, professionals, and, if appropriate, the student that guides the development and implementation of an appropriate education for the students.

Individual family service plan (IFSP) A written document prepared by professionals and the family with an infant or toddler who has disabilities that guides the development and the implementation of an appropriate family service plan.

Individually administered intelligence tests Tests that an evaluator administers to one student at a time to obtain comprehensive data about intellectual ability. Individual tests exist for all age groups, and most individual tests contain subtests that sample various behaviors, including verbal language, motor performance, and visual reasoning.

Informal reading inventories   Commercial and teacher-made instruments for diagnosing reading difficulties, planning instructional intervention, and measuring student progress.

Informant   A teacher, parent, grandparent, teacher aide, or other primary caregiver who provides the information required to rate the items on a scale, such as an adaptive behavior scale.

Inner language   The use of language in thinking, planning, and cognition.

Instructional intervention   The process of developing instructional objectives, establishing intervention priorities, instructing students, and evaluating the effectiveness of the instruction.

Intelligence   A trait or construct associated with cognitive or intellectual capacity that is related to the potential or ability to learn. Intelligence is an abstract quality associated with all types of intellectual processes, including abstract thinking, mental reasoning, using sound judgment, and making rational decisions.

Internal bias   Differences in average scores among two or more groups due to the qualities of a test rather than actual differences between the groups.

Internal scoring   Relies on scorers who have direct contact with the students; this includes teachers who score the work of their own students. See also *external scoring*.

Interrater reliability   Often referred to as *interobserver reliability*, this type of reliability is obtained by comparing the observations of two observers who independently watch or listen to a student in a classroom and in other settings.

Item bias   Unfairness that exists within individual items on a test.

Kinesthetic   The learning modality that relies on a combination of feeling, balance, and motion.

Language   The use of organized voice sounds and written symbols to communicate thoughts and feelings. Language occurs at both receptive and expressive levels of communication.

Learning quotient   This is a specific type of age score that expresses the learning ability of students.

Learning styles   The primary or preferred sensory modes for learning new or difficult information, including visual, auditory, and kinesthetic modalities.

Letter grade   Represents a classic means of describing student performance and is usually derived from a percent correct score and assigned according to a grading scale.

Level grading   With this type of grading, the teacher individualizes grading by indicating the level of difficulty for each grade, such as a "1" for above-grade-level, a "2" for on-grade-level, and a "3" for below-grade-level.

Limited English proficiency (LEP)   Refers to bilingual students who display inadequate skills in understanding and speaking the English language.

Mainstreaming   Educating students with disabilities in regular classes and providing opportunities for students with disabilities to interact with their nondisabled peers in other educational settings.

Mastery level/criterion grading   This type of grading system involves pretesting students to determine performance on specific skills and posttesting to identify skills mastered after instruction.

Mean   The average number in a distribution and the most commonly used measure of central tendency. In most instances, the term *average* refers to the mean rather than to the other specific measures of central tendency. The formula for calculating the mean involves summing all the scores and dividing by the number of scores.

Mean length of utterance (MLU)   An assessment procedure for evaluating the ability to form words, phrases, and sentences. MLU assessment is ideal for measuring the language level of young children. The MLU procedure involves tape recording and later analyzing a spontaneous speech sample containing a minimum of 50 consecutive utterances.

Measurement   The process of determining ability or performance level by using objective information such as numbers, scores, and other quantitative data. Types of measurement include testing, observing behavior, conducting interviews, completing rating scales, filling out checklists, and performing clinical evaluations.

Measures of central tendency   Statistics, including the mean, median, and mode, that describe the typical or representative scores in a group of scores.

Measures of variability   Statistics, including the standard deviation and the standard error of measurement, that summarize the spread or dispersion of test scores.

Measuring progress   Ongoing evaluation and periodic measurement of student performance, program effectiveness, and responsiveness of programs to individual student needs.

Median   The midpoint or middle in a distribution of scores.

Mental age (MA)   A score that estimates mental ability in relation to the average performance of the individuals in the norm group at each successive chronological age.

Miscue analysis   A procedure for systematically measuring and evaluating student reading errors for the purpose of planning remedial reading programs. See also *error pattern analysis*.

Mode   The most frequently occurring score in a distribution.

Momentary time sampling   A behavioral assessment procedure that involves obtaining a sample of the percentage of time in which a target behavior occurs by recording the occurrence or nonoccurrence of the behavior at the end of specified time periods (e.g., at the end of 5 minutes or at the end of every minute).

Morphology   The study of the smallest meaningful units of language, called *morphemes*. For example, the word *boy* has one morpheme, but the plural form of the word (*boys*) has two morphemes because -*s* is a separate language unit.

Motor proficiency   Refers to movement output, especially the efficiency of movements controlled by the muscles of the body. The two major types of motor activity are fine and gross motor movement.

Multiple grading   This grading process enables students to earn more than one grade, such as a grade for effort and a grade for performance.

Multiple intelligences   Different dimensions of intelligence, including unique cognitive behaviors

and cognitive learning styles such as emotional intelligence and interpersonal intelligence.

Multiple-skill achievement tests   Tests that provide an overview of performance in more than one subject area. For example, a multiple-skill test of academic achievement might include subtests for assessing reading, mathematics, and spelling.

Negative response bias   The tendency to respond negatively to questions on self-report inventories and other types of questionnaires.

Nonbiased testing   Testing that minimizes inequalities due to racial, cultural, ethnic, gender, or language background. See also *culture-fair* and *fairness in testing*.

Normal curve equivalent (NCE)   A statistically transformed standard score that fits a normal curve of equal units. NCEs have a mean equal to 50 and a standard deviation equal to 21.06. NCE values within 21.06 points of 50 (50 $\pm$ 21.06, or 28.94 to 71.06) represent average scores. Scores of 28.94 and lower fall more than 1 standard deviation (SD) from the mean of 50 and indicate below-average performance. Scores of 71.06 and higher are more than 1 SD from the mean and represent above-average values.

Normal distribution   A pattern in which scores cluster around the average of a distribution with an even formation of scores above and below the average. Because the shape when graphed looks somewhat like a bell, another name for the normal distribution is the *bell-shaped curve,* or *bell curve*.

Norm-referenced assessment   Assessment that compares an individual score to the scores of those in a comparison group. The comparison group, called the *norm group* or *normative sample,* consists of a carefully selected group of students who take the test in a precise manner.

Norm-referenced score   A score that enables interpretation of student performance in relation to the performance of others by comparing the score of an individual to the scores of those in a norm group.

On-the-job assessment   A specific type of situational evaluation for measuring vocational behavior in actual work settings.

Partial interval recording   A behavioral assessment procedure that involves dividing a period of time into brief intervals (e.g., a 1-minute time period into 10-second intervals or a 10-minute period into 1-minute intervals) and observing whether a target behavior occurs at any time during the interval.

Pass fail grading   This type of grading involves establishing minimum criteria for receiving passing grades and assigning grades of "pass" to students who meet the criteria and grades of "fail" to students who do not meet the criteria.

Peer assessment   Evaluation of students by other students, which if often a part of cooperative learning.

Peer editing   Having other members of the cooperative group review the work of individual students.

Peer tutoring assessment   Evaluation of peer tutoring using strategies for monitoring progress such as having tutors complete daily progress sheets, observing tutor-tutee pairs, conducting interviews, and having tutors and tutees complete simple questionnaires.

Percent correct score   A criterion-referenced score that describes performance as the percentage of correct answers on a test.

Percentile rank   A score that shows relative standing by ranking a student in comparison to those in a corresponding norm group. A percentile is any 1 of 99 scores divided into a distribution of 100 equal ranks ranging from 1 to 99. The 50th percentile signifies the average ranking or average performance.

Perception   The process of comprehending or giving meaning to information received by the senses. Assessment of perception involves measuring the way in which students process information from the senses, especially visual and auditory information.

Perceptual-motor integration   The process of integrating information received by the senses with corresponding movements of the body, including visual-motor, auditory-motor, and tactile-motor movements.

Performance behaviors   Behaviors sampled by intelligence tests that rely primarily on fine motor proficiency and perceptual ability rather than language ability.

Performance measurement   A curriculum-based assessment approach for assessing math and other types of academic achievement. The most common and useful forms of performance measurement are percent correct and performance rate scoring of class worksheets, homework assignments, and class tests. Percent correct is the percentage of correct responses on a worksheet, assignment, or test. Performance rate refers to the number of correct responses in a specified time period.

Performance rate scoring   The use of time probes or tests to measure the number of responses in a specific period.

Performance scale   A subtest of the Wechsler Intelligence Scale for Children-Third Edition (WISC-III) that consists of items requiring responses based on visual reasoning ability and fine motor proficiency.

Personal self-sufficiency   With young children, personal self-sufficiency refers to the ability to perform self-help skills such as dressing eating, hygiene, and toileting. With older children, personal self-sufficiency encompasses a wide range and variety of daily living skills such as selecting and caring for appropriate clothing, eating independently in cafeterias and restaurants, and performing other daily activities.

Personal-social responsibility   A term that encompasses behaviors such as trustworthiness, commitment, appropriate socialization, proper interpersonal interaction, and self-direction. For young children, personal-social responsibility refers to behaviors such as complying with parents, getting along with siblings, and playing constructively. For older children, personal-social responsibility includes behaviors such as taking care of personal items, making friends at school, and completing homework.

Phonology   The study of the smallest units of sound in language, called *phonemes*. American English includes 44 speech sounds or phonemes. Phonemes have no meaning by themselves but contribute to word meaning. For example, the word *boy* includes three phonemes: *b, o,* and *y.*

Point systems   In this grading system, students receive grades corresponding to the number of points earned, with points assigned for completing learning activities, tests, and assignments.

Portfolio assessment   An ongoing process of evaluating the activities and accomplishments associated with reflective teaching and learning that occur in portfolio-based instruction. See also *alternative assessment, authentic assessment,* and *curriculum-based assessment.*

Portfolio conferences   A key element in portfolio assessment that consists of meetings in which students review learning goals and discuss progress.

Portfolio grading   This type of grading involves evaluating student performance based on appraisal of authentic samples of student work that appear in a portfolio.

Practical measurement concepts   Concepts that focus on the applied, functional features and the practical aspects of assessment instruments.

Pragmatics   The use of language in context, especially during social interaction. The essence of pragmatics is the process of sharing intents that occur in a wide variety of contexts, including those involving two people, small groups, and large groups. For example, the verbal sharing of intents includes intimate communication such as whispering as well as formal communication such as introductions at a reception.

Preparing for assessment   The process of reviewing cumulative records, gathering information from others, studying the assessment tool, and organizing an assessment session.

Prevocational skills   The personal, social, and applied academic skills that are necessary for success on any job.

Principles of developmental assessment   Guidelines that professionals follow when they use the developmental approach to assess the behavior and performance of young children with special needs.

Principles of using scores   Practical suggestions for using test scores accurately and effectively with appropriate caution to avoid errors.

Process portfolios   Portfolios that document the stages of learning and provide a progressive record of student growth.

Product portfolios   Portfolios that demonstrate mastery of learning tasks or sets of learning objectives, and contain only the best work.

Progress-measuring process   A term that describes ongoing evaluation and periodic measurement of overall performance to gauge program effectiveness and to ensure that services respond to individual needs.

Progressive improvement grading   Students receive feedback and instruction on tests and learning activities throughout the grading period, but assigning grades from the cumulative tests and learning activities occurring at the end of the term.

Prompting during assessment   Using verbal cues, modeling, and physical prompts while administering a test or conducting another type of assessment procedure.

Quartile   A type of percentile score that expresses percentiles in four equal units, or fourths.

Quotient score   Includes two distinctly different kinds of scores. One type is an age score that expresses performance based on the ratio of functioning age to chronological age. Some older intelligence tests use this score, which is called a *ratio intelligence quotient* (ratio IQ). Similar age-based quotient scores exist for other types of tests. The other kind of quotient score is a standard score that expresses performance on the basis of the relationship between an individual score and the average score in a norm sample group. When used with intelligence tests, it is called a *deviation intelligence quotient* (deviation IQ) Similar deviation quotient scores exist for other types of tests.

Random responses   A validity problem associated with self-report inventories and other assessment tools in which respondents answer questions inconsistently.

Ratio IQ   An age score derived from an intelligence test that expresses mental ability on the basis of the ratio of a student's mental age to chronological age. The formula for calculating a ratio IQ is mental age divided by chronological age multiplied by 100.

Raw score   The simple numerical result of testing, typically the number of items answered correctly. In most situations, evaluators avoid using raw scores to report test results. Instead, they convert raw scores into various types of transformed scores.

Readiness tests   A special category of developmental scales designed to measure a child's knowledge of the basic skills necessary for success in the beginning years of school. Most readiness tests measure the behavior of children between the ages of 4 and 7 years.

Receptive language   The process of understanding and giving meaning to the communication (most often verbal language) of others.

Regular Education Initiative (REI) A proposal advocating that general education accept primary responsibility for educating students with disabilities, which involves complete integration of students with disabilities into regular classes and removal of labels on students with disabilities. REI calls for significant changes in assessment, including the participation of all teachers in evaluating students with special needs.

Reliability An essential technical quality of assessment instruments that refers to the accuracy and consistency of test scores and other measures of the skills, abilities, and behaviors of students. Methods for estimating reliability include test-retest, alternate-form, split-half, and interrater reliability.

Response modes Ways of answering items on a test or other assessment including alternative methods of responding such as using a sign language or a communication board to answer verbal test items.

Rubrics Scoring criteria that describe an array of possible responses and specify the qualities and characteristics that occur at different levels of performance.

Scores The numerical result of testing that summarizes test results using numbers and provides an effective and efficient way to describe student performance in an objective manner.

Screening instruments Brief, easy-to-administer tests, rating scales, checklists, and direct observation techniques that provide an overview or sketch of behavior rather than a detailed analysis.

Screening process The process of determining general levels of performance or behavior through the use of concise, abbreviated tests and evaluation procedures.

Self-assessment Students evaluate their own work especially in cooperative learning and portfolio-based instruction.

Self-concept Refers to students' feelings about themselves in various life situations.

Self-injurious behavior (SIB) Responses that result in physical damage to the student exhibiting the behavior. Although self-injurious behavior takes many forms, common examples include head banging, hand biting, hair pulling, scratching, and eye poking.

Semantics Understanding and expressing word meanings and word relationships. Word meanings and relationships include vocabulary, synonyms, antonyms, word categories, ambiguities, and absurdities. For example, word relationships include the associations that exist between words such as *8:45* and a *quarter to nine,* and between *house* and *home.*

Shared grading This type of grading involves collaboration among two or more teachers in assigning grades.

Showcase portfolios A portfolio displaying a student's best work. Similar to the portfolios professionals use to illustrate their work.

Simple numerical report Criterion-referenced scores that express performance as the number of right and wrong answers on a test, such as 45 of 50 correct responses (i.e., 45/50).

Single-skill achievement tests Tests that are especially useful for gathering in-depth diagnostic information about student performance in a single content area.

Situational assessment The use of systematic observation techniques to evaluate work- and career-related performance on the job or in real or simulated environments such as vocational training settings, simulated workstations, job tryouts in the community, and other community-based settings.

Skewed distribution A distribution that occurs when scores cluster at either the high or the low end rather than in the middle of a distribution. A positive skew occurs when scores cluster around the low end of a distribution; a negative skew results from scores that bunch up at the high end of a distribution.

Social age This is a special type of age score that describes the social skill development of young children.

Sociogram An assessment technique for measuring social acceptance and peer popularity by having students rate each of their classmates in a nonobtrusive manner for the purpose of analyzing the group structure in a classroom and identifying the popularity of individual students.

Splinter skills Behaviors developed in isolation from related skills, such as learning to write the letters of the alphabet without understanding the meaning of the letters. See also *gaps in development.*

Split-half reliability A measure of accuracy based on the correlation between two halves of the same test that is obtained by giving a test once, splitting the test items in half, and comparing the two halves to each other.

Spontaneous language   The candid, unrehearsed verbal expression of students that occurs naturally in real-life situations.

Standard deviation   An estimate of the variability of scores based on the average distance of individual scores from the mean of the distribution. Groups of scores with higher variability yield larger standard deviations than those with lower variability.

Standard error of measurement   An estimate of the variability of individual test scores that testing specialists employ as a measure of the accuracy or reliability of a test.

Standard score   A general term for a variety of scores that express performance by comparing the deviation of an individual score from the average score for students in a norm group of the same chronological age or scholastic grade level. The most widely used standard scores have means of 100 and standard deviations of 15.

Standardization   Refers to structuring test materials, administration procedures, scoring methods, and techniques for interpreting results. Standardization makes it possible to give a test in the same way to a group of students or to the same student more than once. This helps to ensure accuracy and consistency in measuring progress, determining levels of performance, and comparing performance to others.

Standards for scoring   Guidelines for scoring tests and reporting test scores that include recommendations for fairly reporting test results and suggestions for avoiding pitfalls and problems in scoring.

Stanine   A standard score with a mean of 5 and a standard deviation of 2 that is based on a scale of 1 to 9. Average stanines occur around the mean of 5. Stanines above 1 SD from the mean $(5 + 2 = 7)$ fall in the above-average range, and stanines below 1 SD $(5 - 2 = 3)$ fall in the below-average range.

Statistics   Numbers, including test scores, that summarize large groups of data by putting them into manageable form.

Stereotypy   Behaviors characterized by idiosyncratic, highly consistent, repetitive, rhythmic movements of the body or body parts. Also referred to as *stereotypic* or *self-stimulatory behavior,* examples of stereotypy include

head weaving, rocking, arm and finger flapping, posturing, and mouthing hands or objects.

Student behavior   A broad term that encompasses a range of nonacademic behaviors, including social-emotional development.

Student portfolio   A systematic collection of student work and related materials that depicts a student's activities, accomplishments, and achievements in one or more school subjects.

Student self-assessment   A variety of procedures in which students engage in various types of reflections and self-evaluations.

Syntax   The way morphemes or words go together to form phrases and meaningful sentences. For example, the sentence "I am going to the store" is syntactically correct, but the sentence "I going store" is incorrect.

Task analysis   An instructional technique and a curriculum-based assessment procedure that involves breaking down a difficult task into small steps.

Teachable moment   See *critical moment.*

Team approach   A method that provides a way for professionals to combine efforts with parents to obtain the best possible assessment data for meeting the needs of the child and the family. The team approach relies on the expertise of professionals from various disciplines as well as the family.

Team assessment   The use of a small group of professionals with complementary skills who work together to evaluate a student.

Test   A test contains a standard set of questions for the purpose of producing a score, a set of scores, or some other numerical result. Tests are usually given once in a prescribed manner and in a structured setting.

Test anxiety   Nervousness or tension before tests or other important assessment events.

Test directions   Instructions given to students for taking a test, which may include the purpose of the test, the time alotted, the directions for responding, and how to record answers.

Test format   The structure or layout of a test such as multiple choice, essay, short-answer, matching, and true/false.

Test norms   Sets of scores developed from the scores of subjects in the norm group, which includes carefully selected students who take the test in a precise manner. Many types of norms exist, including national, state, and local norms.

Test-retest reliability A process for evaluating accuracy that involves giving a test twice to a carefully selected group and comparing the resulting scores to obtain an estimate of test consistency.

Transition services A coordinated set of activities designed to facilitate movement from school to postschool activities, including postsecondary education, vocational training, integrated employment (including supported employment), continuing and adult education, adult services, independent living, and community participation.

T-score A standard score with a mean of 50 and a standard deviation of 10. A t-score of 50 denotes average performance, whereas a t-score of 40 (1 SD below the mean) suggests below-average performance, and a t-score of 60 (1 SD above the mean) connotes above-average performance.

Validity A term that refers to the effectiveness of assessment instruments and is considered the most important technical characteristic of a test. The basic question of validity concerns "How well does the test measure what it was designed to measure?" or "Does the test do what it is supposed to do?"

Verbal language Behaviors sampled by tests that require students to give verbal responses to oral questions from an evaluator such as answering factual and comprehension questions, defining vocabulary words, identifying similarities, and solving arithmetic problems.

Verbal scale A subtest of the Wechsler Intelligence Scale for Children—Third Edition (WISC-III) that contains orally presented items that a student answers verbally.

Visual-motor processing A term that refers to the process of coordinating sensory information from the eyes with corresponding motor movements such as eye-hand coordination and visual-motor control.

Visual-reasoning behaviors Behaviors that require students to use visual perception ability to make perceptual discriminations that involve simple classifications and abstract manipulation of symbolic concepts. Classification tasks usually consist of discrimination of colors, shapes, numbers, and objects. Abstract manipulation involves tasks such as visual discrimination (e.g., recognizing small differences in objects such as geometric drawings), visual sequencing (e.g., identifying the progressive relationship in a series of geometric figures), and recognition of details (e.g., identifying missing parts in pictures).

Vocabulary diversity The originality, maturity, and variety of words used in writing.

Vocational assessment The process of evaluating the particular skills necessary for success in specific jobs, professions, or trades.

Vocational interest inventories Specialized tests for assessing the job and career preferences of individuals and groups of students.

Work samples Tasks, materials, tools, and equipment taken from real jobs or job clusters and used to measure vocational interest and potential.

Written tests Rating scales, checklists of skills, and inventories that evaluators use to measure performance and behavior. Most written tests are relatively inexpensive, and evaluators can administer and score them in short time periods.

Z-score A standard score with a mean of 0 and a standard deviation of 1. A z-score of 0 denotes average performance, whereas a z-score of +1 (1 SD above the mean) suggests above-average performance, and a z-score of −1 (1 SD below the mean) indicates below-average performance.

Name Index

Subject Index